SIGIR '94

SIGIR '94

Proceedings of the Seventeenth Annual International ACM-SIGIR Conference on Research and Development in Information Retrieval, organised by Dublin City University.

Held in Cooperation with the ACM-SIGIR
AICA-GLIR (Italy)
BCS-IRSG (UK)
CEPIS-EIRSG (Europe)
GI (Germany)
ICS (Ireland)

3–6 July 1994 · Dublin, Ireland

Edited by

W. Bruce Croft and C. J. van Rijsbergen

Springer-Verlag
London Berlin Heidelberg New York
Paris Tokyo Hong Kong
Barcelona Budapest

Bruce W. Croft
Department of Computer Science
University of Massachusetts
Amherst
MA 01003
USA

C. J. van Rijsbergen
Department of Computer Science
University of Glasgow
8–17 Lilybank Gardens
Glasgow, G12 8RZ
Scotland

ISBN 3–540–19889–X Springer-Verlag Berlin Heidelberg New York
ISBN 0–387–19889–X Springer-Verlag New York Berlin Heidelberg

British Library Cataloguing in Publication Data
A catalogue record for this book is available from the British Library

Library of Congress Catloguing-in-Publication Data
A catalog record for this book is available from the library of congress

Printed in Great Britain

Typesetting: Camera ready by author
Printed and bound by Athenæum Press Ltd, Newcastle upon Tyne
34/3830–543210 Printed on acid-free paper

Preface

The papers included in these proceedings were presented at the Seventeenth Annual International ACM-SIGIR Conference on Research and Development in Information Retrieval, held from July 3 to July 6 1993 in Dublin, Ireland. This conference alternates in location between North America and Europe and this year is held in cooperation with the following professional computing societies: ACM-SIGIR, AICA-GLIR (Italy), CEPIS-EIRSG (Europe), GI (Germany) and the Irish Computer Society. With 35 selected papers, 2 keynote talks, 2 panels, 8 tutorials, one ACM-SIGIR award paper and a series of demonstrations, this makes this the biggest SIGIR conference to date.

The 35 selected papers included here were chosen from 129 submitted and all submissions were reviewed by at least three referees from the programme committee. The programme committee was actually composed of two subcommittees, one based in North America chaired by Bruce Croft, the other based in Europe chaired by Keith van Rijsbergen. A meeting was held in the United States and a selection of the best of the papers submitted to that subcommittee was made. At a European meeting following that the final selection of papers, panels and tutorials which comprise this conference, was made. These conference proceedings also include the paper presented by the recipient of the triennial ACM-SIGIR award.

The task of refereeing scientific papers is a demanding one for members of the programme committee and the additional referees but the reward for all to see is a top class scientific programme which makes the SIGIR conference the premiere meeting for the presentation of results in research and development in information retrieval. The breadth of topics covered in this years conference reflects the continued development and advancement of our field within the scientific community.

We are very grateful to the School of Computer Applications at Dublin City University for providing all kinds of resources and support in order to allow this conference to take place. We also acknowledge the support of Bórd Fáilte, Aer Lingus, the National Software Directorate, the ESPRIT IDOMENEUS Network of Excellence and the Commission of the European Communities.

This conference would have been impossible without the great deal of hard work done by many volunteers including John Dunnion (Treasurer), Jennifer Pearson (panels and tutorials) and Fergus Kelledy (local organisation). These and many others who gave freely of their time have contributed much to making this conference a success.

– W. Bruce Croft, programme chair (North and South America, Asia)
– Alan F. Smeaton, conference chair
– Keith van Rijsbergen, programme co-chair (Europe, Africa, Australia)

Conference Organisation

Conference Chair:
Alan F. Smeaton, Dublin City University

Treasurer:
John Dunnion, University College Dublin

Tutorials and Panels:
Jennifer Pearson, Dublin City University

Local Organisation:
Fergus Kelledy, Dublin City University

Programme co-chairs:
Keith van Rijsbergen, Glasgow University, Scotland
W. Bruce Croft, University of Massachusetts, USA

Programme Committee
Ijsbrand Jan Aalbersberg, Phillips, USA
Maristella Agosti, U. Padova, Italy
Rik Belew, UC San Diego, USA
Nick Belkin, Rutgers, USA
David Blair, U. Michigan, USA
Christine L. Borgman, UCLA, USA
Forbes J. Burkowski, U. Waterloo, Canada
Yves Chiaramella, LGI-IMAG, France
Panos Constantopoulos, Greece
Ian Cornelius, UCD, Ireland
E.A. Fox, VPI&SU, USA
H-P Frei, UBILAB, Switzerland
M.E. Frisse, Washington U., USA
Norbert Fuhr, U. Dortmund, Germany
Forbes Gibb, U. Strathclyde, UK
Jane Grimson, Trinity College, Ireland
John Hughes, UUJ, Northern Ireland
Peter Ingwersen, Royal School, Denmark
David Lewis, AT&T, USA
Desai Narasimhalu, ISS, Singapore
Vijay Raghavan, U. SW Louisianna, USA
Stephen Robertson, City U., UK
Ron Sacks-Davis, RMIT, Australia
Gerard Salton, Cornell, USA
Peter Schäuble, ETH, Switzerland
Tengku M.T. Sembok, NUM, Malaysia

Alan Smeaton, Dublin City U., Ireland
Karen Sparck Jones, U. Cambridge, UK
Craig Stanfill, Thinking Machines Corp., USA
Carlo Tasso, Universita' di Udine, Italy
T.P. van der Weide, U. Nijmegen, Netherlands
Peter Willett, U. Sheffield, UK
S K M Wong, U. Regina, Canada

Additional Refereeing

James Allan, Cornell University
Guillermo Averbach, Virginia Tech
Abraham Bookstein, University of Chicago
John Broglio, University of Massachusetts
James P Callan, University of Massachusetts
Iain Campbell, Glasgow University
Fabio Crestani, Glasgow University
Mark Dunlop, University of Paisley
Steven Finch, Edinburgh University
Lenwood S Heath, Virginia Tech
Paul Kantor, Rutgers University
Pekka Kilpelainen, University of Ontario
Bob Krovetz, University of Massachusetts
Mounia Lalmas, University of Windsor
Dario Lucarella, CRA-ENEL
Ted Metcalfe, Washington State University of Medicine
A McEnery, Lancaster University
Joan Morrissey, University of Windsor
Luct Terry Nowell, Virginia Tech
Chris Paice, Lancaster University
Darell Raymond, University of Waterloo
Mark Sanderson, Glasgow University
Hans Schek, ETH
Fabrizio Sebastiani, Glasgow University
Hayri Sever, Cornell University
Amit Singhal, Cornell University
Ulrich Thiel, GMD-IPSI
Stephen Tomlinson, Cornell University
Bill Wake, Virginia Tech

Sponsors:

Dublin City University

Aer Lingus

Bórd Fáilte

Commission of the European Communities

IDOMENEUS ESPRIT Network of Excellence (no:6606)

National Software Directorate

Table of Contents

ROUTING

PASSAGE RETRIEVAL

IMPLEMENTATION

PANEL SESSIONS

Text Categorisation

A Sequential Algorithm for Training Text Classifiers

David D. Lewis and William A. Gale

AT&T Bell Laboratories
Murray Hill, NJ 07974; USA
lewis@research.att.com, gale@research.att.com

Abstract

The ability to cheaply train text classifiers is critical to their use in information retrieval, content analysis, natural language processing, and other tasks involving data which is partly or fully textual. An algorithm for sequential sampling during machine learning of statistical classifiers was developed and tested on a newswire text categorization task. This method, which we call uncertainty sampling, reduced by as much as 500-fold the amount of training data that would have to be manually classified to achieve a given level of effectiveness.

1 Introduction

Text classification is the automated grouping of textual or partially textual entities. Document retrieval, categorization, routing, filtering, and clustering, as well as natural language processing tasks such as tagging, word sense disambiguation, and some aspects of understanding can be formulated as text classification. As the amount of online text increases, the demand for text classification to aid the analysis and management of text is increasing.

One advantage of formulating text processing tasks as classification is that methods from statistics and machine learning can be used to form text classifiers automatically. While using machine learning does require manually annotating training data with class labels, this annotation takes less skill and expense than, for instance, building classification rules by hand [1].

There is often more text available than can be economically labeled, so a subset or *sample* of the data must be chosen to label.[1] Random sampling [3] will usually not be effective. If only 1 in 1000 texts are class members (not atypical), and only 500 texts can be labeled, then a random sample will usually contain 500 negative examples and no positive ones. This will not support training a classifier to distinguish positive from negative examples.

Relevance feedback [4] does a kind of nonrandom sampling. In effect, users are asked to label those texts that the current classifier considers most likely to be class members. This approach, which we might call *relevance sampling*, is a reasonable strategy in a text retrieval context, where the user is more interested in seeing relevant texts than in the effectiveness of the final classifier produced. Relevance feedback has also been proposed for finding examples of unusual word senses [5]. However, relevance feedback has many problems as an approach to sampling. It works more poorly as the classifier improves, and is susceptible to selecting redundant examples.

Relevance sampling is a sequential approach to sampling, since the labeling of earlier examples influences the selection of later ones [6]. This paper describes an alternative sequential approach, *uncertainty sampling*, motivated by results in computational learning theory. Uncertainty sampling is an iterative process of manual labeling of examples, classifier fitting from those examples, and use of the classifier to select new examples whose class membership is unclear. We show how a probabilistic classifier can be trained using uncertainty sampling. A test of this method on a text categorization task showed reductions of up to 500-fold in the number of examples that must be labeled to produce a classifier with a given effectiveness.

2 Learning with Queries

A classifier can often be learned from fewer examples if the learning algorithm is allowed to create artificial examples or *membership queries* and ask a teacher to label them [7, 8].[2] In many learning tasks creation of artificial examples is no problem. However, an artificial text created by a learning algorithm is unlikely to be a legitimate natural language expression, and probably would be uninterpretable by a human teacher.

[1] An exception is when large quantities of previously labeled text are available, as when automated text categorization is being deployed to replace or aid an existing staff of manual indexers [2].

[2] In this paper "queries" always refers to membership queries, not text retrieval queries.

1. Create an initial classifier
2. While teacher is willing to label examples
   (a) Apply the current classifier to each unlabeled example
   (b) Find the b examples for which the classifier is least certain of class membership
   (c) Have the teacher label the subsample of b examples
   (d) Train a new classifier on all labeled examples

Figure 1. An algorithm for uncertainty sampling with a single classifier.

Recently, several algorithms for learning via queries have been proposed that filter existing examples rather than creating artificial ones [9, 10, 11]. These algorithms ask a teacher to label only those examples whose class membership is sufficiently "uncertain". Several definitions of uncertainty have been used, but all are based on estimating how likely a classifier trained on previously labeled data would be to produce the correct class label for a given unlabeled example. Looking at this as a sampling method rather than a querying one, we call this approach *uncertainty sampling.*

Seung, Opper, and Sompolinsky [11] present a theoretical analysis of "query by committee" (QBC), an algorithm that, for each unlabeled example, draws two classifiers randomly from the *version space*, i.e. the set of all classifiers consistent with the labeled training data [12]. An infinite stream of unlabeled data is assumed, from which QBC asks the teacher for class labels only on those examples for which the two chosen classifiers disagree.

Freund, Seung, Shamir, and Tishby extend the QBC result to a wide range of classifier forms [13]. They prove that, under certain assumptions, the number of queries made after examining m random examples will be logarithmic in m, while generalization error will decrease almost as quickly as it would if queries were made on all examples. More precisely, generalization error decreases as $O(1/m)$. Therefore, in terms of the number of queries, generalization error decreases exponentially fast.

This is a provocative result, since it implies that the effect of training on labeled data can be gotten for the cost of obtaining unlabeled data, and labeling only a logarithmic fraction of it. However, the QBC assumptions include that the data is noise free, a perfect deterministic classifier exists, and that it is possible to draw classifiers randomly from the version space, all of which are problematic for real world tasks. The effectiveness of QBC and related methods on real world tasks remains to be determined.

A heuristic alternative to QBC's random drawing of classifiers from the version space is to let the learning algorithm do what it always does—pick a single classifier from the version space. If the classifier can not only make classification decisions, but estimate their certainty, the certainty estimate can be used to select examples.

A single classifier approach to uncertainty sampling has several theoretical failings, including underestimation of true uncertainty, and biases caused by nonrepresentative classifiers [9, 10]. On the other hand, experiments using a single classifier to make arbitrary queries [14] or select subsets of labeled data [8, 15] have shown substantial speedups in learning. Relevance sampling, which has proven quite effective for text retrieval, also uses a single classifier.

3 An Uncertainty Sampling Algorithm

Figure 3 presents an algorithm for uncertainty sampling from a finite set of examples using a single classifier. Ideally b, the number of examples selected on each iteration, would be 1, but larger values may be appropriate if scoring and selecting examples is expensive. This algorithm can be used with any type of classifier that both predicts a class and provides a measurement of how certain that prediction is. Probabilistic, fuzzy, nearest neighbor, and neural classifiers, along with many others, satisfy this criterion or can be easily modified to do so. Perhaps the most difficult requirement is that measurements of relative certainty be produced even when the classifier was formed from very few training examples.

Uncertainty sampling is similar to the strategy of training on misclassified instances [16, 17]. The difference is that when data is not labeled we must use the classifier itself to guess at which examples are being misclassified. Note that the initial classifier plays an important role, since without it there may be a long period of random sampling before examples of a low frequency class are stumbled upon.

4 A Probabilistic Text Classifier

In this section we describe a classifier form which produces estimates of $P(C_i|\mathbf{w})$, the posterior probability that an example with pattern $\mathbf{w}$ belongs to class C_i. Estimates of this probability can be used both to decide when an example should be assigned to a class, and to estimate how likely it is that the classification will be correct. We describe how the classifier is trained and how we use it for uncertainty sampling and classification.

4.1 A Probabilistic Classifier

Classifiers which estimate the posterior probability via Bayes' Rule:

$$P(C_i|\mathbf{w}) = \frac{P(\mathbf{w}|C_i) \times P(C_i)}{\sum_{j=1}^{q} P(\mathbf{w}|C_j) \times P(C_j)} \tag{1}$$

have been applied to a variety of text classification tasks, including text retrieval [18], text categorization [19, 20], and word sense identification [5]. Here the C_i are a disjoint and exhaustive set of classes to which an example may belong, and $\mathbf{w} = (w_1, ..., w_d)$ is an observed pattern.[3] $P(\mathbf{w}|C_i)$ is the conditional probability that an example has pattern $\mathbf{w}$ given that it belongs to class C_i, while $P(C_i)$ is the prior probability that an example belongs to class C_i.

In this paper, we treat only the case $q = 2$, so there are two classes $C_1 = C$ and $C_2 = \bar{C}$, with $P(\bar{C}) = 1 - P(C)$. In this case it is useful to express the relative posterior probabilities of C and $\bar{C}$ as an odds ratio:

$$\frac{P(C|\mathbf{w})}{P(\bar{C}|\mathbf{w})} = \frac{P(C)}{P(\bar{C})} \times \frac{P(\mathbf{w}|C)}{P(\mathbf{w}|\bar{C})} \tag{2}$$

Given the huge number of possible $\mathbf{w}$'s, estimation of $P(\mathbf{w}|C)/P(\mathbf{w}|\bar{C})$ by direct observation of $\mathbf{w}$'s in the training set is futile. By making certain independence assumptions [21], we can make the following decomposition:

$$\frac{P(C|\mathbf{w})}{P(\bar{C}|\mathbf{w})} = \frac{P(C)}{P(\bar{C})} \times \prod_{i=1}^{d} \frac{P(w_i|C)}{P(w_i|\bar{C})} \tag{3}$$

Then, using the fact that $P(\bar{C}|\mathbf{w}) = 1 - P(C|\mathbf{w})$, plus some arithmetic manipulations, we can get the following expression for $P(C|\mathbf{w})$:

$$P(C|\mathbf{w}) = \frac{\exp(\log \frac{P(C)}{1-P(C)} + \sum_{i=1}^{d} \log \frac{P(w_i|C)}{P(w_i|\bar{C})})}{1 + \exp(\log \frac{P(C)}{1-P(C)} + \sum_{i=1}^{d} \log \frac{P(w_i|C)}{P(w_i|\bar{C})})} \tag{4}$$

Equation 4 is rarely used directly in text classification, probably because its estimates of $P(C|\mathbf{w})$ are systematically inaccurate. One reason for this inaccuracy is that the independence assumptions made in producing Equation 3 are always incorrect when the w_i's are words or other features defined from natural language. Another problem is that $P(C)$ is typically small and thus hard to estimate, a problem which is compounded when the training set is not a random sample.

Logistic regression [22] provides a partial solution to these problems. It is a general technique for combining multiple predictor values to estimate a posterior probability. The form of the estimate is:

$$P(C|\mathbf{x}) = \frac{\exp(a + b_1 x_1 + ... + b_m x_m)}{1 + \exp(a + b_1 x_1 + ... + b_m x_m)} \tag{5}$$

A number of approaches to using logistic regression in text classification have been proposed [23, 24, 25]. The similarity between Equation 4 and Equation 5 prompted us to try a particularly simple approach, where the log likelihood ratio from the Bayesian independence formulation is used as the single predictor variable:

$$P(C|\mathbf{w}) = \frac{\exp(a + b \sum_{i=1}^{d} \log \frac{P(w_i|C)}{P(w_i|\bar{C})})}{1 + \exp(a + b \sum_{i=1}^{d} \log \frac{P(w_i|C)}{P(w_i|\bar{C})})} \tag{6}$$

Intuitively, we could hope that the logistic parameter a would substitute for the hard-to-estimate prior log odds in Equation 4, while b would serve to dampen extreme log likelihood ratios resulting from independence violations. We have in fact found this simple formulation to work well for text categorization, though we have not compared it with the more complex formulations suggested by other authors. Note that our approach would probably not be appropriate if documents were of widely varying lengths.

[3] We are careful to distinguish an example e from the corresponding pattern $\mathbf{w}$, since different examples may have the same feature values $w_1, ..., w_d$.

4.2 Training the Classifier

The first step in using Equation 6 is estimating the values $P(w_i|C)/P(w_i|\bar{C})$. We used the following estimator:

$$\frac{P(w_i|C)}{P(w_i|\bar{C})} \doteq \frac{\frac{c_{pi}+(N_p+0.5)/(N_p+N_n+1)}{N_p+d(N_p+0.5)/(N_p+N_n+1)}}{\frac{c_{ni}+(N_n+0.5)/(N_p+N_n+1)}{N_n+d(N_n+0.5)/(N_p+N_n+1)}} \tag{7}$$

Here N_p and N_n are the numbers of tokens in the positive and negative training sets, respectively, c_{pi} and c_{ni} are correspondingly the number of instances of w_i in the positive and negative training sets, and d is the number of features. This is an ad hoc estimator, loosely justified by its analogy to the expected likelihood estimator [26]. The above estimator attempts to avoid extreme estimates of the log likelihood ratio when N_p and N_n are of very different sizes, for instance before our sampling procedure starts finding positive examples.

In text classification there typically is a huge set of potential w_i's, for instance all the types (distinct words) in a collection of documents. Using feature selection to reduce this set (or, equivalently, to lock all but a few values at 0) can improve effectiveness [19]. As a feature quality measure we used:

$$(c_{pi}+c_{ni})\log\frac{P(w_i|C)}{P(w_i|\bar{C})}. \tag{8}$$

We selected features in order of this value until a specified fraction (0.7 in the experiments reported here) of the total score of all training examples was reached. This was done separately for features with positive and negative log likelihood ratios.

After feature selection is performed, the log likelihood values are used to compute:

$$\sum_{i=1}^{d}\log\frac{P(w_i|C)}{P(w_i|\bar{C})} \tag{9}$$

for each training example. Logistic regression is then used to find the values a and b which give the best fit of this value to the probability of class membership.

4.3 Uncertainty Sampling with the Probabilistic Classifier

Uncertainty sampling is simple given a classifier that estimates $P(C|\mathbf{w})$. On each iteration, the current version of classifier can be applied to each example, and those examples with estimated $P(C|\mathbf{w})$ values closest to 0.5 selected, since 0.5 corresponds to the classifier being most uncertain of the class label.

We adopted the slightly more complex method of scoring all examples, and then choosing the $b/2$ examples closest to 0.5 and above it, and the $b/2$ examples closest to 0.5 and below it. This method guarantees that no more than half the examples selected on an iteration are exact duplicates (unless all examples score above 0.5 or all score below 0.5). In addition, there is also some evidence that training on pairs of examples on opposite sides of a decision boundary is useful [14].

4.4 Classification with the Probabilistic Classifier

An advantage of using a classifier which provides accurate estimates of $P(C|\mathbf{w})$ is that, under certain assumptions, decision theory gives an optimal rule for deciding whether an example should be assigned to class C ([27], p. 15). Let l_{ij} be the penalty or *loss* incurred for deciding class i when the true class is j. (We let $i, j = 1$ for C, $i, j = 2$ for $\bar{C}$.) We then should assign the example to class C exactly when:

$$l_{21}P(C|\mathbf{w}) + l_{22}(1-P(C|\mathbf{w})) > l_{11}P(C|\mathbf{w}) + l_{12}(1-P(C|\mathbf{w})) \tag{10}$$

For instance, if we desire minimum error rate (both types of incorrect decisions are equally bad) the appropriate losses would be $l_{12} = l_{21} = 1$ and $l_{11} = l_{22} = 0$.

5 Experiment

We conducted an experiment to see if uncertainty sampling would reduce the amount of labeled data necessary to train a classifier, in comparison with random sampling and relevance sampling. The training method and probabilistic classifier of Section 4 were used. Classifiers were trained to perform a text categorization task on news story titles.

	Training		Test	
Category	Number	Freq.	Number	Freq.
tickertalk	208	0.0007	40	0.0008
boxoffice	314	0.0010	42	0.0008
bonds	470	0.0015	60	0.0012
nielsens	511	0.0016	87	0.0017
burma	510	0.0016	93	0.0018
dukakis	642	0.0020	107	0.0021
ireland	780	0.0024	117	0.0023
quayle	786	0.0025	133	0.0026
budget	1176	0.0037	197	0.0038
hostages	1560	0.0049	228	0.0044

Table 1. The 10 categories used in our experiments, with number of occurrences and frequency of occurrence on training and test sets.

5.1 Data Set

The titles of 371,454 items which appeared on the AP newswire between 1988 and early 1993 were divided randomly into a training set of 319,463 titles and a test set of 51,991 titles. Titles were processed by lower casing text and removing punctuation. Word boundaries were defined by whitespace. Titles were used, rather than the full text of the items, to minimize computation.

Categories to be assigned were based on the "keyword" from the "keyword slug line" present in each AP item ([28], p. 317). The keyword is a string of up to 21 characters indicating the content of the item. While keywords are only required to be identical for updated items on the same news story, in practice there is considerable reuse of keywords and parts of keywords from story to story and year to year, so they have some aspects of a controlled vocabulary.

We defined categories of AP titles according to whether particular substrings appeared in the keyword field. For instance, the following stories were assigned to the *bond* category (the keyword is shown in bold):

SavingsBonds Savings Bond Sale Plunge After Rate Cut
SavingsBonds Treasury Announces 2 Percent Reduction in Savings Rate
SavingsBonds-Flood Flood Victims Permitted to Cash in Savings Bonds Early
MesaBonds Mesa to Begin $600 Million Bond Exchange Offer Wednesday
BondFirms Report: Wall Street Bond Firms To Ban Political Contributions
Obit-Bond James Bond, Ornithologist, Gave Name To Fictional Agent 007
People-Bond Julian Bond: Rights Movement Needs Individuals, Not Charismatic Leaders

while these were not:

Clinton President-Elect Plays Touch Football
Bank-Failures Bank, S&L Failures at Seven-Year Low
Taxes:SavingsBon Taxes: Savings Bonds
TreasuryBorrowing Treasury Shifts Borrowing Away From Long-Term Bonds
MuniProbe Tougher Political Contribution Rules for Muni Bonds Proposed

The categories defined in this fashion were somewhat messy semantically. Julian Bond and James Bond should not be included with savings bonds, while we lose items about financial bonds if the keyword was truncated, misspelled, or emphasized some other aspect of the story. Perfect categorization with these category definitions was therefore not possible. We do not believe this is a serious problem, since we are interested here in the relative rather than absolute effectiveness of categorization methods. Indeed, these categories provide a useful test of the robustness of our methods to errors in the training data.

The 10 categories we defined are shown in Table 1 along with their frequencies in the training and test sets. The categories were chosen to have relatively low frequencies, while still providing a reasonable number of positive examples in both the training and test sets.

5.2 Training

The initial classifier required by the uncertainty sampling algorithm (Figure 3) could be produced from a set of words suggested by a teacher, just as classifiers are constructed from the texts of user requests in text retrieval systems [29]. To avoid experimenter bias, we instead used a starting subsample of 3 positive examples of the category randomly selected from the training set. Feature selection always used the words from these 3 examples in addition to words chosen as described in Section 4.2.

On each run, the 3 starting examples were used to train an initial classifier, after which 249 iterations of uncertainty sampling with a subsample size of 4 were carried out as described in Section 4.3. After each subsample was selected, its category labels were looked up and the examples were added to the set of labeled examples to be used in training the next classifier. The classifier produced on each iteration was used for example selection on the next iteration, as well as being retained for evaluation. In order to study the impact of the starting subsample on the quality of the final classifier, we repeated this process 10 times for each category, each time with a different starting subsample of 3 positive examples.

We compared uncertainty sampling with both relevance sampling and random sampling. Relevance sampling was carried out identically to uncertainty sampling, except that the 4 examples with the highest values of $P(C|\mathbf{w})$ were chosen, rather than 4 with values close to 0.5.

The "random" samples actually combined the starting subsamples of 3 positive examples with truly random samples of various sizes. In this fashion, training sets of the following sizes were produced:

3 6 10 20 40 80 160 320 640 1000 2500 4000 6000 8000 10000 15000 20000 30000 40000 50000 60000 70000 80000 ... (by 20000's) ... 300000 319463

Larger sets included the smaller ones. A classifier was formed from each of these sets using the same training methods used for uncertainty and relevance sampling, but the classifier was used only for evaluation, not to guide sampling. Two runs were done from each of 10 starting subsamples for a category, giving a total of 20 runs per category.

5.3 Evaluation

We treated each of the 10 categories as a binary classification task and evaluated the classifiers for each category separately. Classifiers were evaluated by applying them with the minimum error rate loss parameters ($l_{12} = l_{21} = 1$ and $l_{11} = l_{22} = 0$) to the 51,991 test items and comparing the classifier decisions with the actual category labels. All classifiers trained on the random samples were evaluated. Classifiers formed during the first 10 iterations of uncertainty and relevance sampling, plus every 5th iteration thereafter, were evaluated.

For text categorization, the effectiveness measures of recall and precision are defined as follows:

$$\text{recall} = \frac{\text{Number of test set category members assigned to category}}{\text{Number of category members in test set}} \tag{11}$$

$$\text{precision} = \frac{\text{Number of test set category members assigned to category}}{\text{Total number of test set members assigned to category}} \tag{12}$$

When comparing two classifiers it is desirable to have a single measure of effectiveness. Van Rijsbergen defined the E-measure as a combination of recall (R) and precision (P) satisfying certain measurement theoretic properties ([30], pp. 168-176):

$$E = 1 - \frac{(\beta^2 + 1)PR}{\beta^2 P + R} \tag{13}$$

The parameter β ranges between 0 and infinity and controls the relative weight given to recall and precision. A β of 1 corresponds to equal weighting of recall and precision. To get a single measure of effectiveness where higher values correspond to better effectiveness, and where recall and precision are of equal importance, we define $F_{\beta=1} = 1 - E_{\beta=1}$.

6 Results

Table 2 shows for each category the mean $F_{\beta=1}$ for classifiers formed by uncertainty sampling as well as those formed by relevance sampling and on the full training set. We also show effectiveness using just the 3 starting examples, plus 7 randomly selected examples. This gives a sense of the quality of the initial classifier. For all categories except *tickertalk*, an uncertainty sample of 999 texts resulted in a classifier substantially more effective than the initial classifier or one formed from a relevance sample of 999 texts. The classifier was usually of similar or better effectiveness than one trained on all 319,463 texts. Classifiers trained on a random sample of 1000 texts in most cases had very low effectiveness.

Figure 2 plots effectiveness against sample size for uncertainty sampling, relevance sampling, and random sampling. Results for 9 categories are presented, omitting *tickertalk* on which no strategy worked well.

Category	3 + 996 uncer.		3 + 7 rand.		3 + 996 rel.		3 + 319,460 full	
	mean	SD	mean	SD	mean	SD	mean	SD
tickertalk	.033	(.031)	.018	(.023)	.023	(.039)	.047	(.001)
boxoffice	.700	(.041)	.222	(.172)	.481	(.053)	.647	(.023)
bonds	.636	(.034)	.146	(.134)	.541	(.069)	.509	(.020)
nielsens	.801	(.016)	.291	(.218)	.567	(.132)	.741	(.022)
burma	.653	(.035)	.032	(.033)	.201	(.057)	.464	(.023)
dukakis	.136	(.046)	.101	(.075)	.035	(.021)	.163	(.015)
ireland	.416	(.041)	.050	(.033)	.170	(.038)	.288	(.030)
quayle	.386	(.040)	.081	(.064)	.140	(.072)	.493	(.009)
budget	.290	(.039)	.058	(.046)	.141	(.029)	.235	(.005)
hostages	.477	(.021)	.068	(.042)	.177	(.039)	.498	(.003)

Table 2. Mean and standard deviation of $F_{\beta=1}$ for training on initial 3 examples combined with each of 996 uncertainty selected examples, 7 random examples, 996 relevance selected examples, or 319,460 remaining examples. Means are over 10 runs for uncertainty and relevance sampling, and over 20 runs for random and full sampling.

7 Discussion

As Figure 2 shows, classifier effectiveness generally increases with sample size under all sampling methods, but faster with the two sequential methods. Of the sequential methods, uncertainty sampling substantially outperforms relevance sampling. The results hold across categories with widely varying absolute levels of effectiveness.[4]

The superiority of uncertainty sampling over relevance sampling is particularly notable since the low frequency of the categories used limited the danger that relevance sampling would drown in positive examples. Indeed, the difference between uncertainty sampling and relevance sampling is lower for the less frequent categories. However, even here uncertainty sampling is better, both in its higher mean and in its lower standard deviation.

In most cases effectiveness levels reached by random sampling only with 100,000 or more training examples are reached by uncertainty sampling with less than 1000 examples, while training on 1000 randomly selected examples gives greatly inferior results. In some cases, reaching a given level of effectiveness requires 500 times as many randomly selected examples as examples selected by uncertainty sampling.

Some caution is required in comparing the results for small uncertainty samples with those for large random samples. For 6 of 10 categories, the mean $F_{\beta=1}$ for a classifier trained on a uncertainty sample of 999 examples actually exceeds that from training on the full training set of 319,463 examples. This means that some aspect of our classifier training is not making effective use of large training sets. Feature selection is the most likely villain. Our method produced several thousand features when applied to the full training set, and previous work suggests this is too many [19].

The graphs of average effectiveness hide some variation from run to run. Several of the standard deviations shown in Table 2 amount to 10% or more of the mean effectiveness, meaning that the quality of the final classifiers is somewhat unpredictable.

One source of this variation was our initial subsamples of 3 positive examples. When a subsample was badly unrepresentative of the category, the initial classifier was ineffective, and there was a considerable delay before uncertainty sampling started to find additional positive examples. Even initial classifiers with the same raw effectiveness could lead to different parts of the space of examples being searched first.

Besides influencing early classifier formation, the starting subsamples had an impact on effectiveness through our making their words required features. This can be seen in the standard deviations for the Full column of Table 2 where, since all classifiers were trained on the same set of examples, the only difference among runs for a category is in the required features provided by the initial examples.

A second source of variation was fluctuations in the quality of successive classifiers. The uncertainty sampling process is inherently exploratory, with deficiencies in the classifier produced on one iteration leading to the selection of compensating examples on later iterations.

8 Future Work

Our results demonstrate that effective text classifiers can be created by obtaining large amounts of unlabeled data and labeling only a small fraction of it. While we tested uncertainty sampling on a text categorization task, it can equally well be applied to any classification task.

[4] The variations in absolute levels of effectiveness are to be expected—some categories are simply harder than others, and some of our category definitions were particularly noisy.

Text retrieval is an obvious application, though the tradeoff between retrieving the texts most useful to the user vs. the texts from which the system will learn the most must be considered [31]. The tradeoff is less of an issue in filtering, routing, and information dissemination applications, since the cost of judging nonrelevant examples can be amortized over a longer period of operation.

Uncertainty sampling should also benefit classification-based approaches to natural language processing tasks. A number of projects have annotated or are annotating large corpora to support the training of statistical methods for these tasks. Our results suggest that gathering huge unlabeled corpora, and using uncertainty sampling to annotate a small subset for each task may be cheaper and equally effective. Domains besides text processing where large data sets are available can also benefit.

Many questions remain to be answered about uncertainty sampling. The most important practical ones have to do with how the teacher knows when to stop, and how to form the final classifier for use after they do. Estimates of classifier effectiveness would enable the teacher to track progress, but new methods will be needed to produce such an estimate from a sample which is not random. Effectiveness estimates would also aid in selecting a classifier to use from the classifiers formed on the last few iterations. Alternately, methods for stabilizing the fluctuations from iteration to iteration might be pursued.

A variety of extensions and improvements to uncertainty sampling can be explored. We need to determine the relationship between subsample size and effectiveness, since larger subsamples require less computation. It also seems likely that subsample size can be increased if redundancy within subsamples is decreased. Other efficiency improvements include using a less accurate but more efficiently trained classifier during sampling [32], and picking the first examples satisfying a threshold on uncertainty rather than the most uncertain examples. Simultaneous training of classifiers for multiple classes is also of interest.

As currently formulated, uncertainty sampling requires that the underlying training algorithm produce reasonable classifiers even from very small training sets. This meant we had to tinker with feature selection and parameter estimation to avoid producing pathological behavior on small samples. We are currently exploring variations on uncertainty sampling which would be more robust with respect to problems in classifier training.

9 Summary

Text is cheap, but information, in the form of knowing what classes a text belongs to, is expensive. Automatic classification of text can provide this information at low cost, but the classifiers themselves must be built with expensive human effort, or trained from texts which have themselves been manually classified. We have demonstrated that uncertainty sampling can sharply reduce the amount of text which must be manually labeled to create an effective classifier. Uncertainty sampling has potential applications in a variety of text processing tasks, as well as in other domains where large amounts of unclassified data are available.

10 Acknowledgments

We thank Jason Catlett, William Cohen, Eileen Fitzpatrick, Yoav Freund, Trevor Hastie, Robert Schapire, and Sebastian Seung for advice and useful comments on this work, and Ken Church for making available his text processing tools and his help with them.

References

1. P. J. Hayes. Intelligent high-volume text processing using shallow, domain-specific techniques. In Paul. S. Jacobs, editor, *Text-Based Intelligent Systems: Current Research in Text Analysis, Information Extraction, and Retrieval*, pages 227–241. Lawrence Erlbaum, Hillsdale, NJ, 1992.
2. P. Biebricher, N. Fuhr, G. Lustig, M. Schwantner, and G. Knorz. The automatic indexing system AIR/PHYS—from research to application. In *Proc. SIGIR-88*, pages 333—342, 1988.
3. W. G. Cochran. *Sampling Techniques.* John Wiley & Sons, New York, 3rd edition, 1977.
4. G. Salton and C. Buckley. Improving retrieval performance by relevance feedback. *Journal of the American Society for Information Science*, 41(4):288–297, 1990.
5. W. A. Gale, K. W. Church, and D. Yarowsky. A method for disambiguating word senses in a large corpus. *Computers and the Humanities*, 26:415–439, 1993.
6. B. K. Ghosh. A brief history of sequential analysis. In B. K. Ghosh and P. K. Sen, editors, *Handbook of Sequential Analysis*, chapter 1, pages 1–19. Marcel Dekker, New York, 1991.
7. D. Angluin. Queries and concept learning. *Machine Learning*, 2:319–342, 1988.

8. M. Plutowski and H. White. Selecting concise training sets from clean data. *IEEE Transactions on Neural Networks*, 4(2):305–318, March 1993.

9. D. Cohn, L. Atlas, and R. Ladner. Improving generalization with self-directed learning, 1992. To appear in *Machine Learning*.

10. D. J. C. MacKay. The evidence framework applied to classification networks. *Neural Computation*, 4:720–736, 1992.

11. H. S. Seung, M. Opper, and H. Sompolinsky. Query by committee. In *Proceedings of the Fifth Annual ACM Workshop on Computational Learning Theory*, pages 287–294, 1992.

12. T. M. Mitchell. Generalization as search. *Artificial Intelligence*, 18:203–226, 1982.

13. Y. Freund, H. S. Seung, E. Shamir, and N. Tishby. Information, prediction, and query by committee. In *Advances in Neural Informations Processing Systems 5*, San Mateo, CA, 1992. Morgan Kaufmann.

14. J. Hwang, J. J. Choi, S. Oh, and R. J. Marks II. Query-based learning applied to partially trained multilayer perceptrons. *IEEE Transactions on Neural Networks*, 2(1):131–136, January 1991.

15. D. T. Davis and J. Hwang. Attentional focus training by boundary region data selection. In *International Joint Conference on Neural Networks*, pages I–676 to I–681, Baltimore, MD, June 7–11 1992.

16. P. E. Hart. The condensed nearest neighbor rule. *IEEE Transactions on Information Theory*, IT-14:515–516, May 1968.

17. P. E. Utgoff. Improved training via incremental learning. In *Sixth International Workshop on Machine Learning*, pages 362–365, 1989.

18. N. Fuhr. Models for retrieval with probabilistic indexing. *Information Processing and Management*, 25(1):55–72, 1989.

19. D. D. Lewis. An evaluation of phrasal and clustered representations on a text categorization task. In *Proc. SIGIR-92*, pages 37–50, 1992.

20. M. E. Maron. Automatic indexing: An experimental inquiry. *Journal of the Association for Computing Machinery*, 8:404–417, 1961.

21. W. S. Cooper. Some inconsistencies and misnomers in probabilistic information retrieval. In *Proc. SIGIR-91*, pages 57–61, 1991.

22. P. McCullagh and J. A. Nelder. *Generalized Linear Models*. Chapman & Hall, London, 2nd edition, 1989.

23. W. S. Cooper, F. C. Gey, and D. P. Dabney. Probabilistic retrieval based on staged logistic regression. In *Proc. SIGIR-92*, pages 198–210, 1992.

24. N. Fuhr and U. Pfeifer. Combining model-oriented and description-oriented approaches for probabilistic indexing. In *Proc. SIGIR-91*, pages 46–56, 1991.

25. S. Robertson and J. Bovey. Statistical problems in the application of probabilistic models to information retrieval. Report 5739, British Library, London, 1982.

26. W. A. Gale and K. W. Church. Poor estimates of context are worse than none. In *Speech and Natural Language Workshop*, pages 283–287, San Mateo, CA, June 1990. DARPA, Morgan Kaufmann.

27. R. O. Duda and P. E. Hart. *Pattern Classification and Scene Analysis*. Wiley-Interscience, New York, 1973.

28. N. Goldstein, editor. *The Associated Press Stylebook and Libel Manual*. Addison-Wesley, Reading, MA, 1992.

29. W. B. Croft and D. J. Harper. Using probabilistic models of document retrieval without relevance feedback. *Journal of Documentation*, 35(4):285–295, 1979.

30. C. J. van Rijsbergen. *Information Retrieval*. Butterworths, London, second edition, 1979.

31. A. Bookstein. Information retrieval: A sequential learning process. *Journal of the American Society for Information Science*, 34:331–342, September 1983.

32. David D. Lewis and Jason Catlett. Heterogeneous uncertainty sampling for supervised learning. In *Proceedings of the Eleventh International Conference on Machine Learning*, 1994. To appear.

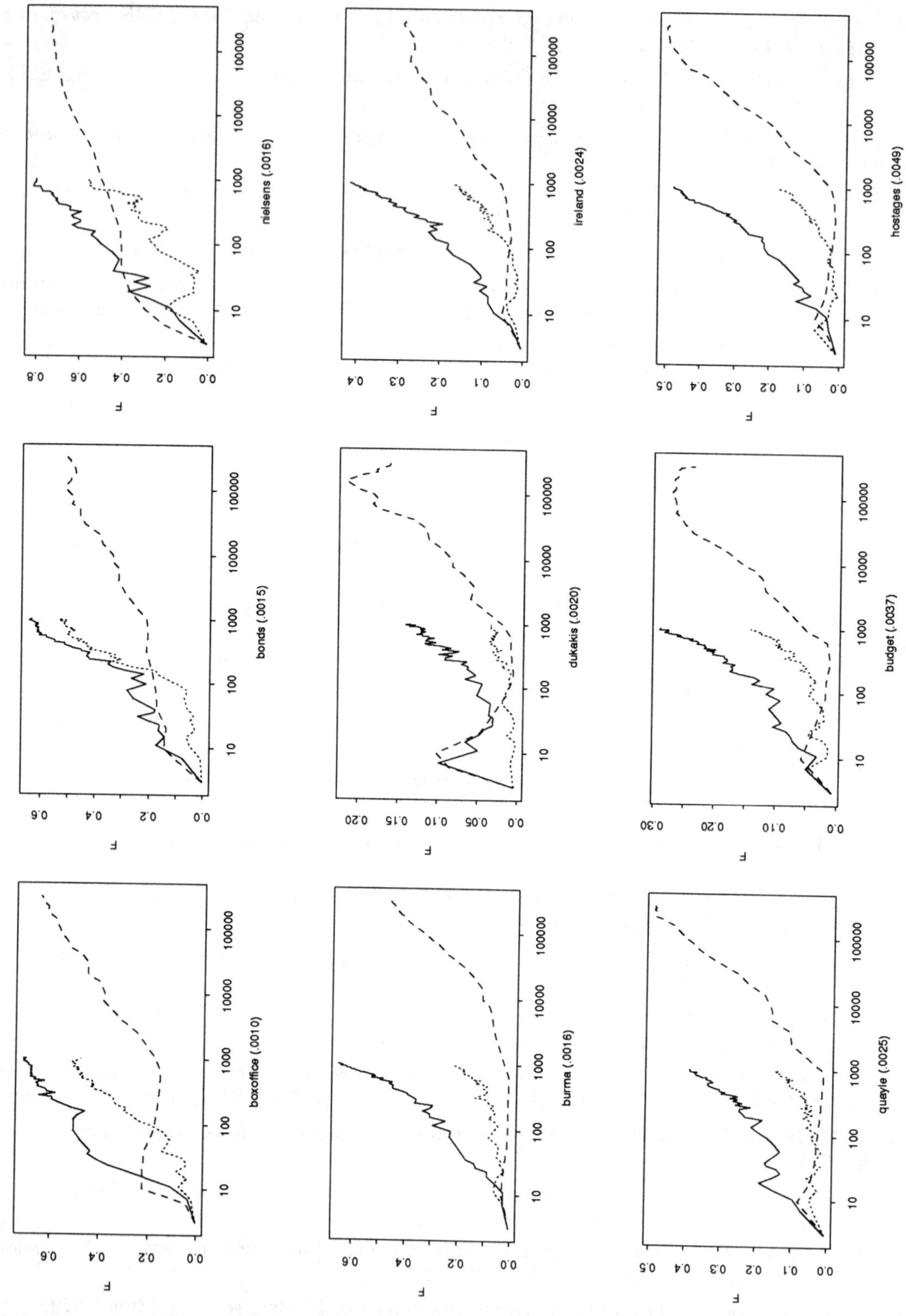

Figure 2. Mean $F_{\beta=1}$ values for text classifiers trained on uncertainty (solid line), relevance (dotted line) and random (dashed line) samples of titles from AP corpus. Means are over 10 runs for uncertainty and relevance sampling, and over 20 runs for random sampling. Results shown for 9 categories. Frequency of category on training set shown in parentheses.

Expert Network: Effective and Efficient Learning from Human Decisions in Text Categorization and Retrieval

Yiming Yang

Section of Medical Information Resources
Mayo Clinic/Foundation
Rochester, Minnesota 55905 USA

Abstract

Expert Network (*ExpNet*) is our new approach to automatic categorization and retrieval of natural language texts. We use a training set of texts with expert-assigned categories to construct a network which approximately reflects the conditional probabilities of categories given a text. The input nodes of the network are words in the training texts, the nodes on the intermediate level are the training texts, and the output nodes are categories. The links between nodes are computed based on statistics of the word distribution and the category distribution over the training set. *ExpNet* is used for relevance ranking of candidate categories of an arbitrary text in the case of text categorization, and for relevance ranking of documents via categories in the case of text retrieval. We have evaluated *ExpNet* in categorization and retrieval on a document collection of the MEDLINE database, and observed a performance in recall and precision comparable to the Linear Least Squares Fit (LLSF) mapping method, and significantly better than other methods tested. Computationally, *ExpNet* has an $O(N \log N)$ time complexity which is much more efficient than the cubic complexity of the LLSF method. The simplicity of the model, the high recall-precision rates, and the efficient computation together make *ExpNet* preferable as a practical solution for real-world applications.

1 Introduction

A major problem in retrieval of natural language texts is the vocabulary differences between humans. Related concepts can be represented by a variety of words. Therefore, retrieval methods based on shared words in queries and texts, which we call "surface-based matching", can be effective only if the authors who write the texts and the users who issue the queries happen to choose the same words for the related concepts; otherwise, poor retrieval results are unavoidable. A common technique for handling the vocabulary differences in practical databases is to use subject categories to index the content of texts. For surface-based matching methods, however, the problem of text categorization is not any easier than the problem of text retrieval, because the vocabulary gap between free texts and indexing categories may be even larger than the vocabulary gaps among the texts themselves. Manual assignment remains the dominant method of text categorization in practical databases. MEDLINE, for example, the world's largest and most frequently used on-line bibliographic database, spends over two million dollars per year for the manual categorization of about 350,000 new entries [1]. There is thus a strong motivation for automatic or semi-automatic text categorization.

It has been recognized that human knowledge is crucial for solving the vocabulary gap problem. The human knowledge can be either invoked from predefined terminology thesauri, or automatically learned from training samples where the related texts of different vocabularies are assigned by humans. A well-observed problem with thesaurus-based matching is that general-purpose thesauri often do not have sufficient vocabulary coverage crossing different applications. Furthermore, subjective decisions in thesaurus development often do not reflect the context sensitivity of word meanings and the application dependent relationship between words. As a result, no reliable improvements have been observed by using general-purpose thesauri compared to surface-based matching [2] [3] [4] [5]. In contrast to relying on human developed thesauri, learning the mapping between different vocabularies from training samples ("example-based matching") has the potential advantage to objectively reflect the application dependent features of word usage. Example-based matching methods include the relevance feedback approach [6], the Darmstadt Indexing Approach (DIA) [7], the Linear Least Squares Fit (LLSF) mapping [3][8], Bayesian belief networks [9] [10], and neural networks [11].

Relevance feedback has the user indicate texts related to a query in an initial retrieval based on surface matching. It then adds the words in the related texts to the query in order to reduce the vocabulary gap between the query and the texts which are not retrieved by the initial query. Relevance feedback has shown significant improvement over surface-based matching and thesaurus-based matching in many cases of text retrieval. However, the limitation is that it requires relevance information for each query, and cannot use the information for predicting the answers to different queries. Such a restriction makes relevance feedback only rarely applicable to text categorization. For example, most documents (abstracts of articles including titles) in a bibliographic database differ from each other, so documents previously categorized by humans cannot be useful for relevance feedback in the categorization of new ones.

The DIA system probabilistically learns term-descriptor associations from manually indexed documents, where "term" means a word or phrase in a document, and "descriptors" are predefined indexing units in the DIA dictionary. DIA uses a technique known as "the least squares polynomial" (LSP) to obtain the term-descriptor associations. The LLSF mapping method is similar to the DIA/LSP approach, in the sense that it also learns from manual assignments of text categorization, and uses a least squares fit technique. A common feature of DIA/LSP and LLSF is that both allow training documents and testing documents to be different, so previously indexed documents can be used to index new documents. A major difference between LSP and LLSF is the context-sensitivity of the mapping. The term-descriptor associations in LSP are computed based on the occurrences of term/descriptor pairs in the training sample. The word-category associations in LLSF are computed based on the occurrences of word-combination/category-combination pairs. The LLSF mapping learned this way is therefore context-sensitive. Further discussions regarding this aspect can be found in a previous paper [12]. While the difference between LSP and LLSF in text categorization is rather subtle, the difference in text retrieval is more fundamental. LSP determines the relevance between a query and a document based on the shared terms, and ignores the non-shared terms. That is, it uses relevance judgements by humans to weight shared terms, not to connect the non-shared terms which are conceptually related. LLSF, on the other hand, uses the relevance judgements to establish connections between the query vocabulary and the document vocabulary (either free words or indexing categories), so the information within non-shared words are also effectively used in the retrieval. In our evaluations of text retrieval, LLSF has shown a performance comparable to relevance feedback, and significant improvements over surface-based matching and thesaurus-based matching [8]. In the evaluations of text categorization (where relevance feedback is not applicable), LLSF has significantly outperformed surface-based matching and thesaurus-based matching [3] [8] [13]. The current problem with LLSF is the cubic time complexity of training, which makes it expensive to apply this method to very large data collections.

Bayesian belief networks and neural networks have also been studied for incorporating human assessments in solving the vocabulary differences. Haines and Croft [9] implemented relevance feedback on simplified inference networks for text retrieval; Tzeras and Hartmann [10] proposed a Bayesian belief network approach to text categorization. The Haines approach inherits the limitation of relevance feedback, i.e. human assessment must be given for every query, and predicting answers for different queries is impossible. Tzeras' evaluation showed a less effective performance of the belief network than the LSP approach, while the computation cost was far higher than LSP. Wong and Cai proposed a neural network [11] for learning term associations, and demonstrated its use on a small retrieval data set (32 queries in the training set, 4 queries in the testing set, and 82 documents in total). The effectiveness of this method on larger text collections is not yet clear, and the intensive computation remains a potential problem when adopting it to real world applications.

Next we will introduce a new example-based approach to text categorization and retrieval, the Expert Network. This method is as effective as the LLSF mapping, and has a time complexity of $O(N \log N)$, far more efficient than LLSF, Bayesian belief networks and neural networks.

2 Method

ExpNet can be applied to either text categorization or text retrieval. We will first describe the model for text categorization, and then introduce its use in text retrieval by an extension. The task of text categorization is to assign the related categories to texts based on their contents. Our strategy is to automatically learn the text-to-category mapping from human assignments. Texts categorized by experts are undoubtedly a rich resource for learning, and such training data are available in most databases. While obtaining the training data is not difficult, the crucial question is how to use a finite training set to predict the categories of arbitrary texts. A text requiring categorization may be different from the

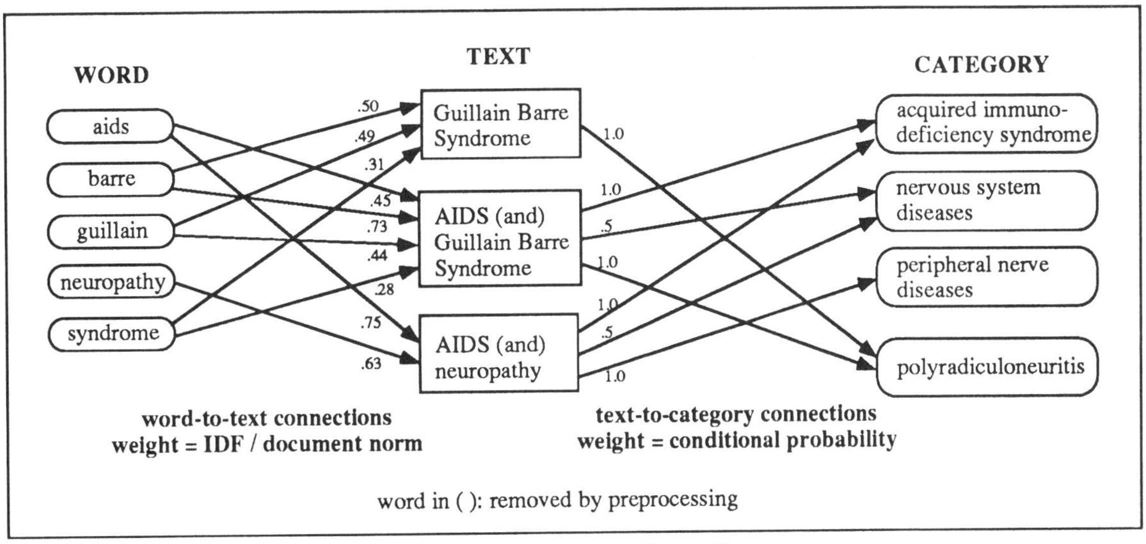

Figure 1. An example of the Expert Network

available training texts, so we must find a way to predict the categories of a new text from the partially matched training texts. For convenience, we will call the text requiring categorization "the request", and a training text "a document" if no specification is given. A request or a document is treated as a set of weighted words in our model.

The Expert Network provides empirical linkages between free words and categories via training documents. Figure 1 shows a simple example of ExpNet. The network consists of three levels of nodes. The input nodes are the unique words in the training documents. The nodes in the intermediate level are the training documents. The output nodes are the categories of the training documents. A word node and a document node are connected if the word occurs in the document. Similarly, a document node and a category node are connected if the category is assigned to the document by humans. These connections facilitate the relevance ranking of categories given an arbitrary request, as described in the following sections.

2.1 Category Ranking via ExpNet

The category ranking of ExpNet consists of two steps. The first step is to measure the similarities between a request and training documents. The second step is to rank the categories based on the similarity scores of the documents, and the conditional probabilities of categories given a document.

We use the conventional similarity measurement, that is, the cosine value of the vectorized request and document, defined as:

$$sim(X, D_j) \stackrel{\text{def}}{=} \frac{\sum_{t_i \in (X \cap D_j)} x_i \times d_{ij}}{||X||_2 \times ||D_j||_2} \tag{1}$$

where

X is a request; D_j is a document; t_i is a word shared by X and D_j;

x_i is the weight of word t_i in request X; d_{ij} is the weight of word t_i in document D_j;

$||X||_2 = \sqrt{x_1^2 + x_2^2 + x_3^2 + \ldots}$ is the norm of X;

$||D_j||_2 = \sqrt{d_{1j}^2 + d_{2j}^2 + d_{3j}^2 + \ldots}$ is the norm of D_j.

For word weighting, we adopted the commonly used schemes as options, including binary weights, term frequency (TF), Inverse Document Frequency (IDF), and the combination TF×IDF [14]. The first layer of ExpNet is constructed for the similarity computation. The weight of the link from word t_i $(i = 1, 2, \ldots, m)$ to document D_j $(j = 1, 2 \ldots, n)$ is set to the normalized weight $\frac{d_{ij}}{||D_j||_2}$. When a request is sent to ExpNet, the word weights (also normalized) in the request are passed through the input nodes, multiplied by the weights of word-to-document links and summed at the document nodes. Such a computation results in a similarity score of each document as specified in Formula (1).

The second step is the novel part of the method. The idea is to estimate the likelihood suggested by each of the training documents and then integrate the local estimates. We define $P_r(c_k|D_j)$ as the conditional probability of category c_k being related to document D_j by human judgement. Given a training sample of categorized documents, the conditional probability can be estimated as

$$P_r(c_k|D_j) \approx \frac{\text{number of times category } c_k \text{ is assigned to document } D_j}{\text{number of times document } D_j \text{ occurs in the training sample}} \tag{2}$$

where $D_1, \ldots, D_n$ are unique training documents, and $C_1, \ldots, C_l$ are unique categories. Note that a document may have more than one occurrence in the training sample. Diagnoses in patient records, for example, often repeat. Abstracts of articles, as another example, are unlikely to repeat in a bibliographic database; however, some may become identical if an aggressive "stoplist" is applied in a preprocessing to remove unimportant or redundant words. Consequently, the number of times a category assigned to a document may also be more than one.

Given a request X, the relevance score of each category is estimated as the weighted sum of the conditional probabilities,

$$rel(c_k|X) \approx \sum_{j=1}^{n} sim(X, D_j) \times P_r(c_k|D_j) \tag{3}$$

Note that $sim(X, D_j)$ is a cosine value, not a probability. Consequently, $rel(c_k|X)$ is not the probability of category c_k being related to request X. Nevertheless, the relevance scores have the functionality of ranking documents similar to what the probabilities would do. The second layer of ExpNet is constructed for computing the relevance scores. The weight of the link from document D_j to category c_k is set to the conditional probability $P_r(c_k|D_j)$. Before the computation, the default score of each category is set to zero. After the similarity values of documents are computed in the first layer of ExpNet, they are propagated to the second layer, multiplied by the weights of the document-to-category links, and summed at the category nodes. This results in a relevance score of each category as specified in Formula (3).

2.2 Optimization of Category Ranking

While using a weighted sum of the conditional probabilities in category ranking is a reasonable idea, further questions can be raised regarding optimal integration. For example, should we count the contributions from all the documents in the relevance ranking? Or should we just count a few top-ranking documents and ignore the remaining ones? Would a threshold setting for document cutoff optimize the category ranking?

To answer these questions, we tested the effect of document cutoff on the category ranking. That is, we sorted the training documents according to their similarity values, and took only n' ($n' \leq n$) top-ranking documents into account in the relevance estimation. Formula (3) is therefore modified as below,

$$rel(c_k|X) \approx \sum_{D_j \in \{n' \text{ top-ranking documents}\}} sim(X, D_j) \times P_r(c_k|D_j) \tag{4}$$

We used MEDLINE documents for the tests, including 586 training documents and 1758 testing documents (refer to Section 3 for details). There is no overlap between the training set and the testing set. For each of the cutoff thresholds n' = 1, 5, 10, 20, 30, ..., 586 (no cutoff at all), we computed a 10-point average precision. That is, we computed the precision values at recalls of 10%, 20%, ..., 100% and averaged them for a global measure. Figure 2(a) shows the testing results. The interesting points are:

(1) the poorest result (12.6%) occurred when $n' = 1$, i.e. only the top-ranking document was selected;

(2) the best result (34.1%) occurred when $n' = 30$, i.e. the 30 top-ranking documents were selected;

(3) for $n' > 30$, the performance slowly decreased and converged to the level of no cutoff ($n' = 586$).

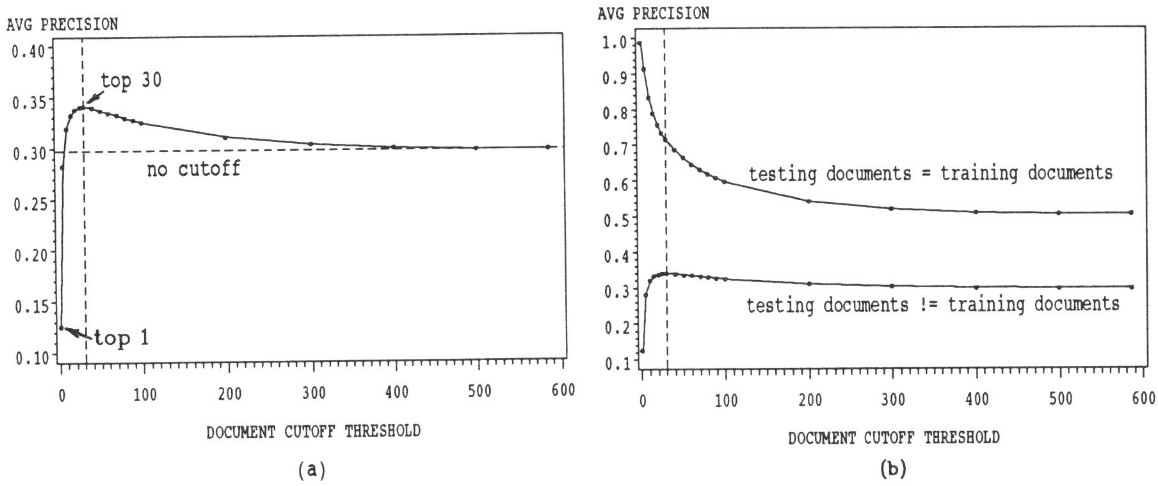

Figure 2. The effect of document cutoff in text categorization.

Our analyses based on the observations are:

(1) The poor result of selecting only the top-ranking document is not surprising. Given that a request and the top-ranking document are partially matched, it is reasonable to assume that they would have some categories in common, but it is misleading to assume that they have exactly the same categories in all cases.

(2) The category ranking based on a few top-ranking documents is relatively reliable, because the categories of these documents, especially the shared categories among them, are informative about the contents of the request.

(3) After a certain point, counting more documents with lower similarity values only contributes noise.

Note that the condition of the above test is that the training documents and the testing documents are different. This is typically true in bibliographic databases where documents are unlikely to be identical to each other. However, in some other applications such as diagnoses or procedure reports in patient records, the texts are relatively short and often repeatedly used. The commonly used texts are likely to occur in a training set. Does the above analysis still hold? To answer this question, we tested a case where every request was included in the training set, that is, we used the MEDLINE training documents as the testing set. Figure 2(b) compares the results of this test and the previous test. The effect of document cutoff in this test is obviously different:

(1) The best result (98.7%) occurred when $n' = 1$, i.e. only the top-ranking document was selected;

(2) for $n' > 1$, the performance monotonically decreased and converged to the level of no cutoff.

This test indicates that when a training document is found to be exactly the same as the request, it is often not helpful to further refer to other training documents which are partially matched. However, the testing condition is rather extreme, where every request is covered by the training set. In reality, a mixture of requests is more likely, that is, some requests are covered by the training set and some are not. For such a situation, a multiple threshold setting would be reasonable:

(1) set the threshold to 1, if the maximal similarity score of the training documents is 1;

(2) set the threshold to constant n' ($n' \leq n$) otherwise.

We are not going to include further details of the optimization. The point is, the optimal threshold(s) can be empirically determined, based on the statistical features of applications.

3 Evaluation

The MEDLINE documents mentioned in Section 2.2 are used for the evaluation. The data set was originally designed for an evaluation of MEDLINE retrieval [15] and has been used for evaluations of other retrieval and categorization systems [5] [8] [12] [13]. The categories of the documents are assigned by MEDLINE indexers. There are about 168 words and 17 categories per document on average. We arbitrarily split the documents (2344) into a training set (586 documents) and a testing set (1758 documents). There are no duplicates in the entire collection, and consequently, no overlap between the training documents and testing documents. The training set contains 7813 unique words and 1832 unique categories. The testing set contains 14339 unique words and 3430 unique categories; about 42% of these words and 46% of the categories are covered by the training set. The total number of unique categories including the training set and the testing set is 4020. So the chance of a random assignment being correct is $\frac{17}{4020}$ or 0.4%.

A preprocessing was applied to the documents for the removal of punctuation, numbers and the non-informative words on a stoplist, and for changing uppercase letters to lowercase; no stemming was applied. For weighting the links of ExpNet, we tested the word weighting options including binary weights, TF (Term Frequency), IDF (Inverse Document Frequency), and the combination TF×IDF. We will refer to the result of the optimal weighting (using IDF) in the comparison of ExpNet with other methods. The document cutoff threshold of ExpNet was set to 30.

We tested the following methods on the MEDLINE testing set for comparison.

(1) **LLSF** is an example-based categorization/retrieval method described in Section 1. It is theoretically different from ExpNet; however, it uses the same training data as ExpNet.

(2) **STR** (STRing matching) is our implementation of word-based matching in which documents and category descriptions are represented using vectors, and words are represented using binary weights. The relevance score of a category with respect to a document is the cosine value of the vectorized document and category description. We use STR to test the effectiveness of basic word-based matching in text categorization.

(3) **SMART**, developed by Salton's group [2], is one of the most representative retrieval systems. We use SMART to test the effectiveness of retrieval techniques in text categorization. The documents and categories are represented using vectors in the same way as in STR, except the binary word weighting is replaced by the statistical word weighting schemes of SMART. We ran the SMART system for category ranking based on the cosine-similarity between documents and category descriptions. The default parameter setting of SMART was used, and word weighting options TF and TF×IDF were tested. We observed a better result of using TF×IDF than using TF, and will refer to the better result in the comparison of SMART with other methods. Relevance feedback of SMART is not applicable to this test because the training documents and the testing documents are different.

(4) **RFW** ("relevance forward") is our modification of relevance feedback, in order to make it possible to use the training data. Recall that relevance feedback adds words in the related documents of each query to the query. RFW takes a symmetric approach of adding words in the training documents to the descriptions of the related categories. We ran the SMART system for relevance ranking of the expanded categories with respect to the testing documents. We observed that using TF weights had a better result than using TF×IDF, and will refer to the better result in the comparison of different methods.

Figure 3 (a) compares the recall-precision curves of ExpNet and the alternative methods. Figure 3 (b) shows the 10-point average precisions. STR had an average precision of 10.0%. SMART had better performance (16.3%) than STR, indicating the advantage of its statistical word weighting over the binary weighting of STR. RFW had a significant improvement over SMART, showing the benefit of employing human experience in text categorization. ExpNet and LLSF had superior performance over RFW, giving evidence of better ways of using human experience. Instead of simply adding document words to category descriptions as RFW did, ExpNet and LLSF used the statistical information in the training sample to optimize the category ranking; this made the difference. By setting SMART as the base of the comparison, the relative improvements are 114.4% for ExpNet, 113.8% for LLSF, 49.0% for RFW, and -32.8% for STR.

It is interesting to see the very close performance of ExpNet and LLSF, as their results differ only by 0.1% in precision on average. Although they are theoretically and mathematically different methods, the testing results show that both made effective use of the statistical information in the training sample. We

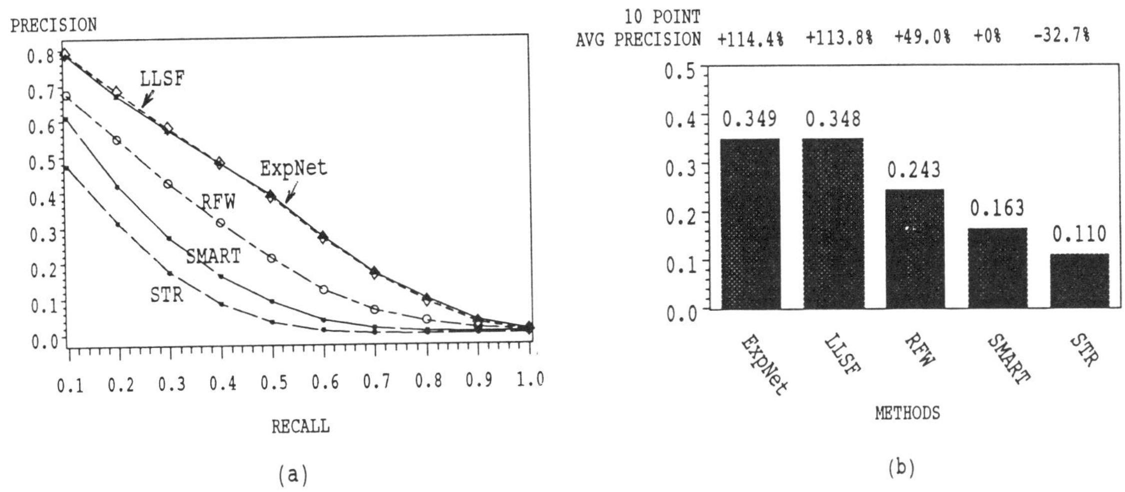

Figure 3. The results of different methods in text categorization of MEDLINE documents.

have tested ExpNet and LLSF in categorization of another text collection which includes 6134 surgical procedures from Mayo patient records [12]. The results were 87.6% for ExpNet and 88.6% for LLSF in the 10-point average precision. The point is, no significant difference between ExpNet and LLSF has been observed in their categorization effectiveness.

4 Computational Complexity

A major attraction of ExpNet is its computational efficiency. ExpNet does not require complex learning or intensive computation. The "learning" of ExpNet is simply the computations of within-document word weights (Section 2.1) and the conditional probabilities of categories (Section 2.2). These computations are based on counting word occurrences and category occurrences in a training set, so the time is proportional to the number of documents, assuming that the average numbers of words and categories per document are constant. In the big-O notation, the time complexity is $O(n)$, where n is the number of training documents. In the construction of ExpNet, we also sort the input nodes (the words) in alphabetical order. The sorting time is $O(m \log m)$ when using a Quick Sort algorithm, where m is the number of unique words in the training set. Together, the time for constructing ExpNet is $O(n) + O(m \log m)$.

Another aspect of the computation is the time for category ranking using ExpNet. For a given query, the category ranking consists of the computations of weighted sums in layers 1 and 2 of the network. The time complexity is $O(N \log N)$, where $N = \max(m, n, l)$, and l is the number of unique categories. This analysis can be explicitly seen in the following algorithm.

initiate the similarity score of documents, $sim(D_j) := 0$ *for* $j = 1, \ldots, n$;

initiate the relevance score of categories, $rel(c_k) := 0$ *for* $k = 1, \ldots, l$;

foreach *word in the request* **do** { # $O(\log m) + O(\frac{n}{m})$

find the corresponding node t_i *for the request word using a binary search;* # $O(\log m)$

foreach *link from node* t_i *to document node* D_j # $O(\frac{n}{m})$

update the similarity score $sim(D_j) = sim(D_j) + \frac{x_i}{\|X\|_2} \times \frac{d_{ij}}{\|D_j\|_2}$;

};

sort $\{D_1, D_2, \ldots, D_n\}$ *by the similarity scores and select the* n' *top-ranking documents;*

$O(n \log n)$

foreach *link from document* D_j *in the* n' *top-ranking documents* # $O(\frac{n}{l})$

update the relevance score $rel(c_k) = rel(c_k) + sim(D_j) \times Pr(c_k|D_j)$;

sort $\{C_1, C_2, \ldots, C_l\}$ *by the relevance scores;* # $O(l \log l)$

The computation time of each step in the above algorithm is indicated after the # sign. In line 4, for example, the binary search through a sorted list of m input nodes takes $O(\log m)$ time. In lines 5-6, the computation of the inner **foreach** loop is proportional to the average number of links per word, which is equal to the average number of unique training documents that contain the word. Let constant k_w be the average number of words per document, then the average occurrences per word is approximately $\frac{k_w \times n}{m}$. Consequently, the upper bound of the average links per word is $O(\frac{n}{m})$. In the outer **foreach** loop of lines 3-6, the time is the product of the number of request words and the time of the inner steps. Since we assume the average number of words per request is constant, the time of the outer loop is $O(\log m) + O(\frac{n}{m})$. The sorting in line 8 takes $O(n \log n)$ time. The computations of the rest of the lines can be estimated in a similar way. To summarize, the time of the category ranking of ExpNet is $O(\log m) + O(n \log n) + O(l \log l) = O(N \log N)$, assuming $O(\log m) \leq O(N \log N)$.

In Section 3, we have shown that ExpNet and LLSF are equally effective in text categorization. From the computational point of view, however, the difference between these two methods is rather significant. Our current implementation of LLSF uses the LINPACK algorithm for singular value decomposition, which requires roughly $O(N^3)$ time [8] (our on-going research shows that the cubic time complexity can be reduced to quadratic). So the training time of LLSF is $O(N^3)$. The categorization time of LLSF is $O(N \log N)$. In our experiments on the training set of 586 MEDLINE documents (containing 7813 unique words and 1832 unique categories), the training of LLSF took 2.25 hours of CPU time on a SUN SPARCstation 10, while the training (network construction) of ExpNet took only 16 seconds. The categorization was 5 seconds per document by LLSF and 0.4 seconds per document by ExpNet. Note that the $O(N \log N)$ time is a necessary cost for any algorithm which requires relative ranking of categories or documents. Hence, ExpNet is optimal.

5 Extension for Text Retrieval

The ExpNet model for text categorization can be easily extended for text retrieval by adding two layers of nodes and links on the network. Figure 4 illustrates such an extension.

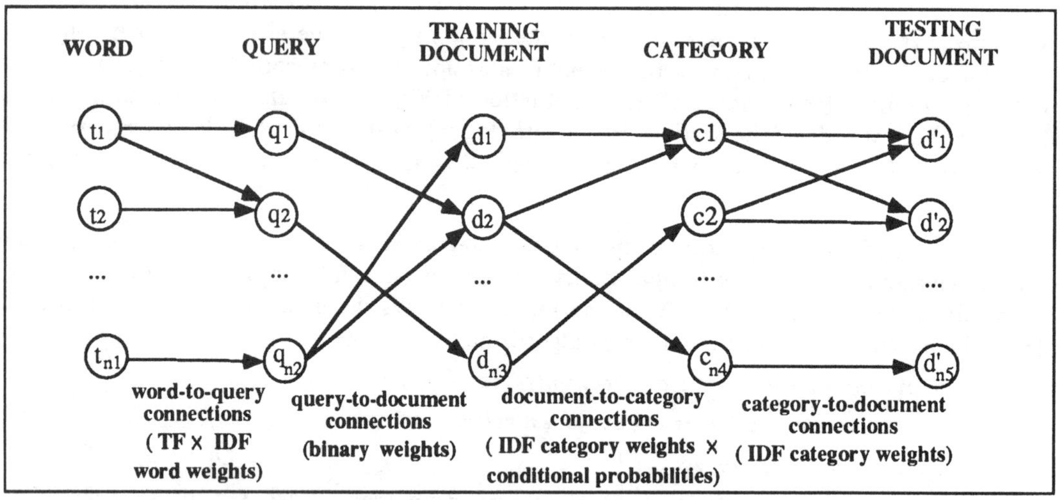

Figure 4. The Expert Network for document retrieval.

The input nodes of the extended ExpNet are the unique words in training queries. The second column of nodes are the training queries. The third and fourth columns are the training documents and their categories, which are the same as in the categorization model. The output nodes are the testing documents which may or may not overlap with the training documents. The first layer of links relates words to training queries, using normalized within-query word weights. The second layer relates training queries to training documents according to human judgements in retrieval. A query-to-document link is established if and only if the document is assigned by humans to the query as being related; all the links have an equal weight of 1. The third layer relates training documents to training categories; the weight of a document-to-category link is the product of the IDF category weight [8] and the conditional

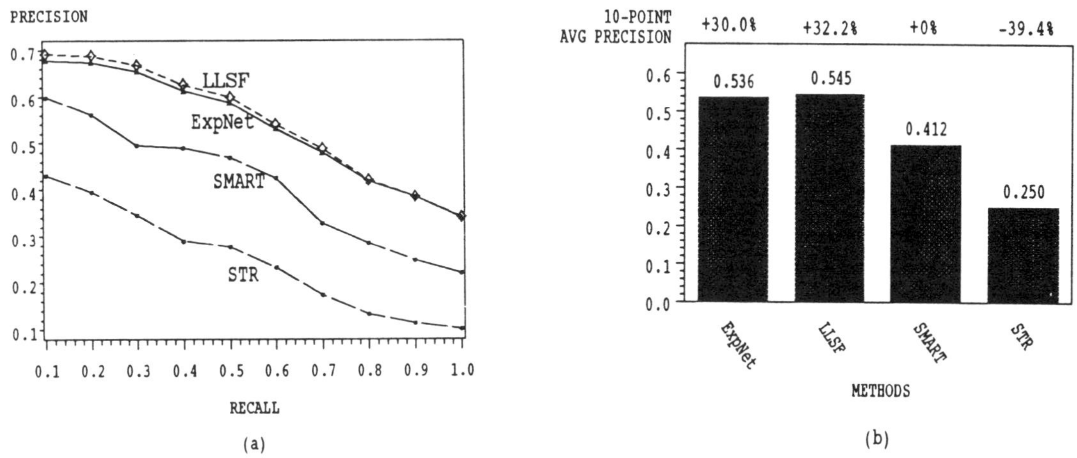

Figure 5. The results of different methods in retrieval of MEDLINE documents.

probability of the category given the document. The fourth layer connects the categories to the testing documents according to human judgements in categorization. A category-to-document link is established if and only if the category is assigned to the document by humans, and is weighted using the IDF value of the category. Such an ExpNet facilitates the relevance ranking of testing documents with respect to an arbitrary query.

We tested the ExpNet retrieval model on the same set of MEDLINE documents which we used in the categorization evaluation. In addition, we used the retrieval queries (75) and the query-document relevance judgements which were available with the documents. We split the data into a training set and a testing set; 88% of the testing queries were covered by the training queries, and none of the testing documents are covered by the training documents. We omit the details of the data set construction due to the space limit of this paper; more description can be found in previous papers [8][12]. Figure 5 shows the retrieval results of ExpNet in comparison with the alternative retrieval methods. ExpNet was only 0.9% less than LLSF in average precision, and significantly outperformed the alternative methods.

6 Discussion

To summarize this paper, a major problem in text categorization and text retrieval is the vocabulary differences between documents and categories, or between user queries and documents. ExpNet, with the capability of learning from human experiences, effectively solves the vocabulary difference problem with a low computation cost. The power of ExpNet comes from the utilization of human judgements about text categorization. The human assignments provide empirical linkages between free vocabularies of documents and a controlled vocabulary of categories. These linkages make ExpNet more effective than word-based matching methods. Furthermore, using categories as semantic units in representing document content is presumably less noisy than using arbitrary words. This would be another reason for the superior performance of ExpNet over word-based matching in document retrieval.

Another characteristic of ExpNet is its use of lexical similarity. In word-based matching, lexical similarity between a query and a document, or a document and a category, is used as the criteria of relevance judgement. In contrast, ExpNet uses lexical similarity for allocating a request in a "neighborhood" of training texts which offer human assigned connections to the target space (categories or documents). In other words, the lexical similarity is used for relating requests to available human knowledge about training texts, and for integrating local relevance estimates into a global measure. Such a use of lexical similarity makes the relevance ranking of ExpNet much simpler than other methods using probabilistic relevance ranking. In Bayesian belief networks, for example, the conditional probabilities for all potential word permutations require an exponential time and space complexity, and independence assumptions therefore have to be made to avoid the intensive computation, i.e. trading context sensitivity for tractability. ExpNet, on the other hand, does not assume word independence in computing the conditional probabilities.

In conclusion, the simplicity of the model, the effective use of human knowledge, and the optimal computational efficiency together make ExpNet a preferable solution for categorization and retrieval of natural language texts. Exploring the capacity of this approach in very large databases and potential limitations remain the focus of our further research.

Acknowledgement

I would like to thank Dr. Kent Bailey for fruitful discussions, and my colleagues in the Natural Language Processing Group at the Section of Medical Information Resources, Mayo Clinic, for help with this project. This work is supported in part by NIH Research Grant LM-05416 to Mayo Clinic, and National Library of Medicine Training Grant LM-07041 in Medical Informatics to the University of Minnesota.

References

1. Hersh WR, Haynes RB. Evaluation of SAPHIRE: an automated approach to indexing and retrieving medical literature. *Proc 15th Ann Symp Comp Applic Med Care* 1991; 15:808–812

2. Salton G. Development in Automatic Text Retrieval. *Science* 1991; 253:974-980

3. Yang Y, Chute CG. A Linear Least Squares Fit mapping method for information retrieval from natural language texts. *Proc 14th International Conference on Computational Linguistics (COLING 92)* 1992; 447–453

4. Harman D. Overview of the first TREC Conference. *Proc 16th Ann Int ACM SIGIR Conference on Research and Development in Information Retrieval* 1993; 36-47

5. Hersh WR, Hickam DH, Leone TJ. Words, concepts, or both: optimal indexing units for automated information retrieval. *Proc 16th Ann Symp Comp Applic Med Care* 1992; 16:644–648

6. Salton G, Buckley C. Improving retrieval performance by relevance feedback. *J Amer Soc Inf Sci* 1990; 41(4): 288–297

7. Fuhr N, Hartmann S, Lustig G, et al. AIR/X - a rule-based multistage indexing systems for large subject fields. *Proceedings of the RIAO'91* 1991; 606-623

8. Yang Y, Chute CG. An application of Least Squares Fit Mapping to text information retrieval. *Proc 16th Ann Int ACM SIGIR Conference on Research and Development in Information Retrieval* 1993; 281-290

9. Haines D., Croft B. Relevance Feedback and inference networks. *Proc 16th Ann Int ACM SIGIR Conference on Research and Development in Information Retrieval* 1993; 2-11

10. Tzeras K, Hartmann S. Automatic indexing based on Bayesian inference networks. *Proc 16th Ann Int ACM SIGIR Conference on Research and Development in Information Retrieval* 1993; 22-34

11. Wong SKM, Cai YJ. Computation of term associations by a neural network. *Proc 16th Ann Int ACM SIGIR Conference on Research and Development in Information Retrieval* 1993; 107-115

12. Yang Y, Chute CG. An example-based mapping method for text categorization and retrieval. ACM Transaction on Information Systems 1994; in press

13. Yang Y, Chute CG. Words or Concepts: the Features of Indexing Units and their Optimal Use in Information Retrieval. *Proc 17th Ann Symp Comp Applic Med Care* 1993; 17:685–689

14. Salton G. *Automatic Text Processing: The Transformation, Analysis, and Retrieval of Information by Computer.* Addison-Wesley, Reading, Pennsylvania, 1989

15. Haynes R, McKibbon K, Walker C, Ryan N, Fitzgerald D, Ramsden M. Online access to MEDLINE in clinical settings. *Ann. Int. Med.* 1990; 112:78–84

Towards Language Independent Automated Learning of Text Categorization Models

Chidanand Apté
IBM Research Division
T.J. Watson Research Center
Yorktown Heights, NY 10598
apte@watson.ibm.com

Fred Damerau
IBM Research Division
T.J. Watson Research Center
Yorktown Heights, NY 10598
damerau@watson.ibm.com

Sholom M. Weiss
Rutgers University
Dept. of Computer Science
New Brunswick, NJ 08903
weiss@cs.rutgers.edu

Abstract

We describe the results of extensive machine learning experiments on large collections of Reuters' English and German newswires. The goal of these experiments was to automatically discover classification patterns that can be used for assignment of topics to the individual newswires. Our results with the English newswire collection show a very large gain in performance as compared to published benchmarks, while our initial results with the German newswires appear very promising. We present our methodology, which seems to be insensitive to the language of the document collections, and discuss issues related to the differences in results that we have obtained for the two collections.

1 Introduction

In many carefully organized text storage and retrieval systems, texts are classified with one or more codes chosen from a classification system. Examples include the NTIS (National Technical Information Service) documents from the US government, news services like UPI and Reuters, publications like the ACM Computing Reviews and many others. Assigning subject classification codes manually to documents is time consuming and expensive. Recent work has shown that in certain environments, knowledge based systems can do code assignment quickly and accurately [Hayes and Weinstein, 1991, Hayes *et al.*, 1990]. Human-engineered rule-based models for assigning subject codes, while relatively effective, are also very expensive in time and effort for their development and continued support. Machine learning methods provide an interesting alternative for automating the rule construction process. This report presents results on experiments to derive the assignment rules automatically from samples of the text to be classified.

A well known example of a knowledge-based system for the classification task is the CONSTRUE system [Hayes *et al.*, 1990] used by the Reuters news service. This is a rule based expert system using manually constructed rules to assign subject categories to news stories, with a reported recall and precision of over 90% on 750 test cases [Hayes and Weinstein, 1991]. While these are exceptionally good results, the test set seems to have been relatively sparse when compared to the number of possible topics. An example of a machine learning system for the same task is a system based on Memory Based Reasoning [Masand *et al.*, 1992], which employs nearest neighbor style classification and has a reported accuracy in the range of 70-80% on Dow Jones news stories.

In considering the problem of categorizing documents, the rule based approach has considerable appeal. While weighted solutions such as the linear probabilistic methods used in [Lewis, 1992b] or nearest-neighbor methods may also prove reasonable, the models they employ are not explicitly interpretable. Since human-engineered systems have been successfully constructed using rule-based solutions, it would be most useful to continue with a model that is compatible with human-expressed knowledge. Because of the parsimonious and interpretable nature of decision rules, we can readily augment our knowledge or verify the rules by examining related categorized documents.

We report here results that we have obtained with using a rule based machine learning approach on two large collections of Reuters' newswires, in English and German. The collections are essentially streams of stories, numbering in the tens of thousands. Each story has associated with it a headline, a date, one or more topics (that have been assigned by Reuters staff), and various fragments of information mainly used for book-keeping purposes. The goal is to have the computer system induce pattern directed rules that can be used for automatically assigning the topics. Amongst our more interesting observations was the fact that our methodology seems to perform almost equally well for both the English and the German collection, suggesting that our approach may be insensitive to language issues, thereby making it a more versatile and portable technique for document classification.

2 Automated Learning of Topic Assignment Models

Machine learning systems solve problems by examining samples described in terms of measurements or features. For machine learning methods to be applicable, the samples of documents must be transformed into this type of representation. For text categorization, an adaptation of a machine learning method must implement the following main processes:

- A preprocessing step for determining the values of the features or attributes that will used for representing the individual documents within a collection. This is essentially the *dictionary* creation process.
- A representation step for mapping each individual document into a *training sample* using the above dictionary, and associating it with a *label* that identifies its category.
- An induction step for finding patterns that distinguish categories from one another.
- An evaluation step for choosing the *best* solution, based on minimizing the classification error or cost.

The initial task is to produce a list of attributes from samples of text of labeled documents, i.e., the dictionary. The attributes are single words or word phrases. Given an attribute list, sample cases can be described in terms of the words or phrases found in the documents. Each case consists of the values of the attributes for a single article, where the values could be either boolean, i.e., indicating whether the attribute appears in the text or does not, or numerical, i.e., frequency of occurrence in the text being processed. In addition, each case is labeled to indicate the classification or topic of the article it represents.

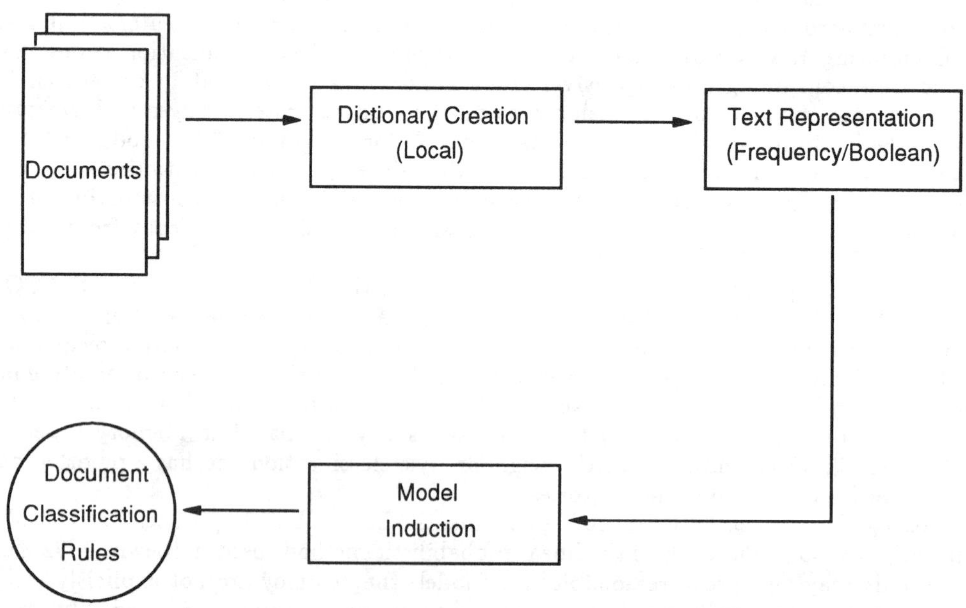

Figure 1: Machine Learning Architecture for Document Classification

For rule induction, the objective is to find sets of decision rules that distinguish one category of text from the others. The best rule set is selected, where "best" is a rule set that is both accurate and not excessively complex. Accuracy of rule sets can be effectively measured on large numbers of independent test cases. Complexity can be measured in terms of numbers of rules or rule components, where smaller rule sets that are reasonably close to the best accuracy are sometimes preferred to more complex rules sets with slightly greater accuracy.

Figure 1 illustrates our strategy. Here a *local* dictionary is created for each classification topic. Only single words found in documents on the given topic are entered in the local dictionary. For each local dictionary, the n most frequently occurring words are used as features. In addition, instead of boolean features, frequency counts of the occurrence of words in a story, or more complicated frequency related measures, can be used.

Research on machine learning from text suggests that the simpler dictionaries of single words give the best performance. This does *not* mean that the best solution ignores phrases and combinations of words. Clearly these combinations are important to understanding text. Rather, the burden is shifted from a preprocessing program that composes a dictionary to a learning program that finds a solution. Thus these research results mostly suggest that it is very difficult to find the right combinations of words independent of the ultimate decision model. The implication of this analysis is that performance can be increased by improved learning methods. These methods should potentially find higher order relationships in the feature space i.e. the dictionary words.

One of the main distinguishing characteristics of our approach is that we will use a rule induction model for our representation. An example of these rules is illustrated in Table 1. Here the problem is posed as a two class problem. If any of these rules is satisfied, the story is classified as "football". Otherwise, the decision reverts to the default class of a "non-football" article. Most applications of text classification involve classes that are not exclusive, and one or more of the categories can occur simultaneously. Thus most problems are handled as multiple two-class problems.

Rule	Class
running back	football article
kicker	football article
injure reserve	football article
award & player	football article

Table 1: Example of an Induced Rule Set

Rule and tree induction methods have been extensively described in published works [Breiman *et al.*, 1984, Weiss and Kulikowski, 1991, Quinlan, 1993]. For our document indexing system, we have used a rule induction technique called Swap-1 [Weiss and Indurkhya, 1993]. Rule induction methods attempt to find a compact "covering" rule set that completely partitions the examples into their correct classes. The covering set is found by heuristically searching for a single best rule that covers cases for only one class. Having found a best conjunctive rule for a class C, the rule is added to the rule set, and the cases satisfying it are removed from further consideration. The process is repeated until no cases remain to be covered. Unlike decision tree induction programs and other rule induction methods, Swap-1 has an advantage in that it uses optimization techniques to revise and improve its decisions. Once a covering set is found that separates the classes, the induced set of rules is further refined by either pruning or statistical techniques. Using train and test evaluation methods, the initial covering rule set is then scaled to back to the most statistically accurate subset of rules.

	TRAINING CASES	
	Football	Not Football
Football	151	10
Not Football	0	1081

	TEST CASES	
	Football	Not Football
Football	135	26
Not Football	12	1069

Table 2: Example of Estimated Performance for a Rule Set

For the document classification application, Swap-1 induces rules that represent patterns, i.e. combinations of attributes, that determine the most likely class for an article. The result of applying Swap-1 to a training set of cases is a set of rules and a table of the associated error rates on the training as well as test samples. The results for applying the rule set of Table 1 are illustrated in Table 2. A detailed discussion of Swap-1 and its use in our document classification experiments appears in [Apté *et al.*, 1993].

3 Results with English Reuters Newswires

To provide an objective basis for comparison of our results with others, particularly [Lewis, 1992a, Lewis, 1992b], we made an extensive number of runs using English Reuters[1] data. These are 21,450 news stories from 1987. All stories beyond April 7th were used as independent test cases, and the remaining data were the training cases. The data consists of 14,704 training cases and 6,746 test cases. There are 135 topics of interest, with 93 of these topics occurring more than once in the training data. Of these newswires, there are 7133 stories with "empty" topic assignments. We chose to ignore these stories, since we can neither learn from them or test on them. As a result, the raw data that we worked with had 10,645 training cases and 3,672 test cases. We derived our own dictionaries and attributes from the raw document training data and applied rule induction machine learning methods (Swap-1). For each experiment for a given topic, a random subset, corresponding to 33% of the training data, was reserved for error estimation. Each of the recursively pruned rule sets was evaluated on these randomly selected cases to help select the best rule set. Estimates on these cases were generally within 2% of the performance of the selected rule sets on the 3,672 independent test cases from after April 7th.

wheat & farm $\longrightarrow$ wheat
wheat & commodity $\longrightarrow$ wheat
bushels & export $\longrightarrow$ wheat
wheat & agriculture $\longrightarrow$ wheat
wheat & tonnes $\longrightarrow$ wheat
wheat & winter & $\neg$soft $\longrightarrow$ wheat

	Test Cases	
	wheat	not wheat
wheat	73	8
not wheat	14	3577

Table 3: Induced Rule Set and Performance on Test Data for Reuters' English "wheat" Category

Dictionaries were created two different ways. First was the approach using the local dictionary procedure, where the 150 most frequent words for the given topic were generated. A brief universal list of stopwords was maintained, and these words were removed from the most frequent 150 words. The second approach was to create a universal dictionary by counting all words in all documents in the training set, except for stop words. Depending on the topic, a variable number of features were derived by an entropy-based feature selection method. From a universal dictionary of approximately 10,000 features, the number of features selected for each category ranged between 30 and 200. For the text representation, we experimented with both frequency and boolean features.

Performance is measured by *recall* and *precision*. Recall is the percentage of total documents for the given topic that are correctly classified. Precision is the percentage of predicted documents for the given topic that are correctly classified. Because the document topics are not mutually exclusive, document classification problems are usually analyzed as a series of dichotomous classification problems, i.e the given topic vs. not that topic. For example, Table 3 illustrates the rule set that was induced for the *wheat* category for a local dictionary with a boolean representation for the text. Also included in the figure is the performance table of this rule set on the Reuters post-April-7-1987 test data. Given the rule evaluation table as in Table 3, one can measure performance using a wide variety of metrics, based on error rates or costs. For the purpose of this study, we have chosen the *microaverage* measure, as used in [Lewis and Ringuette, 1994]. To evaluate overall performance across the entire set of topics, the results are microaveraged, i.e. the performance tables for each of the topics, such as in Table 3, are added and the overall recall and precision are computed. The point at which recall equals precision is the *breakeven* point; it can be used as a single summarizing measure for comparison of results.

The breakeven point for each of the four combinations of dictionaries and features is illustrated in Table 4. In addition, the previously reported breakeven points of 67% for decision trees [Lewis and Ringuette, 1994] and 65% for a probabilistic method [Lewis, 1992a] are listed. If all text is treated uniformly, the breakeven point for the local dictionary with frequency features is 78.9%. However, the newswire stories contain a one line headline that can provide additional clues to the topic. If the words occurring in the headline are given additional emphasis, by counting them twice, instead of a uniform count for words in either the headline or body of an article, then performance for the local dictionary with frequency features is increased by almost 2%, to a breakeven point of 80.5%.

[1] The latter was obtained by anonymous ftp from /pub/doc/reuters1 on ftp.cs.umass.edu. Free distribution for research purposes has been granted by Reuters and Carnegie Group. Arrangements for access were made by David Lewis.

Learning Method	Dictionary	Text Representation	Performance Breakeven (%)
Optimized Rule Induction	Local	Frequency + Headlines	80.5
		Frequency	78.9
		Boolean	78.5
	Universal	Frequency	78.0
		Boolean	75.5
Decision Tree			67.0
Probabilistic Bayes			65.0

Table 4: Breakeven Points for Reuters' English Data

A breakeven point is a combined summary measure, but for text categorization both recall and precision may be of interest. Figure 2 illustrates the overall performance of the rule induction variations. To determine a breakeven point several learning experiments must be performed and some parameter must be varied to elicit the tradeoff of recall and precision. The appropriate technique may vary with the learning method. For rule induction, the traditional goal is to minimize the number of errors. However, this may not occur at the breakeven point. We used the standard approach of substituting costs for errors to vary the recall and precision. For a cost of one, each false negative is counted as one error[2], but for a cost of two, each false negative is counted as 2 errors. The effect of increasing the cost of false negatives is to increase the recall, at the expense of precision. In our experiments with the Reuters data, the breakeven point was achieved near a cost setting of three.

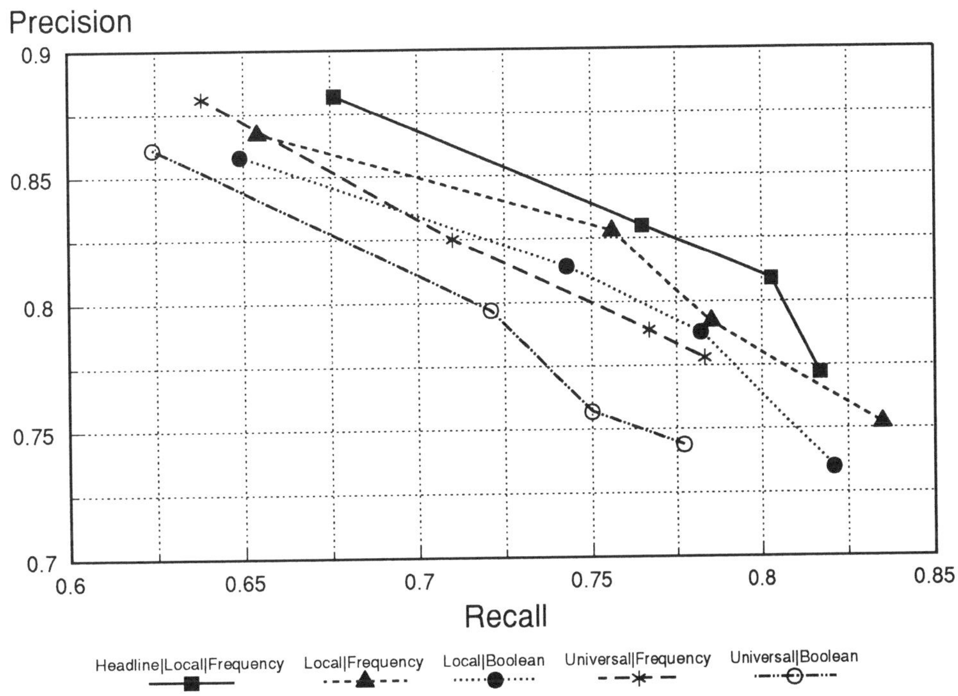

Figure 2: Recall/Precision Tradeoff for Reuters' English Data

4 Results with German Reuters Newswires

From the best results that we obtained with the English Reuters data, we observed the following salient features in our automated learning methodology:

- The usage of local dictionaries for each individual topic.
- A language independent match mechanism for determining the entries in the local dictionary.

[2]A cost of one is equivalent to the usual minimum error criterion.

- The usage of frequency of occurrence of local dictionary entries in the feature vector for representing the news stories.

- Weighting terms encountered in headlines of stories.

Given that our methodology does not rely on any language-specific technique, we hypothesized that it should perform similarly well on document collections in other languages. To provide an objective verification of this hypothesis, we have conducted detailed experiments with German Reuters[3] data. These are 8,367 news stories from 1993. All stories beyond July 1st are used as independent test cases, and the remaining data were the training cases. The data consist of 6,479 training cases and 1,888 test cases. There are 90 topics of interest.

sicherheitsrat(security council) $\longrightarrow$ G131
militaerische(military) $\longrightarrow$ G131
raketen(rockets) $\longrightarrow$ G131
bosnien(Bosnia) $\longrightarrow$ G131
nato $\longrightarrow$ G131
soldaten(soldiers) $\longrightarrow$ G131

	Test Cases	
	G131	not G131
G131	84	43
not G131	7	774

Table 5: Induced Rule Set and Performance on Test Data for Reuters' German "Defence" Category

Unlike the simple list of topics in the English Reuters collection, the topics for the German Reuters formed a taxonomy. There were 4 major topics, and two levels of hierarchies below the major level. At the leaf level of the hierarchy, we encountered very few stories per topic. The German Reuters topics were much broader than the ones we saw in the English Reuters. Our preliminary analysis suggested that there was much more variability in assigning topics to stories. For assigning topics from a taxonomy to a story, a complete assignment should include one or more topic from each level of the taxonomy for a story. However, analysis of our collection indicated that humans assigned fewer topics for a story than we deemed appropriate.

This poses a problem to a classification learning apparatus. Assuming that the system is attempting to learn a topic assignment model for a topic T, there will be in the training cases two sets of examples, the T set, that corresponds to all the newswires that had T as one of their topics, and the $\neg T$ set, that corresponds to all the newswires that did not have T as one of their topics. Given the disparity in topic assignment that we observed in the raw data, there will possibly be present in the $\neg T$ set, stories with topics that are either direct or indirect parents or children of T in the classification taxonomy. This will cause weakening of classification tests that otherwise would have been strong discriminators.

How can we modify our machine learning apparatus so that it can learn topic assignment models in the presence of this uncertainty? The training set that we prepare may be modified in either a simple or an extended fashion;

- simple: remove direct parents or children from the competition with their direct descendants, e.g. for topic T, remove all stories from the $\neg T$ set that have topics that are direct parents or children of T.

- extended: remove all ancestors and descendants from the competition, e.g. for topic T, remove all stories from the $\neg T$ set that have topics that are either direct or indirect parents or descendants of T.

Under the assumption that the extended option will result in categorization models that are more accurate, we ran our experiments with the extended modification option, otherwise using exactly the same apparatus that was used for obtaining the best results with English Reuters. We used a pre-stopword top-300 word local dictionary for each topic, and averaged about 125 words in the post-stopword dictionary. Table 5 illustrates an example of an induced rule set and its performance on topic G131 (Defense). The rules in this example and for other topics as well seem to be intuitively appropriate for the most part. Table 6 illustrates the breakeven performance that we obtained for some variations that have been tried so far. Note that for the lower levels in the taxonomy we tested topics that had more than 180 newswires,

[3]This collection was obtained by IBM Research from Reuters for exclusive use in this ongoing research.

and more than 100 newswires. At the top level we chose all topics since sufficient newswires were available for each of them. We can observe that the performance declines as we include topics with fewer newswires.

Topics Selected	Number of Topics	Performance Breakeven (%)	Breakeven Cost
Top level	4	73	2
Lower levels (> 180 newswires)	31	67	3
Lower levels (> 100 newswires)	43	66	3
All levels (> 180 newswires)	35	70	2-3
All levels (> 100 newswires)	47	69	2-3

Table 6: Breakeven Points for Reuters' German Data

Our current hypothesis for the slightly lower performance as compared to the English Reuters is twofold. First, the sample size that we are working with for the German collection is far smaller than the English collection. Secondly, the uncertainties introduced due to incomplete topic assignments (by the Reuters staff) from a taxonomic viewpoint have not been fully resolved in our existing methodology and will need continued investigation.

5 Discussion

Our methodology for automatic generation of text categorization models seems to perform consistently across document collections in these two languages. It is our hypothesis that our "match" mechanism for creating dictionary tokens and representing text, and the ability of the rule induction process to learn category distinguishing pattern sets using these tokens, are the two principle components that provide this pattern-directed language-independent classification power.

When compared to previous results on the English Reuters data, our new results appear significantly better. Figure 2 suggests that the use of local dictionaries and frequency information were effective and improved the results of our rule induction methods. By far the greatest improvement came from the learning method (Swap-1). While previous experience has shown that the optimization techniques of this rule induction method can often substantially improve results over competitive methods, such as decision trees, text classification has a number of characteristics that make optimized rule induction particularly suitable. The optimization techniques that are employed are quite strong in finding feature dependencies. In terms of text classification this means that given single word dictionaries it can find the key word combination co-occurrences that distinguish between topics.

A source of uncertainty with the German newswires is caused by the hierarchic classification system in use. For the top level classes, there is no problem. However, there is no uniform pattern of human code assignment below the top level. That is, some stories have only a top level code assigned. How is this to be compared to a story with a leaf node code assigned which lies in the same hierarchy? Is the assignment of only a top level code to be considered equivalent to a leaf node code of "other"?. If not, how should such stories be used when computing classification results on the test data set? These issues require continued investigation.

German as a language has two salient major differences from English (although they are both in the same language family and therefore have many resemblances). The first is that German is a more heavily inflected language and one might suppose that it is more important to normalize word forms to stems. Our results do not seem to bear this out, however. It appears that the frequent non-common words which we use as features tend to occur with the same inflection in a topic, for the most part. The second major difference is that German tends to use word formations involving several stems to form a single word where English would use a noun phrase. One might suppose that these would need to be decomposed. Again, our results do not support this. Relatively few of the long compounds occur as features, and those that do might be considered to be specialized idioms which should not be decomposed. For example, in one experiment using the top 150 non-common word stems as features for the category "politics", the only compounds were "aussenminister" = "exterior minister", "menschenrecht" = "human rights", "ministerpraesident" = "minister president", and "mitgliedstaaten" = "partner states", all arguably idioms in this context.

From these experiments, it appears that optimized rule induction is more than competitive with other machine learning techniques [Masand *et al.*, 1992, Lewis and Ringuette, 1994, Lewis, 1992a] for document classification, and very close behind human-engineered systems [Hayes and Weinstein, 1991]. Such conclusions can only be supported by rigorous and exacting comparisons. The 1987 English Reuters stories have recently been widely circulated and should prove to be an important benchmark for objective comparisons. The 1993 German Reuters collection will hopefully provide an additional benchmark as we and others continue to extend our results.

References

[Apté *et al.*, 1993] C. Apté, F. Damerau, and S. Weiss. Automated Learning of Decison Rules for Text Categorization. Technical Report RC 18879, IBM T.J. Watson Research Center, 1993. To appear in ACM Transactions on Office Information Systems.

[Breiman *et al.*, 1984] L. Breiman, J. Friedman, R. Olshen, and C. Stone. *Classification and Regression Trees.* Wadsworth, Monterrey, Ca., 1984.

[Hayes and Weinstein, 1991] P. Hayes and S. Weinstein. Adding Value to Financial News by Computer. In *Proceedings of the First International Conference on Artificial Intelligence Applications on Wall Street*, pages 2–8, 1991.

[Hayes *et al.*, 1990] P.J. Hayes, P.M. Andersen, I.B. Nirenburg, and L.M. Schmandt. TCS: A Shell for Content-Based Text Categorization. In *Proceedings of the Sixth IEEE CAIA*, pages 320–326, 1990.

[Lewis and Ringuette, 1994] D. Lewis and M. Ringuette. A comparison of two learning algorithms for text categorization. In *Symposium on Document Analysis and Information Retrieval*, Las Vegas, NV, April 1994. ISRI; Univ. of Nevada, Las Vegas. To appear.

[Lewis, 1992a] D. Lewis. An Evaluation of Phrasal and Clustered Representations on a Text Categorization Task. In *Proceedings of the Fifteenth Annual International ACM SIGIR Conference on Research and Development in Information Retrieval*, pages 37–50, June 1992. Edited by Nicholas Belkin, Peter Ingwersen, and Annelise Mark Pejtersen.

[Lewis, 1992b] D. Lewis. Feature Selection and Feature Extraction for Text Categorization. In *Procceedings of the Speech and Natural language Workshop*, pages 212–217, February 1992. Sponsored by the Defense Advanced Research Projects Agency.

[Masand *et al.*, 1992] B. Masand, G. Linoff, and D. Waltz. Classifying News Stories using Memory Based Reasoning. In *Proceedings of the Fifteenth Annual International ACM SIGIR Conference on Research and Development in Information Retrieval*, pages 59–65, June 1992. Edited by Nicholas Belkin, Peter Ingwersen, and Annelise Mark Pejtersen.

[Quinlan, 1993] J.R. Quinlan. *C4.5: Programs for Machine Learning.* Morgan Kaufmann, 1993.

[Weiss and Indurkhya, 1993] S. Weiss and N. Indurkhya. Optimized Rule Induction. *IEEE EXPERT*, 8(6):61–69, December 1993.

[Weiss and Kulikowski, 1991] S.M. Weiss and C.A. Kulikowski. *Computer Systems That Learn.* Morgan Kaufmann, 1991.

Using IR Techniques for Text Classification in Document Analysis

Rainer Hoch
German Research Center for Artificial Intelligence (DFKI)
P.O. Box 20 80, D-67608 Kaiserslautern, Germany
E-mail: hoch@dfki.uni-kl.de

Abstract

This paper presents the INFOCLAS system applying statistical methods of information retrieval for the classification of German business letters into corresponding message types such as order, offer, enclosure, etc. INFOCLAS is a first step towards the understanding of documents proceeding to a classification-driven extraction of information. The system is composed of two main modules: the central indexer (extraction and weighting of indexing terms) and the classifier (classification of business letters into given types). The system employs several knowledge sources including a letter database, word frequency statistics for German, lists of message type specific words, morphological knowledge as well as the underlying document structure. As output, the system evaluates a set of weighted hypotheses about the type of the actual letter. Classification of documents allow the automatic distribution or archiving of letters and is also an excellent starting point for higher-level document analysis. [1]

1 Introduction

Document analysis has the task to transform a printed document into an equivalent symbolic representation. Because of their inherent complexity, document analysis systems are usually composed of distinct analysis modules [14].

In [5] we presented a document analysis system that involves four distinct steps of analysis: layout extraction, logical labeling, text recognition, and partial text analysis. *Layout extraction* comprises all low-level processing routines like skew angle adjustment and segmentation to compute the layout structure of a document. *Logical labeling* is used to hypothesize the so-called logical objects of a document, e.g. title, author, chapter, etc. *Text recognition* explores the captured text of logical objects. In this way, word hypotheses are generated, validated by dictionary look-up and redundant word candidates are eliminated. Finally, a *partial text analysis* of selected objects (sender, subject, body) is initiated for classifying the document (invoice, order, enclosure, etc.) and for the extraction of some relevant information.

The system is model-driven and based on the ODA (Office Document Architecture) platform, an international standard for the representation and the exchange of documents [15]. Exemplary, German business letters are analyzed. Figure 1 summarizes the architecture of our document analysis system.

In this paper, we describe our prototypical system INFOCLAS for *indexing and classifying printed business letters*. The paper continues our work being shown in [7]. INFOCLAS has been developed as a tool to provide expectations towards the message possibly conveyed in business letters, such as offer or order. Thus, it guides further text analysis procedures enabling the application-oriented interpretation of documents.

INFOCLAS can be seen as a first step towards the understanding of documents (cf. [2]): Using statistical methods of information retrieval (IR) [23, 24], we differentiate the letters into different classes which are called *message types* according to the EDIFACT standard [16]. More precisely, index terms are extracted, weighted according to their likelihood of relevance and then matched against lists of message type specific words. Considering such words being representative for certain letter types, we are able to analyze five distinct types:

---

[1] This work has been supported by the Germany Ministry for Research and Technology (BMFT).

order, *offer*, *inquiry*, *enclosure*, and *advertisement*. In the near future, other message types will also be modeled, e.g. *invoices*.

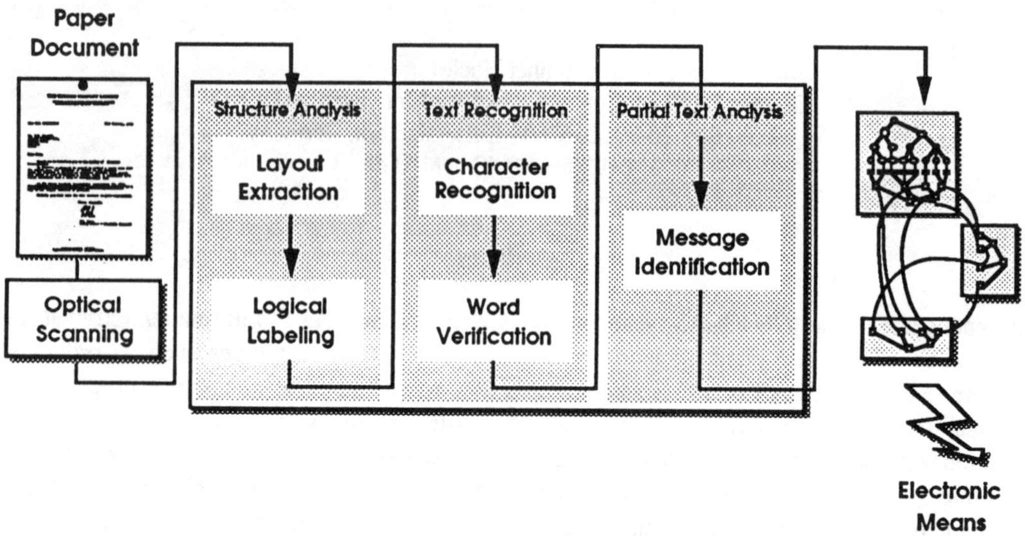

Figure 1: Architecture of document analysis system.

In principle, a classification of electronic documents is advantageous for several reasons. First, the automatic distribution as well as the subsequent processing and archiving of letters is facilitated. In this way, possible application scenarios are: in-house mail or fax distribution, knowledge-based indexing of documents, and automatic task processing. Second, a hypothesis about the type of letter is an excellent starting point for higher-level document analysis [6].

In contrast to classical IR systems, INFOCLAS must deal with incorrect words as well as word alternatives coming up with our OCR (optical character recognition) component. Thus, the question is how OCR results will influence the accuracy of document retrieval [27] and text classification. Strictly speaking, the system must be robust towards different kinds of recognition errors.

The main characteristics of the INFOCLAS system are:

- dealing with noisy OCR results
- combining IR techniques and document analysis for automatic indexing and text classification
- exploitation of document structure (subject, body)
- true morphological analysis to eliminate stop words
- model of message type specific words
- application domain: business letters
- context of larger document routing/database filling task

The remaining sections of the paper are organized as follows: Section 2 explains the two central system components of INFOCLAS, the indexer as well as the classifier. Then, Section 3 describes the training database of business letters and presents the first results of using INFOCLAS dealing with word alternatives of OCR. In Section 4, we compare our approach with other work in the area. Finally, Section 5 concludes the paper with an outline of our current research activities.

2 System Components

INFOCLAS is a simple knowledge-based system enhancing the capabilities of our document analysis system Π_{ODA} [5]. As already mentioned, we analyze German business letters. The two principal tasks of the system are:

- Automatic indexing: the computation of weighted index terms of a document (the "indexer")
- Text classification: the computation of hypotheses about the type of the document (the "classifier")

Automatic indexing includes a true morphological analysis for the German language (no word stemming), the reduction of stop words by using the part-of-speech information, local and global frequency analysis of the remaining stems, and finally index term weighting applying IR techniques. These weighted index terms are a prerequisite for subsequent text classification.

The task of the classifier involves the matching of index terms with word lists that are most characteristic for certain letter classes, or message types, respectively. These lists are called message type specific word lists.

While simple (i.e. well-structured) parts of the letter such as *recipient, sender* and *date* are checked syntactically for verification of recognition results, the INFOCLAS system concentrates on those parts containing free text, especially on the *subject* and the letter's *body*. For these two logical objects, an examination is most promising because statistical methods usually rely on natural language texts in contrast to the well-structured constituents of a letter (e.g. recipient). Moreover, there is also a drastic compression of text when concentrating on the index terms of selected document parts (in total the compression rate is between 3 to 5 [7]).

In the next sections, we will explain the processing steps of the indexer as well as the classifier in more detail.

2.1 Indexer

Applying IR techniques, we extract keywords or phrases from a single business letter. In the IR literature, these keywords are designated as *index terms* or *descriptors*. The process of ascertaining terms is known as *automatic indexing*. Additionally, weights are computed assigning indications of importance to terms [23, 24].

In this way, a letter can be represented by an n-dimensional vector of pairs

$$L_i = ((d_{i1}, w_{i1}), (d_{i2}, w_{i2}), \ldots , (d_{in}, w_{in}))$$

where L_i = letter i, d_{ij} = descriptor j in letter i, and w_{ij} = weight of descriptor d_{ij}.

The external interface and processing model of the indexing specialist are depicted in Figure 2. Initial character recognition yields the needed word candidates for the indexer. In addition, contextual information is provided during logical labeling [5].

Typically, indexing with INFOCLAS is performed on the logical objects *subject* and *body* of a letter. Furthermore, there is no fixed vocabulary for indexing, so all text words are used for content identification (free text indexing).

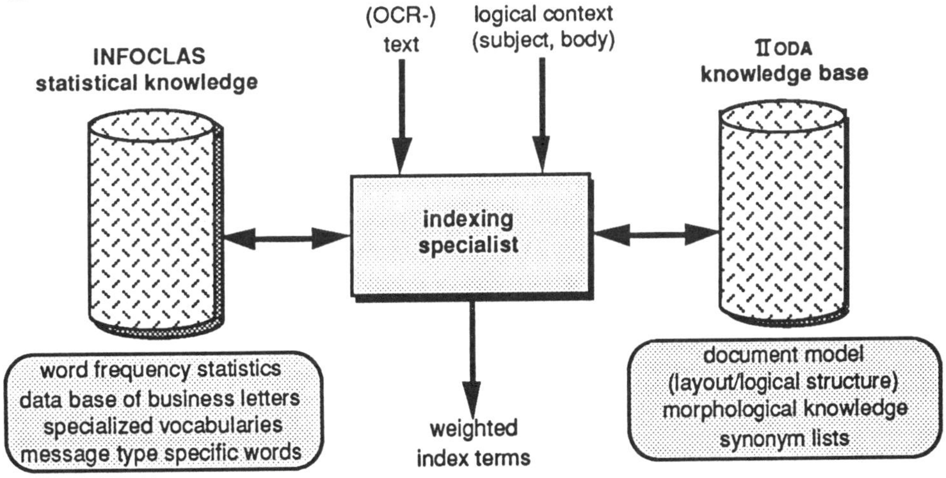

Figure 2: External interface of indexing module.

INFOCLAS engages two kinds of knowledge sources: statistical knowledge as well as the Π_{ODA} knowledge base (see Figure 2). Statistical knowledge comprises common word frequencies of German, some specialized vocabularies (common abbreviations, cities, countries, employee names, etc.), message type specific words, and a database of already analyzed business letters. The Π_{ODA} knowledge base makes use of a document model for the structure of business letters, a tool for morphological analysis and simple synonym lists. All these additional knowledge sources are integrated for improving classification results. For example, using structural information we can concentrate on the subject and the body of the letter to compute the weighted index terms. Especially less important terms of the letter parts "sender", "recipient", "your sign", "company specific data" will not be considered.

Computation with the indexer now proceeds in four steps (Figure 3): morphological analysis, stop word reduction, frequency analysis, and index term weighting.

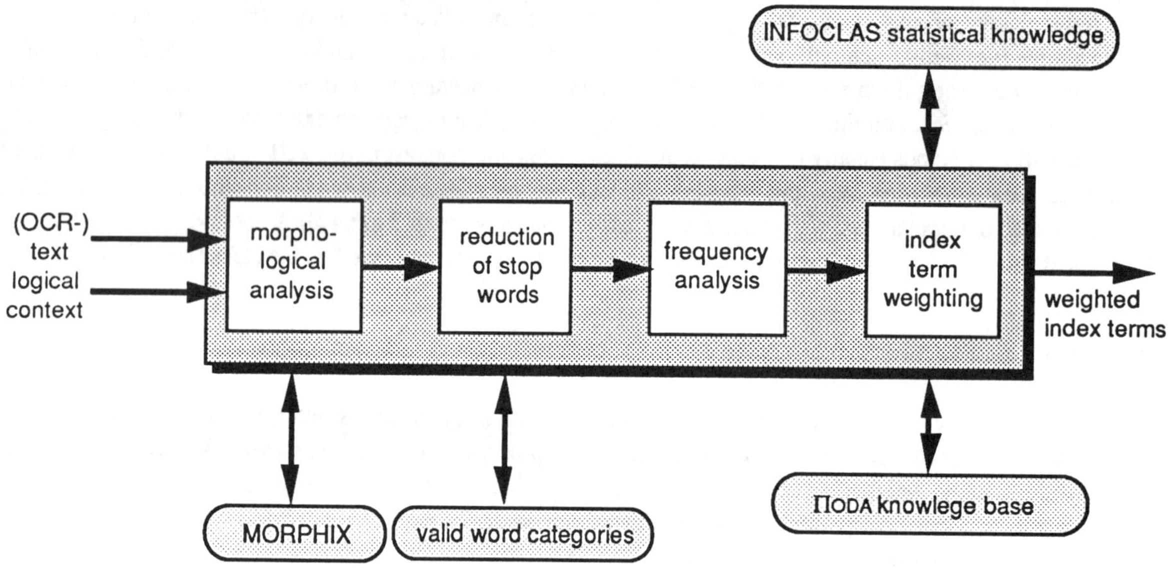

Figure 3: Components of indexing module.

Morphological analysis. First, a morphological tool for German reduces all input words to their respective stems. We use the morphological analysis component MORPHIX 3.0 [8]. MORPHIX handles all inflectional phenomena of the German language by considering morphologic regularities as the basis for defining fine-grained word-class specific subclassification. Besides morphosyntactic features, there are also phonological aspects which are considered in refining the classification. In spite of the complexity of German inflections, the tool is very fast. The average time for analyzing one word lies between 0.01 and 0.02 cpu-seconds, though the system is implemented in Common Lisp.

Because the internal lexicon of MORPHIX was originally small, we enlarged it by defining domain-specific words. Additionally, we improved its I/O-interface to deal with German umlauts (ä, ö, ü) and s-zet (ß). However, one crucial problem still remains: MORPHIX does not handle word composites (compound nouns) which frequently occur in the German language. Rules for word segmentation of composites may solve this problem.

Stop word reduction. As output, MORPHIX yields morphological and syntactical information for each input word form. For instance, word category (part-of-speech), case, gender, number, tense, etc. are conveyed. In contrast to traditional information retrieval systems which initially eliminate stop words and then apply word stemming algorithms (suffix stripping), our approach reverses this order. After morphological analysis we delete irrelevant stop words using the part-of-speech information. Only words of category noun, verb, adjective, and adverbs, or unknown words (e.g. proper names) to MORPHIX, respectively, are further considered.

These *content words* directly correspond to the so-called *open categories* of words in a language which are rather dynamic in opposition to the *closed categories* of articles, conjunctions, prepositions, pronouns, determiners, etc. Latter are also known as *function words* [10]. Our opinion is that only elements of the open categories are significant for content identification of a document.

Frequency analysis. In a third step, the indexer performs a frequency analysis of all remaining word stems, i.e. words of category noun, verb, adjective, and adverb. We distinguish between relative and absolute frequency measures for the identification of content indicators. The *relative frequency* is the number how often an index term occurs within one letter locally. The *absolute frequency* gives the number of term occurrences within the entire database of already analyzed letters (i.e. the document collection). Absolute frequencies are stored in an inverted file of index terms for efficient retrieval.

Note that these frequency measures also represent primitive weighting functions. In practice, however, they are too crude for content identification. For example, an initial phrase often used in German business letters is the salutation “Sehr geehrte Damen und Herren” (Dear Sirs and Madams), but has no deep significance. We apply other IR weighting functions which are derived from these basic frequencies.

Index term weighting. Finally, the central component for index term weighting is invoked. The user can select between three different weighting functions, including either an *inverse document frequency* function, the *information value* of a term suggested by information theory, or, optionally, the *term discrimination value* [23].

The idea behind *inverse document frequency* is to assign high weights of importance to terms occurring in only a few documents. The weight of an index term is proportional to its relative frequency in a letter and inversely proportional to the number of letters containing this term. The following formula mirrors this fact:

$$weight_{ij} = freq_{ij} * \log_2(n) - (\log_2 (docfreq_j) + 1$$

where i = document i, j = index term j, n = total number of documents, $docfreq_j$ = number of documents in collection containing index term j.

As our run time measurements had shown, computation of the term discrimination value was very expensive [7]. The discrimination value computes the degree to which the use of each index term of a document will help to distinguish the documents of each other. In particular, the dynamics of our letter database as well as the usage of a free index term vocabulary leads to computational load, although we have used a centroid for efficient similarity computation [28]. Comparing the information value with the inverse document frequency of a term, classification results are identical [7]. In the following we refer to the inverse document frequency because of its fast computation.

2.2 Classifier

The classifier has the task to generate weighted hypotheses about the message type of a business letter. In fact, we are able to analyze five message types, i.e. order, offer, inquiry, enclosure, and advertisement. Our terminology of message types has its origin in the EDIFACT standard [16]. EDIFACT is an application-driven standard for a common representation to interchange data of transport, commerce and administration. We take just these message types from EDIFACT which were adequate for our initial database consisting of 83 incoming DFKI letters (the learning set). Since the system is open, new message types can easily be integrated.

At the moment, the model of each message type is represented by lists of *primary, secondary and tertiary words* (more precisely, word stems), so-called *message type specific words*. While primary words are most significant and characteristic for one certain message type, secondary words as well as tertiary words may be shared from several messages.

The idea behind this approach is that in business-oriented correspondence certain keywords and phrases are often repeated in association with the message type. Our experience confirms this. Some words are indeed characteristic for particular message types. For example, typical offers include word inflections of the German verb “anbieten” (infinitive form “to offer”), “angeboten” (past participle), “boten <*text*> an” (simple past) or their synonyms. Other examples are the word stems “order”, “refer to”, “deliver”, “submit”, “send”, etc. in orders. Figure 4 sketches all primary and secondary words of the message type “offer”.

```
primary:    (("angebot" "bestell" "bitt" "bezugnehm" "lieferung" "liefer" "netto" "skonto" "zahlungsbedingung"
            "bestellung" "rechnung" "schick" "send")
secondary:  ("auflage" "beschreibung" "verfuegung" "anfertigung" "anlage" "eventuell" "garantie" "rueckfrage"
            "summe" "zahlbar" "adresse" "beabsichtig" "bedingung" "beitrag" "bemuehung" "direkt"
            "einzelpreis" "obig" "rabatt" "telefon" "telefongespraech" "anhang" "auffuehr" "auftrag" "bedarf"
            "beifueg" "beiliegend" "beinhalt" "einzeln" "erbitt" "erhalt" "gesamtsumme" "herstell"
            "lieferbedingung" "moeglich" "moeglichst" "neu" "neuauflage" "probeexemplar" "schnell" "schreib"
            "telefonat" "uebersend" "umfang" "verfuegbar" "version" "vorlieg" "zahlung" "zwischensumme"
            "zahl" "nachfolg")
```

Figure 4: Primary and secondary words for message type “order” (in German).

During the training phase, such message type specific words were evaluated carefully, first by ranking the index terms wrt. to their frequency and then by improving the resulting lists manually (see Section 3.1). The usage of synonym lists or a thesaurus could further improve the quality of these lists.

During the classification of a letter all weighted index terms—computed by the indexer—are matched against specific words of each message type. There are different constants, or multipliers, controlling this matching process. Primary words have a higher multiplier when they match index terms in comparison with secondary and tertiary words (lowest value), thus indicating their greater importance and allowing a fine-tuning of classification. Thus, the formula for this classification process is:

$$class_{ik} = c1 * \sum_{j=1}^{n} p(d_{ij}) * w_{ij} + c2 * \sum_{j=1}^{n} s(d_{ij}) * w_{ij} + c3 * \sum_{j=1}^{n} t(d_{ij}) * w_{ij}$$

$$p(d_{ij}) = \begin{cases} 1, & \text{if } d_{ij} \in \text{primary-word-list} \\ 0, & \text{otherwise} \end{cases}$$

$s(d_{ij})$, $t(d_{ij})$: analogous for secondary and tertiary words

where i = document i, j = index term j, c1, c2, c3 are constants, d_{ij} = descriptor j in letter i, w_{ij} = weight of descriptor d_{ij}, $k \in$ {order, offer, inquiry, enclosure, advertisement}.

In this manner the index terms of a letter are matched against all specific words and multiplied with the respective constants. The resulting values are added and finally normalized by the number of index terms. The process is then repeated for each single message type. As result, the classifier generates an ordered list of weighted hypotheses about the type of message recognized.

Classification results of letter 48 of database:

BEBE (enclosure):	41.81 %	(71.92)
ANGE (offer):	19.52 %	(33.59)
ANFR (inquiry):	15.14 %	(26.05)
BEST (order):	14.86 %	(25.57)
WERB (advertisement):	8.66 %	(14.90)

Table 1: Results of classifying the letter 48 of database.

For instance, Table 1 presents the classification results of letter 48 of our database. On the right side, the absolute weights of computation are shown in parentheses. It reveals that this letter has a high probability of being a enclosure while the three next hypotheses have almost equal probabilities and thus are less probable.

3 Experimental Results

3.1 Training Database

Our training database consists of 83 incoming business letters taken from the daily correspondence of our institute. All these letters are written in German (from the 90 initial letters we discarded the English ones). All letters are typical in some sense: they have one or two pages, do not contain tables or figures in the body (company logos are ignored), have some well-structured parts such as addresses, date, enclosures, company specific information etc. as well as complex ones (subject, body). On average, a letter includes between 100 and 200 words.

The letters were scanned by students with a commercial OCR. Some remaining spelling and recognition errors were eliminated thus yielding a database of correct ASCII letters. Within the letters, we identified five sensible letter types, the so-called message types, according to the EDIFACT standard: *order*, *offer*, *inquiry*, *enclosure*, and *advertisement*. Some letters did not fit into this model, they were gathered in a more general class named *statement*. This manual classification was performed by three person.

For each message type, we collected the respective letters and applied the German morphological tool MORPHIX. Further, we eliminated all word stems which did not belong to nouns, verbs, adjectives, and adverbs. [2] Then, a frequency analysis was started ranking the remaining word stems with respect to their absolute frequency. This ranked list was post-processed by humans to exclude high frequent words which occur in most letters being not relevant for text classification such as salutations, greetings, titles, etc. Finally, we divided the resulting list of each message type into three parts: primary words being most significant for one class, secondary words being significant for a few classes, and tertiary words being less significant.

All in all, a person works for about one month to establish the training database—after initial interface problems have been overcome.

3.2 Classification Results

INFOCLAS has been completely implemented in Common Lisp/CLOS and currently runs on Sun SPARCstation. There are three interfaces to INFOCLAS, a functional programmer's interface, a powerful menu-driven Lisp user interface as well as a comfortable graphical user interface implemented with the Window Tool Kit of Common Lisp. The menu interface allows a change of parameter settings interactively and browsing the actual letter database.

Using INFOCLAS, document classification is very fast: cpu time varies between half a second and two seconds per letter where a letter includes maximal 75 index terms.

Table 2 presents the classification results with a real test sample of 42 arbitrary business letters taken from our OCR. 24 letters (57 %) were classified correctly, i.e. INFOCLAS yields the right message at the first position of the message type hypotheses list. Concerning 8 letters (19 %), the second hypothesis of INFOCLAS is the right one. Classification fails for 10 letters (24 %). Note that the test sample did not contain any order at all, and exactly one offer! Classification of advertisements and inquiries run well because of their typical style of writing, certain phrases and common words (e.g. the word "new" in advertisements; conjunctive forms within inquiries).

document class	first hypothesis	second hypothesis	false
advertisement	13	1	1
inquiry	4	3	1
enclosure	5	4	2
order	0	0	0
offer	1	0	0
no class	1	0	6

Table 2: Classification results wrt. message types.

A closer look at the results reveals some other interesting facts: First, INFOCLAS has problems with letters which do not fit into our model. In this case, the assumption of an equal distribution of classification scores can no longer be maintained. We have to refine our model of message types, either by introducing new types such as statement, invoice, etc. or subclasses of the existing ones (e.g. invitations belonging to statements). Second, the body of three letters was very short containing only a few index terms (3, 6 and 9 terms). In this case, a classification solely based on weighted index terms becomes a hard problem.

Third, some letters directly suffer from the quality of OCR results. Actually, our OCR has a word accuracy of about 80 per cent. Thus, classification fails when index terms are disturbed which are significant for a certain

---

[2] By the way, the problem was that a lot of words are either domain specific, proper names or compound nouns. Hence, we were forced to extend the internal lexica of MORPHIX initially. This problem faded the more letters we analyzed.

message type. One letter *could not be recognized at all* because of the inferior input quality, i.e. the text was written by a needle printer. Next we will start more experiments to investigate how noisy OCR results effect the letter classification.

We have also compared run time measurements of the distinct weighting functions and how they influence classification results. Differences in the quality of classification *were negligible in contrast to run time.* The computation of the term discrimination value is rather expensive in contrast to the other weighting functions (cf. [7]). It correlates with the size of the letter database directly. Thus, we took the inverse document frequency as the default weighting function offering an almost linear complexity.

In addition, there are two inherent problems when indexing letters from our database. On the one hand, the size of business letters is small comprising one or two pages at most. On the other hand, the experimental letter database is currently not very large for reasons of lacking resources, thus implying a small set of reasonable message types being modelled. Typically, between 10 and 25 letters were analyzed to extract specific words of each message type. In [3] the problem of database size for the expressiveness of empirical IR results is also addressed.

4 Related Work

Classical IR techniques including the extraction and weighting of index terms from documents are described in [22, 23, 24, 26] and others.

A newer approach for automatic indexing can be found in [25]. The idea is to incorporate the *context of a word* for automatic indexing instead of the word exclusively. This context may be either a phrase, a sentence, a paragraph, or a section. Moreover, the automatic extraction of links between text units is possible. This approach also applies the classical vector space model.

Latent semantic indexing (LSI) is another statistical method based on singular value decomposition, i.e. a matrix decomposition technique related to factor analysis. Here the terms of a document are represented as points in a 50 to 150 dimensional "semantic" space and matched against user queries [18].

Masand et al. [19] present a k-nearest neighbor method for classifying news stories from the Dow Jones news wire. Features are *single words and capital word pairs* which are typical for company and product names in business-oriented news. Text is also compressed by eliminating stop words, common words, and then weighted applying inverse document frequency. The system does not require any manual knowledge acquisition and runs on a connection machine.

Knowledge-based IR systems are FASTUS [1], FRUMP [4], CODER [9], TCS [12], SCISOR [21], FERRET [20], and others. P. S. Jacobs [17] gives an excellent overview on the current activities in this research area.

While all the above approaches deal with correct ASCII-word input, little work has been done on the combination of IR techniques and document analysis [7].

J. Hull [13] uses the vector space model to locate a set of documents which are similar to the actual document. The vocabulary from these documents is then used to identify correct words from a set of word alternatives improving word recognition results. By this way, the recognition score of each word alternative instead of its local frequency is taken to compute the inverse document frequency weight.

Finally, Taghva et al. [27] describe how noisy OCR results will influence recall and precision of IR queries.

5 Conclusion & Future Work

To summarize, we presented a system called INFOCLAS for the indexing and the classification of German business letters into different message types. The system primarily applies statistical methods of information retrieval, but also employs additional knowledge sources, such as word frequency statistics for German, message type specific words, morphological knowledge, and knowledge about the logical structure of a document. INFOCLAS takes (ASCII-) words either correctly or incorrectly recognized by our document analysis system as input.

Our future work concentrates on several topics:

Word alternatives. Currently, INFOCLAS deals with word alternatives of OCR in a best-first manner. An extension of the indexer may also consider word alternatives, perhaps integrating recognition scores for index term weighting.

Elimination of word alternatives. The classification results of INFOCLAS can be used to prefer word candidates which have a lower credibility wrt. recognition. For instance, in a business letter of a bus travel agency the word "seats" in the context of ordering a bus is much more common than the words "beats" or "seals".

Word contexts. In order to establish a more advanced class hierarchy and to take word collocations, phrases and concepts into account, we are implementing a rule-based approach (called the RULECLAS system). Here, INFOCLAS is used as a very fast and simple pre-processor for the classification task. The rule-based system allows the definition of a concept hierarchy as well as text patterns similar to TCS [12].

Information extraction techniques. We also concentrate on information extraction techniques such as those implemented in the FRUMP system [4], SCISOR [21], or TCS [12]. These systems accurately extract certain conceptual information from texts in selected topic areas, e.g. news stories. Even the FRUMP system proved that an expectation-driven strategy was useful for skimming texts in constrained domains. We belief that our domain of business letters and a corresponding message type model will allow similar skimming techniques for natural language processing (NLP). In particular, our message types are comparable with the sketchy script idea presented in FRUMP. Until now, we did not integrate such NLP tools into our system.

Acknowledgement

I would like to thank Stefan Dittrich who implemented most parts of the INFOCLAS system. Also many thanks to Claudia Wenzel for integrating INFOCLAS into our document analysis system as well as programming its graphical user interface and Hans-Günther Hein for valuable comments on the paper.

References

1. D. E. Appelt, J. R. Hobbs, J. Bear, D. Israel, M. Tyson. FASTUS: A Finite-state Processor for Information Extraction from Real-world Text. Proc. of 13th International Conference on Artificial Intelligence (IJCAI'93), Chambéry, France, 28. Aug.-3. Sept. 1993, pp. 1172-1178.

2. T. Bayer, J. Franke, U. Kressel, E. Mandler, M. Oberländer, J. Schürmann. Towards the Understanding of Printed Documents. In: H. Baird, H. Bunke, K. Yamamoto (eds.), *Structured Document Image Analysis*, Springer-Verlag, 1992, pp. 3-35.

3. W. B. Croft. Retrieval from large text databases. Proc. of *Symposium on Document Analysis and Information Retrieval, Las Vegas*, Nevada, USA, 1992, pp. 96-101.

4. G. DeJong. An Overview of the FRUMP System. In: W. G. Lehnert, M. H. Ringle (eds.), *Strategies for Natural Language Processing*, Lawrence Erlbaum Assoc., Hillsdale, 1982, pp. 149-175.

5. A. Dengel, R. Bleisinger, R. Hoch, F. Fein, F. Hönes. From Paper to Office Document Standard Representation. *IEEE Computer*, vol. 25, no. 7, 1992, pp. 63-67.

6. A. Dengel and R. Hoch. Intelligent Interfaces between Paper and Computer. In: A. H. Rubenstein, H. Schwärtzel (eds.), *Lecture Notes*, Springer-Verlag, Berlin Heidelberg New York, 1992, pp. 122-136.

7. R. Hoch, A. Dengel. INFOCLAS: Classifying the Message in Printed Business Letters. Proc. of *2nd Symposium on Document Analysis and Information Retrieval*, Las Vegas, Nevada, USA, April 26 - 28, 1993, pp. 443-456.

8. W. Finkler, G. Neumann. MORPHIX—A Fast Realization of a Classification-Based Approach to Morphology. Proc. of *4. Österreichische Artificial Intelligence-Tagung*, Springer-Verlag, Berlin, 1988, pp. 11-19.

9. E. A. Fox. Development of the CODER system: A testbed for artificial intelligence methods in information retrieval. *Information Processing & Management*, vol. 23, no. 4, 1987, pp. 341-366.

10. M. D. Harris. *Introduction to Natural Language Processing*. Reston Publishing Company Inc., Reston, Virginia, 1985.

12. P. J. Hayes, P. M. Andersen, I. B. Nirenburg, L. M. Schmandt. TCS: A Shell for Content-Based Text Categorization. Proc. of *6th Conference on AI Applications*, Santa Barbara, CA, 1990, pp. 320-326.

13. J. J. Hull, Y. Li. Word Recognition Result Interpretation Using the Vector Space Model for Information Retrieval. Proc. of *2nd Symposium on Document Analysis and Information Retrieval*, Las Vegas, Nevada, USA, April 26 - 28, 1993, pp. 147-155.

14. *IEEE Computer Magazine*. Special Issue on Document Image Analysis Systems, vol. 25, no. 7, July 1992.

15. ISO 8613. *Information Processing, Text and Office Systems, Office Document Architecture and Interchange Format (ODA/ODIF)*, parts 1-8, 1988.

16. ISO 9735. *Electronic date interchange for administration, commerce and transport (EDIFACT)*, application level syntax rules, 1988.

17. P. S. Jacobs (ed.). *Text-Based Intelligent Systems—Current Research and Practice in Information Retrieval*. Lawrence Erlbaum Associates, Publishers, Hillsdale, New Jersey, 1992.

18. K. E. Lochbaum, L. A. Streeter. Comparing and Combining the Effectiveness of Latent Semantic Indexing and the Ordinary Vector Space Model for Information Retrieval. *Information Processing & Management*, vol. 25, no. 6, 1989, pp. 665-676.

19. B. Masand, G. Linoff, D. Waltz. Classifying News Stories using Memory Based Reasoning. Proc. of *15th Annual International Conference on Research and Development in Information Retrieval (SIGIR'92)*, 1992, pp. 59-65.

20. M. L. Mauldin. Retrieval Performance in FERRET—A Conceptual Information Retrieval System. Proc. of *14th Annual International ACM/SIGIR Conference on Research and Development in Information Retrieval*, 1991, pp. 347-355.

21. L. F. Rau, P. S. Jacobs. Integrating top-down and bottom-up strategies in a text processing system. Proc. of *Second Conference on Applied NLP*, Austin, Texas, 1988, pp. 129-135.

22. C. J. van Rijsbergen. *Information Retrieval*. Butterworths, London, 2nd edition, 1979.

23. G. Salton, M. J. McGill. *Introduction to Modern Information Retrieval*. McGraw-Hill, Inc., 1983.

24. G. Salton. Developments in Automatic Text Retrieval. *Science*, vol. 253, August 1991, pp. 974-980.

25. G. Salton, C. Buckley. Global Text Matching for Information Retrieval. *Science*, vol. 253, 1991, pp. 1012-1015.

26. K. Sparck Jones. *Automatic indexing*. Journal of Documentation, 30, 1974, pp. 393-432.

27. K. Taghva, J. Borsack, A. Condit, S. Erva. The Effects of Noisy Data on Text Retrieval. *Technical Report 93-06*, Information Science Research Institute, University of Nevada, Las Vegas, March 1993, pp. 71-81.

28. P. Willett. An Algorithm for the Calculation of Exact Term Discrimination Values. *Information Processing & Management*, vol. 21, no. 3, 1985, pp. 225-232.

Indexing

An Evaluation Method for Stemming Algorithms

Chris D. Paice

Department of Computing, Lancaster University
Bailrigg, Lancaster LA1 4YR, U.K.

Abstract

The effectiveness of stemming algorithms has usually been measured in terms of their effect on retrieval performance with test collections. This however does not provide any insights which might help in stemmer optimisation. This paper describes a method in which stemming performance is assessed against predefined concept groups in samples of words. This enables various indices of stemming performance and weight to be computed. Results are reported for three stemming algorithms. The validity and usefulness of the approach, and the problems of conceptual grouping, are discussed, and directions for further research are identified.

Introduction

Stemming is a widely-used method of word standardisation designed to allow the matching of morphologically related terms, such as "clusters" and "clustering". The idea is that, in a language like English, a typical word contains a *stem* which refers to some central idea or 'meaning', and that certain affixes have been added to modify the meaning and/or to fit the word for its syntactic role. The purpose of stemming is to strip away the affixes and thus reduce the word to its essence.

In practice, some affixes may alter the meaning of a word so greatly that to remove them would be to discard vital information. In particular, deletion of prefixes is not generally felt to be helpful, except in certain domains such as medicine and chemistry. On the other hand, most suffixes in English are considered to be potentially removable. This paper is concerned with stemming in the restricted sense of suffix removal.

A useful summary of various stemming and conflation algorithms is given in the paper by Lennon *et al.* [1]; further algorithms have been described by Frakes [2] and by Paice [3].

Stemming Errors

There are two particular problems in using stemming for word standardisation. In the first place, pairs of etymologically related words sometimes differ sharply in meaning - for example, consider "author" and "authoritarian". In the second place, the transformations involved in adding and removing suffixes involve numerous irregularities and special cases.

Stemming errors are of two kinds: *understemming errors*, in which words which refer to the same concept are not reduced to the same stem, and *overstemming errors*, in which words are converted to the same stem even though they refer to distinct concepts. In designing a stemming algorithm there is a trade-off between these two kinds of error. A *light stemmer* plays safe in order to avoid overstemming errors, but consequently leaves many understemming errors. A *heavy stemmer* boldly removes all sorts of endings, some of which are decidedly unsafe, and therefore commits many overstemming errors.

There have been several investigations into the effects of stemming on retrieval performance in test collections [1,2,4,5]. In most cases, stemming was found to improve retrieval performance, but not by very much, and there were no consistent differences of performance between different stemmers. Harman was unable to show any consistent benefit over not using stemming at all [6].

We might expect a relationship between the weight of stemming used and the retrieval performance in particular types of search; for instance, it might be supposed that heavy stemming is appropriate when high recall is needed. Lennon *et al.* used the degree of dictionary compression as a measure of the weight, or strength, of each stemmer, but found that this did not correlate clearly with the performance in precision-oriented and recall-oriented searches [1].

Although evaluating stemmers on the basis of their effects on retrieval performance may seem appropriate from an IR viewpoint, it is probably unhelpful in practice, because it gives no insight into the specific causes of errors. Moreover, it ignores the fact that stemmers are not used only in IR systems - for example, they may be used in a natural language interface, or in a frame-instantiation program. IR-based evaluations are irrelevant to such applications.

This paper outlines an approach to stemmer evaluation which is based on detecting and counting the actual under- and overstemming errors committed during stemming of word samples derived from actual texts. This permits the computation of a 'stemming weight' index for each stemmer, as well as indices representing the under- and overstemming error rates and the general accuracy. The method involves manually dividing a sample of words into conceptual groups, and referring the actual stemming performance to these groups.

It may be objected that natural words do not fall into entirely clear-cut semantic groups, and that anyway humans cannot be relied upon to make objective assignments. In fact of course, the very practice of stemming obviously relies on an assumption of semantic grouping, even if it is somewhat approximate. Our assumption here is that careful human judgment can produce groups which are in reasonable agreement with 'reality', and that these can be used for evaluation purposes.

In using a sample of words taken from a natural source, we encounter the question of whether to base the evaluation on all the individual word tokens in the sample, or on only the distinct word types. In the first case, we would determine the frequencies of all the word types and take these into account in computing the performance indices. This is perfectly straightforward, but it is found that the results then obtained tend to be dominated by the way the stemmer handles a quite small number of high frequency word groups - for example, common verbs such as "be"/"being"/"been", "do"/"doing"/"done" etc. This is unfortunate since in practice common and irregular forms are often handled by lexical lookup anyway. Stemmers are mainly required to deal with words of relatively rare and unpredictable occurrence. In view of this, our evaluation method ignores occurrence frequencies, and uses word types rather than tokens. An incidental benefit is that there is no need to remove syntactic function words - nor to worry about what should be included in the stoplist - since it can be shown that inclusion or exclusion of these words has very little effect on the results.

Computation of Performance Indices

Suppose we have a sample of W different words, partitioned into 'concept groups' each containing forms which are both semantically and morphologically related to one another. For each concept group two totals may be computed.

Firstly, since a perfect stemmer should merge every member of a concept group with every other, the number of pairs of different words in the group defines the 'desired merge total' DMT_g for that group. This is given by

$$DMT_g = 0.5\, n_g(n_g - 1)$$

where n_g is the number of words in the group.

Secondly, a perfect stemmer should not merge any member of the present concept group with any word which is not in the group. Thus, for every group there is a 'desired non-merge total' DNT_g given by

$$DNT_g = 0.5 n_g(W - n_g)$$

By summing these two totals over all groups in the word sample, we obtain the *global desired merge total* $GDMT$ and the *global desired non-merge total* $GDNT$ respectively. Each equation contains a 0.5 factor to compensate for double counting of pairs during the summation.

After applying a stemmer to the sample, we are likely to find that some of the groups still contain two or more distinct stems. In such groups there are understemming errors to be counted. Thus, suppose a concept group of size n_g contains s distinct stems after stemming, and that the numbers of instances of these stems are $u_1, u_2, \ldots u_s$. The number of understemming errors for the group (the 'unachieved merge total' UMT_g) is given by

$$UMT_g = 0.5 \sum_{i=1..s} u_i(n_g - u_i)$$

Summing this quantity over all groups we obtain the *global unachieved merge total* $GUMT$; the understemming index UI is now given by the ratio $GUMT/GDMT$.

After stemming, we also expect to find cases where the same stem occurs in two or more concept groups. The procedure here is to gather all cases of a particular stem into a 'stem group'; now any stem group whose members are derived from two or more different concept groups contains overstemming errors which need to be counted.

Consider a stem group which contains n_s items which are derived from t different concept groups, and suppose that the numbers of representatives of these concept groups are $v1, v2, \ldots vt$. The number of overstemming errors for this stem group is represented by the 'wrongly-merged total' WMTs, given by:

$$WMT_s = 0.5 \sum_{i=1..t} v_i(n_s - v_i) \qquad \{1\}$$

Summing this quantity over all stem groups we obtain the *global wrongly-merged total* $GWMT$; the overstemming index OI is now given by the ratio $GWMT/GDNT$.

It is clear that for a heavy stemmer OI will be rather high and UI low, whereas for a light stemmer the situation will be reversed. The ratio of these two quantities may therefore be taken as a measure of the *stemming weight* SW:

$$SW = OI/UI\,.$$

Because we have no precise theory to account for the relationship between the understemming and overstemming tendencies, we lack any satisfactory framework in which to assess particular UI and OI values. It will commonly occur that one stemmer will be better than another in terms of UI, but worse in terms of OI. So is there any way to judge whether one is better than another overall? And does the question even have meaning? Regarding the second question we may observe that, if the difference in weight is quite small and the difference in UI and/or OI is large, then it probably does make sense to talk about the relative general accuracy of the two stemmers, at least for the word sample under consideration.

In order to obtain some kind of baseline against which the general accuracy of a stemmer may be judged, we refer to the process of *length truncation* - that is, reducing every word to just its first q letters (words shorter than q being left unchanged). Length truncation is the crudest method of stemming, and we would obviously expect any rule-based or table-based stemmer to do better. Note however that length truncation refers to not just one but a series of stemmers, each with a different value of q; for IR purposes truncation lengths of 5, 6 and 7 seem to be the most useful.

The idea here is that if we determine values of UI and OI for a series of truncation lengths, the (UI,OI) coordinates define a *truncation line* against which any stemmer can be assessed. Any reasonable stemmer will give a (UI,OI) point between the truncation line and the origin; in general, the further away the point is from the truncation line, the better the stemmer can be said to be. Specifically, a performance measure which we may call the *error rate relative to truncation*, or $ERRT$, can be obtained by extending a line from the origin **O** through the (UI,OI) point **P** until it intersects the truncation line at **T**, as illustrated in Figure 1. $ERRT$ is then simply defined as

$$ERRT = \text{length}(\mathbf{OP})/\text{length}(\mathbf{OT})\,.$$

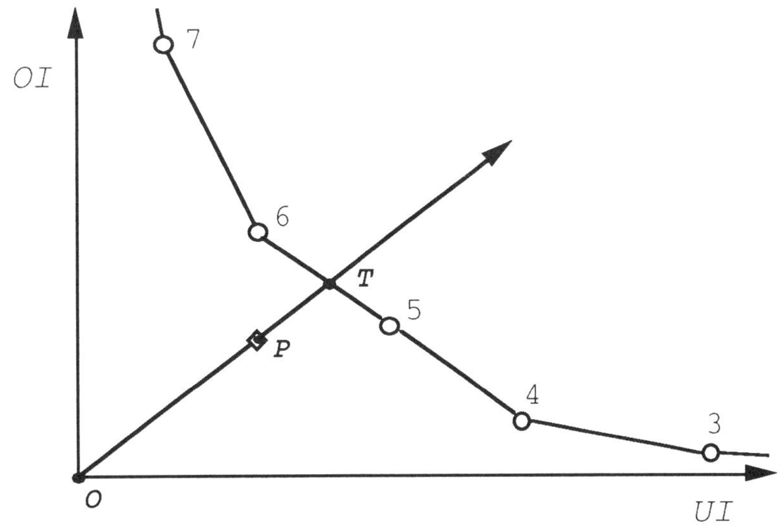

Figure 1: computation of ERRT value

Experimental Arrangements

A suite of computer programs was written to permit computation of the above indices. The processing falls broadly into four parts:

-- conversion of a source text sample into a grouped file;

-- computation of a truncation line for the grouped file;

-- application of one or more stemming algorithms to the words in the grouped file, to obtain values of UI,OI and SW;

-- computation of the $ERRT$ value for each stemmer by comparing its (UI,OI) point to the truncation line.

The only stage where human effort is involved is in the construction of the groups. The grouping program presents to the user an alphabetic display of all the distinct words from the source. The program makes all the obvious decisions on the user's behalf, but for all uncertain cases refers to the user for the decision. Adjacent groups are separated by inserting 'barriers' into the file.

The grouped file thus produced is not likely to be correct. For one thing, some of the 'obvious' decisions taken by the program may in fact be wrong. For another, alphabetic ordering may sometimes split up certain conceptual groups (consider "read", "readily", "reading", "readjust", "reads"). Thirdly, the user may require time to reconsider some of the more difficult groupings. Consequently, a second and perhaps even third scan of the file needs to be performed, using a standard editor, before the grouping will be satisfactory. The grouping is thus a rather laborious process, though once it is finished the grouped file represents a permanent resource for future use.

A question arises over what to do about irregular verbs. It seems natural and proper that "fly" and "flew" should be placed in the same group, but what about "is" and "were", and "go" and "went"? Stemming relies on morphological regularities and similarities, so it seems wrong to penalise it for not merging totally dissimilar forms. In the event, a rule-of-thumb was used that words should only be grouped together if at least the first two letters were the same. This was partly a matter of convenience, since it is awkward to bring together words which are far apart in the alphabetic list. The rule obviously leads to anomalies - e.g., "bring" and "brought" are grouped, but "buy" and "bought" are not - but because the indices are based on word types rather than tokens it has only a tiny effect on the values of the indices.

During the grouping process, the user is presented with individual, isolated words; no context is given, and so there is no chance to allow for the different meanings of ambiguous words. In making a grouping decision, the user is in effect deciding whether two words *typically* refer to the same underlying concept, given a knowledge of the general domain of the source material.

This still leaves the question whether two words which refer to related but not quite identical concepts should be counted as equivalent. It may be that taking a 'strict' view of semantic equivalence will give materially different results than taking a 'loose' view. To investigate this point, groups were actually defined at two levels of 'tightness', using two kinds of inter-group barrier. First, there is a level of possibly large, loose groups, containing words which may be quite weakly related to one another. Secondly, any loose group may be subdivided into two or more tight subgroups, each containing words which refer to more-or-less identical concepts. This approach means that for each stemmer which is evaluated against a given word sample, two separate sets of performance indices are generated.

Some examples of the two-level grouping are shown in Figure 2. The words abstract and addition have been placed in individual subgroups because they are both ambiguous. Thus, one sense of abstract is related to abstractness, the other to literature abstracts. During the grouping, abstracting was assigned to the latter subgroup because the domain of the source was known to be library science.

(abstract) (abstraction, abstractly)
(abstracts, abstracting, abstracted, abstractors)

(addition) (additional, additionally)
(add, adds, adding, added, additive)

(alter, alters, altered, alterations)
(alternate, alternately, alternating, alternations)
(alternative, alternatives, alternatively)

(appropriate, appropriately) (appropriations)

(authur, author's, authors, authorship)

(authoritarian) (authoritative) (authority, authorities)
(authorized, authorization)

(cost, costing, costed, costs) (costly)

(device, devices) (devise, devising, devised)

(element, elements, elemental) (elementary)

(explicate, explicates, explicated, explication, explications)
(explicit, explicitly)

(frame, frames, framing, framed) (framework, frameworks)

Figure 2 : examples of two-level concept groups
Words enclosed within parentheses are grouped tightly together.
A horizontal line is a major barrier between adjacent loose groups.
(All are actual examples taken from CISI source.)

Performance evaluations were carried out for three stemmers whose details (including specific rule tables) are fully described in the IR literature: the Lovins stemmer [7], the Porter stemmer [8] and the Paice/Husk stemmer [3]. To provide a baseline for computing values of $ERRT$, UI and OI values were also obtained for simple truncation using truncation lengths of 4, 5, 6, 7 and 8.

A sample of words was obtained by processing all of the titles and abstracts in the CISI test collection, which is concerned with Library and Information Science. This source contained a total of 184,659 words, reduced to 9,757 after deletion of duplicates. Runs were also carried out using two smaller word samples: 1,527 distinct words (derived from 8,947 source words) from a textbook excerpt concerned with computer storage devices, and 3,559 distinct words (from 32,098 source words) from the texts of 14 papers on agriculture.

In order to investigate the influence of sample size on the performance indices, four subsamples were prepared from the CISI text source, by taking every nth line from complete collection, with n values of 2, 4, 8 and 16, and then preparing grouped files as usual. The resulting word samples contained 7,304, 5,395, 3804 and 2,654 word types respectively, compared with 9,757 for the full CISI vocabulary.

Results

Although the values of the indices were markedly different for the different word samples, the *patterns* of values were much the same in all cases, so that similar conclusions could be drawn for each sample. Table 1 shows the results obtained for the CISI sample. If we compare the corresponding values obtained for the and loose levels of grouping, we find that all four indices vary in the ways we would expect. Understemming will obviously be greater, and overstemming less, for loose than for tight grouping, and this in turn causes considerably smaller SW values for the loose grouping level. The $ERRT$ values are larger with loose grouping; this too is understandable since loose semantic relationships are naturally reflected in weaker and less systematic morphological similarities.

	---- tight grouping ----				---- loose grouping ----			
	UI	*OI*	*SW*	*ERRT*	*UI*	*OI*	*SW*	*ERRT*
trunc(4)	0.062	0.000814	0.013127	------	0.099	0.000706	0.007155	------
trunc(5)	0.176	0.000262	0.001487	------	0.258	0.000183	0.000710	------
trunc(6)	0.337	0.000073	0.000218	------	0.442	0.000022	0.000050	------
trunc(7)	0.527	0.000028	0.000054	------	0.633	0.000002	0.000004	------
trunc(8)	0.700	0.000012	0.000017	------	0.780	0.000000	0.000000	------
Lovins	0.326	0.000063	0.000193	0.92	0.459	0.000020	0.000044	1.00
Paice/Husk	0.121	0.000118	0.000978	0.55	0.257	0.000051	0.000197	0.67
Porter	0.374	0.000028	0.000074	0.76	0.542	0.000004	0.000007	0.88

Table 1 : Stemming performance indices for the CISI word sample

If now we compare the *pattern of values* within the tight and loose sections of Table 1, we can find no marked differences, and this suggests that the properties and validity of the indices are not strongly affected by the level of grouping - provided presumably that a consistent strategy is used.

Comparing the three stemmers with one another, the relative values of the four indices may be summarised as follows:

$$UI(\text{Porter}) > UI(\text{Lovins}) > UI(\text{Paice/Husk})$$

$$OI(\text{Paice/Husk}) > OI(\text{Lovins}) > OI(\text{Porter})$$

$$SW(\text{Paice/Husk}) > SW(\text{Lovins}) > SW(\text{Porter})$$

$$ERRT(\text{Lovins}) > ERRT(\text{Porter}) > ERRT(\text{Paice/Husk})$$

Although the magnitudes of the differences varied a good deal, and in a couple of cases were only marginal, the above inequalities actually held for all of the word samples tested. In terms of the UI index, Lovins was noticeably closer to Porter than to Paice/Husk.

If we take $ERRT$ as a general indicator of performance accuracy, we would have to conclude that Paice/Husk is a better stemmer than Porter, which is in turn better than Lovins. However, the differences in stemming weight between Paice/Husk and Porter are so great that it is probably meaningless to compare their accuracy: Paice/Husk is a heavy stemmer and Porter a light stemmer, and presumably each is suited to a different task.

It is helpful to look at Figure 3, which plots UI vs. OI for the CISI sample at the tight grouping level. This not only highlights the great difference in weight between Paice/Husk and Porter, it also casts light on the performance of Lovins. Notice first that the truncation line is convex towards the origin; this is as expected, given the generally inverse relationship between between UI and OI. However, a line joining the performance points for Paice/Husk, Lovins and Porter is clearly concave towards the origin, suggesting that Lovins is genuinely less accurate than either of the other stemmers. This relationship holds for both tight and loose levels of grouping for all the word samples tested .

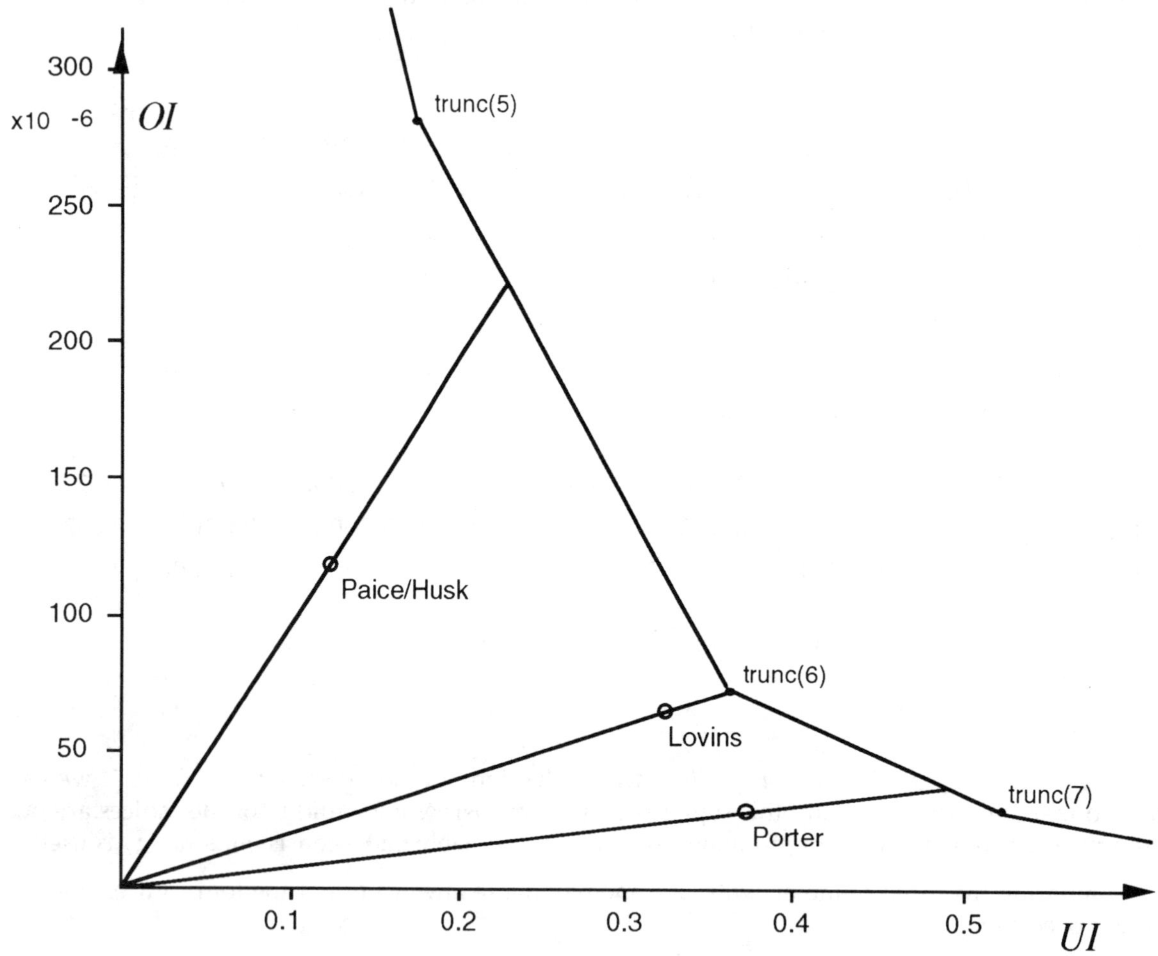

Figure 3 : UI x OI plot for CISI sample (tight grouping)

Lennon *et al.* represented the weights of their stemmers by the dictionary compression each could achieve. Their results for Lovins and Porter are compared with ours in Table 2. Our results from the CISI sample are closest to theirs from the Brown linguistic corpus; oddly, this appeared to be the least similar source to ours. However, our ratio for the compression by Lovins compared to

Porter was 1.14, whilst theirs were all in the range 1.13 to 1.18. Our compression values confirm clearly that Porter is a lighter stemmer than Lovins, and also that Paice/Husk is much heavier.

	--- *this work* ---		--- *Lennon et al. 1981* ---			
	n	CISI	Brown	NPL	Inspec	Cranfield
sample words	9,757	100.0	----	----	----	----
tight groups	5,101	47.7	----	----	----	----
loose groups	4,350	55.4	----	----	----	----
Lovins stems	5,409	44.6	45.8	39.2	39.5	30.9
Paice/Husk stems	4,755	51.3	----	----	----	----
Porter stems	5,964	38.9	38.8	34.6	33.8	26.2

Table 2 : Dictionary compression by three stemmers.
n represents numbers of items;
other values are percentage compression rates.

We now turn to the effect of sample size. It appears that UI, representing the internal structure of the concept groups, is fairly insensitive to sample size. OI however (and consequently SW) falls off sharply as sample size increases. $ERRT$ shows a less consistent tendency: the values for Lovins and Porter reach a minimum at about 5,000 sample words, whereas Paice/Husk decreases throughout, but shows signs of levelling off around 10,000 words.

We may recall that OI is defined as $GWMT/GDNT$. The global desired non-merge total $GDNT$ can be expected to depend on the square of the word sample size W. We may therefore infer that the global wrongly-merged total $GWMT$ increases less fast, and this in turn implies that the average value of formula {1} is less than proportional to W. This can be explained if the average stem-group size shows little or no tendency to increase with W; this is plausible since it is likely that as the source grows, the fresh introductions will increasingly tend to be non-domain-related singleton words.

Findings

The general results of our experiments may be summarised as follows:

-- The specific values of the performance indices vary markedly depending on the source text.

-- For a particular word source, the values of UI are fairly insensitive to sample size, whereas values of OI and SW fall off sharply as sample size increases. $ERRT$ values show modest fluctuations.

-- In terms of the stemming weight SW, Porter is a light stemmer and Paice/Husk a heavy stemmer.

-- The difference in the SW value between Porter and Paice/Husk is so great that it is probably meaningless to compare their performance.

-- The Lovins stemmer seems to be generally less accurate than either of the other two stemmers.

-- The choice of grouping level does not appear to be a critical matter, provided that a consistent strategy is used in each case.

The lightness of the Porter stemmer is in agreement with earlier findings that Porter is significantly lighter than Lovins and several other algorithms [1].

Final Comments

The author is well aware of various doubts and problems with the methods described in this paper. Further work is clearly needed to explore the validity of the approach and to make the programs more useful. One area of difficulty concerns the subjective and fuzzy nature of the grouping operations, and it would be valuable to have some objective evidence to assist in this activity. Rather than basing the grouping on a display of isolated words it might be better if grammatically tagged words could be presented instead. Part-of-speech tags might be of some use, but semantic tags would appear to be of greater value [9]. Use of tagged text would of course mean that a particular word type might be assigned to different groups on different occasions.

Use of these stemmer evaluation tools (whether in the existing or an enhanced form) is not limited to comparing the performance of existing off-the-shelf stemmers: they can also be used for optimising the rule-tables which the stemmers use. The types of changes considered would of course depend on the nature of the stemmer in question. For example, we might try to make Porter's algorithm stem a little more heavily by adding additional rules or by modifying or relaxing some of the contextual constraints.

With Paice/Husk, the emphasis would be on reducing the number of overstemming errors by retracting or modifying some of the more troublesome rules. In this case, it would be desirable to discover which rules are a serious cause of overstemming errors. This could be done by modifying the stemmer to keep a note of each removed ending (or the rule used to remove it) so that this information is available when the under- and overstemming errors are being counted. It should then be possible to compute individual error indices for each different ending.

It would be interesting to apply this evaluation method to dictionary-based conflation in order to investigate the extent and significance of the performance gap between a well-optimised stemmer and a full dictionary operation.

Acknowledgements. I should like to thank Gareth Husk, Chris Danson and Helen Simpson for their invaluable work in developing various parts of the software.

References

1. Lennon, M., Pierce, D.S., Tarry, B.D., Willett, P. An evaluation of some conflation algorithms for information retrieval. *Journal of Information Science* 1981; **3**, 177-183.

2. Frakes, W.B. *Term Conflation for Information Retrieval.* Ph.D. thesis, Syracuse University, NY, 1982.

3. Paice, C.D. Another stemmer. *SIGIR Forum* 1990; **24**, 56-61.

4. Hafer, M.A. and Weiss, S.F. Word segmentation by letter successor varieties. *Information Storage and Retrieval* 1974; ***10***, 371-385.

5. Landauer, C. and Mah, C. Message extraction through estimation of relevance. In: R.N.Oddy *et al.* (Eds.), *Information Retrieval Research.* London: Butterworths, London, 1981, pp.117-138.

6. Harman, D. How effective is suffixing? *Journal of the American Society for Information Science* 1991; **42**, 7-15.

7. Lovins, J.B. Development of a stemming algorithm. *Mechanical Translation and Computational Linguistics* 1968; **11**, 22-31.

8. Porter, M.F. An algorithm for suffix stripping. *Program* 1980; **14**, 130-137.

9. Wilson, A. and Rayson, P. The automatic content analysis of spoken discourse: a report on work in progress. In: Souter, C. and Atwell, A., *Corpus-based Computational Linguistics.* Rodopi, Amsterdam & Atlanta GA, 1993.

On the Measurement of Inter-Linker Consistency and Retrieval Effectiveness in Hypertext Databases

David Ellis, Jonathan Furner-Hines and Peter Willett*
Department of Information Studies, University of Sheffield,
Sheffield S10 2TN, UK

Abstract

An important stage in the process of retrieval of objects from a hypertext database is the creation of a set of inter-nodal links that are intended to represent the relationships existing between objects; this operation is often undertaken manually, just as index terms are often manually assigned to documents in a conventional retrieval system. In this paper, a study is reported in which several different sets of links were inserted, each by a different person, between the paragraphs of each of a number of full-text documents. The degree of similarity between the members of each pair of link-sets (*i.e.*, the degree of inter-linker consistency) was then evaluated. The results indicated that little similarity existed amongst the link-sets, a finding that is comparable with those of studies of inter-indexer consistency, which suggest that there is generally only a low level of agreement between the sets of index terms assigned to a document by different indexers. These latter studies have historically been considered significant on account of their common assumption that there exists a positive relationship between recorded levels of inter-indexer consistency and the levels of retrieval effectiveness that may be achieved by the systems studied. In order to test the validity of making a similar assumption in the context of link-assignment, the paper continues with a description of an investigation into the nature of the relationship existing between (i) the levels of inter-linker consistency obtaining among the group of hypertext databases used in our earlier experiments and (ii) the levels of effectiveness of a number of searches carried out in those databases. An account is given of the implementation of the searches and of the methods used in the calculation of numerical values expressing their effectiveness, and conclusions are drawn regarding the consistency–effectiveness relationship.

1 Introduction

An automated system that enables its users to access quantities of text may be identified as a *hypertext retrieval system* if its components include a database structured in the form of a network, and a retrieval mechanism that is navigational and browsing-based [1]. Hypertext systems provide the facility for any relationship existing between two text representations, or *nodes*, to be represented by a *link*; searchers are able to retrieve individual nodes successively by activating the links between them. Such links may be created by manual or automatic means. In this paper, we report on a study of the manual assignment of inter-nodal links to databases in which the texts represented are the individual paragraphs of a single full-text document. This study has been implemented in two stages as follows.

Firstly, we conducted an experiment in which we measured the degree of similarity between a number of hypertext databases that shared a common set of nodes but whose link-sets had been manually created by different people. Our purpose at this stage was to use the similarity values that we calculated as measurements of the extent to which agreement existed in the choice of hypertext links to be inserted in a full-text database, *i.e.*, as measurements of the degree of *inter-linker consistency* in the work of the originators of the link-sets. In Section 2, we explain in more detail how this study relates to work on inter-*indexer* consistency, and in particular on an assumption that is often made by researchers in this field but for which evidence is scant—namely, that the degree of consistency in the terms assigned to documents by indexers is positively associated with retrieval effectiveness [2, 3]. In Section 3, we describe the methods that we employed in the first stage of our experiment, firstly in the construction of our test databases, and secondly in the calculation of numerical values that express the degree of similarity between the two databases in any pair. Although the calculation of values indicating the degree of similarity between objects is a technique that has been widely used in the fields of textual [4] and chemical [5] information retrieval, *inter alia*, its application to hypertext

* To whom all correspondence should be addressed (e-mail: p.willett@sheffield.ac.uk).

structures is a novel one, and the methodology of these experiments is treated in some detail. In Section 4 we discuss the results of our calculations: our principal conclusions are that the recorded levels of inter-linker consistency were generally low, but that they displayed marked variation.

Secondly, we carried out an investigation of the relationship between, on the one hand, the levels of inter-linker consistency observed amongst the group of databases in which links had been inserted and, on the other, the effectiveness of searches carried out in those databases. We conjectured that the manual creation of sets of inter-nodal links in hypertext databases is analogous in certain respects to the manual creation of sets of index terms in conventional document databases, and wished to test the hypothesis that consistency and effectiveness are related in the former context just as, it is suggested, they are in the latter. The significance of accepting such a hypothesis rests on the results of the first stage of our study. These indicated that levels of inter-linker consistency are low and variable: if we were also to find that consistency and effectiveness are related to some degree, then the simple conclusion would be that the levels of effectiveness that may be achieved by hypertext retrieval systems are correspondingly low and variable. Given the intensive nature of the manual labour required in the creation of sets of hypertext links, such a conclusion might have serious implications for those contemplating the addition of hypertextual characteristics to a conventional document database. In Section 5, we give an account of the methods used in our study's second stage: firstly in the implementation of the searches on the databases, and secondly in the calculation of numerical values expressing the effectiveness of the searches. In Section 6, we report the current status of the work, which involves a comparison of the sets of results produced by the two stages of the study.

Although the methods that we use, in the calculation both of similarity values and of values of retrieval effectiveness, will in their essence be familiar to those experienced in the traditional experimental activities of information retrieval research, their application in the current context is almost wholly novel. The basic directed-graph model of hypertext is considered axiomatic in much of the published work on hypertext structure [6], but few authors have made use of computational graph theory in consideration of the variations in structure that may be observed amongst different hypertext databases, the sole notable example of recent work in this field being that of Botafogo *et al.* [7]. Similarly, few studies of hypertext retrieval systems make more than nominal use of traditional measures of retrieval effectiveness: the experiments described by Al-Hawamdeh *et al.* [8] and by Savoy [9] are conspicuous exceptions. In this paper, therefore, we place particular emphasis on the description of the methodology that we have developed.

2 Inter-Indexer Consistency and Retrieval Effectiveness

The aim of work in the field of *inter-indexer consistency* is the measurement of the extent to which agreement exists among different indexers on the sets of index terms to be assigned to individual documents [3]. Such measurement is possible where two or more sets of terms are assigned to each document, each set constructed by one of two or more individual indexers. Studies of inter-indexer consistency were especially popular in the 1960s [10]; although interest has waned in subsequent decades, reports of experiments continue to appear with some regularity [11]. The principal conclusions of such studies, beyond suggestions as to how consistency might be improved, are normally that recorded levels of consistency display marked variation, and that high levels of consistency are rarely achieved.

For most writers on the subject, the degree of significance that is commonly attributed to the results of studies of inter-indexer consistency appears to derive from the assumption that they are predictive of the levels of retrieval effectiveness that may be attained by the systems studied. Leonard [3, p. 33], for example, states that "interindexer consistency and retrieval effectiveness exhibit a tendency toward a direct, positive relationship, i.e. high interindexer consistency in assignment of terms appears to be associated with a high retrieval effectiveness of the documents indexed." The argument posited in order to account for this relationship generally runs as follows: (i) Studies of inter-indexer consistency provide empirical evidence that indexers asked to index the same document do so inconsistently. (ii) It is reasonable to infer from this evidence that inconsistency also arises in the indexing by different indexers of different documents—in other words, one indexer may well use a term to represent a concept in one document that is different from the term used by another indexer in another document. Studies of *intra*-indexer consistency indicate that the levels of consistency identifiable in the work of a single indexer on a collection of documents are often similarly low [10]. (iii) The larger the number of index terms that are used in a document database to represent the same concept, the more difficult it becomes for the user to represent the concept with search terms that match those used in the indexing, and the less effective their retrieval. As Leonard [3, p.32] puts it, "the greater the agreement among indexers regarding the terms that best describe a document's content, the higher the probability that the index terms will also match terms used in a search for which the document is regarded as a relevant item."

It should be noted that an argument in this form postulates a relationship simply between inter-indexer consistency and the component of retrieval effectiveness known as *recall* (the proportion of all the relevant documents in a database that are retrieved). Although the number of studies of consistency conducted is large, empirical data confirming the existence of such a relationship is notoriously rare. For most authors, the sole source of such data is the study reported in Leonard's unpublished thesis [2]. Leonard's test collection consisted of eighteen groups of ten documents, each group drawn from one of two databases. Within each group, five documents had been judged as relevant to a particular pre-defined query, and five as non-relevant. Each group of documents was indexed by five indexers drawn from a pool of forty, and measurements of inter-indexer consistency for each group were calculated using two separate methods. Searches were undertaken using the pre-defined queries on each of the five 'versions', indexed by a different indexer, of each of the five document groups, and measurements of recall and precision calculated by comparing the results of these searches with the original relevance judgments. Leonard reported that the rank-order correlations between the measurements of consistency and the averaged measurements of recall for each group indicated "a definite trend toward a moderate to strong positive association of variables" [3, p. 32]. Significantly, no such relationship was suggested by the correlations between the measurements of consistency and the averaged measurements of precision.

We believe that the manual insertion of hypertext links between the documents stored in a database is analogous to the manual assignment of index terms to such documents. Just as the performance of a 'conventional' document retrieval system is strongly dependent on the terms used to index documents, the performance of a hypertext retrieval system is strongly dependent on the links inserted between the objects stored in its database, in that a poorly-constructed set of links may render the database of little practical use to those who seek information from it. Moreover, the creation of links, like the creation of sets of index terms, is a time-consuming and skilled process, since it requires the person creating the links to have a clear overview of the contents of the text and of the conceptual relationships that exist between its component parts. It is hence of interest to investigate the hypothesis that there exists a relationship between inter-linker consistency and the effectiveness of hypertext retrieval systems similar to the one that is posited to exist between inter-indexer consistency and effectiveness.

3 Measurement of Inter-Linker Consistency: Methodology

3.1 Creation of the Test Databases

The databases used in our experiments derived from five printed full-text documents (to which references are provided in an Appendix to this paper), each a thesis, journal article or book written by a member of the Department of Information Studies at the University of Sheffield. Each printed document comprised a set of paragraphs, ranging in number from 23 to 347, arranged in a linear sequence. A machine-readable version was produced of each of the documents using the authoring system *GUIDE* [12]; *GUIDE* was chosen for this purpose on account of its widespread availability and use within the academic community in the U.K., and because of its use in a previous study of the effectiveness of retrieval from hypertext that used a similar test collection [8]. Copies of each of the five electronic documents were then allocated to five student volunteers from the Department. Each of the twenty-five volunteers was instructed in the use of an interactive system, developed using *GUIDE*, that allowed them to create explicit representations of links between paragraphs whose contents they decided were related. On completion of the linkers' work, the results were five hypertext versions of each of five different documents, each sharing a common set of *nodes* (*i.e.*, paragraphs) with four others, but each having a different set of *links* inserted amongst the nodes. Each hypertext version of a document was subsequently considered as a one of twenty-five complete and separate hypertext databases.

3.2 Calculation of Similarity Values

Given our intention to calculate values that would indicate the extent of inter-linker consistency amongst the databases in our test collection, we set out to calculate a variety of values for each database-pair that might be said to represent the degree of similarity between the members of that pair. The measurement of the degree of similarity between the objects in our study involved four steps, as follows:

3.2.1 Identification of Objects for Comparison

The objects that we wished to compare were the five databases associated with each document. Each database could be compared with four others, resulting in ten database-pairs per document. The members of each set of links assigned to a database were classified according to the relative position of their source and target nodes, and link-subsets of three types defined on the basis of this classification.

3.2.2 Numerical Representation of Objects

Each link-subset was represented in a number of ways that allowed us to calculate many numerical values quantifying the degree of similarity between them. We drew on ideas developed in the branch of mathematics known as *graph theory* [13], which may be used to model the structural characteristics of any system that is made up of a set of objects and a set of binary relations existing between the members of pairs of those objects. A *directed graph* $\mathcal{G}$ is given by $\mathcal{G} = \langle V,E \rangle$, where V is an object set given by $V = \{v_1,v_2,v_3,\ldots,v_p\}$, each of whose p members is called a *vertex*, and E is a relation set given by $E \subseteq V \times V$, each of whose members is called a directed *edge*. Each edge of a directed graph is defined by an ordered pair of vertices: we may say that an edge 'points' from the first coordinate of the pair to the second coordinate. A hypertext database may be represented in graph-theoretic form, where the objects or nodes stored in the database are mapped to the vertices of a directed graph, and the links between nodes correspond to edges [6].

Graphs may easily be represented diagrammatically, using pictures made up of points and lines: in order that a graph may be analysed by computer, however, it is necessary for it to be represented in a machine-readable format, which normally involves some form of numerical matrix. Each of the three link-subsets of one of our hypertext databases, for example, may be represented in the form of an adjacency, distance or converted distance matrix. For any directed graph $\mathcal{G}$ of p nodes, we can define an *adjacency matrix* $\mathcal{A}$ consisting of $p \times p$ elements of the form a_{ij}. Each of these elements has a value of 1 (if the set of links contains a member pointing from v_i to v_j), 0 (if the set of links does not contain a member pointing from v_i to v_j), or NULL (if $i = j$, *i.e.*, if the node v_i is the same as node v_j). Similarly, we can define a *distance matrix* $\mathcal{D}$ consisting of $p \times p$ elements of the form d_{ij}, where d_{ij} is the length (measured in links) of any shortest path between the nodes v_i and v_j (if those nodes are connected), 0 (if those nodes are not connected), or NULL (if $i = j$). A *converted distance matrix* can also be defined: this modified version of the distance matrix is described by Botafogo *et al.* [7].

3.2.3 Selection of Attributes

The sets of elements contained in the graph-theoretic representations of our link-subsets were thus identified as the object-representations that we wished to compare. The next step involved the selection of those *attributes* of these graph-theoretic representations whose values were to be used to characterise the representations in the course of their comparison. Any set of attribute-values may be expressed in the form of an n-tuple, where n is the number of attributes whose values are used to characterise the object-representation.

We may derive n-tuples of attribute-values from any graph-theoretic representation of a hypertext database $\mathcal{G}$ with p nodes in two ways:

(a) Using the elements of the matrix as attribute-values. We can do this either (i) by representing the matrix as a single n-tuple (where $n = p^2 - p$), or (ii) by representing the matrix as an n-tuple (where $n = p$) of n-tuples (where $n = p-1$).

(b) Using the values of topological indices as attribute-values. The values of topological indices are defined by functions on the elements of matrices [14]. We may identify two classes of such indices: (i) a class of 'node' indices, the values of whose members take the form of an n-tuple of numerical elements; and (ii) a class of 'graph' indices, the values of whose members take the form of single numbers. An example of a node index is N, given by $\langle N_1,N_2,N_3,\ldots,N_p \rangle$, where p is equal to the number of nodes in the database, and N_i is equal to the ratio of the sum of values in all rows of the matrix to the sum of values in the ith row.

3.2.4 Selection of Coefficients

Finally, we needed to select an appropriate measure or *coefficient*, whose values were to be derived from analysis of the various attribute-values of the two object-representations in a pair. Whatever the nature of the attribute-values used, we may use any of a variety of similarity coefficients to compare a pair of n-tuples. Elsewhere, we have reviewed the composition and role of a large number of such coefficients [4]. Any of these may be used for our purposes (and in the course of our experiment we calculated sets of similarity values using over twenty different formulae); most applications in information retrieval, however, display a historical attachment to simple, linear, non-probabilistic *association coefficients* such as those provided by the *Dice* and *cosine* formulae.

4 Measurement of Inter-Linker Consistency: Results

For each database-pair, consistency values were computed using (i) three different types of link-subsets, (ii) three different types of graph-theoretic representation (adjacency, distance and converted distance matrices), (iii) a variety of sets of attribute-values of two types (matrix-element and topological-index), each derived using a different formula, and (iv) over twenty different similarity coefficients. Limitations of space mean that it is not possible for full results to be presented here; a summary, however, is provided in another paper [15], and full details are to appear in a BLRDD report [16]. For our present purposes, this mass of results may be adequately represented by the frequency diagram depicted in Figure 1. Each value of consistency (*C*) whose frequency is recorded in this diagram derives from (i) a pair of link-subsets of a particular type, *viz* that which includes only those links between paragraphs whose contents were identified by the link-creator as being semantically related, rather than those between paragraphs that were adjacent in the linear sequence followed by the original document, (ii) adjacency data, (iii) the single-*n*-tuple matrix-element method, and (iv) the Dice coefficient. Although corresponding frequency diagrams for sets of consistency values derived using other methods of computation depict varying distributions, the conclusions that may be drawn from the great majority of these alternatives are similar to the two principal conclusions that may be drawn from the values recorded in Figure 1. These are:

1. Inter-linker consistency is *low*. Inspection of the frequency diagram, which represents the whole set of values of *C* over all five documents, reveals a highly positively-skewed distribution, with a median of 0.03. In other words, most of the values are found toward the lower limit of the range 0.00 to 1.00. The mean of the values forming such a skewed distribution is less significant; for the record, nonetheless, it is 0.12.
2. Inter-linker consistency is *variable*. A few of the values of *C* recorded for Document 3 are much higher than the median of the whole set of values, reaching 0.50 or above.

These two points are comparable with the principal conclusions of the inter-indexer consistency studies mentioned in Section 2, *viz* that high levels of consistency are rarely achieved, but that recorded levels of consistency do display marked variation.

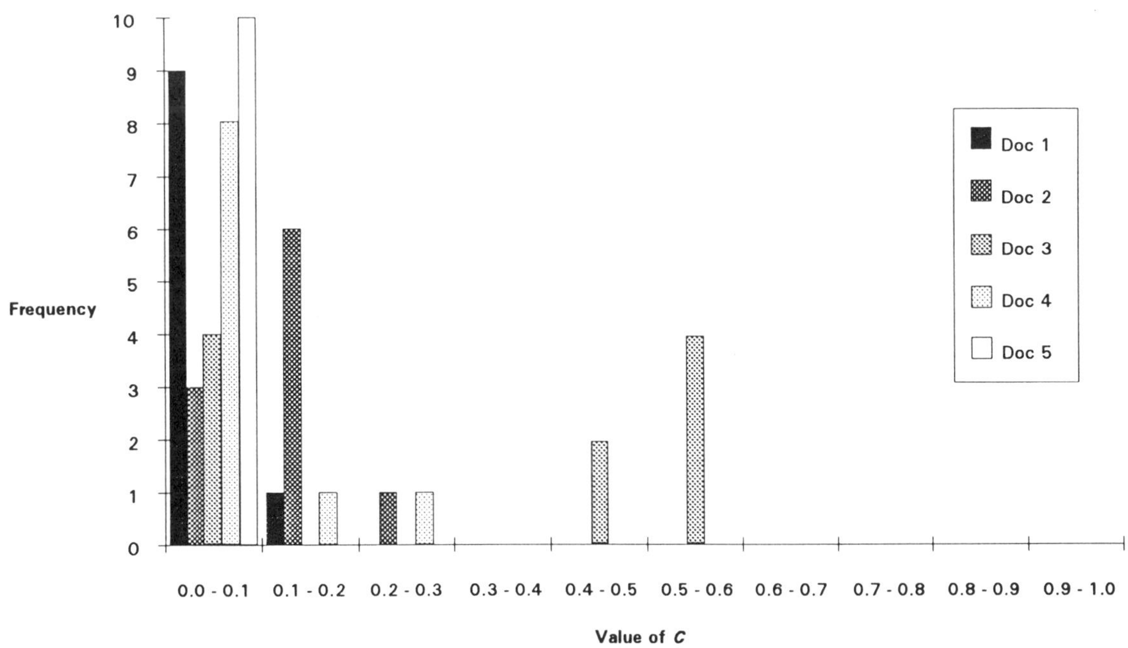

Figure 1. Frequency diagram showing the counts of values of *C* falling in 0.1-wide ranges

5 Measurement of Retrieval Effectiveness: Methodology

5.1 Search Design

In the second stage of the study, a total of forty volunteer searchers was recruited from the group of master's and doctoral students at the Department of Information Studies. In their capacity as students, few of these volunteers had any professional experience of database searching, but all had an understanding of the purpose and operation of online retrieval systems and of the nature of the relationship of 'relevance' that might exist between a query and a document.

Each of these volunteers was instructed in the use of an interactive computer system, again developed using *GUIDE*, that allowed them to access any of the twenty-five databases, to view one node of the database on the screen at a time, and to navigate successively from one individual node of the database to another, thus displaying on the screen the content of the target node on the screen. Searchers were able to navigate in this way by activating on-screen *buttons* of a number of types. The searchers were told that the most important buttons were those embedded in the text of a document's paragraphs, each labelled with the ID number of a target paragraph. Each of these buttons indicated the source of a link that had been inserted by the volunteer linker responsible for the currently-accessed database; the ID number of a paragraph represented its position in the linear sequence adopted in the original printed document. The location of a button was indicated to the searcher by a section of highlighted text chosen for this purpose by the linker: it was by this means that the searcher was given an indication of the potential relevance of the target of the link. As well as buttons enabling the user to change databases, to view a 'Help' screen, and to exit the system, other buttons provided searchers with different navigational options, including a backtracking facility, and a facility to display the paragraphs immediately preceding and succeeding (in the original linear sequence) the currently-displayed paragraph. Whenever a searcher selected any database for access, the first screen to be displayed was that database's table of contents, which comprised a list of the titles of the chapters, sections and subsections of the original printed document, together with the ID numbers of the paragraphs beginning these sections. Each title formed the label of a button on whose activation the paragraph of that number would be displayed.

Each of the volunteers was allocated five databases for searching, one of each of the five versions of each of the five original documents: thus, each database-version was searched by eight different searchers. Each searcher was given the same list of twenty-five queries, five for each of the five databases. These queries derived from those suggested by the authors of the original printed documents for experiments conducted previously in the Department that made use of a similar test collection [8]. The searchers were instructed to identify all and only those paragraphs that, in their opinion, would be relevant to a person with the particular information expressed in the query.

Because each database version had a unique set of links inserted amongst its set of nodes, the navigational options available to a searcher at any stage of the process would be likely to differ from those available to someone at a similar stage of the search in another database version. It was hypothesised that at least a proportion of the variation in the degree of effectiveness observed between searches carried out by different people would be a result of certain differences exhibited in the structures of the link-sets. No attempts were made to control for the effects of variables such as searcher expertise; however, in an attempt to discover variation occurring as a result of the provision or otherwise of a global search facility in addition to a simple navigational mechanism, the experiment was designed so that only half of the searchers were allowed to use a 'Keyword search' facility. This facility enabled the user to search the whole of the currently-accessed database for occurrences of any single- or multi-word string (no wildcard characters, truncation or Boolean combinations).

5.2 Computation of Retrieval Effectiveness

Historically, the majority of evaluative studies of document retrieval systems have included attempts to quantify their *effectiveness*, using measures such as recall and precision that are based on pre-retrieval manual relevance judgments. By way of exception, evaluative studies of systems based on navigational retrieval mechanisms have tended to eschew quantitative techniques in favour of evaluation of a less formal nature, largely as a result of the historical attachment of many hypertext researchers to the field of human–computer interaction rather than to that of information retrieval. In work such as this, the essence of any hypertext system is seen to lie in the peculiarity of its user interface; as a result, any measurement of the quality of a system's performance may generally be equated with evaluation of its *usability* rather than of its performance.

Several recent experiments have focused, from a human-factors perspective, on the usability of the interface to hypertext systems, often in comparison with other media for the presentation of information such as paper [17]. As we indicated in Section 1, studies of hypertext retrieval systems that make more than a passing reference to the use of traditional measures of retrieval effectiveness are few and far between: examples of such studies are provided by Al-Hawamdeh *et al.* [8] and Savoy [9].

It should be made clear, however, that the traditional method of computing the effectiveness of retrieval in an experimental environment, by comparing what is actually retrieved with what a human judging panel determine should be retrieved, is not necessarily the most appropriate for the evaluation of retrieval systems based on navigational mechanisms [18]. In the context of an interactive navigational retrieval system such as the one under consideration in this paper, the 'retrieval' or display of a paragraph as a result of user navigation should not be taken as an indication that that paragraph is necessarily relevant to the user's information need: it is left to the searcher to decide which of the paragraphs retrieved are relevant to their needs. In other words, the effectiveness of a search depends to a large extent on the particular navigational actions of the searcher. Nevertheless, because the range of navigational options open to a searcher at any stage of the process is determined by the nature of the set of links inserted between the nodes of the database, it is also true that a search's effectiveness will be limited to a substantial degree by the opportunities that are provided by the system for the searcher to navigate to relevant nodes. In simple terms, if there is a particular paragraph to which a searcher is never given the chance to navigate, they will never be able to decide whether that paragraph is relevant to their needs or not.

In the light of these observations, we propose that the effectiveness of the retrieval system used in our experiments should be measured in two different ways, using sets of relevance judgments of three types:

(a) *Judge-relevant* paragraphs. A set of relevance judgments, produced in association with the authors of the original printed documents, was assigned to each set of five queries before any of the searches had taken place. Each set consists of the numbers of all and only those paragraphs that the judges believed would be relevant to a person with the information need expressed in the query.

(b) *Searcher-relevant* paragraphs. On completion of the searches, another forty sets of relevance judgments, produced by the volunteers, were assigned to each set of five queries. Eight of these sets of judgments were produced for each of the five database versions. Each set consists of the numbers of all and only those paragraphs that the searcher believed would be relevant to a person with the information need expressed in the query.

(c) *Navigator-relevant* paragraphs. A set of 'judgments' of a third type is that corresponding to the paragraphs 'visited' or retrieved by the user in the course of their navigation. Another forty sets of judgments could be identified in this way, eight for each of the five database versions. Each set consists of the numbers of all those paragraphs through which the searcher navigated. Note that if a paragraph is searcher-relevant, it is also necessarily navigator-relevant, but not *vice versa*.

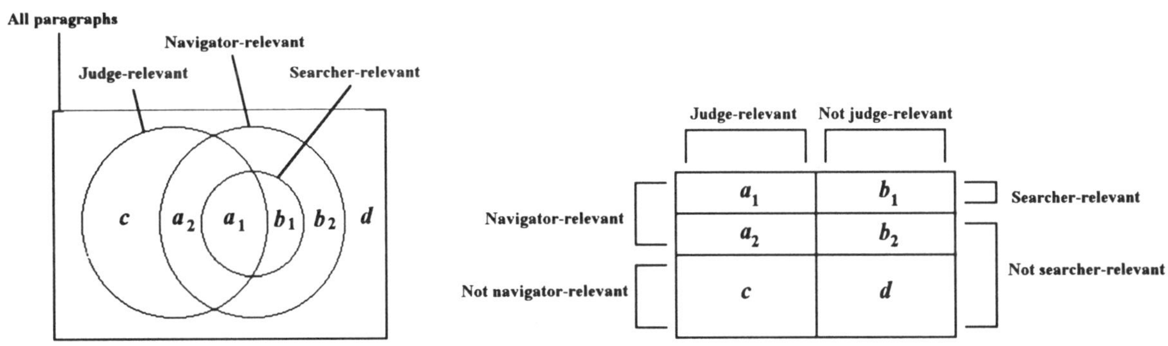

(i) (ii)

Figure 2. (i) Venn diagram, and (ii) table, showing the relationships between sets of judge-relevant, navigator-relevant and searcher-relevant paragraphs

We can now define a modified version of the 2×2 table that is often depicted in discussions of the measures of recall and precision [19, p. 148]. This modified version (see Figure 2) consists of six cells a_1, a_2, b_1, b_2, c, d as follows: a_1 is the number of paragraphs that are judge-relevant and searcher-relevant; a_2 is the number of paragraphs that are judge-relevant and navigator-relevant, but not searcher-relevant; b_1 is the number of paragraphs that are not judge-relevant, but are searcher-relevant; b_2 is the number of paragraphs that are neither judge-relevant nor searcher-relevant, but are navigator-relevant; c is the number of paragraphs that are judge-relevant, but are not navigator-relevant; and d is the number of paragraphs that are neither judge-relevant nor navigator-relevant.

For each set of queries x and for each searcher y, we may define the following measures of recall and precision: $R1_{x,y}$, equal to $a_1 / (a_1+a_2+c)$, the ratio of the number of paragraphs that are both judge-relevant and searcher-relevant, to the total number of those that are judge-relevant; $P1_{x,y}$, equal to $a_1 / (a_1+b_1)$, the ratio of the number of paragraphs that are both judge-relevant and searcher-relevant, to the total number of those that are searcher-relevant; $R2_{x,y}$, equal to $(a_1+a_2) / (a_1+a_2+c)$, the ratio of the number of paragraphs that are both judge-relevant and navigation-relevant, to the total number of those that are judge-relevant; and $P2_{x,y}$, equal to $(a_1+a_2) / (a_1+a_2+b_1+b_2)$, the ratio of the number of paragraphs that are both judge-relevant and navigation-relevant, to the total number of those that are navigation-relevant.

6 Comparison of Consistency with Effectiveness

Our principal research hypothesis (H_1) is that there is a positive association between inter-linker consistency and retrieval effectiveness. The objective of our experiment was therefore to compare the measurements of inter-linker consistency resulting from our use of the methods described in Section 3, with the measurements of retrieval effectiveness resulting from our use of the methods described in Section 5. Because a single consistency value gives an indication of the similarity between two hypertext versions of the same document, then each such value should be compared with a corresponding value that gives an indication of the *average* effectiveness that may be achieved by searching either of those two databases. It is in this way that Leonard [2] compares levels of inter-indexer consistency with retrieval effectiveness, although he calculates his averages over groups of ten documents rather than groups of two.

For the purposes of this experiment, we consider each pair of hypertext databases as an object that may be characterised by a value of each of two attributes, C and M. There are fifty objects in our sample (ten database-pairs per document). Each value of attribute C represents the level of inter-linker consistency between the two members of a database-pair; each value of attribute M represents the mean level of mean effectiveness attained by searches in the two members of a database-pair. A value representing the mean level of effectiveness for a single database may be obtained by taking the average of a set of values, each element of which represents the level of effectiveness of one of the eight individual searches conducted in that database. A value representing the level of effectiveness of a search may be calculated using any of the four different formulae defined in Section 5.2, and in theory it would be of interest to state four experimental hypotheses, each corresponding to a different definition of effectiveness and hence to a different set of values of M. Our one-tailed null hypothesis (H_0) is thus that there is no positive association between the set of values of C and any set of values of M. As Leonard's original hypothesis concerned recall only, however, we are concerned more with values of M derived from the formula for $R1$, and to a lesser extent with those derived from $R2$, than with those derived from values of precision. The scattergram in Figure 3 shows the value of C for each database-pair plotted against its corresponding value of $R1$.

A number of observations should be made before the results of any statistical test of correlation are analysed:

1. The recorded values of C form a distribution that is far from normal. As we noted in Section 4, inspection of Figure 1 reveals a highly positively-skewed distribution.
2. However, again as we noted earlier, a few of the values of C are much higher. The values that are particularly high (within the range 0.45 to 0.60) are to be found amongst those recorded for Document 3, *i.e.*, values of equivalent magnitude to these were not recorded for any of the other documents. This might suggest that each sample of values for a particular document is drawn from a different population. We do not intend to test this hypothesis here (it is doubtful, in any case, that the samples are sufficiently large to allow conclusions to be drawn at an appropriate level of significance), but it is certainly not unreasonable to imagine that those factors having a strong influence on level of consistency include some which may be expressed in terms of the characteristics of the documents under consideration, and that these characteristics (*e.g.*, length, subject, difficulty) vary considerably—with the result that levels of consistency vary accordingly between documents.
3. Similarly, neither of the samples of values of mean recall form a normal distribution, and inspection of Figure 3 would indicate that, again, each sample of values for a particular document is drawn from a different population. Factors influencing the level of mean recall might include not only the same characteristics of documents that affect level of consistency, but also characteristics of the different sets of queries associated with each document (*e.g.*, terminological usage, specificity). Results presented elsewhere [16] also indicate

that the relationship between recorded values of mean recall and those of mean precision is more complex than the inverse relationship commonly observed in studies of conventional full-text retrieval systems.

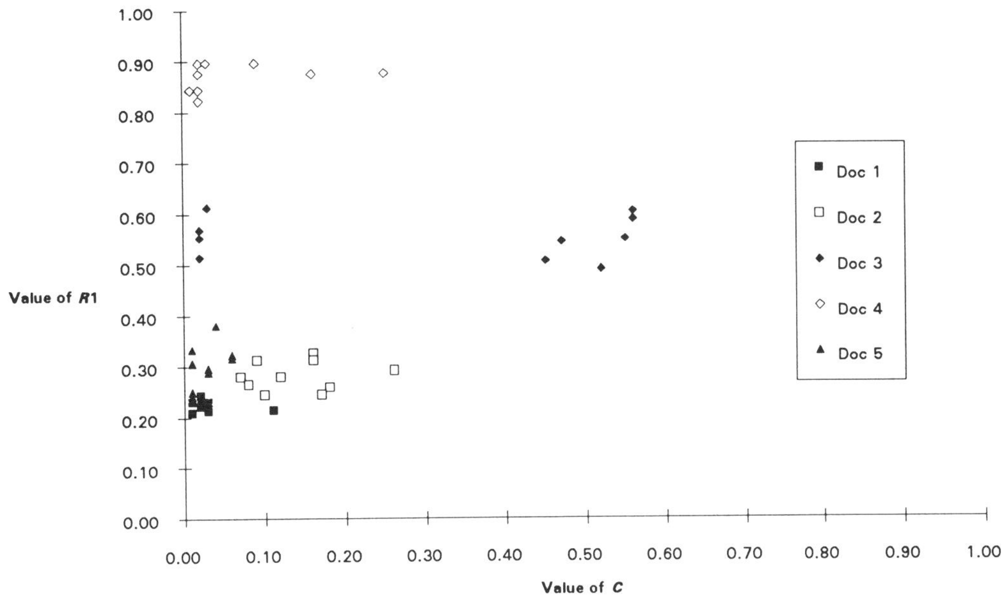

Figure 3. Scattergram showing the value of C for each of fifty database-pairs plotted against its corresponding value of $R1$

The non-normal shape of each of the distributions under consideration precludes the use of Pearson's product–moment correlation coefficient to test the extent of the association between variables: in any case, inspection alone is necessary to confirm that there is no discernible association between the values of C and the values of $R1$ when both samples are taken as wholes. It is instructive, however, to investigate levels of association between the samples of values for a particular document, so that the potentially variable effects of document and query characteristics are controlled. In doing this, we shall consider values of an alternative, non-parametric coefficient, Spearman's rank-order correlation coefficient, that was used by Leonard in his pioneering study of the relationship between consistency and effectiveness.

For a one-tailed test where $n = 10$, the value of the rank-order correlation coefficient ρ must exceed 0.564 for the level of association that it represents to be considered significant at a level of probability of $p \leq 0.05$. If we attempt to correlate the values of C and $R1$ for one document at a time, we find that the value of ρ does not exceed the relevant threshold in any of the five cases. When the values of C for each document are compared with values of $P1$, $R2$ and $P2$, conflicting patterns emerge: the level of positive association between C and $P1$ is revealed to be significant in two cases (Document 1: $\rho = 0.854$, $p \leq 0.005$; Document 2: $\rho = 0.691$, $p \leq 0.025$), while the level of *inverse* association between the same two variables is similarly significant in another case (Document 5: $\rho = -0.812$, $p \leq 0.005$). C and $R2$ are correlated to a significant degree in only one case (Document 4: $\rho = 0.824$, $p \leq 0.005$), and C and $P2$ exhibit an inverse association in one case (Document 3: $\rho = -0.854$, $p \leq 0.005$). Similar results may be found when the values of C used in the comparison are derived from different formulae: in the overwhelming majority of cases, the recorded value of ρ does not suggest the existence of a positive association.

7 Conclusion

Given these results, and those presented elsewhere [16], we are unable to reject the null hypothesis H_0, that there is no positive association between the set of values of C and any of the four sets of values of M. If we had found that levels of inter-linker consistency, like those of inter-indexer consistency, are predictive of levels of retrieval effectiveness, then those results would have had ominous implications for the evaluation of retrieval systems that access databases in which hypertext links have been inserted manually, especially given the intensive nature of the manual labour required in the creation of hypertext links. But we did not find this to be so, and we are therefore not in a position to draw conclusions about the consistency–effectiveness relationship that are equivalent to those drawn by Leonard.

However, our research raises many issues, suitable for further study, that concern the effectiveness of hypertext systems. It would be of interest, for example, to see whether our results were reproducible using (i) other authoring systems with different linking mechanisms to those provided by *GUIDE*, (ii) original hypertexts that are not merely conversions of existing texts, (iii) professional hypertext authors, (iv) links created automatically by means of statistical analysis of term occurrencies, and (v) expert searchers, *inter alia*. A particularly fertile area for future research, however, would be a comparison of the differential effect on retrieval effectiveness of (i) link structure, and (ii) search strategy. If it were found that the precise shape of a link structure is relatively unimportant in terms of its ultimate influence on retrieval effectiveness, then we would yet be forced to draw a disturbing conclusion: that the presumed objective of a manual linker's efforts—to construct link-sets on whose account the effectiveness of future searches will somehow be optimised—is largely doomed to failure.

Acknowledgments

We thank students and colleagues from the Department of Information Studies for their creation of the sets of hypertext links and for conducting the searches used in our experiments, and the British Library Research and Development Department for funding this work under grant number RDD/G/142.

Appendix: Test Collection

1. Ellis D. The derivation of a behavioural model for information retrieval design. PhD thesis, Department of Information Studies, University of Sheffield, 1987
2. Rasmussen EM. Cluster analysis on a highly parallel array processor. PhD thesis, Department of Information Studies, University of Sheffield, 1988
3. Ormerod A, Willett P, Bawden D. Comparison of fragment weighting schemes for substructural analysis. Quantitative Structure–Analysis Relationships 1989; 8:115–129
4. Loughridge B, Sutton J. The careers of MA graduates: training, education and practice. Journal of Librarianship 1988; 20:255–269
5. Ford N. Expert systems and artificial intelligence: an information manager's guide. Library Association, London, 1991

References

1. Waterworth JA, Chignell MH. A model for information exploration. Hypermedia 1991; 3:35–58
2. Leonard LE. Inter-indexer consistency and retrieval effectiveness: measurement of relationships. PhD thesis, Graduate School of Library Science, University of Illinois, Urbana-Champaign, IL, 1975
3. Leonard LE. Inter-indexer consistency studies, 1954–1975: a review of the literature and summary of study results. Graduate School of Library Science, University of Illinois, Urbana-Champaign, IL, 1977 (Occasional paper no. 131)
4. Ellis D, Furner-Hines J, Willett P. Measuring the degree of similarity between objects in text retrieval systems. Perspectives in Information Management 1993; 3:128–149
5. Willett, P. Similarity and clustering in chemical information systems. Research Studies Press, Letchworth, 1987
6. Halasz F, Schwartz M. The Dexter hypertext reference model. In: Moline J, Benigni D, Baronas J (eds) Proceedings of the Hypertext Standardization Workshop. NIST, Gaithersburg, MD, 1990, pp 95–113
7. Botafogo RA, Rivlin E, Shneiderman B. Structural analysis of hypertexts: identifying hierarchies and useful metrics. ACM Transactions on Information Systems 1992; 10:142–180
8. Al-Hawamdeh S, Smith G, Willett, P. Paragraph-based access to full-text documents using a hypertext system. Program 1991; 25:119–131
9. Savoy J. Effectiveness of information retrieval systems used in a hypertext environment. Hypermedia 1993; 5:23–46
10. Hooper RS. Indexer consistency tests—origin, measurements, results and utilization. IBM, Bethesda, MD, 1965
11. Sievert MC, Andrews MJ. Indexing consistency in Information Science Abstracts. Journal of the American Society for Information Science 1991; 42:1–6
12. GUIDE user manual. OWL International, Bellevue, WA, 1990
13. Wilson RJ. Introduction to graph theory (3rd ed). Longman, London, 1985
14. Basak SC, Magnuson VR, Niemi GJ, Regal RR, Veith, GD. Topological indices: their nature, mutual relatedness, and applications. Mathematical Modelling 1987; 8:300–305
15. Ellis D, Furner-Hines J, Willett P. On the creation of hypertext links in full-text documents: measurement of inter-linker consistency. Journal of Documentation 1994; in press
16. Ellis D, Furner-Hines J, Willett P. The manual creation of hypertext links in full-text documents. British Library, London, 1994 (BLRDD report); in preparation
17. Rada R, Murphy C. Searching versus browsing in hypertext. Hypermedia 1992; 4:1–30
18. Su LT. Evaluation measures for interactive information retrieval. Information Processing & Management 1992; 28:503–516
19. van Rijsbergen CJ. Information retrieval (2nd ed). Butterworths, London, 1979

Query Expansion using Lexical-Semantic Relations

Ellen M. Voorhees
ellen@scr.siemens.com

Siemens Corporate Research, Inc.
755 College Road East
Princeton, NJ 08540

Abstract

Applications such as office automation, news filtering, help facilities in complex systems, and the like require the ability to retrieve documents from full-text databases where vocabulary problems can be particularly severe. Experiments performed on small collections with single-domain thesauri suggest that expanding query vectors with words that are lexically related to the original query words can ameliorate some of the problems of mismatched vocabularies. This paper examines the utility of lexical query expansion in the large, diverse TREC collection. Concepts are represented by WordNet synonym sets and are expanded by following the typed links included in WordNet. Experimental results show this query expansion technique makes little difference in retrieval effectiveness if the original queries are relatively complete descriptions of the information being sought even when the concepts to be expanded are selected by hand. Less well developed queries can be significantly improved by expansion of hand-chosen concepts. However, an automatic procedure that can approximate the set of hand picked synonym sets has yet to be devised, and expanding by the synonym sets that are automatically generated can degrade retrieval performance.

1 Introduction

Users of retrieval systems that use word matching as a basis for retrieval are faced with the challenge of phrasing their queries in the vocabularies of the documents they wish to retrieve. This difficulty is especially severe in large, full-text databases since such databases contain many different expressions of the same concept [1]. Yet the ability to retrieve documents from such databases is crucial in a wide range of applications: retrieving documentation in support of a legal case, facilitating the organization and retrieval of correspondence and forms in an office, filtering news feeds for articles of interest, finding relevant passages within the complete manual set of a complex system for the particular problem at hand, etc. One method of easing the user's burden when selecting query words is for the retrieval system to automatically expand the query by adding terms that are related to the words supplied by the user. The new terms can either be statistically related to the original query words (that is, the terms tend to co-occur with one another in documents) or chosen from lexical aids such as thesauri, controlled vocabulary schedules, and the like.

Using statistical relations to expand query vectors is attractive since the the relations are easily generated from the documents at hand, obviating the need for lexical aids, which are expensive to build and maintain. Unfortunately, such methods have had little success in improving retrieval effectiveness when used apart from relevance data [2, 3]. Indeed, Peat and Willett show there are limitations to the effectiveness one can expect from such systems [4]. (Note, however, that methods that exploit statistical relations but do not expand the query, such as Latent Semantic Indexing [5], have been more successful.)

Using lexical aids as a source of related terms has met with some success in small experiments. Salton and Lesk found that expansion by synonyms improved performance but expansion by broader or narrower terms selected from a hierarchical thesaurus was too inconsistent to be generally useful [6]. Wang, Vendendorpe, and Evens found that a variety of lexical-semantic relations improved retrieval performance [7]. However, each of these conclusions was drawn from experiments on very small collections using single-domain thesauri.

This paper examines the utility of query expansion by lexical-semantic relations in a large collection that spans several domains. Queries are expanded using the relations encoded in WordNet [8], a large, general-purpose lexical system built at Princeton University, and are run against the TREC collection [9]. To eliminate the confounding effects of expanding a poor selection of words, the terms that were expanded were chosen by hand. Thus, the results reported here represent an upper bound on the performance to be expected from a completely automatic procedure that uses this expansion strategy. Even in this best-case scenario, the expansion did not improve the effectiveness of queries that were relatively complete at the start. Less complete queries — queries consisting of a single sentence describing the topic of interest — were significantly improved by the expansion.

2 The Retrieval Environment

This section provides the background necessary to understand the context in which the experiments were carried out. The following section describes the experiments themselves, and the remaining section summarizes the conclusions the data support.

2.1 WordNet

The expansion procedure used in this work relies heavily on the information recorded in WordNet, a manually-constructed lexical system developed by George Miller and his colleagues at the Cognitive Science Laboratory at Princeton University [8]. WordNet's basic object is a set of strict synonyms, called a *synset*. Synsets are organized by the lexical relations defined on them, which differ depending on part of speech. For nouns (the only part of WordNet used in this study), the lexical relations include antonymy, hypernymy/hyponymy (*is-a* relation) and three different meronym/holonym (*part-of*) relations. The *is-a* relation is the dominant relationship, and organizes the synsets into a set of approximately ten hierarchies[1]. Figure 1 shows a piece of WordNet. The figure contains all the ancestors and descendents as defined by the *is-a* relation for the six senses of the noun *swing*. Also shown is that one of the senses, a child's toy, is *part-of* a playground.

2.2 The TREC Collection

The TREC collection is a test collection being produced as a result of the TREC and Tipster workshops [9]. The part of the collection used in this work consists of the approximately 742,000 documents on TREC disks one and two, queries 101-150, and the set of relevance judgements produced after the TREC-2 and Tipster-3 evaluations.

The TREC documents consist of English prose obtained from a variety of sources including newspapers, abstracts of technical papers, and the *Federal Register*. There are some SGML-like tags in the documents to delineate the bibliographic parts of the document (document number, title/headline, author, etc.). Other tags that mark special punctuation in the body of a document were ignored in this work. The documents were indexed completely automatically using the standard SMART indexing routines [10] (i.e., tokenization, stop word removal, and stemming) to produce an inverted index of document vectors.

The text of a TREC query or, in TREC parlance, *topic statement*, is a complex natural-language statement of need as shown in Figure 2. Each topic statement has a set of fields flagged by special markers (the words enclosed in angle brackets). The Narrative field provides a particularly detailed description of what constitutes a relevant document; the Concepts field usually lists words and phrases that the creator of the statement thinks are related to the topic. A shorter version of each topic statement is also available. This shorter version, the Summary Statement, is usually a single sentence describing the search request. The Summary Statement for the topic shown in Figure 2 is the sentence given in the Description field. (The Summary Statement is frequently, but not always, identical to the the Description field.)

For this work, I added a new field to the topic statements: a list of hand-selected WordNet synsets containing nouns germane to the topic. My goal in selecting synsets for a particular topic was to pick synsets that emphasized important concepts of the topic. One aspect of the problem is sense resolution, i.e., selecting the synset that contains the correct sense of an ambiguous original topic word. I did not restrict myself to adding only synsets that contain some original topic word, however, since one purpose of the experiments is to investigate the efficacy of lexical-semantic relations assuming good starting concepts. Instead, the choice of synsets was governed by my understanding of the full topic statment and the fact that the selected synsets would be used to expand the query. I added an average of 2.7 (minimum 0, maximum 6) synonym sets per topic.

Topic 122 shown in Figure 2 provides an example of how synsets were selected for a topic. The topic asks for information about bringing cancer fighting drugs to market. The text never mentions 'pharmaceutical', but I added the synset {*pharmaceutical*}, a child of the synset {*drug*}, to the text. Early experiments demonstrated that expansion worked poorly when synsets with very many children in the *is-a* hierarchy were used. In addition to *pharmaceutical*, {*drug*} has children for many different types of drugs (stimulants, intoxicants, sedatives, etc.) that are not related to cancer-fighting. I chose the more

[1] The actual structure is not quite a hierarchy since a few synsets have more than one parent.

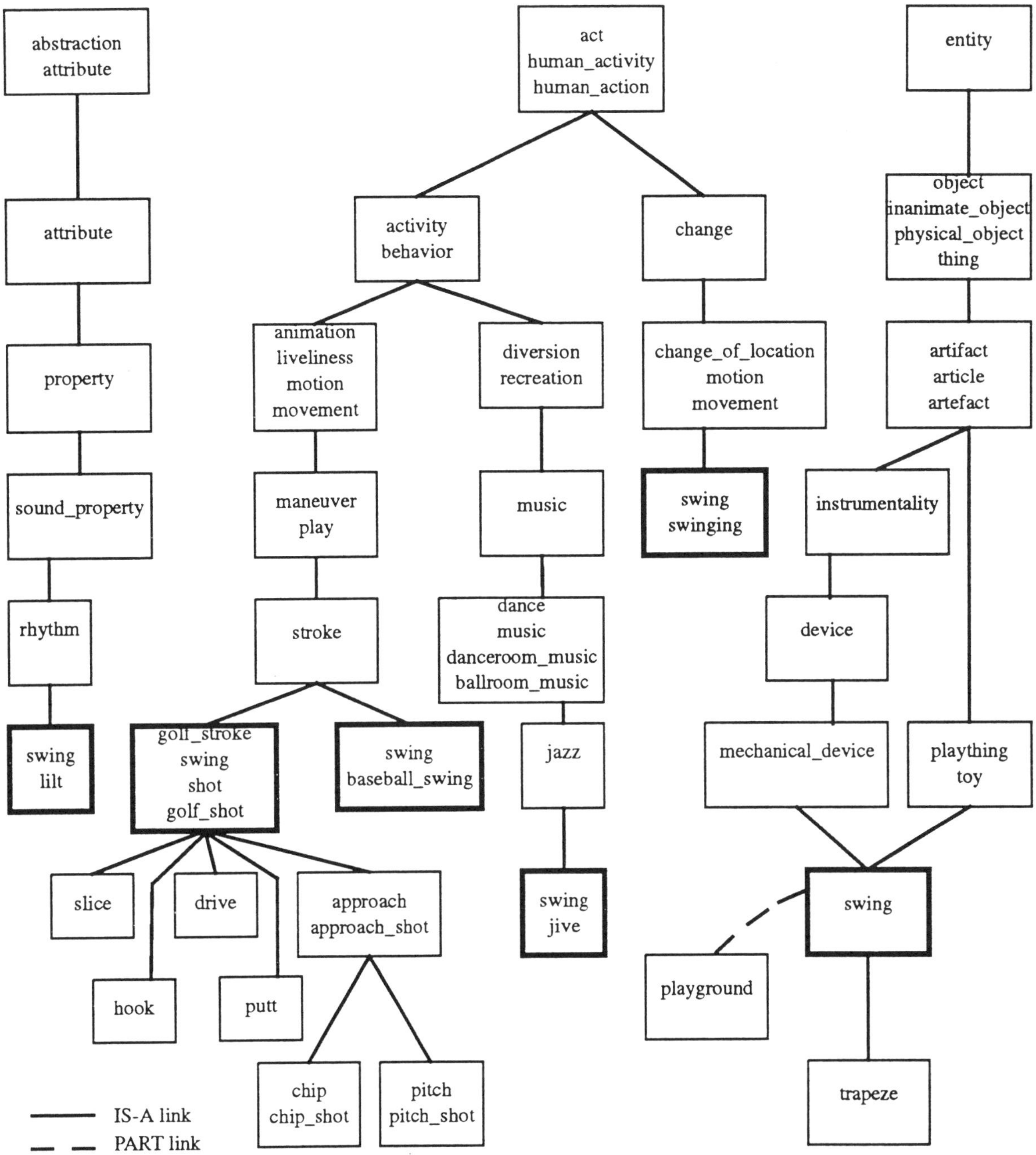

Figure 1. Relations defined for the six senses of the noun *swing* in WordNet.

specific *pharmaceutical* to avoid over-generalizing the expanded query. The complete list of synsets added to topic 122 is {*cancer*}, {*skin_cancer*}, and {*pharmaceutical*}.

Some topics contain important concepts that have no corresponding synset. Occasionally, the missing synset is a gap in WordNet; for example, *toxic waste*, *genetic engineering*, and *sanctions* meaning economic disciplinary measures are not in version 1.3 of WordNet. More often, the important concept was a proper noun or highly technical term that one wouldn't expect to be in WordNet. *SDI* or *Star Wars*, for example, is an important concept for topics 101 and 102 but does not occur in WordNet. Nothing was added to the topic texts for concepts that lacked corresponding synsets in these experiments, although making some provision for them would improve retrieval performance.

2.3 The Expansion Procedure

Once the text of the topics is annotated with synsets, the remainder of the processing is automatic. Selected fields of the original topic statements are indexed using the standard SMART routines. The

```
<dom> Domain: Medical & Biological

<title> Topic: RDT&E of New Cancer Fighting Drugs

<desc> Description:

Document will report on the research, development, testing, and evaluation (RDT&E) of
a new anti-cancer drug developed anywhere in the world.

<narr> Narrative:

A relevant document will report on any phase in the worldwide process of bringing new
cancer fighting drugs to market, from conceptualization to government marketing
approval.  The laboratory or company responsible for the drug project, the specific
type of cancer(s) which the drug is designed to counter, and the chemical/medical
properties of the drug must be identified.

<con> Concept(s):

1. cancer, leukemia

2. drug, chemotherapy
```

Figure 2. Topic statement of query 122.

terms derived from these sections are "original query terms". The expansion procedure is invoked when the synonym set section is reached.

Given a synset, there is a wide choice of words to add to a query vector — one can add only the synonyms within the synset, or all descendents in the *is-a* hierarchy, or all words in synsets one link away from the original synset regardless of link type, etc. The expansion procedure is parameterized to facilitate comparing the effectiveness of a variety of these schemes. The parameter set for a given run specifies for each relation type included in WordNet the maximum length of a chain of that type of link that may be followed. A chain begins at each synset listed in the synset section of the topic text and may contain only links of a single type. All synonyms contained within a synset of the chain are added to the query. Collocations such as *change_of_location* in Figure 1 are broken into their component words, stop words such as *of* are removed, and the remaining words are stemmed. The word stems plus a tag indicating the lexical relation through which the stems are related to the original synset are then appended to the original query terms.

As an example of the expansion process, consider the synsets for *swing* shown in Figure 1. If the synset added to the topic is the synset containing *golf_stroke*, and any number of hyponym (child) links may be traversed, then the stems of *golf, stroke, swing, shot, slice, hook, drive, putt, approach, chip*, and *pitch* would be added to the query vector. If hyponym chains are limited to length one, then *chip* and *pitch* would not be added. If the synset added to the topic is the one containing swing meaning plaything and any link type may be followed for one link, then the stems of *swing, mechanical, device, plaything, toy, playground*, and *trapeze* would be added to the query.

Stems added through different lexical relations are kept separate using the extended vector space model introduced by Fox [11]. Each query vector is comprised of subvectors of different concept types (called *ctypes*) where each ctype corresponds to a different lexical relation. A query vector potentially has eleven ctypes: one for original query terms, one for synonyms, and one each for the other relation types contained within the noun portion of WordNet (each half of a symmetric relation has its own ctype). An original query term that is a member of a synset selected for that query appears in both of the respective ctypes. Similarly, a word that is related to a synset through two different relations appears in both ctypes.

The similarity between a document vector D and an extended query vector Q is computed as the weighted sum of the similarities between D and each of the query's subvectors:

$$sim(D,Q) = \sum_{\text{ctype } i} \alpha_i \times D \cdot Q_i$$

where $\cdot$ denotes the inner product of two vectors, Q_i is the ith subvector of Q, and α_i, a real number, reflects the importance of ctype i relative to the other ctypes. Terms in documents vectors are weighted using the *lnc* weights suggested by Buckley et al. [12]; that is, the weight of a term is set to $1.0 + \ln(tf)$ where tf is the number of times the term occurs in the document and is then normalized by the square root of the sum of the squares of the weights in the vector (cosine normalization). Query terms are weighted using *ltN*: the log term frequency factor above is multiplied by the term's inverse document frequency, and the weights in the ctype representing original query terms are normalized by the cosine factor. Weights in additional ctypes are normalized using the length computed for the original terms' ctype. This normalization strategy allows the original query term weights to be unaffected by the expansion process and keeps the weights in each ctype comparable with one another.

3 Experiments

3.1 Full Topic Statement

The purpose of this investigation is to determine the efficacy of expanding a query by lexical-semantic relations. Given a set of concepts to be expanded, the effectiveness of an expanded run is dependent on the link types followed during the expansion and the relative weight given to each link type (the α's in the similarity function above), so a variety of different schemes must be tested. Table 1 shows the 11-point average precision value and percent difference over the unexpanded run for different combinations evaluated using the full topic statement (except the "Definitions" field) plus synsets. Four expansion strategies were tried: expansion by synonyms only, expansion by synonyms plus all descendents in the *is-a* hierarchy, expansion by synonyms plus parents and all descendents in the *is-a* hierarchy, and expansion by synonyms plus any synset directly related to the given synset (i.e., a chain of length 1 for all link types). The α for the original terms subvector was usually greater than the α for the other subvectors to reflect the assumption that user-supplied terms are generally superior than automatically added ones. The runs in which the original terms α was less than or equal to another α tested this assumption.

Clearly, the expansion is ineffective: none of the expansion strategies significantly improves the performance of the unexpanded query. Indeed, the difference in performance between an expanded and unexpanded run for individual queries is very small for most expanded runs. Individual query performance differs more for more aggressive expansion strategies (i.e., expanding using longer chains of links and weighting added terms more heavily) but across the set of queries the aggregate performance is worse for aggressively expanded queries.

In an earlier set of experiments, the most effective expanded run was the one that expanded a query synset by any synset directly related to it and had $\alpha = .5$ for all added subvectors [13]. While this combination is not optimal for these queries, it has the advantage of being a straight-forward choice of expansion parameters. Thus, this expansion strategy, which will be called the standard expansion strategy, is used for the experiments described in the next section.

3.2 Less Detailed Topic Statements

Query expansion is a recall-enhancing technique designed to overcome some of the problems caused by differing vocabularies. To test the hypothesis that expansion is unhelpful in the TREC collection due to the very complete problem statement provided by a TREC topic, queries derived from shorter versions of the original topic statements were expanded using the standard expansion strategy. One query set was derived using the Summary Statement plus the Concepts field; another query set was derived using only the Summary Statement. Both new versions used exactly the same set of synsets to expand as did the queries derived from the full topic statement.

Table 2 compares the lengths of the different query vectors. The table contains the mean number of original terms and the mean ratio of additional terms to original terms for each of the different versions of queries: derived from full topic (Full), derived from Summary Statement plus Concepts (SmryCon), and derived from Summary Statement (Summary) only. The mean number of additional terms is the same (17.56) for each version since the same set of synsets is expanded each time.

Figures 3 and 4 contain the retrieval results for the two new versions of the queries. The unexpanded run is the same version of the query as the expanded run with no additional terms added. The base case uses the unexpanded queries derived from the full topic statement. Expansion does not improve the Summary Statement plus Concepts version of the queries, but significantly improves the Summary Statement only version (35% improvement in 11-point average precision). Note, however, that the overall level of effectiveness obtained by the expanded Summary queries is less than the unexpanded full topic queries (39% degradation in the 11-point average precision).

3.3 Automatic Selection of Synsets

Given that short queries have the potential to be significantly improved by expansion, it is necessary to see if the potential can be realized by a completely automatic procedure. While it is possible to present

				ave. prec.	% change
Unexpanded queries				.3586	—
Expansion by synonyms only					
orig terms α	synonyms α				
1	.1			.3614	+0.8
1	.3			.3639	+1.5
1	.5			.3634	+1.3
1	.8			.3629	+1.2
Expansion by synonyms plus all descendents					
orig terms α	synonyms α	descendents α			
1	.1	.1		.3617	+0.9
1	.3	.1		.3639	+1.5
1	.3	.3		.3635	+1.4
1	.5	.1		.3635	+1.4
1	.5	.3		.3637	+1.4
1	.5	.5		.3622	+1.0
1	.8	.1		.3614	+0.8
1	.8	.3		.3612	+0.7
1	.8	.5		.3603	+0.5
Expansion by synonyms plus parents and all descendents					
orig terms α	synonyms α	descendents α	parents α		
1	.1	.1	.1	.3617	+0.9
1	.3	.1	.1	.3640	+1.5
1	.3	.3	.1	.3639	+1.5
1	.3	.3	.3	.3647	+1.7
1	.5	.1	.1	.3639	+1.5
1	.5	.3	.1	.3638	+1.5
1	.5	.3	.3	.3646	+1.7
1	.5	.5	.1	.3624	+1.0
1	.5	.5	.3	.3628	+1.2
1	.5	.5	.5	.3627	+1.1
1	.8	.1	.1	.3622	+1.0
1	.8	.3	.1	.3617	+0.9
1	.8	.3	.3	.3614	+0.8
1	.8	.5	.1	.3605	+0.5
1	.8	.5	.3	.3605	+0.5
1	.8	.5	.5	.3609	+0.6
1	1	1	1	.3511	-2.1
1	2	1	1	.3350	-6.6
Expansion by synonyms plus any directly related synset					
orig terms α	synonyms α	other α			
1	.3	.1		.3629	+1.2
1	.3	.3		.3630	+1.2
1	.5	.1		.3624	+1.0
1	.5	.3		.3620	+0.9
1	.5	.5		.3608	+0.6
1	.3	.5		.3604	+0.5
1	1	1		.3491	-2.7

Table 1. Combinations of expansion strategies and relation weights tested.

users with a list of candidate synsets and have them select the ones to expand, choosing correct synsets is a tedious process, and a poor choice can be worse than not expanding [13].

Figure 5 provides a high-level description of the algorithm developed to select the synsets. The algorithm is based on the observation that the synsets need to represent the correct sense of *important* concepts of the query [14]. Using the same reasoning as is used for inverse document frequency weights [15], importance is approximated by the number of documents in which a query term occurs — a term occurring in more than N documents is not expanded. Sense resolution is approximated by requiring a new term to be related to at least two original query terms before it is included in the expanded query.

A series of retrieval runs using the above procedure on the Summary Statements tested the procedure's effectiveness. The experiments tested different values of N: 70,000, approximately 10% of the collection,

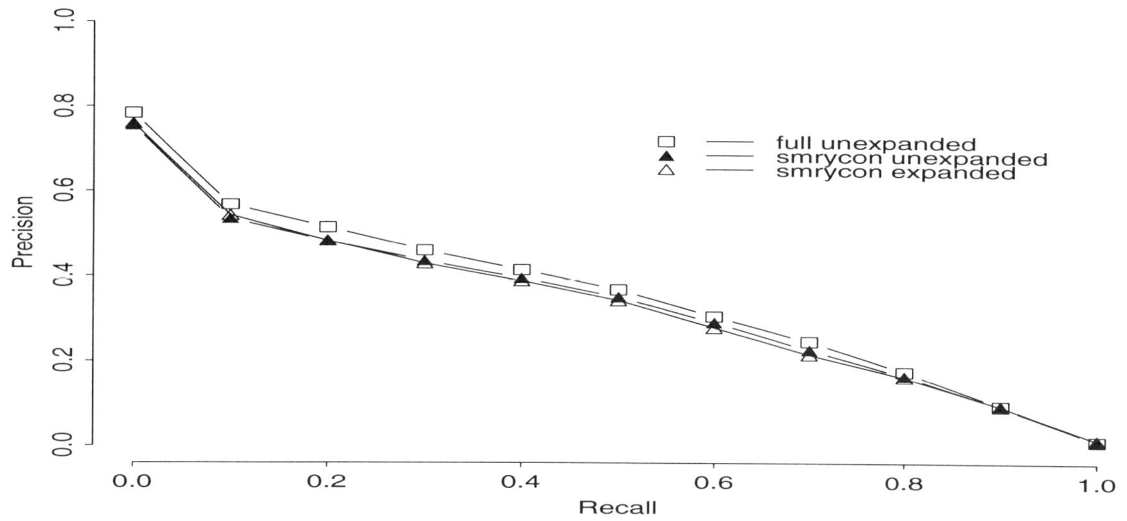

Figure 3. Effectiveness of queries derived from Summary Statement and Concept fields.

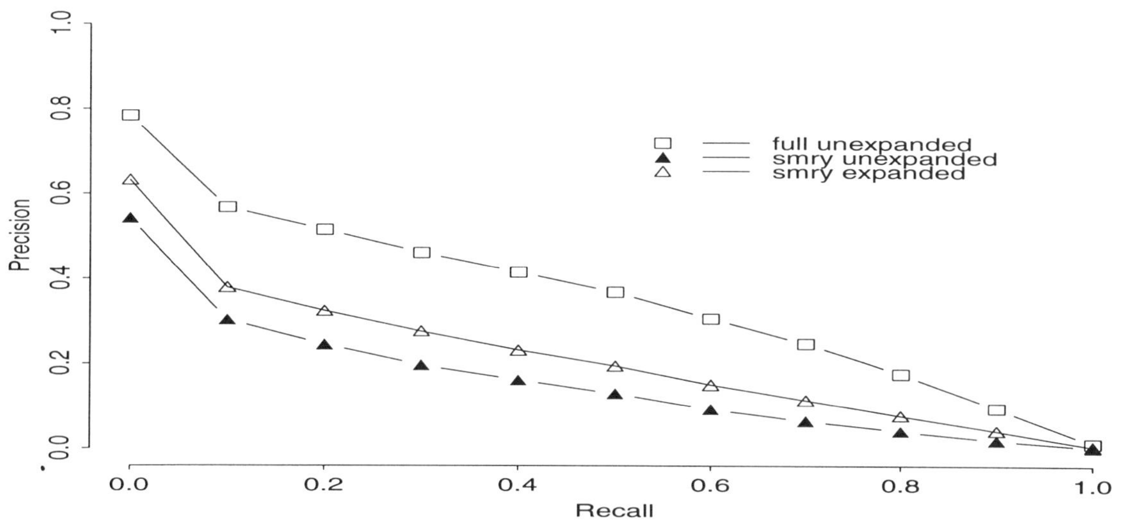

Figure 4. Effectiveness of queries derived from Summary Statement.

and 35,000, approximately 5% of the collection; different limits on the lengths of chains to follow when expanding (all link types were treated identically): 1 and 2; and different α values: .3, .5, and .8. Table 3 shows the 11-point average precision values obtained for these runs. As can be seen, none of the runs materially changes the performance of the unexpanded Summary Statement queries.

Inspection of the queries that resulted from the automatic selection procedure suggests that the requirement that a term appear in two lists is not a good approximation to sense disambiguation. The correct senses of words contained in a short query seldom have common relatives. Instead, the words that

	Full	SmryCon	Summary
Mean number terms	52.54	29.22	11.02
Mean ratio	.36	.77	1.71

Table 2. Length statistics for different versions of queries.

```
for (each query word w) {
        if (w not already expanded and
                    document frequency of w ≤ N ) {
                expand all synsets containing w producing kin list of w
        }
}
for (each relative in the set of kin lists) {
        if (relative occurs in more than 1 list)
                add relative to query vector
}
```

Figure 5. Procedure to automatically select synonym sets to expand.

appear in more than one list are likely to be fairly general terms with more than one sense themselves. For example, since collocations are split into their components during the expansion process, general nouns such as *system* tend to appear in multiple lists.

4 Conclusion

The experiments discussed here demonstrate that expansion by general lexical-semantic relations provides little benefit when a user supplies a detailed query. Since query expansion is a recall-enhancing technique, it is not surprising that longer queries benefit less than shorter queries. However, the longer queries are by no means doing a perfect job of retrieval, and they can be improved by other expansion techniques such as relevance feedback [16]. The success of these other methods suggests that the most useful relations for query expansion are idiosyncratic to the particular query in the context of the particular document collection.

Nonetheless, users frequently do not supply a detailed query. In this case, lexical-semantic relations have the potential to improve an initial query, though this expanded query is unlikely to be as effective as a better formulated user-supplied query. The challenge now lies in finding an automatic procedure that is able to select appropriate concepts to expand.

	ave. prec.	% change
Unexpanded queries	.1634	—
N=70,000; max chain length=1		
$\alpha = .3$	.1627	-0.5
$\alpha = .5$	.1603	-1.9
$\alpha = .8$	.1543	-5.6
N=70,000; max chain length=2		
$\alpha = .3$	.1633	-0.1
$\alpha = .5$	.1557	-4.7
$\alpha = .8$	.1402	-14.2
N=35,000; max chain length=1		
$\alpha = .3$	.1636	+0.1
$\alpha = .5$	.1635	+0.1
$\alpha = .8$	.1639	+0.3
N=35,000; max chain length=2		
$\alpha = .3$	.1645	+0.7
$\alpha = .5$	.1642	+0.5
$\alpha = .8$	.1617	-1.0

Table 3. Effectiveness of expansion strategies on Summary Statement queries when expanding automatically selected synsets.

References

1. David C. Blair and M. E. Maron. Full-text information retrieval: Further analysis and clarification. *Information Processing and Management*, 26(3):437–447, 1990.
2. A. F. Smeaton and C. J. van Rijsbergen. The retrieval effects of query expansion on a feedback document retrieval system. *Computer Journal*, 26:239–246, 1983.
3. C. T. Yu, C. Buckley, and G. Salton. A generalized term dependency model in information retrieval. *Information Technology: Research and Development*, 2:129–154, 1983.
4. Helen J. Peat and Peter Willett. The limitations of term co-occurrence data for query expansion in document retrieval systems. *Journal of the American Society for Information Science*, 42(5):378–383, 1991.
5. Scott Deerwester, Susan T. Dumais, George W. Furnas, Thomas K. Landauer, and Richard Harshman. Indexing by latent semantic analysis. *Journal of the American Society for Information Science*, 41(6):391–407, 1990.
6. G. Salton and M. E. Lesk. Computer evaluation of indexing and text processing. In Gerard Salton, editor, *The SMART Retrieval System: Experiments in Automatic Document Processing*, pages 143–180. Prentice-Hall, Inc. Englewood Cliffs, New Jersey, 1971.
7. Yih-Chen Wang, James Vandendorpe, and Martha Evens. Relational thesauri in information retrieval. *Journal of the American Society for Information Science*, 36(1):15–27, January 1985.
8. George Miller. Special Issue, WordNet: An on-line lexical database. *International Journal of Lexicography*, 3(4), 1990.
9. Donna K. Harman. The first Text REtrieval Conference (TREC-1), Rockville, MD, U.S.A, 4–6 November, 1992. *Information Processing and Management*, 29(4):411–414, 1993.
10. Chris Buckley. Implementation of the SMART information retrieval system. Technical Report 85-686, Computer Science Department, Cornell University, Ithaca, New York, May 1985.
11. Edward A. Fox. *Extending the Boolean and Vector Space Models of Information Retrieval with P-norm Queries and Multiple Concept Types.* PhD thesis, Cornell University, 1983. University Microfilms, Ann Arbor, MI.
12. Chris Buckley, Gerard Salton, and James Allan. Automatic retrieval with locality information using SMART. In D. K. Harman, editor, *Proceedings of the First Text REtrieval Conference (TREC-1)*, pages 59–72. NIST Special Publication 500-207, March 1993.
13. Ellen M. Voorhees. On expanding query vectors with lexically related words. In D. K. Harman, editor, *Proceedings of the Second Text REtrieval Conference (TREC-2)*, 1993. In press.
14. Ellen M. Voorhees and Yuan-Wang Hou. Vector expansion in a large collection. In D. K. Harman, editor, *Proceedings of the First Text REtrieval Conference (TREC-1)*, pages 343–351. NIST Special Publication 500-207, March 1993.
15. Karen Sparck Jones. A statistical interpretation of term specificity and its application in retrieval. *Journal of Documentation*, 28(1):11–21, March 1972.
16. Chris Buckley, James Allan, and Gerard Salton. Automatic routing and ad-hoc retrieval using SMART: TREC 2. In D. K. Harman, editor, *Proceedings of the Second Text REtrieval Conference (TREC-2)*, 1993.

User Modelling

Perceptual Speed, Learning and Information Retrieval Performance

Bryce Allen
University of Illinois
Champaign, IL, USA

Abstract

Although the cognitive ability "perceptual speed" is known to influence search performance by end-users, previous research has not established the mechanism by which this influence occurred. Results from educational psychology suggest that learning that occurs during searching is likely to be influenced by perceptual speed. An experiment was designed to test how this cognitive ability would interact with a system feature designed to enhance learning of search vocabulary, specifically, presenting subject descriptors as the first element in the display of a reference. Results showed significant interactions between perceptual speed and the order of presentation of data elements in predicting both vocabulary learning and search performance. These results indicate that searchers with higher levels of perceptual speed will learn additional search vocabulary, and use that vocabulary to complete higher quality searches, when they use a system designed to optimize scanning of subject descriptors. This outcome supports the idea that cognitive abilities influence information system usability, and that usability is determined by interactions between characteristics of users and system features. The findings also suggest that system features that enhance the learning of search vocabulary, such as query expansion mechanisms, can have a significant positive effect on the quality of end-user searching.

1. Purpose

Perceptual speed is a cognitive ability defined as "Speed in comparing figures or symbols, scanning to find figures or symbols, or carrying out other very simple tasks involving visual perception" [1]. Allen showed that this ability influences performance of untrained users who search information retrieval systems. People who score higher on standard tests of perceptual speed perform higher quality searches (as measured by standard precision and recall ratios) than those who score lower on the tests [2].

This finding is of some interest, and it raises a number of additional research questions. It seems a reasonable assumption that the influence of perceptual speed on search performance occurs primarily in a small number of tasks. In doing a search, a user accomplishes a variety of specific tasks: defining the topic of the search, selecting appropriate search vocabulary, issuing commands or selecting menu choices, viewing retrieved information and making judgments about its relevance or usefulness. The first research problem addressed in this research was identifying the task or tasks most likely to be influenced by perceptual speed.

System designers and programmers make choices that influence the usability of information systems. At the same time, cognitive abilities such as perceptual speed influence the usability of information systems. Specific design features can combine with specific user characteristics to ensure that information systems are more usable by some people than others. Accordingly, the second problem addressed in this investigation was to identify a specific design feature that might be associated with the influence of perceptual speed on retrieval performance. This design feature could be incorporated into information systems that would take advantage of the high levels of perceptual speed of some users.

2. Research Background

2.1 Search Tasks Influenced by Perceptual Speed

One recent attempt to locate the information retrieval task influenced by perceptual speed [3] tested the hypothesis that perceptual speed influences performance in the task of scanning lists of subject terms such as those typically used in "browse" interfaces, and that the resulting difference in browsing leads to the difference in search quality. The results of the experiment did not support that hypothesis. The present investigation was based on the idea that perceptual speed might influence the task of perceiving vocabulary in references that could be used to expand or rephrase queries. This task has a variety of facets, one of which appears to be the learning of new or alternative search vocabulary.

Research into learning shows that perceptual speed influences some types of learning. Meltzer found significant correlations between perceptual speed and achievement in both reading and arithmetic in 6-8 year old students [4]. This cognitive ability was the main predictor of reading comprehension in 7-year olds. Of particular interest was her finding that perceptual speed was not uniformly correlated with achievement across age levels. Her research suggested that there was a stage in the process of learning how to read, or how to do arithmetic, in which perceptual speed plays a major role; but at earlier and later stages perceptual speed has less effect on achievement. This idea is consistent with a model of skill acquisition advanced by Ackerman [5,6]. This model divides skill acquisition into three stages. In the first phase of skill acquisition, an understanding of task requirements is achieved, and general cognitive abilities (verbal, numerical, figural) are most important. In the second phase, performance of the task becomes faster as learners try out various methods of simplifying or streamlining the task. During this phase, perceptual speed has its greatest impact on learning. In the third stage of skill acquisition, performance of the task becomes automatic, requiring little attention, and psychomotor abilities primarily influence performance.

There appear to be at least two different kinds of learning, or skill acquisition, that occur in information retrieval. The first is the learning of general patterns of searching that could be applied to any search, and the second is the learning process associated with doing a search on a specific topic. When acquiring general skill in information retrieval, users may move through all three of Ackerman's phases. If searchers are in the second stage (where perceptual speed has its greatest effect), the model would predict differences in performance associated with different levels of perceptual speed. Similarly, it seems possible that searchers approaching a topic for the first time would move through the same three phases. In this case, the learning would focus less on general strategies and tactics than on aspects of the specific topic. Learning of vocabulary that leads to a more successful search fits into this model of skill acquisition.

There is ample evidence of the importance of this second kind of learning (i.e., learning of new search vocabulary) in information systems. Shenouda demonstrated that some searchers employ vocabulary in later cycles that they have seen in earlier cycles, and recognize this as a distinct search strategy [7]. In a detailed examination of end-user search tactics, Shenouda found that roughly 8% of search tactics involved adding a term because it had appeared in examined references. Although this seems like a small proportion, it represented a significant search tactic. In the design and development of information retrieval systems, this learning of new (and potentially useful) vocabulary from records viewed is called query expansion. Examples of systems that employ query expansion include Dynix, INNOPAC, Silver Platter, INSTRUCT and Muscat [8]. In these systems, users are typically able to highlight or otherwise select a data element from a displayed record, and issue a command that will add that data element (or words derived from it) to the query. Some systems make the process of query expansion more thorough. For example, the MAP command in Dialog automates the process of extracting descriptors (or other relevant data elements) from retrieved references and entering them as new search vocabulary [9]. Here, one command can cause all of the descriptors from a retrieved set to be searched, thus expanding the retrieved set(s) considerably. Other systems, such as OPAKI, use relevance judgments from users as the basis for expanding queries with vocabulary from those relevant references, without further input from users. The fact that a variety of systems have developed features to facilitate the learning of new search vocabulary, and using that newly learned vocabulary in retrieval, attests to the importance of this cognitive task in information retrieval.

2.2 System Features Associated With Perceptual Speed

Selection of a system feature that would be likely to be related to the influence of perceptual speed on search performance was also influenced by learning theory. Researchers have found serial effects in studies of recall of textual materials [10,11,12]. These investigations show that textual materials presented first are learned more thoroughly, and hence recalled more completely. This "primacy effect" is also associated with ideas that are more important, or higher in the logical structure of the text [13]), and it seems likely that effects of primacy in serial position and logical position are linked. The primacy effect suggests that what people see first in a display of bibliographic information will be more likely to contribute to learning. It follows that data elements containing vocabulary that is likely to improve retrieval in subsequent cycles should be presented first. Howard, in an eye-movement study of information retrieval, showed that subject headings received the highest number of fixations per word [14]. This would suggest that subject headings should appear first in the record display, to take advantage of the primacy effect.

Many information retrieval systems have the flexibility to allow users, or system administrators, to establish this order of presentation. For example, Dialog allows users to specify their own display format, and most OPACs permit a library to design the display formats for bibliographic data, at least at the time of installation (C. Hildreth, personal communication, 1 October 1993). It is not clear how many users or system administrators have elected to follow the research on the primacy effect and to place subject headings first. The fact that systems are capable of doing so serves as an indicator that there is at least an intuitive understanding of the potential effect of order of presentation on usability. Accordingly, in this research, the order of presentation of data elements was varied as an element in the design. A very simple design change was introduced into a standard "browse" information retrieval system. One version of this system displayed references in the "usual" order: Author, Title, Source, Subject Headings, Abstract. The second version of this system presented Subject Headings first, then the remaining elements in the usual order. It was anticipated that greater learning would be evident in users of the second version.

2.3 Perspectives from Information Science

This research project derived not only from the specific findings of learning researchers and the experiences of information systems designers, but also from a long tradition of research in information science. A few salient contributions to that tradition highlight its development. Cuadra warned that nascent information retrieval systems would have to attempt to obtain user acceptance if they were to be successful, and pointed to specific areas of improvement in system design that could lead to greater user acceptance[14]. Fenichel drew attention to factors that influence search performance, including cognitive factors such as levels of knowledge and expertise [15]. Her research indicated that "user acceptance" was not a simple concept, and that different users might react differently to systems, searching them with different degrees of effectiveness. Borgman extended the discussion of individual differences among users of information systems to end-users, and considered a wide variety of individual differences that might affect their use of systems [16]. Shneiderman [17] summarized the research tradition when he emphasized the importance of accommodating human diversity, including usage profiles, task profiles and interaction styles, in designing interfaces. The present research was an attempt continue in this research tradition and the associated systems development, by locating the effect of one specific cognitive ability within one specific information retrieval task, in the context of one specific system design feature.

2.4 Statement of Problem and Hypotheses

The hypotheses tested in this investigation arose from an understanding of information system usability that locates usability in the interaction between system performance (as influenced by design features) and user performance (as influenced by personal characteristics). Features of system design that may affect system performance include data storage methods, search engines and user interfaces. Characteristics that may influence user performance include users' skills, knowledge, and cognitive abilities. In this investigation, the user characteristic studied was perceptual speed, the design feature selected was the order of presentation of data elements, and the resulting interaction was studied with the context of a specific information retrieval task, the learning of new search vocabulary. The objective of the research was to investigate experimentally the nature of the interaction between search performance, perceptual speed, and the task of learning vocabulary during searches.

The hypotheses tested by this study were:

H_1. There is a significant interaction between the effects of the system design feature of order of presentation of data elements and the user characteristic of perceptual speed in determining search performance, measured by recall and precision.

This hypothesis was based on the idea that users with higher levels of perceptual speed would be more likely to scan quickly through references, and so would perceive alternate vocabulary that they could use to perform higher quality searches. It was also expected that those who saw the subject headings first would be more likely to learn new headings to use in their searches. The anticipated interaction was that searchers with high levels of perceptual speed who saw subject headings first in references would do the best searches.

H_2. There is a significant interaction between the effects of the system design feature of order of presentation of data elements and the user characteristic of perceptual speed in determining the amount of learning of search vocabulary that occurs during a search.

This hypothesis was based on the idea that the higher levels of search performance in the first hypothesis would be associated with higher levels of vocabulary learning. It was expected that searchers with higher levels of perceptual speed would be more likely to scan quickly through references, and so would learn more search vocabulary. It was also expected that the primacy effect would influence those who saw the subject headings first to learn additional vocabulary. The anticipated interaction was that searchers with high levels of perceptual speed who saw subject headings first in references would learn the most additional search vocabulary.

H_3. Learning is a mediator variable between perceptual speed and search performance.

This hypothesis combined the first two hypotheses, and suggested a causal chain from the individual characteristic (perceptual speed), to performance of a search task (learning additional search vocabulary), to search outcome (measured by precision and recall).

H_4. The effect of perceptual speed on search performance will differ depending on the stage of skill acquisition attained by the searchers, as measured by familiarity with searching and with the topic of the search.

This hypothesis was based on the skill acquisition model discussed above. It was included here as an exploratory element to see if searchers at different stages of skill acquisition would be influenced by perceptual speed in different ways.

H5. There is a significant interaction between the effects of the system design feature of order of presentation of data elements and the user characteristic of perceptual speed in determining the speed with which searches are accomplished.

This hypothesis was suggested by the emphasis on speed of scanning as a factor in learning vocabulary. It seemed reasonable to expect that higher levels of performance would be associated with higher levels of search speed. Specifically, it was expected that searchers with higher levels of perceptual speed who saw subject headings first in displays would complete searches more quickly.

3. Method

3.1 The Test Systems

A small information retrieval system was programmed in Future Basic on an Apple Macintosh computer. This system used subject browsing as the retrieval mechanism. A data file was created by selecting 126 references indexed by subject headings shown (by relevance judgments obtained in previous research) to be relevant to the topic. To this set of references was added 130 references indexed by randomly selected subject headings. The result was a data file that contained a number of references potentially relevant to the topic, along with a number of references of only tangential relevance or of total non-relevance to the topic.

These 256 references, derived from the H. W. Wilson index Reader's Guide to Periodical Literature, contained author, title and source information, as well as a block of subject headings, introduced by the phrase "Subjects Covered:". In addition, 216 or 84% of the references had abstracts, introduced by the term "Abstract:". The references were indexed by a total of 134 subject headings. Participants in the research searched the datafile by browsing through an alphabetical list of these subject headings, and selected headings they thought might be productive. Browsing occurred either by entering a search expression, which caused the list to scroll to the part of the alphabetic list containing the search expression or its nearest match, by scrolling up and down the list using the standard Macintosh scroll bar, or by using "up arrow", "down arrow", "page up" or "page down" keys. Participants selected a subject heading by scrolling to, or clicking on the heading, then hitting the "return" key.

Selection of a subject heading caused the references indexed by that subject heading to be displayed, one at a time, on the screen. At any time during this display, participants could elect to return to the subject heading list and begin again. The system created a time-stamped log of all search activities, and included in this log frequency counts of browse activities.

As described above, one version of this system presented the references in the usual order (Author, Title, Source, Subjects Covered, Abstract), while the second version presented the references with subject headings first (Subjects Covered, Author, Title, Source, Abstract). There were no other differences between the two versions. Participants in the research were randomly assigned to one of the two test systems.

3.2 Materials

The stimulus article was a two-page abridgment of the article: Eron, L. D. (1980). Prescription for reduction of aggression. American Psychologist, 35, 244-252. Allen [2,3] used this article in a number of studies and its Flesch-Kincaid reading ease score of 12.3 shows that it is suitable for undergraduates. Two tests used to assess the perceptual speed of participants were drawn from the Kit of Factor-Referenced Cognitive Tests. The first test was the Number Comparison Test, in which participants inspected pairs of multi-digit numbers and indicated whether the two numbers in each pair were the same or different. The second test was the Identical Pictures Test, in which participants checked which one of five numbered geometrical figures or pictures in a row was identical to the figure given at the left end of the row. In each case, the number of correct answers obtained within a limited time, less a penalty for incorrect answers, was the score recorded for the participant.

A true-false test was designed to show participants' levels of technical knowledge of the research into the effects of television violence viewing on childhood aggression (the topic of the stimulus article). This test, consisting of twelve questions, was shown in pretests to reliably distinguish between people with academic knowledge of the topic and those with only general, background knowledge of the topic.

3.3 Participants

One hundred volunteer participants, drawn from the general student population of the University of Illinois, took part in this research. Demographically, this sample represented a cross-section of the academic community. Students were paid $5.00 for their participation, which lasted about one hour.

3.4 Procedures

Participants began by completing the true-false test that assessed their familiarity with research on television violence viewing and childhood aggression. They then read the stimulus article, preceded by the instructions, "Please read carefully the following article. In a few minutes you will be asked to identify references to additional articles on the same topic." Following the reading of the stimulus article, participants completed the tests of perceptual speed. These tests acted as unrelated interpolated tasks and ensured that long-term memory and understanding were being used in the search rather than short-term or rote memory. The time required to complete the tests, approximately eight minutes, was too brief to erode long-term gist recall of the stimulus material. Following the tests, participants were randomly assigned to one of the two experimental systems. Their instructions were as follows:

> Information Search. A few minutes ago you read an article on a topic. Now, assume that you are doing a term paper on that topic for one of your courses. To do your term paper, you want to find more articles on the topic. You will be searching an experimental information retrieval system to find references to those articles. The researcher will assist you in learning how to use this system. There is no limit to the number of references you can find. Keep searching until you are satisfied that you would have enough information to start your term paper.

The level of motivation of participants in this research, and the expectations they had regarding what constituted a successful search, may have differed from those of ordinary users of information systems. Doing searches on a topic in which one is not vitally interested may be understood to be part of student life, but motivation in the research was supplied by a $5 reward, rather than a grade on a term paper. Similarly, expectations of an information retrieval system encountered in a laboratory and explicitly described as "experimental" may differ from expectations of operational systems encountered in a library. These problems associated with the experimental setting are acknowledged, but since they seemed likely to occur uniformly across all experimental groups, they were disregarded in the analysis of the results reported below.

Training provided by the researcher included how to enter search terms, how to browse the subject heading list, how to select headings, and how to view the references. No instruction was provided on search tactics or vocabulary. Since the problem of researcher-induced bias was recognized as a potential problem, four different researchers interacted with participants in a relatively random manner dictated by individual schedules. This arrangement minimized the likelihood that an individual researcher's instructions or comments would influence the results of the experiment.

As references were displayed, each was followed by the question, "Print this reference?", to which acceptable answers were "Y" or "N". Participants were instructed that they should answer "Y" if they felt that the reference was useful for their term paper. When participants completed their search, they filled out a brief questionnaire that asked them about their academic backgrounds and experience in using computers and libraries. They were also asked about their level of familiarity with the topic and the difficulty they experienced finding references.

3.5 Analysis

3.5.1 Independent Variables

The main independent variables were the scores achieved on the perceptual speed tests, and the order of presentation of data elements in the display of references. Both independent variables figured in Hypotheses 1, 2, and 5, but perceptual speed alone was the independent variable in Hypotheses 3 and 4.

3.5.2 Dependent Variables

The main dependent variables in this research related to search performance. In order to assess recall and precision, the responses to the question "Print this reference?" were analyzed. Thirty-three references were judged to be of potential use by half or more of the participants who saw them. These were accepted as the "relevant" references in the database. Given this list of relevant references, recall and precision ratios were calculated for each search. These variables were used to test hypotheses 1, 3, and 4.

Another important dependent variable was the amount of learning that took place during the searches. This was operationalized as the proportion of subject headings selected that had been seen as part of a reference before being selected. For example, if a participant viewed a reference that used the subject heading "Television and Children" and subsequently selected that subject heading from the list of headings, it was considered at least possible that the subsequent selection was influenced by having seen the heading used as part of an earlier reference. This variable was used in testing Hypotheses 2 and 3.

Selecting a subject heading after seeing it in a reference does not necessarily indicate that learning has occurred. The selection of the heading could be based on background knowledge, recall of the stimulus material, or random choice. If, however, one experimental group consistently selected previously viewed headings more than the other, and if the effects of background knowledge, recall of stimulus material, and random choice were the same in each group, it seems a reasonable conclusion that the first group engaged in more learning than the second group. This method of assessing the amount of learning was considered appropriate in an experimental setting in which groups could be compared. It would not be appropriate in other research settings where thinking-aloud protocols or interviews with searchers would be better indicators of the amount of learning that occurred.

Finally, speed in searching was measured by dividing the number of references viewed by the total time taken to complete the search. This measure of speed, the number of references viewed per minute, gave a measure of search speed that was normalized by total time spent searching, and so evened out differences between those who did brief searches and those who completed much longer searches. This variable was used in testing hypothesis 5.

3.5.3 Control Variables

In order to provide evidence about the extent to which the influence of perceptual speed on search performance depends on the stage of skill acquisition, data were collected on a number of variables. The questionnaire gave self-reports of frequency of library use and microcomputer use, and there were two measures of topic knowledge: the results from the true-false test that provided a measure of level of technical knowledge, and a self-report of familiarity with the topic that gave perceptions of general knowledge. These control variables, although used in all analyses, were particular important in testing hypothesis 4.

4. Findings

4.1 Hypothesis 1.

H_1. There is a significant interaction between the effects of the system design feature of order of presentation of data elements and the user characteristic of perceptual speed in determining search performance, measured by recall and precision.

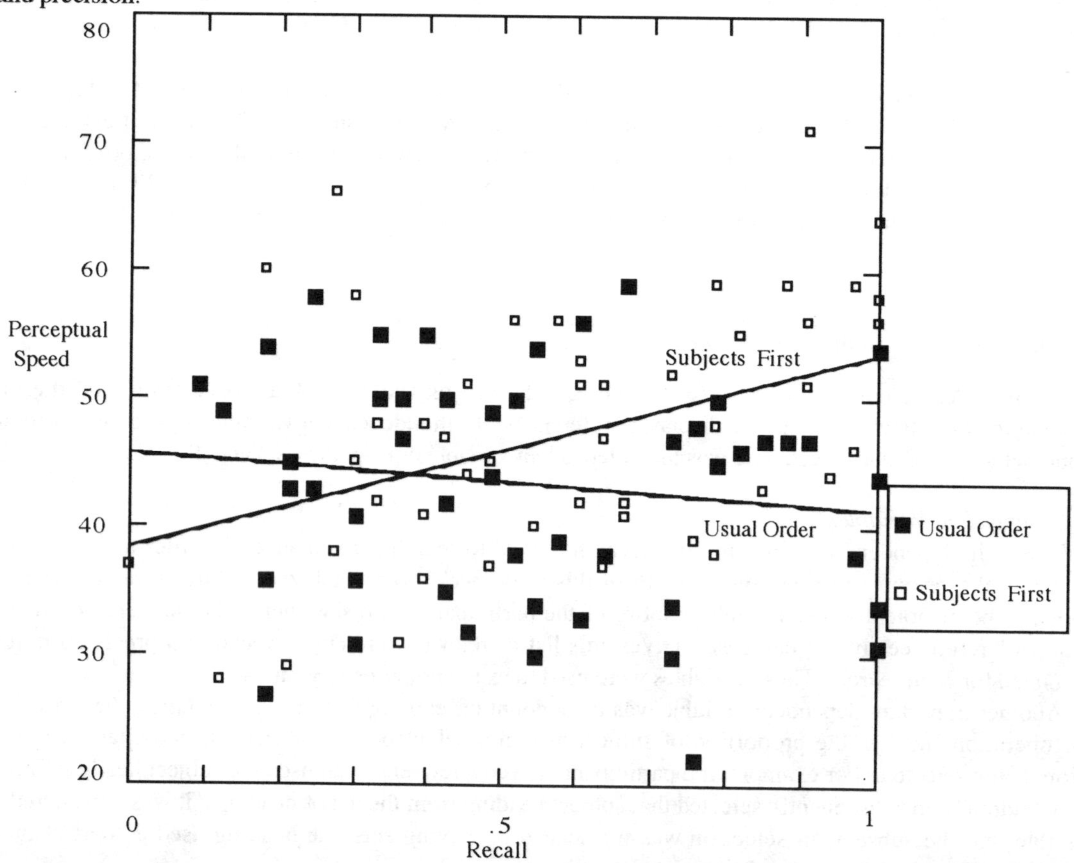

Figure 1: Predictors of Recall

When predictors of recall and precision were analyzed using a general linear model, a significant interaction (p<.02) was found between the scores achieved on one of the tests of perceptual speed, the Number Comparison Test, and the order of presentation of data elements in predicting recall. Figure 1 illustrates the relationship between the predictors of recall.

The correlation between recall and perceptual speed in the system that presented references in the usual order, with subject headings appearing after descriptive data, was r = -.126, p>.38. The correlation between recall and perceptual speed when subject headings were presented first was r = .398, p<.01. This outcome supported Hypothesis 1.

4.2 Hypothesis 2

H_2. There is a significant interaction between the effects of the system design feature of order of presentation of data elements and the user characteristic of perceptual speed in determining the amount of learning of search vocabulary that occurs during a search.

When predictors of learning search vocabulary, operationalized as the proportion of search expressions that had been viewed in references, were analyzed using a general linear model, a significant interaction (p<.05) was found between the scores achieved on one of the tests of perceptual speed, the Number Comparison Test, and the order of presentation of data elements in predicting recall. Figure 2 illustrates the relationship between the predictors of learning. For those participants who saw the references presented in the usual order, with subject headings in the middle of the display, the correlation between perceptual speed and learning was r = -.059, p>.68. For those who saw the references presented with subject headings first, the correlation was r = .358, p<.02. This outcome supported the second hypothesis.

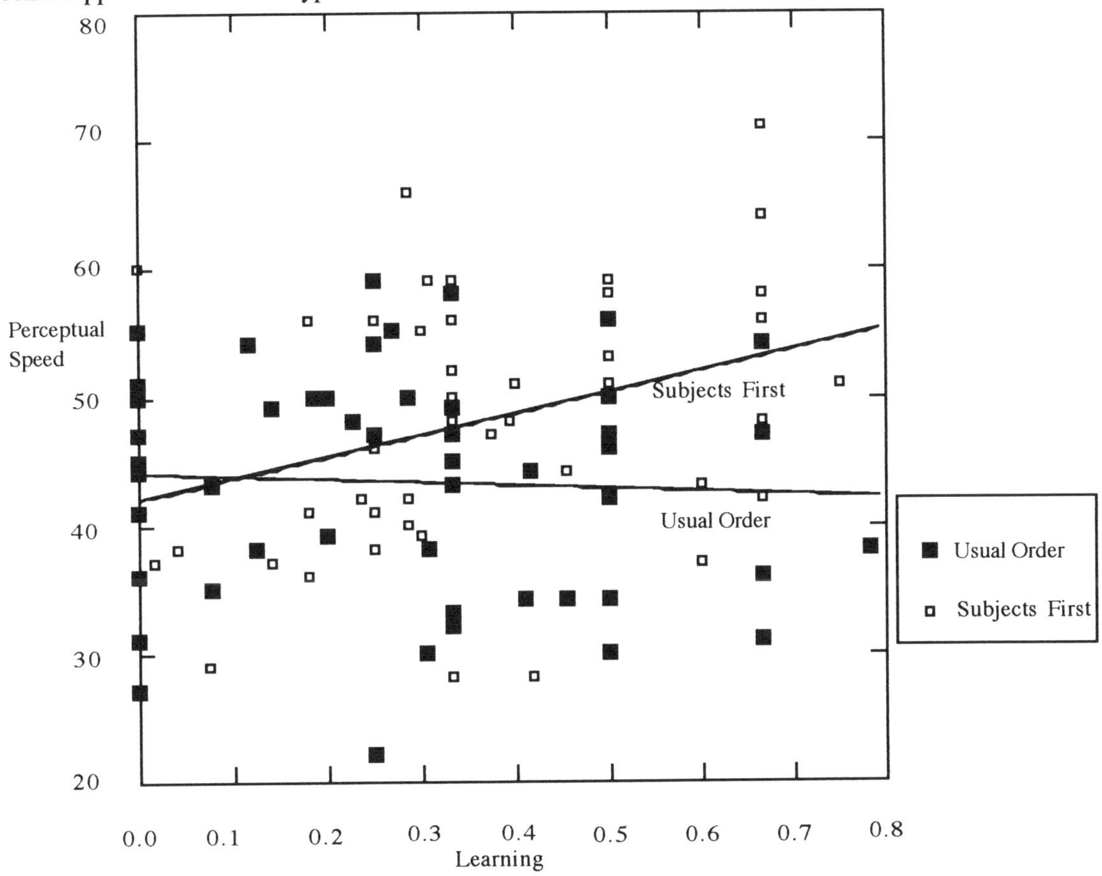

Figure 2: Predictors of Learning

4.3 Hypothesis 3.

H_3. Learning is a mediator variable between perceptual speed and search performance.

This hypothesis was tested using the method described by Baron and Kenney [18], using only the data from those participants who used the version of the information retrieval system in which subject headings were presented first (n=50). The results for the first two hypotheses showed that both perceptual speed and learning influence search performance. The hypothesized order of these effects, based on learning theory, is that perceptual speed influences learning, which in turn influences performance. In other words, learning is a mediator between perceptual speed and search performance. The Baron and Kenny technique for testing this hypothesis requires three regressions: the mediator on the independent variable, the dependent variable on the independent variable, and the dependent variable on both the independent variable and the mediator. These three regressions produced the following results. When the mediator (learning) was regressed on the independent variable (perceptual speed), the predictor was shown to have a significant effect (r^2=.128, p<.02). When the dependent variable (recall) was regressed on the independent variable (perceptual speed), the predictor was shown to have a significant effect (r^2=.158, p<.01). When the dependent variable (recall) was regressed on both the independent variable (perceptual speed) and the mediator (learning), learning was shown to be a significant predictor (p<.01), and the beta for perceptual speed was less than it was in the second regression (.24 as opposed to .398). These results meet the criteria established by Baron and Kenny, and establish that learning mediates between perceptual speed and search performance. This model does not hold for the first (usual) order of presentation, in which learning appears not to be related to perceptual speed. This outcome supports the third hypothesis, but only for participants who used the information retrieval system with the second order of presentation (subject headings first).

4.4 Hypothesis 4.

H_4. The effect of perceptual speed on search performance will differ depending on the stage of skill acquisition attained by the searchers, as measured by familiarity with searching and with the topic of the search.

There was a large difference in the correlation between recall and perceptual speed when level of self-reported library use was taken as the measure of level of skill acquisition. This difference is shown in Table 1.

Low Library Use (less than once/month)	-.011
Moderate Library Use (at least once/month)	.139
High Library Use (at least once/week)	.413

Table 1. Correlations between perceptual speed and recall.

This result supports the fourth hypothesis. It is interesting, however, that no differences of this sort appeared when comparing the correlations based on knowledge (either technical or general) or familiarity with microcomputers.

4.5 Hypothesis 5.

H_5. There is a significant interaction between the effects of the system design feature of order of presentation of data elements and the user characteristic of perceptual speed in determining the speed with which searches are accomplished.

Speed of searching, in this research, was operationalized as the number of references viewed per minute. When predictors of speed were analyzed using a general linear model, no significant interaction was found between the scores achieved on one of the tests of perceptual speed and the order of presentation of data elements in predicting recall. Figure 3 illustrates the relationship between the predictors of search speed.

The correlation between perceptual speed and search speed for those using the version of the information retrieval system that presented references in the usual order of data elements was r=.08, p>.57. The correlation for those who used the version that presented references with subject headings first was r=.469, p<.01. Although the interaction approached significance, this hypothesis was not supported. However, the patterns shown by the data were in the predicted direction.

5. Discussion

Search performance, as a measure of system usability, clearly depends on a complex interaction between user characteristics and system features. In this instance, the measure of search performance that was found to be influenced in such a complex manner was recall. Previous research [2,3] found that precision was the measure of performance that was influenced by perceptual speed. Given the usual inverse relationship between precision and recall, this shift from a positive effect on precision to a positive effect on recall may seem contradictory, and if the information systems used were comparable, this would be the case. However, the information systems for which these results were found were sufficiently different that the shift in the measure of search performance can be discounted. The first research used an operational information retrieval system with a large CD-ROM database, while this research used a small system with an experimental database. These differences in search systems appear to account for the different facet of search performance influenced by perceptual speed. The salient result was the same in all investigations: perceptual speed influenced search performance. It is possible that if these experimental systems used in this research were scaled up to operational size, the impact of perceptual speed would again be found on precision.

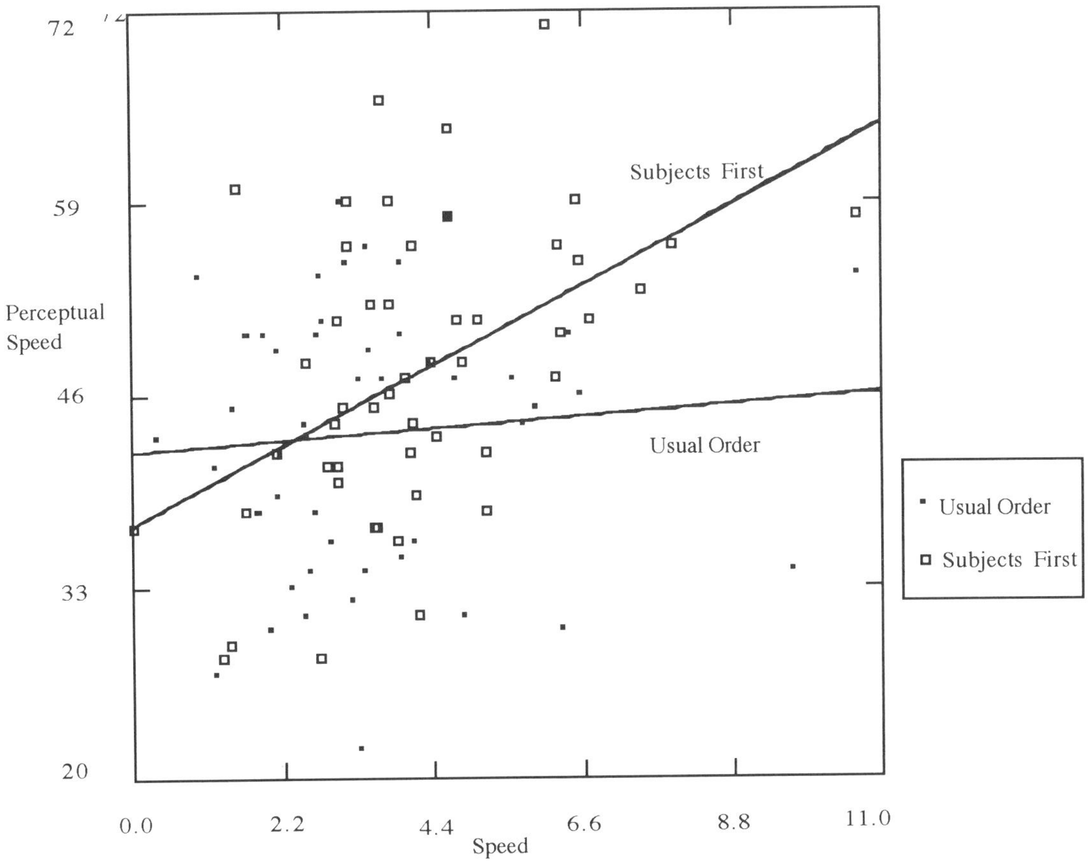

Figure 3: Predictors of Search Speed

The association of perceptual speed with learning is strongly supported by this research. However, this association was not found in participants who used the interface with the usual order of presentation of data elements. Learning was as important for these participants as a determinant of search quality as it was for those participants who saw the alternative order of presentation of data elements. Search quality was highly associated with the amount of learning that occurred, regardless of order of presentation used. It seems clear that learning has a pervasive influence on recall. In some information systems, that influence mediates between the cognitive ability perceptual speed and search performance.

The findings of this experiment may be summarized as follows. When people use an information system designed to enable fast scanning of important subject descriptors, those who have higher levels of perceptual speed are able to take advantage of the design features of that information system. They learn more vocabulary, achieve better search performance, and work more quickly than those with lower levels of perceptual speed. When people use an information system not designed to enable fast scanning of important subject descriptors, perceptual speed does not influence the amount of learning, nor search performance or search speed. In this research, the only variable associated with the amount of learning done by participants using the system with the usual order of presentation was a modest correlation with frequency of microcomputer use (Spearman's $R = -.255$, $p<.05$). It seems reasonable to assume that searchers using a system not designed to enable fast scanning of important subject terms adopt alternative strategies for learning new search vocabulary and thus completing more effective searches. Further investigation will be necessary to determine what those alternative strategies might be.

It also appears that the effect of perceptual speed on search performance, mediated through learning, is governed by the level of skill acquisition achieved by users. The highest, expert, level of skill is unlikely to be achieved by most end users of information retrieval systems. We can, in all likelihood, disregard the third stage of Ackerman's model, and think only about the first and second stages. In the first stage, users are still trying to figure out how to do a search. As they pass this stage, as evidenced in this research by higher levels of self-reported frequency of library use, then perceptual speed becomes more important as a determinant of learning and consequently of search quality.

5. Conclusions

The implications of this research for the design and use of information retrieval systems seem clear. By making a minor change in the way an information system presents data, designers can change the pattern of usability of the system. Simply altering the order of presentation of data elements in a bibliographic display can transform an information system from a "one-size-fits-all" system to one in which certain users, because of their higher levels of perceptual speed, are able to achieve significantly better performance. At the same time, the system change does not appear to disadvantage those with lower levels of perceptual speed: these users scored about the same on precision, recall, amount of learning, and speed regardless of the order of presentation they viewed. The fact that improvements in usability can be generated for some, without placing an additional burden on others, may be taken as an argument that this type of system feature should be incorporated into all information retrieval systems.

This example argues strongly that usability research must continue to provide input into information system design decisions. As indicated above, some systems have the capability to adopt the order of presentation that was associated with search quality improvement for users with high perceptual speed. It is essential that decisions about system features such as order of presentation of data elements be based on a clear understanding of the effect that the design decision will have on system usability, and of the complex nature of the interaction between system features and user characteristics. The task of investigating the effect of interactions between many system design alternatives and many user characteristics is daunting, but this investigation provides further evidence of the importance of tackling this set of problems.

The association between learning of search vocabulary during a search and quality of searching that was found in this investigation emphasizes the importance of search tactics that have been part of the toolbox of professional searchers for years. Clearly, however, not all unsophisticated users of information systems are in a position to make equally good use of this tactic for improving search results. The findings of this experiment indicate the need for additional investigations of vocabulary learning and the role of system design features in enhancing this type of learning, including existing query expansion systems. These findings demonstrate the desirability of incorporating system features that support the learning of search vocabulary, and justify the effort expended by system designers to make this task easier for users.

References

1. Ekstrom RB, French JW, Harman HH, Dermen D. Manual for kit of factor-referenced cognitive tests. Educational Testing Service, Princeton NJ, 1976

2. Allen BL. Cognitive differences in end-user searching of a CD-ROM index. In: 15th international conference on research and development in information retrieval proceedings. ACM, Baltimore, 1992, pp 298-309

3. Allen BL. Cognitive abilities and information system usability. Inf Proc Man in press

4. Meltzer LJ. Visual perception: stage one of a long-term investigation into cognitive components of achievement. Br J Educ Psychol 1982; 52: 144-154.

5. Ackerman PL. Determinants of individual differences during skills acquisition: cognitive abilities and information processing. J Exp Psychol Gen 1988; 117: 288-318.

6. Ackerman PL. Individual differences and skill acquisition. In: Ackerman PL, Sternberg V, Glaser R (eds), Learning and individual differences: advances in theory and research, Freeman, New York, 1989, pp 164-217

7. Shenouda WA. Online search strategy modification by end users. Ph.D. thesis, Rutgers University, 1991

8. Walker S, DeVere R. Improving subject retrieval in online catalogues. 2. Relevance feedback and query expansion. British Library Research and Development Department, London, 1990

9. Ojala MP. In command of business data: using the MAP and GET commands. Online 1989; 13: 83-90

10. Deese J, Kaufman RA. Serial effects in recall of unorganized and sequentially organized verbal material. J Exp Psych 1957; 54: 180-187

11. Freebody P, Anderson RC. Serial position and rated importance in the recall of text. University of Illinois Center for the Study of Reading, Urbana, IL, 1981

12. Rubin DC. A unit analysis of prose memory. J Verb Learn Verb Behav 1978; 17: 599-620

13. Meyer BJF, McConkie GW. What is recalled after hearing a passage? J Educ Psychol 1973; 65: 109-117

14. Cuadra CA. Online systems: promise and pitfalls. J Am Soc Inf Sci 1971; 22: 107-114

14. Howard DL. What the eye sees while predicting a document's pertinence from its citation. In: Griffiths JM (ed) ASIS '91: proceedings of the 54th ASIS annual meeting. Learned Information, Medford NJ, 1991, pp. 87-101

15. Fenichel CH. Online searching: measures that discriminate among users with different types of experiences. J Am Soc Inf Sci 1981; 32: 23-32

16. Borgman CL. All users of information retrieval systems are not created equal: an exploration into individual differences. Inf Proc Man 1989; 25: 237-251

17. Shneiderman B. Designing the user interface: strategies for effective human-computer interaction. Addison-Wesley, Reading MA, 1992

18. Baron RM, Kenney DA. The moderator-mediator variable distinction in social psychological research: conceptual, strategic, and statistical considerations. J Pers Soc Psychol 1986; 51: 1173-1182

Term Relevance Feedback and Query Expansion: Relation to Design

Amanda Spink
School of Library and Information Sciences
University of North Texas

Abstract

To improve information retrieval effectiveness, research in both the algorithmic and human approach to query expansion is required. This paper uses the human approach to examine the selection and effectiveness of search terms sources for query expansion. The results show that the most effective sources were the users written question statement, user terms derived during the interaction and terms selected from particular database fields. These findings indicate the need for the design and testing of automatic relevance feedback techniques that place greater emphasis on these sources.

1. Introduction

Relevance feedback techniques and the selection of search terms for query expansion are major research areas in information retrieval research which seek to improve the effectiveness of interactive information retrieval. Query expansion research can be divided into two major areas. Firstly, extensive research has been conducted into automatic and semi-automatic query expansion techniques [1-7]. Automatic query expansion techniques utilize the text of a user's question and/or retrieved document/s found to be relevant by the user, as input for techniques to derive a set of search terms to retrieve additional relevant documents. The emphasis in automatic query expansion techniques or relevance feedback techniques is on formulating and testing algorithms and automatic techniques which select and weight search terms for query expansion.

Different relevance feedback techniques utilize different search term selection strategies. The Vector Space Model [8-9] automatically expands queries by adding all terms in the retrieved relevant documents. The Probabilistic Model or theory of relevance weights [10] is based on query term distribution in non-relevant and relevant documents. Many modifications to the Probabilistic Model have been developed [11-14]. Significant performance improvement has been found by ranking a union of all terms from retrieved relevant documents using the EMIM measure (Expected Mutual Information Measure) and then selecting terms from the top of the list [3].

Multiple iterations and the addition of only selected terms, between 20 and 40 in number, were found to be more effective than adding all terms from relevant retrieved documents [15]. A recent study evaluated six algorithms for their effectiveness in ranking terms for query expansion, comparing their performance in term ranking for query expansion to rankings by users [1-2]. Other automatic and semi-automatic techniques have also been reviewed [2&4].

Secondly, in contrast to the automatic or "algorithmic" approach, the human approach to query expansion research examines the user's representation of their question and whatever tools eg. thesaurus or experiences they use to derive or modify a set of search terms during query expansion. The human approach emphasizes investigating and observing human decision-making and human behavior, and the variables in the process of search term selection. The human search term selection process involves the user and information retrieval (IR) system. During the mediated situation with a user and human intermediary, the process may involve a user and IR system, intermediary and IR system, or user and intermediary, or all three.

There have been few major research studies within the human approach to search term selection. Recent research has developed categories of search term types, but not based on the source and effectiveness of search terms [16-19]. The study reported in this paper developed a classification of search terms according to source and a categorization based on effectiveness in the retrieval of documents judged relevant by the user. The effectiveness of search terms from different sources in retrieving relevant documents during mediated information retrieval could then be compared.

No previous study has examined the selection, source of search terms and effectiveness of sources for query expansion during mediated information retrieval, nor the process by which users select search terms for query expansion interactively from retrieved documents (referred to as Term Relevance Feedback (TRF)). This is a study of how and from where users select search terms for query expansion to improve retrieval performance.

To improve IR effectiveness research is needed in both the "algorithmic" and "human" streams, and further joint efforts utilizing the results of human studies in interface and system design [20].

2. Research Questions

This paper examines the following research questions: (1) Are TRF search terms selected for query expansion from retrieved documents?, (2) How effective are TRF search terms in retrieving relevant documents, as compared to other sources? (3) What is the role of the user and intermediary in the selection of TRF search terms during mediated information retrieval? and (4) From which database fields are TRF search terms selected? The aim of this study was to observe the human task of term selection for query expansion to provide guidelines for IR system enhancement.

3. Background: Data Collection

The research presented in this paper is part of a human oriented investigation of feedback and search terminology in information retrieval [21]. Data utilized in the study was collected during a pioneering study of mediated information retrieval [22]. Forty users with real requests were videotaped participating in a pre-online interview and online interactive search on DIALOG conducted by a professional search intermediary. The study reported in this paper follows analysis reported previously [21-24].

3.1 Methodology

To determine if search terms were selected through term relevance feedback during mediated information retrieval, the source of each search term was FIRST identified. The method utilized to identify the search terms and their sources is described in detail in previous papers [21-24].

Briefly, for each question the set of search terms was extracted from the search log. Using the user's written question statement, the online search log and the transcript of the discourse between the user and intermediary, the first mention of the search term (or the search concept from which it was derived) was credited to its source.

Provided below is an example of the identification of a new term during TRF from Search Number 8. During the display of 15 retrieved documents, the user identifies the term "school role" in the descriptor field, which is subsequently used as a search term in query expansion. The user comments:

User: Right. Exactly, uh hum. Let's see we have school role, did you see that one.

Each search term was classified according to its source and categorized according to its retrieval of relevant or non-relevant documents. A more detailed methodology was developed to examine the effectiveness of TRF search terms as compared to other sources, including consideration of documents which were retrieved by search statements of two or more search terms with logical connectors between them. The methodology utilized a weighting scheme which distributes credit for retrieval in proportion to search terms in various logical combinations.

Each document retrieved (relevant or non-relevant) was assigned a weighting of 1. Each search term that contributed to the retrieval of that document was identified (matched in the search statement and the displayed relevant documents) and assigned a portion of the weighting of 1. If only one search term was responsible for the retrieval of the relevant document, that term was assigned a retrieval weighting of 1; but, if more than one search term was responsible for the retrieval of a document, each search term was assigned a proportional retrieval weighting. For example, in the search statement "dog and cat", since both terms contributed to the retrieval of the relevant item they both received a proportional retrieval weighting of .5. In the search statement "dog or cat", if both terms were in the item each term was allocated .5, but if only one term retrieved the item, that term was allocated a weighting of 1. The proportional retrieval weighting was then calculated for each search term and then each search term source. This methodology has been further detailed in preceding papers [21]. To determine the role of the user and intermediary in the selection of TRF search terms, a micro-analysis was conducted utilizing each transcript of a user-intermediary dialogue in conjunction with the accompanying search log, to determine the TRF search terms identified by the user or intermediary during the online interaction. The database field from which each TRF search term was identified was also determined during the micro-analysis.

4. Results

The results of the study are provided in the following sections corresponding to the four research questions.

4.1. Sources of Search Terms

The forty online searches contained 593 search terms distributed in descending order as to its source as shown in Table 1. Five sources of search terms were identified:

1. **User Question Statement (QS):** included in or derived from the written statement submitted by the user at the beginning.
2. **User-interaction (UI):** suggested by the user during interaction with the intermediary prior or during the online search.
3. **Intermediary (IN):** suggested by the intermediary prior or during the online search.
4. **Thesaurus (TH):** derived from the thesaurus, when not suggested apriori by any other source. (Eg., if a search term has already appeared in the question statement and was later translated directly into a descriptor from a thesaurus, the thesaurus was NOT credited as a source, the question statement was.)
5. **Term Relevance Feedback (TRF):** extracted by the user or intermediary during the online interaction after examination of documents retrieved for query expansion.

Table 1 shows that term relevance feedback (TRF) was a source of search terms during the 40 mediated information retrieval interactions. Although not as large in number as search terms provided by the user, from the question statement or during user-interaction, TRF contributed a total of 67 (11%) search terms.

Table 1. Sources of search terms. (N searches = 40)

Sources	Number	%	Cum.%
User			
a. Question statement	227	38%	38%
b. User interaction	134	23%	61%
Sub total user	361	61%	61%
Thesaurus	113	19%	80%
Term Relevance Feedback	**67**	**11%**	**91%**
Intermediary	52	9%	100%
TOTAL	593	100%	

Average search terms per search = 14.8 Maximum = 43. Minimum = 4. Standard deviation = 8.77.

TRF terms were selected for query expansion during 22 (55%) of the 40 mediated interactions.

Table 2 shows the number of searches which used each source of search terms.

Table 2. Number of searches which used each search term source.

Source	No. of Searches	% of Searches
Question statement	40	100%
User-interaction	28	70%
Term Relevance Feedback	**22**	**55%**
Intermediaries	20	50%
Thesaurus	20	50%

4.2. Sources of Terms and Relevance of Retrieved Items

Table 3 gives the distribution of search terms in relation to the relevance of retrieved documents. A number of search terms were found to have retrieved both relevant and non-relevant documents within the same search, therefore the categories are not mutually exclusive. Four categories of search terms based on retrieval effectiveness were identified:

1) **T(R):** search terms which retrieved relevant documents only, and nothing but relevant documents.
2) **T(R + N):** search terms which retrieved at times relevant and at other times not relevant documents, that is, the retrieval of these search terms as to relevance was mixed.
3) **T(N):** search terms which retrieved not relevant documents only, nothing but not relevant documents.
4) **T(Z):** search terms which had zero retrievals, that is, retrieved nothing at all.

The first two categories of search terms T(R) and T(R + N), represent the positive retrievals and were responsible for the retrieval of all relevant documents, even though these included at times not relevant as well as relevant documents. The categories T(N) and T(Z), or the negative retrievals, were responsible for not relevant only and zero retrievals.

Table 3 presents the number and percentage of the total search terms within the four categorizations based on effectiveness.

Table 3. Search terms and relevance of retrieved documents. (N searches = 40; Relevant documents = 3565; Not Relevant documents = 2660).

Documents Retrieved	No. of Terms	%
Relevant documents only, T(R)	25	4%
Relevant and not relevant, T(R + N)	353	60%
Subtotal with any R (Positive retrieval)	378	64%
Not relevant only, T(N)	147	24%
Zero retrieval, T(Z)	68	12%
Subtotal T(N) + T(Z) (Negative retrieval)	215	36%
Total	593	100%

4.2.1. *Effectiveness of Term Relevance Feedback Search Terms*

Table 4 shows the sources of terms and relevance of retrieved documents, providing a comparison for all five sources.

Table 4. Sources of Terms and Relevance of Retrieved Documents

QS (Question Statement) UI (Users) IN (Intermediaries)
TH (Thesaurus) TRF (Term Relevance Feedback)

Search Term Categories/	Sources					
	QS	UI	IN	TH	**TRF**	Total
T(R)	11	7	3	2	**2**	25
	4.8%	5.2%	5.8%	1.8%	**3%**	4.2%
T(R + N)	174	63	21	50	**45**	353
	76.7%	47%	40.4%	44.2%	**67.2%**	59.5%
T(N)	30	51	16	34	**16**	147
	13.2%	38.1%	30.8%	30.1%	**23.8%**	24.8%
T(Z)	12	13	12	27	**4**	68
	5.3%	9.7%	23%	23.9%	**6%**	11.5%
Source	227	134	52	113	**67**	593
Totals	38.3%	22.6%	8.8%	19.1%	**11.3%**	100%

Table 4 shows that TRF search terms represented: 67 (11.3%) of all 593 search terms, 2 (10%) of **T(R)** (Relevant Only) terms, 45 (13%) of **T(R + N)** (Mixed Retrieval) terms, 16 (11%) of **T(N)** (Not Relevant Only) terms and 4 (6%) or **T(Z)** (No Retrieval) terms.

TRF search terms represented a small proportion of the total search terms and the categories of search terms. Table 4 shows that a major proportion (3% + 67.2% = 70.2%) of the 67 TRF search terms contributed to the positive retrievals. That is, fully 70% of terms derived during the term relevance feedback process contributed to the retrieval of relevant documents.

Table 5 shows the number and percentage of terms from each source that contributed to the retrieval of relevant documents.

Table 5. Percentage of search terms from each source which retrieved relevant documents (N searches = 40).

Source	No. Relevant Terms	Total From Source		%
Question Statement	186	227		82%
User Interaction	72	134		54%
Total for Users	258	361	Mean	71%
Term Relevance Feedback	**48**	**67**		**72%**
Intermediaries	25	52		48%
Thesaurus	50	113		44%

Table 5 shows that 48 (72%) out of the 67 TRF search terms contributed to the retrieval of documents judged relevant by the user.

Table 6 shows the mean percentage of documents retrieved per search retrieved by search terms from each source.

Table 6. Mean percentage of relevant documents per search retrieved by search terms from each source. (N searches = 40).

Source	No. Searches	Range (%)	Mean (%)
Question Statement	37	1 - 100	70%
User Interaction	26	2 - 91	22%
Thesaurus	19	2 - 58	21%
Intermediary	19	2 - 30	14%
Term Relevance Feedback	**14**	**1 - 26**	**9%**

Table 6 shows that TRF search terms contributed a mean percentage of 9% of relevant documents per search.

4.3. Selection of Term Relevance Feedback Search Terms: User or Intermediary

Table 7 shows the number of TRF search terms selected by the user and intermediary during the 22 mediated online interactions were utilized.

Table 7. Term relevance feedback search terms. (Number Searches = 22)

	Total TRF Search Terms	%	Relevant TRF Search Terms	%
Users	25	37%	15	31%
Intermediaries	42	63%	33	69%
Total RF Terms	67	100%	48	100%

Users derived a total of 25 (37%) TRF search terms and 15 (60%) of those terms contributed to the retrieval of relevant documents. Thus, users contributed 15 (31%) of the 48 relevant TRF search terms utilized. Intermediaries derived a total of 42 (63%) of the TRF search terms; 33 (79%) of those terms contributed to the retrieval of relevant documents. Thus intermediaries contributed 33 (69%) of the relevant TRF search terms.

A majority of users and intermediaries utilized term relevance feedback to identify search terms from the displayed documents. Despite the user's greater domain knowledge, intermediaries were more effective in selecting TRF search terms which contributed to the retrieval of relevant documents. This may be a function of the intermediary's greater experience in utilizing the interactive capabilities of information retrieval systems.

4.4. Field Selection of Term Relevance Feedback Search Terms

TRF search terms were selected by either the user or intermediary during the online interactions for query expansion. During the 40 online interactions the title, author, journal name and descriptor fields were generally displayed, with 55% of the formats requested also displaying the abstract. Table 8 shows the DIALOG formats utilized during the 40 mediated searches and the 22 searches that utilized term relevance feedback. Table 9 provides the fields included in each format.

Table 8. DIALOG formats utilized. (Number Searches = 40)

Format	No. of Items 40 Searches	%	No. of Items 22 TRF Searches	%
2	461	7%	207	5%
3	1484	24%	841	21%
5	1631	26%	1333	34%
6	222	4%	261	7%
7	1541	25%	837	21%
8	904	15%	485	12%
Total	6225	100%	3964	100%

Table 9 provides a listing of the bibliographic fields displayed in each DIALOG format. Most searches utilized several formats, particularly format 3, format 5 and format 7.

Table 9. DIALOG Formats and bibliographic fields displayed.

Format	Content - Bibliographic Fields Displayed
2	Full Record except Abstract(TI/AU/SO/DE/ID/SH)
3	Bibliographic Citation (TI/AU/SO)
5	Full Record (TI/AU/SO/AB/DE/ID/SH)
6	Title (TI)
7	Bibliographic Citation and Abstract (TI/AU/SO/AB)
8	Title and Indexing (TI/DE/ID/SH)

Table 10 shows the percentage of records in the 40 searches and 22 searches that utilized TRF, that displayed each field.

Table 10. Bibliographic fields and percentages (Number Searches = 40 & 22).

Bibliographic Field	% 40 Searches	% 22 TRF Searches
Title	100%	100%
Author	87%	81%
Source	78%	91%
Abstracts	54%	55%
Descriptors	48%	51%
Identifiers	48%	51%
Subject Headings	44%	45%

Table 11 shows the field from which search terms were derived during term relevance feedback and the retrieval effectiveness of those terms.

Table 11. TRF search terms and database fields. (Number Searches = 22)

Field Name	No. of TRF Terms Selected	%	No. of Relevant TRF Terms Selected	%
Title	18	27%	16	33%
Journal Name	3	3%	2	4%
Abstract	2	3%	1	2%
Descriptor	39	58%	25	52%
Identifier	2	3%	2	4%
Subject Heading	3	3%	2	4%
Total	67	100%	48	100%

Table 11 shows that 85% of the 67 TRF search terms were selected from the title or descriptor field. 88% of the title selections and 62% of the descriptor selections contributed to the retrieval of relevant documents. Although many of the searches included the display of the full abstract (55% items displayed), only a small number (3%) of TRF search terms were selected from the abstract field. The data indicates that users and intermediaries selected TRF terms from titles and descriptors, rather than abstracts.

5. Summary of Findings

Question 1: Are search terms selected during relevance feedback for query expansion?

The majority (55%) of users and intermediaries utilized term relevance feedback to identify search terms for query expansion, but these terms represented only 11.3% of the total search terms. Thus the total number of TRF search terms (67) represented only a small proportion of the total number of search terms (593) when compared to other sources (less than user and thesaurus terms, but slightly more than intermediary terms).

Question 2: How effective are TRF search terms in the retrieval of items judged relevant by the user, as compared with other search term sources?

Due to their small number, TRF search terms were not as significant as other sources in retrieving relevant items. On average, these terms only contributed to the retrieval of 9% of relevant items per search. Additional analysis (Table 4) presented a different picture, showing that a high proportion of TRF search terms were quite productive in retrieving relevant items. The proportion of these terms which contributed to the retrieval of relevant items was high (72%), higher than the intermediary (48%) or thesaurus (44%) terms, slightly higher than user interaction terms (71%), but lower than question statement terms (82%).

Question 3: What is the role of the user and intermediary in the selection of TRF search terms?

The intermediaries identified the major proportion of the relevant TRF search terms, with the users identifying about one third. Of the intermediaries TRF search terms, 79% contributed to the retrieval of relevant items and of the users TRF search terms, 59% (15/26) contributed to the retrieval of relevant items. The results indicate that intermediaries selected a greater number of TRF search terms and selected more effective terms. Users should be encouraged to utilize the interactive capability of the IR system and identify TRF search terms to enhance query expansion and strategy reformulation.

Question 4: From which database fields were TRF search terms selected?

The major proportion of the TRF search terms were selected from the title and descriptor fields, and only 3% were selected from abstracts, despite the 55% of documents that included the display of the abstract. The data indicates that users and intermediaries did not utilize abstracts for TRF search term selection, possibly due to the complex and lengthy nature of many of the abstracts. The degree to which abstracts were utilized for relevance judgements and the selection of search terms is an area for further analysis.

6. Design Conclusions

The results of this study show that users select effective search terms for query expansion from retrieved items, but other sources are also important. The most effective sources of search terms for query expansion were firstly, terms from the users written question, then terms from the user during the interaction and terms selected from the titles and descriptor fields of the retrieved documents.

Research studies indicate that more effective automatic techniques or relevance feedback techniques for query expansion are based on the selection of between 20 - 40 terms from the relevant retrieved documents [15]. Results of this study of human behavior suggest the need for design and testing of automatic relevance feedback techniques that select, or weight more heavily, terms for query expansion from; (1) title and descriptor fields of retrieved relevant documents, or (2) user's knowledge domain terms from a question statement or during the interaction.

Terms from the users written question statement were found to be the most effective in query expansion. During interactive information retrieval, users and intermediaries makes notes and record ideas on paper. If users could record these notes and ideas interactively, they could be used as a source of terms and information by an intelligent information retrieval system.

A facility could be designed which allows the user to enter a user information problem statement (UIPS) in natural language, preceding the initial search statement. This UIPS could be continuously modified by the user interactively, reflecting changes in the user's information problem and the identification of new search terms (resulting from term relevance feedback or user-interaction with an intermediary, thesaurus or terms the user derives from their own domain knowledge during the interaction). Terms identified by user's from their knowledge domain and term relevance feedback during the interaction were found to be effective in the retrieval of relevant documents. The UIPS or working document could be utilized by the IR system (in an automatic process) or by the user (in a semi-automatic process) to identify search terms for query expansion.

Results also highlight the need for IR interfaces that encourage the user to utilize their own domain knowledge and examine the documents retrieved as a source of search terms for query expansion. The surprisingly low utilization of abstracts for the selection of new search terms during bibliographic database searching indicates that further research is needed to examine the role of abstracts and full text documents in relevance judgements and search term selection for query expansion.

This study investigated the human approach to the selection of search terms and TRF search terms for query expansion. Term relevance feedback (TRF) search terms are of significant interest in information retrieval research as they result from the interactive process between human and IR system. They represented a small proportion of the total search terms utilized during the 40 online searches and contributing to the retrieval of a small number of relevant items, but they were highly productive in contributing to the retrieval of relevant items.

Research is currently in progress examining the utilization of term relevance feedback for query expansion by end-users, which will be compared with the results of this study of mediated information retrieval.

Acknowledgements

The author would like to acknowledge the contribution of Dr. Tefko Saracevic to the development of this paper and Zhwei Zhang for his contribution to the data analysis.

References

1. Efthimiadis EN. Interactive query expansion and relevance feedback for document retrieval systems. PhD thesis, City University, London, UK, 1992

2. Efthimiadis EN. A user-centered evaluation of ranking algorithms for interactive query expansion. Proceedings 16th Annual International ACM SIGIR Conference of Research and Development in Information Retrieval 1993;16:146-159

3. Harper DJ. Relevance feedback in document retrieval systems: An evaluation of probabilistic strategies. PhD thesis, Jesus College, Cambridge, England, 1980

4. Harman D. Relevance feedback revisited. Proceedings of the 15th International Conference on Research and Development in IR, SIGIR 1992, Copenhagen, Denmark, June 21-24, 1992

5. Robertson SE. On term selection for query expansion. Journal of Documentation 1990;46(4):359-364

6. Sparck Jones K. (Ed.) Automatic keyword classification for information retrieval. London: Butterworths, 1971

7. van Rijsbergen CJ, Harper DJ, Porter MF. The selection of good search terms. Information Processing and Management 1981;17(2):77-91

8. Rocchio JJ. Relevance feedback in information retrieval. In: Salton G (ed) The SMART Retrieval System Prentice-Hall, Englewood NJ, 1971 pp 313-323

9. Salton G, Buckley C. Improving retrieval performance by relevance feedback. Journal of the American Society for Information Science 1990;41(4):288-297

10. Robertson SE, Sparck Jones K. Relevance weighting of search terms. Journal of the American Society for Information Science 1976;27(3):129-146

11. Croft WB, Harper DJ. Using probabilistic models of document retrieval without relevance information. Journal of Documentation 1979;35(4):285-295

12. Harper DJ, van Rijsbergen CJ. An evaluation of feedback in document retrieval: Using co-occurrence data. Journal of Documentation 1978;34(3):189-216

13. Robertson SE. On relevance weight estimation and query expansion. Journal of Documentation 1986;42(3):182-188

14. Wu H, Salton G. The estimation of term relevance weights using relevance feedback. Journal of Documentation 1981;37(4):194-214

15. Harman D. Towards interactive query expansion. Proceedings ACM SIGIR Conference on Research and Development in Information Retrieval, Grenoble, France, 1988

16. Fidel R. Searchers' selection of search keys: I. The selection routine. Journal of the American Society for Information Science 1991;42(7):490-500

17. Fidel R. Searchers' selection of search keys: II. Controlled vocabulary or free-text searching. Journal of the American Society for Information Science 1991;42(7):501-514

18. Fidel R. Searchers' selection of search keys: II. Searching styles. Journal of the American Society for Information Science 1991;42(7):515-527

19. Bates MJ, Wilde BN, Siegfried S. An analysis of search terminology used by humanities scholars: The Getty Online Searching Project Report Number 1. The Library Quarterly 1993;63(1):1-39

20. Belkin NJ, Marchetti PG, Cool C. BRAQUE: Design of an interface to support user interaction in information retrieval. Information Processing and Management 1992;29(3):325-344

21. Spink A. Feedback in information retrieval. PhD thesis. Rutgers University, School of Communication, Information and Library Studies, 1993

22. Saracevic T, Mokros H, Su L, Spink A. Interaction between users and intermediaries in online searching. Proceedings 12th Annual National Online Meeting 1991;12:329-341

23. Spink A, Saracevic T. Sources and uses of search terminology in mediated online searching. Proceedings 55th Annual Meeting American Society for Information Science 1992;29:249-255

24. Spink A, Saracevic T. Dynamics of search term selection during mediated online searching. Proceedings of 56th Annual Meeting American Society for Information Science 1993:30:63-72

Modelling Information Retrieval Agents with Belief Revision

Brian Logan, Steven Reece* and Karen Sparck Jones

Computer Laboratory, University of Cambridge
New Museums Site, Pembroke Street, Cambridge CB2 3QG, UK
(sparckjones@cl.cam.ac.uk)

Abstract

This paper describes the development and computational testing of a model of the information intermediary based on an AI theory of belief revision. We describe the theoretical foundations of the work in a general account of the way an agent's beliefs and intentions are formed and modified, and in an analysis of the functional tasks an intermediary has to carry out; we indicate the specific developments required to automate and integrate both aspects of intermediary behaviour, as determinants of interactive dialogue with the user; and report, with illustrations, on tests and findings. The research shows that such approaches can be implemented in an essentially principled manner, though there are many large problems still to be overcome, and our experiments are only the first, extremely simple, trials of the basic strategy for intermediary simulation.

1 Introduction

We have sought to model the information intermediary by combining a general theory of belief revision, due to Galliers, with the functional characterisation of the intermediary proposed by Belkin and his colleagues. We have developed and tested a computational implementation showing that our model supports simple information-seeking dialogue with the adaptive and cooperative properties of real ones. Our experiments validate some, though not all, of the major claims of the belief revision theory; they also suggest that while Belkin at al's functional account of the intermediary's skills is rational, modelling the intermediary as a collection of independent agents is not. Galliers' theory underpins communication between agents, but effective communication between user and librarian requires dialogue control that an unconstrained distributed agent architecture does not provide. This paper describes our development and implementation of the two theories as a single integrated system, and presents illustrative results. These lay foundations for further research, though a great deal more work is needed before such a sophisticated approach to interaction between user and intermediary could be expected to issue in any practical interface. A full account of this work is given in [1].

2 Background

We described the motivation for our work, and both Galliers' and Belkin et al's theories from this point of view, in some detail in [2]. Galliers' theory itself is presented in [3] and the MONSTRAT model work by Belkin, Brooks, Daniels and others in [4], [5], [6], [7] and [8] (hereafter collectively called BBD).

As an illustrative starting point here, our aim is to model the librarian's capacities in such a dialogue as:

```
U:  I am looking for books on Classical architecture.
L:  Are you more interested in Greek or Roman architecture?
U:  No, like the British Museum.
L:  Ah, you mean Classical Revival architecture.
    .....
```

The key features of Galliers' theory are that agents are autonomous but also knowledge and resource limited, so cooperative interaction with other agents, notably by dialogue communication, is required to reach an agent's goals. Formulating and achieving goals, as in literature seeking, is based on belief revision: thus formulating an adequate statement of information need and a corresponding retrieval strategy involves communication, driven by current intentions and plans, aimed at resolving conflicts of belief due to inadequate knowledge and obtaining a solid base for action. Belief revision is determined

*Present addresses: Brian Logan, Martin Centre for Architectural and Urban Studies, Department of Architecture, University of Cambridge; Steven Reece, Department of Engineering Science, University of Oxford.

by how ground assumptions are endorsed, derived beliefs are connected, and change is minimised. In the revision process a new belief is evaluated in terms of preferences among the alternative consistent sets of beliefs that adopting or rejecting the candidate belief imply. In general agents are evaluating many competing belief sets in order to establish which one(s) are superior in terms of stronger *endorsement*, greater *connectivity* (proofs), and *minimal change*.

BBD's intermediary/librarian model, based on a detailed study of real interviews, treats the intermediary as a collection of specialised functional experts, agents engaged with subtasks of the overall task of satisfying the user's information need. These experts include 'Problem Description', 'User Model', 'Retrieval Strategy' etc, each operating as an autonomous agent requesting and passing information among themselves and also communicating with the user. BBD noted that in the real dialogues there was no overall protocol, but that different segments, or 'foci', in the dialogues concentrated on a specific expert agent's goals within a flexible and varied flow visiting and revisiting subtasks. They thus viewed the intermediary as a distributed system, and initially advocated an open, blackboard architecture.

It appeared that these two theories could be very effectively combined to obtain the required full intermediary model, since Galliers' belief revision theory seemed to provide the mechanism for driving both the individual functional experts and their joint 'collective' operating as a single agent vis-a-vis the user.

2.1 Required Developments

While Galliers' and BBD's theories appeared to fit well together, applying them together required not only computational implementation, but significant development of both in order to supply missing pieces and ensure effective integration. It was necessary to extend Galliers' account of operations on beliefs to treat intentions and planning, and to provide for inference, in order both to get the inputs required to choose which beliefs and intentions to adopt and to pursue these through action. The computational modelling itself called for a specific mechanism to manage the data and processes of revision.

It was necessary to supplement BBD's account of the intermediary, on the other hand, with some means of sustaining and organising dialogue with more power than the BBD 'Response Generator' and 'Explanation' modules. Though Belkin and his colleagues (cf [4]) report experiments with the internal architecture of the intermediary, they did not address the question of dialogue management. However it is clearly necessary to decide when to ask the user for information, and maintaining effective interaction with the user implies that dialogue content has to be ordered and grouped: system outputs cannot simply be triggered, as separate items, by independent internal prompts. Moreover, as discussed in [2], BBD's model needed development to integrate dialogue management and overall control and to substantiate the metafunctions 'Plan' and 'Match' BBD do not analyse. Though Ingwersen in [9] has proposed a much more elaborate model, essentially subsuming BBD's, he has not tackled these issues either.

3 Implementation of Belief Revision

In Galliers' theory ground assumptions (relative to a context) are endorsed as communicated, given ('innate'), or hypothetical. Belief communication may be first-hand or second-hand, positive or negative, so e.g. a strongly communicated belief from a highly reliable source may be endorsed *2c-pos*. The options for given are either specific (*spec*) or default (*def*) generalisation. Any beliefs not otherwise endorsed are hypothetical (*hypoth*). Thus beliefs (which may themselves be propositions or their negations) can be ordered by the difficulty of disbelieving them, from those endorsed *1c-pos* down to *hypoth*. Beliefs are related to other beliefs, forming internally consistent sets, so one set may be more strongly endorsed than another. Sets may also be more or less strongly connected, or internally dense: thus individual beliefs, especially *core beliefs* independently defined as important in some context, may have more or less derivational (proof) support in different belief sets. So if an agent is entertaining a candidate belief, adopting or rejecting it (i.e. adopting its negation) involves examining all the different maximally consistent belief sets containing either it or its negation, and preferring those that are better endorsed and more connected (*mc*). In addition, since the whole approach is a conservative one based on the principle that agents are reluctant to change their beliefs without good reason, if other things are equal sets that make minimal change over the previous state are preferred. These types of reason for preferring belief sets are considered in order, first by connectivity, then endorsement, then minimal change: however any may determine the final outcome. This will normally be a set of equally preferred belief sets requiring further resolution through the acquisition of new information.

Intentions depend on beliefs, and revising beliefs entails revising intentions. We have therefore incorporated intentions into an extended account of cognitive *attitudes*: cognitive states are combinations of propositional attitudes, with derivational links between beliefs, intentions, and predicted future states. The general process of belief revision applied to all attitudes then handles intention revision either directly in the face of conflict with communicated intentions or indirectly as a result of conflicts between motivating beliefs. Connectivity applies to intentions in a straightforward way. Commitment, the key feature of intention, is captured in part by the strength of endorsements on supporting beliefs, and in part by characterising intentions directly according to the utility of their goal states and the effort required to reach these. Thus goal states are either *desire-pos* or *desire-neg* and either *effort-pos* or *effort-neg* (on simple heuristic definitions). The difference between beliefs and intentions is that the strengths of beliefs depend on their sources, the commitment to intentions on their (expected) outcomes. Then in choosing between competing sets of attitudes involving both beliefs and intentions, these are rated first by the belief preference criteria and then the intention ones.[1]

It is further necessary to provide for inference and planning. This is straightforward. Normal inference mechanisms (e.g. modus ponens) add derived beliefs or intentions to existing attitude sets, resulting in either conflict or additional support for existing attitudes and therefore provoking revision. Planning is also handled by inference, applying intention generation rules along with planning operators to existing attitudes. There is thus a basic *agent action cycle*: incorporating new information in existing attitude sets, firing deductive inference rules over existing attitudes to obtain new ones, performing revision to obtain preferred sets, and executing preferred intended actions. This is the way an agent responds to communicated input in a dialogue, modifying its attitudes and itself taking communicative action.

3.1 Computational Apparatus

The computational implementation requires an apparatus for constructing and evaluating all the attitude sets constituting responses to input. Our approach, the 'Increased Coherence Model' (ICM) is based on de Kleer's ATMS [10, 11]: for a full account see [1]. An agent has a message interception unit (MIU) for storing incoming and outgoing messages and a cognitive unit (CU) reading from and writing to the MIU board. The CU has a database, an attitude revision (i.e. ATMS-based) component, an inference engine, and a planner: the engine contains axiomatic rules operating on the information in the database which consists of derived attitudes and their supports; the revision component does belief and intention revision given the available justifications, taking the attitudes as ATMS assumptions; the planner constructs and assesses plans, working on intentions derived from beliefs and resulting in actions. As an agent's cognitive state covers believed, intended, or uncertain attitudes, and the agent's commitments to its attitudes, the engine and planner use this information to guide their choice of inferences and plans, and the ATMS to maintain consistent sets of attitudes.

Notationally, we refer to an agent's attitude to a proposition or state of affairs, the time of holding the attitude and the endorsement of or commitment to it (for convenience we may refer to individual attitudes as possible attitudes). For convenience we refer to commitments to beliefs, i.e. to the strength with which we hold them, as well as to commitments to intentions: commitments to beliefs are heuristically computed from their endorsements and may be strong, weak or uncertain. Then if an agent's belief state is its set of preferred belief sets, a given proposition can figure in these in various ways reflecting the agent's degree of commitment to it. As noted, intentions are based on beliefs but are explicitly marked, and there are intention sets analogous to belief sets. Belief and intention are linked by rules to the effect that an agent cannot intend a state it believes true. Overall, revision results in consistent sets of interdependent beliefs and intentions characterised by the agent's commitments to these attitudes. We say an agent believes a belief or intends an intention if these attitudes occur in every preferred set, i.e. are *pervasive*; attitudes in some sets only are uncertain.

Internally, commitments are handled as a form of endorsement: the various types of commitments are included in the endorsement orderings for beliefs and intentions respectively, and can therefore be used in preference evaluation to determine, as a consequence of revision, what the agent's new commitments to its attitudes are. Individual attitudes can be multiply endorsed, and may also be *definite*, i.e. ascribed to another agent and treated as premises. An agent's database thus consists of all the agent's attitudes, their endorsements (including commitments), and their justifications, i.e. inference supports. In processing via the ATMS, preferences between sets in terms of their attitude endorsements are computed by the procedure described in [1]: as endorsements are not propagated through to *derived* attitudes, the effect of the algorithm is to test whether attitudes should be retained or adopted by seeing if they remain viable when their weakest ground assumption is removed. Evaluating attitude sets for connectivity (for core attitudes) is easily done via the ATMS: this records minimal proofs via justification chains and these can be checked to see whether one set includes all the proofs in another set plus additional ones, and so should be preferred. Finally, the ATMS can be used to evaluate for minimal change by checking to see which sets preserve most of their previous pervasive beliefs.

Inference rules are applied to obtain new justifications for attitudes. These are general rules, with endorsements, that are not part of the database. However when they are instantiated via the rule binding algorithm they become specific attitudes providing justifications in the database and therefore subject to defeasible inference. Given the many possible inferences that can be drawn relating to new attitude,

[1] Note that previous states may emerge as still preferred.

e.g. a communicated belief, we constrain inference by concentrating on the current task, as defined by *recency* and modelled by a stack: thus inference is applied to attitude sets from the top of the stack. The inference algorithm (described in [1]) exploits *relevance* relations between attitudes, where commitment to one attitude depends on that to another.

As mentioned earlier, for action (as in dialogue) to satisfy intentions, planning is needed. This is done in STRIPS style, implemented via rules applied through the inference engine and exploiting the belief revision mechanism to choose preferred plans. The rules include desire rules determining the leading intention and utility of a plan, and planning rules to decompose intentions: the planning rules in turn operate on *action schemata* embodying primitive agent actions, which may be 'internal' (e.g. perform an inference) or 'external' (e.g. send a message to the MIU for communication to another agent).

Computationally therefore, the agent's cognitive architecture is operationalised with the ATMS, working on the database, supporting the belief revision mechanism, which plays a central role: it supplies attitude information to, or receives it from, the inference engine, and it supports planning both via inference in plan formation and through plan assessment. Agent processing in an action cycle is provoked by MIU messages stimulating possible beliefs.

For example, in the dialogue fragment presented in the previous section, it turns out U is mistaken about the meaning of the term 'Classical architecture'. This involves two changes of belief: L revises her original assumption about the period U is interested in; and U revises his belief about the meaning of the term 'Classical'. U's initial belief sets contain the pervasive belief

(*bel U* (*problem-desc classical-architecture*) *strong*)

i.e. U is strongly committed to the belief that *classical-architecture* is a suitable problem descriptor, and the intention

(*p-int U* (*bel L* (*problem-desc classical-architecture*)) *desire-pos*)

i.e. U intends to share his problem description with L. U generates a plan to achieve this intention, which results in his first utterance. U's utterance causes L to revise her beliefs to include the fact that the topic of U's query is 'Classical architecture'. Immediately after U's utterance, L believes

(*p-bel L* (*bel U* (*problem-desc classical-architecture*)) *2c-pos*)

and, following inference and belief revision, L adopts U's belief as her own:

(*bel L* (*problem-desc classical-architecture*) *strong*).

L does this because she has no reason to believe that 'Classical architecture' is not a good description of U's problem (e.g. U has not previously stated he is writing an essay on fish farming). L constructs a plan from this new belief to determine whether U is more interested in Greek or in Roman architecture (perhaps because L infers that the problem description 'Classical architecture' is too general). However U's response to L's question leads L to realise that there has been a misunderstanding and that the appropriate problem description is 'Classical Revival architecture', not 'Classical architecture'. L therefore abandons her plan to determine if U is more interested in Greek or in Roman architecture.

4 Implementing the BBD Model

As mentioned earlier, implementing the BBD model required a decision about the specific architecture to be used, provision of a dialogue management capability, and a supply of actual IR task knowledge (data and rules). The version of the BBD model we have used for reference is that given in [7]

The architecture design problems of distributed systems are well known, particularly the challenges presented by a full-blown open-access blackboard approach with multiple agents interacting under an uncontrolled, 'evolutionary' regime. As noted in [12], this view of the intermediary, as originally suggested by BBD, presents great difficulties in the face of unpredictable inputs from arbitrary agent sources, only very general prior definitions of task and task satisfaction, and the need for communicatively effective (i.e. coherent) dialogue with the user. In these circumstances viable system operation calls for a controller with so much knowledge and power that it actually subsumes the individual expert agents.

The comparative experiments reported in [5] simulating various architectures indeed showed that some degree of control was necessary, though they concluded that a blackboard architecture was still preferable to an actor one. The various implementations of expert intermediaries done by [13], [14] and [15] have all been of a quite strongly controlled kind, with experts distinctly subordinate to a controller rather than working as a collective of equals.

We carried out our own comparative simulations with alternative blackboard and actor architectures [16]; these showed somewhat better performance for actors, but again emphasised the need for control. But more importantly, when we came to implement dialogue management in detail, which neither BBD nor any of the other systems mentioned had significantly addressed, we found it too difficult, at least for our 'Mark 1' system, to work with a set of functional expert agents. We therefore not merely abandoned the original blackboard proposal, but the idea of a multi-*agent* implementation for the intermediary. We adopted a much more conventional approach with a single control module and the functional expert agents replaced by distinct specialised rule sets. The BBD model had some ten functional experts, which could be grouped as central and support processors, the former including e.g. Problem Description and Retrieval Strategy, the latter e.g. Input Analysis; but the nature and relations of the support processors are not well-developed in BBD's account. We wanted to concentrate on belief revision, and not to engage with language processing per se. Our Mark 1 architecture therefore had a controlling Dialogue module managing both interaction with the user and the other specialised retrieval task modules, which was thus the locus of the intermediary agent's belief revision. The system does not do any actual natural language processing: the (notional) input/output interface receives and sends communications in a simple propositional language with speech act operators, which we assume current NLP interpretation and generation could handle; we also assume that communication at the strictly linguistic level is transparent, i.e. that librarian and user agents correctly 'hear' and 'parse' messages they receive.

4.1 Dialogue Modelling

We have had to develop and implement a specific model of dialogue pragmatics suited both to the way agents are motivated by belief and to the nature of information-seeking dialogues as illustrated by BBD, and hence designed both to achieve dialogue goals and to maintain proper dialogue flow. We have drawn, as obviously appropriate, on the theory of speech acts, where communication depends both on an agent's own beliefs about the world and on its beliefs about its interlocutor(s), and is strategically motivated to reach end states that the dialogue participants have cooperated to define and attain. Within this framework each individual dialogue contribution is motivated by a desire to change participants' cognitive states, i.e. beliefs and intentions; but it is also, to ensure effective communication, constrained by the need to maintain dialogue coherence which relies on the use of recognised structures for interaction, like question-answer, as well as topic continuity.

The primitive speech acts we use are conventional in their general style, but have been defined to reflect our need to capture the actual conditions of dialogue participation (where little can be assumed) rather than advance planning (as in [17]). We have three speech acts, *tell*, *ask* and *answer*, with specific preconditions and effects expressed primarily in terms of the agent's beliefs about its own and its interlocutor's states. For simplicity, the propositional language used to communicate is that also used for the internal representation of attitudes; however, reflecting the real case, it does not follow that the internal 'meanings' of linguistic terms are the same for all participants: e.g. what the predicate *'classical'* denotes in the architectural domain. Communication includes an indication of the speaker's commitment to the attitude being communicated, which may be *strong* or *weak*.[2]

In our implementation successful communication is guaranteed at the basic level, i.e. where the hearer recognises the speaker wishes the hearer to have a belief (though the speaker may not themselves hold it). However at the higher level speech acts may be successful or not for various reasons. An act succeeds if the hearer not merely recognises but adopts the speaker's intention, i.e. if the speaker's intention for the hearer is satisfied, and fails otherwise. However these outcomes have to be specifically characterised in belief revision terms. Thus success implies that all of preconditions, communication, and effects must be achieved. Failure may occur e.g. when the hearer does not believe what the speaker supposes the hearer believes; it may be from speaker's or hearer's point of view, and may be 'obvious' or involve misunderstanding. By extension, a communicative plan will be successful if each speech act step succeeds.

To maintain dialogue coherence (or *d-coherence* to distinguish it from coherence of belief), we have found it sufficient to work with simple conventions in the spirit of dialogue games [18], which both participants know. Thus if each takes turns, there are legal responses to each of the three possible outcomes for each speech act. The responses are of *continuation* type or *repair* type, with the former depending on context and the latter on perceived failure. Thus we have a transition table, so e.g. a *tell* may be continued by a *tell* or *ask* or repaired by a *tell* or *ask*, while *ask* is continued only by *answer* and repaired only by *tell*. This table ensures d-coherence (at least over relatively short segments), and also naturally supplies segmentation analogous to the 'foci' of BBD's dialogue analysis, in a simple model of task-oriented dialogue structure. Specifically, continuation must lead to segmentation, which may or may not be on the same subject, while repair may lead to a new segment, but must be on the same subject; thus segmentation occurs when agents disagree or the dialogue subject changes.

The foregoing provide the basic dialogue apparatus. Dialogue is driven by the action schemata an agent has for planning, in this case for planning dialogue communication, supported by its desire and planning rules and also by specific dialogue rules. The desire rules, triggered by attitude conflict, provoke planning to resolve the conflict, say by one agent giving the other a justification for its belief. We have three schemata: `tell`, `adopt` and `infer`. These are complex objects characterising agents, attitude types, preconditions, effects, constraints etc. The `tell` schema is used for communication about attitudes; the `adopt` schema allow an agent to adopt an attitude held by another agent; and the `infer` schema drives

[2]"Speaker" and "hearer" are conventional dialogue terms: there is of course no actual speech processing in our system.

inference from a rule. To support these schemata there are further rules for ascription, so e.g. the hearer assumes the speaker believes the dialogue preconditions hold; for attitude adoption, so e.g. if the speaker is strongly committed to a belief, this is reason for the hearer to adopt it; and for prediction, so e.g. the speaker knows that if it communicates a strong commitment to an attitude, this is reason for the hearer to adopt it. Specifically, for instance, if the speaker communicates commitment *strong*, the prediction is that the hearer will endorse the communicated belief *2c-pos* or communicated intention *desire-pos*.

Prediction is complex, and to implement it adequately we have introduced finer levels of endorsement distinguishing an agent's predictions about its own (*auto*) attitudes from its predictions about another agent (*alter*)'s attitudes. These endorsements allow justifications like *auto* taking *alter's* strong endorsement of a belief as ground for assuming that *alter* will continue to hold the belief, so *auto* can plan on this basis. These *auto* and *alter* endorsement types are ordered, like the others, so prediction can be extended over combinations of current and predicted attitudes in the calculation of preferences between attitude sets. Supported by desire rules to identify leading intentions, and planning rules for intention decomposition, the rules just described support an enriched version of the agent action cycle allowing for prediction and action based on it, as well as just choice among attitudes.

All of these rule types are essential for planned action, and hence for the formulation and expression of communications as one kind of action. However this apparatus not only generates speech acts. Our approach as a whole also ensures stability of behaviour under dialogue, partly through minimal change in belief revision, partly through the desire to minimise effort, and partly through a general predisposition to avoid conflict.

For instance, in the earlier example dialogue fragment U's first utterance, a *tell* act, leads to a continuation response, an *ask* act by L on the same topic. U's first utterance successfully communicates U's intention and and appears successful in changing L's cognitive state. However U and L attach different meanings to the term 'Classical architecture'. Thus in contrast, while L's first utterance is successful in communicating L's intention, it does not result in the desired communicative outcome (an answer to L's question). The attitude conflict that is now evident leads instead to a repair response and a new segment. (Note that L predicted that the performance of the *ask* act would be successful in achieving the goal of determining whether U was more interested in Greek or in Roman architecture, otherwise L would not have asked her question.)

4.2 The IR Functional Component

As mentioned, the task experts are not fully independent agents in our actual implementation, but rather data and rule sets. In our experiments so far, moreover, they have been extremely simple. It is clear from studies like [7] that a Problem Description agent in particular, if intended for a practical implementation, would have to have ramified knowledge of a kind that is very hard to capture; and this is also implied by the amount of resource required even for a domain-limited system like [19]'s expert. However our primary aim has been to evaluate the mechanism of belief revision within the IR task context, and thus for our Mark 1 implementation we provided only enough task knowledge to see whether the system could simulate the *kind* of cooperative interaction, with a mutual exchange of information and development of a search specification, that BBD's transcripts exhibit. But even so, as the computational complexity of the mechanism, which has to work on many attitude sets, makes computation very effortful, we could only provide very simple task resources. Thus as described further below, we have only replicated human behaviour in an extremely limited way, and whether we have demonstrated either the adequacy of the model or the long-term practical viability of the approach is therefore a matter for discussion.

Taking [7] as our guide, as mentioned earlier, we have explored an architecture with all of BBD's five central experts: Problem State (PS), Problem Mode (PM), User Model (UM), Problem Description (PD) and Retrieval Strategy (RS). The crucial problem is in defining each module's goals in a way that makes satisfaction specifiable and attainable. We have treated the first three of these modules in a straightforward way in terms of limited attributes e.g. early or middle for PS, document type for PM, and novice or expert for UM, which can be checked by simple system questions if not supplied, and which are not mandatory for searching. PD and RS, especially the former, are more challenging even for a very limited intermediary but realistically-intended task modelling, and we were particularly concerned that both individual module knowledge bases and the 'translation' relationships between them should not be completely obvious.

For test purposes we chose architecture as our subject domain. Problem descriptions have several components: *topic, subject area, document type* and *document level.* Retrieval strategies have *term, database* and *document type* components. These components essentially correspond to BBD subfunctions as given in [7]. Document type and level do not exactly match 'slit', but they are clearly natural notions for retrieval, and having several components met our requirement to model satisfaction. We assume, partly for clarity in distinguishing various aspects of literature searching and partly as reflecting a common real situation, that searching uses a controlled indexing language (thesaurus). Thus while for topic components the PD module works with a *description* of the user's need in a simple *descriptor* meaning language, the RS module works to provide a *request* with Boolean operators linking *terms*. Then to guide the search development task we have definitions of *valid*, *minimal* and *good* descriptions/requests. Thus for our experiments we have naively defined a minimal description as one with a topic component with at least three descriptors, collectively neither too general nor too specific; and a good description as one with such a topic component and also document type and document level components (search area is inferred from topic). Requests are similarly defined, so a minimal request has a term component (with at least three terms), a good request has term, database, and document level components. Descriptors are organised in hierarchies, tagged with broad *subject* labels, and are supplied with *synonym* alternatives (reflecting natural language variation of concept reference). We assume that user and librarian have overlapping, but not identical, descriptor vocabularies. The essential business of forming a sound problem description is thus of choosing a useful number of descriptors from hierarchies with the appropriate subject orientation, at the right hierarchical levels.

As noted, though the PD descriptors may look like index terms, we wanted to allow both for the common separation of user language from search terms and for the task of formulating search strategies. We therefore require a mapping of description onto request which also satisfies our RS goals for requests. (For our simple experiments, however, we have stopped at the point of actual search and do not revise requests after retrieval feedback.)

Like the descriptors, our terms are organised in hierarchies, with subject labels and with descriptors as *entry words*. But we do not have a simple-minded one-one mapping between elements or structures. There are three possible descriptor-term mappings: direct; or synonym to term; or 'shift' to less or more general term. These data resources supply one part of the task apparatus: the other is provided by rules for obtaining descriptions and requests meeting the goal criteria, and especially the RS goal. The architecture thus assumes processing driven from the RS goal, with top-down goal resolution done heuristically (by abduction). The mechanisms for PS, PM and UM are quite simple, essentially asking basic questions. The system then has to derive an appropriate request from the PD description which may, e.g., mean getting a modified description from the user. The system has to work over both description and request attempting to satisfy the PD and RS goal criteria in the mapping transformation from description to request.

All of this seems quite straightforward from the retrieval point of view. It is however necessary to relate all these operations specifically to those of the belief-revision apparatus: they have to be expressed in terms of attitudes, embedded in planning etc. In particular, the task goals have to be stated not just as desires, but in such a way that they force the development of a satisfactory request. This is done by the need to achieve a balance between effort cost for the librarian and relevant retrieved benefit for the user.

Thus in our illustrative dialogue fragment, L's question about the type of architecture U wants is motivated by a desire to improve the problem description, since U's initial topic component, the single descriptor 'Classical architecture', does not constitute even a minimal problem description and would result in a poor search request. To achieve L's goal of a good request (to serve U's goal for information), L must devise a plan to modify U's cognitive state, but one which also does not consume too many computational resources.

We simulated the specific task model for PD using OPS5 and showed it was acceptable. However when we attempted the actual implementation we found further simplification beyond that described above was needed and we therefore reduced the task modules to three: UM, PD and RS, with UM and RS very rudimentary.

5 Computational Testing

The main problem computationally is the cost of manipulating all the very many attitude sets that may have to be considered: quite modest propositional proposals very naturally and plausibly generate large numbers of alternative responses for assessment. For instance with a simple three-turn interchange and small knowledge bases and rule sets, thousands of attitude sets may be produced. Our initial runs were extremely time consuming, but with 'optimisations' of various sorts (see below) we reduced the time required to a reasonable level, i.e. from days to minutes.[3]

Our test methodology was to see whether we could replicate example dialogue phenomena, i.e. forms of information exchange from both topic content and pragmatic points of view. Thus we ran the system in 'duplication' mode, i.e. simulating two agents, one the librarian and one the user. We could not of course,

[3]Note that we can't reduce the number of belief sets by eliminating those sets which are least preferred. Not only would this make major revisions in the agent's beliefs impossible (the agent having discarded the necessary 'improbable' belief sets), it causes problems when an intended state is achieved or when the world changes even in predictable ways. Presumably the agent is reasonably sure a state it intends does not currently hold, otherwise it would not have been trying to achieve it. However this means that the intended state will always be least preferred and therefore will be discarded.

with 'free', 'intelligent' agents expect that our system behaviour would simply copy that of the source examples, as it were word for word: we were looking for similar behaviour. We also lacked the knowledge sources to replicate the topics of dialogue examples taken from the BBD transcripts. What we did was identify specific types of phenomenon which could be convincingly described as e.g. showing a failure of a default assumption, and then, by providing an appropriate start state in out architecture domain, run the agents to see what happened. Thus given a simple architecture domain version of a transcript dialogue fragment, F, we sought a system-produced analogue F'. Altogether we ran four such simulations, covering a range of phenomena including 'failed inform', the case where one agent's knowledge is incomplete and the agent knows it is; 'misunderstanding', where an agent lacks knowledge but does not realise it; and 'failed prediction', i.e. by an agent about the effects of an utterance. The simulations utilised a total of 11 domain-specific rules and 33 dialogue rules.

5.1 An Extended Example

So, for instance, for the exemplar fragment for a 'failed inform'

```
U: I'm looking for books on Wren.
L: Who is Wren?
U: He designed St Paul's Cathedral.
```

we obtained the two-agent system dialogue in our 'message' language

U : (*tell U L* (*bel U* (*problem-desc wren*) *strong*))

L : (*tell L U* (*int L* (*exists !x* (*bel L* (*class wren !x*)) *strong*)))

U : (*tell U L* (*bel U* (*class wren designed-st-pauls*) *strong*))

(where we omit books for simplicity, abbreviate *user* and *libr* to *U* and *L*, and use *!x* as existential quantifier): this may be glossed in English as

```
U: my problem descriptor is wren
L: I want a problem descriptor class for wren
U: the problem descriptor class for wren is designed st pauls
```

The way this works, heavily abbreviated and simplified, is as follows. U is initialised with beliefs about *wren* including the belief that *wren* is a good problem descriptor, and with the possible intention to share this descriptor with L:

(*p-int U* (*bel L* (*problem-desc wren*)) *desire-pos*)

From this intention U constructs a plan to communicate with L, issuing in U's first message above. The plan has 5 steps, covering both telling the message content and doing so strongly enough to ensure L adopts U's problem description. At the point of 'utterance' U has 10 belief-type attitudes and 67 intention-type ones, in 4 candidate sets of beliefs and 12 of intentions. L infers U's strong commitment to *wren* and hence cooperatively adopts it as U's problem descriptor. But as L cannot find *wren* in a descriptor hierarchy, as needed to develop a sound problem description, L instantiates a rule to ask U for *wren's* class. L's plan for finding out about *wren* from U has 14 steps, including e.g. one from the conjunction of L's belief that she does not know what class U believes *wren* to be and L's intention to `adopt` (i.e. to come to believe) what class U believes *wren* to be, to the intention that L should come to know what U's class for *wren* is. This is represented as (step 3):

(*not* (*bel L* (*exists !x* (*bel L* (*bel U* (*class wren !x*)))))) &

(*p-int L* (*exists !x* (*action* (*adopt U L* (*bel L* (*class wren !x*))))) *effort-pos* ⇒

(*p-int L* (*exists !x* (*bel L* (*bel U* (*class wren !x*)))))

Another, later step (step 13) from L's prediction that U will `tell` L what class U believes *wren* to be to L's prediction that she will know what class U believes *wren* to be has the form

(*f-p-bel L* (*exists !x* (*action* (*tell U L* (*bel U* (*class wren !x*))))) ⇒

(*f-p-bel L* (*exists !x* (*bel L* (*bel U* (*class wren !x*)))))

f-p-bel denotes a future possible belief, i.e. a prediction. L's plan is based on the belief that U has a class for *wren*, which is justified by a rule exploiting the fact that U produced this descriptor. L's output utterance strongly conveys L's intention to discover U's class information, and U therefore adopts this as an intention to satisfy which, as U already has *wren's* class, leads to U's reply.[4] At this point, after a 4-step plan, U has 179 propositions under consideration with 4 candidate belief sets and no less than 1152 candidate intention sets. The plans involve many rule applications, e.g. for step 13 above the rule

[4] When an intention is achieved, the intended state switches from disbelieved to believed, and the intention becomes distintended. This change is propagated to higher-level states and intentions that depend on the intended state. For example if, immediately prior to L's utterance, U were to add "... and his design for St Paul's", L's goal is achieved and her plan is therefore aborted.

(*f-p-bel ?A* (*exists ?X* (*action ?ACT*))) &
(*action-schema ?PRECOND ?ACT* (*?EFFECT*) *?CONSEQ ?EFFORT*) ⇒
(*f-p-bel ?A* (*exists ?X ?EFFECT*))

i.e. if an agent *?A* predicts that an action *?ACT* will be performed, then it believes that the effects *?EFFECT* of that action will be true in the future, is instantiated, and the whole seems extremely top-heavy for such a minimal exchange between two agents. However it correctly demonstrates that when such reasoning is properly decomposed, as it has to be, many non-trivial steps are needed to make even the most obvious transitions from one attitude to another.

We had two problems with the computational testing. The first was that we could not identify natural core beliefs, required for applying the connectivity (*mc*) preference criterion, and so could not evaluate this important part of the basic theory properly. The second was that the system could only be radically speeded up by not preserving previously planned, but unsupported, intentions, which also weakens our claims for the theory. Subject to these qualifications, however, we found that our experiments did, on an intuitive assessment (the only one practicable), deliver cooperative, problem-solving interaction of the kind required for the task.

6 Assessment

Though computationally expensive, the tests were very limited in relation to the extent of task knowledge and scope of dialogue found in the real IR case, as illustrated by e.g. [20] or [21], or as compared with the computational dialogue modelling envisaged for the TRAINS project (see [22]). The problems that emerged from our modelling study as a whole were with computational complexity; connectivity; prediction both of world states and intentions; communicating commitment; and focusing in dialogue, so e.g. a topic shift is recognised. Reducing complexity needs some way of limiting revision by e.g. taking some attitudes as fixed; connectivity needs refinement to allow for quality as well as quantity of proof; predictability needs a theory of common sense reasoning (a tall order); communicating commitment requires another intensional layer in the system; and focusing needs at least something like recency. These are all tough problems, with complexity and dialogue focusing as most pressing. Further, to get a working implementation even for trivial dialogue examples, we had to introduce many rather specific endorsement types. This conflicts both with the claim for a general approach and seems unsatisfactory in itself. It is possible that the correct response is to operate on two levels, with a few universal types subsuming a set of more particular, task and domain specific endorsements. This requires further study.

But we nevertheless believe that, limited though our experiments have been in many ways, they do demonstrate that the sophisticated approach to attitude revision proposed by Galliers does lead to appropriate communicative interaction between agents in an information-seeking situation like the library one, and as such provides a deeper account of the intelligent intermediary than any hitherto proposed or implemented. This may appear paradoxical given the rich, cognitively-motivated account of intermediary functions that [9] gives. Our general approach is sympathetic to Ingwersen's call for open interfaces that support the user; and from one point of view our implementation falls within Ingwersen's model, since the explicit functions implemented are those Ingwersen and BBD share. We have also implemented, though with elementary substance, other implicit functions. But we have done this in ways that cut across Ingwersen's function block structure. Moreover the specific requirement, for computation, to model operational *processing* in detail has meant that we have not only begun to fill in key blanks in Ingwersen's and the BBD models: we have also made them more genuinely dynamic.

Acknowledgement

This work was supported by the UK Tri-Council Initiative on Cognitive Science and Human-Computer interaction, under Grant SPG 8930752: we are grateful for this funding. Dr Alison Cawsey, now of the Department of Computer Science, University of Glasgow, worked on this project in its first years, and Dr Julia Galliers, of the Computer Laboratory, has been associated with it throughout.

References

1. Logan, B. et al. "Belief revision and dialogue management in information retrieval". Technical Report, Computer Laboratory, University of Cambridge, 1994
2. Cawsey, A. et al. "Automating the librarian: belief revision as a base for system action and communication with the user". *The Computer Journal* 1992; 35:221-232

3. Galliers, J. R. "Autonomous belief revision and communication". In: Gärdenfors P. (ed) *Belief revision.* Cambridge University Press, Cambridge, 1992, pp 220–246
4. Belkin, N. J., Seeger, T. and Wersig, G. "Distributed expert problem treatment as a model for information systems analysis and design". *Journal of Information Science* 1983; 5:153–167
5. Belkin, N. J., Hennings, R. D. and Seeger, T. "Simulation of a distributed expert-based information provision mechanism". *Information Technology* 1984; 3:122–141
6. Brooks, H. M., Daniels, P. J. and Belkin, N. J. "Problem descriptions and user models: developing an intelligent interface for document retrieval systems". In: *Informatics 8: Advances in intelligent retrieval.* Aslib, London, 1985
7. Brooks, H. M. *An intelligent interface for document retrieval systems: developing the problem description and retrieval strategy components.* PhD Thesis, City University, London, 1986
8. Daniels, P. J. *Developing the user modelling function of an intelligent interface for document retrieval systems.* PhD Thesis, City University, London, 1987
9. Ingwersen, P. *Intermediary functions in information retrieval interaction.* PhD Thesis, Copenhagen Business School, 1991.
10. De Kleer, J. "An assumption-based truth maintenance system". *Artificial Intelligence* 1986; 28:127–162
11. De Kleer, J. "Extending the ATMS". *Artificial Intelligence* 1986; 28:163–196
12. Cawsey, A. et al. "Automating the librarian: a fundamental approach using belief revision", Technical Report 243, Computer Laboratory, University of Cambridge, 1992
13. Brajnik, G., Guida, G. and Tasso, C. "User modelling in expert man-machine interfaces: a case study in intelligent information retrieval". *IEEE Transactions on Systems, Man, and Cybernetics* 1990; 20:166–185
14. Fox, E. A., Weaver, M. T., Chen, Q.-F. and France, R. K. "Implementing a distributed expert-based information retrieval system". In: *Proceedings of RIAO 88 Conference on User-Oriented, Content-Based Text and Image Handling.* MIT Press, Cambridge MA, 1988, pp 708–726
15. Croft, W. B. and Thompson, R. H. "I3R: a new approach to the design of document retrieval systems". *Journal of the American Society for Information Science* 1987; 38:389–404
16. Cawsey, A. et al. "A comparison of architectures for multi-agent communication'. In: *ECAI-92, 10th European Conference on Artificial Intelligence,* 1992, pp 249-251
17. Allen, J. *Natural Language Understanding.* Benjamin/Cummings Publishing Company, Menlo Park CA, 1987
18. Kowtko, J.C., Isard, S.D. and Doherty, G.M. "Conversational games within dialogue". Research Paper HCRC/RP-31, Human Communication Research Centre, University of Edinburgh, 1992
19. Vickery, A. et al. "A reference and referral system using expert system techniques". *Journal of Documentation.* 1987; 43:1–23
20. Bates, M.J. "Where should the person stop and the information search start?". *Information Processing and Management* 1990; 26:575-591
21. Shute, S.J. and Smith, P.J. "Knowledge-based search tactics". *Information Processing and Management* 1993; 29:29-45
22. Traum, D.R. "The discourse reasoner in TRAINS-90". TRAINS Technical Note 91-5, Department of Computer Science, University of Rochester, 1991

Polyrepresentation of Information Needs and Semantic Entities
Elements of a Cognitive Theory for Information Retrieval Interaction

Peter Ingwersen
Royal School of Librarianship
Copenhagen Denmark

Abstract

The paper outlines the principles underlying the theory of polyrepresentation applied to the user's cognitive space and the information space of IR systems, set in a cognitive framework. By means of polyrepresentation it is suggested to represent the current user's information need, problem state, and domain work task or interest in a structure of causality as well as to embody semantic full-text entities by means of the principle of 'intentional redundancy'. In IR systems this principle implies simultaneously to apply different methods of representation and a variety of IR techniques of different cognitive origin to each entity. The objective is to aproximate as close as possible text retrieval to retrieval of information in a cognitive sense.

1.Introduction

The aim of this paper is to apply the cognitive point of view to IR theory which, by application of the *cognitive structures* of different origin involved in IR, may improve the intellectual access to information sources and provide an enriched contextual platform to be applied by IR systems to support the users' information seeking [1]. The objective is to point to the potential value of matching the multidimensional variety of representations inherently existing in or extracted from information objects *and* from the cognitive space of a user. Further, it attempts to demonstrate that by making adequate and combined use of empirical and analytic evidence from mainstream IR research as well as from operational and information seeking investigations, it is possible to approximate text retrieval to retrieval of information in the proper sense of the concept.

The following section presents and defines the concepts required for the establishment of a cognitive framework for IR. Based on existing empirical evidence, the section analyses the information need variation during IR interaction and the possibility of incorporating polyrepresentation of the cognitive space of users, that is, their information need formation and underlying work and problem situation. The following section takes a global view of information seeking and retrieval by pointing to the use of the variations of representations of texts and IR techniques in systems, already well-known to operational and laboratory IR research, and explores the introduced principle of intentional redundancy associated with text entities, IR system and users. The concluding section discusses the global model of polyrepresentation in IR and outlines briefly its theoretical consequencies.

2. The Cognitive Approach to IR Theory

From the cognitive point of view in information science each act of information processing - whether perceptual or symbolic - is mediated by a system of categories and concepts which, for the information processing device, are a model of his/its world [2]. In human information processing the world model constitutes the cognitive space which, consisting of highly dynamic and changeable cognitive structures, controls the perception and further processing of external input, e.g. during communication and IR interaction. The individual cognitive space and, in particular, the current cognitive/emotional structures and states are determined by the experiences gained through time in a social context [1]. In automatic information processing the world model is dynamic but not self-contained. It consists of the human cognitive structures embedded in the system prior to processing. Its individual cognitive structures, e.g. in form of algorithms or textual symbolic strings, may interact with one another and with structures generated by humans external to the system - when ordered and capable to do it. However, the processing will constantly take place at a linguistic sign level of communication - never at a cognitive one. Only to human recipients of communicated signs the perception may *also* take place at a cognitive/emotional level, actually transforming the current cognitive states into new states, conceivably providing information transformed into knowledge and novel cognition. During any act of human or computerized communication the viewpoint regards all communicated messages as signs transferred at a linguistic level which, only via perception and mediation by the individual recipient´s current cognitive state, may transform into information at a cognitive level. Consequently, this view implies that any intentionality and meaning underlying the communicated messages are lost and has to be rebuild, i.e. interpreted, by the recipient by means of those pre-suppositions which make him/it participate in the communication act. Computers (or books for that matter) hold pre-defined and fixed pre-suppositions, whilst those of humans are individually unpredictable, formed as they are by episodic, semantic and emotional experiences. We may hence observe three fundamental characteristics of crucial importance to IR: 1) the *uncertainties* and *unpredictabilities* inherent in IR interaction and associated with interpretation, on the side of the user and on the side of the IR system - both as senders, recipients and processors. From a different perspective Sparck Jones has likewise pointed to similar uncertainty factors [3]; 2) the *pre-suppositions* and *intentionality* underlying the communicated messages are vital for the perception and understanding of such messages; 3) direct and real information retrieval - as opposed to text retrieval performed at a linguistic level - is only possible by the individual user himself. IR systems may consequently only be most successful by acting as supportive means to retrieval by humans.

In order to reduce the uncertainties as well as the unpredictabilities in IR and ease the perception and interpretation the cognitive viewpoint suggests to provide and make use of *different cognitive structures* during acts of communication, i.e. structures of *different cognitive and functional origin* - on both sides of the communication channel. As far as possible such structures ought to demonstrate *contextual properties*. From this perspective *all* the participating cognitive structures in IR are of potential value and should be available for IR interaction purposes, that is, the structures of the current user and those embedded in textual information objects and system architectures, see Fig. 1. For instance, this means also to explore further the supportive potentials of combinations of the mainstream partial match techniques with relevance feedback functionality.

From this perspective the paper proposes to apply a principle of *intentional redundancy* to IR interaction by means of *polyrepresentation* of both contextual *semantic entities* of texts and of *user need characteristics* as its necessary components, in order to reduce the uncertainties constantly present in the IR interaction processes.

2.1 Cognitive Structures in IR

In this framework *cognitive structures* are manifestations of human cognition, reflection or ideas. In IR they take the form of transformations generated by a variety of human actors belonging to a variety of different *cognitive origins*: systems designers and producers, IR thechnique developers, indexing rule constructors, indexers, authors of texts and images (note 1), intermediary mechanism designers, and users in a domain-related context. Consequently, in an IR system designers´ cognitive structures may be represented by specific database structures or one or several matching algorithms, e.g. the vector space and probability formulars - see Fig. 1, left-hand side. Human indexers´ cognitive structures are represented by the index terms added to records, essentially being the result of an intellectual interpretation of an author´s text or images, often guided by pre-defined rules and a thesaurus for which the structure and knowledge representation other humans are responsible. In automatic indexing the weighting function applied signifies in itself a transformed cognitive structure. The author´s text, incl. titles, captions and headings, are representations of cognitive structures intended to be communicated. Specidic portions of the texts, e.g. titles, captions, and the full-text, demonstrate *different functional origin*. An intermediary mechanism´s manipulation of user requests into query formulations during request model building represents additional cognitive structures.

The user´s own request formulation is a representation of his current cognitive state concerned with an information need. Similarly, conceivable problem statements and work task or interest descriptions are representations of intrinsic cognitive structures underlying the user´s information seeking. Such intrinsic cognitive structures of users are more or less variable and transformable, as opposite to system and text representations which, in a cognitive sense, always are invariable. From this perspective, intrinsic information needs may indeed be stable as well as well-defined in realistic terms, as is the case in the present Tipster/Trec projects and in the earlier Cranfield experiments. As empirical evidence demonstrates below, information needs in real-life IR situations become indeed quite stable at a certain point of a session. But rather often IR sessions are exploratory throughout long initial phases. Real-life information needs are commonly variable, vaguely stated or ill-defined. Well-defined intrinsic wishes for information seem to be a special case.

What interests us here is consequently to establish methods founded in theory to support such intrinsically ill-defined and variable information needs. In the laboratory experiments IR research attempts to maximize the performance of a variety of retrieval techniques and methods of representation of information objects - essentially the left-hand side of Fig. 1. The experimental laboratory settings generally force the researchers to apply well-defined information needs. What is attempted in this contribution is to view these experimental results in combination with evidence concerned with research on real-life information seeking behaviour, that is, the totallity of Fig. 1.

The difficult task is to cope with the unpredictability associated with vague information needs which yield badly constructed, twisted or one-two word request formulations at the initial phases of IR interaction. The assumption to exploit the underlying cognitive structures of users in order to improve the situation is not unknown in user-oriented IR research. Below are outlined the investigative results supporting *the explicit use* of such underlying structures.

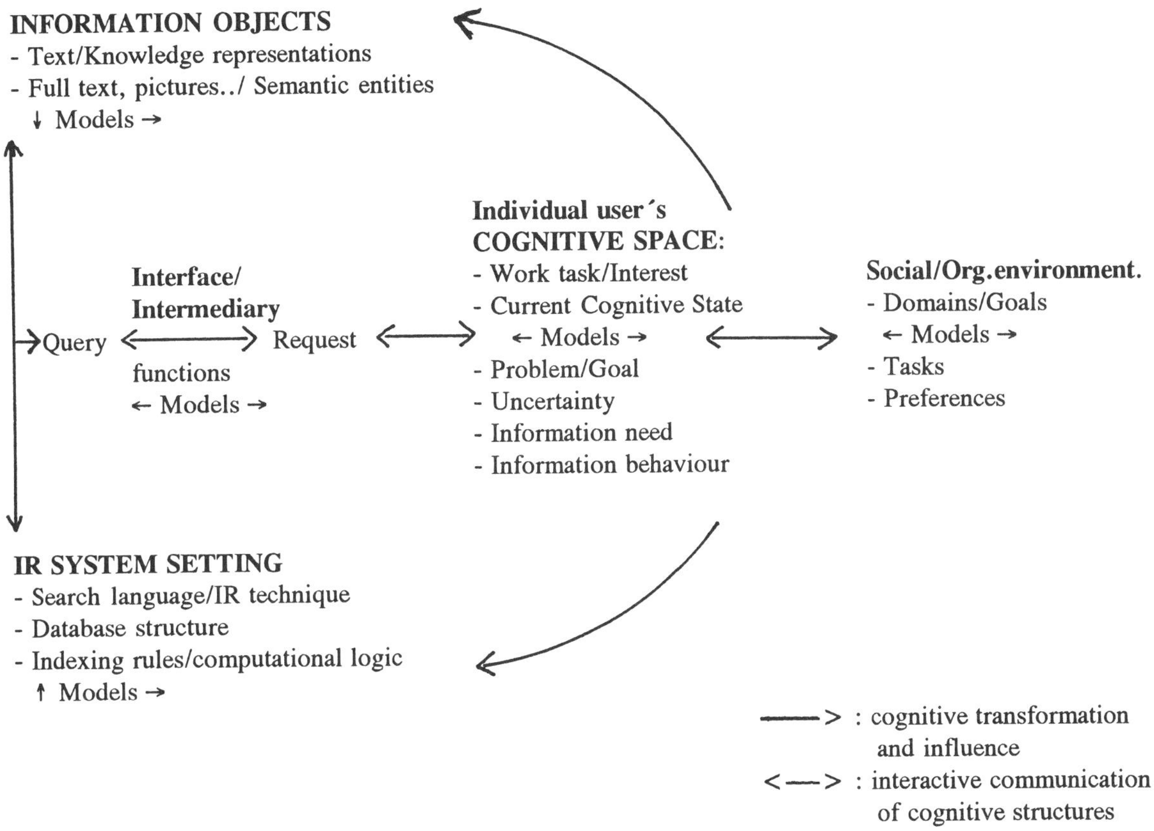

Fig. 1. Cognitive communication model of information interaction in information science. From [1, p. 33].

At the centre, Fig. 1, the cognitive structures embedded into intermediary mechanisms are, for example, the Monstrat functions [4,5], based on the extraction of underlying problem descriptions or the Mediator Model functionalities [1], such as the Domain Model and the Request Model Builder, also found in the I3R system [6].

At the right-hand side, Fig. 1, are outlined the major different cognitive structures of individual users which may be represented to intermediary mechanisms and IR systems, e.g. the actual work task or interest leading to a current cognitive state which may end up in a problem or goal for the actual user. The cognitive situation in the user´s problem space may produce a certain degree of uncertainty, e.g. as to how to reach a goal, finally generating a wish for external information, i.e. the intrinsic information need. According to the current cognitive state, the model of the IR system and the intentionality, this wish for information is represented in form of a request. These mental activities take place in the context of a domain of epistemic, social or organisational nature which, aside from influencing the current searcher in a 'historical´ sense, in addition constantly influence the authors of texts and systems design attitudes - the left-hand side, Fig. 1. This assumed intrinsic *causality* associated with the formation of the information need signifies an extension of the ASK hypothesis [7] as well as the sense-making theory by Dervin and Nilan [8] by making use of cognitive task analysis approaches to systems design [9,10], placed in the framework of the cognitive viewpoint.

Prior to Belkin, Dervin and Nilan and other scholars´ analytic contributions to understanding information need formation D.M. Mackay stated in 1960 an often cited conception of the issue: ".. a certain incompleteness in his [the inquirer's] picture of the world -an inadequacy in what we may call his 'state of readiness' to interact purposefully with the world around him *in terms of a particular area of interest*" [11]. Fundamentally, both Belkin, Dervin and Nilan as well as R.S. Taylor in his analysis from 1968 [12] regard the recognized 'incompleteness´, 'inadequacy' or 'anomaly´ as the mental trigger for the proceeding internal cognitive activities related to the development of the information need. The point here has always been that the user is only capable of describing what he knows at a given point in time according to his current cognitive state, but not what he does not know yet and is actually searching for. Hence, the user may consequently only vaguely formulate a request for information by formulating fragments of his current cognitive state. However, what he might be able to do, in theory, is to state his *underlying problem* or motive. Quite importantly, already Mackay points to a reason or *causality* underlying this incompleteness, uncertainty state, ASK or problem situation: 'the area of interest'. We regard this area of interest as identical to the individual's current *work task.* This task may deal directly with a person's actual work within a specific domain, e.g. designing databases for AI purposes. It may also simply be concerned with an 'interest' not directly related to working conditions, but e.g. be associated with entertainment, hobby or leasure domains.

Belkin et al.'s investigations (protocol analyses) of the 'problem space' provide us with insight into two basic underlying phenomena: the *vagueness* or uncertainty also associated with *problem statements* made during intermediary-user interaction, i.e. pre-search interviewing [5,7] - and the possibility of actually *acquireing data* concerning 'cognitive state', 'domains' and 'tasks' during human interaction. Saracevic and Su's large-scale investigations of online system-intermediary-user interaction incorporate in addition the *feedback* from the system [13]. One may observe that the mentioned structures surface in more rich forms and evolve through the interactive IR processes.

From a re-analysis of Ingwersen's sets of original thinking-aloud protocols (14) identical patterns emerge. The protocols contain a great amount of assessments and relevance feedback based on the retrieved and presented full-text material. By means of the experimental setting, which initially made the users browse the shelves with their own needs while thinking aloud prior to a system-librarian-user interaction, we may *observe the cognitive evolution of the information need.* In some cases the starting point is a very vaguely formed need which develops into an information need quite known to the user (and the experimentors) when finally encountering the intermediary. However, such internally quite well-defined needs become very often twisted or reduced at the initial point of search interviewing. This problem of reduction is mainly caused by the imcompatibility of the models the participants hold of one another.

The vital points during interaction seem to be when parts of information sources, indexes, tables of contents, etc. are confronted by the user and the intermediary, since such triangular situations *force the user to reformulate* an already conscious need and the problem statements, and the intermediary to ask certain types of questions. The protocols demonstrate clear-cut statements and assessments associated with the underlying elements of 'work task' and 'domain'. For instance, in a protocol concerned with searching for an appropriate form of 'Boolean logic formulars' the user initially puts up with request labels consisting of synonyms for 'Boolean Logic'. Via feedback from the system the user decides to move on to other possible domains or aspects of 'Boolean logic' - from a philosophical one to a mathematical one. During this process several text entities are judged relevant to the 'topic' of 'Boolean logic', but only partially relevant to the actual need/problem and the work task. Since his preferred mode of formular is not displayed in a suitable form in these full-text sources, the intermediary asks for the user's current 'field of interest'. The answer, 'applied computer science', signifies the 'domain' and triggers the user to explain his underlying 'work task': the appropriate form of the formular is associated with 'electronic circuits *when repairing and designing computer systems*'. Since a question like 'what are you going to use the information for?' never occured during the search interview, the user did not supply any details of his existing intrinsic knowledge about his task.

Kuhlthau has very recently reported empirical results supporting the idea that the initial *state of uncertainty* concerned with an information need momentarily becomes even more uncertain during the initial phases of information seeking [15]. Also in relation to *complex work task operations* Murtonen and Järvelin [16] have found that the types of information needs may be very different, ranging from well-defined ones in less complex tasks to vague or non-defined needs (and problems/goals) in case of very complex tasks. What seems defined are alone the task itself and the domain concerned with the task. This tentative result coincide with investigations of why EIS and SIS systems do not work properly when traditional solutions of information provisions are applied.

Together with other re-analyses of similar protocols, these investigations of operational information seeking demonstrate that 1) aside from the 'current cognitive state' additional underlying cognitive structures are indeed present, often in well-defined forms and their potential values should be used to guide the system towards possible ranges of information sources; 2) that *relevance assessments* and *relevance feedback* may be carried out in relation to core cognitive elements different from the 'topicality' of the information need (e.g. the topic "Boolean logic") [17]. It is not only the 'what', but more importantly the 'why' which determine assessments. For example, assessments are related to the underlying problem (i.e. the adequate form of the formular in a design process), the work task (i.e. design and repair of computer circuits), or the domain (i.e. applied computer science). This phenomenon of *differentiated relevance* may be related to the 'utility' values introduced by Cooper

[18]. For instance, all the domain-related philosophical, mathematical, logical, and computer science texts concerned with the request on 'Boolean logic' would be regarded topically relevant. Only very few texts in the actual library collection were in fact useful to the user's work task and problem. With reference to the discussion by Salton [19] a differentiated assessment would have provided the system with a high performance ratio concerning the work task and problem fulfilment - and a very low traditional recall ratio.

2.2 Intentional Redundancy as the Principle for Polyrepresentation

The principle of *intentional redundancy* applied to polyrepresentation in IR originates from the arguments put forward by Sparck Jones concerned with the necessity of "working through redundancy, that is, *different ways of referring* to the same concept and of linking different concepts in form of a conceptual network thrown over the underlying information objects" [3, p. 9]. The generic inference network proposed by Turtle and Croft [20] follows similar lines of thinking. We call this redundancy "intentional", since general and non-estimated redundancy in relation to representations of information objects may not always be productive in IR. The degree, mode and function of redundancy should be determined by knowledge of the current user´s information behaviour, e.g. as inferred or believed by the intermediary mechanism, based on a elaborate model of searcher behaviour.

In other words, from a cognitive perspective as many and as different cognitive structures as possible should be made available and applied during IR interaction, however, in accordance with an estimation which allows for a controlled or calculated selection of exactly such structures that are regarded most appropriate to the current retrieval situation. This issue of estimation is not necessarily seen as a mathematical one but rather a behavioural and psychological issue.

Simplified intentional redundancy has been attempted for decades in the operational online environment by means of different forms of indexing and thesaurus support applied to the same bibliographic record collection. Conceptual inference networking is a more subtle and dynamic form of redundancy. However, with intentional redundancy in the context of the cognitive viewpoint we propose to *extend the principle into the user´s cognitive space*, exploiting its different cognitive structures, Fig. 1, right-hand side. These are constituting a more powerful inference network with truely dynamic properties and based on human intentionality. Intentional redundancy on both the systems and user side is assumed to provide improved access structures for both participants during IR interaction.

The principle is proposed carried out by *polyrepresentative* means. By polyrepresentation is meant the representation in a variety of different forms of one information object, e.g. of an information requirement or a text entity. Fundamentally, they are forms of the different cognitive structures as defined above, and are generated via a variety of well-known methods applied to IR systems. Different indexing methods applied to the same text collection yields different sets of text or document entities for the same query, e.g. natural language vs. controlled vocabulary methods. Several empirical investigations of the matter [21,22,23] carried out in the operational exact match environment demonstrate clearly that the combination - *the overlap* - of controlled index *phrases* and natural language representations from basic index yields the best retrieval results, better than the two separately. The more variety in cognitive origin of method, the more different results. Human indexing will result in retrieved sets rather different from automatically indexed collections of texts. Inter-indexer inconsistencies and inter-linker inconsistency for hypertext link-creation are, not surprisingly, quite high [24].

One of the very few investigations of the *alternative overlap* between index term retrieval of journal articles and searching via *citation indexing* has been carried out by McCain [25]. For the same queries in Medline and the ISI databases the result was as expected from a cognitive viewpoint: The two *very* different cognitive structures of indexers and authors, the latter group interpreting the texts with completely different intentions than the former, yielded an overlap of only 11 % on average. As above, the two representative methods are *complementary* to one another. In addition, the degree of overlap between natural language representations of full-text and citation indexing (as well as the NL representations of such citations) ought to be explored further. As instruments for such investigations the ISI databases are insufficient. The prediction for the outcome is that the two sets of retrieved text entities are similarly complementary. With respect to overlap between sets of texts retrieved via *different partial* (and exact match) *techniques* for the same query, the picture is identical. A more detailed outline of the characteristic retrieval power of the variety of matching techniques is provided by Belkin and Croft [26] and by Croft in relation to ´intelligent´ IR [27]. From a cognitive perspective this evidence of variety is obvious - and should be directly exploited.

Not surprisingly, recent TREC investigations of the retrieval performance of *combined query versions* generated by several searchers, but deriving from the one and same well and pre-defined information need, demonstrate a performance similar to that of the best performing query. This latter query version is, of course, always unknown beforehand and hence unpredictable [28]. This interesting research on inter-searcher consistency, similar to the inter-indexer consistency experiments, strongly indicates the individual cognitive nature of request formulation rooted in intrinsic causality. It seems unrealistic to assume that several real-life searchers may initiate IR based on identical and well-defined needs for information. The realistic alternative proposal is consequently to obtain *simultaneous but cognitively different representations* of the current user´s information need situation - framed by the principle of intentional redundancy.

2.2.1 Polyrepresentation of Semantic Entities of Full-Text.

Adequate semantic entities of full-text are defined as the smallest unit of a given text which provides a recipient with a semantically confined context. Such entities may thus range from sentences over paragraphs, to encyclopaedia entries, news release units and sub-sub-sections in journal articles and books. The suggestion to apply such smaller parts of traditional documents for representation and retrieval purposes is not novel. For monographs the principle of using chapter headings and table captions was proposed and tested in relation to the SAP-Projects for library online catalogs for more than a decade ago [29,30]. Use of paragrahs in full-text retrieval of encyclopaedia settings has recently been made by the Salton et al. [31,32]. Similarly, paragraphs are used in hypertext link-creation experiments [24]. In linguistic based IR sentences are the preferred semantic entity for analysis and retrieval [33] and are also proposed by van Rijsbergen to form the kernel to which to apply the principle of logical uncertainty [34,35]. The SIMPR indexing machine makes use of chapter and section headings as well as full-text sentences in order to produce indexing concepts automatically by linguistic analysis and to point to potentially relevant sub-sections and paragraphs in large monographic material [36,37]. One may here observe a structural or syntactic approach to representation as well as to retrieval which tends to approximate a contextual level in IR research.

Regardless the document type in question it seems adequate to assume that text *paragraphs* and single figures or tables provide the smallest semantically confined unit of documents that may produce the information searched for. Empirical experiences tell us this as well as intuition. If we, for instance, observe how authors directly cite other text entities in their own texts, it seems very probable that one or a few related paragraphs provide the vital context embodying and giving meaning to the cited sentence.

Negative consequences exist for IR when using smaller units of full-text. The variation of representation methods may be reduced. No 'paragraph header' normally exists in addition to the full-text terms and concepts. However, it is still functionally relevant, for instance, to claim that a section or news item header may cover several sequential paragraphs of text.

Other negative aspects of introducing semantic entities is the difficulty of applying human indexer interpretations to the entities in order to assign representations mainly concerned with elements *not mentioned* in the text, but of reasonable value to retrieval and users. This issue concerns indexing methods similar to those suggested by Blair [38] or by Hjorland [39], in which the domain and the text's cognitive potentials play vital roles. Representations of, for instance, treatment, author intent or situational dependent task-relationships, and alike aspects of a text incl. domain-related class codes, may only be possible to assign to the total document text - not to individual semantic entities. However, if assigned to the entire document, such representations do provide access to the context of entities belonging to the document. This and other relationships of conceptual dependency between the whole and its entities and between entities and their forms of representation may be exploited in a structured manner, e.g. as attempted by Schmeltz Pedersen by application of lattice theory [40].

Finally, one may note that the *writing style* manifested in the various forms of entities is influencing the parameters for retrieval. Paragraphs from Introductions are slightly different in style from the corresponding abstracts, and rather different from the entities embedded in the remaining text body. Every document type has its independent style which vary from domain to domain.

To summarize the application of the intentional redundancy principle to paragraphs as the selected semantic entity, polyrepresentation may take may take several different forms. As a minimum, three cognitively different structures of representation and retrieval modes may be involved:

1) the authored *text itself* incl. overlying headings, and the citations to other texts in certain document types; 2a) the *method(s) applied to representing* the paragraph via form(s) of automatic indexing and linguistic text analysis; 2b) the *retrieval technique(s)* applied to the original text and the representations. The representations and the techniques may be identical, since each partial match technique also may serve as means to automatic indexing at single-term level; 3) the domain-dependent *thesaurus structure* (if existing) applied to and supporting the representations. In addition, structures of *other authors* actually citing the paragraph - or at least the page holding it - may be involved. This latter representation is only applicable for certain document types.

For each different origin mentioned, we may anticipate at least one version of representative structure to be present in relation to the same semantic entity - but *several different simultaneous versions* may actually be expected. For instance, several different methods of automatic representation may be applied simultaneously:

a) single term extraction and weighting, combined with b) linguistic analysis producing concepts - as in SIMPR - which may c) be validated via a thesaurus structure, producing 'controlled' index terms not present in the analysed text. *Several retrieval principles* may be applied in parallel: vector space, probability, clustering, spreading activation, logical uncertainty, etc. - each on the different versions of representations if required. Each version will retrieve different sets of paragraphs with a varying degree of overlap in a calculated and intentional manner. One is free to manipulate the search outcome, for example by producing a variety of overlapping sets, to create conceptual network structures, or simply to ignore some of the structures in action. This *bottom-up approach* to representation and retrieval of semantic entities makes it in addition possible to view larger parts of the entire document in light of the retrieval power of its own entities. The mode of manipulation will depend on the intentionality of the current user - as perceived by the system.

3. Polyrepresentation in IR - the Global Model

Fig. 2 displays the global model of polyrepresentation of semantic entities in information space and the user's intrinsic cognitive structures following the principle of intentional redundancy. At the right-hand side the model attempts to visualize the participating cognitive elements responsible for the formation of the individual intrinsic information need and the resulting request versions. In this respect, the elements form the polyrepresentative entities of the user's cognitive space in a vertical bottom-up mode of causality, leading towards the information need. Combined, the representations extracted by interface functionalities, such as the Request and User Model Builder functions in the Mediator Model [1, p. 209-216] or similar model builders suggested elsewhere [5,6], provide a *structured context* of statements and descriptions to be applied to or by the IR system. Each cognitive element may form the basis for further elaboration in a horizontal dimension by structured questioning via an interface functionality, as suggested in [41]. Both dimensions may hence form the context necessary for applying the principle of logical uncertainty as an alternative retrieval principle [34,35].

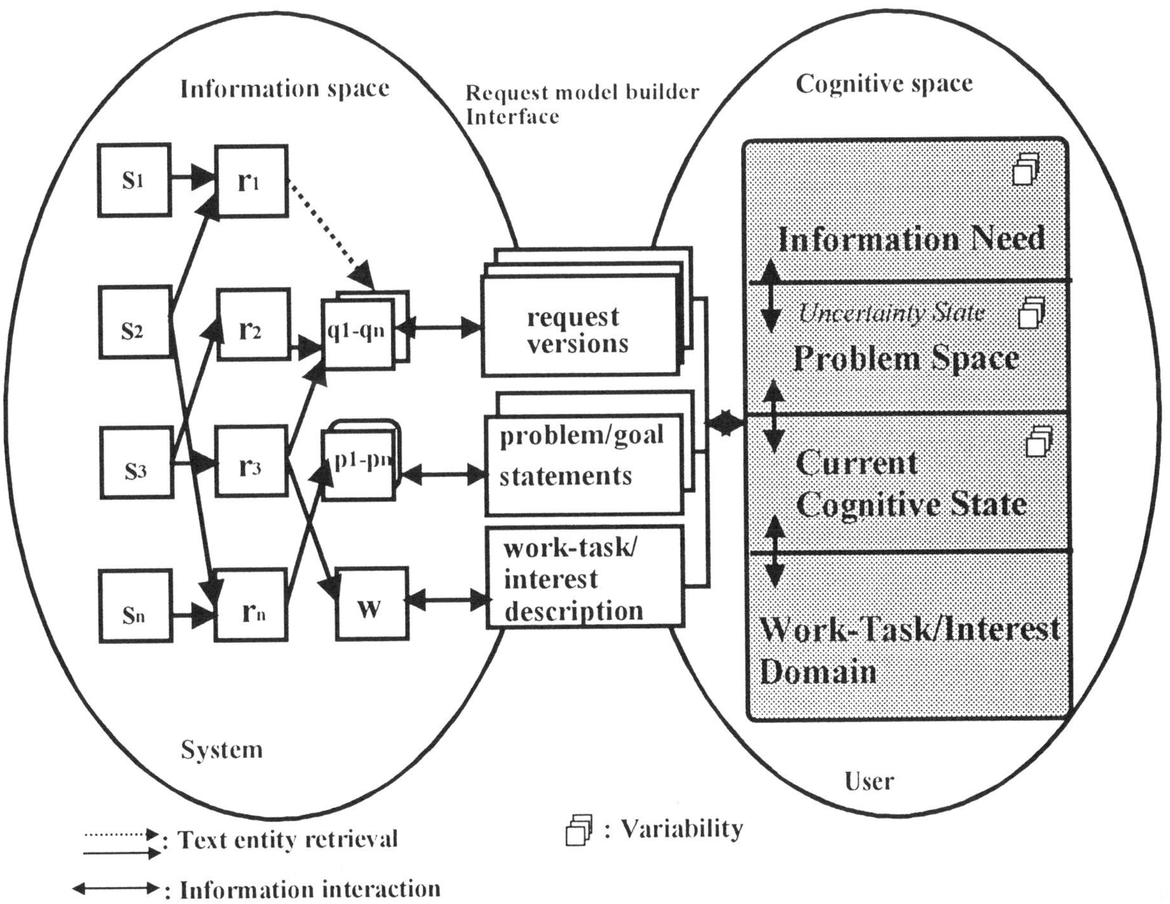

Fig. 2. The Global Model of Polyrepresentation in IR, extending the generic inference network of information space by Turtle and Croft [20] to incorporate representations of the user's cognitive space and interface functionality.

A third dimension of context is made up by the degree of conceptual background knowledge of the user, associated with his 'current cognitive state'. Again, various interface models have suggested functional solutions to extract this type of knowldge from the user which is essential for estimating the nature and quality of the current intrinsic information need [1,6,42]. Naturally, a fourth dimension of time exist during any retrieval session, signified by the variability and versioning of statements demonstrated on the model.

The *interface* plays a key-role in this scenario, since its outlined functionalities assure that the intentional redundancy principle may be inforced. The aforementioned estimations as to which representative methods and retrieval techniques to apply, and under which circumstances, are based on the the interface's perception of the retrieval situation of the user. The crucial point is the estimation of the cognitive nature and quality of the information need. For instance, if it is perceived that the user simply wish to *verify and locate* items already explicitly known, the intention of the interface would be to abandon redundancy and apply exact match retrieval on simplified representations of entities in information space. On the other hand, if the need seems to be of topical nature, there exist two basic alternatives: 1) the information need is intrinsicly *vague, ill-defined* or *non-existent*, and consequently *variable*; 2) the intrinsic need is rather *well-defined and stable*. According to the cognitive view it would be mandatory in case of the first possibility to allow the user to *explore* the information space in a multidimensional way. This exploratory behaviour constitutes an extention and specification of Bates' so-called 'Berry-picking seeking behaviour' [43,44]. We extend this 'Berry-picking' metaphor also to encompass the conceivable (re)formation of the underlying problem or goal which, as stated above, also may be vaguely developed internally to the user.

At the left-hand side of the model the (*r*..) notation signifies nodes of concepts derived from different representative methods (-> *r*..) applied to the semantic entity nodes (*S*..). The (S..) notation may also signify sets or clusters of semantic entities. As the figure stands it demonstrates the application of *one retrieval technique*, e.g. the probability-based method. In relation to each representation of the user's cognitive space, i.e. (q.., p.., w), incl. the domain, the retrieval of semantic entities is based on the probability that an entity satisfies these representations individually or in combination with one another (r.. -> q.., p.., w) - as discussed above. However, only real assessments can be carried out by the actual user in relation to his intrinsic cognitive representations. A similar model would represent another retrieval technique in action, e.g. vector-space, in principle *yielding different nodes* or (sets of) semantic entities for the same (q..), (p..), etc., and for the same semantic entities (S..) embodied by the same methods of representations (r..) as before. (r1 - rn) might, for instance, be matching concepts validated by a domain thesaurus (r1), simple concepts extracted by linguistic text analysis (r2), single text terms (r3), or personal names extracted from the entities (rn).

In case of an ill-defined or vague intrinsic information need, the interface should concentrate on the *remaining* cognitive elements, internal to the user, in order to allow for browsing and explorative behaviour in the information space by *following different conceptual pathes* in the system. These pathes are associated with the aforementioned different structures of representation - the left-hand side of Fig. 2. The idea is that for each element of the user's own cognitive space, the right-hand side, Fig. 2, there should exist a corresponding network of concepts (r..) and semantic entities (S..) which may be explored by the user. For *each such element*, say the 'work task', a path is constituted by at least one of several different methods of representation (r3) matching the user description extracted by the interface (w). The resulting semantic entities are signified by (S3). In total, the model demonstrates that by introducing statements of 'problem space' and 'work task/domain', additional pathes for exploration and retrieval are made available - pathes which might never be reached via the query versions alone. By means of this additional information from the system, relevance judgment and query expansion is possible (r1 ----> q2) during the proceeding part of the session.

Not demonstrated on the model is the additional intentional possibility to combine, or concentrate, all the retrieved sets of entities (e.g. S2 - Sn), regardless to which cognitive structure they belong in the user's cognitive space. Fundamentally, this procedure implies to view request, problem and task statements and domain dscription as *one large manifestation* of the information need. This is the recommended strategy to follow if the initial request, problem statement and work task/domain descriptions are rich, conceivably signifying a well-defined and stable intrinsic information need. In addition to traditional relevance assessments resulting in relevance feedback to the system, this intentional strategy allows also for assessments directly associated with each of the user's different cognitive structures. It is thus possible to separate 'utility values' from 'topicality'.

It would be possible to implement the model, Fig. 2, into several ongoing experiments, e.g. the OKAPI project [45]. The user response to each element, extracted by the interface, will in realistic terms consist of few conceptual structures. The virtue of OKAPI so far has been its conscious dedication to a realistic user environment in which searchers do not carry stable and well-defined information needs. In contrast to the TREC experiments, real-life experimentation takes place involving human searchers and real information requests. The advantage for OKAPI would conceivably be that the total amount of potentially relevant data for (initial) probability retrieval would be augmented *and* in addition be structured, that is, available for various forms of manipulation by the system in supporting the user's proceeding exploration and expansion of statements.

In relation to the TREC experiments the model of polyrepresentation could be implemented by enhancing the description of the pre-defined ´information needs´, already supplied by the project. At present the information needs in TREC contain a 'Domain description´ and a 'request version´ of the need. In addition, this request is explained in more depth by a 'description´. For each need is given a detailed essay on the kind of material which is supposed to be relevant. This essay, or assessment background, is corresponding to the notion of *'preference´*, Fig. 1, right-hand side. Hence, it is suggested to add a realistic *Problem/Goal Statement* as well as a *Work Task/Interest Description*. This enhancement would make it possible during the relevance judgment and human query expansion processes [46] to know *why* an item ought to be relevant according to the mentioned assessment essay.

4. Concluding Discussion

This cognitive approach to IR theory is supported by empirical evidence from both the information seeking research as well as from studies made in the operational environment. In addition, it does not contradict the IR developments achieved so far associated to partial matching. It attempts to incorporate them in a global framework.

Polyrepresentation of the user's knowledge space signifies to represent not only the current information need, but in addition, and more importantly, to reach into the underlying problem space, actual work task or interest, and the dominating work domain. These elements are associated with the information need formation by following a principle of causality, that is, the intentionalty underlying the fact of having such a need at all. Information needs internal to the user are basically regarded being of vague and variable nature, but may also exist in stable and well-defined forms, according to the nature of the current problem state of the user in the situation. The nature of the representations of all elements in terms of request, problem and work task formulations may point to the actual condition of the intrinsic information need.

The ongoing laboratory experimental settings are found valid, but confined to investigations of invariable information needs represented by well-formulated and predefined requests for information. In realistic terms this Cranfield approach conforms to a limited case of retrieval. In this confined experimental scenario it is suggested also to monitor problem and work task relationships, by adding simulated elements for each already defined experimental query.

For relevance assessment the theory suggests and allows for *relative*, but statistical significant assessments. This is already the case in the TREC and Tipster experiments. In addition, *partial relevance* of documents is made available following the presented approach, since the semantic entities are the main objective of assessment and retrieval. Hence, the theory also encourages to include differentiated relevance, implying that 'topicality´ relevance is supplied with work task and problem relevance or rather, *utility*: Several semantic entities may be topically relevant, but only partially relevant or irrelevant for the actual work task and problem - and vice versa. In realistic terms, and in order to investigate the exploratory quality of partial match and different methods of representation, one may in addition apply ill-defined queries with rich problem and task definitions.

Such enhanced but still simulated experimental situations are assumed to improve the reliability of results, although, of course, the number of experimental variables will increase further compared to today´s research setting. Ideally, real-life situations should not only be simulated but actually be applied in the research design. The significance is to take a methodological step further by incorporating the problems concerning concepts like reliability and validity, known from the social sciences in general and marketing research in particular. Indeed, these concepts, e.g in terms of experimental question design [47], are important components of any type of relevance or utility assessment.

Note 1: Throughout the paper 'Text' signifies textand all other media-borne messages, such as images, video, films, etc.

References

1. Ingwersen, P. Information Retrieval Interaction. Taylor Graham, London, 1992.
2. De Mey, M. The relevance of the cognitive paradigm for information science. In. Harbo, O. et. al. (eds.). Theory and Application of Information research. Mansell, London, 1980, pp. 48-61.
3. Sparck Jones, K. Retrieving information or answering questions. The 8th British Annual Research Lecture. British Library, 1989 (BLRD/c/130)
4. Belkin, N.J., Seeger, T., Wesig, G. Distributed expert problem treatment as a model for information systems analysis and design. J. of Inf.Sc., 1983; 5:153-167.

5. Belkin, N.J., Brooks, H., Daniels, P.J. Knowledge elicitation using discourse analysis. Int. journ. of Man-machine Studies, 1987; 27:127-144.
6. Croft, W.B. and Thomson, R. I3R: A new approach to the design of document retrieval systems. JASIS, 1987; 38(6): 389-404.
7. Belkin, N.J., Oddy, R., Brooks, H. ASK for information retrieval. J. of Doc., 1982; 38:61-71; Part II: 145-164.
8. Dervin, B. and Nilan, M. Information needs and uses. ARIST, 1986;21:3-33.
9. Rasmussen, J., Pejtersen, A.M., Goodstein, L.P. Cognitive Engineering: Concepts and Applications. Wiley, 1992.
10. Wood-Harper, A.T., Antill, Lyn, Avison, D.E. Information Systems Definition: The Multiview Approach. Blackwell Scientific Publ., Oxford, 1985.
11. Mackay, D.M. What makes the question. The Listener, 1960; 63:789-790.
12. Taylor, R.S. Question negotiation and information seeking in libraries. Coll. and Res. Libr., 1968; 29:178-194.
13. Saracevic, T., Mokros, H., Su, L.T. Nature of interaction between users and intermediaries in online searching: a qualitative analysis. ASIS Proc., 1990, 27 p.
14. Ingwersen, P. Search procedures in the library analysed from the cognitive pointof view. J. of Doc., 1982;38:165-191.
15. Kuhlthau, C. Seeking Meaning. Ablex Publ., New York, 1993.
16. Murtonen, K. and Järvelin, K. Task Complexity Affects Information Seeking and Use. Tampere, Finland, University of Tampere, dept. of Information Studies, Research Notes (RN-1992-2), 1992.
17. Schamber, L., Eisenberg, M., Nilan, M. A re-examination of relevance: toward a dynamic, situational defintion. Inf. Proc.& Managm., 1990; 26(6):755-776.
18. Cooper, W.S. The paradoxal role of unexamined documents in the evaluation of retrieval effectiveness. Inf.Proc.& Managm., 1976;12:367-375.
19. Salton, G. The state of retrieval system evaluation. Inf.Proc. & Managm., 1992; 28(4):441-449
20. Turtle, H. and Croft, W.B. Inference methods for document retrieval. In: Vidick, J. (ed). ACM-Sigir Conf. Proc.Bruxelles, Bruxelles University, 1990, pp. 1-24.
21. Tenopir, C. Issues in Online Database Searching. Englewood Cliffs, NJ, Libraries Unlimited, 1989.
22. Katzer, J. et al. A study of the overlap among decument representations. Information Technology: Res.and Dev., 1982:2, 261-274.
23. Lancaster, F.W. Indexing in Theory and Practice. Library Association, London, 1991.
24. Ellis, D., Furner-Hines, J. and Willett, P. On the creation of hypertext links in full-text documents: Measuring of inter-linker consistency. J. of Doc. (in press).
25. MacCain, K.W. Descriptor and citation retrieval in the medicine behavioural sciences literature: Retrieval overlaps and novelty distribution. JASIS, 1989;40:110-114.
26. Belkin, N.J. and Croft, W.B. Retrieval techniques. ARIST, 1987; 22:109-145.
27. Croft, W.B. Approaches to intelligent information retrieval. Inf. Proc. & Managem., 1987, 23(4), 249-254.
28. Belkin, N.J. Cool, C., Croft, W.B. and Callan, J.P. The effect of multiple query representations on information retrieval performance. Proceedings of the 16th SIGIR Conf. New York, NY: ACM Press, 1993, pp. 339-346.
29. Atherton-Cochrane, P. Books are for Use: Final Report of the Subject Acess Project. Syracuse, N.Y., Syracuse University, School of Information Studies, 1979.
30. Wormell, I. Subject Access Project - SAP: Improved Subject Retrieval for Monographic Publications. Doctoral Dissertation. Lund: Lund University, 1985.
31. Salton, G. and Buckley, C. Automatic text structuring and retrieval. Experiments in automatic encyclopedia searching. In: 14th Int. Conf. of ACM-Sigir. New York, ACM Press, 1991, pp. 21-30.
32. Salton, G., Allan, J. and Buckley, C. Approaches to passage retrieval in full text information systems. In: Proceedings of the 16th SIGIR Conf., Pittsbourg. New York, NY: ACM Press, 1993, pp. 49-58.
33. Smeaton, A. Progress in the application of natural language processing to information retrieval tasks. The Computer Journal, 1992:35, 268-278.
34. van Rijsbergen, C. A new theoretical framework for information retrieval. ACM-Sigir Conf. Proc., Pisa, IEI, 1986, pp. 194-200
35. van Rijsbergen, C. The science of information retrieval: its methodology and logic. In: Conf. Informatienvetenschap in Nederland. Haag, Rabin, 1990, pp. 20-38.
36. Smeaton, A., Voutilainen, A., Sheridan, P. The application of morpho-syntactic language processing to effective text retrieval. Esprit '90 Conf. Dordrecht, Klüver, 1990, pp. 619-635.
37. Bookstein, A. Towards a multi-disciplinary Bradford Law. 4th In. Conf. on Bibliometrics, Informetrics, and Scientometrics. Berlin, 1993. (extended abstract).
37. Gibb, F. Knowledge-based indexing in SIMPR: Integration of natural language processing and principles of subject analysis in an automated indexing system. J. of Doc. and Text Managem., 1993, 2:131-154.
38. Blair, D.C. Language and Representation in Information retrieval. Oxford, Elsevier, 1990.
39. Hjorland, B. The concept of 'subject' in information science. J. of Doc. 1992;48:172-200.
40. Schmeltz Pedersen, G. A browser for bibliographic information retrieval, based on an application of lattice theory. In: Proceedings of the 16th SIGIR Conf., Pittsbourgh. New York, NY: ACM Press, 1993, 270-280.
41. Ingwersen, P. and Wormell, I. Ranganathan in the perspective of advanced information retrieval. Libri, 1992;42(3):184-201.
42. Brajnik, G., Guida, G., Tasso, C. User modelling in intelligent information retrieval. Inf. Proc. & Managm., 1987:23(4), 305-320.
43. Bates, M. An exploratory paradigm for online information retrieval. In: Brookes, B.C. (ed.). Intelligent Information Systems for the Information Society. London, North-Holland, 1986, pp. 91-99.
44. Bates, M. The design of browsing and berry-picking techniques for the online search interface. Online Review, 1989; 13(5):407-424.
45. Hancock-Beaulieu, M. Query expansion: advances in research in online catalogues. J. of Inf.Sc., 1992;18:99-103.
46. Callan, J.P. and Croft, W.B. An evaluation of query processing strategies using the TIPSTER collection. Conf. Proc. of the 1993 ACM-Sigir, Sigir Forum, New York, ACM Press, 1993, pp.347-355.
47. Fowler, F.J. Survey Research Methods. 2. ed. Sage, London, 1993.

Theory and Logic

Investigating Aboutness Axioms using Information Fields

P.D. Bruza*
School of Information Systems
Queensland University of Technology
GPO Box 2134
Brisbane Q 4001
Australia
bruza@qut.edu.au

T.W.C. Huibers
Department of Computer Science
Utrecht University
P.O. Box 80.089
3508 TB Utrecht
The Netherlands
theo@cs.ruu.nl

Abstract

This article proposes a framework, a so called information field, which allows information retrieval mechanisms to be compared inductively instead of experimentally. Such a comparison occurs as follows: Both retrieval mechanisms are first mapped to an associated information field. Within the field, the axioms that drive the retrieval process can be filtered out. In this way, the implicit assumptions governing an information retrieval mechanism can be brought to light. The retrieval mechanisms can then be compared according to which axioms they are governed by. Using this method it is shown that Boolean retrieval is more powerful than a strict form of coordinate retrieval. The salient point is *not* this result in itself, but *how* the result was achieved.

1 Introduction

The logic based approach to information retrieval has been around for some time now. So far, a number of inference mechanisms, both strict and plausible, have been proposed for driving the retrieval process [15, 6, 4, 12]. Furthermore, the expressive power of the approach has been demonstrated by several authors [14, 13, 7, 2]. We feel, however, that its real potential has not yet been tapped. Research has not yet produced a powerful enough framework whereby information retrieval systems can be compared *inductively* instead of *experimentally*. A breakthrough in this area would mean that a theorem could be proven stating, for example, that vector space retrieval is more effective that Boolean retrieval. Such a result would not only spare us the efforts of experimentation, but more importantly, it would allow us to side step the controversies surrounding the experimental process. This paper is an attempt at laying some ground work for an inductive theory of information retrieval.

2 Informational Fundamentals

In information retrieval, the question of aboutness appears in a number of guises. For example, in order to drive the retrieval mechanism aboutness is studied as a relation between a document and a query. Sometimes, the question whether one document is about another document arises, for example, in document clustering. Aboutness between descriptors occurs within the framework of a characterization language, for example, a term independence assumption is just another way of expressing that two terms aren't about each other.

We begin by abstracting from notions such as descriptors, documents and queries and introduce the notion of an *information carrier*. The central theme of this paper is to axiomatize the notion of when one information carrier is about another one. A rather strict notion of aboutness will be employed:

> an information carrier i will be said to be *about* information carrier j if the information born by j holds in i

This definition can be found explicitly or implicitly in several papers on logic-based information disclosure [8, 15, 2]. The intuition behind it closely approximates the notion of a *model* in logic, for this reason the notation $i \models j$ will be used to denote that information carrier i is about carrier j. Note that this conception of aboutness is not applicable for document clustering where aboutness is determined by the overlap between respective document characterizations. The definition is however useful for studying aboutness between a document and a query.

*This work was performed while at Utrecht University

Information Carriers

Information carriers are descriptions of situations, real or possible worlds etc. These descriptions may be long and detailed, for example, a document, or may be short, for example, a query. Some information carriers convey more information about a situation(s) than others. According to Landman [11] and Barwise [1] information can be partially ordered with respect to information containment (denoted by $\rightarrow$):

$i \rightarrow j$ iff the information which i carries already *contains* the information which j carries

In other words, carrier i bears more information that carrier j. Bear in mind that carrier i "is less than" carrier j in the ordering. Information containment is related to specificity. For example, the information carrier little green martians is more specific than green martians which is more specific than martians. Note that little green martians $\rightarrow$ green martians $\rightarrow$ martians. The information containment relation $\rightarrow$ is reflexive, antisymmetric and transitive. Transitivity in the context of information containment is also known as the Xerox Principle [1].

Information Composition

A document can be seen as a composition of various pieces of information. It can therefore be viewed as a complicated description of a diverse range of situations, for example, an encyclopedia. The way information carriers can be composed to form complexer information carriers functions according to rules. At lower levels of information granularity, composition is typically governed by linguistic considerations, for example, how subelements of a sentence may be combined to form a sentence. Above the level of sentences, composition rules become structural in nature. For example, how sentences are composed to form paragraphs and paragraphs to sections etc. Document specification languages such as SGML are specifically designed to provide the rules for governing such structural composition.

As an illustration of information composition, consider the information carriers green martians and little martians. These can be composed to form the carrier little green martians. Note how the latter carrier bears precisely the information furnished by the combination of the two previous carriers. This is the fundamental property of information composition. More formally,

$i \oplus j$ is the largest (as defined by $\rightarrow$) information carrier that precisely contains the information born by i and by j.

Recent work with index expressions also shows how connectors can be used to combine characterizations [4, 2]. For example, river $\circ$ pollution and pollution in australia can be composed to render the carrier river $\circ$ pollution in australia. Within Boolean retrieval $\oplus$ is embodied by $\wedge$.

If one carries information composition to the extreme one attains total information, which according to Landman is *too much information* [11]. Imagine if all the information carriers of mankind were to be composed into a single carrier! The total information carrier will be denoted by ∞ which constitutes the bottom element of the partial order of information carriers. As a consequence, all information carriers are informationally contained in ∞. The carrier ∞ is intuitively similar to *falsum* in the context of the propositional calculus in the sense that all formulae can de derived from it.

Information Preclusion

Not all information carriers can be meaningfully composed. The reason for this is that they are incompatible; the information they share clashes, or is contradictory. In other words, carriers i and j are said to preclude each other, denoted $i \perp j$. It is natural to assume that facts (viewed as information carriers) preclude their negation, for example martians are green $\perp$ martians are not green. Information preclusion, however, is not restricted to being a relation over facts. It can be argued that green martians precludes blue martians because martians are either blue or green, but not both. This intuition behind this phenomenon can be explained in terms of possible worlds: After characterizing a world as being a "green martian" world, it cannot be re-characterized as a "blue martian" world. Note that little martians does not preclude green martians. Several authors regard information preclusion as being fundamental to a theory of information [11, 1].

Even though green martians precludes blue martians this does not necessarily mean that their composition isn't an information carrier. One can imagine an information carrier formed from the composition of the previous two carriers but the information it bears is discordant:

green martians	$\oplus$	blue martians	$\rightarrow$	green martians	and
green martians	$\oplus$	blue martians	$\rightarrow$	blue martians	*but*
green martians	$\perp$	blue martians			

An information carrier k is termed *harmonious* if and only if it doesn't bear discordant information. That is, there are no information carriers i, j such that $k \rightarrow i$ and $k \rightarrow j$ where $i \perp j$.

Information preclusion is sometimes defined in terms of composition [11]: Two information carriers i and j are deemed to preclude each other if and only if their composition results in total information: $i \perp j$ iff $i \oplus j = \infty$. In other words, non-harmonious information carriers are synonymous with total information. To illustrate this definition index expression based information carriers will be used [2].

Example 2.1

Figure 1 depicts a partial ordering of index expressions under information containment. In the context of this ordering and using the above definition of preclusion air ∘ poll ⊥ riv ∘ poll *and* aus ⊥ holl, *but* poll $\not\perp$ aus. □

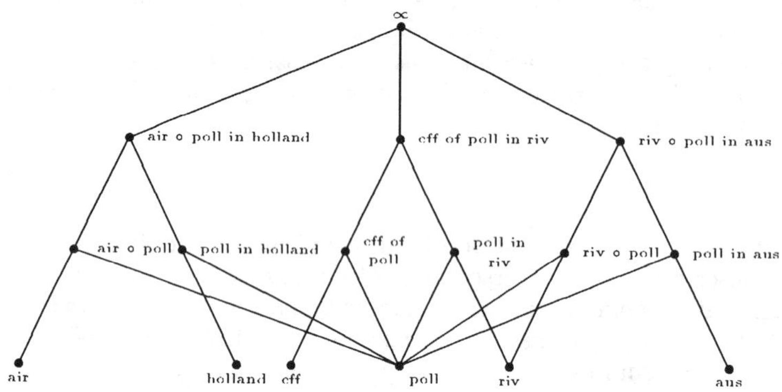

Figure 1. Example poset index expression carriers

Preclusion is interesting for information disclosure because if it is known that two information carriers preclude each other, then this may be used to determine aboutness. For example, if we know that a document is about green martians and that green martians precludes blue martians, we may then be able to infer that the document is *not* about blue martians.

Information Degradation

The converse of information composition is information degradation. The interesting facet of this notion is that it is related to uncertainty. For example, when one wants to retrieve all documents about i or j in Boolean retrieval systems, the expression $i \vee j$ is used. The uncertainty comes in as follows: if a given document is about $i \vee j$ it need not be about i. The expression $i \vee j$ can be considered to be a carrier which bears vague information, hence the term *information degradation.* We will not further deal with information degradation, although it does play a role in information retrieval. Instead, attention will be focussed on how aboutness behaves in the light of information containment, composition and preclusion.

Information Fields

To summarize, a framework has been proposed in which the notion of information carrier is fundamental. Such a framework is termed an *information field.* An information fields draws its underlying concepts from theories of information being currently developed in situation theory (specifically infon algebras [1]) and data semantics [11]. The intention is that an information field offers the necessary building blocks to axiomatize the the notion of aboutness employed in a given information retrieval mechanism. More about this in the next section.

Definition 2.1 (Information Field)

An information field *is a structure* $(\Im, \rightarrow, \oplus, \perp, \infty)$ *such that*

1. $\Im$ *is a non-empty set of information carriers*
2. $(\Im, \rightarrow)$ *is a poset*
3. $\infty \in \Im$ *and for all* $i \in \Im$, $\infty \rightarrow i$
4. *if* $i, j \in \Im$ *then* $i \oplus j \in \Im$, *where* $i \oplus j$ *is the largest information carrier such that* $i \oplus j \rightarrow i$ *and* $i \oplus j \rightarrow j$
5. $\perp \subseteq \Im \times \Im$

□

3 Axiomatizing Aboutness

We sometimes speak about information retrieval theory, but what are the axioms that govern this theory? Certainly they exist because the researchers who propose a retrieval mechanism entertain some assumptions as to what produces "good" retrieval. The problem is that these assumptions are often not expressed, and when they are, they tend not to be expressed in a general enough way to determine whether two different retrieval mechanisms are governed by the same or similar sets of assumptions. At the moment, the question as to whether the assumptions behind coordinate retrieval are the same as those that govern vector space retrieval cannot be satisfactorily answered. If it could, the two systems could be formally compared, for example, by using representation theorems. Such an approach has been used with success in comparing non-monotonic reasoning systems.

This section proposes a system of axioms expressed in terms of concepts from the information field. The term "axiom" should not be interpreted in a strict logical sense, but rather in a more intuitive fashion: The axioms are intended to characterize the *assumptions* inherent within a given retrieval mechanism with regard to aboutness. Retrieval mechanisms can then be compared according to which axioms they are governed by. The notion of aboutness is embodied by a binary relation $\models$ over the set of information carriers $\Im$. The first axiom posits that an information carrier is about itself.

Axiom 1 (Reflexivity (R))

$$i \models i$$

An information carrier is about the information it contains. This is the premise behind the Containment Axiom.

Axiom 2 (Containment (C))

$$\frac{i \to j}{i \models j}$$

Say we have a document d which is about green martians. It is natural to assume green martians $\to$ martians. Therefore, d is about martians. This is an example of Right Containment Monotonicity.

Axiom 3 (Right Containment Monotonicity (RCM))

$$\frac{k \models i \quad i \to j}{k \models j}$$

Right Containment Monotonicity is fundamental to many systems proposed in situation theory [1]. Note that Left Containment Monotonicity is not a sensible axiom for governing aboutness.

$$\frac{k \models j \quad i \to j}{k \models i}$$

For example, let d be a document which is about martians and green martians $\to$ martians. Left Containment Monotonicity permits the conclusion that d is about green martians, which does not necessarily have to be the case. Left Containment Monotonicity lurks behind the lack of precision in a recently proposed context free plausible inference mechanism [3].

Axiom 4 (Context-Free And (C-FA))

$$\frac{k \models i \quad k \models j}{k \models \; i \oplus j}$$

Boolean retrieval, for one, is founded on this axiom. For example, if a document d is about river and the same document is about pollution it is assumed that d is about river $\wedge$ pollution. Recent research has shown that this can be a dubious assumption, particularly at lower levels of information granularity [5, 16]. The problem lies in the fact that the carrier river $\wedge$ pollution bears implicitly the assumption that river and pollution are related which doesn't have to be the case. By way of illustration, river valleys $\oplus$ air pollution is about both river and pollution, but the carrier is not about river pollution. In order to alleviate this problem, a context sensitive approach can be adopted.

Axiom 5 (Context-Sensitive And (C-SA))

$$\frac{i \to c \quad c \models j \quad c \models k}{i \models \; j \oplus k}$$

The idea is that information composition may only occur if the component carriers j, k are a part of the same informational context c. As a matter of passing, the carrier c may be of a different type than i, as is demonstrated by the following example based on Farradane's relational indexing [9]. Farradane introduced nine relationship types between terms, for example, air **A** pollution denotes an *action* relationship type between the terms air and pollution. This carries the information that pollution is something which affects, or acts on the air. The relationship type can be considered as a context which relates two terms, so with $d =$ river valleys $\oplus$ air pollution, the following would be a valid application of CS-A within Boolean retrieval:

$$\frac{d \rightarrow \text{air } \mathbf{A} \text{ pollution} \quad \text{air } \mathbf{A} \text{ pollution} \models \text{air} \quad \text{air } \mathbf{A} \text{ pollution} \models \text{pollution}}{d \models \text{air} \wedge \text{pollution}}$$

Note that it is not possible to affirm river $\wedge$ pollution as these terms are unrelated in the carrier d. Current retrieval systems tend only to support syntactic contexts, for example, the terms must appear in the same paragraph. Finally, the Context-Free And axiom is in fact derivable from the Context-Sensitive And by choosing the broadest possible context ($i = c$).

If a document is not about pollution, then it can't be about river pollution. This is the intuition behind the so called Negation Rationale.

Axiom 6 (Negation Rationale (NR))

$$\frac{k \not\models i}{k \not\models i \oplus j}$$

It has been recently proven that inference network models implicitly embody this property if the topology of the network is determined by the information containment relation [4].

If it can established that a component part of an information carrier i is about another carrier k, then composing i with another carrier j will not violate this, provided no preclusions are apparent. In other words, aboutness is preserved under composition.

Axiom 7 (Compositional Monotonicity (CM))

$$\frac{i \models k \quad j \not\perp k}{i \oplus j \models k}$$

Note that the carrier j must not preclude k in order to avoid paradoxes of aboutness. Assume that green martians $\models$ space creatures and earth creatures $\perp$ space creatures. Application of Compositional Monotonicity without looking at preclusion relations would allow the following:

$$\frac{\text{green martians} \models \text{space creatures}}{\text{green martians} \oplus \text{earth creatures} \models \text{space creatures}}$$

The paradox arises as follows: It follows from the definition of an information field that

$$\text{green martians} \oplus \text{earth creatures} \quad \rightarrow \quad \text{earth creatures}$$

and therefore, via the Containment Axiom:

$$\text{green martians} \oplus \text{earth creatures} \quad \models \quad \text{earth creatures}$$

but Rational Negation (see later) allows this result and the preclusion to yield:

$$\text{green martians} \oplus \text{earth creatures} \quad \not\models \quad \text{space creatures}$$

which is a contradiction of the unprecluded compositional monotonicity axiom. This example also demonstrates how the axioms can interact with each other in quite complex ways.

If information carriers preclude each other, then it doesn't seem unreasonable to assume that they are not about each other. Applications of this assumption can be readily found in information retrieval. For example, in Boolean retrieval the formula α precludes $\neg\alpha$ and certainly $\alpha \not\models \neg\alpha$ and vice versa. Furthermore, term vectors in vector space retrieval are orthogonal to each other. This is a geometric expression of information preclusion. These examples are concrete cases of the so called Preclusion Axiom:

Axiom 8 (Preclusion (P))

$$\frac{i \perp j}{i \not\models j \textit{ and } j \not\models i}$$

For *harmonious* information carriers, an axiom governing when a carrier is *not* about another carrier can be stated. This axiom is illustrated as follows. Given that $d =$ little green martians is harmonious. Furthermore, d is (via Containment) about green martians. Assuming, as before, that green martians $\perp$ blue martians, then Rational Negation permits the conclusion that d is *not* about blue martians.

Axiom 9 (Rational Negation (RN))

$$\frac{i \models j \quad j \perp k}{i \not\models k}$$

Last in the list of axioms pertinent to determining aboutness is the rather infamous *Closed World Assumption* which bedevils a number of retrieval models, most notably Boolean retrieval [14, 2].

Axiom 10 (Closed World Assumption (CWA))

$$\frac{i \not\models j \quad j \perp k \quad i \not\perp k}{i \models k}$$

There are a number of issues that deserve attention. Do the axioms capture all the properties of aboutness desirable for information retrieval? Are they complete? Are they sound? In the rest of this section, these important questions will be addressed.

One method to examine the soundness and completeness of the axioms is to examine them within the context of an existing logic. For this purpose, the propositional calculus is chosen. The basic idea is to treat propositional formulae as information carriers. Within this realm the notion of aboutness between formulae can neatly be mapped onto entailment. Information containment is captured by the inference mechanism of the propositional calculus. This corresponds to the intuition that the information contained by a given formula is all the theorems provable from it. Information composition is embodied by conjunction. Furthermore, a formula is deemed to preclude its negation. More specifically, let $\mathcal{B}(P)$ be the set of formulae based of the atomic propositions P and the connectives $\neg, \wedge, \Rightarrow$ and where $f \in P$ denotes *falsum*. Let $\vdash_{PC}$ and $\models_{PC}$ respectively denote the inference and entailment relations of propositional calculus. Furthermore, let $(\mathcal{B}(P), \vdash_{PC}, \wedge, \perp, f)$ be an information field such that $i \perp \neg i$ for $i \in \mathcal{B}(P)$.

To investigate soundness is it sufficient to prove that the axioms preserve the truth of $\models_{PC}$. Well known theorems for the propositional calculus can be applied. For example, the following is the proof for Right Containment Monotonicity:

$$\begin{array}{lll} & k \models_{PC} i \quad i \rightarrow j & \langle \texttt{completeness} \rangle \\ \Longrightarrow & k \vdash_{PC} i \quad i \rightarrow j & \langle \texttt{definition} \rangle \\ \Longrightarrow & k \vdash_{PC} i \quad i \vdash_{PC} j & \langle \texttt{cut} \rangle \\ \Longrightarrow & k \vdash_{PC} j & \langle \texttt{soundness} \rangle \\ \Longrightarrow & k \models_{PC} j & \end{array}$$

It turns out that, barring the Closed World Assumption, all other axioms examined within an information field based on the propositional calculus preserve truth. That is, the axiomatization is not sound in the context of this logic. As a consequence, the notion of aboutness cannot be mapped onto truth. The fact that the first nine axioms are sound is disappointing in the sense that it reveals that the axiomatization does not extend much further than the propositional calculus. In particular, non-monotonic behaviour, which is surely inherent in information retrieval, needs to be axiomatized.

The axioms are complete, that is: if $i \models_{PC} j$ then $i \models j$. This means that within the propositional calculus, truth can be mapped directly onto aboutness. The proof is as follows:

$$\begin{array}{lll} & i \models_{PC} j & \langle \texttt{completeness} \rangle \\ \Longrightarrow & i \vdash_{PC} j & \langle \texttt{definition} \rangle \\ \Longrightarrow & i \rightarrow j & \langle \texttt{containment} \rangle \\ \Longrightarrow & i \models j & \end{array}$$

4 Boolean Information Fields

In order to illustrate the axioms of the previous section in the context of information retrieval, we will first consider Boolean retrieval due to its simplicity and close relation with logic. To distill the axioms which govern Boolean retrieval requires a definition which establishes aboutness within this model. This definition functions as a foothold which can be used to examine which axioms are valid within the associated information field.

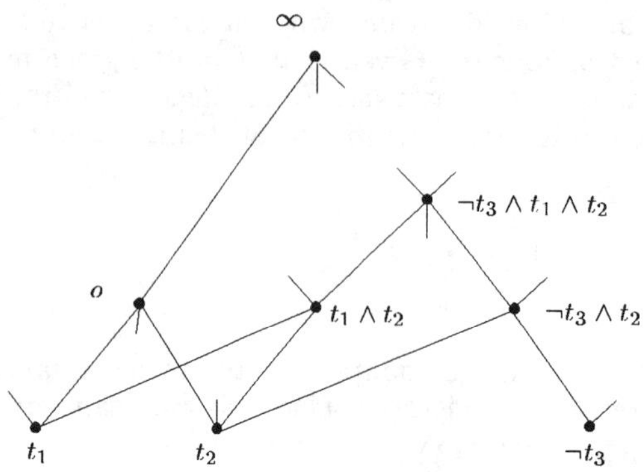

Figure 2. Part of a Boolean Information Field

Definition 4.1 (Boolean Aboutness)

Let T be a vocabulary (set of terms) and $\mathcal{B}(T)$ the Boolean language defined on T using the logical connectives $\neg, \vee, \wedge$. Furthermore, let $_{\text{BR}}$ be a set of strict inference rules defined on $\mathcal{B}(T)$. Let $\mathcal{O}$ be a set of objects (documents) whereby for $o \in \mathcal{O}, \chi(o)$ $(\chi(o) \subseteq T)$ denotes the characterization of o. Let $\alpha \in \mathcal{B}(T)$, then

$$o \models \alpha \quad \textit{iff} \quad \chi(o) \vdash_{\text{BR}} \alpha$$

□

In other words, a query α holds in a document o if and only if the query can be deduced from o's characterization using the strict inference rules which are defined as follows. For simplicity, only rules involving $\neg$ and $\wedge$ are specified:

1. if $\alpha \in \chi(o)$ then $\chi(o) \vdash_{\text{BR}} \alpha$
2. if $\chi(o) \vdash_{\text{BR}} \alpha,\ \chi(o) \vdash_{\text{BR}} \beta$ then $\chi(o) \vdash_{\text{BR}} \alpha \wedge \beta$
3. if $\chi(o) \not\vdash_{\text{BR}} \alpha$ then $\chi(o) \vdash_{\text{BR}} \neg\alpha$

The basis of this inference mechanism (clause 1) can be explained in terms of information containment: $\alpha \in \chi(o)$ is nothing more than an affirmation that the index term α is *informationally contained* in o, hence $o \rightarrow \alpha$. Therefore, both objects and terms are considered information carriers in the Boolean Information Field. This demonstrates that information fields can consist of information carriers of different types. Furthermore, clause 1 and definition 4.1 imply $o \models \alpha$, hence a Boolean Information Field supports the Containment Axiom.

Complex Boolean formulae are also considered to be information carriers and are ordered informationally in a natural way whereby information composition $\oplus$ is modelled by $\wedge$: $\alpha \wedge \beta \rightarrow \alpha$ and $\alpha \wedge \beta \rightarrow \beta$. Note that in this set up information composition is only defined for formulae. There is no composition operator for objects. This is consistent with the view held in the Boolean retrieval model that objects are disjoint, amorphous things with no operators defined on them. As a consequence, the Compositional Monotonicity axiom is not applicable. To complete the Boolean Information field, all formulae are deemed to informationally preclude their negation: $\alpha \perp \neg\alpha$. An illustration of a part of the Boolean Information Field is depicted in figure 2.

Thus far we have established that Boolean Information Fields embody the Containment Axiom. Furthermore, it can directly shown that clause 2 functions according to the Context-Free And axiom as follows:

$$\dfrac{\dfrac{\dfrac{o \models \alpha}{\chi(o) \vdash_{\text{BR}} \alpha}\,\text{Def 4.1} \qquad \dfrac{o \models \beta}{\chi(o) \vdash_{\text{BR}} \beta}\,\text{Def 4.1}}{\chi(o) \vdash_{\text{BR}} \alpha \wedge \beta}\,\text{Def 4.1}}{o \models \alpha \wedge \beta}\,\text{Def 4.1}$$

In a similar way, it can be shown that clause 3 cloaks the Closed World Assumption and that the Right Containment Monotonicity (RCM) axiom is also supported. Using RCM it can quickly be demonstrated that the Negation Rationale is also supported by proceeding *reductio ad absurdum*: Given there are carriers i, j, k and $k \not\models i$, $k \models i \wedge j$ is assumed. By definition, $i \wedge j \rightarrow i$, and applying RCM

$$\frac{k \models i \wedge j \quad i \wedge j \rightarrow i}{k \models i}$$

leads to a contradiction. Therefore, $k \not\models i \wedge j$ must have been the case.

In order to investigate the Rational Negation axiom, we must first insure that all objects are *harmonious* information carriers. This turns out to be the case because $o \rightarrow t$ and $o \rightarrow \neg t$ cannot occur ($t \in \chi(o)$ and $\neg t \in \chi(o)$ is not possible in Boolean retrieval). It can then be shown that the Rational Negation property is supported by a Boolean Information Field. Analysis of the remaining aboutness axioms leads to the following theorem which states which axioms are supported by a Boolean Information Field.

Theorem 4.1 Let BF be a Boolean Information Field with $\models \subseteq \mathrm{BF}_{\Im} \times \mathrm{BF}_{\Im}$ and $\models$ defined as in Definition 4.1, then BF satisfies the axioms *C,CF-A,CWA,RCM,NR,RN.*

5 Strict Coordinate Information Fields

When providing a foothold definition for studying coordinate retrieval care must be taken not to confuse two different notions of aboutness. The match function which drives coordinate retrieval measures overlap, for example, between the set of terms characterizing a document d and the set of terms comprising the query q. One way of interpreting aboutness is to deem that d is about q if and only if the overlap between their respective characterizations is non-null. This interpretation of aboutness is adopted to promote recall, however, this is *not* the aboutness being investigated here. Remember q must hold in d, and this is the case when $q \subseteq \chi(d)$. Adopting this interpretation of aboutness allows the investigation of coordinate retrieval, but in a narrower sense. For this reason it will be referred to as *strict* coordinate retrieval.

Definition 5.1 (Strict Coordinate Aboutness)
Let T be a vocabulary, with $\alpha \subseteq T$. Furthermore, let $\mathcal{O}$ be a set of objects whereby for $o \in \mathcal{O}, \chi(o)$ ($\chi(o) \subseteq T$) denotes the characterization of o. Then,

$$o \models \alpha \quad \textit{iff} \quad \alpha \subseteq \chi(o)$$

□

The mapping of strict coordinate retrieval to an information field proceeds in a similar way to Boolean retrieval. Both object characterizations and queries are modelled as information carriers consisting of a set of terms. Information containment within this framework is modelled by the subset relation over $\wp(T)$. Furthermore, the indexing relation once again determines an information containment relation between objects and terms: if $t \in \chi(o)$ then $o \rightarrow \{t\}$. The information composition operator $\oplus$ is realized by set union. The notion of information preclusion is foreign to coordinate retrieval, hence $\perp = \emptyset$. It can be shown that the Strict Coordinate Information Field embodies the following axioms.

Theorem 5.1 Let CF be a Strict Coordinate Information Field with $\models \subseteq \mathrm{CF}_{\Im} \times \mathrm{CF}_{\Im}$ and $\models$ defined as in Definition 5.1, then CF satisfies the axioms *C,CF-A,RCM,NR*

Comparing the representation theorems from Boolean retrieval and strict coordinate retrieval, we see that the axioms supported by a Strict Coordinate Information Field is a subset of the axioms supported by a Boolean Information Field. Stated otherwise; a Boolean Information Field is more powerful than a Strict Coordinate Information Field. In terms of information retrieval this means that whatever object a strict coordinate retrieval mechanism can deliver can also be delivered by a Boolean retrieval mechanism. It seems that this result is also reflected in an algebraic setting as there exists a homomorphism from a Strict Coordinate field to a Boolean Field. The homomorphism h is defined as follows assuming the same underlying set of objects O and vocabulary T. First, the information carriers of the Strict Coordinate Information Field CF are mapped to the information carriers of the Boolean field BF.

$$\begin{aligned} h(\infty^{\mathrm{CF}}) &= \infty^{\mathrm{BF}} \\ h(o^{\mathrm{CF}}) &= o^{\mathrm{BF}} \\ h(t^{\mathrm{CF}}) &= t^{\mathrm{BF}} \end{aligned}$$

Information carriers consisting of a set of terms are mapped to a conjunction of those terms:

$$h(\{t_1, \ldots, t_n\}^{\mathrm{CF}}) = \bigwedge_{1 \leq i \leq n} h(t_i^{\mathrm{CF}})$$

Furthermore, if α, β are information carriers in the Strict Coordinate Field, information composition can be mapped as follows:

$$h(\alpha \cup \beta) = h(\alpha) \wedge h(\beta)$$

Algebraic properties are a potentially powerful tool for the comparison of information fields, and thus the associated information retrieval mechanisms.

6 Conclusions and Further Research

The theme of this article is the theoretical comparison of information retrieval mechanisms. Such a comparison occurs as follows: Both retrieval mechanisms are first mapped to an associated information field. Within the field, the axioms that drive the retrieval process can be filtered out. In this way, the implicit assumptions governing an information retrieval mechanism can be brought to light. The retrieval mechanisms can then be compared according to which axioms they are governed by. Using this method it is shown formally that Boolean retrieval is more powerful than a strict form of coordinate retrieval. The salient point is *not* this result in itself, but *how* the result was achieved.

As the theoretical comparison of retrieval mechanisms is in its infancy, there are many avenues for further research. To begin with, the investigation of more existing retrieval mechanisms is needed. We envisage that an ordering of retrieval mechanisms could result. The effectiveness of a new retrieval mechanism could then be examined, not by running experiments, but by mapping it appropriately into the ordering. Detailed investigation into aboutness axioms is also needed. In particular, the axioms presented here should be extended to model non-monotonic aspects of aboutness. It should be possible to investigate under which conditions axioms preserve aboutness within the context of a given information field. This could open the door to soundness results similar to those found in logic. Furthermore, representation theorems (like those used to compare non-monotonic reasoning systems [10]) backed by algebraic comparisons are an interesting avenue for further exploration. The ultimate goal is an inductive theory of information retrieval.

Acknowledgements

The authors thank Bernd van Linder for the interesting discussions on (modal) logic and for his keen and critical eye.

References

1. J. Barwise and J. Etchemendy. Information, Infons, and Inference. In R. Cooper, K. Mukai, and J. Perry, editors, *Situation Theory and its Applications*, volume 1 of *CSLI Lecture Note Series*, pages 33–78. CSLI, 1990.
2. P.D. Bruza. *Stratified Information Disclosure: A Synthesis between Information Retrieval and Hypermedia.* PhD thesis, University of Nijmegen, 1993.
3. P.D. Bruza and L.C. van der Gaag. Efficient Context-Sensitive Plausible Inference for Information Disclosure. In *Proceedings of the Sixteenth ACM SIGIR Conference on Research and Development in Information Retrieval*, pages 12–21, 1993.
4. P.D. Bruza and L.C. van der Gaag. Index Expression Belief Networks for Information Disclosure. *International Journal of Expert Systems*, 1994. (To appear).
5. J.P. Callan and W. Bruce Croft. An Evaluation of Query Processing Strategies using the TIPSTER collection. In *Proceedings of the Sixteenth ACM SIGIR Conference on Research and Development in Information Retrieval*, pages 347–355, 1993.
6. Y. Chiaramella and J. Nie. A Retrieval Model based on an Extended Modal Logic and its Application to the RIME Experimental Approach. In *Proceedings of the 13th International ACM SIGIR Conference on Research and Development in Information Retrieval*, pages 25–43, 1990.
7. Y. Chiarmarella and J.P. Chevallet. About Retrieval Models and Logic. *The Computer Journal*, 35(3):233–242, 1992.
8. W.S. Cooper. A Definition of Relevance for Information Retrieval. *Information Storage and Retrieval*, 7:19–37, 1971.
9. J. Farradane. Relational Indexing Part I. *Journal of Information Science*, 1(5):267–276, 1980.
10. S. Krauss, D. Lehmann, and M. Magidor. Nonmonotonic Reasoning, Preferential Models and Cumulative Logics. *Artificial Intelligence*, 44:167–207, 1990.

11. F. Landman. *Towards a Theory of Information.* Foris, 1986.

12. M. Meghini, F. Sebastiani, U. Straccia, and C. Thanos. A Model of information Retrieval based on Terminological Logic. In *Proceedings of the Sixteenth ACM SIGIR Conference on Research and Development in Information Retrieval*, pages 298–307, 1993.

13. J. Nie. An Outline of a General Model for Information Retrieval Systems. In *Proceedings of the Ninth ACM SIGIR Conference on Research and Development in Information Retrieval*, pages 495–506, 1986.

14. C.J. van Rijsbergen. A New Theoretical Framework for Information Retrieval. In *Proceedings of the Ninth International ACM SIGIR Conference on Research and Development in Information Retrieval*, pages 194–200, 1986.

15. C.J. van Rijsbergen. A non-classical logic for information retrieval. *The Computer Journal*, 29(6):481–485, 1986.

16. G. Salton, J. Allan, and C. Buckley. Approaches to Passage Retrieval in Full Text Information Systems. In *Proceedings of the Sixteenth ACM SIGIR Conference on Research and Development in Information Retrieval*, pages 49–58, 1993.

A Probabilistic Terminological Logic for Modelling Information Retrieval*

Fabrizio Sebastiani†

Istituto di Elaborazione dell'Informazione
Consiglio Nazionale delle Ricerche
Via S. Maria, 46 - 56126 Pisa (Italy)
E-mail: fabrizio@iei.pi.cnr.it

Abstract

Some researchers have recently argued that the task of Information Retrieval (IR) may successfully be described by means of mathematical logic; accordingly, the relevance of a given document to a given information need should be assessed by checking the validity of the logical formula $d \rightarrow n$, where d is the representation of the document, n is the representation of the information need and "$\rightarrow$" is the conditional connective of the logic in question. In a recent paper we have proposed *Terminological Logics* (TLs) as suitable logics for modelling IR within the paradigm described above. This proposal, however, while making a step towards adequately modelling IR in a logical way, does not account for the fact that the relevance of a document to an information need can only be assessed up to a limited degree of certainty. In this work, we try to overcome this limitation by introducing a model of IR based on a *Probabilistic* TL, i.e. a logic allowing the expression of real-valued terms representing probability values and possibly involving expressions of a TL. Two different types of probabilistic information, i.e. *statistical information* and *information about degrees of belief*, can be accounted for in this logic. The paper presents a formal syntax and a denotational (possible-worlds) semantics for this logic, and discusses, by means of a number of examples, its adequacy as a formal tool for describing IR.

1 Introduction

In recent years, researchers in Information Retrieval (IR) have devoted an increasing amount of work to the search for *models* of IR, i.e. for theoretical descriptions of the IR process that could serve both as specifications for building running systems, and as theoretical tools for abstractly investigating the relative efficiency of systems built along their guidelines.

The attention of researchers seems lately to have concentrated on the so-called *Logical Model*, first introduced by van Rijsbergen [11]. According to the Logical Model, IR may be seen as the task of retrieving, in response to an information need on the part of the user, all the documents that belong to a given document base and that make the formula $d \rightarrow n$ valid (according to the notion of validity of the chosen logic $\mathcal{L}$), where d and n are the representations of the document and of the information need in the language of $\mathcal{L}$, and "$\rightarrow$" is the "conditional" connective of $\mathcal{L}$.

In fact, the Logical Model does not go as far as specifying *which* logic has to be chosen for modelling IR. As a consequence, the key problem of this research paradigm is the selection of an adequate logic for this task; a number of proposals have thus recently appeared that, with varying degrees of success, attempt to instantiate the Logical Model by means of an appropriate logic.

In a recent paper [9], we have argued that a family of logics suitable (at least, at a first approximation) for modelling relevance of documents to information needs along the guidelines of the Logical Model is that of *Terminological Logics* (TLs); we have gone further to propose one such logic (which we have dubbed MIRTL) that we deemed particularly suited to IR purposes.

However, TLs do not deal with *uncertain information* and *statistical information*. Because of this, our model does not make provisions for the fact that the system is not normally able to assess the relevance of a document to an information need with certainty. Actually, van Rijsbergen stresses that, given that the system cannot reasonably expect to determine relevance "objectively", we should think in terms of the the *probability* that the system attributes to d being relevant to n. In the logical model, IR then

*This work has been carried out in the framework of project FERMI 8134 - "Formalization and Experimentation in the Retrieval of Multimedia Information", funded by the European Community under the ESPRIT Basic Research scheme.

†Current address: Department of Computing Science, University of Glasgow, G12 8QQ Glasgow, United Kingdom. E-mail: fabrizio@dcs.glasgow.ac.uk

becomes the task of computing, for each document d, the real number r such that $P(d \to n) = r$ is valid, and ranking documents in terms of the associated r.

In this paper, we attempt to solve this problem by extending TLs in a *probabilistic* way. Two different types of probabilistic information will be supported in our framework: probabilistic information as *statistical information*, and probabilistic information as *information on the degree of belief* that the system has in other information. Quite obviously, our framework will also allow the combination of these two types of probabilistic information, i.e. it will allow the representation of the degree of belief that the system has in some piece of statistical information.

One interesting result of this approach is that the resulting logic allows the expression of conditional probabilities involving expressions of a TL; it will then be possible, as advocated by van Rijsbergen, to model the probability of relevance of a document to an information need in terms of a conditional probability. But the interesting facet of this is that this will be possible while staying within the confines of classical logic[1], thus relying on a semantic apparatus that is more intuitive and less controversial than that of the conditional logic advocated by van Rijsbergen.

The paper is structured as follows. In order to make it reasonably self-contained, in Section 2 we give a brief introduction to TLs and to the role they play in the model introduced in [9]. In Section 3 we argue that, for IR purposes, it would be useful to endow TLs with primitives for expressing both statistical information and information about degrees of belief. In Section 4 we go on to specify in full formal detail how both types of probability can actually be embedded in TLs; we do this by specifying a formal syntax and a denotational semantics for a language that allows the expression of real-valued terms representing probability values and possibly involving expressions of a TL. We will call the resulting logics *Probabilistic Terminological Logics* (PTLs); we will also see one example of them, i.e. a probabilistic version of MIRTL, that we will call $\mathcal{P}$-MIRTL. Section 5 concludes.

2 An introduction to Terminological Logics and their use in IR modelling

The basic claim of our previous paper [9] is that Terminological Logics:

1. provide a representation language rich enough to accommodate, in an intuitive "object-oriented" syntax, complex descriptions of documents. This language is rich enough to account for the *multifaceted nature* of documents, i.e. for the fact that documents have a number of "orthogonal" properties (such as content, structure, graphical characteristics, etc.) that users might want to use in referring to them within queries;
2. can accommodate, *in the same representation language, and with the same intuitive "object-oriented" syntax*, descriptions of user information needs complex enough to address the above mentioned multifaceted nature of documents;
3. can accommodate, *in the same representation language, and with the same intuitive "object-oriented" syntax*, the expression of "lexical" information, i.e. the kind of information that IR systems usually store in thesauri;
4. provide for an interesting, semantically clean, and natural way of thinking of the relevance of a document to an information need in terms of the "$d \to n$ view" put forth by van Rijsbergen.

The primary syntactic expressions of TLs are *terms*. In TLs a term is an expression that denotes either an individual, or a unary or binary relation on the domain of discourse. Terms denoting individuals are called *individual constants* (hereafter indicated by metavariables i, i_1, i_2, ...), while terms denoting unary relations are called *concepts* (indicated by metavariables C, C_1, C_2, ...) and terms denoting binary relations are called *roles* (indicated by metavariables R, R_1, R_2, ...). In the same manner as complex sentences of classical sentential logics are formed by the recursive application of connectives to sentential letters, complex terms of TLs are formed by the recursive application of *term-forming operators* to individual constants, unary predicate symbols (indicated by metavariables M, M_1, M_2, ...) and binary predicate symbols (indicated by metavariables D, D_1, D_2, ...). Each TL has its own set of operators; the one included in MIRTL are detailed in Footnote 2.

In the model of IR developed in [9], a document is represented by an individual constant, while a class of documents is represented by a concept. For example, the individual constant `paper666` might represent a particular document contained in the document base under consideration. Given the unary predicate symbols `paper` and `tl`, the binary predicate symbols `author`, `appears-in`, `affiliation` and `deals-with`, and the individual constants `SIGIR93` and `IEI-CNR`, the expression

```
(and paper
     (func appears-in (sing SIGIR93))
```

[1] TLs may in fact be regarded as fragments of first-order logic.

    (all author (func affiliation (sing IEI-CNR)))
    (c-some deals-with tl))

is a concept that (under the obvious interpretation for predicate symbols and individual constants, and under the interpretation of term-forming operators detailed in [9]) denotes the class of all those papers that appear in the SIGIR93 proceedings, all of whose authors are affiliated with IEI-CNR, and that deal with TLs[2]. Note that, in describing this class of documents, we have freely interspersed "contextual" information about these documents (i.e. their authors, the affiliation of these authors, the volume in which the papers appear) and information about their "semantic content" (i.e. what these papers deal with); quite obviously, different types of information have the same semantic importance, as they are conveyed in the same, uniform language.

Terminological Logics also allow for *instance assertions* (or simply *assertions* – indicated by metavariables γ, γ_1, γ_2, ...), by means of which one can state that a given individual constant is an instance of a given concept (or that a pair of individual constants is an instance of a given role). In the model of IR developed in [9], an assertion is used to represent the membership of a document with a class of documents, and hence to *describe* the document itself; for instance, the assertion

(and paper
    (func appears-in (sing SIGIR93))
    (all author (func affiliation (sing IEI-CNR)))
    (c-some deals-with tl)) [paper666]

states that **paper666** is a paper that appears in the SIGIR93 proceedings, all of whose authors are affiliated with IEI-CNR, and that deals with TLs. The assertion mechanism also allows to represent the fact that a document may itself be a part of a larger document, as in the following example:

(and conference-proceedings
    (all (inv appears-in) (c-some deals-with (sing IR)))) [SIGIR93]

This assertion states that **SIGIR93** is a volume containing the proceedings of a conference, and that all of the papers appearing therein have information retrieval as their common topic. Note, incidentally, that this states something about **paper666** too, because in the previous assertion it had been stated that **paper666** appears in **SIGIR93**; about **paper666** we now also know that it deals with information retrieval.

TLs also allow stating (by means of *axioms* – indicated by metavariables δ, δ_1, δ_2, ...)) that either a relation of "conceptual containment" ($\dot{<}$) or of "conceptual equivalence" ($\doteq$) holds between two terms. In the model of IR developed in [9], axioms are used to make lexical, "thesaural" knowledge available to the reasoning mechanism in a transparent way. For example, the expression

tl $\doteq$ (and logic
        (func syntax term-oriented-syntax)
        (func semantics extensional-semantics))

defines TLs to be logics with a term-oriented syntax and an extensional semantics.

It is now easy to see how issues 1÷3 are addressed within the model we have proposed: individual documents are represented by individual constants, and are described by stating, by means of assertions, their membership with classes of documents, which, in turn, are represented by means of concepts. Also information needs, given that they can be viewed as identifying sets of documents (i.e. the set of documents that the user states to correspond to his/her information need), are represented by concepts.

---

[2] For reasons of space we will not give the formal semantics of the term-forming operators of MIRTL here; the interested reader is referred either to [9] or to the full paper [10]. The *informal* meaning of these operators is the following:

- (top) and (bottom) denote the set of all individuals of the domain of discourse and the empty set, respectively;
- (a-not M) denotes the set of all individuals of the domain that are not denoted by M;
- (sing i) denotes the set containing only the individual denoted by i; this construct (its name standing for "singleton") is included in order to be able to have individual constants as sub-components of concepts;
- (and C_1 C_2 ... C_n) denotes the set of those individuals that are denoted by C_1 and, at the same time, by C_2 and ... C_n;
- (all R C) denotes the set of those individuals whose R's are all C's; for instance, (all author italian) denotes the set of individuals whose authors are all italians;
- (c-some R C) denotes the set of those individuals having at least one R that is a C; for instance, (c-some author italian) denotes the set of individuals that have at least one author who is an italian;
- (atleast n R) (resp. (atmost n R)) denotes the set of those individuals having at least (resp. at most) n R's;
- (inv R) denotes the set containing the inverses of those pairs that are denoted by R; for instance, (inv husband) will be, under the obvious interpretation, equal to the role wife.

We will also use the following shorthands:

- (exactly n R) will be used in place of (and (atleast n R) (atmost n R));
- (func R C) will be used in place of (and (all R C) (exactly 1 R)).

The only issue we have not yet hinted to is how to accommodate the matching function between queries and documents. In the model described in [9] this was done via the notion of ***subsumption*** (i.e. "hierarchical domination") between terms. For better compatibility with what is to come in the rest of this paper, we can restate the result in terms of the notion of *validity*, familiar from classical logic: the terminological model sees IR as the task of retrieving, as a response to a query C, all and only those documents i such that $C[i]$ is valid in Ω, i.e. such that the denotation of i belongs to the denotation of C in all interpretations satisfying the ***knowledge base*** Ω, i.e. the set of assertions describing documents and their membership with document classes and axioms describing thesaural knowledge. In the case of TLs, then, the "instance assertion" operator "[ ]" plays the role of van Rijsbergen's "$\rightarrow$" conditional connective.

3 The need for probabilities

In the previous section we have described how van Rijsbergen's "$d \rightarrow n$" model can be instantiated in the case of TLs. It now remains to be seen how we can extend this model in order to account for van Rijsbergen's recommendation that the logical model of IR should hinge on the computation of the *probability* that $d \rightarrow n$. In order to tackle this problem in our model, we should endow our representation language with the possibility of attributing probabilities to the expressions that are to describe documents, lexical knowledge and queries, and upon which the computation is to be based.

There are at least two different senses in which probabilities are used in IR. One is concerned with the *degrees of belief* (or *degrees of confidence*) that the system (or the indexer) "subjectively" has in some facts, such as the fact that a given document might be relevant to a given information need on the part of the user. The second is concerned with "objective" *statistical* information that the system (or indexer) has, and that is brought to bear in the decision process.

3.1 Information about degrees of belief

The first issue to take into consideration is the possiblity of attributing a probability to an assertion. For instance, the indexer (whether human or machine) might judge that the likelihood that **paper666** would be deemed relevant by a user formulating his/her information need by means of the query

(**and paper** (**c-some deals-with tl**))

is greater than or equal to 0.8. In doing this, the indexer is expressing his/her *degree of belief* in the relevance of the document to the query. Accordingly, the representation language of our logic will allow the expression of formulae such as

w((**and paper** (**c-some deals-with tl**)) [**paper666**]) ≥ 0.8

and, in general, of formulae of type $(w(\gamma)\ relop\ t)$, where γ is an assertion, t is an expression which evaluates to a real number, and *relop* is one of the relational operators "$=$", "$\neq$", "$\leq$", "$\geq$", "$<$" and "$>$".

Suppose now we want to express the fact that, if we believed that **paper666** is a document that deals with logics, our degree of belief in the fact that **paper666** deals with TLs would be greater or equal than 0.8. This is actually a *conditional probability* notion. But once we have the possibility of representing the degree of belief in an assertion, this is easily expressible, as what this actually means is

```
w(and document                        ≥ 0.8 ·   w(and document
      (c-some deals-with tl)                          (c-some deals-with logic))
      (c-some deals-with logic))
```

In keeping with the usual notation for conditional probabilities, we will abbreviate the latter formula as

$w_{(x)}$((**c-some deals-with tl**) | (**and document** (**c-some deals-with logic**))) ≥ 0.8

In semantic terms, along with [4], we will model degrees of belief by relying on a "possible worlds semantics" (PWS) [7], i.e. by viewing the different states of affairs (or "worlds", in PWS jargon) that the system considers in principle possible, as grouped into structures. We will postulate the existence of a probability distribution on the set of worlds belonging to a given structure; in a given world, the formula $w(\gamma)$ *relop* t will be true just in case the probability of the set of worlds belonging to the same structure and in which γ is true "relop's" the value of t at that world. Hence, the formula in the above example will be true at world x just in case the probabilities of the worlds which are possible relative to x (i.e. that belong to the same structure as x), and in which **paper666** is indeed a paper that deals with TLs, sum up to at least 0.8.

It goes without saying that the same mechanism can also be used for representing the degree of belief of the system in an axiom. Our representation language will then allow the expression of formulae such as

w(**tl** $\prec$ (**and logic** (**func syntax term-oriented-syntax**))) ≥ 0.8

It should be noted that, given the possible-worlds interpretation we have given above, this actually means that the degree of belief that the system has in the fact that *all* TLs have a term-oriented syntax is at least 0.8; it does *not* mean, instead, that the system firmly believes that more than 80% of all TLs have a term-oriented syntax! There is a fundamental difference in these two statements, to the extent that they should be seen as encoding *two different kinds of knowledge*: the truth of the latter statement depends on the objective state of the world, but the truth of the former depends instead on the subjective state of a cognitive agent.

Indeed, the possibility to express a sentence of the latter, "statistical" type is of paramount importance in a model of IR, as statistical notions play a central role in IR. In order to do this, however, we have to introduce further semantic mechanisms.

3.2 Statistical information

As we said in the previous section, the possibility of expressing statistical information would prove of paramount importance in our model. For instance, the indexer might want to express the fact that 80% of the documents in the document base under consideration deal with computer science.

In order to do this, however, we have first to introduce the notion of assigning a probability to a concept (or to a role). By "probability of a concept C" (resp. of a role R) here we mean the probability that a randomly picked individual i (resp. pair of individuals $\langle i_1, i_2\rangle$) turns out to be a C (resp. a R). This interpretation is in keeping with the fact that here we want to model a *statistical* notion of probability: we intend to describe either a chance setup, or the statistical information that we might possess as a result of experimentation on this chance setup. The real-valued quantity "the probability that a randomly picked individual is a C" (resp. that a pair of randomly picked individuals are a R) will be expressed by the probability term $w_{\langle x\rangle}C$ (resp. by the probability term $w_{\langle x_1,x_2\rangle}R$).

Suppose now we want to express the fact that 80% of the documents in the document base under consideration deal with computer science. What this actually means is that the probability that an individual which has been randomly picked out of the set of documents is about computer science is 0.8. This is, again, a conditional probability notion, which is easily expressible, as it may be written as

$w_{\langle x\rangle}$(**and document** (**c-some deals-with** (**sing CS**))) $= 0.8 \cdot w_{\langle x\rangle}$(**document**)

Similarly to the case of degrees of belief, we will abbreviate the latter formula as

$w_{\langle x\rangle}$((**c-some deals-with** (**sing CS**)) | **document**) $= 0.8$

In semantic terms, we will have to take a radically different approach from the one based on "possible worlds" of the previous section. Here we do not want to model the system's uncertainty about the truth value of a (non-probabilistic) proposition; rather, we want to model the system's certainty about the truth value of a probabilistic proposition! What we need here is to "stay in a fixed world", and postulate a probability distribution on the domain of discourse of that world: the probability of a concept will then be the sum of the probabilities of the elements in the domain that belong to the denotation of that concept. If the probability distribution is *uniform*, this corresponds to checking the *relative cardinality* of the concept, i.e. the percentage of individuals of the domain that belong to the denotation of that concept [1]. For instance, the probability of the concept (**c-some deals-with** (**sing CS**)) will be the sum of the probabilities of those individuals that belong to its denotation, i.e. that deal with computer science.

4 A Probabilistic Terminological Logic

In the previous section we have informally argued how the introduction of probabilities into our "terminological model" would allow the expression of a number of notions interesting to IR. In this section we proceed to specify in full detail the syntax and semantics of a particular PTL, that we have dubbed $\mathcal{P}$-MIRTL. Actually, $\mathcal{P}$-MIRTL consists of an extension of the MIRTL logic by means of probabilistic features. It goes without saying that $\mathcal{P}$-MIRTL should serve only as an example of the potentialities of PTLs in modelling IR; other TLs different from MIRTL might be "plugged" in the framework without any added work.

The semantics of our logic will be given in the style of *denotational semantics*. For the logically uninitiated, we should say that denotational semantics (also known as *model-theoretic* or *Tarskian semantics*) is the standard way of formally specifying the meaning of logical languages. Such a specification is accomplished by postulating the existence of a number of "ways the world could be" (*interpretations*), and of systematically specifying in which of these interpretations the expressions of the language are true; "systematically" here means that the semantic specification mirrors the recursive structure of the syntactic BNF specification, with one semantic clause for each syntactic clause. Inference is then defined as the derivation of only those formulae that are true in all the interpretations in which the premises are also true. The specification that follows fully conforms to this systematic pattern.

For reasons of space, we will not specify the semantics of MIRTL in full detail, but will limit our discussion to its probabilistic extension; the interested reader may consult either [9] or the full paper [10].

4.1 Syntax

The syntax of $\mathcal{P}$-MIRTL extension hinges on the notions of "formula" and "probability term". These will be defined in a mutually recursive way.

Definition 1 *A* probability term *is either a rational constant* z*, or is an expression of the form* $w_{\langle x\rangle}C$*, or of the form* $w_{\langle x_1,x_2\rangle}R$*, or of the form* $w(\phi)$ *(with* ϕ *a* formula*), or of the form* $(t_1 \; mathop \; t_2)$*, where both* t_1 *and* t_2 *are probability terms and "mathop" is an operator in the set* $MATHOP=\{+,-,\cdot,\div\}$*.*

A formula *is either an axiom* δ*, or an assertion* γ*, or an expression of the form* $(t_1 \; relop \; t_2)$*, where both* t_1 *and* t_2 *are probability terms and "relop" is an operator in the set* $RELOP=\{=,\neq,\geq,\leq,<,>\}$*.*

We will use metavariables $\phi, \phi_1, \phi_2, \ldots$ ranging on formulae and metavariables $t, t_1, t_2, \ldots$ ranging on probability terms. As hinted in Section 3, we will use the notation $w_{\langle x\rangle}(C_1|C_2) \; relop \; t$ as shorthand for the expression $w_{\langle x\rangle}(\textbf{and} \; C_1 \; C_2) \; relop \; (t \cdot w_{\langle x\rangle}C_2)$, and the notation $w(C_1[i]|C_2[i]) \; relop \; t$ as shorthand for the expression $w(\textbf{and} \; C_1[i] \; C_2[i]) \; relop \; (t \cdot w(C_2[i]))$.

Note that our language is indeed much more powerful than the examples of Section 3 show[3]. For instance, in formulae of type $(t_1 \; relop \; t_2)$, term t_2 is not restricted to be a numeric expression; it is therefore possible to compare, by means of a relational operator, two "complex" probability terms, as in

```
w⟨x⟩(and document                    w⟨x⟩(and document
        (c-some deals-with      <            (c-some deals-with
                (sing CS)))                          (sing Mathematics)))
```

Also, it is possible to "nest" probability operators, e.g. to express how strongly the system believes in some proposition of a statistical nature. For example, it is possible to write two formulae like

$$w(w_{\langle x\rangle}(\texttt{multimedia-document} \mid \texttt{document}) \geq 0.7) = 0.1$$

$$w(w_{\langle x\rangle}(\texttt{multimedia-document} \mid \texttt{document}) \geq 0.2) = 0.8$$

whose combined effect is to assert that the system is not inclined to believe (i.e. its degree of belief is 0.1) that more than 70% of the documents in the collection are multimedia documents, but is definitely more inclined to accept (i.e. its degree of belief is 0.8) that this percentage might only be above 20%.

4.2 Semantics

Now that we have completely detailed the syntax of the probabilistic features of $\mathcal{P}$-MIRTL, we may switch to discussing its semantics (a semantics that will follow the guidelines of Halpern's $\mathcal{L}_3$ logic [4]). As previously hinted, a denotational semantics for a logical language is obtained by postulating the existence of a number of "ways the world could be"; these are usually called *interpretations*. In our case, these will exactly be the "interpretations" of MIRTL as defined and characterised in Definitions 1÷5 of [9]. Such interpretations consist of mappings of individual constants into individuals of the domain, and of predicate symbols into relations on the domain, that are "well-behaved" with respect to the intuitive meaning of the operators of the language (i.e. the term-forming operators, the assertion operator "[ ]" and the axiom operators "$\dot{<}$" and "$\doteq$".).

In order to give semantics to the probabilistic features of $\mathcal{P}$-MIRTL, we will adopt a version of "possible world semantics" (PWS); as in all versions of PWS, we will see the set of interpretations as partitioned into structures, that we will call *PTL structures*[4]. A PTL structure is a 4-uple $M = \{\mathcal{D}, I, \nu_{dom}, \nu_{int}\}$, where $\mathcal{D}$ is a nonempty set of individuals, I is a set of MIRTL interpretations on $\mathcal{D}$, ν_{dom} is a discrete probability distribution on the domain $\mathcal{D}$, and ν_{int} is a discrete probability distribution on the set I of interpretations.

[3] In the full paper [10] we also consider formulae of type $w_{\langle x_1,x_2\rangle}R$ where either x_1 or x_2 may be an individual constant. This allows the expression of probability terms such as $w_{\langle x,\text{SIGIR93}\rangle}$(appears-in), which expresses the "probability that a randomly picked x appears in the SIGIR93 proceedings".

[4] In most approaches based on PWS, interpretations are called "possible worlds"; we avoid using this terminology here, both because it has often given rise to misunderstandings about the meaning of "possible", and because we want to highlight the relationship of containment between the semantics of MIRTL and the semantics of $\mathcal{P}$-MIRTL. It is worthwhile to notice that, in the same way that possible worlds for e.g. sentential modal logic are truth value assignments (to the formulae of sentential logic) that comply with the intuitive meaning of the connectives of sentential logic, interpretations are assignments of "extensions" (to concepts, roles and individual constants) that comply with the intuitive meaning of the operators of MIRTL. It is thus clear that "classical" (sentential) possible worlds stand to sentential logic as our interpretations stand to MIRTL.

The notion of *extension* of a probabilistic term t in an interpretation $\mathcal{I}$ of M, written $[t]_{(M,\mathcal{I})}$, and the notion of *truth* of a formula ϕ in an interpretation $\mathcal{I}$ of M, written $(M,\mathcal{I}) \models \phi$, are defined, in a mutually recursive way (this is obvious, given that the syntax of probabilistic terms and formulae is also mutually recursively defined), by means of the following clauses:

1. $[z]_{(M,\mathcal{I})} = \mathbf{z}$
2. $[w_{(x)}C]_{(M,\mathcal{I})} = \sum_{d \in \mathcal{I}(C)} \nu_{dom}(d)$
3. $[w_{(x_1,x_2)}R]_{(M,\mathcal{I})} = \sum_{(d_1,d_2) \in \mathcal{I}(R)} \nu_{dom}(d_1) \cdot \nu_{dom}(d_2)$
4. $[w(\phi)]_{(M,\mathcal{I})} = \sum_{\mathcal{J} \in I \,:\, (M,\mathcal{J}) \models \phi} \nu_{int}(\mathcal{J})$
5. $[t_1 \; mathop \; t_2]_{(M,\mathcal{I})} = [t_1]_{(M,\mathcal{I})} \; \mathbf{mathop} \; [t_2]_{(M,\mathcal{I})}$
6. $(M,\mathcal{I}) \models \delta$ iff $\mathcal{I}$ satisfies δ
7. $(M,\mathcal{I}) \models \gamma$ iff $\mathcal{I}$ satisfies γ
8. $(M,\mathcal{I}) \models t_1 \; relop \; t_2$ iff $[t_1]_{(M,\mathcal{I})} \; \mathbf{relop} \; [t_2]_{(M,\mathcal{I})}$

We will now comment on the meaning of each of these clauses and then give a comprehensive example of their use. Clause 1 simply states that the extension of a rational constant is always (i.e. in any interpretation $\mathcal{I}$ of any PTL structure M) the rational number it obviously represents (e.g. the constants 0.25, $\frac{1}{4}$ and $\frac{4}{16}$ all represent the number **0.25**). Analogously, Clause 5 states that the extension of a term $(t_1 \; mathop \; t_2)$ is always obtained by the application of the real-valued operation **mathop** which the symbol "*mathop*" obviously represents (e.g. the "+" symbol representing addition), to the extensions of the two terms involved; similar considerations apply to Clause 8.

Probabilities come in with Clause 2: in order to compute the extension, at a given interpretation $\mathcal{I}$ of M, of the probability that a randomly picked x be a C, we first check what individuals belong to the interpretation of C under $\mathcal{I}$, and then sum up the probabilities that the distribution ν_{dom} attributes to them. The case of Clause 3 is completely analogous, the only difference being that pairs of individuals (and, consequently, the product of their probabilities) have to be considered instead of single individuals.

Things are quite different with Clause 4; this clause aims to specify the semantics of formulae involving the system's degrees of belief, so a reference must be made to the interpretations that the system "believes in principle possible" and to their respective probabilities. In order to compute the system's degree of belief in a formula, we first check what are the interpretations in which that formula is true, and then sum up the probabilities that the distribution ν_{int} attributes to them[5].

Finally, things are quite simple for Clauses 6 and 7; MIRTL assertions and axioms are true in an interpretation $\mathcal{I}$ just if they are satisfied by $\mathcal{I}$ in the sense of Definitions 2 and 3 of [9].

Let us now work out a simple example in order to see how all this works.

Example 1 *Suppose we have a PTL structure $\mathcal{M} = \{\mathcal{D}, I, \nu_{dom}, \nu_{int}\}$, where:*

- *$\mathcal{D}$ is the set containing the three individuals a, b and c;*
- *I is the set consisting of the two interpretations $\mathcal{I}_1$ and $\mathcal{I}_2$, which, given the two unary predicate symbols* d *and* md *(which we might take to stand for "document" and "multimedia document", respectively), are such that $\mathcal{I}_1(\mathtt{d}) = \{a,b\}$, $\mathcal{I}_1(\mathtt{md}) = \{a,b\}$, $\mathcal{I}_2(\mathtt{d}) = \{a,b,c\}$ and $\mathcal{I}_2(\mathtt{md}) = \{a\}$;*
- *ν_{dom} is a discrete probability distribution on $\mathcal{D}$ such that $\nu_{dom}(a) = 0.1$, $\nu_{dom}(b) = 0.3$ and $\nu_{dom}(c) = 0.6$;*
- *ν_{int} is a discrete probability distribution on I such that $\nu_{int}(\mathcal{I}_1) = 0.65$ and $\nu_{int}(\mathcal{I}_2) = 0.35$.*

Suppose we want to know what is the extension of the term

$w(w_{(x)}(\mathtt{md}|\mathtt{d}) \geq 0.8)$

(i.e. what is the system's degree of belief in the fact that 80% of the documents in the collection are multimedia) in interpretation $\mathcal{I}_1$. This term is shorthand for the term

[5] Readers familiar with PWS for modal logic might have noticed that, unlike what normally happens for formulae whose interpretation depends on a multiplicity of "possible worlds", there is no "accessibility relation" involved in the computation of degrees of belief. This is not inconsistent with the principles underlying PWS, as it is well-known (see e.g. [5, pages 334–335]) that using the set of all worlds belonging to a modal structure is equivalent to using only the set of worlds that are "accessible" through an equivalence relation. $\mathcal{P}$-MIRTL is then conceptually similar to the S5 modal logic; analogously to what happens in S5, terms representing degrees of belief have the same extension in all interpretations belonging to the same PTL structure.

$$w(w_{(x)}(\textbf{and md d}) \geq 0.8 \cdot w_{(x)}(\mathtt{d}))$$

According to Definition 1 of [9], $\mathcal{I}_1((\textbf{and md d})) = \{a,b\}$ *and* $\mathcal{I}_2((\textbf{and md d})) = \{a\}$*. It follows that* $w_{(x)}(\textbf{and md d})$ *evaluates to* $\nu_{dom}(a) + \nu_{dom}(b) = 0.4$ *in* $\mathcal{I}_1$*, and to* $\nu_{dom}(a) = 0.1$ *in* $\mathcal{I}_2$*. Given that* $w_{(x)}(\mathtt{d})$ *obviously evaluates to* $\nu_{dom}(a) + \nu_{dom}(b) = 0.4$ *in* $\mathcal{I}_1$*, and to* $\nu_{dom}(a) + \nu_{dom}(b) + \nu_{dom}(c) = 1$ *in* $\mathcal{I}_2$*, the formula*

$$w_{(x)}(\textbf{and md d}) \geq 0.8 \cdot w_{(x)}(\mathtt{d})$$

is true in $\mathcal{I}_1$ *but false in* $\mathcal{I}_2$*. Hence, the extension of the term*

$$w(w_{(x)}(\mathtt{md}|\mathtt{d}) \geq 0.8)$$

in $\mathcal{I}_1$ *is equal to* $\nu_{int}(\mathcal{I}_1) = 0.65$*.*

Notice that this term has the same extension also in interpretation $\mathcal{I}_2$*; as we have already noticed in Footnote 5, terms expressing degrees of belief evaluate to the same value in all interpretations belonging to the same PTL structure.*

Similarly to what happens in all applications of logical reasoning, we are hardly interested in what is the truth value of a given formula, or the extension of a given term, at a *particular interpretation* $\mathcal{I}$; loosely speaking, we cannot know which interpretation is *the* correct one, i.e. the one that corresponds to the "real world", since we always have *partial* (and often *erroneous*) knowledge about the real world (in our case: about the documents in our collection and about what they are about), and much of what is true in the real world is unknown to us. Because of this, we are rather interested in what is the truth value of a given formula, or the extension of a given term, at all those interpretations that are "consistent" with our partial and erroneous knowledge about the world; this corresponds to the logical process of *inferring* those formulae whose truth is a consequence of the truth of the formulae that constitute our knowledge about the world. As in all other logics, in $\mathcal{P}$-MIRTL this is formalised by the notion of *validity in a theory*.

Definition 2 *A* theory *of* $\mathcal{P}$*-*MIRTL *is a set* Φ *of formulae which is closed under logical consequence; i.e.* Φ *is such that, if* $\phi \in \Phi$ *and* ϕ' *is true in all the interpretations in which* ϕ *is true, then also* $\phi' \in \Phi$*.*

Definition 3 *A formula* ϕ *is* valid *in a theory* Φ *of* $\mathcal{P}$*-*MIRTL*, written* $\models_\Phi \phi$*, iff* ϕ *is true in all interpretations* $\mathcal{I}$ *(of all PTL structures* M*) in which all formulae in* Φ *are also true.*

Note that the above observations on partial and erroneous knowledge apply to probability distributions too. By relying on the notion of validity in a theory Φ, we free ourselves from the problem of knowing, in all details, which probability distribution on the domain (resp. on possible worlds) is *the* correct one. This is reasonable, as we could not hope to know the truth value of every (probabilistic) formula expressible in our language: also our *probabilistic* knowledge is partial, and often erroneous too! A set of formulae Φ does not specify a probability distribution in full detail, but has the effect of putting a number of constraints on how probability distributions "consistent" with Φ should be; these constraints identify a whole family of distributions, and the formulae valid in Φ are exactly those formulae that are true in all the interpretations characterised by these distributions.

An interesting side-effect of introducing the notion of probability distribution into the semantics of our logic is that our logic will obey the familiar laws of the probability calculus; this will be true both for formulae representing information about degrees of belief, and for formulae representing statistical information. For example, Bayes' Theorem is valid in our logic, i.e. all formulae of type

$$w_{(x)}(C_1|C_2) \cdot w_{(x)}(C_2) = w_{(x)}(C_2|C_1) \cdot w_{(x)}(C_1)$$

or of type

$$w(C_1[i]|C_2[i]) \cdot w(C_2[i]) = w(C_2[i]|C_1[i]) \cdot w(C_1[i])$$

will be valid in any theory Φ, as can easily be seen by applying our definition of conditional probability.

According to the model of IR that we are proposing in this paper, a document i is then deemed to be relevant to an information need C with probability r, with r a real number, iff the formula $w(C[i]) = r$ is valid in Φ, where Φ is the (consequential closure of) the set of formulae representing the documents in the collection and the lexical, "thesaural" knowledge of the system.

5 Concluding remarks

In this paper we have presented a logical model for information retrieval based on a probabilistic terminological logic. In this model, IR is seen as the task of 1) computing, for a given information need (represented by the concept) C and for each document (represented by an individual constant) i, the real number (represented by the constant) r such that $w(C[i]) = r$ is valid in Φ (i.e. in the theory representing the document base and the lexical, "thesaural" knowledge), and 2) ranking documents in terms of their associated r.

Besides enjoying the numerous properties that accrue from the adoption of a TL (properties that are more fully described in [9]), this model takes advantage of the considerable expressive power provided by our probabilistic extension to the terminological framework. This extension allows the distinct expression of two radically and conceptually different kinds of probabilistic information that feature in the IR task, i.e. *statistical* information, and information about the *degrees of belief* that the IR system being modelled has in other information.

Although statistical information and information about degrees of belief are conceptually different, it is clear that there is a relationship between the two. Our work so far has aimed at providing a framework in which both could be expressed and reasoned upon in a principled, semantically clear way. A further step in this direction should be the investigation of mechanisms for allowing information about degrees of belief to be directly *derivable* from statistical information. For instance, ifthe system has no belief at all (i.e. to no degree) whether a given assertion $C[i]$ is true, but at the same time knows that 80% of all individuals of the domain are C's, it might plausibly decide to believe with a 0.8 degree of confidence that i, a particular individual in the domain, is a C. This approach to the derivation of degrees of belief, well known in actuarial reasoning, is known as *direct inference* (see e.g. [8]). Other approaches exist however, yielding different results, and based on principles as diverse as the *maximum entropy principle* (see e.g. [3]), the *centre of mass principle* or the *maximal independence principle* (see e.g. [2]). Unfortunately, in all of these approaches, degrees of belief are *completely determined* by statistical information, to the extent that two formulae such as $w(C[i]) = r_1$ and $w_{(x)}(C) = r_2$ would jointly imply that $r_1 = r_2$; instead, it is clear that we would like to be able to entertain such beliefs without this implying that $r_1 = r_2$. Investigating mechanisms that allow statistical information to determine degrees of belief *only when these latter are not already determined* is the next research task that this work opens up.

Acknowledgements

I would like to thank Mark Sanderson for reading an earlier draft and providing useful comments.

References

1. F. Bacchus. *Representing and reasoning with probabilistic knowledge.* MIT Press, Cambridge, MA, 1990.
2. F. Bacchus, A. Grove, J. Y. Halpern, and D. Koller. From statistics to beliefs. In *Proceedings of AAAI-92, 10th Conference of the American Association for Artificial Intelligence*, pages 602–608, San Jose, CA, 1992.
3. A. Grove, J. Y. Halpern, and D. Koller. Random worlds and maximum entropy. In *Proceedings of the 7th annual IEEE Symposium in Logic in Computer Science*, pages 22–33, Santa Cruz, CA, 1992.
4. J. Y. Halpern. An analysis of first-order logics of probability. *Artificial Intelligence*, 46:311–350, 1990.
5. J. Y. Halpern and Y. O. Moses. A guide to completeness and complexity for modal logics of knowledge and belief. *Artificial Intelligence*, 54:319–379, 1992.
6. W. L. Harper, R. Stalnaker, and G. Pearce, editors. *Ifs. Conditionals, belief, decision, chance and time.* Reidel, Dordrecht, NL, 1981.
7. S. A. Kripke. Semantical analysis of modal logic. *Zeitschrift für Mathematische Logik und Grundlagen der Mathematik*, 9:67–96, 1963.
8. H. Kyburg. The reference class. *Philosophy of science*, 50:374–397, 1983.
9. C. Meghini, F. Sebastiani, U. Straccia, and C. Thanos. A model of information retrieval based on a terminological logic. In *Proceedings of SIGIR-93, 16th ACM International Conference on Research and Development in Information Retrieval*, pages 298–307, Pittsburgh, PA, 1993.
10. F. Sebastiani. A model of information retrieval based on a probabilistic terminological logic (extended version). Technical report, Istituto di Elaborazione dell'Informazione, Consiglio Nazionale delle Ricerche, Pisa, Italy, 1994. Forthcoming.
11. C. J. van Rijsbergen. A non-classical logic for information retrieval. *The Computer Journal*, 29:481–485, 1986.
12. C. J. van Rijsbergen. Probabilistic retrieval revisited. *The Computer Journal*, 35:291–298, 1992.

Natural Language Processing

Retrieving Terms and their Variants in a Lexicalized Unification-Based Framework

Christian JACQUEMIN
Institut de Recherche en Informatique de Nantes, IUT
3, rue du Maréchal Joffre
F-44041 NANTES Cedex 01, FRANCE

Jean ROYAUTE
Programme de Recherche Indexation, INIST – CNRS
2, allée du Parc de Brabois
F-54514 VANDOEUVRE-lès-NANCY, FRANCE

Abstract

Term extraction is a major concern for information retrieval. Terms are not fixed forms and their variations prevent them from being identified by a match with their initial string or inflection. We show that a local syntactic approach to this problem can give good results for both the quality of identification and parsing time.

A specific tool, *FASTR*, is developed which handles an identification of basic terms and a parser of their variations as well. Terms are described by logic rules automatically generated from terms and their categorial structure. Variations are represented by metarules. The parser efficiently processes large size corpora with big dictionaries and mixes lexical identification with local syntactic analysis. We evaluate the accuracy of results produced by these metarules and improve these results with filtering metarules.

1 A Natural Language Processing Front-End to Automatic Indexing

Complex terms represent important chunks of information in full-text documents and their identification plays a crucial role in information retrieval [1] :

- Words in multiword terms are less ambiguous than in regular syntactic structures. An *artery* can be either a road or a blood vessel while a *Coronary artery* only corresponds to the second meaning.
- The entries of a thesaurus mainly consist of multiword terms. Their detection is an important clue for assigning pointers to or postings for the documents to the thesaurus entries.
- Technical sublanguages use large lexicons of complex terms which refer to precise concepts in their domain. Their specificity makes them good candidates for the representation of the content of a text.

In this study, we focus on the identification of complex terms through natural language processing (NLP) techniques. Unfortunately, such descriptors accept a wide range of variations which have to be accounted for. These variations have three reasons: temporal evolution, language domain and style of writing. Three main categories of variations can be observed: morphology, syntax and semantics. It is reasonable to assume that semantic variation can be efficiently processed by the inference module [2]. Conversely, morphological [3] and syntactic variations are two main issues for descriptor extraction through NLP. In this study, we focus on the second one. We define a local syntactic variation of a lexical entry [4] as one of its occurrences which cannot be identified through the sole considerations of inflection or hyphenation: for example *hepatic veno-occlusive disease* is a variation of *Hepatic disease* in this sense. The lexical variations are also interesting in other fields of computational linguistics and information retrieval such as lexical acquisition. As depicted in Figure 1, the variations may change an exceptional event (the occurrence of a lexical item) into a frequent one (the occurrence of the same item or one of its variants).

The statistical approach to information retrieval shows good performances when compared with NLP techniques as reported by the TREC–2 Program Committee [5]. However, a statistical tool can take advantage of a linguistic preprocessor aimed at retrieving complex terms from documents [6]. The statistical extraction of complex lexical entries has difficulties in coping with rare but significant occurrences. This is the reason why statistical [7] approaches to lexical acquisition relate occurrences including similar content words. But a precise observation of variation such as the one proposed in this paper is much more accurate than methods only depending on the distance or relying on blind deletion of empty words. For example, *cells from her skin and peripheral blood* can be filtered out as an incorrect variant of *blood cell* through syntactic considerations. In contrast *cells from peripheral blood* is confidently accepted as a correct variant of *blood cell* as will be further explained in 3.1.

Moreover, when identified as a coordination or an insertion, a variation is an opportunity for acquiring a new lexical entry. For example, the coordination *blood and bone marrow cell* which is a variation of *Blood cell* allows for the acquisition of *Bone marrow* and *Bone marrow cell.* Variation also can help with the acquisition of noun phrase interpretation as proposed in [8]. For example, the permutations of *Blood cell* exemplified in Figure 1 mainly introduce two prepositions: *in* and *from.* They denote a semantics of spatial inclusion between both nouns schematized by *cells* INCLUDED-IN *blood* [9] where *cells* is a 'trajector' with respect to the 'landmark' *blood.*

When considering syntactic variation as a specific topic, tools have to be provided to describe and process it efficiently. In this aim, this study presents *FASTR* (a contraction of *FAST* and *PATR* that stands for *FASt Term Recognizer*) a computationally and conceptually tractable front-end to automatic indexing which is composed of a grammar generator and a parser. The generator transforms a list of terms into grammar rules with the help of an on-line dictionary. The rules are used by the parser together with a list of frequent words and a set of metarules to retrieve descriptors and their variants from untagged corpora. The estimations are illustrated through a joint experiment between the natural language laboratory of the *Institut de Recherche en Informatique de Nantes* and the documentation center of *INIST/CNRS.* A list of 80,000 multi-domain terms and two large corpora of scientific abstracts are used for this test: a 100,000-word corpus on metallurgy (METAL) and a 1.5 million-word medical corpus (MEDIC).

The rest of the paper is organized as follows. Part 2 is a presentation of the formalism and the parser. Part 3 is an evaluation of the efficiency of metarules in the extraction of the different kinds of variations.

2 Coordinations	**40 Permutations**	**40 Permutations (continued)**
blood and bone marrow cells	cells (TLCs) from peripheral blood	cell frequency in the peripheral blood
blood and cerebrospinal fluid t cell	cells) (lysed whole blood	cells from blood
	cells) detected in a fetal blood	cells from her skin and peripheral blood
	cell activity of peripheral blood	cells from peripheral blood
14 Insertions	cells among circulating blood	cells from the peripheral blood
blood CD4+, CD8+ cells	cell and blood	cell homogenates of peripheral blood
blood b cell	cells available in the cord blood	cells in blood
blood b cells	cells collected from the peripheral blood	cells in bone marrow and peripheral blood
blood borne cells	cells could be detected in peripheral blood	cells in his peripheral blood
blood contained cells	cells could be enhanced in peripheral blood	cells in paired samples of peripheral blood
blood from a cell	cell count in venous blood	cells in peripheral blood
blood hematopoietic progenitor cells	cells detected in the peripheral blood	cells in the blood
	cells differed between tumour and blood	cells in the peripheral blood
blood leukemic cells	cell infiltration in the retina to blood	cell proliferative responses of peripheral blood
blood monocluclear cells	cells into the peripheral blood	cell saver for intraoperative blood
blood mononuclear cell	cell lines were prepared from peripheral blood	cell strains) and from peripheral blood
blood mononuclear cells	cell nuclear antigen and blood	cell suspensions from the peripheral blood
blood monuclear cells	cells observed in peripheral blood	cells was made in the peripheral blood
blood stem cell	cells on the blood	cells was measured in paired peripheral blood
blood t cells	cell populations were investigated in the blood	cells which are primarily derived from blood

Figure 1. The 56 different variations of *Blood cell* observed in the [MEDIC] corpus.

2 *FASTR*: From Terms to Descriptors

Two convincing arguments can be settled about the application of NLP techniques to automatic indexing. First, [10] compares statistically selected 'phrase discriminators' with syntactically selected ones for information retrieval. Fagan notes the limitations of non-syntactic methods to retrieve some good phrase descriptors such as the ones involving conjunctions. For such phrases, he has to incorporate a syntax-based phrase construction which relates semantically close constructions. Instead of such a hybrid approach, [11] use a selective NLP technique together with a thesaurus and show that it performs as well as human indexing. A second argument is that most of the NLP formalisms are adaptable enough to represent any desirable additional information such as semantic or derivational links between complex lexical entries. Both arguments have led us to the choice of a general unification-based formalism for *FASTR* stemmed from *PATR-II* [12]. *PATR-II* is used to represent various kinds of unification-grammars as well as complex lexical data [13].

2.1 Automatic Tagging of Terminological Data

The *FASTR* application needs a tagged indexing lexicon. We have applied this tagging phase to the *PASCAL* lexicon of *INIST*, but it can be extended to other terminological or indexing lexicons. This automation shortens the linguistic engineering process. We name lexicon tagging the operation which attributes to each word of this lexicon a single syntactic category. The on-line dictionary *DELAF** [14] is used in the process. Tagging is independent of the word context because it is very difficult to detect word ambiguities in the terminological noun phrase. Three principles are retained in the case of multiple ambiguities: (a) if the ambiguity is with an infinitive verb, gerund verb or past-participle verb and any other syntactic category, only the verb category is retained; this choice is justified by our desire to keep the morphological trace with a verb in order to facilitate the integration of more complex morphological properties; (b) if the ambiguity is with the noun and any other categories, it is the noun category that is retained ; (c) residual cases concern ambiguities with adjective/adverb: in this case we give priority to adjectives; (d) the most frequent words like prepositions, conjunctions, pronouns are allocated to the category which is most probable in an indexing lexicon. All the words not recognized by the *DELAF* dictionary receive a Noun category.

2.2 The Formalism: Stemming from *PATR–II*

The formalism of *FASTR* takes from *PATR–II* the decomposition of syntactic rules into a context-free portion and a set of equations. The context-free portion constrains the concatenation of constituents, while the equations constrain the information of the constituents. Rule (3) of Figure 2 describes the term *Concentration effect* which is a noun phrase composed of the concatenation of two nouns. The inflection number describes the affixes which are added to the stem for the different inflections of the lemma described by rules (1) and (2) of Figure 2.

2.3 The Formalism: Additional Features

The description given in 2.2 is a general description of lexical entries by syntactic rules with a flat syntactic structure. In the frequent case where lexical entries are embedded one in another, the formalism of *FASTR* allows to take advantage of a structured representation as outlined for *Lexicalized Tree Adjoining Grammars* [15]. Moreover it can be convenient to gather in a single rule several related terms with common lemmas. This corresponds to the possibility of disjunction in the structure of the rule which is exemplified by rule (4) of Figure 3. This rule represents both lexical entries *Right (pulmonary artery)* and *Left (pulmonary artery)* with a disjunction on the adjective and an embedded term *Pulmonary artery*. The sign → stands for the concatenation of constituents, while the sign = stands for the alternative between several constituents.

```
(1) Word 'concentration':
      <cat> = N
      <inflection> = 1.
(2) Word 'effect':
      <cat> = N
      <inflection> = 1.

(3) Rule N1 → N2 N3:
      <N1 lexicalisation> = 'N3'
      <N1 label> = '025972'
      <N2 lemma> = 'concentration'
      <N2 inflection> = 1
      <N3 lemma> = 'effect'
      <N3 inflection> = 1.
```

Figure 2. Rules representing *Concentration effect*.

```
(4) Rule N1 → (A2 = A3 + A4) (N5 → A6 N7):
      <N1 lexicalisation> = 'N7'
      <N1 label> = '006431'
      <A3 lemma> = 'left'
      <A3 inflection> = 1
      <A4 lemma> = 'right'
      <A4 inflection> = 1
      <A6 lemma> = 'pulmonar'
      <A6 inflection> = 3
      <N7 lemma> = 'arter'
      <N7 inflection> = 3.
```

Figure 3. Rule representing *Left (pulmonary artery)* or *Right (pulmonary artery)*.

* The *DELAF* dictionary is a dictionary of inflected forms of words developed by the LADL laboratory (CNRS - University of Paris 7). The *Programme de Recherche Indexation* laboratory of *INIST* use this dictionary for their R&D application.

The main difference between the formalisms of *FASTR* and *PATR–II* is the availability of metarules in *FASTR* to represent term variations. Metarules in *FASTR* are composed of a left-hand side matching with the initial rule and a right-hand side yielding the transformed rule. As for the rules, a set of equalities can constrain the information in both these context-free portions. Metarule (5) of Figure 4 corresponds to the permutation of the first and the second constituent of a 2-constituent term and the insertion of two words (X means *any lexical category*). When applied to rule (3) of Figure 2, this metarule yields a rule describing the strings *effect* W_1 W_2 *concentration* where W_1 and W_2 are any words. It allows for the extraction of *effect of glucose concentration*. In contrast, metarule (6) of Figure 4 corresponds to permutations where the first inserted word is the preposition *of*.

```
(5) Metarule Perm( X1 → X2 X3 ) = X1 → X3 X4 X5 X2:
      <X1 metaLabel> = 'XX'.

(6) Metarule Perm( X1 → X2 X3 ) = X1 → X3 P4 D5 X6 X2:
      <P4 lemma> = 'of'
      <X1 metaLabel> = 'XX'.
```

Figure 4. Two metarules in *FASTR* used t retrieve variations.

2.4 The Parser: Lexicalization and Optimization

The organization of the application is a classic one for an NLP tool, except for the rule generator which is a specific device. First the grammar (rules of terms and lemmas) is automatically generated from the list of terms and then compiled in the application. This automation avoids errors due to human writing and ensures a very quick updating in case of modification. Then the text is parsed in two steps. A morphological step is needed for segmentation and stemming as *FASTR* is working on raw untagged corpora. The second step is the syntactic parse of the texts using the rules activated during the stemming phase. The rules which fail to be parsed are transformed through metarules and tried again.

An eye must be kept on the optimization of the application. The parser must be scalable to the size of industrial lexical resources and textual data. The first and major improvement consists of a bottom-up filtering of the grammar through lexicalization links as suggested in [15] for top-down parsing of lexicalized grammars. The parsing algorithm can take advantage of this lexicalization by only working on the rules corresponding to the lemmas in the input sentence.

Data access also has to be optimized in order to allow for short access time whatever the size of data. Stop words are memory resident and are accessed through a Hash Code table (approx. 100 words). The single words residing in the disk dictionary are accessed through a B-tree (approx. 30,000 words).

The conceptual and computational devices presented in this section are more detailed in [16]. They ensure a good computational tractability of the application as will be shown in the following section.

2.5 The Parser: Bench Marks

The speed of the parser in *FASTR* strongly depends on the size of the grammar of term rules and weakly depends on the size of the metagrammar. Let us study these different factors separately. First, in Figure 5, the parsing speed is depicted as a function of the logarithm of the number of rules. These results confirm that the speed remains acceptable, even for a large grammar: the speed is 18,300 words per minute with a grammar of 8,000 term rules and 2,900 words per minute with a grammar of 80,000 term rules. Secondly, the speed also depends on the number of metarules. The parser only spends a small proportion of its time on the generation of transformed rules and their application. Therefore the incidence of the number of metarules on the parsing speed is less crucial than the number of rules was (Figure 6).

By exemplifying the parsing speed on different tasks in Figure 7, we illustrate the amount of time spent by the application on the three different processes involved in parsing: the core processing (stemming and rule loading), the parsing of terms (basic rules) and the parsing of term variants (transformed rules). The three tasks illustrated by Figure 7 are (1) the general indexing (extraction of terms and their variants), (2) the indexing restricted to basic terms and (3) the extraction of term variants only.

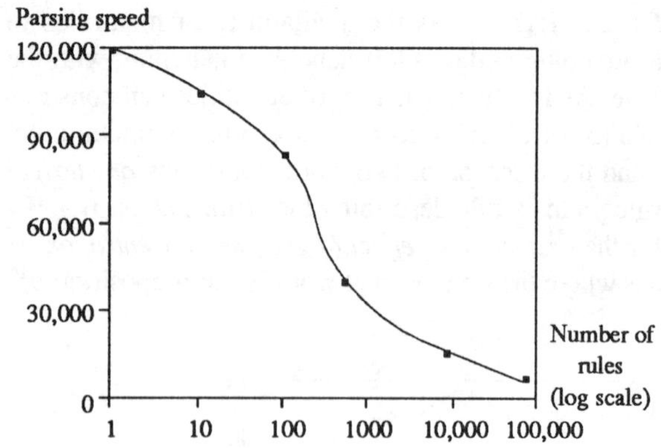

Figure 5. Parsing speed of *FASTR* as a function of the number of rules (with 110 metarules).

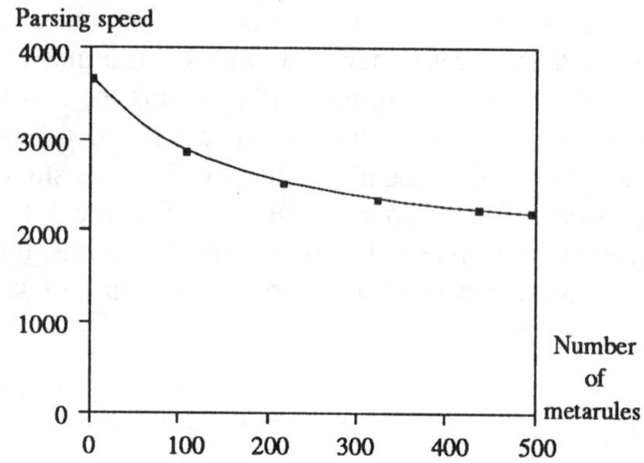

Figure 6. Parsing speed of *FASTR* as a function of the number of metarules (with 80,000 term rules).

Size of the terminological lexicon	80,000 terms	8,000 terms	1 term
Task 1: extraction of terms and variants	2,900 (2,600)	18,300	120,000
Task 2: extraction of terms	3,100 (2,800)	19,800	120,000
Task 3: extraction of variants	4,900 (5,000)	20,500	117,000

Figure 7. The parsing speed of *FASTR* on Sun Sparc-2 Workstation as a function of the tasks achieved by the parser.

The very slight difference between the values of the first and second line of Figure 7 indicates that *FASTR* only spends 10% of its time in extracting variations. The quality improvement induced by this extraction considerably makes up for its computational cost. Therefore, it is worth enhancing the number of metarules because it increases precision and only slightly reduces the parsing speed. The values between parentheses indicated in Figure 7 represent the parsing speed when giving up unification (when working only on the context-free portion of the rules). As this gain is very small, we can assume that an addition of syntactic features will have no incidence on the performances. Such an addition can be used for representing the semantic or derivational links.

In short, the parsing speed depends mainly on the size of the lexical data. The values obtained by testing the application on a workstation show that this kind of hardware is well suited for working with *FASTR* on such large corpora as [MEDIC] of *INIST*.

3 Metarules and Term variants Retrieval: An Evaluation

This part presents more precisely the extraction of term variants in two steps. First a set of paradigmatic metarules is given. The results of the induced indexing of the [MEDIC] corpus is evaluated. Then a set of more filtering metarules is proposed to rule out some of the incorrect variations of the first step. A second evaluation is realized.

The three kinds of variations studied are insertion, permutation and coordination. Elision is intentionally left aside although being an important source of variation** because it cannot be handled properly through metarules only [17]. Elision calls for a handling of the reference between sentences as well as the existence of generic links between terms.

The connection between terms and their variants is described in [4]. The authors use a syntactico-semantic parser to detect compound terms in queries and conflate terms with a similar semantic interpretation. The variations of the terms included in a query are then systematically generated in order to match them with a text database. The generation is restricted to inflections and simple permutations which do not modify the interpretation. This definition is probably too restrictive because it would not account for variations such as *cells from peripheral blood* stemming from *Blood cell*. This approach points out how important and common syntactic variation is but calls for an exhaustive semantic description of single words.

In order to remedy the high human cost of conceptual information retrieval, [6] completes a classic syntactic

** A study of the [METAL] corpus reported in [17] shows that 2.6% of the multi-word term occurrences are elliptic.

analysis by a statistical observation in order to extract head/modifier relations from texts. Reduction to a basic syntactic structure and word stemming account for a wide range of variations similar to the ones detected by *FASTR*. However, it requires a sentence parser which may be difficult to maintain and to modify due to the high number of interdependent rules. When using a partial parser such as *FASTR* or [11], precision is weaker and candidate terms must be filtered accurately. [11] matches candidate terms with controlled terms through substring comparisons. It yields a score of similarity and a degree of confidence which are used to classify and accept new terms. Our approach is close to the one of [11] because we look for syntactic variants of controlled terms. The variants observed in [11] are mainly elisions and embedded terms, we focus rather on permutations, insertions and coordinations.

3.1 Paradigmatic Metarules and Filtering Metarules

Metarules presented in this part are said to be paradigmatic for they do not filter the category of the inserted words, except for the requirement of a conjunction inside a coordination. Therefore the corresponding metarules are given by their context-free portion only without any additional constraints on the constituents. Metarules are grouped into classes corresponding to the rules whose roots have the same number of daughter constituents. For example, metarule (5) of Figure 4 applies to terms composed of two constituents such as *Gene expression* or *Low (melting point)*. Although being slightly noisy, these metarules which do not require any specific tuning work very well on the [MEDIC] corpus. The following is an example of metarules corresponding to 3-constituent terms. Each metarule is followed by an example of variation and the basic term :

Metarule **Coor**(X1 → X2 X3 X4) = X1 → X2 <u>C5 X6</u> X3 X4:.
inflammatory <u>and erosive</u> joint disease [Inflammatory joint disease]

Metarule **Ins**(X1 → X2 X3 X4) = X1 → X2 <u>X5</u> X3 X4:.
impaired <u>intravenous</u> glucose tolerance [Impaired glucose tolerance]

Metarule **Perm**(X1 → X2 X3 X4) = X1 → X4 <u>X5 X6 X7</u> X2 X3:.
diseases <u>of the central</u> nervous system [Nervous system diseases]

Paradigmatic metarules do not constrain syntactic features of words (category, gender, number). One of the ways of increasing the precision of metarules consists in constraining the syntactic category of these words. For example, we observe that the permutation variation requires a 'pivot' element such as the preposition *of* (*<u>fraction</u>* ***of*** *<u>cells</u>* → *Cell fraction*), but also other prepositions (*<u>cells</u>* ***in*** *unperturbed <u>tumors</u>* → *Tumor cell*) or else a verbal sequence (*<u>cell</u> lines* ***have been*** *<u>isolated</u>* → *Isolated cell*). But the recognition of terms in variant forms, for reasons of robustness, uses words unknown by the terminological lexicon and it is more natural to define metarules which forbid some categories of words than metarules which constrain the syntactical category of words which can be unknown. We have named them negative metarules because they are activated prior to the other metarules. They aim at causing a spurious analysis by giving it a specific label in order to keep track of it during the tuning stage and to ignore it during result developments.

3.1.1 Negative Metarules of Insertion

Insertion marks the presence of one or several words within a term. It is probably the least constrained variation because it is difficult to prevent the presence of one or more words within a term. We define a set of negative metarules as follows:

Metarule **NIns** (X1 → X2 X3) = X1 → X2 (X6 = Pu7 + Pc8 + P9) X10 X3:
<P9 lemma> = 'of'.

This metarule identifies as spurious analysis of the X2 X3 term any sequence of text with an inserted X6 element that is a punctuation mark (Pu7), a subordinating coordination (Pc8) or the preposition *of* (P9). It identifies the following sequence *concentration ; baseline measurement* as spurious analysis of the *Concentration measurement* term. This leads us to reject the sequences with the preposition *of* because they can only be used with permutation variations: *basis of live weight* cannot be linked to the term *Basis weight*. Figures 8 and 9 show the effect of negative metarules to identify relevant terms and reject bad analyses of terms.

Textual sequences	Terms (2, 3, 4 words)
vitamin d deficiency	Vitamin deficiency
arterial blood pressure	Arterial pressure
left common coronary artery	Left coronary artery
polymerase chain amplification reaction	Polymerase chain reaction
premature rupture of the membranes	Premature rupture of membrane
farnsworth munsell 100 hue test	Farnsworth 100 Hue test
granulocyte macrophage colony stimulating factor	Granulocyte colony stimulating factor

Figure 8. Relevant term variants corresponding to insertions (`Metarule` **`Ins`**).

Textual sequences	Spurious analysis of terms
coronal angle , slice	Coronal slice
comparison **of** the measurements	Comparison measurement
concentration **and** gradient	Concentration gradient
concentration ; baseline measurement	Concentration measurement
hips , superolateral bone	Hip bone

Figure 9. Terms rejected through filtering insertion metarules (`Metarule` **`NIns`**).

3.1.2 Negative Metarules of Permutation

Generally speaking, the permutation variations are carried out around the prepositions (*of, in, with, on, from,* etc.) as *fractions of cells [Cell fraction]*, or verbal sequences as *enzyme is a serine [Serine enzyme]*. We give more examples of these in Figure 10.

The most frequent spurious analyses (see Figure 11) are permutations around conjunctions. *Identification or specific* cannot be linked to the term *Specific identification*. Another factor of spurious analyses is due to the presence of punctuation in sequences capable of leading to permutation.

Textual sequences	Terms
Preposition of	
fusion **of** tumorigenic heLa cells	Cell fusion
formation **of** insoluble proteinaceous deposits	Deposit formation
localization **of** the dural defect	Defect localization
Preposition in	
fluctuations **in** mean arterial blood pressure	Pressure fluctuation
cells **in** unperturbed tumors	Tumor cell
cell **into** a metastatic tumor	Tumor cell
cell lines **into** nude mice permits tumor	Tumor cell
Preposition with	
pressure **with** normoxic blood	Blood pressure
cell DNA **with** the ultimate tumor	Tumor cell
spectrometry **with** selected ion	Ion spectrometry
treatment **with** either sterile water	Water treatment
Verbal sequences	
cell line **have been** isolated	Isolated cell
applicator **using** microwaves	Microwave applicator

Textual sequences	Terms
Preposition from	
fractions **from** AML cells	Cell fraction
cells **from** peripheral blood	Blood cell
cultures **from** six different tissues	Tissue culture
fiber loss **from** animal	Animal fiber
Preposition for	
method **for** three dimensional measurement	Measurement method
hospital **for** sick children	Children hospital
factor **for** small cell	Cell factor
center **for** health	Health center
test **for** our hypothesis	Hypothesis test
Preposition at/on/above	
viscosity **at** varying shear	Shear viscosity
transition **at** nucleotide	Nucleotide transition
contrast **on** clinical MR images	Image contrast
units **above** control	Control unit
volume reduction **on** fetal plasma	Plasma volume
Verbal sequences	
enzyme **is** a serine	Serine enzyme
gene **may be** a negative regulator	Regulator gene

Figure 10. Relevant term variants corresponding to permutations (`Metarule` **`Perm`**).

Textual sequences	Spurious analysis of terms
motility in epithelial **and** carcinoma cell	Cell motility
results , **and** 1 was negative	Negative result
regurgitation , TEE identified all 14 mitral	Mitral regurgitation
factors , ie , environmental	Environmental factor
effect of body position on	On effect

Figure 11. Terms rejected through filtering permutation metarules (`Metarule` **`NPerm`**).

For this type of variation, punctuation makes it difficult to identify the term because it establishes borderlines within the sentence. Punctuation is often linked to a coordination. Thus, the sequence *cell, colonic polyps tumor* cannot be linked from a syntactic point of view to *Tumor cell* even though from a semantic point of view, any occurrence of *tumor* makes the term *Tumor cell* valid. Negative metarules reject sequences with presence of punctuation, of subordinating conjunctions and coordinating conjunctions:

```
Metarule NPerm (X1 → X2 X3) = X1 → X3 (X6 = Pu7 + C8 + Pc9) X5 X2:.
```

this metarule identifies the sequence *age and preoperative mental,* where `X6` corresponds to the coordinating conjunction *and,* as a spurious analysis of the term *Mental age*. It also rejects *analysis, our data* as non-linked to the term *Data analysis* since `X6` corresponds to a comma.

A few terms, such as *On effect, On line* have a Preposition–Noun structure. Since the occurrences of *effect* and *line* followed by *on* at a distance of a few words are frequent, we create the following negative metarule:

```
Metarule NPerm (X1 → P2 X3) = X1 → X3 X4 X5 P2:.
```

which identifies *effect of calcium on*, where P2 is a preposition as not being linked to the term *On effect.*

3.1.3 Negative Metarules of Coordination

We distinguish two types of coordination (see Figure 12 the table of relevant coordinations): coordinations that concern the head of a noun phrase, and coordinations that concern the modifier part (to the right of the head–noun). The following sequence: *renal hemodynamics and function* coordinates the two head nouns *hemodynamics* and *function.* In this other sequence: *apical and basolateral membrane*, the coordination concerns the two modifiers *apical* and *basolateral.* We show in Figure 12 that coordinating elements are: comma and conjunctions *and* and *or*. The distinction of these two types of coordination makes it possible to reject all of the sequences with a plural noun in a modifier position, since a modifier noun cannot generally take on a plural form. Subsequently, we reject the following sequence: *cells or fetal cultures* as linked to the term *Cell culture* since the plural noun *cells* and the adjective *fetal* cannot be coordinated elements. The following negative metarule:

```
Metarule NCoor (X1 → X2 X3) = X1 → X2 C4 X5 X3:
         <X2 number> = plural.
```

recognizes the following sequence: *cells or fetal cultures* as not being related to the term *Cell cultures* since the plural noun *cells* and the adjective *fetal* cannot be coordinated elements. In the case of a determination, coordinations in noun phrases require that the noun sequence that follows the conjunction be not preceded by a non-possessive determiner. *Tissue or its cell culture* is a correct variant of the term *Tissue culture*. With the following metarule, we reject the sequence *relaxation and the time* as a possible variation of the term *Relaxation time*:

```
Metarule NCoor (X1 → X2 X3) = X1 → X2 C4 Dd5 X5:.
```

We give in Figure 13 the most frequent examples of bad analyses of coordination variations

Textual sequences	Terms (2, 3, 4 words)
Coordination of heads	
cell growth and differentiation	Cell differentiation
cell differentiation and proliferation	Cell proliferation
hemoglobins s and c	Hemoglobin C
interleukins 1 , 2 , and 3	Interleukin 1
Coordination of modifiers	
apical and basolateral membrane	Apical membrane
duchenne or becker muscular dystrophy	Duchenne muscular dystrophy
middle and posterior cerebral arteries	Middle cerebral artery
somatosensory and brainstem auditory evoked potentials	Somatosensory evoked potential

Figure 12. Relevant term variants corresponding to coordinations (`Metarule Coor`).

Textual sequences	Spurious analysis of terms
Coordination with non-possessive determiners	
production **and the** formation rate	Production rate
relaxation **and the** time	Relaxation time
fluids **and the** synovial fluid	Fluid fluid
Coordination with plural nouns in modifier position	
cells and a higher cloning	Cell cloning
cells and purified fractions	Cell fraction
concentrations and colonic epithelial cell	Concentration cell

Figure 13. Terms rejected through filtering coordination metarules (`Metarule NCoor`).

3.2 Indexing a large medical corpus: an evaluation

Indexing experimentation focused on the [MEDIC] corpus which is a bibliographical medical corpus of more than 9 MB of textual abstracts. We have carried out an initial evaluation over the whole corpus using paradigmatic metarules. Out of 17,304 abstracts, we have identified 31,428 pluriterms without variations, and 10720 with variations. Concerning pluriterms, there is a 34% increase in relation to pluriterms without variations. The distribution of the diverse variations is the following: Permutation (57%), Insertion (37,6%) and Coordination (5,4%). The examination of these results allows us to detect the principal causes of spurious analyses of paradigmatic metarules. We have tested the set of negative metarules defined in 3.1 on a more restrained number of abstracts (1,650). In this subset of the corpus, paradigmatic metarules are the least productive of all the corpus. We only obtain an increase of 25%. After filtering, this figure drops to 20.4%. The new distribution of the variation is as follows: Permutation (47.9%), Insertion (43.1%) and Coordination (9%). Examination of results after filtering shows that all the terms rejected with negative metarules are linguistically justified. However, they do not allow us to reject all the spurious analyses. In the long permuted sequences, results are random because there is no control on the words exterior to the terms. For insertion and coordination variations, negative metarules are very efficient and reject all the spurious analysis.

Finally, with a view to understanding why certain terms are not recognized, we have tried to qualitatively evaluate automatic indexing compared with manual indexing. In this analysis, we distinguish the terms which cannot have an occurrence in a text whose retrieval can result from an inference process in an indexing system [18] (for example generic terms formed with the head noun *disease* such as *Urinary system disease*, *Abdominal disease*, etc.). Out of 100 abstracts taken randomly, we observe 292 terms that are common to both manual and automatic indexing, which represents about 2.9 shared terms in a bibliographic reference. A large number of simple words in automatic indexing are irrelevant. This is due to two types of cases: simple words are more polysemous than pluriterms and many terms are general adjectives (such as *acute*, *low*, *high*, etc.) which modify another term in the indexing record of bibliographical references (such as *acute* which can qualify the term *infarct*). This polysemy is important because the *PASCAL* lexicon is a multidisciplinary indexing lexicon. We identify four types of 'non-analysis' of pluriterms. First, morphological variations: the term *myocardium* is not recognized in presence of the adjective *myocardial*. Secondly, elision variations: in the structure of a term, many head nouns yield little information such as in the *PASCAL* term *Pressure volume ratio* where the noun *ratio* is deleted. Thirdly, we notice that the presence of an acronym in a term (frequent in scientific texts) blocks recognition; for example, in place of the *PASCAL* term *Magnetic Resonance Imaging* we encounter *MR imaging*. The last type of non-analysis is linked to the variation of the head term within a semantic paradigm (the term *Transgenic animal* and the textual sequence *transgenic mouse*). It is possible to include in the definition of the head noun of the rule of this term a list of possible *transgenic animals*.

Conclusion

FASTR is a NLP front-end which links texts to descriptors in an efficient way. The representation of variations by metarules makes this parser more powerful than statistical methods and classical parsers with a pattern-matching algorithm. Analysis speed is a function of the number of terms; this makes it usable in industrial contexts with a large terminological volume. We show how the utilization of paradigmatic metarules makes it possible to obtain an acceptable indexing with variations. We adjoin to these paradigmatic metarules a set of negative metarules which aim at increasing the accuracy of results. We consider filtering results satisfying when all inaccurate analyses are justified linguistically and when linguistic engineering development time is short. The comparison made with human indexing shows which elements must be taken into account for future work.

References

1. Sparck Jones K. Assumptions and Issues in Text-Based Information Retrieval. In: Jacobs PS (ed) Text-Based Intelligent Systems, Lawrence Erlbaum Associates, Hillsdale, 1992.
2. Krovetz R, Croft WB. Word Sense Disambiguation Using Machine-Readable Dictionaries. In: Proceedings, 12th Annual ACM SIGIR Conference on Research and Development in Information Retrieval, 1989, pp 127–136.
3. Krovetz R. Viewing Morphology as an Inference Process. In: Proceedings, 16th Annual International ACM SIGIR Conference on Research and Development in Information Retrieval, 1993, pp 191–203.
4. Sparck Jones K, Tait JI. Automatic Search Term Variant Generation. Journal of Documentation, 40(1), 1984, pp 50–66.
5. Harman D, Buckley C, Dumais S et al. Report on TREC–2 (Text REtrieval Conference). SIGIR Forum, 27(3), 1993, pp 14–18.
6. Strzalkowski T, Vauthey B. Information Retrieval Using Robust Natural Language Processing. In: Proceedings, 30th Annual Meeting of the Association for Computational Linguistics, 1992, pp 104–111.
7. Enguehard C, Malvache P, Trigano P. Indexation de textes: l'apprentissage de concepts. In: Proceedings, 14th International Conference on Computational Linguistics, 1992, pp 1197–1202.
8. Jacquemin C. A Coincidence Detection Network for Spatio-temporal Coding: Application to Nominal Composition. In Proceedings, 13th International Joint Conference on Artificial Intelligence, 1993.
9. Langacker RW. Foundations of Cognitive Grammar. Vol I. Theoretical Prerequisites. Stanford University Press, Stanford, 1987.
10. Fagan JL. Automatic Phrase Indexing for Document Retrieval: An Examination of Syntactic and Non-Syntactic Methods. In: Proceedings, 10th Annual ACM SIGIR Conference on Research and Development in Information Retrieval, 1987, pp 91–101.
11. Evans DA, Ginther-Webster K, Hart M, Lefferts RG, Monarch IA. Automatic Indexing Using Selective NLP and First-Order Thesauri. In: Proceedings, RIAO'91, 1991, pp 624–643.
12. Shieber SN. An Introduction to Unification-Based Approaches to Grammar. CSLI Lecture Notes 4, CLSI, Stanford, 1986.
13. Boguraev B, Briscoe T. Large Lexicons for Natural Language Processing: Utilizing the Grammar Coding System of LDOCE. Computational Linguistics 13(3–4), 1987, pp 203–218.
14. Courtois B. Un système de dictionnaires électronique pour les mots simples du français. Langue Française 87, Larousse, Paris, 1990, pp 11–22.
15. Schabes Y, Joshi AK. Parsing with Lexicalized Tree Adjoining Grammar. In: Tomita M (ed) Current Issues in Parsing Technologies, Kluwer Academic Publisher, Dordrecht, 1990.
16. Jacquemin C. FASTR: A Unification Grammar and a Parser for Terminology Extraction from Large Corpora. In: Proceedings of IA'94, EC2, Paris, 1994. *Forthcoming*.
17. Jacquemin C. Representing and Parsing Terms with Acceptability Controlled Grammar. In: Proceedings, Terminology and Knowledge Engineering 93, Indeks Verlag, Cologne, 1993, pp 235–244.
18. Royauté J, Schmitt L, Olivetan E. Les expériences d'indexation a l'INIST. In: Proceedings, 14th International Conference on Computational Linguistics, 1992, pp 1058–1063.

Word Sense Disambiguation and Information Retrieval

Mark Sanderson
Department of Computing Science,
University of Glasgow,
Glasgow G12 8QQ
United Kingdom
(email: sanderso@dcs.gla.ac.uk)

Abstract

It has often been thought that word sense ambiguity is a cause of poor performance in Information Retrieval (IR) systems. The belief is that if ambiguous words can be correctly disambiguated, IR performance will increase. However, recent research into the application of a word sense disambiguator to an IR system failed to show any performance increase. From these results it has become clear that more basic research is needed to investigate the relationship between sense ambiguity, disambiguation, and IR.

Using a technique that introduces additional sense ambiguity into a collection, this paper presents research that goes beyond previous work in this field to reveal the influence that ambiguity and disambiguation have on a probabilistic IR system. We conclude that word sense ambiguity is only problematic to an IR system when it is retrieving from very short queries. In addition we argue that if a word sense disambiguator is to be of any use to an IR system, the disambiguator must be able to resolve word senses to a high degree of accuracy.

1 Introduction

Word ambiguity is not something that we encounter in every day life, except perhaps in the context of jokes. Somehow, when an ambiguous word is spoken in a sentence, we are able to select the correct sense of that word without considering alternative senses. However, in any application where a computer has to process natural language, ambiguity is a problem. For example, if a language translation system encountered the word 'bat' in a sentence, should the translator regard the word as meaning: an implement used in sports to hit balls; or a furry, flying mammal?

The field of IR is no exception to this problem. For example, a manager of an on-line news retrieval system reported (in a personal communication with the author) that the recent change in British Prime Minister has caused problems. A number of users had tried to retrieve articles about the Prime Minister using the query 'major'. This query caused many articles about 'John Major' to be retrieved. However, in addition many more articles were retrieved where 'major' was used as an adjective or as the name of a military rank.

From this example, it seems reasonable to assume that an IR system will improve its performance if the documents it retrieves are represented by word senses rather than words. Recently, research was conducted to investigate this method of document representation. The researchers used a word sense disambiguator (a program that attempts to resolve the senses of ambiguous words) to disambiguate an IR test collection. However, experiments using this disambiguated collection showed a drop in retrieval performance.

As a consequence of this unexpected result, it was clear that a more basic investigation of the significance of ambiguity to IR was required. It is the results of this investigation that are presented here.

The structure of this paper is as follows. A brief review of previous research is presented in Section 2, followed by an outline of the experimental objectives. Section 3 describes the experimental methods used. This is followed in Section 4 by a description of results. Finally, Section 5 covers conclusions and future work.

2 Previous Research

The automatic disambiguation of word senses is a problem that has been studied for many years - Gale, Church and Yarowsky [1] cite work dating back to 1950. Early attempts to build disambiguators [2, 3, 4] relied on a combination of hand built lexicons and rules. Although working well for the examples they were programmed for, researchers were never able to 'scale up' the disambiguators to work on large disambiguation problems.

However in 1986 Lesk [5] built a disambiguator that used the textual definitions of word senses in an on-line dictionary to provide sense evidence. By using this large reference work, Lesk's disambiguator had the potential to be applied to large scale problems. The disambiguation technique Lesk used is in fact similar to techniques used in IR. To disambiguate a word *w* appearing in a certain context (for example, the 20 words surrounding *w*), the definitions of all the potential senses of *w* were looked up in the online dictionary. These definitions could be thought of as a small collection of documents. Disambiguation was a ranked retrieval of the definitions using the context as a query. The sense defined by the top ranked definition was chosen as the sense of *w*.

Since Lesk's paper a bewildering array of disambiguators have been built: Cowie [6], Black [7], Wallis [8] and Demetriou [9] have made further use of dictionaries; Zernik [10] built a disambiguator using a morphological analyser; Hearst [11] used learning based on human evidence; Dagan [12] used bilingual corpora; Church [13] tried aligned bilingual corpora; Voorhees [14] and Sussna [15] used the WordNet thesaurus; and Yarowsky [16] used a combination of Roget's thesaurus and Grollier's encyclopaedia to produce one of the better performing disambiguators to date.

2.1 Disambiguation and IR

The first attempt to use a disambiguator with an IR system was by Weiss [2]. Using his disambiguator to resolve the senses of five ambiguous hand picked words in the ADI collection, Weiss reported a 1% improvement in IR performance.

Some of the most extensive research on ambiguity and IR was performed by Krovetz and Croft [17], who used the CACM and TIME test collections. For each of the standard queries in these collections, they performed a retrieval. For each retrieval, they examined the match between the intended sense of each query word and that word's sense in a number of the retrieved documents. This manual investigation involved the study of thousands of these query/document word sense matches (or mismatches). Amongst other things, the study found that: a sense mismatch was more likely to happen when the document was not relevant to the query; and further, that sense mismatches occurred more often when there were a small number of words in common between the query and document. They concluded that the impact of sense ambiguity on IR was not dramatic, but that disambiguating word senses was probably beneficial to retrieval when there were few words in common between the document and the query.

The first large scale tests of applying a disambiguator to an IR system were performed by Voorhees [14] and Wallis [8]. Voorhees built a sense disambiguator based on the WordNet thesaurus [18]. She applied the disambiguator to the CACM, CISI, CRAN, MED and TIME collections. Unfortunately retrieval experiments run on these disambiguated collections resulted in a drop in IR performance.

Wallis used a disambiguator as part of a more elaborate experiment which replaced the words in a text collection by the text of their dictionary definitions. This was done so that synonymous words (which have similar dictionary definitions) would be represented in a similar manner, and therefore documents containing these synonymous words would be retrieved together. When replacing a word by its definition, a disambiguator was used to select the definition that most represented the word. Wallis performed tests on the CACM and TIME collections, but found no significant improvement in IR performance.

The results of both Voorhees and of Wallis are surprising as it would seem reasonable that if ambiguity were resolved, IR performance would increase. One of the problems faced by them was a lack of reliable performance figures for their disambiguators: for example, Voorhees reported problems establishing the correct (ie the intended) sense of some of the words in the standard queries. Such problems make it difficult to establish just what went wrong.

2.2 Evaluation of Disambiguators

Evaluation has always been a problem in disambiguation research, as the only way to evaluate a disambiguator's performance has been through the manual checking of its output. As this is such a time consuming process, most disambiguators have only been evaluated on a handful of words.

Yarowsky [19] reported on a novel technique for evaluating disambiguators that is completely automatic. The method involved the introduction to a text collection, of artificially created ambiguous words, called pseudo-words. The creation of such a word (in this case a size 2 pseudo-word) is performed by replacing all occurrences of two words, for example 'banana' and 'kalashnikov', by a new ambiguous word 'banana/kalashnikov'. The source of evidence used by the disambiguator (eg lexicon) would be updated to reflect the union of the two words. The disambiguator is then applied to each occurrence of the new word. Evaluation of the disambiguator's output is a trivial matter as we know beforehand the correct sense of each occurrence of the word.

However, like any simulation, there are limitations. The method chosen to form pseudo-words from individual words is one of random selection. Therefore, the various senses of a pseudo-word are unlikely to be closely related. This differs from a proportion of actual ambiguous words whose senses are related in some manner. The significance of this difference is unclear, and therefore it can not be claimed that the ambiguity introduced exactly matches the ambiguity found in real situations.

Note that the technique of introducing ambiguity is not new to the field of IR, the transformation that word stemmers perform can be thought of as introducing ambiguity to a collection. Although of course, unlike the process presented here, the aim of a stemmer is to improve performance.

3 The Experimental Technique

Although Yarowsky invented psuedo-words solely for the purpose of evaluating disambiguators, his method would seem well suited to the examination of the relationship between sense ambiguity and IR. To conduct this examination, the performance of an IR system retrieving from a test collection is first noted. Then, ambiguity is introduced into the collection using pseudo-words. The performance of the IR system retrieving from this additionally ambiguous collection can be compared to the performance figures gained from the initial retrieval.

Pseudo-words allow the experimenter to vary, at will, the precise amount of ambiguity in a collection. So for example, levels of ambiguity that far exceed the levels in standard test collections could be studied. However, the primary advantage of using pseudo-words is that the disambiguation of the pseudo-words can be precisely controlled by the experimenter. Therefore the effects on retrieval performance of a disambiguator operating at varying levels of accuracy can also be studied. It is this use of pseudo-words to simulate ambiguity in a test collection that forms the basis of the experiments presented in this paper.

4 Test Collection

Before explaining experimental detail and results, it is necessary to describe the test collection that was used. The collection chosen for the experiments was the Reuters text categorisation collection (created to test the Construe system [20], later modified by Lewis [21]) which consists of 22,173 documents taken from the Reuters newswire. The Reuters collection was chosen in preference to the standard IR test collections (CACM, Cranfield, LISA, TIME, NPL etc.) because it is significantly larger than them and in addition, it was felt that the usage of English in Reuters was less specialised than in many of the test collections. The latter is an important factor for planned disambiguation experiments which will use a standard English dictionary to provide evidence of word senses.

The main difference between Reuters and an IR test collection is that Reuters doesn't have a set of standard queries with corresponding relevant documents. However each document in Reuters is tagged with a number of manually assigned subject codes. It is these codes that allow us to use Reuters as a test collection for comparing document representation methods. This use of Reuters was first described by Lewis and it is his method, with some modifications, that is described here.

First, **R** is defined as the set of all documents in the Reuters collection. This set is then partitioned into two subsets of equal size: **Q** (the query set) and **T** (the test set). The method used to partition **R** was chosen to be a random assignment of documents into one of the two subsets. This method ensured that groups of documents covering common themes would be evenly distributed to both **Q** and **T***.

Next, **S** is defined as the set of all subject codes that have been assigned to at least one document in **Q** and at least one document in **T**. If we pick one of the subject codes from **S**, we can now perform a retrieval. (The retrieval system used in these experiments was developed specifically for this work. It is based upon the probabilistic weighted term model as described in [22].)

For example suppose we perform a retrieval for the subject code 'crude'. First, all documents in **Q** tagged with 'crude' are selected. Then by performing relevance feedback using the selected documents, word/weight pairs are generated to form a query. This query is used to retrieve from the **T** set. The resulting ranked document list is examined to see where in the ranking, documents tagged with 'crude' appear. The position of the tagged documents is used to produce precision/recall figures. A conservative interpolation technique (outlined in [23]) is used to transform these figures into precision values at ten standard recall levels (0.1, 0.2, ..., 1.0).

This process is repeated for each subject code in **S**, each time producing another set of precision values. These precision values are then averaged to give an overall set of values for each of the ten standard recall levels.

So by partitioning Reuters and using the subject codes, all the components of a classic IR test collection are created.
• the collection to be searched - **T**
• a set of queries - generated from **Q**, for each element of **S**
• a set of relevant documents for each query - documents in **T** tagged with the respective element of **S**.

The use of relevance feedback to generate the queries in place of verbose user generated queries means that the form of retrieval can be likened to an iteration of relevance feedback during a retrieval session.

4.1 Data Reduction

When performing a retrieval experiment using Reuters the question arises, how many query words should be generated by the relevance feedback process? It is clear from the work of Hughes [24] and Harman [25] that in a given situation there is an optimum number of words to use. As it was thought that such optimum numbers may be dependent on the amount of introduced ambiguity, the number of query words added was made a variable of the retrieval experiments. Therefore, the experimental results are expressed in three variables: precision (*p*), recall (*r*) and the number of query words added (*w*). The results can be plotted on a three-dimensional graph as shown in Figure 1. From the graph we can see that for all recall levels, the precision is low at *w*=1, with a rapid rise peaking at around *w*=5, before falling away as *w* increases.

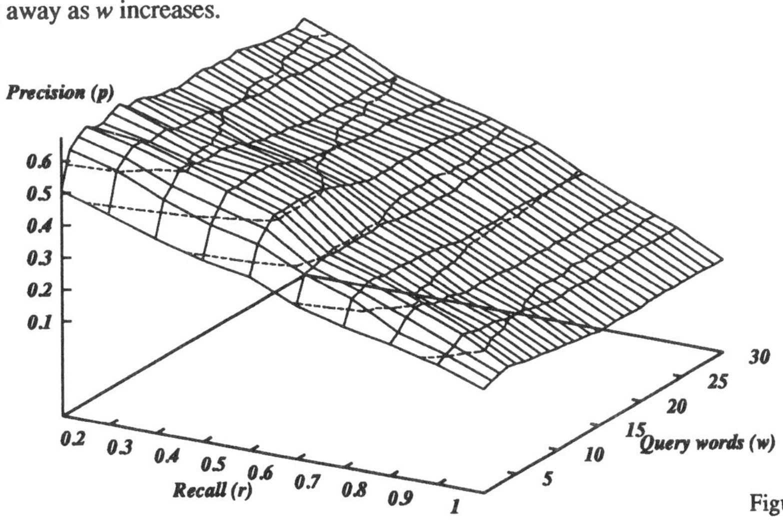

Figure 1

* This differs from Lewis who partitioned the collection based on the document's creation date. Such a partitioning was necessary for testing a newswire categorisation system, however this was not a factor of the experiments presented here.

Unfortunately it was found that three-dimensional graphs become difficult to read when the results of several retrieval experiments were plotted together. What was needed was a two dimensional plot of *w* against a variable expressing retrieval performance, in other words reduce the *p/r* figures to a single number. The method used to calculate this number is illustrated with the following example. To calculate the retrieval performance of the *p/r* figures tabulated in Figure 2, for each of the ten pairs of *p/r* numbers a corresponding *f* measure is calculated. The formula for *f* is,

$$f = \frac{1}{1/2(1/p) + 1/2(1/r)}$$

This measure is discussed in detail in [23]*.

Recall (*r*)	Precision (*p*)	F-measure (*f*)
0.1	0.592995	0.171140
0.2	0.544545	0.292552
0.3	0.472835	0.367091
0.4	0.432949	0.415823
0.5	0.398068	0.443249
0.6	0.326031	0.422488
0.7	0.278630	0.398600
0.8	0.224293	0.350358
0.9	0.165700	0.279872
1.0	0.107376	0.193929

Figure 2

Of the ten *f* measures calculated (Figure 2), the maximum (f-max) is selected as the retrieval performance figure. Applying this data reduction method, the graph in Figure 1 can now be plotted in two dimensions (Figure 3).

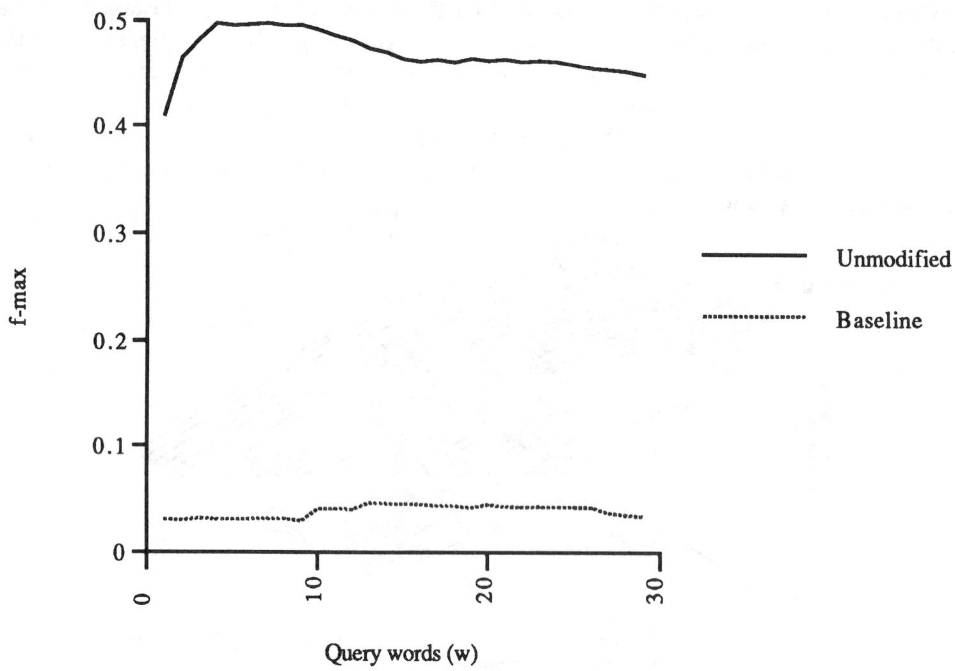

Figure 3

* In fact van Rijsbergen defines a measure called E, however F is simply defined as 1-E.

4.2 Random Case Test

Before any retrieval experiments were performed, it was necessary to establish how well the Reuters subject codes indicated document content. In other words, are the documents in set **Q**, marked with the subject code 'crude', good sources of evidence for retrieving similarly marked documents in set **T**?

The experimental method used to test this was identical to the method outlined above except for an additional step: when documents tagged with a certain subject code were selected from the set **Q**, a random set of documents were selected (from **Q**) and used to form the query instead. Figure 2 shows the result of this 'random case' experiment along with the result of an experiment using the subject codes as normal. As can be seen the random case is significantly worse than the method using the subject codes. In addition to establishing the utility of the subject codes as document content indicators, this experiment provides a 'baseline' which gives a scale to compare the differences between subsequent experimental results.

5 Experimental Results

Two sets of experiments were run: the first were concerned with the effect on IR performance of the introduction of additional ambiguity into the Reuters collection using pseudo-words; the second set of experiments studied the effect on IR performance of disambiguating pseudo-words (introduced into the collection) with a disambiguator operating at varying levels of accuracy.

5.1 Effects of Ambiguity on Performance

In the first experiment all words in the Reuters collection were paired to produce size 2 pseudo-words. The result of the retrieval experiment run on this additionally ambiguous collection is shown in Figure 4. As can be seen, when the result is compared to the retrieval experiment run on the unmodified collection, there is little difference in retrieval performance.

As this experiment showed only a small drop in performance, it was decided that more ambiguity needed to be introduced into the collection by creating larger pseudo-words. The creation of such pseudo-words is no different to the method outlined above. For example, to create a size three pseudo-word, all occurrences of the words: 'banana', 'kalashnikov', and 'anecdote' would be replaced by the pseudo-word 'banana/kalashnikov/anecdote'.

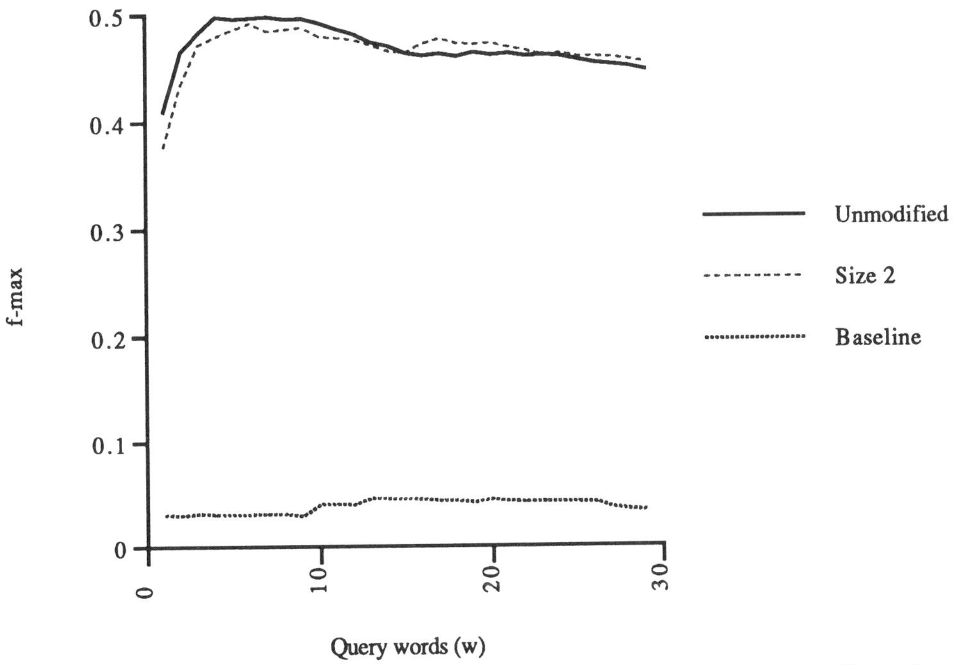

Figure 4

Four further experiments were run where ambiguity was introduced into the collection using pseudo-words of sizes three, four, five and ten. The results of these experiments are shown in Figure 5. As can be seen, IR performance is remarkably resistant to the introduced ambiguity. This is quite a striking result when we consider that in the final experiment (size ten pseudo-words) the number of distinct words in the Reuters collection was reduced from around 40,000 to 4,000.

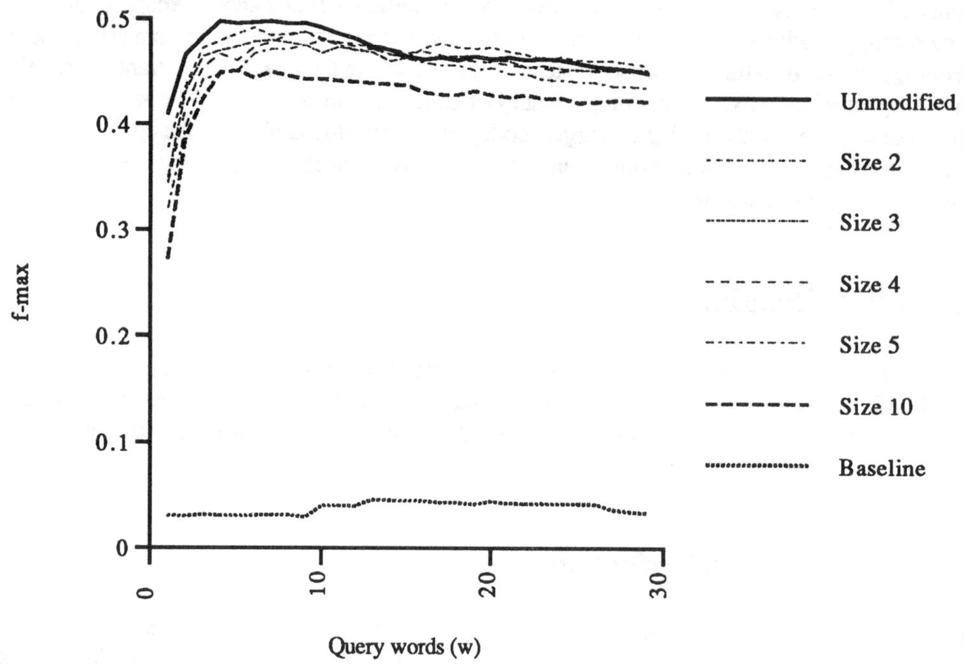

Figure 5

When comparing in detail the difference in performance between retrievals from the unmodified collection and retrievals from an ambiguous collection (Figure 6), we can see that the difference is greatest for retrievals based on queries of one or two words. Once the number of words in the query increases, the difference in performance quickly reduces. This result would seem to indicate that the degree of word collocation (ie the number of query words

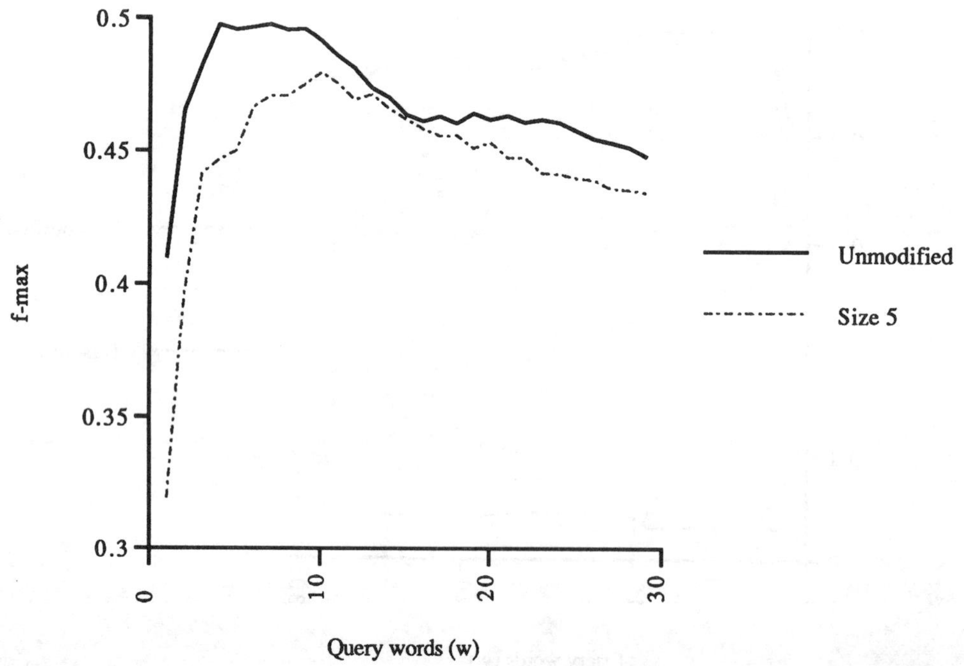

Figure 6

occurring in a retrieved document) plays an important role in the impact of sense ambiguity to IR. This concurs with the findings of Krovetz and Croft. Intuitively this is perhaps not too surprising, after all, if a document is retrieved by matching on the query words: 'mammal', 'flying', 'vampire' & 'bat', it is unlikely that this particular use of 'bat' refers to the sporting implement.

5.2 Disambiguating Ambiguity

The final set of experiments investigated the effects on performance of a pseudo-word disambiguator operating at varying levels of accuracy. For these experiments ambiguity was introduced into the collection using size five pseudo-words. This additionally ambiguous collection was then disambiguated, but with a controlled amount of error. A retrieval was then run on the 'erroneously disambiguated' collection.

This experiment was performed a number of times, each time with the percentage of correct disambiguations set to a different value. The results of two of these experiments are shown in Figure 7. As can be seen from the graph,

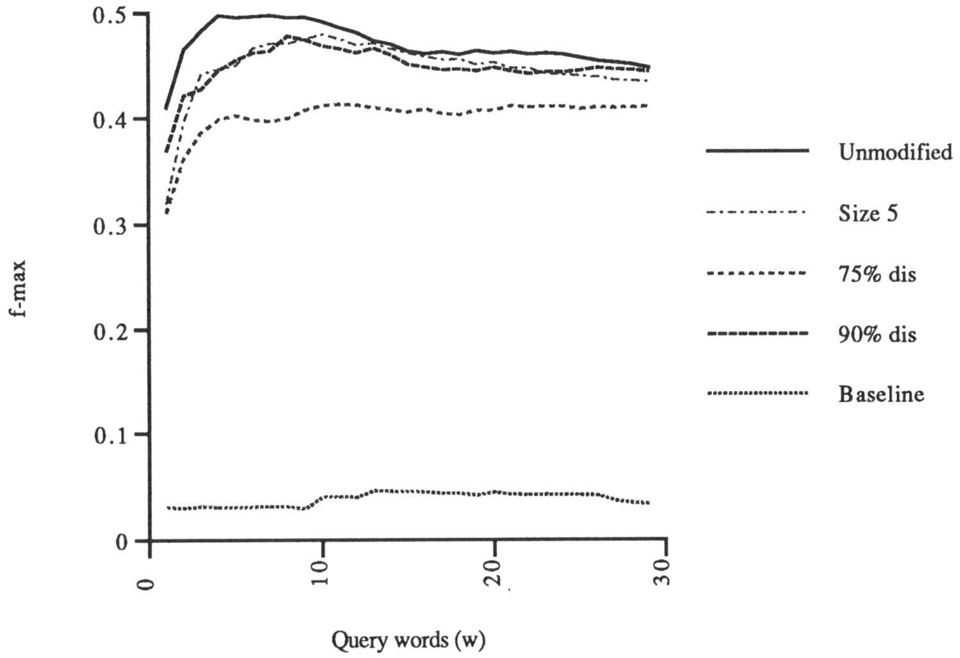

Figure 7

disambiguation accuracy has a dramatic effect on performance. When the introduced ambiguity is disambiguated with an accuracy of 75%, the retrieval performance is actually worse than performance using the ambiguous collection. With disambiguation at 90% accuracy, performance is similar to that of the ambiguous collection, although a small improvement can be seen for retrievals based on queries composed of one or two words. There is some anecdotal evidence to suggest that in general, tools built for computational linguistics tasks need to operate at, at least 90% accuracy before they are of practical use.

6 Conclusions

Using the novel experimental technique of introducing and removing ambiguity into a test collection in a controlled manner, insights into the significance of ambiguity to IR have been gained. In general, we can conclude that the performance of such systems is insensitive to ambiguity but very sensitive to erroneous disambiguation.

One area to which these results may be pertinent is that of bilingual IR systems. Such systems consist of document collections written in a foreign language but searched with queries constructed in a user's native language. Such an approach is of obvious interest in the common situation where a person's ability to read a foreign language is greater than their ability to write it. It may be thought that the amount of ambiguity introduced by the automatic translation process would adversely affect the retrieval performance. However, the results presented here suggest that this introduced ambiguity may not, in fact, be such a problem.

Overall, the results presented in this paper appear to confirm 'common sense' beliefs, such as the ability of collocation to resolve word sense ambiguity and the high accuracy required of a disambiguator, with perhaps a little surprise as to the degree to which IR systems are resilient to ambiguity. It is hoped that this refining of the general appreciation of word sense ambiguity may be useful in identifying which areas justify further investigation within the context of IR.

7 Acknowledgements

Thanks go to: Fabrizio Sebastiani, Alison Cawsey, Keith van Rijsbergen, Bob Krovetz and especially Iain Campbell for their constructive comments on earlier drafts of this paper.

8 References

1. Gale W, Church KW, Yarowsky D. Estimating upper and lower bounds on the performance of word-sense disambiguation programs. Proceedings of the ACL, 1992; 30:249-256

2. Weiss SF. Learning to disambiguate. Information Storage and Retrieval, 1973; 9:33-41

3. Kelly E, Stone P. Computer recognition of English word senses. North-Holland Publishing Co., Amsterdam, 1975

4. Small S, Rieger C. Parsing and comprehending with word experts (a theory and its realisation). In: Strategies for Natural Language Processing, Lehnert WG, Ringle MH (Eds), LEA, 1992, pp 89-148

5. Lesk M. Automatic sense disambiguation: how to tell a pine cone from an ice cream cone. Proceedings of the SIGDOC Conference 1986; 24-26

6. Cowie J , Guthrie J, Guthrie L. Lexical disambiguation using simulated annealing. Proceedings of COLING Conference, 1992;359-365

7. Black E. An experiment in computational discrimination of English word senses. IBM Journal, 1988; 32:185-194

8. Wallis P. Information retrieval based on paraphrase. Proceedings of PACLING Conference, 1993

9. Demetriou GC. Lexical disambiguation using constraint handling in Prolog (CHIP). Proceedings of the European Chapter of the ACL, 1993; 6:431-436

10. Zernik U. TRAIN1 vs. TRAIN2: Tagging word senses in corpus. Proceedings of RIAO 91, Intelligent Text and Image Handling, 1991; 567-585

11. Hearst MA. Noun homograph disambiguation using local context in large text corpora. Proceedings of the 7th conference, UW Centre for the New OED & Text Research Using Corpora, 1991; 7

12. Dagan I, Itai A, Schwall U. Two languages are more informative than one. Proceedings of the ACL, 1991: 29:130-137

13 Church KW. Using bilingual materials to develop word sense disambiguation methods. Proceedings of ACM SIGIR Conference, 1992; 15: 350

14. Voorhees EM. Using WordNet™ to disambiguate word sense for text retrieval. Proceedings of ACM SIGIR Conference, 1993;16:171-180

15. Sussna M. Word sense disambiguation for free-text indexing using a massive semantic network. Proceedings of CIKM, 1993

16. Yarowsky D. Word sense disambiguation using statistical models of Roget's categories trained on large corpora. Proceedings of COLING Conference, 1992; 454-460

17. Krovetz R, Croft WB. Lexical Ambiguity and Information Retrieval. ACM Transactions on Information Systems, 1992;10

18. Miller G. WordNet: an on-line lexical database. International Journal of Lexicography, 1990; 24:513-523

19. Yarowsky D. One sense per collocation. Proceedings of ARPA Human Language Technology Workshop, 1993

20. Hayes PJ. Intelligent high volume text processing using shallow, domain specific techniques. Working Notes, AAAI Spring Symposium on Text-Based Intelligent Systems, 1990:134-138

21. Lewis DD. Representation and learning in information retrieval. PhD Thesis, COINS Technical Report 91-93 Department of Computer and Information Science, University of Massachusetts, Amherst, MA 01003, 1991

22. Robertson SE, Sparck-Jones K. Relevance weighting of search terms. Journal of the American Society for Information Science, 1976;27:129-146.

23. van Rijsbergen CJ. Information retrieval (second edition). London: Butterworths, 1979

24. Hughes GF. On the mean accuracy of statistical pattern recognisers. IEEE Transactions on Information Theory, 1968;14:55-63

25. Harman D. Relevance feedback revisited. Proceedings of ACM SIGIR Conference, 1992;15:1-10

A Full–Text Retrieval System with a Dynamic Abstract Generation Function

Seiji Miike Etsuo Itoh Kenji Ono Kazuo Sumita

{miike,etsuo,ono,sumita}@isl.rdc.toshiba.co.jp

Research and Development Center
Toshiba Corporation
Komukai-Toshiba-cho 1, Saiwai-ku, Kawasaki, 210, Japan

Abstract

We have developed a Japanese full-text retrieval system named BREVIDOC* that enables the user to specify an area within a text for abstraction and to control the volume of the abstract interactively. This system analyzes a document structure using linguistic knowledge only and thus is domain-independent. In its text structure analysis, the system determines relations among paragraphs and sentences, based on linguistic clues such as connectives, anaphoric expressions, and idiomatic expressions. The system analyzes and stores the text structure in advance so that it can generate an abstract in real time by selecting sentences according to relative importance of rhetorical relations among the sentences. The retrieval system works on an engineering workstation.

*Broadcatching System with an Essence Viewer for Retrieved Documents

1 Introduction

Retrieval of documents from very large data collections or very large text databases may soon come into wide use (e.g. [1]). In order to make such retrieval more feasible, a document retrieval system must provide an efficient interface. In the research of human-computer interaction, visualizing and presenting information is one of the major topics. At present, concrete and abstract objects with hierarchical relations, such as a work space or directories, are the target of visualization (e.g. [2]). However, visualizing and presenting information and documents by analyzing and structuring their contents have not been realized so far. This will be important in document processing since information and documents continue to increase and text plays an important role in multimedia.

To realize the aforesaid visualization and presentation, a method for analyzing and structuring contents of documents needs to be established. In computational linguistics, although efforts have been applied to analyze text structure and discourse structure (e.g. [3], [4], [5], [6]), little practical application has been presented, because of difficulties in building large lexicons and grammars as well as computational complexity in analyzing texts from the standpoint of practical use. In comparison, most of knowledge-based systems tend to show good performance in limited domains, such as M&A in financial news stories (e.g. [7]).

This paper first presents our approach to the design and construction of a full-text retrieval system with a dynamic abstract generation function and the system configuration. Next, the component subsystems of the retrieval system are described: the document structure analyzer and the dynamic abstract generation function. Finally, an example of the operation of the retrieval system is shown.

2 Approach

It is a burden on the user of a document retrieval system to select documents that she/he truly needs from the documents retrieved by the system. For content-based retrieval, robustness and extendability are important, especially for a practical use.

If documents have abstracts, users can easily grasp their outline. Research has been carried out on automatic abstract generation. Here, the widely used simplified method is based on types of words or phrases in the sentences, and further progress in developing effective methods to represent knowledge and to analyze and understand language must be made [8].

For interaction between a human and a document retrieval system, the system is desired to interactively generate and modify an abstract from the viewpoint of the user, which is not realized by the conventional method of preparing an abstract in advance by a human or computer.

Keeping these points in mind, we have constructed a prototype of a full-text retrieval system named BREVIDOC that analyzes a document structure and interactively generates an abstract. The document structure analysis is based on linguistic knowledge only, therefore, the system is domain-independent. Moreover, since an abstract is generated according to relative importance of rhetorical relations among the sentences in a text, the abstract is coherent and qualitatively better than those generated through word-frequency-based abstraction [9].

In order to make it efficient for the user to select documents she/he needs, the system provides a dynamic abstract generation function which enables the user to specify an area within a text for abstraction and to control the volume of the abstract interactively. In abstract generation, real-time processing is crucial to system performance from the viewpoint of human interface; however, the computational power of current workstations is insufficient for this purpose. To meet the demands of real-time response, the document structure analyzer extracts document structures and stores them in advance.

3 System Configuration

Based on the approach described above, we have constructed a prototype of a full-text retrieval system with a function for dynamic abstract generation. Our prototype retrieval system consists of a document structure analyzer, a full-text search engine, and a dynamic abstract generation function. The system configuration is shown in Figure 1. In Figure 1, the dashed-line box represents the module executed before the real-time retrieval process, and the dashed-line arrows represent their data flow. The modules indicated by the solid lines are active in the retrieval process. We used the full-text search engine developed by Nakamoto et al.[10].

In advance, the document structure analyzer (Figure 2), described in the next chapter, extracts document structures from Japanese documents that are free of descriptive markup like SGML, and stores them in the document database. In a real-time retrieval process, the system retrieves documents which contain the given words. The system then generates an abstract of the retrieved document and presents it to the user.

The retrieval system has been implemented on a UNIX-based engineering workstation, and applied to technical papers of monthly *Toshiba Review* and newspaper editorials of *Asahi*.

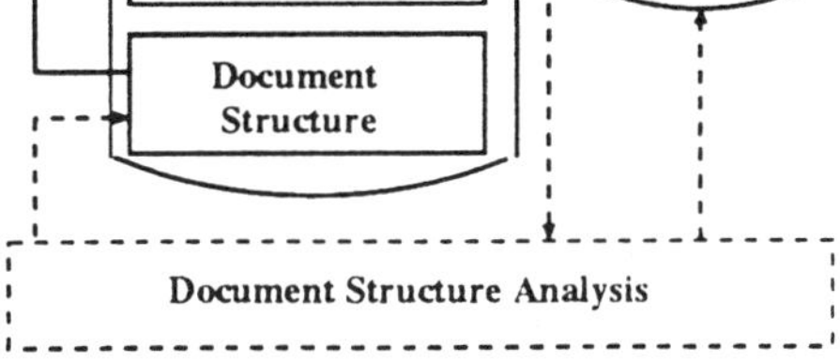

Figure 1. System Configuration

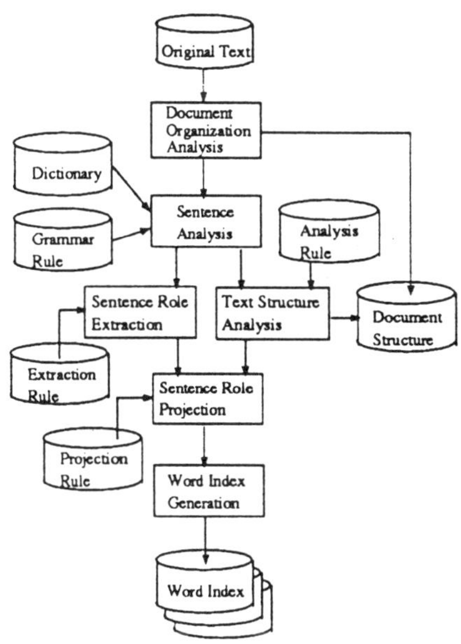

Figure 2. Configuration of Document Structure Analyzer

4 Document Structure Analyzer

Figure 2 shows the document structure analyzer which realizes four major processes:
(1) document organization analysis
(2) sentence analysis
(3) text structure analysis
(4) semantic role extraction and word indexing

4.1 Document Organization Analysis

A document composed of several sections has a structure. A technical paper, for example, consists of a preface, a set of sections and references, and a section consists of a heading and a text.

In order to analyze the organization of sections the system finds a heading of each section based on the morphological characteristics of headings, e.g., they begin with a number or symbol character, they do not end by a period, they follow and procede a null line [11]. It also detects a space character at the beginning of a line to recognize the boundary of each paragraph in sections.

The output of each document in the document organization analysis consists of the heading of each section, the scope of the body of the section, and the position of each paragraph in the section.

4.2 Sentence Analysis

Each phrase or sentence is analyzed by a morphological analyzer and a syntactic analyzer [12], with a dictionary which has about 60,000 entries. The morphological analyzer constructs word lattice for input sentences and produces a sequence of word structures, which in turn will be the input of the syntactic analyzer. Since Japanese language is one of agglutinative languages, which means that there are no blanks between adjoining words within a sentence, the morphological analyzer utilizes word connection information to eliminate morphologically implausible word sequences. The syntactic analyzer which employs an ATN-like fashion derives a syntactic structure for a string of categories in a sentence. Lexical ambiguities are resolved by eliminating category values that do not permit coherent word category combination. The sentence analysis speed is about 20,000 words per hour on an engineering workstation.

4.3 Text Structure Analysis

This process analyzes the internal structure of the body of each section. In an ordinary text, rhetorical patterns are often used to clarify the argument. The typical connective expressions are connectives and sentence predicates. We have divided them into 34 categories as in Table 1. Here, connective expressions include not only connectives such as 'therefore', but also idiomatic expressions stating relations to other part of text such as "in addition" and "here ... is described."

A text structure is represented by a binary tree analogous to a syntactic tree of a natural language sentence. The text structure analysis is composed of the following four major steps ([3], [13]).

(1) Rhetorical relation extraction

Rhetorical relations, some of which are shown in Table 1, are detected by matching with connective expressions described by 1,350 regular expressions and a sequence of sentence identifiers and relations is constructed. For a sentence without any explicit connective expressions, the extension relation <EX> is set to the sentence.

(2) Segmentation

Rhetorical expressions between distant sentences which define the text structure are detected by 150 *if-then* rules. The *if*-part corresponds to linguistic surface patterns, e.g. "... follows. First ... Second ...." The *then*-part represents a connection sequence embedded with constraint operators which are added onto the sequence produced in step (2) and put restrictions on structures to be generated in step (4). In addition, anaphoric expressions and their referents are extracted for segmenting the sequence.

(3) Candidate generation

All possible text structures are generated, using the binary trees which do not violate segmentation restrictions. The generation is performed in a bottom-up manner of sentence parsing by the CYK algorithm. For an example of a text composed of 6 sentences, only 6 candidates are generated, while 42 binary trees would be produced without the segmentation rules.

(4) Preference judgment

The structure candidate with the lowest penalty score is selected by determining by 600 preference rules for every two neighboring relations in the candidate. For example, the sequence [[P <EG> Q] <SR>

Table 1. Example of Rhetorical Relation

relation	expression
serial <SR>	"*yotte*" (thus), "*sokode*" (then)
summarization	"*kekkyoku*" (after all), "*matomeru to*" (in summary)
reason	"*naze nara*" (because), "*sono wake wa*" (the reason is ...)
rephrase	"*sunawachi*" (that is ...), "*iikaeru to*" (in other words)
negative	"*shikashi*" (but), "*daga*" (although)
example <EG>	"*tatoeba*" (for example), "... *nado de aru*" (and so on)
background	"*juurai*" (previously), "*kore made*" (until now)
direction	"*koko dewa ... wo noberu*" (here ... is described), "*konkai*" (this time)
parallel	"*douji ni*" (at the same time), "*mata*" (in addition)
supplement <SP>	"*nao*" (besides), "... *wa iu made mo nai*" (Needless to say ...)
contrast	"*ippou*" (however), "*hanmen*" (on the contrary)
repetition	"*to iu noha*" (in other words), "*sore wa*" (it is ...)
topic shift	"*sate*", "*tokorode*" (well, now)
first	"*dai ichi ni*" (first), "*mazu*" (first)
extension <EX>	"*kore wa*" (This is), "*sono youna* ..." (Such ...)

R] is more preferable than [P <EG> [Q <SR> R]], where each of P, Q and R represents a sentence (see Table 1).

After the analysis of intra-paragraph structures, the analyzer analyzes inter-paragraph structures. In both analyses, the same steps are taken; the only difference is that the latter uses a rhetorical relation of the first sentence of each paragraph.

Figure 3 shows a paragraph from an article titled "A Zero-Crossing Rate Which Estimates the Frequency of a Speech Signal," where underlined words indicate connective expressions. Although the fourth and fifth sentences are clearly exemplifications of the first three sentences, the sixth is not. Also, the sixth sentence is the concluding sentence for the first five. Thus, the text structure for this text can be represented by a binary tree as shown in Figure 4.

1: In the context of discrete–time signals, zero–crossing is said to occur if successive samples have different algebraic signs.
2: The rate at which zero crossings occur is a simple measure of the frequency content of a signal.
3: <u>This is</u> particularly true of narrow band signals.
4: <u>For example</u>, a sinusoidal signal of frequency F_0 sampled at a rate F_s, has F_s/F_s samples per cycle of the sine wave.
5: Each cycle has two zero crossings so that the long–term average rate of zero–crossings is $Z = 2F_0/F_s$.
6: <u>Thus</u>, the average zero–crossing rate gives a reasonable way to estimate the frequency of a sine wave.

(L.R.Rabiner and R.W.Schafer, *Digital Processing of Speech Signals*, Prentice–Hall, 1978, p.127.)

Figure 3. Text Example

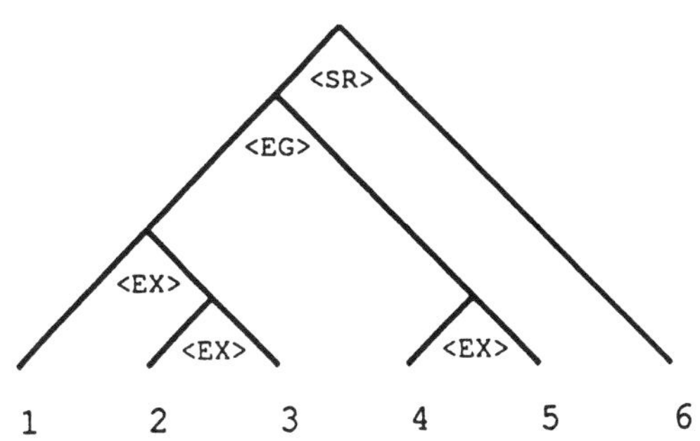

Figure 4. Tree Structure for the Text in Figure 3

4.4 Semantic role extraction and word indexing

A document includes a number of predictable subtopics. Types of subtopics to be included in a document depend on the category of the document. For example, a research paper usually includes the background and the purpose of the research, the approach taken, and the conclusion, whereas a newspaper editorial includes the background and the writer's opinion.

The purpose of this procedure is to improve retrieval precision by recognizing the semantic role of sentences which include query words. The procedure is composed of the following three major steps [14].

(1) Semantic role extraction

The system extracts the semantic role of each sentence in every document based on the semantic role extraction rules in a *if-then* form. The conditional parts give syntactic patterns corresponding to the semantic roles and are matched with sub-trees obtained by morphologiclly and syntactically analyzing sentences. If the matching succeeds, the semantic roles of the sentences are determined.

We have prepared 122 extraction rules with the semantic roles shown in Table 2 for analysis of technical papers. Table 2 also shows examples of linguistic expressions corresponding to the semantic roles. The variety of semantic roles necessary and sufficient to alanyze document structures must be determined through further experimentation.

Table 2. Example of Semantic Roles

semantic role	expression
topic	"... *nitsuite kaisetsu suru*" (... is explained), "*nitsuite noberu*" (... is described)
purpose	"... *wo mokuteki ni*" (for the purpose of ...), "... *wo mezasu*" (... aim at...)
background	"*juurai* ..." (previously ...), "*kinnen* ... *te iru*" (recently ... has been – ing)
feature	"*tokuchou ga aru*" (... has the merits ...), "*chuumoku ni atai suru*" (... is worth notice)
conclusion	"... *wo hakatta*" (... has been achieved), "... *ga wakatta*" (... has been confirmed)
remaining problems	"*kongo* ... *tai*" (in the future we wish to ...), "*tsutome te iki tai*" (we intend to ...)

In the current system, the result of systactic analysis of sentences are only used for extracting semantic roles. However the framework can be used for extracting semantic relations of the words in documents, and we plan to utilize such word relations in addition to the current word-based approach.

(2) Semantic role projection

This step projects the semantic role of a sentence extracted in step (1) onto the neighboring part of the text, by looking at the text structure. The projection is executed when a sub-text structure defined in the conditional part of the projection rule matches with an input text structure. For example, in a context such as "The feature ... as follows. First ... Second ...," the semantic role 'feature' extracted from the first sentence is projected to the second and third sentences referencing the local text structure. Typical rhetorical relations used for the semantic role projection are parallel, example, supplement, summarization, rephrase and first.

(3) Word indexing

For every semantic role, a word index is generated from document ID's and words obtained by morphological analysis of sentences with that role. This word index is utilized for fast retrieval.

5 Dynamic Abstract Generation Function

The abstract generation function looks at the analyzed text structure for each section, and then generates an abstract based on relative importance of rhetorical relations. The relative importance of rhetorical relations are categorized into three types as shown in Table 3.

For the relations categorized as *RightNucleus*, the right node is more important than the left node from the viewpoint of abstract generation, than the left node. In the case of *LeftNucleus* relations, the situation is reversed, while both nodes of the *BothNuclei*relations are equal in their importance. For example, since the right node of the serial relation (e.g., *'yotte'* (thus)) is the conclusion of the left node, the relation is categorized into *RightNucleus*, as the right node is more important than the left node.

In order to determine important text segments, the system imposes penalties on a node for each rhetorical relation according to its relative importance. The system imposes a penalty on the left node for the *RightNucleus* relation, and also on the right node for the *LeftNucleus* relation. In the current system, the penalty is always one. It then adds penalties from the root node to the terminal nodes, to calculate the penalties of all nodes. Then, it recursively cuts off the nodes, from the terminal nodes, which are imposed the highest penalty. The list of terminal nodes of the final structure becomes an abstract for the original document. If that abstract is longer than the expected length, the system cuts off terminal nodes of the last sentences, which have been imposed the same penalty score.

Figure 5 is the result of carrying out the aforementioned penalty calculation on the tree structure in Figure 4.

Table 3. Relative Importance of Rhetorical Type

Relation Type	Relation	Import. Node
RightNucleus	serial, summarization, direction, contrast, negative, ...	right node
LeftNucleus	example, reason, background, supplement, first, ...	left node
BothNuclei	parallel, extension, rephrase, repetition, topic shift, ...	both nodes

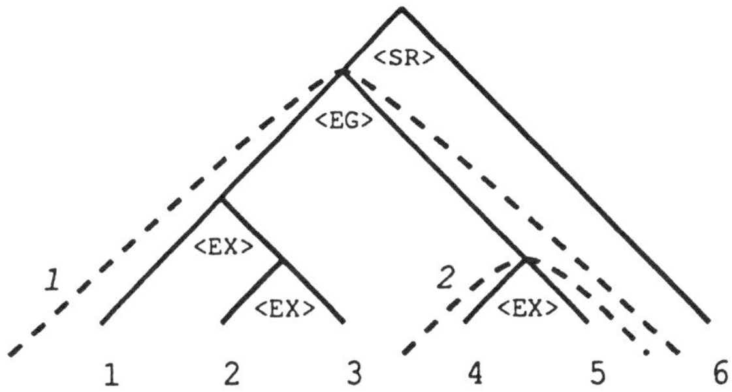

Figure 5. Penalties on Relative Importance for the Text Structure in Figure 4

In Figure 5, the italic numbers are the penalties the system imposed on each node of the structure, and the broken lines are the boundaries between the nodes with different penalty scores. The figure shows that the sentences four and five have penalty score two, that the sentences one, two and three have one, and that the sentence six has no penalty score. In this case, the system selects sentence six as the shortest abstract. It could also select the sentences one and six as a longer abstract.

6 Example

Retrieval from 386 analyzed documents of *Toshiba Review* and abstract generation are described.

(1) Analysis of the user's query

The user can input her/his query sentence in Japanese as shown in Ex.1. The query is analyzed by the same morphological and syntactic analyzer as in the document structure analyzer. The sentence analyzer analyzes the query and extracts a semantic role and content words. Ex.2 shows the semantic role and the content words extracted by analyzing the sentence in Ex.1. The user can modify them if necessary, and set sementic roles and words explicitly.

EX.1 被曝の低減を目指したもの。
Documents whose aim is to reduce human exposure to radiation. (in translation)

EX.2 目的：被曝／低減
purpose: exposure to radiation / reduction (in translation)

(2) Retrieval

The system retrieves documents according to the content words in Ex.2 based on boolean search, using the word index for the semantic role "purpose." As the result of retrieval, the system shows a list of retrieved documents in the left window, an abstract of a document at the top of the list in the middle window, and its original text in the right window as shown in Figure 6. In the left window, the title, the authors and the first part of the shortest abstract generated from the original abstract for each retrieved document are shown. Figure 7 shows the translation of the content of the left window. In the middle window, the system first shows the title, authors, a sentence selected from the original abstract, and headings of the chapters and sections as shown based on the extracted document structure of the retrieved document. Figure 8 shows the translation of the content of the middle window.

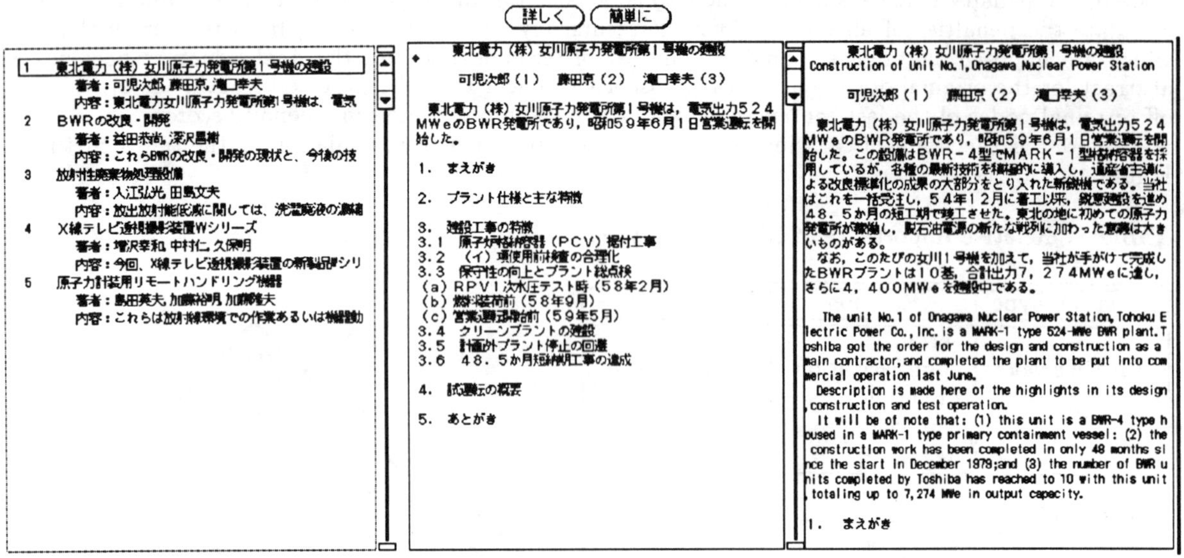

Figure 6. Retrieval Result

1 Construction of Unit No.1, Onagawa Nuclear Power Station
AUTHOR: Kago, J., Fujita, K. and Takiguchi, Y.
CONTENT : The unit No.1 of Onagawa Nuclear Power Station, Tohoku Electric
2 Improvement and Development of Boiling Water Reactor
AUTHOR: Masuda, K. and Fukazawa, M.
CONTENT : Current status of the improvement and development of these BWR
3 Liquid and Solid Radwaste Management
AUTHOR: Irie, H. and Tajima, F.
CONTENT : As for the reduction of radiation condensation of laundry wastes
4 X-Ray-TV Diagnostic Tables, W Series
AUTHOR: Masuzawa, Y., Nakamura, H. and Kubo, A.
CONTENT : W series which is the new product of the TV fluoroscopic system
5 Remote Handling Equipment for Nuclear Instrumentation
AUTHOR: Shimada, H., Kato, H. and Kato, T.
CONTENT : These, for operations performed in a radioactive environment

Figure 7. Translation of the List shown in the Left Window in Figure 6

Since the first document has the expression underlined in its text in Figure 9 (the underlines are drawn by the authors of this paper), it is included among the retrieved five documents.

(3) Abstract generation

The system provides the user with an abstract of any specified area within the text, such as a chapter or a section, and in this way the length of the abstract can be controlled interactively. Moreover, sentences which are being displayed in the abstract window are colored in the original text window, so that the correspondance between the two windows can easily be seen. When the user points at any position in the abstract window with a mouse, and then clicks the button '詳しく (*kuwashiku*, in detail)' or '簡単に (*kantanni*, in short)', the system identifies a chapter or section where the pointed position is contained and generates an abstract of the chapter or section. When the button '詳しく (in detail)' is chosen, the system lowers the threshold by which an abstract is generated. In the case that the button '簡単に (in short) is chosen, the situation is reversed.

Figure 10 shows the abstract generated by pointing at an area above chapter 1 and clicking '詳しく (in detail)' once. Figure 11 shows what happens when '詳しく (in detail)' is clicked again. Figure 12 (in detail) (in short)

Construction of Unit No.1, Onagawa Nuclear Power Station

Kago, J., Fujita, K. and Takiguchi, Y.

The unit No.1 of Onagawa Nuclear Power Station, Tohoku Electric Power Co., Inc. is a MARK-I type 524-MWe BWR plant and was put into commercial operation in June 1, 1984.

1. Introduction
2. Organization and Main Features of the Plant
3. Construction Steps
3.1 Setting the Primary Containment Vessel
3.2 Rationalizing the Inspection
3.3 Maintenance and the Overall Inspection of the Plant
(a)RPV Water Pressure Test
(b)Before Loading the Fuel
(c)Before Commercial Operation
3.4 Construction of a Clean Plant
3.5 Avoiding Emergency Halt of the Plant
3.6 Completing the Construction in Only 48 Months
4. Test Run
5. Conclusion

Figure 8. Translation of the Abstract shown in the middle window in Figure 6

3．4　クリーンプラントの建設
女川１号機は建設当初から試運転まで一貫してきれいなプラントの建設を目ざして“クリーンプラント作戦”を展開した。クリーンプラント作戦では放射性廃棄物発生量の低減のためのクラッド低減および系統機器配管内面の清浄度維持による炉内へのクラッド流入の抑制および運開後の被曝低減を目的とするもので、図４に示す具体的な施策を計画的に実施した。

3.4 Construction of the Clean Plant
From the construction to the test run of Onagawa I Power Station, we consistently followed the Clean Plant Strategy in the hope of building a clean plant. The clean plant strategy aims at reducing clads for reducing the amount of radioactive wastes, suppressing the inflow of clads into the furnace by keeping the inner surface of the apparatus tubes clean, and reducing exposure to radiation when the plant is in operation. We carried out our concrete plans shown in Fig.4.

Figure 9. Text in the First Document and its Translation

shows the translation of the sentences shown in Figure 10, and Figure 13 shows the translation of those in Figure 11. In Figure 11 and 13, one sentence is inserted. The user can skim retrieved documents interactively using this function.

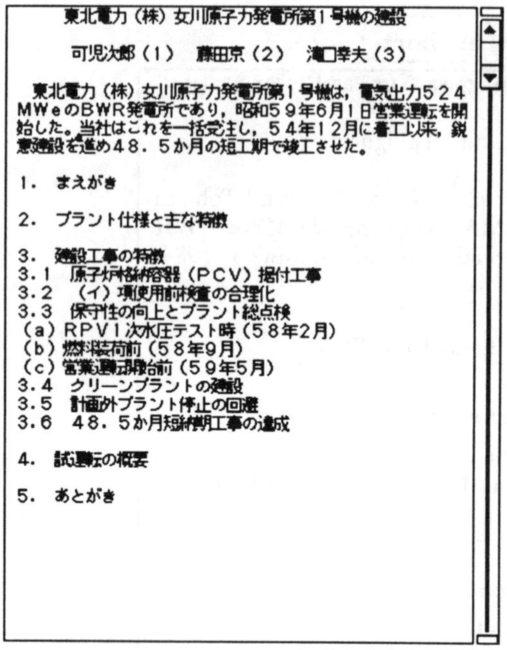

Figure 10. The 2nd Abstract

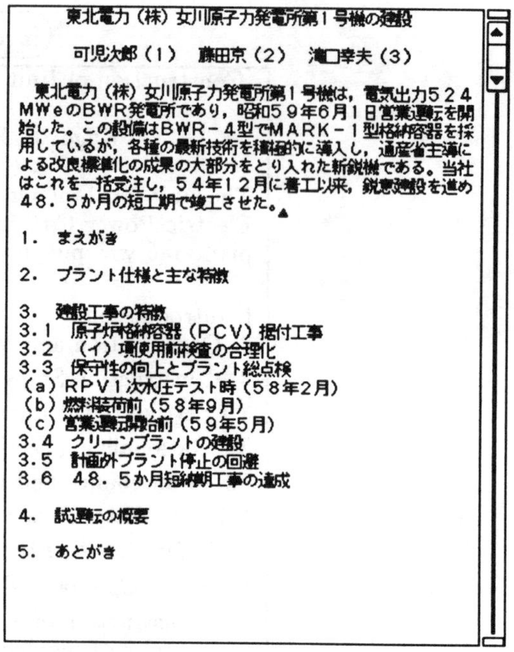

Figure 11. The 3rd Abstract

The unit No.1 of Onagawa Nuclear Power Station, Tohoku Electric Power Co., Inc. is a MARK-1 type 524-MWe BWR plant and was put into commercial operation in June 1, 1984. Toshiba got the order for the design and construction as a main contractor, and completed the plant to be put into commercial operation in only 48.5 months since the start in December 1979.

Figure 12. Translation of Sentences in Figure 10

The unit No.1 of Onagawa Nuclear Power Station, Tohoku Electric Power Co., Inc. is a MARK-1 type 524-MWe BWR plant and was put into commercial operation in June 1, 1984. This unit, a BWR-4 type housed in a MARK-1 type primary containment vessel, incorporates several newest techniques and most of the results obtained during the reform standardization which was led by the Ministry of International Trade and Industry. Toshiba got the order for the design and construction as a main contractor, and completed the plant to be put into commercial operation in only 48.5 months since the start in December 1979.

Figure 13. Translation of Sentences in Figure 11

7 Preliminary Experiment

(1) Text structure analysis

114 paragraphs among 18 papers of *Toshiba Review* were analyzed, and correct text structures were produced for about 74% of the man-made structures [3].

(2) Key sentence coverage

The generated abstracts of 42 papers of *Toshiba Review* and 30 editorials of *Asahi* were compared with their key sentences selected by a hand. As for 24%-abstracts (the percentage signifies the ratio of the number of sentences in the abstract to that in the original text), the coverages of the key sentences and the most important key sentence were 51% and 74% respectively. Whereas, as for 30%-abstracts, the coverages were 41% and 60%. On the other hand, as for the papers, the coverages of key sentences and the most important key sentence selected by three subjects were 60% and 80%. As for the editorials, the coverages were 60% and 60%.

(3) Abstract browsing

The time for selecting retrived editorials of *Asahi* with the dynamic abstract generation function and only with the original text browsing function was compared. In each case, five subjects selected editorials among several ten editorials retrieved by each of some queries. The time using the abstract generation function was about 80% of the time using only the original text browsing function, while precision and recall remained more or less the same.

8 Conclusion

A full-text retrieval system with a dynamic abstract generation function has been developed. The abstract is generated based on rhetorical relations among sentences extracted by analyzing a document structure. The dynamic abstract generation function enables the user to skim through each of the retrieved documents and judge whether it is really required or not efficiently. A preliminary experiment shows that this function is effective. We plan to improve it by incorporating semantic roles of sentences and extra-linguistic knowledge in order to generate an abstract from a viewpoint of the user.

Acknowledgment

The authors would like to thank Isamu Iwai, Yukio Nakamoto, Hideki Hirakawa and Kimihito Takeda for productive discussions; Yumi Mizutani and Tetsuya Sakai for their help with the system implementation.

References

1. Harman, D.: "The DARPA TIPSTAR Project", *SIGIR Forum*, Vol.26, No.2, pp.26–28, 1992.
2. Card, S.K., Robertson, G.G., Mackinlay J.D.: "The Information Visualizer, An Information Workplace", *Proc. of CHI'91*, pp.181–187, 1991.
3. Sumita, K., Ono. K., Chino, T., Ukita, T. and Amano, S.: "A Discourse Structure Analyzer for Japanese Text", *Proc. Int. Conf. Fifth Generation Computer Systems 1992 (FGCS'92)*, pp.1133–1140, 1992.
4. Cohen, R.: "Analyzing the Structure of Argumentative Discourse", *Computational Linguistics*, Vol.13, pp.11–24, 1987.
5. Mann, W.C., Thompson, S.A.: "Rhetorical Structure Theory: A Framework for the Analysis of Texts", *USC/Information Science Institute ResearchReport*, RR-87-190, 1987.
6. Grosz, B.J., Sidner, C.L.: "Attention, Intentions and the Structure of Discourse", *Computational Linguistics*, Vol.12, pp.175–204, 1986.
7. Jacobs, P., Rau, L.: "SCISOR: Extracting information from on-line news", *CACM*, Vol.33, No.11, pp.88–97, 1990.
8. Salton, G.: *Automatic Text Processing*, Addison-Wesley Publishing Company, pp.439–448, 1989.
9. Chino, T., Ukita, T., Ono, K., Sumita, K.: "Implementation and Evaluation of Automatic Text Skimming System for Japanese Explanatory Texts (in Japanese)", *Proc. of IPSJ 46th National Conf.*, Vol.3, pp.189–190, 1993.
10. Nakamoto, Y., Nogami, K., Yajima, M., Tanosaki, Y.: "An Experiment of Full Text Retrieval by Japanese Analysis Method (in Japanese)", *Proc. of IPSJ 46th National Conf.*, Vol.3, pp.125–126, 1993.
11. Sumita, K., Ono, K., Miike, S.: "Document Structure Extraction for Interactive Document Retrieval Systems", *Proc. of SIGDOC'93*, pp.301–310, 1993.
12. Hirakawa, H., Nogami, H., Amano, S: "EJ/JE Machine Translation System ASTRANSAC - Extensions toward Personalization", *Proc. of MT SUMMIT III*, pp.73–80, 1991.
13. Ono, K., Sumita, K., Chino, T., Ukita, T.: "Discourse Structure Analysis for Automatic Text Skimming System for Japanese Explanatory Texts (in Japanese)", *Proc. of IPSJ 46th National Conf.*, Vol.3, pp.187–188, 1993.
14. Sumita, K., Ono, K., Miike, S.: "Document Structure Extraction for Interactive Full-Text Retrieval", *Proc. of Natural Language Processing Pacific Rim Symposium(NLPRS) '93*, pp.144–152, 1993.

Statistical Models

A Document Retrieval Model Based on Term Frequency Ranks

IJsbrand Jan Aalbersberg *
Philips Laboratories, Briarcliff Manor, NY, USA

Abstract

This paper introduces a new full-text document retrieval model that is based on comparing occurrence frequency rank numbers of terms in queries and documents.

More precisely, to compute the similarity between a query and a document, this new model first ranks the terms in the query and in the document on decreasing occurrence frequency. Next, for each term, it computes a local similarity between the query and the document, by calculating a weighted difference between the term's rank number in the query and its rank number in the document. Finally, it collects all those local similarities and unifies them into one global similarity between the query and the document.

In this paper we also demonstrate that the effectiveness of this new full-text document retrieval model is comparable with that of the standard vector-space retrieval model.

1 Introduction

Most of the advanced full-text document retrieval models associate *term weights* or *term probabilities* with the terms in queries and documents. Of those models, the most generally accepted are the *vector-space* and the *probabilistic* retrieval models (see, e.g., [14] and [9]). Common to both (and to other) retrieval models is the use of term *occurrence frequencies* to calculate the term weights or the initial term probabilities (see, e.g., [10]).

Already in 1949 G.K. Zipf formalized a relation between the occurrence frequency of a term in a text (or a set of texts) and its rank number, when all terms in the text (or texts) are ranked according to decreasing occurrence frequency (see [17]). This so-called *rank-frequency law of Zipf* expresses that, for a given text (or set of texts), the product of such an occurrence frequency and such a rank number is approximately constant.

Since then, occurrence frequency rank numbers have been the topic of research in a number of theoretical studies (see, e.g., [4] and [5]). However, in information retrieval (and, more specifically, in full-text document retrieval) its application has mainly been in computing the text-size reduction achieved by text compression or in estimating storage requirements for term lists and dictionaries (see, e.g., [3]).

One of the few exceptions to the above is the proposal of D. Blair to use the rank-frequency law of Zipf to measure the effectiveness of full-text document retrieval models (see [2]). Blair suggests that Zipf's law can be used to compare the language of a document indexer with that of a document inquirer: "The closer the rank-frequency distribution of indexer and inquirer usage is to the Zipfian distribution, the better the evidence that inquirers and indexers are using search terms in substantially the same way" (page 193). And, according to Blair, the latter is favorable for the effectiveness of a full-text document retrieval model.

Another exception is the suggestion of IJ.J. Aalbersberg to apply the rank-frequency law of Zipf in posting compression and term-weight approximation (see [1]). By storing postings on decreasing term occurrence frequency (but without storing the term frequencies themselves) a reduction of the index size by 25% to 50% can be achieved. Using this compression technique in combination with the vector-space retrieval model, Aalbersberg demonstrates that term occurrence frequencies can easily be approximated from occurrence frequency rank numbers, resulting in a retrieval effectiveness that is almost equal to that of standard vector-space retrieval (without the compression technique).

In this paper we continue the research started in [1], by searching for a full-text document retrieval model that better corresponds with the compression technique introduced there. In other words, instead of the vector-space retrieval model that translates occurrence frequency rank numbers back into term occurrence frequencies, we try to identify a full-text document retrieval model that directly uses those rank numbers themselves. Of course, the required retrieval model should provide a retrieval effectiveness that is at least as good as the one obtained using the vector-space retrieval.

*On temporary leave from Philips Research Laboratories, Eindhoven, The Netherlands.

The paper is organized as follows. Firstly, Section 2 recalls the vector-space retrieval model (Section 2.1) and a method to evaluate the effectiveness of full-text document retrieval models (Section 2.2). Secondly, Section 3 reviews the rank-frequency law of Zipf (Section 3.1) and its applicability to approximate term weights (Section 3.2). In Section 4, the main section of the paper, we introduce, investigate, and evaluate a new rank-based full-text document retrieval model: Section 4.1 presents an introduction, Section 4.2 overviews the theory, Section 4.3 provides some variations on the theory, and Section 4.4 investigates its retrieval effectiveness. Finally, the paper concludes with a brief discussion on the results in Section 5.

2 Full-Text Document Retrieval

2.1 Vector-Space Full-Text Retrieval

In term-weighted full-text document retrieval (see, e.g., [13]), a *term weight* becomes associated with each term that occurs in a (document or query) text. A term weight w of a term s in a text t indicates the descriptive value of s for t: 0 for no value and 1 for a maximal value. Term weights are used to compute the *text similarity* between documents and queries. A query will be answered by listing documents in decreasing text similarity to it, and thus listing the most relevant documents first.

The computation of term weights and text similarities can be done along various lines (see, e.g., [14]). The *vector-space* retrieval model represents the term weights of the terms in a text as a vector, and it does term-weight vector calculations to compute text similarities. The model basically calculates term weights in one of the following ways (for slightly different calculations, see, e.g., [1]). For a text t and a term s in t, let $frq(s,t)$ be the *occurrence frequency* of s in t. Then the *simple term weight* of s in t is

$$s\_wght(s,t) = \frac{frq(s,t)}{\sqrt{\sum_{r \in t}(frq(r,t))^2}} \tag{1}$$

and the *modified term weight* of s in t is

$$m\_wght(s,t) = \frac{\log \frac{N}{n_s} \cdot frq(s,t)}{\sqrt{\sum_{r \in t}(\log \frac{N}{n_r} \cdot frq(r,t))^2}}. \tag{2}$$

Here N is the total number of documents and n_x is the number of documents that contain the term x. Note that $\log N/n_x$ is the so-called *inverse document frequency* of x (see, e.g., [15]).

In the vector-space retrieval model a *text similarity* between a query q and a document d, denoted by $sim(q,d)$, is calculated as the inner product of the query term-weight vector and the document term-weight vector:

$$sim(q,d) = \sum_{s \in q} wght(s,q) \cdot wght(s,d) \tag{3}$$

(clearly, $wght(s,x)$ should actually be replaced by the term weight in discussion). Since the query term-weight vector and the document term-weight vector are length normalized, the text similarities always are between 0 and 1: 0 for no similarity and 1 for a maximal similarity.

2.2 Effectiveness of Full-Text Retrieval

Evaluation of full-text document retrieval models is based on *relevance ranking* and it measures *recall* and *precision* for test collections (see, e.g., [14]). Relevance ranking means that the result of a query is an ordered list of relevant documents, recall is the fraction of the relevant documents (stored in the document base) that are retrieved upon a query, and precision is the fraction of the retrieved documents that are relevant. Clearly, a full-text document retrieval model that computes text similarities provides relevance ranking. Furthermore, the effectiveness of such a retrieval model can be indicated by average recall and precision: the higher they are the more effective the retrieval model is. The test collections used are the collections CACM, CISI, CRAN, and MEDLARS (see, e.g., [14] and [16]).

For every test collection and for every query in it we first compute the associated result list. Next we compute for every query the precision values at those points whenever the recall value equals or exceeds 25%, 50%, and 75% for the first time. We then take the mean of these precision values per query and finally we take the mean and the median per test collection.

For the vector-space retrieval model that uses Formula 1 and/or 2 (and Formula 3) we reported the average precision figures in Table 1. Here, the row header "Fx Fy" denotes the retrieval model in which the query term weights and the document term weights are calculated using Formula x and y, respectively. In these evaluations we used a slightly adapted version of the stop word list as presented in [6] (see also [7]). Furthermore, we also used a slightly adapted version of the Lovins' stemming algorithm as outlined in [12] (see also [8]). Finally, apart from words we also indexed numbers.

q	d		CACM	CISI	CRAN	MEDL	average
F1	F1	mean	21.07	14.96	35.37	46.72	29.53
F1	F1	median	13.58	12.74	28.44	45.11	24.97
F1	F2	mean	30.34	19.31	38.01	50.91	34.64
F1	F2	median	23.09	14.20	33.75	47.26	29.58
F2	F1	mean	31.05	23.30	39.80	52.76	36.73
F2	F1	median	24.31	17.04	36.09	49.24	31.67
F2	F2	mean	35.88	24.10	39.01	53.44	38.11
F2	F2	median	30.09	18.48	32.73	51.75	33.26

Table 1. Average Precision Figures

3 Rank-Frequency Law of Zipf

3.1 Theory

The different components of linguistic text do not at all occur at random (see, e.g., [11]). Already in 1949 George Kingsley Zipf established a relation between the occurrence frequency of a term in a text (or a set of texts) and its rank number, when all terms in the text (or texts) are ranked according to decreasing occurrence frequency (see [17]). Informally speaking, Zipf noticed that the product of such an occurrence frequency and such a rank number is approximately constant.

More formally, this *rank-frequency law of Zipf* is as follows. For a text t and a term s in t, let $frq(s,t)$ be the occurrence frequency of s in t. Let t be a text containing $n \geq 1$ different terms $s_1, \ldots, s_n$ and, without loss of generality, assume that these terms are ranked such that $frq(s_1,t) \geq \ldots \geq frq(s_n,t)$ holds. Then the rank-frequency law of Zipf claims that there exists a constant $zpf(t)$, such that, for every $1 \leq i \leq n$, $i \cdot frq(s_i,t) \approx zpf(t)$, i.e., the product of the rank number i of s_i and the occurrence frequency $frq(s_i,t)$ of s_i is approximately constant. The Zipf constant $zpf(t)$ depends on the text t: when the size of t increases, the occurrence frequency of the most frequent term as well as the number of different terms increase – Zipf's law says that they increase evenly – and thus $zpf(t)$ increases.

3.2 Application

It was observed in [1] that the rank-frequency law of Zipf can be applied to compress postings and to approximate term weights in those full-text document retrieval models that compute term weights out of term occurrence frequencies. For the vector-space retrieval model this approximation technique was illustrated as follows.

First, for a text t and a term s in t, the *approximated occurrence frequency* of s in t was defined as $afrq(s,t) = zpf(t)/rnk(s,t)$, where $zpf(t)$ is the Zipf constant of t and $rnk(s,t)$ is the rank number of s when all terms in t are sorted on decreasing occurrence frequency. Next, the *approximated simple term weight* of s in t was defined as

$$as\_wght(s,t) = \frac{\sqrt{afrq(s,t)}}{\sqrt{\sum_{r \in t}(\sqrt{afrq(r,t)})^2}} = \frac{1/\sqrt{rnk(s,t)}}{\sqrt{\sum_{r \in t}(1/rnk(r,t))}} \tag{4}$$

and the *approximated modified term weight* of s in t was defined as

$$am\_wght(s,t) = \frac{\log \frac{N}{n_s} \cdot \sqrt{afrq(s,t)}}{\sqrt{\sum_{r \in t}(\log \frac{N}{n_r} \cdot \sqrt{afrq(r,t)})^2}} = \frac{\log \frac{N}{n_s} / \sqrt{rnk(s,t)}}{\sqrt{\sum_{r \in t}((\log \frac{N}{n_r})^2 / rnk(r,t))}}, \tag{5}$$

with again N the number of documents and n_x the number of documents that contain the term x. Formula 4 and 5 were obtained out of Formula 1 and 2, respectively, by substituting $\sqrt{afrq(s,t)}$ for $frq(s,t)$. The reason for not just substituting $frq(s,t)$ by $afrq(s,t)$ and thus for the presence of the additional square root was the empirical observation that without the square root the term weights were approximated too high for the high-frequent terms and too low for the low-frequent terms.

Evaluation of the effectiveness of the thus obtained full-text document retrieval model results in the precision figures depicted in Table 2. From a comparison with the exact term-weight calculation F2/F2, it is found that the retrieval effectiveness with the Zipf-based term-weight approximation technique F5/F5 shows a deterioration of at most 6%. However, using Formula 4 or 5 to approximate only the term weights of the terms in the documents, while still using Formula 2 to calculate the term weights of the terms in the queries, the resulting precision figures conclude that the setback in retrieval effectiveness now decreases to slightly more than 1%.

q	d		CACM	CISI	CRAN	MEDL	average
F4	F4	mean	16.79	15.10	28.22	42.72	25.71
F4	F4	median	8.63	10.98	19.17	44.39	20.79
F5	F5	mean	31.73	23.73	37.47	50.88	35.95
F5	F5	median	26.80	17.07	32.79	51.90	32.14
F2	F4	mean	31.06	23.21	38.90	53.21	36.60
F2	F4	median	22.05	16.41	33.84	50.05	30.59
F2	F5	mean	33.62	24.03	38.75	54.39	37.70
F2	F5	median	27.38	17.47	33.85	52.46	32.79

Table 2. Average Precision Figures

4 A Rank-Based Retrieval Model

4.1 Introduction

In the standard vector-space retrieval model a text is represented by a term-weight vector (see Section 2.1). For each term in a text such a term-weight vector provides a term weight, calculated out of the occurrence frequency of the term in the text. The text similarity between a query text and a document text is then computed by applying a vector operation on the query term-weight vector and the document term-weight vector.

In other words, the vector-space retrieval model computes the text similarity $sim(q, d)$ between a query q and a document d as follows.

1. Calculate the occurrence frequency vectors $frq(q)$ of q and $frq(d)$ of d.
2. Out of $frq(q)$ and $frq(d)$, calculate the term-weight vectors $wght(q)$ of q and $wght(d)$ of d.
3. Out of $wght(q)$ and $wght(d)$, calculate the text similarity $sim(q, d)$.

The resulting value usually lies between 0 (for no similarity at all) and 1 (for maximal similarity).

It can be learned from [1] that the occurrence frequency rank orders of terms in texts can be very useful for posting compression. It was also demonstrated there that these occurrence frequency rank orders can be easily combined with (vector-space) full-text document retrieval (see Section 3.2). In fact, it was shown that each term weight in a (vector-space) term-weight vector can be calculated out of its rank number in the frequency-based rank order, instead of out of the occurrence frequency itself.

Thus, this alternative (vector-space) full-text document retrieval model computes the text similarity $sim(q, d)$ between a query text q and a document text d as follows.

1. Calculate the occurrence-frequency vectors $frq(q)$ of q and $frq(d)$ of d.
2. Out of $frq(q)$ and $frq(d)$, calculate the rank-number vectors $rnk(q)$ of q and $rnk(d)$ of d.
3. Out of $rnk(q)$ and $rnk(d)$, calculate the term-weight vectors $wght(q)$ of q and $wght(d)$ of d.
4. Out of $wght(q)$ and $wght(d)$, calculate the text similarity $sim(q, d)$.

Again, the resulting value usually lies between 0 (no similarity) and 1 (maximal similarity).

However, when using occurrence frequency rank orders in the posting compression technique described in [1], the question arises whether we can get rid of the intermediate calculation of the term-weight vectors. In other words, is there a way to calculate the text similarity between a query text q and a document text d directly out of their occurrence frequency rank orders? It turns out that there indeed is such a method, which can be schematically described as follows.

1. Calculate the occurrence frequencies of all terms in q and d.
2. Sort the terms in q and d on decreasing occurrence frequency, obtaining the rank-based term sequences $rbts(q)$ and $rbts(d)$.
3. Replace in $rbts(q)$ and $rbts(d)$ each term by a unique symbol, obtaining the rank-based image strings $rbis(q)$ and $rbis(d)$.
4. Use a weighted string-comparison function, to compute the rank-based similarity between $rbis(q)$ and $rbis(d)$.
5. Set the rank-based text similarity $rbsim(q, d)$ between q and d to the rank-based string similarity just computed.

The range of the resulting value depends on the weighted string-comparison function used. In the next section we illustrate the algorithm sketched above with a string-comparison function that results a value between 0 (no similarity) and 1 (maximal similarity).

4.2 Theory

In this section we formalize a full-text document retrieval model that is based on the rank order of term occurrence frequencies. Given a query text q, the model calculates the rank-based text similarity $rbsim(q,d)$ for a document text d. This rank-based text similarity ranges between 0 and 1, reflecting a low query-document similarity between q and d when $rbsim(q,d)$ is near 0 and a high similarity when $rbsim(q,d)$ is near 1.

In the sequel we use the following terminology and notations. Let T be the set of all nonempty finite texts, let S be the set of all (relevant) terms occurring in at least one of the texts in T, and let $\prec$ be a linear ordering on S. Let Σ be a set of symbols such that there exists a bijection from S into Σ, and let f be such a bijection. Let R be the set of all nonempty finite strings over Σ that consist of different symbols only (i.e., each string in R has no two or more occurrences of the same symbol). For a string ρ in R, let $|\rho|$ denote the length of ρ (i.e., the number of symbols in ρ) and let $\phi(\rho)$ denote the set of symbols occurring in ρ (note that, by definition, the length of ρ equals the size of $\phi(\rho)$). For a string ρ in R and an $1 \leq i \leq |\rho|$, let $\rho[i]$ denote the i-th symbol in ρ.

Let t be a text in T and let, for $n \geq 1$, $s_1, \ldots, s_n \in S$ be the terms in t such that $frq(s_1,t) \geq \ldots \geq frq(s_n,t)$ and such that, for all $1 \leq i,j \leq n$, $frq(s_i,t) = frq(s_j,t) \Longrightarrow s_i \prec s_j$ holds. Then the term sequence $(s_1, \ldots, s_n)$ is called the *simple rank-based term sequence* of t, denoted by $s\_rbts(t)$. Furthermore, the *simple rank-based image string* of t, denoted by $s\_rbis(t)$, is the string $f(s_1)\ldots f(s_n)$ over Σ. Note that the linear ordering $\prec$ guarantees that the simple rank-based term sequence and the simple rank-based image string of t are both unique. Furthermore, note that, by definition, the simple rank-based image string of t is an element of R.

Example 4.1. Let t_1 be the document text

"Where is the cat? The cat is in the tree.
Can the cat sleep there? Yes, it can sleep on the branches of the tree,"

let t_2 be the document text

"Where is the dog? The dog and the cat are in the house.
Where is the house? The house is next to the tree,"

and let q be the query text

"What about the cat and the tree?"

Let $S = \{tree, cat, sleep, branch, dog, house\}$ be the set of relevant terms in t_1, t_2, and q, and let $\prec$ be the linear ordering on S such that

$$tree \prec cat \prec sleep \prec branch \prec dog \prec house.$$

Let $\Sigma = \{t,c,s,b,d,h\}$ and let f be the bijection from S into Σ such that $f(tree) = t$, $f(cat) = c$, $f(sleep) = s$, $f(branch) = b$, $f(dog) = d$, and $f(house) = h$. Then, if we remove the stop words (i.e., the terms not in S) from t_1, t_2, and q, we obtain $s\_rbts(t_1) = (cat, tree, sleep, branch)$, $s\_rbis(t_1) = ctsb$, $s\_rbts(t_2) = (house, dog, tree, cat)$, $s\_rbis(t_2) = hdtc$, $s\_rbts(q) = (tree, cat)$, and $s\_rbis(q) = tc$. □

Now the full-text document retrieval question of "what is the document d in $D \subseteq T$ that matches the query q in T the best?" leads to the question "what is a string-comparison function on $s\_rbis(q)$ and $s\_rbis(d)$ such that it nears 0 if and only if q and d have a low similarity and such that it nears 1 if and only if q and d have a high similarity?" We now provide such a string-comparison function *comp* on strings in R, which, whenever applied to $s\_rbis(q)$ and $s\_rbis(d)$, equals 0 if q and d have no terms in common, grows from 0 to 1 when q and d get more terms in common and in a more similar ordering on occurrence frequency, and equals 1 if q and d have the same terms in the same ordering on occurrence frequency.

The string-comparison function *comp* is based on the following assumptions, observations, and their corollaries:

1. for any text t, high-frequent terms in t reflect more-descriptive terms for t than low-frequent terms in t (assumption),
2. for any text t, early terms in the simple rank-based term sequence $s\_rbts(t)$ are higher frequent terms in t than late terms in $s\_rbts(t)$ (observation), and thus
3. for any text t, early symbols in the simple rank-based image string $s\_rbis(t)$ correspond to more-descriptive terms for t than late symbols in $s\_rbis(t)$ (corollary);
4. for any query text q and document text d, a term s is equally descriptive for q as for d if and only if s occurs at the same position in $s\_rbts(q)$ as in $s\_rbts(d)$ (assumption), and thus
5. for any query text q and document text d, a term s is equally descriptive for q as for d if and only if the symbol $f(s)$ occurs at the same position in $s\_rbis(q)$ as in $s\_rbis(d)$ (corollary).

The string-comparison function *comp* has as starting point that if two strings ρ_1 in R and ρ_2 in R are identical, then the string comparison $comp(\rho_1, \rho_2)$ between ρ_1 and ρ_2 should be 1, its maximal value. From that the string-comparison function penalizes deviations from equality, using the following two "penalty" elements.

- $1/\sqrt{i \cdot j}$: a symbol σ occurs in ρ_1 at position i and in ρ_2 at position j (i.e., $\rho_1[i] = \rho_2[j]$). This causes a high penalty whenever $\rho_1 = s\_rbis(q)$, $\rho_2 = s\_rbis(d)$, and σ is positioned late in ρ_1 or in ρ_2 (i.e., the term associated with σ is not very descriptive for q or for d, see the corollary 3 above).
- $(i-j)^2$: a symbol σ occurs in ρ_1 at position i and in ρ_2 at position j (i.e., $\rho_1[i] = \rho_2[j]$). This causes a high penalty whenever $\rho_1 = s\_rbis(q)$, $\rho_2 = s\_rbis(d)$, and σ is positioned very different in ρ_1 than in ρ_2 (i.e., the descriptiveness of the term associated with σ is very different for q than that for d, see the corollary 5 above).

The functionality of these "penalty" elements is illustrated as follows.

Example 4.2. Let t_1, t_2, q, S, $\prec$, Σ, and f be as in Example 4.1. Then the "penalty" elements for comparison of *cat* in the query q with *cat* in the documents t_1 and t_2 consist of:

- $1/\sqrt{2 \cdot 1} = \sqrt{2}/2$ and $(2-1)^2 = 1$ in comparing q with t_1, and
- $1/\sqrt{2 \cdot 4} = \sqrt{2}/4$ and $(2-4)^2 = 4$ in comparing q with t_2.

Thus, since *cat* is ranked higher in $s\_rbts(t_1)$ than in $s\_rbts(t_2)$ (i.e., it is more descriptive for t_1 than for t_2), the associated (first) "penalty" element is higher for t_1 than for t_2. Furthermore, since the ranking of *cat* in $s\_rbts(q)$ is more similar to its ranking in $s\_rbts(t_1)$ than to its ranking in $s\_rbts(t_2)$ (i.e., its descriptiveness is more similar to that in t_1 than to that in t_2), the associated (second) "penalty" element is lower for t_1 than for t_2. □

Combining the "penalty" elements described above, the string-comparison function $comp(\rho_1, \rho_2)$ between two strings ρ_1 and ρ_2 in R is defined as follows. Let the position function

$$pos : \Sigma \times \{\rho_1, \rho_2\} \rightarrow \{1, \ldots, 1 + 2|\rho_1| + 2|\rho_2|\}$$

be such that, for $\sigma \in \Sigma$ and $\rho \in \{\rho_1, \rho_2\}$,

$$pos(\sigma, \rho) = \begin{cases} j & \text{if } \rho[j] = \sigma \text{ for } 1 \leq j \leq |\rho|, \text{ and} \\ 1 + 2|\rho_1| + 2|\rho_2| & \text{if } \rho[j] \neq \sigma \text{ for all } 1 \leq j \leq |\rho|. \end{cases}$$

Then:

$$comp(\rho_1, \rho_2) = 1 - \alpha(\rho_1, \rho_2)/\beta(\rho_1, \rho_2), \tag{6}$$

where

$$\alpha(\rho_1, \rho_2) = \sum_{\sigma \in \phi(\rho_1) \cup \phi(\rho_2)} \frac{(pos(\sigma, \rho_1) - pos(\sigma, \rho_2))^2}{\sqrt{pos(\sigma, \rho_1) \cdot pos(\sigma, \rho_2)}} \tag{7}$$

and

$$\begin{aligned} \beta(\rho_1, \rho_2) \;=\; & \sum_{\sigma \in \phi(\rho_1) \cap \phi(\rho_2)} \frac{(1 + 2|\rho_1| + 2|\rho_2|)^2}{\sqrt{pos(\sigma, \rho_1) \cdot pos(\sigma, \rho_2)}} \\ & + \sum_{\sigma \in \phi(\rho_1) - \phi(\rho_2)} \frac{(1 + 2|\rho_1| + 2|\rho_2| - pos(\sigma, \rho_1))^2}{\sqrt{(1 + 2|\rho_1| + 2|\rho_2|) \cdot pos(\sigma, \rho_1)}} \\ & + \sum_{\sigma \in \phi(\rho_2) - \phi(\rho_1)} \frac{(1 + 2|\rho_1| + 2|\rho_2| - pos(\sigma, \rho_2))^2}{\sqrt{(1 + 2|\rho_1| + 2|\rho_2|) \cdot pos(\sigma, \rho_2)}}. \end{aligned} \tag{8}$$

Here, $\alpha(\rho_1, \rho_2)$ aggregates all "penalty" elements mentioned before and $\beta(\rho_1, \rho_2)$ is a normalization component, guaranteeing that the string-comparison function always lies between 0 and 1.

Example 4.3. Let t_1, t_2, q, S, $\prec$, Σ, and f be as in Example 4.1. Let $\rho = s\_rbis(q) = tc$, $\rho_1 = s\_rbis(t_1) = ctsb$, and $\rho_2 = s\_rbis(t_2) = hdtc$. Then $|\rho| = 2$, $|\rho_1| = 4$, and $|\rho_2| = 4$. Furthermore, reflecting the contributions of t, c, s, and b, respectively,

$$\alpha(\rho, \rho_1) = 1^2/sqrt(2) + 1^2/sqrt(2) + 10^2/sqrt(39) + 9^2/sqrt(52) = 28.66,$$

$$\beta(\rho, \rho_1) = 13^2/sqrt(2) + 13^2/sqrt(2) + 10^2/sqrt(39) + 9^2/sqrt(52) = 266.25,$$

and thus $comp(\rho, \rho_2) = 0.89$. Similarly, reflecting the contributions of t, c, h, and d, respectively,

$$\alpha(\rho, \rho_2) = 2^2/sqrt(3) + 2^2/sqrt(8) + 12^2/sqrt(13) + 11^2/sqrt(26) = 67.39$$

$$\beta(\rho, \rho_2) = 13^2/sqrt(3) + 13^2/sqrt(8) + 12^2/sqrt(13) + 11^2/sqrt(26) = 220.99,$$

and thus $comp(\rho, \rho_2) = 0.70$. □

Apart from normalizing onto a value between 0 and 1, $\beta(\rho_1, \rho_2)$ also ensures that the string-comparison function between ρ_1 and ρ_2 equals 0 if and only if ρ_1 and ρ_2 have no common symbols and that it equals 1 if and only if ρ_1 and ρ_2 are identical. All of this is shown as follows.

Claim 4.1. $0 \leq comp(\rho_1, \rho_2) \leq 1$.

Proof. Since $\alpha(\rho_1, \rho_2) \geq 0$ and $\beta(\rho_1, \rho_2) > 0$, it follows from Formula 6 that $0 \leq comp(\rho_1, \rho_2) \leq 1$ if and only if $\alpha(\rho_1, \rho_2) \leq \beta(\rho_1, \rho_2)$. Partitioning the set $\phi(\rho_1) \cup \phi(\rho_2)$ into the three disjoint subsets $\phi(\rho_1) \cap \phi(\rho_2)$, $\phi(\rho_1) - \phi(\rho_2)$, and $\phi(\rho_2) - \phi(\rho_1)$, Formula 7 and 8 above imply that $\alpha(\rho_1, \rho_2) \leq \beta(\rho_1, \rho_2)$ if and only if

$$\sum_{\sigma \in \phi(\rho_1) \cap \phi(\rho_2)} \frac{(pos(\sigma, \rho_1) - pos(\sigma, \rho_2))^2}{\sqrt{pos(\sigma, \rho_1) \cdot pos(\sigma, \rho_2)}} \leq \sum_{\sigma \in \phi(\rho_1) \cap \phi(\rho_2)} \frac{(1 + 2|\rho_1| + 2|\rho_2|)^2}{\sqrt{pos(\sigma, \rho_1) \cdot pos(\sigma, \rho_2)}}.$$

The latter holds, because, by definition of pos, for all $\sigma \in \phi(\rho_1) \cap \phi(\rho_2)$, $pos(\sigma, \rho_1) \leq |\rho_1|$ and $pos(\sigma, \rho_2) \leq |\rho_2|$, and thus also

$$(pos(\sigma, \rho_1) - pos(\sigma, \rho_2))^2 \leq (1 + 2|\rho_1| + 2|\rho_2|)^2.$$

Consequently, $\alpha(\rho_1, \rho_2) \leq \beta(\rho_1, \rho_2)$. □

Claim 4.2. $comp(\rho_1, \rho_2) = 0$ if and only if $\phi(\rho_1) \cap \phi(\rho_2) = \emptyset$.

Proof. Since $\beta(\rho_1, \rho_2) > 0$, it follows from Formula 6 that $comp(\rho_1, \rho_2) = 0$ if and only if $\alpha(\rho_1, \rho_2) = \beta(\rho_1, \rho_2)$. Partitioning the set $\phi(\rho_1) \cup \phi(\rho_2)$ into the three disjoint subsets $\phi(\rho_1) \cap \phi(\rho_2)$, $\phi(\rho_1) - \phi(\rho_2)$, and $\phi(\rho_2) - \phi(\rho_1)$, Formula 7 and 8 above imply that $\alpha(\rho_1, \rho_2) = \beta(\rho_1, \rho_2)$ if and only if

$$\sum_{\sigma \in \phi(\rho_1) \cap \phi(\rho_2)} \frac{(pos(\sigma, \rho_1) - pos(\sigma, \rho_2))^2}{\sqrt{pos(\sigma, \rho_1) \cdot pos(\sigma, \rho_2)}} = \sum_{\sigma \in \phi(\rho_1) \cap \phi(\rho_2)} \frac{(1 + 2|\rho_1| + 2|\rho_2|)^2}{\sqrt{pos(\sigma, \rho_1) \cdot pos(\sigma, \rho_2)}}.$$

However, by definition of pos, for all $\sigma \in \phi(\rho_1) \cap \phi(\rho_2)$, $pos(\sigma, \rho_1) \leq |\rho_1|$ and $pos(\sigma, \rho_2) \leq |\rho_2|$, and thus

$$(pos(\sigma, \rho_1) - pos(\sigma, \rho_2))^2 < (1 + 2|\rho_1| + 2|\rho_2|)^2.$$

Consequently, $\alpha(\rho_1, \rho_2) = \beta(\rho_1, \rho_2)$ if and only if $\phi(\rho_1) \cap \phi(\rho_2) = \emptyset$. □

Claim 4.3. $comp(\rho_1, \rho_2) = 1$ if and only if $\rho_1 = \rho_2$.

Proof. Since $\beta(\rho_1, \rho_2) > 0$, it follows from Formula 6 that $comp(\rho_1, \rho_2) = 1$ if and only if $\alpha(\rho_1, \rho_2) = 0$. Hence, it follows from Formula 7 that $comp(\rho_1, \rho_2) = 1$ if and only if

$$pos(\sigma, \rho_1) = pos(\sigma, \rho_2)$$

for all $\sigma \in \phi(\rho_1) \cup \phi(\rho_2)$, which clearly is equivalent with $\rho_1 = \rho_2$. □

Another property of the string-comparison function $comp(\rho_1, \rho_2)$ between ρ_1 and ρ_2 is that, for any symbol $\sigma \in \phi(\rho_1) \cup \phi(\rho_2)$, the "penalty" element $(pos(\sigma, \rho_1) - pos(\sigma, \rho_2))^2$ is always smaller whenever σ occurs in both ρ_1 and ρ_2 than in only one of them. This can be deduced from the following claim and its proof.

Claim 4.4. For $\sigma \in \phi(\rho_1) \cap \phi(\rho_2)$,

1. $(pos(\sigma, \rho_1) - pos(\sigma, \rho_2))^2 < (pos(\sigma, \rho_1) - (1 + 2|\rho_1| + 2|\rho_2|))^2$ and
2. $(pos(\sigma, \rho_1) - pos(\sigma, \rho_2))^2 < ((1 + 2|\rho_1| + 2|\rho_2|) - pos(\sigma, \rho_2))^2$.

Proof. By definition of pos, $pos(\sigma, \rho_1) < 1 + 2|\rho_1| + 2|\rho_2|$, and thus the first part of the claim holds if

$$|pos(\sigma, \rho_1) - pos(\sigma, \rho_2)| < 1 + 2|\rho_1| + 2|\rho_2| - pos(\sigma, \rho_1),$$

which, again by definition of pos, holds when $pos(\sigma, \rho_1) \leq pos(\sigma, \rho_2)$. Moreover, if $pos(\sigma, \rho_1) \geq pos(\sigma, \rho_2)$, then the first part of the claim holds if

$$2pos(\sigma, \rho_1) < 1 + 2|\rho_1| + 2|\rho_2| + pos(\sigma, \rho_2),$$

which again holds by definition of pos.

The second part of the claim is proven similarly. □

A final property of the string-comparison function is that it is symmetric.

Claim 4.5. $comp(\rho_1, \rho_2) = comp(\rho_2, \rho_1)$.

Proof. Since

$$(pos(\sigma, \rho_1) - pos(\sigma, \rho_2))^2 = (pos(\sigma, \rho_2) - pos(\sigma, \rho_1))^2$$

and since product, addition, union, and intersection are commutative, this directly follows from Formula 6 through 8 above. □

After the definition of the string-comparison function $comp$, we finally can define the *simple rank-based text similarity* between a query text q and a document text d, denoted by $s\_rbsim(q, d)$, as follows:

$$s\_rbsim(q, d) = comp(s\_rbis(q), s\_rbis(d)). \tag{9}$$

Note that the simple rank-based text similarity is, however only slightly, dependent on the linear ordering $\prec$ on the set of terms S. Furthermore, it follows from Claim 4.1 that $0 \leq s\_rbsim(q, d) \leq 1$, from Claim 4.2 that $s\_rbsim(q, d) = 0$ if and only if q and d have no terms in common, and from Claim 4.3 that $s\_rbsim(q, d) = 1$ if and only if q and d have exactly the same terms in exactly the same ordering on occurrence frequency. Finally, it follows from Claim 4.4 that $s\_rbsim(q, d)$ increases from 0 to 1 when q and d are getting more terms in common.

Example 4.4. Let t_1, t_2, q, S, $\prec$, Σ, and f be as in Example 4.1. Then $s\_rbsim(q, t_1) = 0.89$ and $s\_rbsim(q, t_2) = 0.70$, which shows that t_1 is more relevant to q than t_2 is. □

As we have seen in the literature (see, e.g, [14]) as well as in Section 2.2 and 3.2, the use of inverse document frequencies highly improves the effectiveness of full-text document retrieval models. Incorporating inverse document frequencies in the retrieval model described above can be done as follows.

Let t be a text in T and let, for $n \geq 1$, $s_1, \ldots, s_n \in S$ be the terms in t such that $frq(s_1, t) \cdot \log N/n_1 \geq \ldots \geq frq(s_n, t) \cdot \log N/n_n$ and such that, for all $1 \leq i, j \leq n$, $frq(s_i, t) \cdot \log N/n_i = frq(s_j, t) \cdot \log N/n_j \Longrightarrow s_i \prec s_j$ holds. As before, N is the number of documents stored and n_i is the number of these documents that contain the term s_i ($1 \leq i \leq n$). Then the term sequence $(s_1, \ldots, s_n)$ is called the *modified rank-based term sequence* of t, denoted by $m\_rbts(t)$. Furthermore, the string $f(s_1) \ldots f(s_n)$ over Σ is called the *modified rank-based image string* of t, denoted by $m\_rbis(t)$. Finally, the *modified rank-based text similarity* between a query q and a document d in $D \subseteq T$, denoted by $m\_rbsim(q, d)$, is:

$$m\_rbsim(q, d) = comp(m\_rbis(q), m\_rbis(d)). \tag{10}$$

Also the modified rank-based text similarity is slightly dependent on the linear ordering $\prec$ on the set of terms S. Furthermore, again by Claim 4.1 through 4.4, $0 \leq m\_rbsim(q, d) \leq 1$, $m\_rbsim(q, d) = 0$ if and only if q and d have no terms in common, $m\_rbsim(q, d) = 1$ if and only if q and d have the same terms in the same ordering (on product of inverse document frequency and occurrence frequency), and $s\_rbsim(q, d)$ increases when q and d are getting more descriptive terms in common.

4.3 Variations

It is easily understood that the simple and modified rank-based text similarities as defined in Section 4.2 above are only two examples out of a potential multitude of different ways in which the rank order of term occurrence frequencies can be used in full-text document retrieval. And of course, it is impractical to report and investigate many of the other possible ways to define rank-based text similarities in one and the same paper. Nevertheless, we would like to make some remarks and present some variations on the full-text document retrieval model introduced.

As shown in Claim 4.5, the string-comparison function and thus also the simple and modified rank-based text similarities all are symmetric. However, one could argue that a query and a document are two completely different objects, and thus that it is not logical that the rank-based text similarities between a query and a document should be symmetrical. For instance, one could argue that $\alpha(\rho_1, \rho_2)$ and $\beta(\rho_1, \rho_2)$ should be defined as

$$\alpha(\rho_1, \rho_2) = \sum_{\sigma \in \phi(\rho_1)} \frac{(pos(\sigma, \rho_1) - pos(\sigma, \rho_2))^2}{\sqrt{pos(\sigma, \rho_1) \cdot pos(\sigma, \rho_2)}} \tag{11}$$

and

$$\begin{aligned}\beta(\rho_1, \rho_2) &= \sum_{\sigma \in \phi(\rho_1) \cap \phi(\rho_2)} \frac{(1 + 2|\rho_1| + 2|\rho_2|)^2}{\sqrt{pos(\sigma, \rho_1) \cdot pos(\sigma, \rho_2)}} \\ &+ \sum_{\sigma \in \phi(\rho_1) - \phi(\rho_2)} \frac{(1 + 2|\rho_1| + 2|\rho_2| - pos(\sigma, \rho_1))^2}{\sqrt{(1 + 2|\rho_1| + 2|\rho_2|) \cdot pos(\sigma, \rho_1)}}\end{aligned} \tag{12}$$

or

$$\beta(\rho_1, \rho_2) = \sum_{\sigma \in \phi(\rho_1)} \frac{(1 + 2|\rho_1| + 2|\rho_2| - pos(\sigma, \rho_1))^2}{\sqrt{pos(\sigma, \rho_2) \cdot pos(\sigma, \rho_1)}}, \tag{13}$$

instead of as defined in Formula 7 and 8. Next to the fact that these approaches indeed yield non-symmetric rank-based text similarities, computationally they have the advantage that for all the symbols that are in ρ_2 but not in ρ_1 no calculation has to be made. And when ρ_2 is the rank-based image of a large document while ρ_1 is the rank-based image of only a small query, this makes quite a difference.

Furthermore, although the string-comparison functions as defined by Formula 6 and Formula 11 through 13 satisfy Claim 4.1, 4.2, and 4.4, they do not satisfy Claim 4.3. In other words, for these newly defined functions it does not hold that the string comparison between ρ_1 and ρ_2 equals 1 if and only if ρ_1 equals ρ_2. This is caused by the facts that ρ_1 could be a prefix of ρ_2 and that symbols in ρ_2 but not in ρ_1 are not taken into account in Formula 11 through 13. However, this flaw can be repaired by also incorporating the length of ρ_1 and ρ_2 into the definition of $\alpha(\rho_1, \rho_2)$ and $\beta(\rho_1, \rho_2)$, for instance as follows:

$$\alpha(\rho_1, \rho_2) = \frac{(|\rho_1| - |\rho_2|)^2}{\sqrt{(|\rho_1| + 1) \cdot (|\rho_2| + 1)}} + \sum_{\sigma \in \phi(\rho_1)} \frac{(pos(\sigma, \rho_1) - pos(\sigma, \rho_2))^2}{\sqrt{pos(\sigma, \rho_1) \cdot pos(\sigma, \rho_2)}} \tag{14}$$

α	β		CACM	CISI	CRAN	MEDL	average
F7	F8	mean	35.63	22.25	39.92	55.24	38.26
F7	F8	median	27.53	17.54	36.62	55.09	34.20
F11	F12	mean	37.77	22.82	38.77	54.27	38.41
F11	F12	median	34.02	16.47	35.54	56.72	35.69
F11	F13	mean	36.61	23.10	38.03	53.53	37.82
F11	F13	median	31.14	17.05	33.96	55.29	34.63
F14	F15	mean	37.91	22.88	38.95	54.33	38.52
F14	F15	median	33.42	16.46	36.11	56.78	35.69
F14	F16	mean	36.95	23.08	38.28	53.70	38.00
F14	F16	median	31.19	16.90	33.88	57.04	34.75

Table 3. Average Precision Figures

and

$$\begin{aligned}\beta(\rho_1,\rho_2) &= \frac{(|\rho_1|-|\rho_2|)^2}{\sqrt{(|\rho_1|+1)\cdot(|\rho_2|+1)}} \\ &+ \sum_{\sigma\in\phi(\rho_1)\cap\phi(\rho_2)} \frac{(1+2|\rho_1|+2|\rho_2|)^2}{\sqrt{pos(\sigma,\rho_1)\cdot pos(\sigma,\rho_2)}} \\ &+ \sum_{\sigma\in\phi(\rho_1)-\phi(\rho_2)} \frac{(1+2|\rho_1|+2|\rho_2|-pos(\sigma,\rho_1))^2}{\sqrt{(1+2|\rho_1|+2|\rho_2|)\cdot pos(\sigma,\rho_1)}} \qquad (15)\end{aligned}$$

or

$$\begin{aligned}\beta(\rho_1,\rho_2) &= \frac{(|\rho_1|-|\rho_2|)^2}{\sqrt{(|\rho_1|+1)\cdot(|\rho_2|+1)}} \\ &+ \sum_{\sigma\in\phi(\rho_1)} \frac{(1+2|\rho_1|+2|\rho_2|-pos(\sigma,\rho_1))^2}{\sqrt{pos(\sigma,\rho_2)\cdot pos(\sigma,\rho_1)}}. \qquad (16)\end{aligned}$$

And indeed, along the same lines of proof, it is not difficult to see that the string-comparison functions as defined by Formula 6 and Formula 14 through 16 satisfy all of Claim 4.1 through 4.4.

4.4 Evaluation

We now evaluate the effectiveness of the full-text document retrieval model described in Section 4.2 and 4.3 above. Again (see also Section 3.2) the evaluation method is the one recalled in Section 2.2. Thus, applying Formula 6 through 16 above, for each query in each of the test collections CACM, CISI, CRAN, and MEDL, we made ten retrieval runs and computed the associated precision figures. The resulting average precision figures related to the modified rank-based text similarities (Formula 10) are presented in Table 3. The average precision figures related to the simple rank-based text similarities (Formula 9) are much lower (average mean is between 27 and 28 and average median is between 22 and 23) and therefore they are not shown here. In Table 3, "Fx" in the column headed by α or β denotes the retrieval model in which the modified rank-based text similarities are calculated using Formula x for $\alpha(\rho_1,\rho_2)$ or $\beta(\rho_1,\rho_2)$, respectively.

From these (and the omitted) precision figures it follows that the use of inverse document frequencies (using Formula 10 instead of Formula 9) considerably improves the effectiveness of the rank-based full-text document retrieval model. In relation with what is known from the literature, this is not at all surprising (see, e.g., [14]). However, it is more interesting to compare these precision figures with the ones previously presented in Table 1 and 2. In comparison with the precision figures resulting from the standard vector-space retrieval model (Formula 1 through 3) it is found that, on the average, the effectiveness of the modified rank-based retrieval model does not show a deterioration. Moreover, in comparison with the best-performing vector-space retrieval model F2/F2, a slight increase in effectiveness can even be noticed (from a precision mean of 38.11 to one of at most 38.52 for F14/F15). Finally, looking at the precision figures of the Zipf-based retrieval model described in Section 3.2 (Formula 3 through 5), the effectiveness of the modified rank-based retrieval increases as well (from a precision mean of 37.70 for F2/F4 to one of 38.52 for F14/F15).

Note however that, because of the direct dependency on inverse document frequencies, the retrieval model based on modified rank-based text similarities can only be used in static retrieval environments. Although simple rank-based text similarities do not suffer from this problem, the retrieval model based on simple rank-based text similarities performs much worse than the best-performing vector-space or Zipf-based retrieval model that is suited for dynamic environments (F2/F1 and F2/F4, respectively).

5 Discussion

In this paper we have proposed a new full-text document retrieval model that is based on the direct comparison of occurrence frequency rank numbers of the terms in queries and documents. We also showed that for this new retrieval model there was no loss in retrieval effectiveness when compared with the standard vector-space retrieval model. In a narrow context, this result can be nicely applied in combination with the compression technique presented in [1], our initial motivation for the research presented. However, in a broader context, we have also demonstrated that exact occurrence-frequency information does not always seem to be crucial in the process of full-text document retrieval.

In this paper we did not concentrate on the computational complexity of the new full-text document retrieval model. However, for those variants that do not require a calculation for those terms in a document that are not in the query, we do expect that the computational complexity is comparable with that of, e.g., the vector-space retrieval model.

Finally, this paper did not yet provide a conclusive investigation into all variations on the use of term occurrence frequency rank orders in full-text document retrieval. There might be other models based on occurrence frequency rank numbers that are much more effective, and which thus keep up with the increase in effectiveness caused by add-ons on the standard vector-space retrieval model. For instance, quite some more variations can be made on the string-comparison function. Nevertheless, despite of this inconclusiveness, this paper illustrated the usefulness of looking beyond term occurrence frequencies, for instance by concentrating on term occurrence frequency rank numbers.

References

1. IJ.J. Aalbersberg, Posting Compression in Dynamic Retrieval Environments, Proc. 14th International Conference on Research and Development in Information Retrieval SIGIR 91, Chicago, IL (October 1991), 72 - 81.
2. D.C. Blair, *Language and Representation in Information Retrieval*, Elsevier, Amsterdam, The Netherlands (1990).
3. A.D. Booth, A Law of Occurrence for Words of Low Frequency, *Information and Control* 10 (1967), 386 - 393.
4. B.C. Brookes, Ranking Techniques and the Empirical Log Law, *Information Processing and Management* 20 (1984), 37 - 46.
5. L. Egghe, On the Classification of the Classical Bibliometric Laws, *Journal of Documentation* 44 (1988), 53 - 62.
6. C. Fox, A Stop List for General Text, *SIGIR Forum* 24, No. 1 - 2 (1989/1990), 19 - 35.
7. C. Fox, Lexical Analysis and Stoplists, in *Information Retrieval: Data Structures and Algorithms*, W.B. Frakes and R. Baeza-Yates (eds.), Prentice-Hall, Englewood Cliffs, NJ (1992), 102 - 130.
8. W.B. Frakes, Stemming Algorithms, in *Information Retrieval: Data Structures and Algorithms*, W.B. Frakes and R. Baeza-Yates (eds.), Prentice-Hall, Englewood Cliffs, NJ (1992), 131 - 160.
9. N. Fuhr, Probabilistic Models in Information Retrieval, *The Computer Journal* 35 (1992), 243 - 255.
10. D. Harman, Ranking Algorithms, in *Information Retrieval: Data Structures and Algorithms*, W.B. Frakes and R. Baeza-Yates (eds.), Prentice-Hall, Englewood Cliffs, NJ (1992), 363 - 392.
11. H. Kucera and W.N. Francis, *Computational Analysis of Present-day American English*, Brown University Press, Providence, RI (1967).
12. J.B. Lovins, Development of a Stemming Algorithm, *Mechanical Translation and Computational Linguistics* 11 (1968), 22 - 31.
13. G. Salton, *Automatic Text Processing: The Transformation, Analysis, and Retrieval of Information by Computer*, Addison-Wesley, Reading, MA (1989).
14. G. Salton and C. Buckley, Term-Weighting Approaches in Automatic Text Retrieval, *Information Processing and Management* 24 (1988), 513 - 523.
15. K. Sparck Jones, A Statistical Interpretation of Term Specificity and its Application in Retrieval, *Journal of Documentation* 28 (1972), 11 - 21.
16. Virginia Disc One, CD-ROM from Virginia Polytechnic Institute and State University, Blacksburg, VA (1990).
17. G.K. Zipf, *Human Behavior and the Principle of Least Effort*, Addison-Wesley, Reading, MA (1949).

Automatic Combination of Multiple Ranked Retrieval Systems

Brian T. Bartell† bbartell@eb.com

Garrison W. Cottrell‡ gary@cs.ucsd.edu

Richard K. Belew‡ rik@cs.ucsd.edu

†Advanced Technology Group
Encylopædia Britannica, Inc.
3252 Holiday Court, Ste. 208
La Jolla, California 92037

‡Department of Computer Science & Engineering-0114
University of California, San Diego
La Jolla, California 92093-0114

Abstract

Retrieval performance can often be improved significantly by using a number of different retrieval algorithms and combining the results, in contrast to using just a single retrieval algorithm. This is because different retrieval algorithms, or retrieval *experts*, often emphasize different document and query features when determining relevance and therefore retrieve different sets of documents. However, it is unclear how the different experts are to be combined, in general, to yield a superior overall estimate. We propose a method by which the relevance estimates made by different experts can be automatically combined to result in superior retrieval performance. We apply the method to two expert combination tasks. The applications demonstrate that the method can identify high performance combinations of experts and also is a novel means for determining the combined effectiveness of experts.

1 Introduction

In text retrieval, two heads are definitely better than one. Retrieval performance can be greatly improved by using a number of different retrieval algorithms (or *experts*) and combining their results, in contrast to using just a single retrieval algorithm. Each expert contributes its estimates of which documents are likely to be relevant to the user's query, and the combined set is typically more valuable than any single expert's estimates.

Part of the benefit may be due to the increased recall resulting from a combination of experts. It has been observed that different experts often retrieve different documents; e.g., Katzer et al. [10] found that very different sets of documents were retrieved using different document representation methods, and Harman [9] observed that the systems in the 1993 Text REtrieval Conference (TREC-1) retrieved substantially different sets of documents, even though most systems performed at the same approximate level. Since different experts can retrieve different documents, the perceived performance of the combined system may be higher because of the increased levels of recall that are attainable.

Not all of the performance benefit can be attributed to enhanced recall in the combined system. For example, Saracevic & Kantor [13] demonstrated that the odds of a document being relevant to a query increase monotonically with the number of experts that retrieve the document. A possible explanation is offered by a recent study by Belkin et al. [3]. This study demonstrated that the retrieval results based on different query formulations can be combined to result in performance that is better than any single formulation. Belkin et al. suggest that each expert's relevance estimates may be interpreted as sources of evidence of the true relevance. Additional experts provide additional evidence resulting in a more accurate estimate of the true probability of relevance.

The principal difficulty with combining experts, however, is in deciding how the multiple experts are to be combined to generate an overall retrieval score. In this work, we provide a method by which multiple experts can be automatically combined into a single retrieval system. The technique is applicable to *ranked retrieval* systems, in which the overall performance goal is to correctly rank the documents in the order of their relevance to the user's query. For these systems, the method automatically determines a combination of experts that is optimized to rank relevant documents before less relevant ones. We will demonstrate that this automatically derived combination of experts performs much better than any of the individual experts when applied to two different problems.

In addition, we demonstrate that the method is a useful and novel analytic tool. Belkin et al. [3] made the important observation that a different query formulation (or expert) can contribute to improved performance in the combined system even when it performs poorly on its own. The consequences of this observation are significant: A candidate retrieval method cannot be discounted simply because it does not perform well relative to alternative methods. This same method might still enhance performance when combined with others. This poses a dilemma for system designers: How can a candidate method be evaluated to determine whether it should be added to the system, when simple evaluation of the method (with comparison to other techniques) does not predict its actual utility? The approach we present here can potentially offer insights into this dilemma, as it offers a method for evaluating the performance of experts in combination with others rather than in isolation.

In the next section, we outline our method for automatically combining experts. The approach is based on the general rank optimization method developed in previous work [1] [2]. Sections 3 and 4 present the results of two applications, Section 5 compares the method to an alternative, and Section 6 discusses the method's strengths and limitations.

2 Expert Combination Algorithm

A number of methods for combining retrieval experts have been proposed. Perhaps the most common approach is by manual search of a small set of possible combination strategies. The system designer evaluates one or more candidate combination strategies using a set of queries with relevance-tagged documents, and the strategy resulting in the best performance is selected. Typical of this approach are: Belkin et al.'s [3] analysis of alternative query formulations on the TREC database, Lewis & Croft's [11] comparison of term, phrase, and concept clustering approaches, and Turtle & Croft's [16] inference network framework, in which manual search is used to find the best weighted average of experts. A limitation of manual search is that typically only a small number of strategies are examined.

Alternatives to search include Fox et al.'s [5] Similarity Merge approach, in which a document's overall relevance score is the maximum of all expert's relevance estimates, and Thompson's [15] evaluation method in which each expert is weighted based on its individual utility. In this second approach, each expert is evaluated independently to determine its relative performance level. During retrieval, the experts' relevance estimates are combined in proportion to their performance level. Weighting experts based on their individual performance does not clearly address how they will perform together. Indeed, Thompson found that the combined experts, weighted by performance level, performed no better than a combination using uniform weights. Another alternative is Thompson's Combination of Expert Opinion (CEO) model [14]. CEO is a Bayesian model of the combination of evidence from a set of experts. Experts are combined to yield a more reliable overall estimate of a document's relevance to a query. The method assumes that the experts are statistically independent, though work continues to make this model more generally applicable [15].

Our approach differs from these approaches in that 1) a large space of possible combinations is heuristically searched, 2) the ability of the *combined* system to rank documents based on their relevance is explicitly optimized, and 3) the only restriction on the experts is that they generate numerical estimates of the relevance of documents to the query – the experts need not be statistically independent.

2.1 Parameterized Mixture of Experts

To automatically combine the retrieval experts, we define a model specifying how the experts may be combined. The model takes the individual experts' estimates of document relevance and combines them into a single estimate. In common with a number of the approaches identified above, we use a *linear* combination model throughout this paper. In the linear model, the overall estimate is the sum of scaled estimates from the individual experts. For example, the overall estimate for document d and query q for a system with 3 experts is:

$$R_{\Theta,q}(d) = \Theta_1 E_1(q,d) + \Theta_2 E_2(q,d) + \Theta_3 E_3(q,d) \quad (1)$$

where $R_{\Theta,q}(d)$ is the overall estimate, $E_i(q,d)$ is the relevance estimate of expert i, and Θ_i is the scale on expert i. The set of Θ_i, denoted by Θ, are free parameters in the model. The goal of our method is to automatically determine values for these parameters so that the overall estimates result in the best ranking of documents possible. Though we emphasize the linear model here, non-linear models (neural networks) have yielded positive results [1].

2.2 Optimizing Ranking Performance

To find values for the parameters, we use a criterion which measures how well the model is ranking documents for a set of training queries. We numerically optimize the criterion in order to heuristically search for parameter values which result in superior ranking performance. The criterion we use is a variation on Guttman's Point Alienation [8], a statistical measure of rank correlation. Our criterion is:

$$J(R_\Theta) = \frac{-1}{\mid Q \mid} \sum_{q \in Q} \frac{\sum_{d \succ_q d'} (R_{\Theta,q}(d) - R_{\Theta,q}(d'))}{\sum_{d \succ_q d'} \mid R_{\Theta,q}(d) - R_{\Theta,q}(d') \mid} \tag{2}$$

Here, Q is the set of training queries and d and d' are documents retrieved by at least one of the experts for query q. It is assumed that we either know the relevance of all retrieved documents for the training queries, or we restrict the optimization to those documents that are known. This knowledge is represented by the binary relation $\succ_q$ (a notation adopted from Wong & Yao [17]). $\succ_q$ is a preference relation over document pairs, interpreted as:

$$d \succ_q d' \iff \text{the user prefers } d \text{ to } d' \tag{3}$$

This preference relation is an alternative to the more standard two-valued relevance in which a document is either *relevant* or *irrelevant* to a query. Two-valued relevance can serve as the basis for a preference relation when such a relation can not be obtained from users. In this case, the two-valued relevance judgements are interpreted as a preference order between the relevant (preferred) set and the irrelevant (not preferred) set. The preference relations used in the experiments reported in the next sections were derived from two-valued relevance judgements in this fashion.

We use Conjugate Gradient, a gradient-based numerical optimization technique, to minimize J. Conjugate Gradient is preferred over other gradient methods because it is parameter-free for most applications and source code is readily available (see [12]). Criterion J is not differentiable everywhere (e.g., J is singular if $R_{\Theta,q}(d) = R_{\Theta,q}(d')$, for $d \succ_q d'$) and therefore might be resistant to gradient-based optimization. However, other work has demonstrated that the singularities do not generally cause difficulties [1], and Conjugate Gradient has been quite effective throughout our experiments.

The goal of the optimization is to find parameter values such that the system ranks document d higher than document d' whenever d is preferred by the user to d'. The criterion J defined in equation (2) is a particular mathematical formalization of this goal. There are numerous alternatives, however, to the particular criterion we have used. For example, other criteria have been proposed to solve similar rank-order problems in the field of Multidimensional Scaling (MDS) [4]. We have selected this variation of Guttman's Point Alienation because it is amenable to gradient-based optimization, it is general enough to handle arbitrary user preference relations, and because the measure has been shown to correspond well empirically to average precision, a more standard measure of retrieval effectiveness in Information Retrieval [2]. We have chosen not to explicitly optimize average precision because it is a discrete measure and is therefore not amenable to gradient-based optimization. However, methods do exist for optimizing such non-differentiable criteria, and some methods have been applied to tasks in Information Retrieval [7]. This may be a fruitful direction for further research.

3 Learning Weights on Phrases and Terms

Our first application of the method involves combining two experts. This application demonstrates that the method can be used to evaluate expert performance in combination with other experts, in contrast to the more standard individual analysis.

The first of the two experts (the "term" expert) is a standard vector-space retrieval system using white-space delimited terms. The second expert (the "phrase" expert) is a phrase identifier. It retrieves documents which contain phrases appearing in the query. The phrase expert identifies phrases using a trivially simple algorithm: Any bigram (adjacent word pair) not containing a high-frequency noise word and not crossing a sentence boundary is accepted as a phrase. The phrase expert will never retrieve any documents not already retrieved by the term expert (since any phrase which causes a document to be retrieved by the phrase expert is composed of terms which would cause the same document to be retrieved by the term expert). Thus, the usefulness of the phrase expert in the combined system stems solely from its ability to improve the term expert's document ranking.

Retrieval System	Average Precision Performance Avg Precision	% over Phrases
Phrase Expert	.1672	-
Term Expert	.2340	+40%

Table 1. The phrase expert has very low performance relative to the term expert.

Retrieval System	Truncated Precision for the k Top-Ranked Documents $k=5$	$k=10$	$k=15$	$k=30$
Phrase Expert	.1571	.1365	.1237	.1094
Term Expert	.2132	.1871	.1761	.1602

Table 2. The phrase expert performs worse than the term expert even for the small set of highest ranked documents retrieved.

3.1 Test Collection

To train and test this combination model, we use portions of the Encylopædia Britannica, an edited collection widely regarded as the premier English language general reference work. Articles in the Encylopædia Britannica (EB) have been semantically organized by editors into a hierarchical topic tree, called the Propædia. Our test collection is composed of the 8,006 Micropædia articles categorized by the editors as pertaining to Part 5, Human Society.

The queries used to train and test the system are also derived from the Propædia topic tree. Each node in the topic tree represents a refinement of the topic in the parent node. For example, the root node of Part 5 of the Propædia is "Human Society". Its children are "Social Groups: Peoples and Cultures", "Politics and Government", etc. Further down the tree one finds the more refined topic "Social Differentiation and Stratification". Associated with each of these nodes, both internal and leaf nodes, is a set of articles that discuss aspects of the topic of the node. This structure naturally permits interpretation of the node topics as queries, and their associated documents as the relevant set. We are able to extract 356 queries in this manner. These 356 queries have an average of 7.2 relevant documents per query. The set of 356 queries are partitioned into two subsets, the training set and the test set. The training set, with 128 queries, is used in equation (2) to optimize the model; the remaining 228 queries are used to test the performance of the optimized system.

3.2 Results

Tables 1 and 2 provide a summary of the performance (measured by average precision) of the two experts evaluated independently using the 228 test queries. As the tables illustrate, the term expert performs much better than the phrase expert, topping the phrase expert's average precision performance by 40%. We might expect that much of this effect is because the term expert retrieves many more documents, and therefore can achieve higher performance through much higher levels of recall. For example, the term expert retrieves an average of 2,019 documents per query, whereas the phrase expert retrieves only 28! However, we have found that this difference in recall is not a complete explanation. Even when only the highest ranked documents are used to examine performance, the term expert still outperforms the phrase expert. This performance is summarized in Table 2. In addition, for all of 11 levels of recall between 0.00 and 1.00 the term expert has higher precision than the phrase expert.

In light of these results, it would seem that we should readily reject this phrase expert as a candidate for inclusion in any retrieval system. After all, it does not perform very well, even on the small set of documents it does retrieve. However, the results of our optimization suggest otherwise. The optimized combined system performs 12% better than the best individual expert (the term expert). This result

Retrieval System	Optimized Performance on 228 Test Queries Avg Precision	% over Phrases	% over Terms
Phrase Expert	.1672	-	-
Term Expert	.2340	+40%	-
Optimized Combination	.2618	+57%	+12%

Table 3. The phrase expert still contributes to improved overall performance despite its very low individual performance.

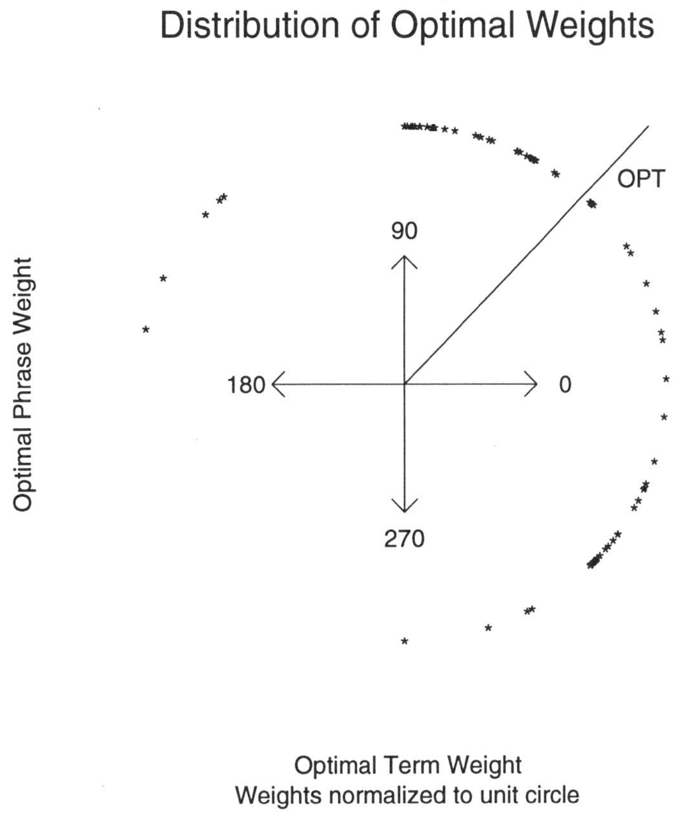

Figure 1. The optimal weights for each independent query vary greatly. Each point above identifies the optimal weights for one of the 128 queries. The optimal weights (OPT) when all 128 queries are optimized together is also shown.

is summarized in Table 3[1]. Thus, the combined system is able to use the two experts' scores to result in a ranking of documents that is better than any single expert's. Note that this comparison is made using the 228 test queries, not the 128 queries used by the method to optimize the model. Thus, the performance scores represent an estimate of how well the optimized model will perform when deployed in the real world accepting queries which it has never before seen. Interestingly, the optimized combination actually weights the phrase expert slightly higher than the term expert: The optimized phrase weight is found to be 0.738, and the term weight is 0.675. This is despite the phrase expert's much lower individual performance.

The reason the phrase expert can contribute to the overall system is evident in a query-by-query analysis. Figure 1 depicts the optimized weights for each of the 128 training queries optimized separately. The weights have been normalized to fall on the unit circle as this does not affect the rank order of documents and clarifies the analysis. The large number of points in the lower right quadrant illustrates that the optimized phrase weight is negative for almost as many queries as it is positive. This suggests that for many queries, the best strategy is to *subtract* the phrase estimate from the term estimate – that is, the phrase expert is identifying irrelevant documents better than relevant documents. However, for those queries for which the phrase parameter is positive, the ratio of the phrase parameter to term parameter is very large. Thus, for these queries, the phrase expert is *very* accurate – the best strategy is to rank documents first using the phrase expert score, and then use the term expert to rank the documents which were not retrieved by the phrase expert. In summary, the phrase expert often performs poorly; however, when the phrase expert is good, it can be very good, resulting in a net positive contribution to the model.

[1] We have used average precision scores to make comparisons between retrieval systems rather than criterion scores even though the optimization procedure only uses the criterion scores. We report average precision because it is a standard measure for comparison in Information Retrieval and because it can be difficult to draw conclusions about absolute system performance from the criterion scores (cf. [4, p. 47]).

Average Precision on Test Set, By Partition					
Query Partition	Phrase Expert	Count Expert	Vector Expert	Optimized System	Improvement over Count Expert
1	.2315	.3235	.2162	.5121	+58%
2	.2989	.3766	.3093	.5559	+48%
3	.3761	.4610	.3173	.6373	+38%
4	.2675	.3344	.2611	.5161	+54%
5	.3600	.4810	.3013	.6011	+25%
6	.1729	.3369	.3338	.5153	+53%
7	.3402	.3248	.2018	.5732	+76%
8	.3124	.4468	.2999	.5629	+26%
Average	.2949	.3856	.2801	.5592	+47%

Table 4. The optimized combination model performs much better than the best individual (the count expert).

4 Optimal Performance in a Commercial System

The second application of our method involves optimization of three experts in a commercial system, *SmarTrieve*, developed by Compton's New Media, Inc. In this application, we emphasize the performance enhancements which are attainable using the method. Part of the retrieval algorithm employed by SmarTrieve entails consulting three experts. These experts provide the following relevance estimates: A traditional vector space estimate (the vector expert); a count of the number of query terms in the document (the count expert); and an estimate of the number of query phrases in the document (the phrase expert).

4.1 Test Collection

We use the Compton's MultiMedia Encyclopedia (CMME) to train and test the combination model. The CMME consists of 20,701 documents along with additional associated multimedia objects (such as short video, sound clips, etc.). All 20,701 full-text documents are used in the experiments.

The training and test queries are derived from a set of questions found in the printed version of the CMME. In each of the 25 volumes, the editors have provided a set of questions which can be answered by one of the articles in that volume. For example, a question in volume 1 is: "What sport may have given rise to the myth of the Minotaur?" (Answer: acrobatics, found in the article titled "Aegean Civilization"). We divide these queries into 8 partitions, each partition having a set of approximately 60 training queries and a set of approximately 60 test queries. We optimize the model separately for each of the 8 partitions, and then evaluate the optimized model using the corresponding test set. The optimization is repeated over these 8 partitions in order to avoid any bias due to the particular queries in one group. To avoid local minima in training, 5 different randomly initialized models are optimized for each partition. The model with the best average precision performance on the training queries is selected as the representative for each partition. Even though we select the model which performs best on the training set, we will evaluate the model using the reserved set of test queries so as not to bias the comparison in favor of the optimized model.

When optimizing the model for each partition, we do not use the relevance judgements for all 20,701 documents. Rather, for each query we identify the 15 documents ranked highest by the unoptimized SmarTrieve system. Relevance judgements for only these top-ranked 15 documents are used for each query in training. Using only the top-ranked 15 documents simulates the scenario in which the relevance judgements are acquired from actual sessions with users of the system – it would be unlikely to convince users to provide feedback on all 20,701 documents in the collection! 15 was chosen arbitrarily as a reasonably small though nevertheless informative subset size.

4.2 Results

The performance of the optimized system and a comparison to the individual experts is illustrated in Table 4. As in the previous section, we compare the performance of the different systems using the sets of test queries and not the queries used to optimize the model. The improvement is at least 25% over the best individual expert (the count expert) for all partitions, and the average improvement is 47%. The difference in performance between the count expert and the optimized system is statistically significant (with $p < 0.0005$, determined by an analysis of variance (ANOVA) of the average precision scores across the 8 partitions). The optimized weights themselves do vary somewhat over the 8 partitions, but are generally stable. The average optimized weights (over the 8 partitions), normalized to have unit sum squared length, are: $\Theta_{\text{Phrase}} = 0.305$, $\Theta_{\text{Count}} = 0.946$, and $\Theta_{\text{Vector}} = 0.112$. The average angle between weight vectors[2] in the different partitions is 13.9°, with standard deviation 7.9. This variation between partitions suggests that the roughly 60 training queries used in each partition do not completely determine the theoretically optimal model, in which the model performs the best on average over all possible queries. Rather, the optimized model is still somewhat specialized to the characteristics of the training set. However, the small average angle between weight vectors and the high retrieval performance on the sets of test queries indicate that different selections of training queries do not lead to wildly different or over-specialized optimized solutions.

Interestingly, the performance improvement of the optimized system is much smaller (only +6%) when the model is optimized using all retrieved documents for each query instead of just the top-ranked 15. This was initially surprising to us, since the additional documents should provide additional information with which to select good parameter values. We have found, however, that using all documents instead forces the model to overcompensate for a few relevant documents which are very poorly ranked by the unoptimized system. That is, for a few queries, the relevant documents are ranked at the end of the retrieved list instead of near the beginning. It is impossible for the linear model to compensate for these difficult queries without sacrificing performance for the other queries, so the optimized model performs unsatisfactorily overall. Restricting optimization to only the top-ranked 15 documents effectively ignores these problematic documents. This behavior appears to be a characteristic of the linear model – other work has demonstrated that some non-linear neural network models do not suffer from this sensitivity to problematic documents [1].

5 Comparison to a Supervised Learning Algorithm

There are alternatives to the particular rank order criterion we have used in this work. One supervised criterion that is very popular in pattern classification and neural networks is the squared error criterion:

$$S(R_\Theta) = \sum_q \sum_d (y_{q,d} - R_{\Theta,q}(d))^2 \tag{4}$$

where $y_{q,d}$ is 1 if document d is relevant to query q, and 0 otherwise. Minimizing this criterion will make the system's relevance estimates more like the true probabilities of relevance. A similar squared error criterion has been used recently by Fuhr & Buckley [6], though they use the criterion to optimize relevance estimates based on single terms rather than to optimize the overall retrieval performance as we do here.

We have applied the squared error criterion to the three expert task in the previous section and have found that it does not perform as well as our rank order criterion. The best improvement to average precision over the count expert, for a number of different linear and non-linear models and training environments, is 2%. A possible explanation for squared error's low performance is that it imposes constraints on the system's relevance estimates which are stronger than are needed for good ranked retrieval. The main goal in a ranked retrieval system is to order the documents in the order of their relevance. Squared error goes well beyond this goal by requiring that the system's estimate be 1.0 for all relevant documents, 0.0 for the others. Certainly any solution that satisfies these constraints also satisfies the rank constraints; however, it appears difficult to satisfy these stronger squared error constraints in practice.

6 Discussion

We have demonstrated a method for combining experts which is effective and applicable to a range of common experts in information retrieval. The method uses well understood numerical optimization techniques to optimize the combination of experts leading to an overall system specifically configured to rank relevant documents before less relevant ones. The method is an alternative to a number of techniques for combining experts that have been proposed recently, in particular the manual search method, weighting by individual performance, and Thompson's CEO method [14]. Each of these alternatives has certain strengths, such as their foundation in probability theory for combining evidence and their potential intuitive appeal. However, the proposed method has certain alternative advantages. Foremost, the method is applicable to a wide range of possible text retrieval approaches. Any approach that estimates the correct relevance ranking of documents by generating a relevance score for each document is a potential

[2] Angle between vectors is used because the fundamental calculation performed with a weight vector is inner product with the vector of expert scores. Magnitude of the weight vector is irrelevant to the overall document ranking; therefore, the only important consideration is the direction (angle) of the weight vector.

expert to be combined using the method. The approach is also sufficiently efficient to be applicable to large collections. Optimization of the 34 Megabyte CMME collection takes only a few seconds using the top-ranked 15 documents and approximately 20 minutes using all retrieved documents on a low-end Sparc IPC. In addition, the method explicitly optimizes the ability of the overall system to correctly rank documents. This is in contrast to alternatives such as the supervised learning approach examined in the previous section.

The improvements to performance demonstrated in this work are very encouraging. However, we must make clear that the amount of possible improvement depends on a number of problem-specific factors. For example, the particular experts used, the characteristics of the collection, and the quality of the training queries can all affect the performance of the optimized system. In addition, factors such as the number of documents included in training can also significantly affect the optimized performance, as the experiments demonstrated. Finally, the level of improvement may be closely tied to how representative the training queries are of typical queries to the system. If the training queries are not representative, then a system may be learned which performs well for the training queries but does not generalize well in the deployed environment.

We have demonstrated that the method can provide a novel means for analyzing the performance of experts when combined with other experts. Typical approaches for evaluating a retrieval method's performance evaluate the method in isolation. This allows for comparison between methods, but does give the system designer the information needed to decide whether a particular method should be included in the system. Echoing Belkin et al.'s [3] findings, we have demonstrated that experts which perform poorly in isolation can still contribute positively to a combined solution. Nevertheless, the issue of analyzing combinations of experts is far from resolved. First, a complete analysis must include the cost (implementation, maintenance, run-time) of including an expert; we have not considered this here. In addition, it is unclear how the best *subset* of a collection of experts can be selected, as different combinations of experts may result in different performance/cost trade-offs. These are interesting directions for future research.

7 Summary

A method for automatically finding a high performance combination of retrieval experts has been proposed. The method uses examples of past queries to learn a combination optimized to rank relevant documents before less relevant ones. The method is applicable to experts which compute ranked retrieval scores indicating the relevance of documents to queries. The method is validated by applications to two expert combination tasks. In the first task, the optimized combination of term and phrase experts performs 12% better than the best individual (the term expert), even though the phrase expert performs very poorly on its own. This illustrates the importance of evaluating experts in the context of other experts in addition to in isolation. In the second task, the optimized combination of three experts in a commercial retrieval system performs 47% better than the best individual.

Acknowledgements: This work was supported in part by NSF grant IRI-9221276. The authors thank Amy Steier for her help in developing the term/phrase experiments, and Encylopædia Britannica Inc. for access to their collections. Address all correspondence to the first author.

References

1. Brian T. Bartell. *Optimizing Ranking Functions: A Connectionist Approach to Adaptive Information Retrieval.* PhD thesis, Department of Computer Science & Engineering, The University of California, San Diego, 1994.
2. Brian T. Bartell, Garrison W. Cottrell, and Richard K. Belew. Learning the optimal parameters in a ranked retrieval system using multi-query relevance feedback. In *Proceedings of the Symposium on Document Analysis and Information Retrieval*, Las Vegas, 1994. in press.
3. Nicholas J. Belkin, C. Cool, W. Bruce Croft, and James P. Callan. Effect of multiple query representations on information retrieval system performance. In *Proc. SIGIR 1993*, pages 339–346, Pittsburgh, PA, June 1993.
4. I. Borg and J. Lingoes. *Multidimensional Similarity Structure Analysis.* Springer-Verlag, New York, 1987.
5. Edward A. Fox, M. Prabhakar Koushik, Joseph Shaw, Russell Modlin, and Durgesh Rao. Combining evidence from multiple searches. In Donna K. Harman, editor, *The First Text REtrieval Conference (TREC-1)*, pages 319–328, March 1993. NIST Special Publication 500-207.
6. Norbert Fuhr and Chris Buckley. A probabilistic learning approach for document indexing. *ACM Transactions on Information Systems*, 9(3):223–248, 1991.

7. Michael Gordon. Probabilistic and genetic algorithms in document retrieval. *Communications of the ACM*, 31(10), October 1988.
8. L. Guttman. What is not what in statistics. *The Statistician*, 26:81–107, 1978.
9. Donna Harman. Overview of the first Text REtrieval Conference. In *Proceedings of the ACM SIGIR*, pages 36–48, Pittsburgh, PA, June 1993.
10. J. Katzer, M. J. McGill, J. A. Tessier, W. Frakes, and P. DasGupta. A study of the overlap among document representations. *Information Technology: Research and Development*, 1(4):261–274, Oct 1982.
11. David D. Lewis and W. Bruce Croft. Term clustering of syntactic phrases. In *Proceedings of the ACM SIGIR*, Brussels, Sept 1990.
12. William H. Press, Brian P. Flannery, Saul A. Teukolsky, and William T. Vetterling. *Numerical Recipes in C: The Art of Scientific Computing.* Cambridge University Press, 1988.
13. T. Saracevic and P. Kantor. A study of information seeking and retrieving. III. Searchers, searches, overlap. *Journal of the ASIS*, 39(3):197–216, 1988.
14. Paul Thompson. A combination of expert opinion approach to probabilistic information retrieval, part 1: The conceptual model. *Information Processing & Management*, 26(3):371–382, 1990.
15. Paul Thompson. Description of the PRC CEO algorithm for TREC. In Donna K. Harman, editor, *The First Text REtrieval Conference (TREC-1)*, pages 337–342, March 1993. NIST Special Publication 500-207.
16. Howard Turtle and W. Bruce Croft. Evaluation of an inference network-based retrieval model. *ACM Transactions on Information Systems*, 9(3):187–222, july 1991.
17. S. K. M. Wong, Y. J. Cai, and Y. Y. Yao. Computation of term associations by a neural network. In *Proceedings of SIGIR*, Pittsburgh, PA, June 1993.

Properties of Extended Boolean Models in Information Retrieval

Joon Ho Lee
Korea Research and Development Information Center
Korea Institute of Science and Technology
P.O. Box 1, Yusung, Taejon 305-600, Korea

Abstract

The conventional boolean retrieval system does not provide ranked retrieval output because it cannot compute similarity coefficients between queries and documents. Extended boolean models such as fuzzy set, Waller-Kraft, Paice, P-Norm and Infinite-One have been proposed in the past to support ranking facility for the boolean retrieval system. In this paper, we analyze the behavioural aspects of the previous extended boolean models and address important mathematical properties to affect retrieval effectiveness. We concentrate our description on evaluation formulas for AND and OR operations and query weights. Our analyses show that P-Norm is the most suitable for achieving high retrieval effectiveness.

1 Introduction

The conventional boolean retrieval system has been most widely used among commercially available Information Retrieval (IR) systems because of easy implementation and efficient retrieval. Documents are indexed with a set of terms, and queries are represented by a legitimate boolean expression composed of index terms and logical operators AND, OR and NOT. The system presents to users the documents satisfying the expression given in a query.

The conventional boolean retrieval system cannot provide ranked retrieval output in decreasing order of query-document similarities. Such a ranked output is useful because controls are now available over the size of the retrieved document set, and iterative retrieval strategies based on successive query reformulations are simplified. Extended boolean models such as fuzzy set, Waller-Kraft, Paice, P-Norm and Infinite-One have been proposed in the past to support ranking facility for the boolean retrieval system. They exploit document term weights reflecting the importance of individual terms in a document to calculate query-document similarities.

Although the fuzzy set model [1, 2, 3], which is a logical extension of the boolean model, overcomes the problem of the conventional boolean retrieval system, it has been criticized to generate incorrect ranked output in certain cases [4, 5]. This is because MIN and MAX operators used for AND and OR operations do not well correspond with human behaviour for document ranking. The Waller-Kraft [6], Paice [7], P-Norm [8] and Infinite-One [9] models have been developed to overcome the problem of the fuzzy set model. Note that they provide n-ary operators for AND and OR operations because binary forms of their operators do not satisfy associativity.

In the area of fuzzy set theory a variety of fuzzy operators have been proposed for AND and OR operations [10]. We have analyzed the effect of the fuzzy operators on retrieval effectiveness and have defined a class of binary operators called *positively compensatory operators* giving high retrieval effectiveness [11, 12, 13]. In this paper, we give mathematical properties of the operators used for AND and OR operations in the previous extended boolean models. We prove the binary operators derived from the Waller-Kraft, Paice, P-Norm and Infinite-One models are included in positively compensatory operators. We also analyze their n-ary operators, and describe the problem of Waller-Kraft, Paice and Infinite-One, i.e. *unequal importance problem.* We define an operator class called *n-ary soft boolean operators* providing high quality ranked output, and show the operators of P-Norm belong to n-ary soft boolean operators.

It has been known that retrieval effectiveness can be improved by assigning importance factors or weights to terms and clauses in queries [1, 4, 8]. Although the Waller-Kraft and Paice models do not provide a way of evaluating query weights, the fuzzy set, P-Norm and Infinite-One models have their own methods. In this paper, we analyze the previous evaluation methods for query weights. Query weights can reflect *absolute* or *relative* importance of terms and clauses. In general users can write a query with relative query weights more easily than with absolute query weights. We describe the fuzzy set model assumes absolute query weights implicitly and the P-Norm and Infinite-One models assume relative query weights.

The remainder of this paper is organized as follows. Section 2 gives the description of extended boolean models. We analyze the binary and n-ary operators of the previous extended boolean models in sections 3 and 4, respectively. We also describe mathematical properties of the operators suitable for achieving high retrieval effectiveness. In section 5 we investigate and analyze evaluation methods for query weights. Finally, concluding remarks are given in section 6.

2 Extended Boolean Models

Extended boolean models such as fuzzy set, Waller-Kraft, Paice, P-Norm and Infinite-One have been developed to support ranking facility for the conventional boolean retrieval system [3, 9, 14]. They use document term weights to calculate query-document similarities, and can be explained within the same framework. An IR system based on extended boolean models is defined by the quadruple <T, Q, D, F>, where

(1) T is a set of index terms used to represent queries and documents.

(2) Q is a set of queries that can be recognized by the system. Each query $q \in Q$ is a legitimate boolean expression composed of index terms and logical operators AND, OR and NOT. (All the description of query weights will be presented in section 5.)

(3) D is a set of documents. Each document $d \in D$ is represented by $\{(t_1, w_{d1}), ..., (t_n, w_{dn})\}$ where w_{di} designates the weight of term t_i in d and w_{di} may take any value between zero and one, i.e. $0 \leq w_{di} \leq 1$.

(4) F is a ranking function

$$F: D \times Q \rightarrow [0, 1]$$

which assigns to each pair (d, q) a number in the closed interval [0, 1]. This number is a measure of similarity between document d and query q, and is called the *document value* for document d with respect to query q. Evaluation formulas for the logical operators are the most important factors to determine the quality of document ranking. Figure 1 shows the evaluation formulas used for AND and OR operations, and F(d, NOT t_i) is evaluated as $1 - w_{di}$.

Note that the formulas of the fuzzy set model are binary functions having only two operands and those of the Waller-Kraft, Paice, P-Norm and Infinite-One models are n-ary functions having two or more operands. This is due to the fact that MIN and MAX operators satisfy associativity whereas the operators of Waller-Kraft, Paice, P-Norm and Infinite-One do not. The use of binary functions not to satisfy associativity results in the problem of generating different document values for two logically equivalent queries (t_1 AND t_2) AND t_3 and t_1 AND (t_2 AND t_3). This problem will be detailed in section 4.1.

3 Analysis of Binary Operators for High Retrieval Effectiveness

3.1 Properties Adverse to Retrieval Effectiveness

The fuzzy set model uses MIN and MAX operators for the evaluation of logical operators AND and OR, respectively. It has been argued that the fuzzy set model generates in certain cases incorrect ranked output not to agree with human behaviour [4, 5]. This is because MIN and MAX operators give the resulting values that depend on only one operand without considering the other. In the area of fuzzy set theory a variety of fuzzy operators have been developed, which can replace MIN and MAX operators. We have analyzed the behavioural aspects of the fuzzy operators and have described two problems, i.e. *single operand dependency* and *negative compensation* to decrease retrieval effectiveness [11, 12, 13].

<u>Single Operand Dependency Problem</u> : If an operator θ has a single operand dependent property, then $\theta(x, y) = x$ or y for some $x, y \in [0, 1]$ such that $x \neq y$. When an extended boolean model uses for AND or OR operations an operator having the single operand dependent property, it causes the single operand dependency problem. For example, suppose that we have two documents d_1, d_2 and a query q_1 shown below. The documents are represented by two pairs of an index term and its weight.

d_1 = { (Information, 0), (Retrieval, 0) }
d_2 = { (Information, 1), (Retrieval, 0) }
q_1 = Information AND Retrieval

When the product operator is used for AND operation, the document values of d_1 and d_2 for query q_1 are the same, i.e. zero. Most people, however, will obviously decide that d_2 rather than d_1 is more similar to q_1. This undesirable result is due to the fact that the product operator has the single operand dependent property, that is, $x \cdot 0 = 0$ for all $x \in (0, 1]$.

$$F(d, t_1 \text{ AND } t_2) = MIN(w_{d1}, w_{d2})$$
$$F(d, t_1 \text{ OR } t_2) = MAX(w_{d1}, w_{d2})$$

(a) The fuzzy set model

$$F(d, t_1 \text{ AND } \ldots \text{ AND } t_n) = (1-\gamma) \bullet MIN(w_{d1}, \ldots, w_{dn}) + \gamma \bullet MAX(w_{d1}, \ldots, w_{dn}), \quad 0 \le \gamma \le 0.5$$
$$F(d, t_1 \text{ OR } \ldots \text{ OR } t_n) = (1-\gamma) \bullet MIN(w_{d1}, \ldots, w_{dn}) + \gamma \bullet MAX(w_{d1}, \ldots, w_{dn}), \quad 0.5 \le \gamma \le 1$$

(b) The Waller-Kraft model

$$F(d, t_1 \text{ AND } \ldots \text{ AND } t_n) = \frac{\sum_{i=1}^{n} (r^{i-1} \bullet w_{di})}{\sum_{i=1}^{n} r^{i-1}}, \quad 0 \le r \le 1 \text{ and } w_{di}\text{'s are considered in ascending order}$$

$$F(d, t_1 \text{ OR } \ldots \text{ OR } t_n) = \frac{\sum_{i=1}^{n} (r^{i-1} \bullet w_{di})}{\sum_{i=1}^{n} r^{i-1}}, \quad 0 \le r \le 1 \text{ and } w_{di}\text{'s are considered in descending order}$$

(c) The Paice model

$$F(d, t_1 \text{ AND } \ldots \text{ AND } t_n) = 1 - \left(\frac{\sum_{i=1}^{n} (1 - w_{di})^p}{n} \right)^{1/p}, \quad 1 \le p \le \infty$$

$$F(d, t_1 \text{ OR } \ldots \text{ OR } t_n) = \left(\frac{\sum_{i=1}^{n} w_{di}^{\ p}}{n} \right)^{1/p}, \quad 1 \le p \le \infty$$

(d) The P-Norm model

$$F(d, t_1 \text{ AND } \ldots \text{ AND } t_n) = \gamma \bullet (1 - MAX(1 - w_{d1}, \ldots, 1 - w_{dn})) + (1-\gamma) \bullet \frac{\sum_{i=1}^{n} w_{di}}{n}, \quad 0 \le \gamma \le 1$$

$$F(d, t_1 \text{ OR } \ldots \text{ OR } t_n) = \gamma \bullet MAX(w_{d1}, \ldots, w_{dn}) + (1-\gamma) \bullet \frac{\sum_{i=1}^{n} w_{di}}{n}, \quad 0 \le \gamma \le 1$$

(e) The Infinite-One model

Figure 1. Evaluation formulas for AND and OR operations

Negative Compensation Problem : If an operator θ has a negatively compensatory property, then $\theta(x, y) < MIN(x, y)$ or $\theta(x, y) > MAX(x, y)$ for some $x, y \in [0, 1]$. When an extended boolean model uses for AND or OR operations an operator having the negatively compensatory property, it causes the negative compensation problem. For example, suppose a document d_3 and two queries q_2, q_3 are given as follows:

d_3 = { (Information, 0.70), (Retrieval, 0.70) }
q_2 = Information AND Retrieval
q_3 = Information

When the product operator is used for AND operation, the document values of d_3 with respect to queries q_2 and q_3 are evaluated as 0.49 and 0.70, respectively. The similarity between q_2 and d_3 is less than that between q_3 and d_3, which clearly does not agree with most people's decision. This is because the product operator has the negatively compensatory property as well as the single operand dependent property, that is, $x \bullet y < MIN(x, y)$ for all $x, y \in (0, 1)$.

3.2 Positively Compensatory Operators

We have defined an operator class called *positively compensatory operators*, which provide high retrieval effectiveness [11, 12, 13]. The positively compensatory operators are functions of the form

$$p : [0, 1] \times [0, 1] \rightarrow [0, 1].$$

They satisfy at least the following properties:

Property p1. $p(x, x) = x$; that is, p is *idempotent.*
Property p2. $\text{MIN}(x, y) < p(x, y) < \text{MAX}(x, y)$ where $x \neq y$.

We can easily know from the definition that positively compensatory operators do not have either the single operand dependent property or the negatively compensatory property. Therefore, an extended boolean model using positively compensatory operators can avoid the single operand dependent and negative compensation problems.

In the area of fuzzy set theory many researchers have proposed a variety of fuzzy operators to evaluate AND and OR operations. We have found the following two pairs of positively compensatory operators in the literature.

$$(A_2) \qquad (1-\gamma) \bullet \text{MIN}(x, y) + \gamma \bullet \text{MAX}(x, y), \quad 0 \leq \gamma \leq 1$$

$$(A_{4.\text{AND}}) \qquad \gamma \bullet \text{MIN}(x,y) + (1-\gamma) \bullet \frac{(x+y)}{2}, \quad 0 \leq \gamma \leq 1$$

$$(A_{4.\text{OR}}) \qquad \gamma \bullet \text{MAX}(x,y) + (1-\gamma) \bullet \frac{(x+y)}{2}, \quad 0 \leq \gamma \leq 1$$

It has been shown that the A_2 and A_4 operators are mathematically equivalent though they are independently developed by different researchers at different time [13].

3.3 Binary Soft Boolean Operators

Figure 2 presents the binary operators derived from the Waller-Kraft, Paice, P-Norm and Infinite-One models. The operators are functions of the form

$$b : [0, 1] \times [0, 1] \rightarrow [0, 1].$$

All of them satisfy at least the following properties:

Property b1. $b(x, x) = x$; that is, b is *idempotent.*
Property b2. If $x < x'$ then $b(x, y) < b(x', y)$, and if $y < y'$ then $b(x, y) < b(x, y')$; that is, b is *strictly monotonic* on each operand.
Property b3. b is a *continuous* function.
Property b4. $b(x, y) = b(y, x)$; that is, b is *commutative.*

The first property indicates that a document is retrieved with the same document values with respect to the queries $q_1 = t_1$ AND t_1, $q_2 = t_1$ OR t_1 and $q_3 = t_1$. The second property is the natural requirement that an increase in an document term weight produces an increase in the document value. The property of continuity prevents a situation in which a very small increase in an document term weight produces a large change in the document value. The property of commutativity insures that a document is retrieved with the same strength for the request t_1 AND t_2 as for the request t_2 AND t_1, and similarly for t_1 OR t_2 and t_2 OR t_1. In the remainder of this paper an operator satisfying properties b1 through b4 will be called the *binary soft boolean operator.*

Theorem 1. If an operator θ satisfies the properties b1 and b2, then $\text{MIN}(x, y) < \theta(x, y) < \text{MAX}(x, y)$ for all $x, y \in [0, 1]$ such that $x \neq y$.

Proof: By the property of strict monotonicity we have that

$$\theta(\text{MIN}(x, y), \text{MIN}(x, y)) < \theta(x, y) < \theta(\text{MAX}(x, y), \text{MAX}(x, y)),$$

and by the property of idempotency we have that

$$\theta(\text{MIN}(x, y), \text{MIN}(x, y)) = \text{MIN}(x, y),$$
$$\theta(\text{MAX}(x, y), \text{MAX}(x, y)) = \text{MAX}(x, y).$$

Hence, $\text{MIN}(x, y) < \theta(x, y) < \text{MAX}(x, y)$, which concludes the proof.

$$F(d, t_1 \text{ AND } t_2) = (1-\gamma) \bullet \text{MIN}(w_{d1}, w_{d2}) + \gamma \bullet \text{MAX}(w_{d1}, w_{d2}), \quad 0 \le \gamma \le 0.5$$
$$F(d, t_1 \text{ OR } t_2) = (1-\gamma) \bullet \text{MIN}(w_{d1}, w_{d2}) + \gamma \bullet \text{MAX}(w_{d1}, w_{d2}), \quad 0.5 \le \gamma \le 1$$

(a) The Waller-Kraft model

$$F(d, t_1 \text{ AND } t_2) = \frac{1}{1+r} \bullet \text{MIN}(w_{d1}, w_{d2}) + \frac{r}{1+r} \bullet \text{MAX}(w_{d1}, w_{d2}), \quad 0 \le r \le 1$$
$$F(d, t_1 \text{ OR } t_2) = \frac{1}{1+r} \bullet \text{MAX}(w_{d1}, w_{d2}) + \frac{r}{1+r} \bullet \text{MIN}(w_{d1}, w_{d2}), \quad 0 \le r \le 1$$

(b) The Paice model

$$F(d, t_1 \text{ AND } t_2) = 1 - \left[\frac{(1-w_{d1})^p + (1-w_{d2})^p}{2}\right]^{1/p}, \quad 1 \le p \le \infty$$
$$F(d, t_1 \text{ OR } t_2) = \left[\frac{w_{d1}^{\ p} + w_{d2}^{\ p}}{2}\right]^{1/p}, \quad 1 \le p \le \infty$$

(c) The P-Norm model

$$F(d, t_1 \text{ AND } t_2) = \gamma \bullet (1 - \text{MAX}(1 - w_{d1}, 1 - w_{d2})) + (1-\gamma) \bullet \frac{w_{d1} + w_{d2}}{2}, \quad 0 \le \gamma \le 1$$
$$F(d, t_1 \text{ OR } t_2) = \gamma \bullet \text{MAX}(w_{d1}, w_{d2}) + (1-\gamma) \bullet \frac{w_{d1} + w_{d2}}{2}, \quad 0 \le \gamma \le 1$$

(d) The Infinite-One model

Figure 2. Binary evaluation formulas for AND and OR operations

We know from Theorem 1 that a binary soft boolean operator belongs to positively compensatory operators. Therefore, the binary operators of Waller-Kraft, Paice, P-Norm and Infinite-One overcome the single operand dependency and negative compensation problems. It should be noted that the A_2 and A_4 operators satisfy the properties b1 through b4 and are binary soft boolean operators. Closer investigation shows that the binary operators of the Waller-Kraft, Paice and Infinite-One models and the A_2 and A_4 operators are mathematically equivalent. Note that $\text{MIN}(w_{d1}, w_{d2}) = 1 - \text{MAX}(1-w_{d1}, 1-w_{d2})$.

4 Analysis of N-ary Operators for High Retrieval Effectiveness

4.1 Necessity of N-ary Operators

AND operations combine terms into term phrases and OR operations treat two terms as effectively synonymous. Thus, we often use consecutive AND operations such as "fuzzy AND set AND theory" and consecutive OR operations such as "human OR people OR person OR man". Unfortunately, a binary soft boolean operator cannot satisfy associativity.

Theorem 2. If an operator θ satisfies the properties b1 and b2, θ cannot be associative.

Proof: Let x and y be such that $x < y$. From the proof of Theorem 1, we know that

$$\theta(x, y) > x.$$

Hence, through strict monotonicity on the first component we have that

$$\theta(\theta(x, y), y) > \theta(x, y).$$

However, if θ is associative

$$\theta(\theta(x, y), y) = \theta(x, \theta(y, y)) = \theta(x, y).$$

Therefore, the associativity of θ entails a contradiction, which completes the proof.

No satisfaction of associativity implies that different document values may be obtainable for logically equivalent queries such as $q_1 = t_1$ AND (t_2 AND t_3) and $q_2 = (t_1$ AND $t_2)$ AND t_3. For example, suppose a document d is represented by three pairs of an index term and its weight $\{(t_1, 1), (t_2, 0.7), (t_3, 0.5)\}$. An extended boolean model using $A_{4.AND}$ ($\gamma = 0.3$) gives 0.721 and 0.607 as document values of document d with respect to queries q_1 and q_2, respectively.

Given a query $q = t_1$ OR t_2 OR t_3, users assume that query terms t_1, t_2 and t_3 have equal importance in query q. However, we cannot preserve this basic assumption in evaluating query q if we use binary soft boolean operators. Consider two ways of evaluating query q, that is, (t_1 OR t_2) OR t_3 and t_1 OR (t_2 OR t_3). The document value for (t_1 OR t_2) OR t_3 is more dependent on term t_3 than terms t_1 and t_2 while that for t_1 OR (t_2 OR t_3) is more dependent on term t_1 than terms t_2 and t_3.

Suppose a document $d = \{(t_1, w_{d1}), (t_2, w_{d2}), ..., (t_n, w_{dn})\}$ and a query $q = t_1$ OR t_2 OR ... OR t_n. We can calculate the similarity between query q and document d by applying the operator $A_{4.OR}$ (γ=0) from the left of query q to the right as follows:

$$F(d,q) = \frac{w_{d1}}{2^{n-1}} + \frac{w_{d2}}{2^{n-1}} + \frac{w_{d3}}{2^{n-2}} + \frac{w_{d4}}{2^{n-3}} + \ldots + \frac{w_{dn}}{2}$$

$$= \frac{1}{2}\left(\frac{w_{d1}}{2^{n-2}} + \frac{w_{d2}}{2^{n-2}} + \frac{w_{d3}}{2^{n-3}} + \frac{w_{d4}}{2^{n-4}} + \ldots + w_{dn}\right)$$

The above expression shows that the document value is more affected by the weight of term t_i than the weight of term t_j where i is greater than j.

4.2 N-ary Soft Boolean Operators

The Waller-Kraft, Paice, P-Norm and Infinite-One models have avoided the problem of not satisfying associativity by expanding their operators into n-ary forms. Waller-Kraft, Paice and Infinite-One, however, have undesirable properties of generating incorrect ranked outputs in certain cases. They violate the usual assumption that all the terms given in a query are equally important, which results in the following *unequal importance problem.*

Unequal Importance Problem (Type I) : The Waller-Kraft model considers only two operand values, i.e. the minimum and maximum operand values in calculating query-document similarities. For example, suppose that we have two documents d_4, d_5 and a query q_4 shown below.

$d_4 = \{ (t_1, 0), (t_2, 0.9), (t_3, 0.9), ..., (t_{99}, 0.9), (t_{100}, 1) \}$
$d_5 = \{ (t_1, 0), (t_2, 0.1), (t_3, 0.1), ..., (t_{99}, 0.1), (t_{100}, 1) \}$
$q_4 = t_1$ AND t_2 AND ... AND t_{100}

Waller-Kraft decides that document values of d_4 and d_5 for query q_4 are the same. Most people, however, will obviously decide that d_4 is more similar to q_4 than d_5.

Unequal Importance Problem (Type II) : The Paice model avoids the first type of the unequal importance problem by reflecting all operand values on document values. It, however, gives different importance to each term in a query. For example, suppose two documents d_6, d_7 and a query q_5 are given as follows:

$d_6 = \{ (t_1, 0.1), (t_2, 0.3), (t_3, 0.3), (t_4, 0.3), (t_5, 0.3), (t_6, 0.3) \}$
$d_7 = \{ (t_1, 0.1), (t_2, 0.7), (t_3, 0.3), (t_4, 0.3), (t_5, 0.3), (t_6, 0.2) \}$
$q_5 = t_1$ AND t_2 AND t_3 AND t_4 AND t_5 AND t_6

Since Paice ($r = 0.7$) evaluates document values of d_6 and d_7 for q_5 as 0.2319 and 0.2310, respectively, d_6 would be retrieved with a higher rank than d_7. That is, the small reduction in the weight of term t_6 dominates the large increase in the weight of term t_2, which does not agree with human behaviour.

Unequal Importance Problem (Type II) : The Infinite-One model also avoids the first type of the unequal importance problem by reflecting all operand values on document values. It, however, generates the document value that is more affected by minimum and maximum values for AND and OR operations, respectively. For example, suppose that we have two documents d_8, d_9 and a query q_6 shown below.

$d_8 = \{ (t_1, 0), (t_2, 1), (t_3, 1), ..., (t_{100}, 1) \}$
$d_9 = \{ (t_1, 0.4), (t_2, 0.6), (t_3, 0.6), ..., (t_{100}, 0.6) \}$
$q_6 = t_1$ AND t_2 AND ... AND t_{100}

Infinite-One ($\gamma = 0.5$) decides that the similarity between d_8 and q_6 is equal to that between d_9 and q_6. Note that the increase in the weight of term t_1 corresponds to the reduction in the weights of all the remaining terms t_2 through t_{100}. Most people, however, will obviously decide that d_8 is more similar to q_6 than d_9.

Since the P-Norm model takes into account all operand values with equal importance, it does not cause the unequal importance problem. Its n-ary operators are functions of the form

$$n : [0, 1] \times \ldots \times [0, 1] \to [0, 1].$$

They satisfy at least the following properties:

Property n1. $n(x, x, \ldots, x) = x$; that is, n is *idempotent*.
Property n2. n is *strictly monotonic* on each operand.
Property n3. n is a *continuous* function.
Property n4. $n(x_1, x_2, \ldots, x_n) = n(y_1, y_2, \ldots, y_n)$ where $y_1, y_2, \ldots, y_n$ is any permutation of $x_1, x_2, \ldots, x_n$; that is, n is a *symmetric* function.
Property n5. n considers all operands *equally important*.

The first property indicates that the queries $q_1 = t_1$ AND ... AND t_1, $q_2 = t_1$ OR ... OR t_1 and $q_3 = t_1$ generate the same document values. The second property implies that an increase in an document term weight produces an increase in the document value. The property of continuity prevents a situation in which a very small increase in an document term weight produces a large change in the document value. The symmetry property insures that the request t_1 AND t_2 AND t_3 AND t_4 generates the same document value as the requests made by the permutation of the terms t_1 through t_4, e.g. t_2 AND t_1 AND t_4 AND t_3. The fifth property of equal importance reflects the usual assumption that all operands are equally important. Note that Waller-Kraft does not satisfy the properties n2 and n5, and Paice and Infinite-One do not satisfy the property n5. In the remainder of this paper an operator satisfying properties n1 through n5 will be called the *n-ary soft boolean operator*. Since the operators of P-Norm belong to n-ary soft boolean operators, they are more effective than those of any other extended boolean models.

The binary operators A_2 and A_4 do not satisfy associativity because they are included in binary soft boolean operators. Their n-ary forms are presented in the area of fuzzy set theory as follows [15]:

$$(A_{2.N}) \qquad \gamma \bullet \mathrm{MAX}(w_1, \ldots, w_n) + (1-\gamma) \bullet \mathrm{MIN}(w_1, \ldots, w_n),\ 0 \le \gamma \le 1$$

$$(A_{4.N.AND}) \qquad \gamma \bullet \mathrm{MIN}(w_1, \ldots, w_n) + (1-\gamma) \bullet \frac{(w_1 + \ldots + w_n)}{n},\ 0 \le \gamma \le 1$$

$$(A_{4.N.OR}) \qquad \gamma \bullet \mathrm{MAX}(w_1, \ldots, w_n) + (1-\gamma) \bullet \frac{(w_1 + \ldots + w_n)}{n},\ 0 \le \gamma \le 1$$

Although the binary operators A_2 and A_4 are mathematically equivalent, the n-ary operators $A_{2.N}$ and $A_{4.N}$ are not. Moreover, $A_{2.N}$ and $A_{4.N}$ are equivalent to the n-ary operators of Waller-Kraft and Infinite-One, respectively.

5 Analysis of Evaluation Methods for Query Weights

5.1 The Previous Schemes for Query Weights

In the previous sections we have considered only non-weighted queries in which all terms and clauses included in the queries are assumed to carry equal importance. It has been known that retrieval effectiveness can be improved by assigning importance factors or weights to the terms and clauses attached to queries. For example, a weighted boolean query q is represented by $(((t_1, w_{q1})$ OR $(t_2, w_{q2})), w_{q1\ OR\ q2})$ AND (t_3, w_{q3}) where w_{qi} is the weight of term t_i in q and $w_{q1\ OR\ q2}$ is the weight of clause t_1 OR t_2. The query weights such as query term weight and query clause weight may take any value between zero and one, e.g. $0 \le w_{qi}, w_{q1\ OR\ q2} \le 1$. A non-weighted boolean query is equivalent to a weighted boolean query in which all query weights are one.

Although the Waller-Kraft and Paice models do not provide a way of evaluating query weights, the P-Norm and Infinite-One models have effective query weighting schemes. Figure 3 shows their evaluation formulas for query weights.

Many methods have been proposed to incorporate query weights in the fuzzy set model. They are classified into two groups such as relevance weighting approaches and threshold approaches [1]. In this paper we only investigate relevance weighting schemes. One is to multiply the weights of query and document terms. Specifically, the value of $F(d, (t_i, w_{qi}))$ is defined as

$$F(d, (t_i, w_{qi})) = w_{di} \bullet w_{qi}.$$

$$F\left(d,\left(t_1,w_{q1}\right) \text{ AND } \ldots \text{ AND } \left(t_n,w_{qn}\right)\right) = 1 - \left(\frac{\sum_{i=1}^{n}\left(\left(1-w_{di}\right)^p \bullet w_{qi}^{\;p}\right)}{\sum_{i=1}^{n} w_{qi}^{\;p}} \right)^{1/p}, \quad 1 \le p \le \infty$$

$$F\left(d,\left(t_1,w_{q1}\right) \text{ OR } \ldots \text{ OR } \left(t_n,w_{qn}\right)\right) = \left(\frac{\sum_{i=1}^{n}\left(w_{di}^{\;p} \bullet w_{qi}^{\;p}\right)}{\sum_{i=1}^{n} w_{qi}^{\;p}} \right)^{1/p}, \quad 1 \le p \le \infty$$

(a) The P-Norm model

$$F\left(d,\left(t_1,w_{q1}\right) \text{ AND } \ldots \text{ AND } \left(t_n,w_{qn}\right)\right) =$$

$$\gamma \bullet \left(1 - \frac{\mathrm{MAX}\left(\left(1-w_{d1}\right)\bullet w_{q1},\ldots,\left(1-w_{dn}\right)\bullet w_{qn}\right)}{\mathrm{MAX}\left(w_{q1},\ldots,w_{qn}\right)}\right) + (1-\gamma) \bullet \frac{\sum_{i=1}^{n}\left(w_{di} \bullet w_{qi}\right)}{\sum_{i=1}^{n} w_{qi}}, \quad 0 \le \gamma \le 1$$

$$F\left(d,\left(t_1,w_{q1}\right) \text{ OR } \ldots \text{ OR } \left(t_n,w_{qn}\right)\right) =$$

$$\gamma \bullet \frac{\mathrm{MAX}\left(w_{d1}\bullet w_{q1},\ \ldots,\ w_{dn}\bullet w_{qn}\right)}{\mathrm{MAX}\left(w_{q1},\ldots,w_{qn}\right)} + (1-\gamma) \bullet \frac{\sum_{i=1}^{n}\left(w_{di} \bullet w_{qi}\right)}{\sum_{i=1}^{n} w_{qi}}, \quad 0 \le \gamma \le 1$$

(b) The Infinite-One model

Figure 3. Evaluation formulas for query weights

The weight of zero indicates the term is to have no impact, that is, to act as if it were omitted from the query. For notational convenience, we would in practice omit terms with zero weight and omit an explicit weight indication if the weight is one. Hence, a relevance weighting scheme should satisfy the following two conditions.

$F(d, (t_1, 1) \text{ AND } (t_2, 0)) = F(d, (t_1, 1))$
$F(d, (t_1, 1) \text{ OR } (t_2, 0)) = F(d, (t_1, 1))$

The P-Norm and Infinite-One models satisfy these conditions. However, the fuzzy set model based on MIN and MAX violates the first condition. In order to overcome this problem, the following definitions have been proposed [4].

$F(d, (t_i, w_{qi})) = w_{di} / w_{qi}$ when term t_i appears in an AND clause
$F(d, (t_i, w_{qi})) = w_{di} \bullet w_{qi}$ when term t_i appears in an OR clause

5.2 The Meaning of Query Weights

In this section we describe the meaning of query weights in detail. Let's consider the following question "Do query weights reflect *relative* importance of the terms and clauses given in a query or *absolute* importance?". This question is analogous to the question "Is $q_1 = (t_1, 1)$ AND $(t_2, 1)$ equivalent to $q_2 = (t_1, 0.1)$ AND $(t_2, 0.1)$ or not?". If query weights reflect relative importance of query terms t_1 and t_2 in the queries, query q_1 is equivalent to q_2. However, if query weights correspond to absolute importance, query q_1 is not equivalent to q_2.

There has been no explicit distinction between absolute query weights and relative query weights in developing evaluation schemes for query weights. The fuzzy set model, however, assumes absolute query weights implicitly whereas the P-Norm and Infinite-One models assume relative query weights. For example, suppose a document d_{10} and queries q_7 and q_8 as follows:

d_{10} = {(information, 0.8), (document, 0.8)}
q_7 = (information, 1) OR (document, 1)
q_8 = (information, 0.1) OR (document, 0.1)

The fuzzy set model evaluates document values of d_{10} for queries q_7 and q_8 as 0.8 and 0.08, respectively. Meanwhile, P-Norm and Infinite-One give the same document values for queries q_7 and q_8, that is, q_7 is equivalent to q_8. This is accomplished by the normalization of query weights, which implies that query weights in P-Norm and Infinite-One reflect relative importance of query terms and clauses. In general users can write a query with relative query weights more easily than with absolute query weights.

6 Concluding Remarks

A major role of IR systems is to present to users a sequence of documents ranked in decreasing order of query-document similarities. Users are able to minimize their time spent to find useful information by reading the top-ranked documents first. Although conventional boolean retrieval systems based on inverted files have the advantages of easy implementation and efficient retrieval, they cannot rank the documents retrieved. Extended boolean models such as fuzzy set, Waller-Kraft, Paice, P-Norm and Infinite-One have been developed to provide ranked output in the boolean retrieval systems.

In this paper we have analyzed mathematical properties of the operators used in the previous extended boolean models for AND and OR operations, and have addressed important issues to affect retrieval effectiveness. We have defined an operator class called n-ary soft boolean operators providing high quality ranked output, and have shown the operators of P-Norm belong to n-ary soft boolean operators. We have also analyzed the previous evaluation methods for query weights. Query weights can reflect absolute or relative importance of terms and clauses. We have described the fuzzy set model assumes absolute query weights implicitly and the P-Norm and Infinite-One models assume relative query weights. In general weighting a query with relative weights is easier than weighting a query with absolute weights. Consequently, our analyses have shown that P-Norm is more suitable for achieving high retrieval effectiveness than any other extended boolean models.

References

1. Buell DA. A general model of query processing in information retrieval system. Information Processing & Management 1981; 17(5):249-262
2. Radecki T. Fuzzy set theoretical approach to document retrieval. Information Processing & Management 1979; 15(5):247-259
3. Sachs WM. An approach to associative retrieval through the theory of fuzzy sets. Journal of the American Society for Information Science 1976; 27:85-87
4. Bookstein A. Fuzzy requests: an approach to weighted boolean searches. Journal of the American Society for Information Science 1980; 31(4):240-247
5. Lee JH, Kim MH, Lee YJ. Ranking documents in thesaurus-based boolean retrieval systems. Information Processing & Management 1994; 30(1):79-91
6. Waller WG, Kraft DH. A mathematical model of a weighted boolean retrieval system. Information Processing & Management 1979; 15:235-245
7. Paice CP. Soft evaluation of boolean search queries in information retrieval systems. Information Technology: Research and Development 1984; 3(1):33-42
8. Salton G, Fox EA, Wu H. Extended boolean information retrieval. Communications of the ACM 1983; 26(11):1022-1036
9. Smith ME. Aspects of the p-norm model of information retrieval: syntactic query generation, efficiency, and theoretical properties. PhD thesis, Cornell University, 1990.
10. Zimmermann HJ. Fuzzy set theory and its applications, 2nd edition. Kluwer Academic Publishers, 1991
11. Lee JH, Kim MH, Lee YJ. Enhancing the fuzzy set model for high quality document rankings. In: Proceedings of the 19th Euromicro Conference. 1992, pp. 337-344
12. Kim MH, Lee JH, Lee YJ. Analysis of fuzzy operators for high quality information retrieval. Information Processing Letters 1993; 46(5):251-256
13. Lee JH, Kim WY, Kim MH, Lee YJ. On the evaluation of boolean operators in the extended boolean retrieval framework. In: Proceedings of the 16th Annual International ACM SIGIR Conference on Research and Development in Information Retrieval. 1993, pp. 291-297
14. Fox EA, Betrabet S, Koushik M, Lee W. Extended boolean models. In: Frakes WB, Yates RB (ed) Information Retrieval Data Structures & Algorithms. Prentice Hall, 1992, pp. 393-418
15. Zimmermann HJ. Fuzzy sets, decision making, and expert systems. Kluwer Academic Publishers, 1987

Performance Evaluation

OHSUMED: An Interactive Retrieval Evaluation and New Large Test Collection for Research

William Hersh, Oregon Health Sciences University
Chris Buckley, Cornell University
TJ Leone, Oregon Health Sciences University
David Hickam, Oregon Health Sciences University

Abstract

A series of information retrieval experiments was carried out with a computer installed in a medical practice setting for relatively inexperienced physician end-users. Using a commercial MEDLINE product based on the vector space model, these physicians searched just as effectively as more experienced searchers using Boolean searching. The results of this experiment were subsequently used to create a new large medical test collection, which was used in experiments with the SMART retrieval system to obtain baseline performance data as well as compare SMART with the other searchers.

1 Introduction

Information retrieval systems, once the purview of search intermediaries in libraries, are increasingly becoming tools for professionals, such as physicians, lawyers, and educators. This is a timely advent for these tools, since many professional fields are facing unprecedented growth in quantity of information, resulting in significant information management problems. This has led to increased advocacy for end-user retrieval applications that are fast and easy-to-use.

We undertook a study to evaluate the use of one such system in a medical practice setting, the General Medicine Clinic at Oregon Health Sciences University. An Apple Macintosh IIsi computer was installed with several applications, one of which was Knowledge Finder (KF) (Aries Systems, North Bedford, MA), a CD-ROM retrieval system featuring a primary care subset of the MEDLINE database covering 270 journals for five years. It features a "natural language" searching interface and relevance ranking based on the vector space model [1]. The usage frequency and user satisfaction of this system have been reported elsewhere [2]. We subsequently created a new large test collection from the searches. This collection, called OHSUMED, was used to conduct further experiments with the SMART retrieval system.

The main objectives for the experiments described here were to:
1. Compare the use of a vector space-like system with novice end-users in an operational setting.
2. Build a large medical test collection for further medical information retrieval research
3. Obtain baseline results from a well-known retrieval system (SMART) and compare its results with that of human searchers.

Interactive comparison of advanced retrieval systems has rarely been done. There have been many batch-style evaluations of experimental retrieval systems [3, 4] as well as studies using user-generated search strategies [5-9]. However, with the exception of the CIRT experiments [10], there have been no "head-on" comparisons of interactive Boolean and natural language/weighting systems.

KF does not feature all of the advanced features seen in systems like SMART (such as relevance feedback and automatic phrase generation), but it does provide an easy-to-use natural language interface that allows searchers to begin with a minimal amount of training. KF also allows traditional Boolean searching with the MeSH vocabulary as well as searching on specific fields in the MEDLINE record, such as journal titles, publication dates, and author names. Of these, only author names were used by any of our searchers.

The second objective, building a large test collection for medical information retrieval research, was designed in the spirit of the TREC Project [11], aiming to bring real world-sized test collections to the experimental retrieval systems. Although TREC is already providing researchers with such a test collection, other large collections must be developed in different domains to determine which results can be generalized.

The final motivation was to perform runs with SMART, generating baseline performance levels with the OHSUMED collection and carrying out some experiments comparing SMART with human searchers using other systems. In particular, we analyzed variation in recall and precision while simulating the advantages that human searchers have, such as ability to control retrieval set size and modify the search based on terms in the documents.

2 Interactive search study methods

The Macintosh workstation was placed in the workroom of the General Medicine Clinic at Oregon Health Sciences University. Users were given minimal training with the system, as little as 10-15 minutes, although they were offered more if they desired it. Each was also given an instruction packet with screen pictures and examples, which was also available, along with user manuals for each of the applications, beside the computer. Most users had previous experience searching the MEDLINE database in different implementations.

2.1 Query generation and replication

User queries were captured by requiring an on-line questionnaire to be completed before an application could be launched. Searchers were required to give a brief statement of their patient and their information need. In addition, the KF application logged the natural language search statement. KF does not, however, log the documents that the user actually views. After the ten month period of the experiment, all KF searches were reviewed, and a subset consisting of all searches where the user entered adequate information for replication (more than three words each of patient information and topic specification) was designated. After elimination of duplicate topics and author searches, the subset contained 106 searches.

For replication of the searches, 11 medical librarians and 11 physicians experienced with MEDLINE were recruited. Each librarian had to be a reference librarian who used MEDLINE at least several times per week. Each physician had to use MEDLINE more than once a month for more than 2-3 years as well as be clinically active in an ambulatory setting. The replicated searches were randomized so that each was searched by two physicians and two librarians, with one of each pair searching with the full MEDLINE feature set and the other using just text words. Searching was done on the ELHILL computer of the NLM, a traditional command line-oriented Boolean system. Searchers were required to search the last six years of the database (current MEDLINE file and first back-file). A reference was considered retrieved if it was displayed to the screen or returned by their last search statement.

2.2 Relevance judgments

References retrieved in the MEDLINE searches that were not in the test database were discarded for performance assessment. Every reference in the test database retrieved for a given query was judged for relevance by physicians who were clinically active and were current fellows in general medicine or medical informatics or senior medical residents. The judges used the patient information and topic designation from the original searcher as the information need of the user, with part of the MEDLINE record (title, source, authors, abstract, and publication type) as the reference. They were encouraged to seek the original articles when relevance could not be assessed from the title and abstract. The reviewers were blinded as to which searcher retrieved which articles. Relevance was judged on a three-point scale: definitely relevant (article provided highly relevant information for clinician faced with the recorded patient data and information need), possibly relevant (article might provide useful information to the clinician), and not relevant (article did not provide any relevant information for this information need). Reviewers were asked to judge relevance from the standpoint of a clinician seeking an answer to the question posed. About 11% of the judgments were duplicated to assess interobserver reliability as measured by the kappa statistic.

3. Interactive searching results

Searching quality was assessed by the measures of relative recall (hereafter referred to as recall) and precision. The test database for the calculation of recall and precision consisted of all MEDLINE references from the 270 journals in the current KF subset spanning from 1987 through 1991, which contained 348,566 references.

The study design provided results for five searches on each query: the original KF search, two MEDLINE searches (librarian and clinician) using the full MEDLINE feature set (MeSH terms and text words), and two searches (librarian and clinician) using text words only. Searching performance was characterized for each of the five groups by the mean relative recall and precision for each of the queries.

Statistical analysis of the results was performed using repeated measures analysis of variance. Post-hoc t-tests for paired observations were performed using the Bonferroni correction.

3.1 Retrieval

Table 1 shows the total number of references and average number of references per query retrieved by the five searching groups for all of the queries, along with the proportion of those references that were in the test database. Only a quarter of all the references retrieved by replicated searches were in the test database. There were also a small number of references retrieved by KF (0.5%) which were not in the test database, due to journals that were added or dropped over time on the actual KF CD-ROM. A total of 15,859 references (149.6 per query) were retrieved by all searchers from the test database, 12,565 (118.5 per query) of which were unique query-reference pairs.

3.2 Relevance judgments

There were 8,714 (69.3%) references judged as not relevant, 2,053 (16.3%) judged as possibly relevant, and 1,798 (14.3%) judged as definitely relevant. The mean number of definitely relevant references per query was 17.0 (median 9, range 0-100). The mean number of possibly relevant references per query was 19.4 (median 13, range 0-81). There were 1,435 (11.4%) pairs judged in duplicate, with 1,003 agreements and 432 disagreements. Table 2 shows the interobserver agreement for duplicated relevance judgments. The kappa score of 0.41 was comparable with other experiments of this type [12-14]. The majority of the disagreements were relevance threshold disagreements; i.e., one judge marked relevant almost all of the other judge's relevant documents plus other additional documents.

There were five queries without definitely relevant references. Because recall and precision are meaningless when there are no relevant documents, and the SMART evaluation program used below ignores queries with no relevant documents, we eliminated these five queries from further analysis.

3.3 Recall and precision results

Recall and precision values for each group were calculated in two ways: using only definitely relevant references (DR) and using definitely plus possibly relevant references (D+PR) (Table 3). For both levels of relevance, the KF searchers obtained recall that was significantly ($p < .0001$) higher than each of the other search groups. In turn, precision was significantly higher ($p < .0001$) for each of the non-KF groups. Librarians obtained better recall and precision using the full MEDLINE feature set than with text words, but the differences between the two were not statistically significant. Physicians obtained better recall with text words and better precision with the full feature set, but these differences were also not statistically significant. Librarians using the full feature set did have significantly ($p < .02$) higher recall than physicians using the full feature set (but not text words) for D+PR articles.

Since the searchers using KF retrieved so many more references per search, an additional searching group was added to the table, which was the KF searches cut off at a maximum of 15 references per search (as opposed to the program's default operation of 100 references per search), which was the average number of references retrieved per query in the test database by all the non-KF searchers. With this definition of retrieval, recall was not significantly different from either librarian or expert physician searchers. However, the precision of the KF searches based only on the top 15 articles was significantly worse than searches using the full MEDLINE feature set conducted by librarians ($p < .01$ for DR articles and $p < .0001$ for D+PR articles) and by expert physicians ($p < .01$ for DR articles and $p < .02$ for D+PR articles).

3.4 Retrieval overlap

Since a number of studies have shown that searchers tend to find non-overlapping sets of relevant references, we also looked at the proportions of relevant references retrieved by one searcher, two searchers, and so on. Over half of the 1,798 DR references were retrieved by only one of the five searchers (Table 4). Another quarter were retrieved only by two searchers. Less than ten percent of all DR references were retrieved by four or five searchers. When the KF retrieval set was reduced to 15 references per search, the number of DR references not retrieved by any searcher was 23.9%. Table 5 shows the proportions of singly retrieved relevant references by search group which retrieved them. For the full KF retrieval set, over one-quarter of definitely relevant references were retrieved by KF alone. With the reduced KF set, librarians ranked highest for unique retrievals.

Table 1 -- References retrieved in test database.

Group	References retrieved	References retrieved per search	Percent of references in test database
Clinic Physicians	9470	89.3	99.5
Librarians-Full MEDLINE	7032	66.3	27.1
Librarians-Text words only	7027	66.3	25.7
Physicians-Full MEDLINE	4550	42.9	25.3
Physicians-Text words only	5897	55.6	26.6

Table 2 -- Interobserver agreement of definitely relevant (DR), possibly relevant (PR), and not relevant (NR) relevance judgments.

		Rater 1		
		DR	PR	NR
	DR	127	112	96
Rater 2	PR		97	224
	NR			779

Table 3 -- Mean recall (R) and precision (P) results for interactive searching.

	Mean number of documents retrieved	Definitely relevant only		Definitely and possibly relevant	
Group		R	P	R	P
Clinic Physicians-using KF	88.9	68.2	14.7	72.5	30.8
Clinic Physicians-KF top 15	14.6	31.2	24.8	25.5	43.8
Librarians-Full MEDLINE	18.0	37.1	36.1	30.8	59.4
Librarians-Text words only	17.1	31.5	31.9	27.0	50.3
Physicians-Full MEDLINE	10.9	26.6	34.9	19.8	55.2
Physicians-Text words only	14.8	30.6	31.4	24.1	48.4

Table 4 -- Number of searchers who retrieved relevant references.

Relevant references retrieved by:	Full KF retrieval	Reduced KF retrieval
0 searchers	n/a	429 (23.9%)
1 searcher	957 (53.2%)	788 (43.8%)
2 searchers	474 (26.4%)	355 (19.7%)
3 searchers	190 (10.6%)	121 (6.7%)
4 searchers	99 (5.5%)	73 (4.1%)
5 searchers	42 (2.3%)	32 (1.8%)

Table 5 -- Sources of retrieval among references retrieved only by one searcher.

Relevant references retrieved by only:	Full KF retrieval	Reduced KF retrieval
Clinic Physicians-using KF	503 (28.0%)	110 (6.1%)
Librarians-Full MEDLINE	195 (10.9%)	282 (15.7%)
Librarians-Text words only	128 (7.1%)	173 (9.6%)
Physicians--Full MEDLINE	63 (3.5%)	93 (5.2%)
Physicians-Text words only	68 (3.8%)	130 (7.2%)

3.5 Interpretation of interactive searching results

This study looked at the quality of searching from two perspectives that had not been taken before: the comparison of a system like KF in the hands of novice searchers to traditional tools used by more experienced searchers, and the comparison of the full MEDLINE feature set to searches based only on title and abstract words. The significantly higher recall obtained by the clinic physicians, even at the cost of diminished precision, shows that end-users can effectively access the medical literature with tools such as KF.

There are some aspects of the study which could explain the significantly better recall by novice searchers besides just the value of KF's innovative approach. To begin with, both the experienced clinician and librarian searchers faced the handicap of having limited information, usually a brief sentence on the patient and information need. It has been shown that librarians perform better searches when they can interview the information seeker, getting more detail on the exact information request [15]. Second, the experienced searchers may have searched differently if their database only contained the references on the KF CD-ROM. While the 42.9 to 66.3 references retrieved per search indicated appropriate strategies for the database they were searching (six years of full MEDLINE), the experienced searchers may have broadened their searches if the initial retrievals led to just the 10.9 to 18.0 references per search present in the test database. Broadening the search could have led to higher recall. Indeed, the higher recall of the novices may have been a function of their much larger retrieval sets as shown by their more modest recall levels when their retrieval set was limited in quantity to the average size of the retrieval sets of the experienced searchers (Table 5).

The other previously unexplored perspective was the comparison of using the full MEDLINE feature set versus just the use of text words by the experienced searchers. The differences between the two types of searching were small and statistically insignificant, indicating that at least for the types of searches done in this study, the full MEDLINE feature set did not confer any strong advantage in retrieving relevant references. When comparing physicians with librarians in using the full feature set, there was a statistically significant advantage in recall for librarians, suggesting that advanced MEDLINE features are a tool of most benefit to librarians.

4 The test collection

The test collection is a subset of the MEDLINE database, which is a bibliographic database of important, peer-reviewed medical literature maintained by the National Library of Medicine (NLM). There are currently over seven million references in MEDLINE dating back to 1966, with about 250,000 added yearly. While the majority of references are to journal articles, there are also a small number of references to letters to the editor, conference proceedings, and other reports. About 75% of the references contain abstracts, while the remainder (including all letters to the editor) have only titles. Each reference also contains human-assigned subject headings from the 17,000-term Medical Subject Headings (MeSH) vocabulary.

4.1 Current collection

The OHSUMED collection contains 348,566 references, which are derived from the subset of 270 journals covered in the KF MEDLINE Primary Care product covering the years 1987 to 1991. The test collection contains the 101 queries that were generated by actual physicians in the course of patient care and had at least one DR document. Each query contains a brief statement about the patient, followed by the information need. The queries are generally terse, more like the older test collections and unlike the long queries from the TREC collection. The collection also contains the relevance judgments for two levels of relevance, as described above: definitely relevant (DR) and definitely or possibly relevant (D+PR).

The NLM has agreed to make this test collection available to information retrieval researchers provided they do not make it available in actual (clinical or library) settings, use it only for research, and inform the users that the database itself is out of date. The files are available via FTP by contacting the first author of this paper.

4.2 Future plans

There are future plans to enhance this collection in two directions. The first is to do at least one additional round of relevance judgments. The SMART experiments described below led to retrieval of documents not already judged for relevance for a given query. Continued experimentation with the collection by other researchers will undoubtedly identify even more unjudged documents. In addition, there will likely be disagreements with the existing relevance judgments.

The second future plan is to build a parallel collection of the full text documents from as many as the references in the collection as possible. Full text is desirable both as a delivery vehicle to the end-user (who does not subsequently need to go to the library to obtain the article in the reference) and as a source for more text to process in indexing. Over a dozen major journals have been available in full-text electronic form since the beginning of the time interval of this test collection (1987), and the publishers are being contacted about their use. The publisher of one of these journals, Annals of Internal Medicine, has already agreed and delivered text.

5 Experiments with SMART

Additional experiments were run using SMART version 11 to obtain baseline performance levels with a well-known experimental retrieval system as well as to compare that system's performance with the human searchers in the original experiment. Five sets of experiments were carried out:

1. Comparison of SMART weighting approaches
2. Effect of documents retrieved by SMART which were not judged for relevance
3. Alternative query and document formulations
4. Relevance feedback
5. Comparisons of SMART and human searchers

Except for as noted in specific experiments, the queries for the SMART experiments were the statements of information need (IN) by the original searcher. Likewise, except as noted, the documents for the SMART experiments consisted of the title, abstract (when present), and MeSH heading fields. All of the experiments reported in this section were done using DR documents only. Experiments were also done with D+PR documents, but while the magnitude of recall and precision levels changed, their relative values did not. For all experiments, recall and precision is shown at levels of 5, 15, and 100 documents retrieved. The latter two levels represent the average level of non-KF and KF human retrieval in the original experiments.

5.1 Comparison of SMART weighting approaches

A comparison of 16 different document weighting methods by 8 query weighting methods (using the IN as the query) yielded a wide range of performance. (The usual SMART weighting triples were used, as shown in Table 6.) A sampling of these results is shown in Table 7. The best document-query weighting was ann.atn, indicating that the only beneficial weighting component for documents was the normalized non-logarithmic term frequency. The cosine normalization did not prove beneficial for documents. Given no normalization, the IDF factor could appear in the document or query without affecting results. However, including it in both the document and query led to mildly decreased effectiveness.

The lack of benefit for the IDF with documents parallels the results of SMART in TREC 2, where the IDF also was not of benefit. The IDF is, however, known to be beneficial with smaller document collections [3, 13], but its benefit seems to wane with larger collection size. The lack of benefit for the cosine normalization was clearly due to a peculiarity in MEDLINE, which in addition to journal citations also contains references to letters to the editor, which have no associated text beyond the title and for this collection were almost always deemed nonrelevant. Normalization leads to higher ranking of these "shorter" documents, markedly lowering recall and precision values. The non-letter documents are also all approximately the same length, as MEDLINE (until recently) imposed a limit of 250 words per abstract and most articles pushed this limit as much as possible. Thus there was no advantage to normalization even for the longer documents.

5.2 Effect of non-judged documents

One problem with the above experiment is one that commonly occurs when new retrieval systems are used with a test collection, in that many documents that have not been judged for relevance are retrieved. Table 8 shows the same runs as in Table 7, but with non-judged documents eliminated from recall-precision calculations. There are substantial improvements in both recall and precision, indicating the maximum possible detrimental effect that non-judged documents have on results. In SMART's performance with TREC (which also has this problem), the maximum detrimental effect after 100 potentially unjudged documents was between 2% and 5%. For the rest of the experiments (with exceptions described below), we included non-judged (assumed nonrelevant) documents in recall-precision calculations.

5.3 Alternative query and document formulations

We also tested variations in both the query and document representations. The original queries contained statements about the patient (BIO) and IN. The results of this baseline query, using the best weighting from Table 7, are given in the first row of Table 9. The results in the next row show the value of adding the BIO statement to the query. This improved the results, but showed maximum benefit when the words in the patient information statement were given only 0.25 of the weight given to words in the IN statement. This is most likely due to the fact that patient information is helpful but not central to the information need.

For the next analysis, we used the original user's natural language query entered into the KF system itself (hereafter referred to as the KF statement). This also provided a modest performance benefit over the baseline at higher document cut-off levels. The major difference between the IN and KF statements was that the latter tended to be more terse. That is, the user typed more information into the pre-search questionnaire than the KF query box. This may be an artifact of the users' past experience with Boolean searching, where one must be careful in entering search terms to avoid output overload.

The one alternate document formulation appears in the last row of Table 9. In this experiment, we compared the results with and without indexing of the human-assigned MeSH terms. In the original experiments, we found that experienced searchers, especially physicians, did not achieve substantial benefit from using MeSH terms in their queries. But this experiment did not address a more fundamental question, which is whether there was benefit to MeSH terms in documents. Our runs indicated that the MeSH terms did confer some benefit, most likely by providing words that were in user queries but not in document titles or abstracts.

5.4 Relevance feedback

We also assessed the performance of relevance feedback by using the Ide method [4]. For each feedback run, the query was expanded by adding 30 terms that occurred in the top five or 10 relevant documents. In order to allow comparison with the other results generated, we did not use residual sets or frozen ranks. The results (see Table 10), indicate better results at the level of fewer documents retrieved (i.e., 15 but not 100).

5.5 Comparisons of SMART and human searchers

The final experiments were an attempt to compare SMART directly with human searchers. This was done by comparing the recall and precision of SMART and the human searcher for each query by having SMART retrieve the exact number of documents retrieved by the human, somewhat analogous to the original SMART-MEDLARS study [7]. For example, if a human searcher retrieved 100 documents for a given query, then we calculated recall and precision for SMART at 100 documents, whereas if a human searcher retrieved only 15 documents, we calculated results for SMART at 15 documents.

The paired comparisons for each of the original searcher groups is shown in Table 11. The first column contains the original searching results. The second column contains the recall and precision values for SMART at the same number of retrieved documents using the IN statement. The third column contains values at the same number of documents using the KF statement, while the last column uses the IN statement with judged documents only. Statistical analysis was done for each searcher group, utilizing a repeated measures analysis of variance with post hoc comparisons done using a t-test with Bonferroni correction.

In general, the R and P values for the original searchers were intermediate between SMART with all documents and with judged documents only. There were, however, some exceptions. For the two original searcher groups that used the MEDLINE feature set, the original values were higher than any of the SMART groups, including those using judged documents only, although the differences from the latter did not achieve statistical significance. This could be interpreted as a tendency for the full MEDLINE feature set to confer some benefit over SMART. However, this group also represents the most experienced searchers, and the results could also be reflecting their advanced skill.

Table 6 -- SMART weighting nomenclature.

triple <term_freq x idf x normalization>

term_freq:
- b - binary (always 1)
- a - term_freq normalized between 0.5 and 1.0 (i.e., 0.5 + 0.5 * tf/max_tf_in_doc)
- l - 1 + ln(term_freq)
- n - term_freq (i.e., number of times term occurs in doc)

idf:
- t - ln (N/n) where N = no. docs in collection and n = no. docs in which term occurs
- n - no idf factor

normalization:
- c - cosine normalization
- n - no normalization

Table 7 -- SMART comparison of weighting approaches based on information need statements and DR documents. Mean percent recall (R) and precision (P) are shown at 5, 15, and 100 documents. Average P represents the 11-point average of precision at each recall point on the recall-precision table.

	5 documents		15 documents		100 documents		Average
	R	P	R	P	R	P	P
anc.atn	8.9	14.3	17.3	11.6	41.8	5.9	12.7
ann.atn	15.2	29.1	29.8	23.4	59.8	9.5	25.3
atn.atn	14.6	27.3	27.2	21.5	58.5	9.2	23.9
bnn.btn	13.9	21.8	23.8	17.0	52.2	8.0	19.7
nnn.ntn	5.0	12.3	10.6	9.7	31.8	5.1	9.6

Table 8 - SMART comparison of weighting approaches based on information needs statements and DR documents, with unjudged documents removed.

	5 documents		15 documents		100 documents	
	R	P	R	P	R	P
anc.atn	16.7	28.4	32.0	23.2	69.8	10.9
ann.atn	19.4	35.8	36.2	28.3	79.2	13.1
atn.atn	17.9	32.5	35.3	27.2	76.6	12.9
bnn.btn	16.1	28.7	31.9	24.1	68.6	11.4
nnn.ntn	11.5	24.7	25.2	21.4	53.5	9.1

Table 9 - Alternative formulations in queries and documents.

	5 documents		15 documents		100 documents		Average
	R	P	R	P	R	P	P
IN query statements	15.2	29.1	29.8	23.4	59.8	9.5	25.3
0.25 * BIO + IN	15.3	29.7	31.4	23.8	62.2	9.8	26.1
KF query statements	15.0	27.9	31.1	23.4	64.1	9.9	26.3
IN on docs without MeSH	15.0	29.1	27.0	22.1	54.5	8.5	23.1

Table 10 -- Relevance feedback.

	5 documents		15 documents		100 documents		Average
	R	P	R	P	R	P	P
After 5 docs	19.3	39.6	33.4	26.2	60.9	10.0	33.0
After 10 docs	25.6	49.1	35.3	28.8	63.7	10.5	39.9

5.6 Assessment of human searcher features

The next set of experiments attempted to simulate the features that could assist the human searcher, in particular the skilled medical librarian. Table 12 starts with the best run from Table 11, librarians using full MEDLINE, and examines differences in the environment caused by the searcher for that run and the SMART IN run. The original searcher and SMART runs start out with the same information need statement. The factors differing in the two environments are:

1. Retrieval set size determined by searcher.
2. Searcher added new query terms.
3. Searcher performed intermediate runs and refined original query.
4. Searcher's retrieved set was fully evaluated for relevance.

Runs 2-4 of Table 12 illustrate the difficulty of effectively comparing retrieval runs when the size of the retrieved set varies on a query-by-query basis, even if the average number of retrieved documents is kept constant. These runs are exactly the same SMART run with the same ranking of documents and each retrieving the same number of total documents. The only difference is in the number of retrieved documents for individual queries. Run 2 retrieves the same number for each query as Run 1, while run 3 always retrieves 18 documents, the average of librarians using full MEDLINE in the original experiments. Run 4 is a manually optimized run, where the number of documents for each query is chosen to maximize the overall recall-precision. (In a real ranked output environment, a user would be able to stop retrieval at any desired point, but undoubtedly would not be able to achieve the recall and precision of run 4.)

For recall and precision, run 1 is significantly better than run 2, while run 4 has a tendency (though not statistically significant) towards improvement over run 1. The power of a user (or system evaluator) to set the retrieval set size has an enormous impact on evaluation. If at all possible, a comparative evaluation of two methods needs to keep the retrieval set size constant at a value neutral to the two methods.

Run 5 is an attempt to emulate the multiple iterations and increased vocabulary of the librarian searchers. A standard automatic feedback run was done, looking at the top 5 documents. Up to 30 terms from the relevant documents were added to the query. Unlike most feedback evaluations, the seen documents were retrievable on the feedback iteration (i.e., no frozen ranking or residual collection). This was done to more closely approximate the multiple iterations of the Boolean searchers. Run 5 is much closer to run 1, but still less effective. Run 6, evaluating using only the documents that had been judged, is again much better than the original run, but still less effective than run 1.

Table 12 demonstrates the difficulty of comparing Boolean searches done by trained intermediaries with ranked output searches. Each of the latter three runs is an attempt to equalize one factor in the differences between the two environments. Together they would achieve much better performance than the MEDLINE searchers. However, each of these runs is an upper bound on the effect of the factor. All that can really be said is that the "true" performance of the ranked system is somewhere between this upper bound and run 2.

Table 11 -- Comparison of original searchers with SMART.

Searcher Group	Original		SMART IN		SMART KF		SMART-IN-judged	
	R	P	R	P	R	P	R	P
Original KF	68.2	14.7	57.5	11.8	61.7	13.7	75.6	19.2
Librarians - MEDLINE	37.1	36.1	24.4	22.7	26.3	24.8	32.2	29.1
Librarians - Text-words	31.5	31.9	27.9	25.3	25.4	26.1	34.1	31.6
Physicians - MEDLINE	26.5	34.9	19.9	23.5	18.9	25.4	24.1	30.6
Physicians - Text-words	30.5	31.4	24.0	25.7	26.0	25.5	30.0	31.9

Table 12 -- Comparisons of Librarians - MEDLINE search group with SMART features.

Run	Retrieval Set Size	R	P
1. Librarians - MEDLINE	searcher set (avg. 18)	37.1	36.1
2. SMART IN	searcher set	24.4	22.7
3. SMART IN	always 18	32.7	21.9
4. SMART IN	optimized (avg. 18)	41.1	38.4
5. SMART IN feedback 5	always 18	35.6	24.3
6. SMART IN (remove non-judged)	searcher set	32.2	29.1

6 Conclusions

This first part of this study showed that novice physicians could effectively use a vector space-like retrieval system for searching MEDLINE in a clinical setting. This provides evidence against the notions that this approach is not effective in operational settings and cannot scale to large document collections. Further interactive experiments in different domains are necessary to see whether this success can be generalized.

This study also resulted in a new large test collection for medical information retrieval research. From both the interactive and SMART experiments, baseline performance data is available, which will allow experimenters and system builders to evaluate new approaches with a real world-sized collection from the medical domain. Experiments with SMART also showed the difficulty of comparing Boolean and ranked searches, especially in the interactive searching environment.

Acknowledgments

This work was supported in part by Grant LM05307 of the U.S. National Library of Medicine.

References

1. Knowledge Finder Reference Manual.North Andover, MA: Aries Systems Corp., 1988
2. Hersh W, Hickam D. Impact of a computerized information system in a university general medicine clinic. Clinical Research 1992;40:567A.
3. Salton G, Buckley C. Term-weighting approaches in automatic text retrieval. Info Proc Mgmt 1988; 24(5):513-523.
4. Salton G, Buckley C. Improving retrieval performance by relevance feedback. J Am Soc Info Sci 1990; 41:288-297.
5. Belkin N, Cool C, Croft W, Callan J. Effect of multiple query representations on information retrieval system performance. In: Korfhage R, Rasmussen E, Willett P, ed. Proceedings of the 16th Annual International ACM Special Interest Group in Information Retrieval. Pittsbrugh, PA: ACM Press, 1993: 339-346.
6. Fuhr N, Knorz G. Retrieval test evaluation of a rule-based automatic indexing (AIR/PHYS). In: vanRijsbergen C, ed. Research and Development in Information Retrieval. Cambridge: Cambridge University Press, 1984: 391-408.
7. Salton G. A new comparison between conventional indexing (MEDLARS) and automatic text processing (SMART). J Am Soc Info Sci 1972; 23(2):75-84.
8. Salton G, Fox E, Wu H. Extended boolean information retrieval. Comm Assoc Comp Mach 1983; 26:1022-1036.
9. Turtle H, Croft W. Evaluation of an inference network-based retrieval model. ACM Transactions on Information Systems 1991; 9:187-222.
10. Robertson S, Thompson C. Weighted searching: The CIRT experiment. Informatics 10: Prospects for Intelligent Retrieval. York: ASLIB, 1990: 153-166.
11. Harman D. Overview of the first Text REtrieval Conference. In: Korfhage R, ed. Proceedings of the 16th Annual International ACM Special Interest Group in Information Retrieval. Pittsburgh: ACM Press, 1993: 36-47.
12. Hersh W, Hickam D. A comparison of two methods for indexing and retrieval from a full-text medical database. Proceedings of the 55th Annual Meeting of the American Society for Information Science. 1992: 221-230.
13. Hersh W, Hickam D. A performance and failure analysis of SAPHIRE with a MEDLINE test collection. Journal of the American Medical Informatics Association 1994; 1:51-60.
14. Haynes R, McKibbon K, Walker C, Ryan N, Fitzgerald D, Ramsden M. Online access to MEDLINE in clinical settings. Ann Int Med 1990; 112(1):78-84.
15. Saracevic T, Kantor P. A study of information seeking and retrieving. III. Searchers, searches, and overlap. J Am Soc Info Sci 1988; 39:197-216.

Results of Applying Probabilistic IR to OCR Text

Kazem Taghva
taghva@cs.unlv.edu

Julie Borsack
jborsack@isri.unlv.edu

Allen Condit
condit@isri.unlv.edu

Information Science Research Institute
University of Nevada, Las Vegas
Las Vegas, NV 89154 USA

Abstract

Character accuracy of optically recognized text is considered a basic measure for evaluating OCR devices. In the broader sense, another fundamental measure of an OCR's goodness is whether its generated text is usable for retrieving information. In this study, we evaluate retrieval effectiveness from OCR text databases using a probabilistic IR system. We compare these retrieval results to their manually corrected equivalent. We show there is no statistical difference in precision and recall using graded accuracy levels from three OCR devices. However, characteristics of the OCR data have side effects that could cause unstable results with this IR model. In particular, we found individual queries can be greatly affected. Knowing the qualities of OCR text, we compensate for them by applying an automatic post-processing system that improves effectiveness.

1 Introduction

Anyone who has performed research in either optical character recognition (OCR) or information retrieval (IR) will attest that each process is complex in its own right. To presuppose what will occur when the two systems are combined would be injudicious at best. The studies we describe, in both this paper and our previous work[1, 2], show the actual effects OCR-generated data has on the IR systems used in our experiments.

In our first study [1], we ran a set of queries against two databases. Each database contained the same document collection, but one database had been manually corrected to a level of 99.8% correctness while the other database had been automatically generated by an OCR device with no manual correction. In this original set of experiments, we used a boolean exact-match system for our IR environment. We believe using different IR systems for this kind of experimentation can influence the results. Since no relevancy information had been found for this collection, our evaluation consisted only of a comparison between the retrieved query sets.

The purpose of our current experiment is to broaden our preliminary testing. The collection we use is larger and rather than using a single OCR device, we use three devices at graded accuracy levels. Our current experiments incorporate a form of the probabilistic IR model and apply a natural language interface[3]. Furthermore, we have collected relevancy information for our larger collection so that precision and recall can be used for evaluation.

Expanding our testing in the ways described is one reason for repeating the retrieval experiment. But another reason is the correctness of the documents we use in our tests. Our assumption in our original accuracy study was that the quoted 99.8% level of correctness was accurate. To make our study more thorough, for all the pages in our expanded collection, we do a manual verification of the corrected text against each hard copy page. This comparison gave us insight into what can be expected from manually corrected document sets. We report on our findings in Section 2.1.

2 Document Collection

Our collection consists of 674 documents (26,467 pages) which are part of a larger collection that was given to the Information Science Research Institute (ISRI) by the Department of Energy (DOE) for continued study in the areas of optical character recognition and information retrieval. The full collection consists of approximately 2,600 (104,000 pages) documents together with their corrected ASCII and page images. These documents make up the Licensing Support System (LSS) prototype. The LSS will capture and track documents that pertain to the site licensing proceedings of the Nuclear Regulatory Commission.

As would be expected from this kind of collection, most of the documents deal with technical, scientific topics. The set we use is full of maps, charts, formulas, and comparable graphical material. Although the documents tend toward the scientific, within this domain the collection is diverse. Our set includes topics from rock mining to safety issues for the transportation of nuclear waste. The set we use covers all sixteen established subject areas designated for the LSS.

Characteristics of this document collection which make it particularly useful for demonstrating the ramifications of using OCR data, is its lack of uniformity in page format, its diverse set of font styles, and its varying grades of hard copy quality. There are almost as many different authoring sources as there are documents. So although the collection is mostly scientific, the broad range of source input gives us a rich collection for the kind of testing we do. This collection consists of full-text documents. The average document length is forty pages and the median length is sixteen pages. For more information about the complete document collection, see [4].

All of the 674 documents were recognized by three different OCR devices to generate the OCR text for our experiment. Our selection criterion for these devices was their level of character accuracy. The three devices we chose reflected the highest accuracy (98.14%), an intermediate accuracy (97.06%), and the lowest character accuracy (94.63%) of the devices we test at ISRI[5]. For clarity, we use the following designations for the three devices respectively: *best*, *middle*, and *worst*. These designations refer to character accuracy only—the qualities of other device features were not considered. The fourth database, designated as *correct*, consists of the 99.8% corrected ASCII for these 674 documents. Our hypothesis was that at some unknown accuracy level, retrieval rates would become unacceptable.

The purpose of our experiments is to see what effects the OCR data will have on the IR systems we use in our testing. To do this kind of evaluation, we must first know the characteristics of not only the OCR-generated text, but also the corrected text to which we compare it. The analysis of our database sets became a considerable part of our experimentation. There are two parts to our analysis: ASCII/OCR document verification and statistical examination of the IR system collections.

2.1 Document Verification

The correspondence of the ASCII document to its original hard copy version, and therefore to its image, is essential to our testing. We found from our first set of experiments that this correspondence may not always be what we expect. So for every document in our text database, we compared each hard copy page, its image page, and its ASCII page.

Correspondence between a hard copy and an image page is simple to detect since an image is an electronic duplicate of its hard copy. Correspondence between a hard copy and its ASCII equivalent is more difficult to judge. Certain qualities and components of a document cannot be duplicated in its ASCII version, such as enlarged print or a photograph. But at some point, the rules for inclusion or exclusion of document elements must be made. These rules were in place for the corrected ASCII generated for the LSS. Unfortunately, with four different contractors these rules were left up to interpretation. Further, whenever human discretion is incorporated into projects of this magnitude, the results are difficult to predict. We found some unexpected differences when we did our comparison. The most significant difference affecting our experimentation was the exclusion of text from the ASCII files. In some cases, this exclusion was purposeful while in others it was due to negligence. For example, one of the editing rules for the LSS was to replace tables and graphics with a `<see image>` tag. In a number of cases, these elements contained a good portion of text. Other discrepancies include the addition of text not part of the original document, erroneous columnization, incorrect page ordering, and deletion of main body text. In a few cases, documents had to be excluded from our testing due to their lack of similarity to the original hard copy version. Although in most cases the corrected ASCII is quite good, the differences we found show that whenever human intervention is introduced, even for correction, some errors and inconsistencies should be expected. For a complete report on our verification procedure and our findings, see [6]. We made no changes to any of the ASCII files in the "99.8% corrected" set. We assume that problems similar to these are inherent in any manual correction procedure and therefore are an integral part of our experimentation.

ASCII verification establishes the usefulness of the corrected document collection. We should also examine the qualities of our OCR collections to understand how they affect our results. OCR technology is a complex process whose results are difficult to predict, especially when its input is as multifarious as the collection we use[7, 8]. Further, the algorithms designed for recognition devices are proprietary, making an educated conjecture difficult. To determine the characteristics of the OCR data, each image was compared to its hard copy and the corresponding generated text was inspected. In general, we looked for gross differences between the image and the generated text. For example, if an OCR generated page had blocks of meaningless characters, it could indicate possible problems with the image. These irregularities were checked for all the OCR-generated pages used in our collection. The most notable difference between the recognized document sets and the 99.8% correct version was the size of the data collections (prior to loading). The largest OCR-generated collection was 169% larger (in megabytes) than the corrected set. We attribute this difference to the exclusion of text in the corrected collection and the interjection of what we call *graphic text*, or strings introduced through mistranslation of graphical

page images	best	middle	worst
26,467	26,445	26,409	26,406

Table 1. Number of recognized pages for the three OCR collections

statistic	correct	best	middle	worst
database size (bytes)	15,686,772	37,080,489	40,918,148	42,247,537
average number of terms per document	6,114	9,321	8,583	7,925
number of unique indexed terms	78,494	320,338	387,276	414,715
terms occurring only once	36,742	223,058	278,907	296,572
terms occurring more than once	41,752	97,280	108,369	118,143
correctly spelled words	22,833	25,241	24,728	23,552

Table 2. Statistics for correct, best, middle, and worst collections

material.

A variance found among the OCR collections was the pages that could be recognized by each of them. With a total of 26,467 page images, the recognized pages of one device were not necessarily a subset of the others. The number of pages recognized by each device can be found in Table 1.

Another difference among the devices is their ability to recognize and "zone out" graphics[7]. If an OCR device has an automatic *zoning* capability, it should differentiate between text and non-text sections (i.e. photographs, maps, etc.); it should translate only those that have been designated as text "zones." We found through our testing that this proficiency can be consequential for some IR systems. The lack of accurate zoning not only adds to overhead, it may also limit IR effectiveness. These repercussions will be discussed in more detail later in this paper. All the devices produced good quality output from good quality page images. Divergence in output accuracy became more apparent among the three devices as the quality of the images dropped.

2.2 Collection Statistics

In our original experiment with a boolean exact-match system, certain statistics about our collections were interesting but not necessarily a determinant in our results. This is not true for the model we use in this set of tests. In Table 2 we present statistics about each of the four collections. We believe these statistics had an impact on our results. First, note the difference in the database size of the correct set versus any of the OCR collections. All three OCR collections are more than twice the size of the correct set. We attribute a good portion of this inflated size to graphic text, but also for every misspelled word in the OCR collections, there exists a certain amount of overhead. This overhead contributes to its size.

The average number of terms per document is another measure of increased magnitude. This number illustrates the average length of the documents in words; it is the total of all occurrences excluding stopwords. Besides correctly spelled words, this is the only decreasing statistic for the best, middle and worst collections respectively. We can explain this downtrend by remembering that the best device recognizes more words correctly. So even though the total number of terms occurring more than once in the best database is lower than the other OCR-generated databases, the total occurrences of these terms is higher. Also, it seems the best database had more duplications of single and double character text strings which were probably generated by graphics.

The number of unique indexed terms is a good indicator of the amplified size of the OCR databases. There is a huge discrepancy between the corrected set and the three OCR collections. But even among the OCR databases, there is noticeable variability. Of the OCR collections, the best database has the fewest unique entries; as the accuracy of the device drops, the number of unique index terms increases. These unique term counts demonstrate the amount of overhead required for OCR-generated text: the IR system may have to store 5 times as many terms. Further, these "terms" will probably be of little use to the user since many are misspellings and graphic text strings that will never be query terms.

In the correct database, the number of terms occurring only once is about 47% of the total number of indexed terms. This percentage is comparable to the statistics found for the collections used in TREC-1[9]. The percentage of terms occurring only once in the OCR collections are disproportionate when compared to the corrected set's percentage. The percentage for these three collections are quite close to each other at above 70%. Terms occurring more than once is simply the complement of those terms occurring once. Of course the fraction of these to the total number of indexed terms is much smaller than what we found in our corrected set.

Another interesting anomaly is the *increase* in the number of correctly spelled words found in the OCR collections compared to the corrected collection. This peculiarity shows that information contained in the documents is actually being removed from the manually corrected collection. Also, if we compare the last two rows of Table 2, there seems to be a considerable gap between the number of words occurring more than once and correctly spelled words. The basis for this difference can be attributed to more than one factor. First, there are certainly legitimate words that were missed due to lack of completeness of our dictionary, proper names, acronyms, and the like. Another factor is that misspellings can be duplicated. In Section 3.2, we show this is particularly true with the OCR collections. We use the intersection of the set of correctly spelled words and the set of words occurring more than once as the starting point for our automatic post-processing system described in Section 3.4. Collectively, these statistics show OCR text has distinct characteristics. For IR to work advantageously with OCR, compensation for these characteristics should be made.

3 Experimental Environment

The document collection we use has considerable bearing on our experiments. The scientific content and diversity of the set makes it a challenge for our experimentation. Other aspects of our testing environment also influence the eventual outcome. The scanner, the recognition devices, the retrieval system, and the queries all affect the results. Following is a brief description of each of these components and how they might affect or be affected by the OCR-generated text.

3.1 Scanning and Recognition

Scanning refers to the digitization of an input page into an electronic bit-mapped image[10]. The most commonly used scanners for text documents are those which *binarize* the input page. Binarization is the conversion of grey levels to either black or white. The binarization is controlled by a given threshold value. Another setting that can be controlled at scan time is the resolution. These settings will affect the ability of the OCR device to recognize the page[11]. For our experiments we used the most commonly applied values for the purpose of character recognition. The images we generated were scanned on the Fujitsu Image Scanner, model number M3096G, at 300 dpi resolution with a median threshold of 127. We are uncertain about the scanning procedures applied for those images generated by the government contractors for the LSS. We do know these images were scanned with either a Ricoh or Fujitsu scanner at 300 dpi[4].

Wherever possible, we used the images generated by the contractors of the LSS. But in a good portion of the documents, the images were either missing or corrupt. For these documents, we scanned the hard copy pages using the settings described to complete our image set.

Each of these page images was automatically zoned and recognized by the three OCR devices. Our environment at ISRI provides a vendor-independent interface that controls all OCR settings and selections. Thus, all parameters remained constant for all the devices throughout our testing. For a full description of this interface, refer to [12]. As pointed out in our first paper [1], reduced accuracy should be expected with automatic zoning. But with such a large number of pages and the inability to duplicate the zoning rules prescribed by the LSS, manual zoning would not have been feasible.

Automatic zoning influenced other aspects of our experiment. We mentioned that graphic text inflates the size of the database index. This is only one of its side effects. If there is enough "noise" in a document, it can affect an IR system's ability to determine meaningful document frequencies. Its effect on the IR system we use is described in Section 3.2.

3.2 INQUERY Retrieval System

The INQUERY Retrieval System applies the foundations of the probabilistic IR model and the notion of *inference networks* to determine document to query relevance. In general, the probabilistic approach tries to determine this relevance from a priori information about term distributions. Inference nets are specific probabilistic representations that attempt to model document and query content. The belief that documents are relevant to a given query is based on the concepts that have been inferred by the system. The method of assigning concepts to documents and to queries is the fundamental component of INQUERY's architecture. In their simplest form, concepts correspond to terms in the document or

query	document	correct		best		middle		worst	
	j	$maxtf_j$	rank	$maxtf_j$	rank	$maxtf_j$	rank	$maxtf_j$	rank
14	193	73	1	714	32	630	27	109	1
28	468	96	27	94	22	179	> 600	396	453

Table 3. Relationship between $maxtf_j$ and $document_j$ ranking

document	correct		best		middle		worst	
j	term	$maxtf_j$	term	$maxtf_j$	term	$maxtf_j$	term	$maxtf_j$
9	image	177	hsf	4364	hsf	1932	m	687
14	stress	76	stress	122	stress	118	stress	88
77	veins	196	n	1835	n	1607	veins	193
87	ore	88	ore	90	ore	90	fhe	129
199	nevada	64	m	293	nevada	68	nevada	63
221	population	16	population	18	population	18	populakion	10
583	test	94	e	100	ihe	256	thc	176
610	doe	81	doe	81	doe	81	doe	81

Table 4. Most frequent terms and disparity in their $maxtf_j$

query[3]. Whether a concept is associated with a specific document depends on both document and collection term frequencies. Formula 1 is a simplification of the formula used by INQUERY to assign concept i to document j[13].

$$k + \left[(1-k) * \frac{\log t_{ij}}{\log maxtf_j} * \frac{\log \frac{c}{f_i}}{\log c} \right] \qquad (1)$$

where

$c \equiv$ collection size
$f_i \equiv$ number of documents in which concept i occurs
$t_{ij} \equiv$ frequency of concept i in document j
$maxtf_j \equiv$ maximum concept frequency in document j

The parameter k serves to bias the initial belief of term relevance and can be adjusted by the user to fit the collection. We use the default belief value of $k = 0.4$ in our tests. The other four values (c, f_i, t_{ij}, $maxtf_j$) govern concept assignment. We found, by analyzing queries with very different document ranking results across the four collections, that collection frequencies, f_i, and document frequencies, t_ij, did not show enough deviation among the databases to adversely affect concept assignment.[1] We did find however, that $maxtf_j$ was inconsistent among the databases and the greater the inconsistency, the more erratic the ranked results. Table 3 shows the ranking of two relevant documents to two selected queries. Note the disparity in document ranking. The $maxtf_j$ values are a major contributor to this discrepancy.

Since the $maxtf$ frequencies seem to dominate concept assignment and therefore document to query relevance, their frequencies within an OCR collection is crucial to understanding the effect of this kind of data. Some of the widely discrepant $maxtf$ terms and their frequencies are listed in Table 4.

Document 9 has two interesting anomalies. The most obvious one is the disproportionate maximum term frequencies for each of the databases. Referring to Formula 1, one can see how these differing values would influence concept assignment and produce unpredictable results. The second item to note is the word `image` that had the maximum term frequency for this document in the correct database. Document 9 is 207 pages and contains much tabular information. The word `image` had replaced these tables and became the $maxtf$ for this document. Document 9 was not the sole example of this phenomenon; there were 65 other documents with "inserted" $maxtf$s.

Document 14 shows a common problem we encountered in our experiments. One would expect the corrected database, in general, to have the highest term frequencies for correctly spelled words. In both our experiments, in most cases, the correct database had *fewer* instances of the correctly spelled words. This observation motivated our in depth verification of the corrected collection and our discovery of "missing text".

Documents 77 and 199 demonstrate another unanticipated effect of using automatic zoning to generate the OCR collections. Although the worst OCR device may not be as effective in character recognition, we found that its ability to ignore non-textual material worked to its advantage in some instances. Because the best device was more resistant to excluding any part of the document that might contain textual

[1] In general though, the best and middle databases had higher frequencies than the worst database.

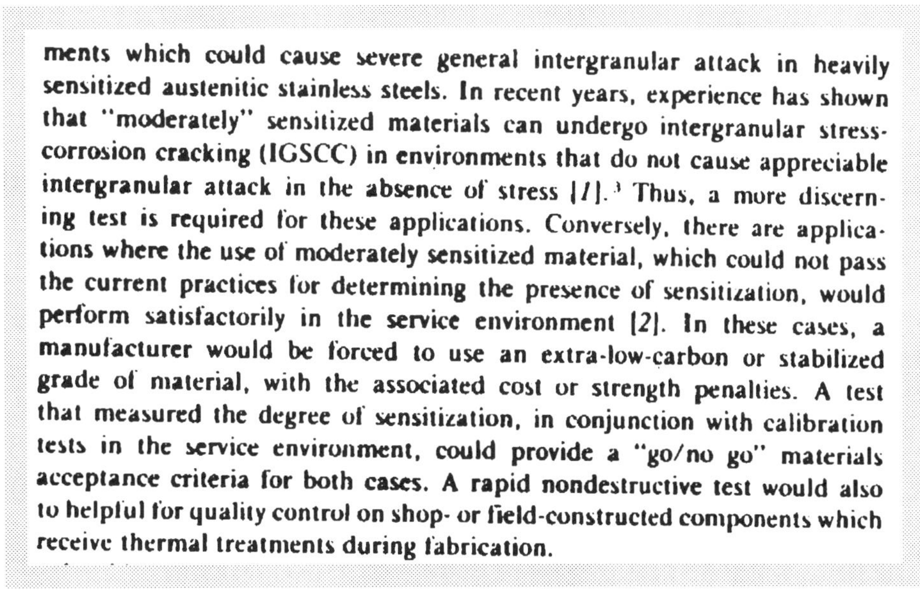
ments which could cause severe general intergranular attack in heavily sensitized austenitic stainless steels. In recent years, experience has shown that "moderately" sensitized materials can undergo intergranular stress-corrosion cracking (IGSCC) in environments that do not cause appreciable intergranular attack in the absence of stress [1].[3] Thus, a more discerning test is required for these applications. Conversely, there are applications where the use of moderately sensitized material, which could not pass the current practices for determining the presence of sensitization, would perform satisfactorily in the service environment [2]. In these cases, a manufacturer would be forced to use an extra-low-carbon or stabilized grade of material, with the associated cost or strength penalties. A test that measured the degree of sensitization, in conjunction with calibration tests in the service environment, could provide a "go/no go" materials acceptance criteria for both cases. A rapid nondestructive test would also to helpful for quality control on shop- or field-constructed components which receive thermal treatments during fabrication.

Figure 1. Image zone of document 583

material, it generated more graphic text than the other devices. Many of these strings are one or two characters long, causing a substantial increase in term occurrences. These terms are sometimes the most frequent terms, which determine the $maxtf$, as can be seen in these two examples. We believe that these irregularities are the principal reason for slightly higher precision values for the worst database.

Documents 87 and 583 exhibit an unforeseen side effect that alters frequencies. In these documents, the middle and the worst devices consistently misrecognized the stopword `the`, causing it to become the highest occurrence term. The images for these documents were not extremely poor; a clip of document 583 appears in Figure 1.

Document 221 shows an expected result of using OCR text. The term `population` was misrecognized by the worst OCR device more than half the time, causing the misspelling `populakion` to become this document's $maxtf$. The last document, 610, was added because it was one of very few documents where both the term and the $maxtf$ were the same for all four databases. `DOE` is the acronym for the Department of Energy.

The frequency changes induced by using OCR text have a broader significance than is apparent from this limited list. All the words contained in the text have the potential for being altered in some way. One of the ramifications is the inconsistency of document ranking caused by erratic maximum term frequencies. Other changes to term counts may cause more subtle effects.

3.3 Queries and Relevancy Judgements

The 68 queries in our current test were a subset of those used in our first experiment. Three queries which requested documents written by named authors were removed. We felt these were unfair queries for a probabilistic system using solely the text of the document. We describe the source of these queries in detail in [1].

Since INQUERY provides a natural language interface, we use this query form for our testing. We made minor modifications to the phrasing to eliminate insignificant words. An example query appears in Figure 2. There were approximately 270 unique search terms (after removal of stopwords) applied in the INQUERY internal query forms. The same set of queries was batch run on each of the four collections.

The relevancy judgements were not part of the collection we received from the DOE. We have been collecting this information since we began our original accuracy experiments. The queries were examined and the complete set of documents was divided among a group of geology graduate students to determine relevance. The students made binary relevancy judgements, classifying documents as either relevant or not relevant. No relevancy ranking was assessed. Excluding seven of the queries having no relevant documents in the collection, the average number of relevant documents per query is 10.

INQUERY provides an automatic evaluation program designed to calculate precision and recall based on relevancy information collected. We use INQUERY's *deval* program to compute average precision over the 68 queries[3].

Test Query INJA-T1-Q1

LSS Prototype Test Question: You have been asked to find out if the Environmental Assessment for the Yucca Mountain Site contained any information on how the repository might affect the economic and social conditions of Nye County. If so, your requestor would like to see those portions.

Inquery natural language translation: *Find documents about the Environmental Assessment for the Yucca Mountain Site that discuss how the repository might affect economic and social conditions of Nye County;*

Figure 2. Example test query translation

3.4 Post-processing

In preparation for our previous experiment, we constructed an automatic OCR post-processing system[14]. This system was designed to correct OCR errors in the text without human intervention. After we loaded our three OCR databases, we ran the post-processing system on all three of these collections to see what improvements we could attain.

Our original post-processing system consisted of numerous steps. We started with a full-text database of documents and obtained an index listing all the unique indexed words in the database. Then, using word frequency information, an English dictionary[2], and an auxiliary domain-specific dictionary, we divided the words into a list of what we call *centroids*, and a list of misspellings. The centroids were the words which were spelled correctly and had high frequency (greater than 1). We then clustered the misspellings around the centroids using approximate pattern matching techniques. We call each pair of matched centroids and misspellings *clusterings*. The idea was that if we could find misspelled words that were close to a centroid word, then we would equate those misspelled words to its centroid. This procedure worked for the most part, but sometimes a misspelled word would be close to more than one centroid. We developed two heuristics to alleviate this problem. The first involved using document frequency information about the words (as opposed to collection frequency). The second process took information about the kinds of mistakes the OCR device was likely to make, and eliminated clusterings that were unlikely to occur. Finally, a list of misspelled words and their correct words was produced, the replacements were made, and the database was reloaded.

The post-processing system we used for the experiment described in this paper is based on our original system[1]. Some changes were added to improve the post-processing system in general, while other changes were added to help rectify problems specifically related to the probabilistic system. In our first experiment we noticed that hyphenated words caused problems for post-processing as well as retrieval. One of the steps that improves OCR text is the removal of end-of-line hyphens and the concatenation of word parts. This step was made smarter. We also increased the number of clustered misspellings by increasing the edit distance for longer words. Further, the accuracy of centroid selection was increased by taking into consideration certain suffixes.

The most notable problem we found with using OCR text with the probabilistic system was the amount of "junk" in the text, and subsequently in the index, that caused unreliable term frequencies. One difficulty is determining which terms are "junk" and which terms are misspellings that could be rectified by the post-processing system. After analyzing the list of indexed words we implemented the following heuristics. We set limits on the minimum and maximum lengths of words (3 and 27 respectively) and removed words with four or more identical consecutive characters. We also ignored strings that had a high ratio of non-alphabetic characters or an irregular vowel-to-consonant ratio. These words were not indexed. The results from running the best database through the post-processing system are compared to its original version in Section 4.2.

4 Retrieval Results and Evaluation

Before presenting the results of our experiments, the context within which these tests were run should be stated. Our purpose was not to increase recall or precision for any of the document collections. Therefore, we did not use all the capabilities INQUERY offers. We used INQUERY version 1.5 with a minimized stopword list of 148 words. We did not apply stemming for purposes of our post-processing system so all the databases are in unstemmed form. Other options provided by INQUERY were ignored and any default values were exploited. Our most basic requirement was consistency throughout our testing. We present two precision and recall tables for each of the experiments run. These are presented in Sections 4.1 and 4.2.

[2]We use *ispell*[15]

Recall	Precision (% change) – 68 queries						
	correct	best		middle		worst	
10	53.5	53.1	(−0.7)	52.9	(−1.0)	54.0	(+1.0)
20	46.0	44.8	(−2.6)	45.7	(−0.5)	47.6	(+3.4)
30	38.6	38.9	(+0.8)	40.8	(+5.7)	39.7	(+2.9)
40	33.8	33.8	(+0.1)	35.3	(+4.5)	35.6	(+5.4)
50	30.4	30.5	(+0.4)	31.0	(+2.2)	31.9	(+5.1)
60	23.3	24.6	(+5.9)	24.6	(+5.9)	24.7	(+6.2)
70	17.8	17.3	(−2.8)	17.5	(−1.6)	18.5	(+4.0)
80	14.7	13.5	(−8.5)	13.2	(−10.8)	14.1	(−4.2)
90	12.7	11.1	(−12.2)	10.8	(−14.6)	11.6	(−8.6)
100	11.8	10.5	(−10.7)	10.2	(−13.9)	10.6	(−10.5)
average	28.2	27.8	(−1.5)	28.2	(−0.1)	28.8	(+2.1)

Table 5. Precision at standard recall points for the corrected document collection and the three OCR collections

Recall		Precision (% change) – 68 queries					
	correct	best-pps		middle-pps		worst-pps	
10	53.5	54.6	(+2.1)	55.8	(+4.3)	54.0	(+0.9)
20	46.0	48.0	(+4.4)	48.7	(+5.8)	47.4	(+3.1)
30	38.6	39.8	(+3.3)	40.1	(+3.9)	38.8	(+0.6)
40	33.8	34.7	(+2.8)	34.8	(+3.0)	34.2	(+1.1)
50	30.4	30.8	(+1.5)	30.2	(−0.5)	30.0	(−1.2)
60	23.3	24.4	(+4.9)	23.4	(+0.6)	24.4	(+4.9)
70	17.8	18.0	(+1.2)	17.7	(−0.8)	18.4	(+3.1)
80	14.7	15.3	(+3.8)	14.5	(−1.4)	15.5	(+4.9)
90	12.7	12.3	(−2.5)	11.5	(−9.2)	12.5	(−1.5)
100	11.8	11.4	(−3.4)	10.8	(−8.7)	11.5	(−2.5)
average	28.2	28.9	(+2.5)	28.7	(+1.8)	28.7	(+1.5)

Table 6. Precision at standard recall points for the corrected document collection and the three OCR collections after post-processing

4.1 Results: Experiment 1

Experiment 1 examines the run of the 68 queries described on the four database collections. Table 5 shows precision and recall results for this experiment. It compares the three OCR collections to the corrected document set at 10 standard recall points. The percentage of difference at each recall point can be found in parentheses.

The results in Table 5 are counterintuitive. The worst collection has the highest average precision and the best collection has the lowest. On the surface it seems as the accuracy of the device improves, the lower the ranking of the relevant documents in its generated collection.

In some respects this is true. As mentioned in Section 3.2, the best device recognized zones aggressively. If there was a possibility of text within a figure or graph, the zone would be recognized. This maximized the maximum term frequencies and in turn suppressed the weight, and therefore the importance, of query terms in relevant documents. The worst device, on the other hand, applies a more passive approach, skipping zones it assumed were not text zones. These differing methods of recognition had an amplified effect on the $maxtf$ and a less significant effect on other term frequencies in the documents. So even though in most cases more terms were recognized correctly by the best device, their significance was weakened by the normalization techniques INQUERY applies.

From an IR perspective though, since the precision results are so close, the differences we see are considered insignificant. Possibly with a minor change in the way we conducted our testing, the results would fluctuate. However, the average values over the 68 queries conceal large individual differences arising from OCR artifacts.

4.2 Results: Experiment 2

Experiment 2 demonstrates the usefulness of our automatic post-processing system (pps). The precision values in Table 6 are what we would anticipate for the three levels of OCR accuracy. Although the averages are still considered insignificant in comparison to the correct database, there is a decided improvement in the best post-processed version when compared to its original version in Table 5. The increase in average precision is over 4%.

query 8	document ranking									
best	1	4	5	16	22	29	32	51	85	99
best after post processing	1	2	3	5	7	22	38	47	61	99

query 11	document ranking					
best	113	115	152	228	275	309
best after post processing	12	58	75	166	243	297

query 14	document ranking			
best	24	32	44	106
best after post processing	1	30	51	93

Table 7. Improvements in relevant document ranking after applying post-processing system

We attribute this improvement to an extreme shift in document ranking for a few queries. In Table 7 we list three queries that show this improvement for the best database over its raw original version. Query 8 ranks every relevant document higher except the 7th. Query 11 shows a considerable upward shift in all the documents, but in particular, the document ranked 1st. Query 14 shows a more acceptable ranking of document 193. We pointed out in Table 3 that document 193 had an exceptionally high $maxtf$. In the best collection this document was ranked 32nd; after post-processing it is ranked 1st.

Note that the average precision for the worst-pps collection (Table 6) has actually decreased. We attribute this decrease to the artificially inflated precision values calculated for the worst collection in experiment 1. These were stabilized after post-processing by increasing the number of correctly spelled words; in particular, the $maxtf$s for the documents in the collection.

5 Conclusion

IR systems use different methods to construe the content of a document. Whatever method is applied, the words of the document are an essential element. For a boolean system, as long as a single term occurrence is found, the document is returned. Our first experiment showed that for a simple boolean system, the problems caused by OCR error could be overcome by redundancy in the document text. As the IR model becomes more sophisticated and tries to extract information from a document's words, their role in the outcome becomes more evident. The level of confidence that could be placed in a presumably correct collection, can no longer be assumed with OCR text; the information extracted may not be reliable. OCR collections then, have an impact on the information the system infers. From our analysis, this impact is more apparent with statistical-based systems.

The impact we see is more specific than what Table 5 shows. Although the average differences seem insignificant, individual queries can be greatly affected by OCR text. Further, when ranking is so disparate, the user's ability to filter through irrelevant documents might be all but impossible. For these reasons, we believe the results of the post-processing system are consequential. Note that the post-processing system[14] we use for this experiment is an enhanced version of the system we used in our original work[1]. We have tuned our post-processing system to deal with the problems we encountered using a probabilistic system. Its goal though is the same: to minimize OCR error and acquire text that is more compatible with the applied form of IR.

With fairly good images, care taken during each of the processes, and automatic post-processing, the results show OCR-generated text can be equivalent to manually typed and corrected text. This happens in part because manually handled text is not as precise as we had hoped and in part because IR systems and the methods for evaluating them are resilient to irregularities in the text. This is especially true for longer documents. As the length of the document decreases the effect on recall and precision may be more apparent[2, 16].

We pointed out in our first paper that we do not view our experiments as a means of evaluating IR systems. We are combining two technologies that, until very recently, were being tested and judged in two separate domains. Our experiments have given OCR evaluation a new perspective. In general, OCR devices have been tested at the character and word level. We have enhanced this objective by testing OCR generated text at the document and collection level which should contribute to research in both the OCR and IR disciplines.

6 Acknowledgments

We would like to thank Chris Buckley, Donna Harman, Bob Korfhage, and George Nagy for reading an earlier draft of this paper. Their comments and suggestions have greatly improved the quality of this work. We would also like to give special thanks to Jamie Callan for his technical support throughout this project.

References

1. Kazem Taghva, Julie Borsack, Allen Condit, and Srinivas Erva. The effects of noisy data on text retrieval. *Journal of the American Society for Information Science*, 45(1):50–58, January 1994.
2. W. B. Croft, S. Harding, K. Taghva, and J. Borsack. An evaluation of information retrieval accuracy with simulated OCR output. In *Proceedings of the Third Annual Symposium on Document Analysis and Information Retrieval*, Las Vegas, NV, April 1994. (to appear).
3. J. P. Callan, W. B. Croft, and S. M. Harding. The INQUERY retrieval system. In *Proceedings of the Third International Conference on Database and Expert Systems Applications*, pages 78–83, 1992.
4. T. A. Nartker, R. B. Bradford, and B. A. Cerny. A preliminary report on UNLV/GT1: A database for ground-truth testing in document analysis and character recognition. In *Proceedings of the First Symposium on Document Analysis and Information Retrieval*, Las Vegas, NV, March 1992.
5. Stephen V. Rice, Junichi Kanai, and Thomas A. Nartker. An evaluation of OCR accuracy. Technical Report 93-01, Information Science Research Institute, University of Nevada, Las Vegas, April 1993.
6. Brian Huey, Jeff Gilbreth, John Goetz Jr., and J. Borsack. Verification of GT1. Technical Report 93-10, Information Science Research Institute, University of Nevada, Las Vegas, December 1993.
7. Richard G. Casey and Kwam Y. Wong. *Image Analysis Applications*, chapter 1, pages 1–36. Marcel Dekker, Inc., 1990.
8. Simon Kahan, Theo Pavlidis, and Henry S. Baird. On the recognition of printed characters of any size and font. *IEEE Transactions on Pattern Analysis and Machine Intelligence*, Pami-9(2):274–288, 1987.
9. D. Harman. Overview of the first TREC conference. In *Proceedings of the Sixteenth Annual International ACM/SIGIR Conference on Research and Development in Information Retrieval*, pages 36–47, Pittsburgh, PA, June 1993. ACM Press.
10. G. Nagy. Optical scanning digitizers. *IEEE Computer*, pages 13–24, 1983.
11. S. N. Srihari. Document image understanding. In *Proceedings of the ACM-IEEE Computer Society*, Dallas, TX, 1986. 1986 Fall Joint Computer Conference.
12. Stephen V. Rice. The OCR experimental environment. Technical Report 92-01, Information Science Research Institute, University of Nevada, Las Vegas, March 1992.
13. W. Bruce Croft and Howard R. Turtle. Text retrieval and inference. In Paul S. Jacobs, editor, *Text-based Intelligent Systems*, pages 127–155. Lawrence Erlbaum Associates, 1992.
14. Kazem Taghva, Julie Borsack, and Allen Condit. An expert system for automatically correcting OCR output. In *Proceedings of the IS&T/SPIE 1994 International Symposium on Electronic Imaging Science and Technology*, San Jose, CA, February 1994.
15. R. E. Gorin, Pace Willisson, Walt Buehring, Geoff Kuenning, et al. Ispell, a free software package for spell checking files. The UNIX community, 1971-present. version 2.0.02.
16. Chris Buckley. Personal communication.

Natural Language vs. Boolean Query Evaluation: A Comparison of Retrieval Performance

Howard Turtle
West Publishing Company
Eagan, MN 55123
turtle@research.westlaw.com

Abstract

The results of experiments comparing the relative performance of natural language and Boolean query formulations are presented. The experiments show that on average a current generation natural language system provides better retrieval performance than expert searchers using a Boolean retrieval system when searching full-text legal materials. Methodological issues are reviewed and the effect of database size on query formulation strategy is discussed.

1 Introduction

Experimental results dating back to the 1970's have shown that simple natural language query techniques are at least as effective as Boolean techniques on comparable retrieval problems [1]. Despite these results, until recently all major commercial search services offered only Boolean query access to their collections. There are many reasons why commercial services were slow to adopt natural language queries, but one major reason was the size of the test collections on which the experimental results were based. Results based on a test collection of a few megabytes were not convincing when commercial search services routinely offered access to collections of many tens of gigabytes [2, 3]. Commercial services were aware that the difficulty of Boolean query formulation increased with collection size and were not convinced that natural language queries would scale up any better than Boolean.

Natural language searching has recently become available on WESTLAW, a large commercial system that provides access to U.S. legal materials [4, 5, 6, 7]. This system is a commercial implementation of the inference network retrieval model described in [8, 9]. Natural language queries now account for a significant portion of all WESTLAW searching (users can easily switch between Boolean and natural language) and, by implication, for a significant portion of all online access to U.S. legal materials.

For the purposes of this paper, a natural language search system is one that accepts as input a description of an information need in some natural language (such as English) and produces as output a list of documents ranked by the likelihood that they will be judged to match the information need. A Boolean search system accepts Boolean queries as input and uses the normal interpretation of first-order logic augmented with proximity operators to select a set of documents that satisfy the query. As discussed later, the set of documents retrieved in a Boolean search may be ranked. Retrieval models that accept Boolean queries but do not use first-order logic (e.g., [10, 11, 8]) are not considered. All commercial Boolean retrieval systems use first-order logic.

Development of the WESTLAW product involved direct comparison of natural language and Boolean query performance on test collections ranging in size from 250 megabytes to 6 gigabytes. In these tests, natural language results are significantly better than those obtained using "equivalent" Boolean queries formulated by expert searchers. These tests also show that natural language queries do, in fact, scale up better than Boolean – a natural language query offers similar performance across a wide range of collection sizes whereas a Boolean query must be refined when moved from a small collection to a large collection in order to produce result sets of manageable size.

What follows describes the methodology used to compare the performance of natural language and Boolean queries (Section 2) and presents and discusses the results of the experiments (Sections 3 and 4).

2 Methodology

In order to compare the retrieval performance of natural language and Boolean queries a set of natural language issue statements was developed by West attorneys. These issue statements represent the kinds of legal problems that lawyers would research using cases decided in the U.S. Federal Courts. These

```
Natural language:

    What factors are important in determining what constitutes a vessel
    for purposes of determining liability of a vessel owner for injuries
    to a seaman under the Jones Act (46 USC 688)?

Boolean:

    (741 +3 824) FACTOR ELEMENT STATUS FACT /P VESSEL SHIP BOAT /P (46 +3 688)
    "JONES ACT" /P INJUR! /S SEAMAN CREWMAN WORKER

Modified Boolean:

    "JONES ACT VESSEL" (MEAN*** /3 VESSEL) (741 +3 824) (STATUS CONSTITUT!
    DETERMIN! DEFINITION /5 VESSEL) /P "JONES ACT" (46 +3 688) /P INJUR!
    /S SEAMAN CREW! WORKER WORKMAN
```

Figure 1: Sample queries

	FSupp	Fed
collection size (docs)	11,953	410,883
collection size (Mb)	254	6,053
unique stems	196,707	1,465,675
maximum stem frequency	11,947	336,000
stem occurrences	21,798,833	507,319,045
max within document frequency	1,309	2,119
mean document length (words)	1,823	1,235
queries	44	44
docs judged relevant per query	35	56
docs judged nonrel. per query	134	27

Table 1: Collection Characteristics

statements are generally a single sentence consisting of an average of just over 17 words. A representative query is shown in Figure 1.

A collection of cases decided in the Federal courts was drawn as a random sample from West's Federal Supplement database. This sample consists of roughly 250 megabytes of text and 12,000 federal cases. The characteristics of this FSupp collection are shown in Table 1.

A group of expert searchers was then asked to formulate Boolean queries for each of the natural language issue statements. The expert searchers were West editors and reference attorneys – all are attorneys and all have considerable experience in searching WESTLAW. Searchers were asked to produce the "best" query that they could for each issue statement. During query formulation they were allowed to conduct as many searches of the test collection as desired. Searchers were allowed to expand the query to include information that was not contained in the original issue statement. Searchers spent an average of 12.5 minutes formulating each Boolean query and conducted an average of 6.7 iterations to arrive at the final query form. A sample Boolean query is shown in Figure 1.

In many experimental studies, Boolean results are assumed to be unordered. In most commercial systems, Boolean results are ranked (ordered) using some document characteristic that is query independent (e.g., by date, alphabetically by author or title, or in some classification order). The Boolean results reported here are ranked in reverse chronological order, which is the presentation order used for virtually all Boolean searches on WESTLAW. Chronological or date ranking is surprisingly effective for legal materials where later decisions often interpret or supersede earlier decisions. Indeed, many users retrieve documents using relevance ranking, then sort the top n documents by date.

The result sets for these Boolean queries contained an average of 22.5 documents (the median result set contains 16 documents). All documents retrieved were evaluated for relevance by attorneys (not necessarily the attorney who formulated the query) on a three point scale: *on point*, *relevant*, and *not relevant*. *On point* cases address exactly the issue raised in the original issue statements, *relevant* cases deal less directly with the issue, but are still considered to be relevant. For the purposes of evaluation, documents rated as *on point* or *relevant* were combined to form the set of relevant documents.

The natural language issue statements were used as input to a number of different commercial and prototype search engines. Many of these tests were conducted under the terms of non-disclosure agreements, but tests were also conducted using the INQUERY software at the University of Massachusetts, the SMART system at Virginia Polytechnic Institute, and using the Personal Librarian software developed by Personal Library Systems. For each natural language search, the top twenty documents were captured and rated for relevance (if they had not been previously rated). The union of all judgments from all experiments was used in the evaluation. On average, 169 documents have been rated for each query of which 35 were judged to be relevant.

The retrieval algorithms were tested extensively with the FSupp test collection. This collection is large by traditional test collection standards, but it is small when compared to many of the collections available on WESTLAW. To test the effectiveness of the retrieval model on large collections a second test collection was selected from a database containing all U.S. Federal cases. This collection contains roughly 6 gigabytes of text and 410,000 documents. The documents in this collection have content similar to those in the FSupp collection, but there are no documents common to the two collections. The characteristics of this Fed collection are shown in Table 1.

A new set of 91 queries was developed for this test collection, but the experiments reported here make use of the same query set developed for the FSupp collection. Because the content of the cases in the two collections are similar, the original issue statements apply equally well to both collections.

2.1 Evaluation

The comparison of retrieval performance between ranked and unranked systems raises a number of difficult problems [1, 12, 13]. The two main problems are: 1) how can ranked versus unranked lists be compared, and 2) how can differences in the size of the returned set be reconciled?

With regard to the first problem, we take the view that the Boolean result is, in fact, ranked. The ranking is based on a document characteristic (date) that is independent of the query, but the ranking certainly is not random and users strongly prefer date ranking to an unordered presentation. While IR research has not yet produced experimental results that would allow us to quantify the degree to which users prefer good rankings to bad (i.e., we don't know how much an $x\%$ improvement in precision is worth to a typical user), the assumption that users prefer to see relevant documents first is plausible and pervasive, if unproven. Even in cases where the result is unordered we would argue that it is reasonable to compare rankings because the rankings determine what the user sees. Further, we are primarily interested in that portion of the ranking that an interactive user will see. For our purposes, a ranking that does well in the first twenty documents is to be preferred to a ranking that does poorly in the top twenty ranks but does very well at high recall levels.

A second problem in comparing the performance of Boolean and natural language queries arises because the techniques generally do not retrieve the same number of documents for a given query. The size of the sets returned by Boolean queries is highly variable. Some ranking algorithms also produce variable size results, but in WESTLAW, a fixed number of documents are retrieved for each natural language query. A user may request additional documents and may choose to alter the number of documents retrieved, but by default, twenty documents are returned. One solution to this problem is to use the size of the Boolean result set as the basis of comparison. If, for a given query, the Boolean result contains n documents then only the top n ranks for the natural language result are used for the comparison. There are several problems with this approach. First, it tends to favor the Boolean query and, in particular, it favors high precision Boolean queries. An adversary that knew how the evaluation was to be done could construct an unbeatable Boolean query by identifying a single document that was certain to be judged relevant and then constructing a query that retrieved only that document. Since Boolean queries tend to favor precision over recall [14] fixing on the Boolean result size would bias the evaluation.

A second problem with using the Boolean result size is that the set is often much larger than any interactive user is prepared to browse. On small collections it may be possible to produce Boolean results that are of manageable size, but on large collections this is often not possible. For example, the mean Boolean result set size on the FSupp collection was 22.5 documents. As will be discussed later, the same queries run on the Fed collection retrieved an average of 206 documents. Even after revision to improve performance on Fed the Boolean queries still retrieved an average of 126 documents and some queries retrieved several hundred documents. These result sets are far larger than most users are willing to browse.

Another solution to the result set size problem is to pick an arbitrary rank cutoff that is close to what an interactive user is willing to browse and to restrict evaluation to those ranks. This approach favors the natural language query if the Boolean result retrieves fewer documents than the cutoff. The Boolean searchers could be told to always retrieve result sets of at least a given size, but this would introduce further biases.

No single evaluation tool provides results that are truly unbiased, so we used four different measures in our tests: precision at standard recall points, raw precision and recall at a fixed rank cutoff, the relative performance of individual queries in the test set, and precision at all ranks up to some maximum value.

Average precision. We use an eleven point average precision with pessimistic interpolation [12] (see Table 3 for an example). For the Boolean queries we assume that the entire collection is ranked. The actual Boolean result fills in the top ranks for each query. All unretrieved documents are sorted by date and inserted in the ranks below the retrieved set, newest document first. Average precision is widely used and allows our results to be compared with earlier work but it tends to favor the natural language result at high recall levels because documents that are not retrieved by the Boolean query tend to appear well down in the ranking. Because the Boolean queries tend to exhibit relatively low recall, the precision values in the lower portion of the precision/recall table are probably not meaningful, especially for the FSupp collection where the Boolean results are small and the relevance judgments are fairly complete.

Raw precision and recall. A fixed rank cutoff of 20 documents is used. This number was originally selected because it is slightly smaller that the mean Boolean result on FSupp and because it is close to the number of documents that a typical user is willing to browse. We report raw precision (the percentage of documents in the top 20 that are relevant) and raw recall (the percentage of all relevant documents that are contained in the top 20). These numbers are easy to interpret since they are a direct indication of the number of relevant documents in the top 20, but they ignore the effect of ranking within the top 20.

We also report the maximum possible precision and recall figures that could be achieved given the set of relevance judgments. If every query had at least 20 relevant documents the maximum possible precision would be 100%. If every query had twenty or fewer relevant documents the maximum possible recall would be 100%.

Individual query performance. In addition to averages for the entire query set, we also report the number of queries for which one technique is superior. For each query we look at both the average precision and the top 20 precision. If both of these measures favor one technique by 10% or more, that technique is declared to be superior. If either difference is less than 10% or if each measure favors a different technique then the difference is declared to be insignificant.

Precision in the top n ranks. We will occasionally report raw precision for all ranks up to some fixed value. This is similar to top twenty precision, but it allows finer comparison. When averaged over a large number of queries precision values tend to monotonically decrease as rank increases. When the performance of two techniques is similar it is often possible to determine where in the ranking the precision curves cross.

2.2 Relevance judgments

It is generally not possible to assemble exhaustive relevance judgments for any but the smallest test collections. As a result, one major variable that affects nearly all information retrieval research is the quality and exhaustivity of the relevance judgments used. The most common technique for assembling relevance judgments is "pooling" in which actual results from several different retrieval tests are used to select documents to be judged for relevance [15, 16]. For the results reported here, all previously unevaluated documents in the top twenty ranks are pooled and submitted for evaluation. The only exception to this policy is that all documents retrieved by Boolean queries on FSupp have been evaluated regardless of the result size. The use of a twenty document cutoff is small when compared to the TREC evaluation where a cutoff of 100 is used [17]. The smaller cutoff reflects our focus on interactive retrieval rather than retrieval to support routing and filtering applications.

The FSupp collection has been used extensively at West Publishing and by a number of other research groups and the relevance judgments represent a pooling of the results of a large number of experiments using different retrieval techniques (including several relevance feedback techniques). While we have made no attempt to estimate the number of relevant but undetected documents that remain in the collection, the FSupp relevance judgments are "reasonably" complete. New experiments often turn up unevaluated

	NL better	No difference	Boolean better
FSupp	36	3	5
Fed	33	6	5
Fed – enhanced queries	29	8	7

Table 2: Per Query performance of natural language vs. Boolean queries

documents, but most of these are judged to be nonrelevant. The set of known relevant documents for the FSupp collection grows slowly.

The Fed collection is much newer and has not been used extensively outside of West. As a result, the number of documents that have been evaluated is much lower than for FSupp, both in terms of the number of documents per query (169 for FSupp versus 83 for Fed), and especially in terms of the percentage of the collection evaluated for each query. The number of relevant documents in the Fed collection is probably much larger than in FSupp and a reasonably high percentage of newly evaluated documents are judged to be relevant, so we regard the Fed judgments as relatively incomplete.

A second point with regard to relevance judgments is that experiments using standard test collections should report the number of unevaluated documents encountered in the top ranks. Most experiments report precision and recall figures that assume unevaluated documents are not relevant. If, however, a new ranking includes many unevaluated documents these results will generally be biased in favor of the retrieval technique(s) upon which the original relevance judgments are based. If any of the highly ranked but unevaluated documents are, in fact, relevant then the reported performance of the new ranking will be understated, sometimes substantially. A bit less obvious is the fact that the reported performance of the original ranking will generally be overstated if previously unevaluated documents are, in fact, relevant – the new relevant documents will occur relatively low in the original ranking which means that the original precision points occur at lower recall values. This shifts the precision/recall curve to the left which, in turn, reduces the area under the precision/recall curve.[1]

The effect of incomplete relevance judgments can be quite pronounced. Early in the testing of West's natural language search engine we ran a series of experiments which showed a new technique produced a ranking that was 5% worse than the baseline in terms of average precision. The unevaluated documents in the top twenty ranks were pooled with other results and submitted to our reference attorneys for evaluation. With complete relevance judgments the new technique was determined to have produced a ranking that was, in fact, 15% better than the baseline. Since that time, one of the factors we examine in experimental results is the number of unevaluated documents in the top n ranks which gives a direct indication of how much the reported precision could be understated.

All of this suggests that test collections with fixed but incomplete sets of relevance judgments have a built-in bias that favors the techniques used to create the relevance judgments. The only real solution to this problem is to create mechanisms to allow documents to be evaluated on an ongoing basis. This is exactly the approach that has been adopted as part of the TREC evaluations [17] and is the approach used at West and in several other industrial research groups.

3 Results

3.1 FSupp Results

The baseline results on the FSupp collection are shown in Table 3. In terms of average precision, the natural language queries perform significantly better than the Boolean queries at all but the lowest recall level. When comparing precision at fixed rank cutoffs, Boolean queries retrieved a relevant document as the highest ranked document more often than did natural language (93.2% precision at rank one versus 84.1% for natural language). At ranks 2 and higher, however, the precision of the natural language query equals or exceeds that of the Boolean query. As discussed earlier, the low precision at high recall levels for Boolean queries arises in part because of the way that the Boolean rankings are constructed – if a document is not retrieved by the Boolean query it is likely to be assigned a relatively low rank.

Focusing on the top twenty documents retrieved, 42.3% of the documents retrieved by the Boolean queries are relevant whereas 57.0% of the documents retrieved by the natural language queries are relevant,

[1] Average precision at standard recall levels approximates the area under the precision/recall curve.

	Precision (% change) – 44 queries		
Recall	Boolean	Natural Language	
0	98.1	92.8	(−5.4)
10	77.9	87.4	(+12.2)
20	67.6	80.5	(+19.1)
30	39.7	71.9	(+81.3)
40	27.8	67.3	(+142)
50	14.9	62.7	(+321)
60	8.5	54.5	(+541)
70	6.5	47.3	(+627)
80	2.5	38.6	(+1471)
90	2.4	25.9	(+977)
100	0.3	13.7	(+4328)
average	31.5	58.4	(+85.6)
P20	42.3	57.0	(+34.9)
Max P20	87.3	87.3	
R20	24.4	32.9	(+34.9)
Max R20	50.3	50.3	

Table 3: Retrieval Performance on FSupp

an improvement of nearly 35% (given the set of relevance judgments, the maximum top twenty precision that could be achieved is 87.3%). These precision figures translate directly into top twenty recall figures of 24.4% for Boolean queries and 32.9% for natural language with a maximum possible recall of 50.3%.

Looking at individual queries (Table 2), natural language outperformed Boolean on 36 queries, Boolean outperformed natural language on 5 queries, and there was no significant difference on 3 queries.

	Precision (% change) – 44 queries		
Recall	Boolean	nl	
0	85.1	94.0	(+10.5)
10	76.1	84.7	(+11.3)
20	67.7	80.4	(+18.7)
30	54.7	72.3	(+32.2)
40	47.5	65.0	(+36.7)
50	37.3	54.5	(+46.0)
60	33.1	43.1	(+30.3)
70	26.8	35.3	(+31.4)
80	21.1	27.1	(+28.3)
90	13.2	18.8	(+41.5)
100	6.2	7.4	(+18.0)
average	42.6	53.0	(+24.2)
P20	61.1	75.9	(+24.2)
Max P20	97.8	97.8	
R20	21.7	26.9	(+24.2)
Max R20	34.7	34.7	

Table 4: Retrieval performance on Fed

3.2 Fed results

When the same Boolean query sets are run on the larger Fed collection the number of documents retrieved increases substantially. The mean result set size for the FSupp collection is 22.5 documents whereas the mean results set size on the Fed collection for the same query set is 206 documents (median of 144 documents). Increasing the collection size by a factor[2] of roughly 24 increases the mean result set size by a factor of roughly 9.

[2]This ratio is based on the number of bytes of text. Fed contains roughly 34 times as many documents as FSupp.

The performance of these query sets on the Fed collection is shown in Table 4. Because of the large Boolean result set sizes and the relatively incomplete relevance judgments, the precision values are more nearly comparable at all standard recall levels than they are on FSupp. In effect, the queries that were formulated for the FSupp collection become high recall searches when moved to Fed. Most of the documents retrieved by the natural language queries are contained somewhere in the Boolean result set although the density of relevant documents in the top ranks is higher for natural language than for Boolean queries. In terms of average precision, natural language queries improve performance by 24.2%.

Using only the top twenty documents, the Boolean queries achieved 61.1% precision and 21.7% recall (maximum possible values are 97.8% precision and 34.7% recall). The natural language queries achieved 75.9% precision and 26.9% recall, an improvement of 24.2%.

	Precision (% change) – 44 queries		
Recall	Boolean	nl	
0	91.7	94.0	(+2.6)
10	80.3	84.7	(+5.5)
20	70.2	80.4	(+14.5)
30	62.2	72.3	(+16.3)
40	51.3	65.0	(+26.5)
50	38.2	54.5	(+42.5)
60	31.2	43.1	(+38.2)
70	20.6	35.3	(+70.8)
80	17.3	27.1	(+56.7)
90	11.2	18.8	(+67.4)
100	3.4	7.4	(+119.8)
average	43.4	53.0	(+22.0)
P20	69.2	75.9	(+9.7)
Max P20	97.8	97.8	
R20	24.5	26.9	(+9.7)
Max R20	34.7	34.7	

Table 5: Retrieval Performance on Fed with modified queries

With a mean result set size of over two hundred, it was clear that attorneys would not examine all of the cases retrieved by the Boolean queries. West's reference attorneys were asked to review the original queries and to revise any that they thought were inappropriate for use on the Fed collection. Seven of the original 44 queries were retained, the remaining 37 were modified. We had expected that the modifications would be to further restrict the Boolean queries developed on FSupp, but this was not always the case. Many of the queries were altered so that they would retrieve additional documents that would have been excluded by the initial formulation. Overall, the effect was to reduce the mean result set size from 206 documents to 126 documents. This result set size is still too large to allow most users to review all of the cases, but the reference attorneys felt that restricting the queries further would produce unacceptably low recall.

The modified Boolean queries do perform better than the originals, but still not as well as the natural language queries (Table 5). The modified Booleans have slightly higher average precision than the original Booleans. The improvement is significant at the low recall levels but performance falls off at high recall levels, primarily because modifications to reduce the result set size have also lowered recall. Looking at the top twenty documents, the modified Boolean queries have improved both precision and recall when compared to the original Booleans, but the natural language results still contain nearly 10% more relevant documents than the enhanced Boolean queries.

Looking at individual queries (Table 2), natural language outperformed the enhanced Booleans on 29 queries, Boolean outperformed natural language on 7 queries, and there was no significant difference on 8 queries.

4 Conclusion

Despite the methodological problems associated with comparing the performance of Boolean and natural language searching, the results of these experiments clearly support the assertion that, at least for full text court opinions, natural language searching will present users with more relevant documents and will present these documents to the user in ranks that are likely to be browsed. On all of the evaluation metrics discussed here, natural language searches consistently produced better rankings. West has tested these techniques extensively on other material types (e.g., statutes, law review articles, administrative codes). Natural language searching performs consistently better than Boolean for all of the material types tested.

These performance comparisons are based on Boolean queries formulated by expert searchers that are intimately familiar with the collections involved, which suggests that the improvements over an "average" or novice searcher would be even more pronounced. Further, the Boolean queries were developed iteratively and incorporate information that is not contained in the natural language queries. The natural language queries were run without modification even though natural language queries can also be iteratively improved.

These results also point up some of the problems associated with searching large full-text collections using Boolean queries. As the size of the collection increases it becomes increasingly difficult to formulate a Boolean query that will produce a manageable result set. The natural language results are surprisingly consistent across the two collections. On both collections, natural language searches achieve 80 – 90% precision at the top ranks with average precision of over 50%. In some ways, natural language performance improves in large collections. Large collections often have more relevant documents for a given query so that precision in the top ranks actually increases with collection size. On FSupp just over half (57%) of all documents in the top 20 ranks were judged to be relevant. On Fed, three out of every four documents in the top twenty ranks were judged to be relevant.

Despite the strong performance of natural language searching, Boolean query languages will not disappear anytime soon. For some queries and some kinds of materials Boolean techniques give better results. Further, some users prefer to use Boolean queries. Commercial systems will need to support both query types to be successful. At the same time, for the average searcher a natural language query will, on average, give better results than a Boolean query. Over time the performance differential can be expected to increase – there is a lot of room for improvement of current generation natural language systems.

References

[1] Karen Sparck Jones. Retrieval system tests 1958-1978. In Karen Sparck Jones, editor, *Information Retrieval Experiment*, chapter 12, pages 213–255, Butterworth, 1981.

[2] Donald R. Swanson. Information retrieval as a trial and error process. *Library Quarterly*, 47(2):128–148, 1977.

[3] David C. Blair. *Language and Representation in Information Retrieval.* Elsevier Science Publishers, Amsterdam, 1990.

[4] Laura Duncan. New research net drops computerese. *Chicago Daily Law Bulletin*, 2, September 16 1992.

[5] IDP Report. West unveils new natural language interface. *Information and Database Publishing Report*, 13(35):1,6, September 18 1992.

[6] Cary Griffith. WESTLAW's WIN: not only natural, but new. *Information Today*, 9–11, October 1992.

[7] Cary Griffith. WESTLAW's winning ways. *Law Office Computing*, 31–38, February/March 1993.

[8] Howard Turtle. *Inference Networks for Document Retrieval.* PhD thesis, Computer Science Department, University of Massachusetts, Amherst, MA 01003, 1990. Available as COINS Technical Report 90-92.

[9] Howard Turtle and W. Bruce Croft. Evaluation of an inference network-based retrieval model. *ACM Transactions on Information Systems*, 9(3):187–222, July 1991.

[10] Edward A. Fox. *Extending the Boolean and Vector Space Models of Information Retrieval with P-Norm Queries and Multiple Concept Types.* PhD thesis, Cornell University, 1983.

[11] Edward A. Fox and Mathew B. Koll. Practical enhanced Boolean retrieval: experiences with the SMART and SIRE systems. *Information Processing and Management*, 24(3):257–267, 1988.

[12] E. M. Keen. Evaluation parameters. In Gerard Salton, editor, *The SMART Retrieval System – Experiments in Automatic Document Processing*, chapter 5, pages 74–111, Prentice Hall, 1971.

[13] Lynn Evans. An experiment: search strategy variation in SDI profiles. In Karen Sparck Jones, editor, *Information Retrieval Experiment*, chapter 14, pages 285–315, Butterworth, 1981.

[14] D. C. Blair and M. E. Maron. An evaluation of retrieval effectiveness for a full-text document retrieval system. *Communications of the ACM*, 28(3):290–299, 1985.

[15] Karen Sparck Jones and C. J. van Rijsbergen. *Report on the Need for and the Provision of an 'Ideal' Information Retrieval Test Collection.* Technical Report British Library Research and Development Report 5266, Computer Laboratory, University of Cambridge, 1975.

[16] Karen Sparck Jones and R. G. Bates. *Report on a Design Study for the 'Ideal' Information Retrieval Test Collection.* Technical Report British Library Research and Development Report 5428, Computer Laboratory, University of Cambridge, 1977.

[17] Donna Harman. Overview of the first text retrieval conference (TREC-1). In Donna K. Harman, editor, *The First Text Retrieval Conference (TREC-1)*, pages 1–20, National Institute of Standards and Technology, March 1993. Proceedings available as NIST Special Publication 500-207.

Probabilistic Models

Inferring Probability of Relevance Using the Method of Logistic Regression

Fredric C. Gey
UC Data Archive and Technical Assistance
University of California, Berkeley USA
e-mail: gey@sdp2.berkeley.edu

Abstract

This research evaluates a model for probabilistic text and document retrieval; the model utilizes the technique of *logistic regression* to obtain equations which rank documents by probability of relevance as a function of document and query properties. Since the model infers probability of relevance from statistical clues present in the texts of documents and queries, we call it *logistic inference*. By transforming the distribution of each statistical clue into its standardized distribution (one with mean $\mu = 0$ and standard deviation $\sigma = 1$), the method allows one to apply logistic coefficients derived from a training collection to other document collections, with little loss of predictive power. The model is applied to three well-known information retrieval test collections, and the results are compared directly to the particular vector space model of retrieval which uses term-frequency/inverse-document-frequency (tfidf) weighting and the cosine similarity measure. In the comparison, the logistic inference method performs significantly better than (in two collections) or equally well as (in the third collection) the tfidf/cosine vector space model. The differences in performances of the two models were subjected to statistical tests to see if the differences are statistically significant or could have occurred by chance.

1. Introduction

We can consider the central task of Information Retrieval to be that of providing *intellectual access* to the contents of a collection of texts or documents. The heart of this task is the concise representation of the meanings of the texts contained in the collection. In the vector space model developed by Gerard Salton and associates at Cornell University [1] [2] [3] both documents and queries are represented as vectors in the "m"-dimensional term space assuming that the indexing vocabulary of nontrivial terms is of size "m". For this model, we have a clear geometric interpretation for both the query and document and can choose distance measures which measure the degree to which the document vector deviates from the query vector. One such well-know measure computes the cosine of the angle between document and query vector. In the sparsest form of the vector space model, query vectors and document vectors only indicate the presence or absence of a vocabulary term in either the query or the document. This can be easily generalized by adding weights to the query or document. These weights, interpreted geometrically, merely show the magnitude and direction of the appropriate vectors.

Weights may be mechanically derived from attributes of terms. For example, for terms in the query or the document, the attribute 'absolute frequency' is the count of occurrences of that term in either the query (QAF) or the document (DAF). For terms t_j used in documents, the attribute 'inverse document frequency' (IDF) is the ratio, $\frac{N}{n_{t_j}}$ where N is the number of documents in the collection and n_{t_j} is the number of documents for which term t_j occurs in the document's text or has been used to index the document. The attribute IDF, which is usually logged, was first suggested by Karen Sparck-Jones [4]. Two well-known weights, used in the SMART retrieval system, are the term frequency for the query terms (QAF), and, for the document terms, the term frequency- inverse document frequency product ($DAF \cdot IDF$). Salton and Buckley in 1988 identified a number of these factors and computed performance measurements for multiple weighting schemes against several test collections. Their experiments show that a simple retrieval weight, which only accounted for the occurrence of the term in the document and the occurrence of the term in the query, performed worst in their retrieval comparisons [5].

By a *probabilistic search system* we mean one whose query specification, indexing processes, and retrieval rules are derived from the formal application of the theory of probability to the logic of the information retrieval problem. Such a system will return documents to the user in an order ranked by probability of satisfying the user's information need. The primary focus of this paper is to test a probabilistic search system which is both theoretically sound and practical. Probabilistic models of text and document retrieval attempt to place the computation of retrieval status value on a sound theoretical footing. If retrieval status value can be computed as the probability of satisfying the user's information need, then the *probability ranking principle* [6] states that the optimal retrieval will be achieved if documents are returned to the user in order of their probability of relevance. This leads to the so-called "Binary Independence" model of probabilistic retrieval [7], which was generalized to the "Linked Dependence model by Cooper [8] Unfortunately experiments with this *relevance feedback* approach have encountered problems of insufficient statistical evidence to predict relevance, even when half the collection is used as a training set. Improved methods for statistical estimation in the face of this insufficient sample size have only been partially successful [9].

2. The logistic inference model

If no assumptions are made about the character of the probabilities of relevance which associate between a query-document pair $r = f(q_i, d_j)$, but we merely allow that a text retrieval system exists and that associated with each query term t_{q_i} and document term t_{d_j} there are a finite set of attributes about the term $(v_1, \cdots, v_n)$ from the query (such as count of occurrences of the term in the query), from the document (such as count of occurrences of the term in the document), and from the collection (such as the total number of documents in the collection divided by the number of documents indexed by the term), and that attribute values vary statistically with the collection, then we have a "Model 0" system, i.e. one which exists before introducing particular models.

The *logistic inference model* says that we can use a *random sample* of query-document-term triples for which binary relevance judgments have been made, and compute the logarithm of the odds of relevance for term t_k which is present in both document d_j and query q_i by the formula:

$$\log O(R \mid q_i, d_j, t_k) = c_0 + c_1 v_1 + \cdots + c_l v_n$$

and further that the logarithm of the odds of relevance for the ith query $q_i = <t_1, \cdots, t_q>$ is the sum of the logodds for all terms:

$$\log O(R \mid q_i, d_j) = \sum_{k=1}^{q} [\log O(R \mid q_i, d_j, t_k) - \log O(R)]$$

where O(R), known as the *prior odds of relevance* is the odds that a document chosen at random from the collection will be relevant to query q_i. The coefficients of individual query and document term properties are derived by using the method of *logistic regression* [10] which fits an equation to predict a dichotomous independent variable as a function of (possibly continuous) independent variables which show statistical variation.

Once log odds of relevance is computed from a simple linear formula, the inverse logistic transformation may be applied to directly obtain the probability of relevance of a document to a query:

$$P((R \mid q_i, d_j) = \frac{1}{1 + e^{-\log(O(R \mid q_i, d_j))}}$$

Once the coefficients of the equation for logodds of relevance have been derived within a document retrieval system for a particular collection from a random sample of query-document-term-relevance quadruples, these coefficients may be used to predict odds of relevance for other query-document pairs (past or future).

Regression models which approximate the dependent variable, document *relevance* by linear combinations of multiple clues such as term frequency, authorship, and co-citation, were first introduced, with some success by Ed Fox [11]. More recently Fuhr and Buckley [12] [13] used polynomial regression to approximate relevance. There are two well-known major problems with the application of ordinary regression approaches to probability of relevance approximation:

- The outcome variable is dichotomous rather than continuous, hence

- the error distribution is binomial rather than normal, as is usually assumed by ordinary regression.

An alternative approach is to use Bayesian inference networks as developed by Turtle and others [14] [15] [16].

3. Sampling for logistic regression

One of the computational problems in using logistic regression is the computational size necessary to compute logistic regression coefficients. Even supposing that only half the document collection is used as a training set the number of query-document-term triples which are to be used for computation becomes astronomical. Naturally, a sampling approach is necessary. Since the number of relevant documents is, for each query, naturally a very small fraction of the total documents in the collection, it is incumbent upon us to attempt to construct a sample which encompasses a significantly higher proportion of relevant documents than non-relevant ones. To assure adequate representation of relevant documents, we would sample most, if not all, of the relevant documents while sampling a significantly smaller proportion of non-relevant documents, and adjusting for non-relevant documents in the regression process by a weight factor which compensates for the differential. Since relevant documents are typically 1/100th fewer than non-relevant documents, it is reasonable to take into the sample, say, every thirtieth non-relevant query-document-term triple and factor it into the logistic regression computation by applying a weighting factor of 30.

We have chosen the Cranfield test collection upon which to fit our model. The Cranfield collection is a long-standing collection used in information retrieval for numerous experiments beginning with the Cranfield's experiments. It does have some deficiencies as outlined by Swanson [17], but it offers the following desirable properties. First, it has 225 queries, which seems to be a sufficient number to afford a reasonable fit to our logistic model. Second, while it only has 1,400 documents, both the documents and the queries seem to possess a better fit to the characteristics of an ideal test collection.

The characteristics of an ideal test collection should be:

- queries are in natural language form, so that query statistics can be collected as well as document statistics,

- the documents have both titles and abstracts present (abstracts are missing from some of the CACM collection),

- The queries are a random sample from some larger query population. There must be a sufficiently large number of queries in order to achieve some statistical significance.

- Documents are a random sample from a larger document collection and,

- That relevance judgments be made for all query-document pairs in the collection. If this is not possible (as it cannot be for million document collections), then the relevance judgments are a carefully crafted sample of all possible relevance judgments, and that the sample size be known.

We will later apply our fit to the CACM collection (52 queries, 3204 documents) and the CISI collection (76 queries, 1460 documents)

4. Logistic regression for six term attributes

Our particular *logistic inference model* has the following additional elementary clues: relative frequency in the query (QRF), relative frequency in the document (DRF) and relative frequency of the term in all documents (RFAD). The complete formula for logodds of relevance, given the presence of term t_j is then:

$$Z_{t_j} = \log O(R \mid t_j) = c_0 + c_1 log(QAF) + c_2 log(QRF)$$

$$+ c_3 log(DAF) + c_4 log(DRF) + c_5 log(IDF) + c_6 log(RFAD)$$

Query absolute frequency (QAF has been previously defined. Query relative frequency (QRF) is equal to query absolute frequency (QAF) query divided by the total number of term occurrences of all terms in the query. Similarly, document relative frequency (DRF) is document absolute frequency divided by the total number of occurrences of all terms in the document. Relative frequency in all documents (RFAD) is the total number of term occurrences of the term in the collection divided by the total number of occurrences of all terms in the entire collection, i.e., collection length.

You will note that all terms in the formula are logged. One reason for using logarithms is to dampen the influence of frequency information. It is unrealistic to assume that 50 occurrences of a term in a document is five times more important than 10 occurrences. Another reason for taking the logs is that the logarithm, in general, smooths out a skewed distribution to one which has nice behavioral properties. Finally, sums of logged variables behave as products of the same variables after an anti-logarithm is applied. Indeed, in comparing the fit for logged and non-logged items, in general (at least for these clues) a higher maximum likelihood is attained for logged clues than for raw clues.

The fit for this extended clues logistic model is done against the same 20,246 query-document-term sample taken from the Cranfield collection. The following coefficients are then derived from this fit:

$$Z_{t_j} = \log O(R \mid t_j) = -0.2085 + -0.2036 log(QAF) + 0.19143 log(QRF)$$

$$+ 0.16789 log(DAF) + 0.57544 log(DRF) - 1.5967 log(IDF) + 0.75033 log(RFAD)$$

What remains is to compute $log(O(R))$ the prior odds of relevance for this collection. This is estimated by counting the number of query-document pairs for which a judgment of relevance has been assigned (for the Cranfield collection this is 1838 pairs) and then dividing by the total number of query-document pairs (for Cranfield 225 queries times 1400 documents). Hence:

$$prior = \frac{1838}{225 \cdot 1400} = .005835$$

becomes the prior probability of relevance, and

$$logprior = \log \frac{prior}{1 - prior} = -5.138$$

and the final formula for ranking is:

$$log(O(R \mid \vec{Q})) = -5.138 + \sum_{j=1}^{q} (Z_{t_j} + 5.138)$$

5. Performance evaluation: statistical significance tests

A key part of this paper is to compare performances of two major methods: our logistic regression probabilistic method, which ranks documents according to probability of relevance against the vector space model, which ranks documents according to the cosine of the angle between the query vector and the document vector. Performance evaluation is usually described in terms of the recall and precision measures. **Recall** is the fraction of relevant documents retrieved at a certain retrieval point in the retrieval process while **precision** is the fraction of retrieved documents which are relevant. These measures can be computed for a single query but are usually averaged over all queries in the collection. It is our intent to use recall and precision as one measure of performance; however, it is our intention to also subject performance differences to a statistical test to determine whether the difference is significant or could have occurred by chance.

The reason one wishes to test statistical significance is that on a particular query one method may be better than another and yet the performance could be reversed for the next query posed. In our model of retrieval, we assume that a query is chosen at random, and our method ranks documents according to probability of relevance to the randomly chosen query. It might be that next set of randomly chosen queries would have an entirely different performance profile. Thus, if we are attempting to compare the performance of two methods (such as logistic inference versus tfidf/cosine vector space) we need to establish a statistical test which will show that the results obtained for the randomly chosen set of queries are statistically significant.

Such a test, well-known in the literature, would be a T-test which would compare the differences between performance for each query, and we determine whether these differences in ranking or in precision are statistically significant. Our approach, therefore, for testing for statistical significance will be:

- For each query take the ranking of relevant documents by each method and compute an average precision value over all ranks (all levels of recall). This will give a unique number for each query for each method.

- Compute the difference in average precision between the two numbers found with each method for the two methods being compared. Thus, in applying the T-test, the sample size will equal the number of queries in the test collection.

- Apply a T-test to these differences under the null hypothesis that the methods perform identically and hence their mean difference should be zero and their standard deviation not significantly different.

[18] provides a summary of possible statistical tests which might be used to evaluate retrieval experiments.

6. Logistic model performance for the Cranfield collection

For the logistic inference model on Cranfield the following table

Logistic Inference versus tfidf/cosine Vector Space Performance Cranfield Collection: Averages over 225 queries		
Recall	Logistic Precision	Vector Space Precision
0.00	0.8330	0.7787
0.10	0.8116	0.7440
0.20	0.7129	0.6434
0.30	0.6021	0.5301
0.40	0.5161	0.4380
0.50	0.4503	0.3814
0.60	0.3698	0.2994
0.70	0.2859	0.2267
0.80	0.2280	0.1882
0.90	0.1640	0.1379
1.00	0.1464	0.1251
11-pt Avg:	0.4655	0.4084
% Change:		-12.3

displays the recall-precision performance results. If we further compute the difference in average precision for each of the 225 queries for the two methods (cosine and logistic) we find that the results are statistically significant at the one tenth of one percent significance level:

Hypothesis Test: two-tail t on Precision Differences between Logistic inference and Tfifdf/cosine methods						
N	null mean	sample mean	sample SE	df stat	test	P
225	0.0000	-0.059885	0.0072063	224	-8.31	.0000

Thus we can see that making use of the full probabilistic model of logistic regression on the set of six term property clues, we obtain a statistically significant improvement over the tfidf/cosine vector space model.

7. A criticism of the Cranfield results

The above results obtained for the logistic inference model have a fundamental difficulty. The entire set of queries, documents and terms from the relevant set is included within the sample used as the training set for the logistic regression. Naturally, when the resulting logistic coefficients are used to rank documents based on relevance, we have a chicken and egg process, whereby the test is applied to the sample which was used for fitting. In past tests of probabilistic models where this approach has also been used [19], the next step in testing such models has been to train on half the number of queries and then use that training to predict the results of the other half of the queries. We feel that a large number of queries is necessary in order to train for a decent logistic regression approach to document retrieval. Our approach, instead, will be to apply the coefficients obtained from using the Cranfield collection as a training set to other collections in our test repertoire, in particular the CACM and CISI collections.

8. Logistic inference for CACM

If we apply the logistic regression equation fitted for the Cranfield sample to the CACM collection, we obtain the following result:

Cranfield Logistic versus Tfidf/cosine Vector Space Performance CACM Collection: Averages over 52 Queries		
Recall	Logistic Precision	Vector Space Precision
11-pt Avg:	0.3322	0.3148
% Change:		-5.2

While it may **seem** that the extended logistic model performs 5.2 percent better than the tfidf/cosine vector space model for the CACM collection, if we apply the same hypothesis test:

CACM Hypothesis test: 2-tail T on Precision Differences between Logistic inference and Tfidf/cosine methods						
N	null mean	sample mean	sample SE	df	test stat	P value
52	0.0000	-0.020528	0.015866	51.0	-1.29	.2016

we find again that this difference of performance is not statistically significant and hence we cannot reject a null hypothesis that, in fact, given another set of queries the tfidf/cosine vector space model might perform as well or better than the extended logistic model.

9. Cranfield logistic model for CISI

Applying the Cranfield fitted regression equation to the CISI collection, we find:

Cranfield Logistic versus Tfidf/cosine Vector Space Performance CISI Collection: Averages over 76 Queries		
Recall	Logistic Precision	Vector Space Precision
11-pt Avg:	0.2088	0.2137
% Change:		4.4

While this seems to indicate better vector space performance, when we apply the statistical test on the average precision and recall measures for 77 CISI queries:

Hypothesis Test: 2-tail T on Precision Differences between Logistic inference and Tfidf/cosine for CISI collection						
N	null mean	sample mean	sample SE	df	test stat	P value
76	0.0000	0.0056973	0.0087791	75.0	0.65	.5183

we find that there can be no statistically significant difference between performance on the vector space model as against the extended logistic model. While the application of the Cranfield-derived coefficient directly to both the CACM collection and the CISI collection produce comparable results on these collections to the vector space model, for neither collection can we find the difference between vector space and extended logistic to be statistically significant.

The blind application of coefficients derived from the statistical distribution of one collection to another collection clearly leaves something to be desired. In the next section, we apply some clever thought to the transformation of coefficients from one collection, in order to adapt them to the statistical clues of the other collections.

10. Standardized variables

The direct application of coefficients derived from a query-document-term sample from one document collection and one set of queries to another document collection and yet another set of queries makes the following assumption. It assumes that all the clues which are being used as sensitive indicators of probability of relevance have *the identical statistical distribution* from collection to collection. By *identical statistical distribution* we mean not only do the clues come from the same underlying probability distribution, but they also have the identical mean and standard deviation for each clue as the original collection on which the logistic regression fitting has been done.

Even though each clue might derive from the same underlying probability distribution, it seems highly unlikely that, from collection to collection, there would be no variation in either the mean and standard deviation of the clue being used for indication of probability of relevance. This gives us insight into the possible adaptation of coefficients which fit one collection to another collection. It is well known that one can take the mean and standard deviation of any statistical distribution and transform that distribution (even though the actual underlying probability density function is not known) into a standardized distribution, i.e., one which has mean zero ($\mu = 0$) and standard deviation one ($\sigma = 1$).

If we obtain coefficients for such a standardized distribution, then we can also apply the coefficients of this standardized distribution to compute coefficients for the standardized distribution of yet another collection which uses the same clues to indicate probability of relevance. The underlying assumption of such an adaptation is the following:

- *For each clue the underlying probability distribution of that clue remains identical from collection to collection changing only in its mean and standard deviation, i.e., only the mean and standard deviation of the particular collection-dependent distribution will change while the underlying standardized probability distribution remains constant over all collections.*

One might well question this assumption on the following grounds:

- *Suppose the mean* μ_i *and standard deviation* σ_i *for clue* i *varies meaningfully from collection to collection, and that these differences have predictive power with respect to relevance. Then the application of standardization of distributions will remove this predictive power.*

In the face of such thinking, the best approach is to experimentally test the assumption. If we accept, for purposes of testing, the assumption and we derive the standardized coefficient for a first collection (in our case the Cranfield collection) we can directly compute the adjusted coefficient for the standardized distribution of any other collection to which we wish to apply our logistic regression technique. In terms of formulae, we obtain the coefficients c_0, c_1, and c_2 for the equation (here we assume two clues, x and y):

$$log(O(R \mid x_1,y_1)) = c_0 + c_1(\frac{x_1-\mu_{x_1}}{\sigma_{x_1}}) + c_2(\frac{y_1-\mu_{y_1}}{\sigma_{y_1}})$$

Given the equation above, for the source collection, if we then look at the equation for the target collection, assuming that we would apply the same coefficients to a standardized distribution, we can then derive the equation for the second collection. If the standardized distribution remains constant from collection to collection, we have for collection two, the same equation,

$$log(O(R \mid x_2,y_2)) = c_0 + c_1(\frac{x_2-\mu_{x_2}}{\sigma_{x_2}}) + c_2(\frac{y_2-\mu_{y_2}}{\sigma_{y_2}})$$

and we wish to derive the coefficients c_0', c_1', and c_2' for the equation:

$$log(O(R \mid x_2,y_2)) = c_0' + c_1'x_2 + c_2'y_2$$

but if we multiply out the first equation above we obtain

$$log(O(R \mid x_2,y_2)) = c_0 - c_1\frac{\mu_{x_2}}{\sigma_{x_2}} - c_2\frac{\mu_{y_2}}{\sigma_{y_2}} + \frac{c_1}{\sigma_{x_2}}x_2 + \frac{c_2}{\sigma_{y_2}}y_2$$

and hence

$$c_0' = c_0 - c_1\frac{\mu_{x_2}}{\sigma_{x_2}} - c_2\frac{\mu_{y_2}}{\sigma_{y_2}}$$

$$c_1' = \frac{c_1}{\sigma_{x_2}}$$

and

$$c_2' = \frac{c_2}{\sigma_{y_2}}$$

Thus to find the logistic coefficients for the target collection, we need only determine the mean, μ_v, and standard deviation, σ_v for each clue v, compute the new coefficients, and apply them directly to clue values for the new collection.

This methodology was first applied by Cooper, Gey and Chen [20] to the queries of the NIST text retrieval conference (TREC1) [21]. This paper provides a more complete analysis of the method.

11. Applying to CACM and CISI collections

In order to obtain means and standard deviation for all clues for the new collection, we must obtain a new sample from each of those collections. If we obtain a small sample (of 1 in 125) query document term triples and all associated clues values, we can compute the following standard deviations for CACM and CISI.

Coll.	st.	log q.af	log d.af	log q.rf	log d.rf	log idf	log rfad
CISI	mean	0.3031	0.4093	-3.5450	-3.7922	1.9045	-5.5303
CISI	std dev	0.5153	0.5795	0.9110	0.6944	0.8333	1.0675
CACM	mean	0.1763	0.3900	-2.7644	-3.4976	2.0968	-5.2434
CACM	std dev	0.3347	0.5855	0.5612	0.7999	1.1378	1.2146

We then use these means and standard deviations together with the Cranfield coefficients to obtain the following new logistic or logodds coefficients for the CACM and CISI collections.

Coll.	const.	log q.af	log d.af	log q.rf	log d.rf	log idf	log rfad
CRAN	-4.125	-0.03229	0.1059	0.06910	0.4193	1.4515	0.7734
CACM	-1.341	-0.08412	0.1520	0.11993	0.5391	1.0933	0.5507
CISI	-0.934	-0.061660	0.1622	0.0663	0.5572	1.5325	0.6680

If we then apply the fit in order to obtain rankings for all queries for both the CACM and CISI collections, we obtain first for CACM the following recall-precision results:

Standardized Logistic vs. Tfidf/cosine Vector Space Performance CACM Collection: Averages over 52 Queries		
Recall	Standardized Logistic Precision	Vector Space Precision
0.00	0.7452	0.6985
0.10	0.6040	0.5683
0.20	0.5338	0.4830
0.30	0.4392	0.3887
0.40	0.3683	0.3210
0.50	0.3128	0.2761
0.60	0.2682	0.2306
0.70	0.1846	0.1770
0.80	0.1388	0.1441
0.90	0.0961	0.1018
1.00	0.0694	0.0735
11-pt Avg:	0.3419	0.3148
% Change:		-7.9

Note that the average precision has increased approximately another 3 percent over the tfidf cosine vector space method of ranking documents. The recall-precision table makes it quite clear that except for the tail of recall-precision, the standardized extended logistic model performs substantially better than the tfidf/cosine vector space model for the CACM collection.

Indeed, if we once again go through our process of computing average precision from all points of recall for each of the 52 significant queries for CACM, and then do a statistical test of the difference from standardized logistic method and tfidf/cosine vector space average precision, we find this improvement is now statistically significant at the 2 percent level.

CACM Hypothesis Test: 2-tail T on Precision Differences between Standardized Logistic and Tfidf/cosine						
N	null mean	sample mean	sample SE	df	test stat	P value
52	0.0000	-0.030180	0.012335	51.0	-2.45	.0179

That is to say, we would only expect in less than two percent of all samples of queries applied to the CACM collection, for the vector space model to perform better than the standardized logistic model. In this way, we can reject the null hypothesis that there is no difference in the performance in the CACM collection and accept the clear indication that standardized logistic regression performs better than the vector space model for the CACM collection.

On the other hand, if we apply this correction factor and standardization to the CISI collection, we find that there is a slight worsening in the performance results.

Standardized Logistic vs. Tfidf/cosine Vector Space Performance CISI Collection: Averages over 76 Queries		
Recall	Standardized Logistic Precision	Vector Space Precision
11-pt Avg:	0.2042	0.2137
% Change:		4.7

When comparing this result with the non-standardized extended logistic model for CISI we see that the precision changes occur in the third decimal place. We can conclude that the difference between the two is certainly not statistically significant, nor is that between CISI standardized and tfidf/cosine. Among reasons for this failure to achieve performance improvement in the CISI collection are the different prior probability of relevance for the collections. [22] gives more detail on the sensitivity of the model to the proper estimation of prior probability of relevance.

12. Conclusions

In this research we have investigated a new probabilistic text and document search method based upon logistic regression. This *logistic inference* method estimates probability of relevance for documents with respect to a query which represents the user's information need. Documents are then ranked in descending order of their estimated probability of relevance to the query.

1. The *logistic inference* method has been subjected to detailed performance tests comparing it (in terms of recall and precision averages) to the traditional tfidf/cosine vector space method, using the same retrieval and evaluation software (the Cornell SMART system) for both methods. In this way the test results remain free of bias which might be introduced from different software implementations of evaluation methods. In terms of recall and precision averages, the logistic inference method outperforms the tfidf/cosine vector space method on the Cranfield and CACM test collections. The methods seem to perform equally well on the CISI test collection (for an appropriately estimated prior probability).

2. Statistical tests have been applied to ascertain whether these performance differences between the two methods are statistically significant. The performance improvement of the logistic inference method over the tfidf/cosine vector space method for the Cranfield and CACM collection is statistically significant at the five percent level. Performance differences for the CISI collections are not statistically significant, for the most plausible estimate of prior probability.

3. The use of standardized variables (statistical clues standardized to mean $\mu = 0$ and standard deviation $\sigma = 1$) seems to enable the training of and fitting for logistic regression coefficients to take place on the queries and documents of one collection and to be applied directly to the queries and documents of other collections.

13. Acknowledgments

The work described was part of the author's dissertation research at the School of Library and Information Studies at the University of California, Berkeley. Many of the ideas contained herein were jointly formulated with my dissertation advisor, Professor William S. Cooper, whose clarity of thinking and relentless persistence made this research both possible and doable. My outside committee member, Professor of Biostatistics Steve Selvin, provided much helpful advice on statistical techniques.

References

1. Salton G et al. The SMART retrieval system: Experiments in automatic document processing. Prentice-Hall, Englewood Cliffs, NJ, 1971

2. Salton G. Text processing: the transformation, analysis and retrieval of information by computer. Addison Wesley, Reading, MA-Menlo Park, CA, 1989

3. Salton G, McGill M. Introduction to modern information retrieval. McGraw-Hill, New York, 1983

4. Sparck-Jones K. A statistical interpretation of term specificity and its application in retrieval. Journal

of Documentation 1972; 28:11-21

5. Salton G Buckley C. Term weighting approaches in automatic text retrieval. Information Processing and Management 1988; 24:513-523

6. Robertson, S. The probability ranking principle in IR. Journal of Documentation 1977; 33:294-304

7. Robertson S Sparck-Jones K. Relevance weighting of search terms. Journal of the ASIS 1976; 27:129-145

8. Cooper W. Inconsistencies and misnomers in probabilistic IR. In: Proceedings of the Fourteenth Annual International ACM/SIGIR Conference on Research and Development in Information Retrieval, Chicago, Ill, Oct 13-16, 1991, pp 57-61

9. Fuhr N Huther H. Optimum probability estimation from empirical distributions. Information Processing and Management 1989; 25:493-507

10. Hosmer D Lemeshow S. Applied logistic regression. John Wiley & Sons, New York, 1989

11. Fox E. Extending the Boolean and Vector Space Models of Information Retrieval with P-Norm Queries and Multiple Concept Types. PhD dissertation, Computer Science, Cornell University, 1983

12. Fuhr N. Optimal polynomial retrieval functions based on the probability ranking principle. ACM Transactions on Informations Systems 1989; 7:183-204

13. Fuhr N Buckley C. A probabilistic learning approach for document indexing. ACM Transactions on Informations Systems 1991 9:223-248

14. Haines D Croft B. Relevance feedback and inference networks. Proceedings of the 1993 SIGIR International Conference on Information Retrieva l, Pittsburgh, Pa, June 27-July 1, 1993, pp 2-12

15. Turtle H. Inference networks for document retrieval. PhD Dissertation, University of Massachusetts, COINS Technical Report 90-92, February, 1991

16. Fung R Crawford S Appelbaum L Tong R. An architecture for probabilistic concept-bases information retrieval. In: Proceedings of the 13th international conference on research and development in information retrieval. Brussels, Belgium, September 5-7, 1990, pp. 455-467

17. Swanson D. Information retrieval as a trial-and-error process. Library Quarterly 1977; 47:128-148

18. Hull D. Using statistical testing in the evaluation of retrieval experiments. Proceedings of the 1993 SIGIR international conference on information retrieval. Pittsburgh, Pa, June 27-July 1, 1993, pp.329-338

19. Yu C Buckley C Lam H Salton G. A generalized term dependence model in information retrieval. Information Technology: Research and Development 1983; 2:129-154

20. Cooper W Gey F Chen A. Information retrieval from the TIPSTER collection: an application of staged logistic regression. In: Proceedings of the First NIST Text Retrieval Conference, National Institute for Standards and Technology, Washington, DC, November 4-6, 1992, NIST Special Publication 500-207, March 1993, pp 73-88

21. Harman, D. Overview of the first TREC conference. In: Proceedings of the 1993 SIGIR international conference on information retrieva l, Pittsburgh, Pa, June 27-July 1, 1993, pp 36-47

22. Gey F. Probabilistic dependence and logistic inference in information retrieval. PhD dissertation, University of California, Berkeley, 1993

Some Simple Effective Approximations to the 2–Poisson Model for Probabilistic Weighted Retrieval

S.E. Robertson — ser@is.city.ac.uk
S. Walker — sw@is.city.ac.uk

Centre for Interactive Systems Research, Department of Information Science, City University
Northampton Square, London EC1V 0HB, UK

Abstract

The 2–Poisson model for term frequencies is used to suggest ways of incorporating certain variables in probabilistic models for information retrieval. The variables concerned are within-document term frequency, document length, and within-query term frequency. Simple weighting functions are developed, and tested on the TREC test collection. Considerable performance improvements (over simple inverse collection frequency weighting) are demonstrated.

1 Introduction

This paper discusses an approach to the incorporation of new variables into traditional probabilistic models for information retrieval, and some experimental results relating thereto. Some of the discussion has appeared in the proceedings of the second TREC conference [1], albeit in less detail.

Statistical approaches to information retrieval have traditionally (to over-simplify grossly) taken two forms: firstly approaches based on formal models, where the model specifies an exact formula; and secondly ad-hoc approaches, where formulae are tried because they seem to be plausible. Both categories have had some notable successes. A more recent variant is the regression approach of Fuhr and Cooper (see, for example, Cooper [3]), which incorporates ad-hoc choice of independent variables and functions of them with a formal model for assessing their value in retrieval, selecting from among them and assigning weights to them.

One problem with the formal model approach is that it is often very difficult to take into account the wide variety of variables that are thought or known to influence retrieval. The difficulty arises either because there is no known basis for a model containing such variables, or because any such model may simply be too complex to give a usable exact formula.

One problem with the ad-hoc approach is that there is little guidance as to how to deal with specific variables—one has to guess at a formula and try it out. This problem is also apparent in the regression approach—although "trying it out" has a somewhat different sense here (the formula is tried in a regression model, rather than in a retrieval test).

The approach in the present paper is to take a model which provides an exact but intractable formula, and use it to suggest a much simpler formula. The simpler formula can then be tried in an ad-hoc fashion, or used in turn in a regression model. Although we have not yet taken this latter step of using regression, we believe that the present suggestion lends itself to such methods.

The variables we have included in this paper are: within-document term frequency, document length, and within-query term frequency (it is worth observing that collection frequency of terms appears naturally in traditional probabilistic models, particularly in the form of the approximation to inverse collection frequency weighting demonstrated by Croft and Harper [4]). The formal model which is used to investigate the effects of these variables is the 2–Poisson model (Harter [5], Robertson, van Rijsbergen and Porter [6]).

2 Basic Probabilistic Weighting Model

The basic weighting function used is that developed in [6], and may be expressed as follows:

$$w(\underline{\mathbf{x}}) = \log \frac{P(\underline{\mathbf{x}}|R)\ P(\underline{0}|\overline{R})}{P(\underline{\mathbf{x}}|\overline{R})\ P(\underline{0}|R)}, \tag{1}$$

where $\underline{\mathbf{x}}$ is a vector of information about the document, $\underline{0}$ is a reference vector representing a zero-weighted document, and R and $\overline{R}$ are relevance and non-relevance respectively.

For example, each component of $\underline{\mathbf{x}}$ may represent the presence/absence of a query term in the document or its document frequency; $\underline{0}$ would then be the "natural" zero vector representing all query terms absent.

In this formulation, independence assumptions (or, indeed, Cooper's assumption of "linked dependence" [7]), lead to the decomposition of w into *additive* components such as individual term weights. In the presence/absence case, the resulting weighting function is the Robertson/Sparck Jones formula [8] for a term-presence-only weight, as follows:

$$w = \log \frac{p(1-q)}{q(1-p)}, \tag{2}$$

where $p = P(\text{term present}|R)$ and $q = P(\text{term present}|\overline{R})$.

With a suitable estimation method, this becomes:

$$w = \log \frac{(r+0.5)/(R-r+0.5)}{(n-r+0.5)/(N-n-R+r+0.5)}, \tag{3}$$

where N is the number of indexed documents, n the number containing the term, R the number of known relevant documents, and r the number of these containing the term. This approximates to inverse collection frequency (ICF) when there is no relevance information. It will be referred to below (with or without relevance information) as $w^{(1)}$.

If we deal with within-document term frequencies rather than merely presence and absence of terms, then the formula corresponding to 2 would be as follows:

$$w = \log \frac{p_{tf}\, q_0}{q_{tf}\, p_0}, \tag{4}$$

where $p_{tf} = P(\text{term present with frequency } tf|R)$, q_{tf} is the corresponding probability for $\overline{R}$, and p_0 and q_0 are those for term absence.

2.1 Eliteness

The approach taken in reference [6] is to model within-document term frequencies by means of a mixture of two Poisson distributions. However, before discussing the 2–Poisson model, it is worth extracting one idea which is necessary for the model, but can perhaps stand on its own. (This idea was in fact taken from the original 2–Poisson work by Harter [5], but was extended somewhat to allow for multi-concept queries.)

We hypothesize that occurrences of a term in a document have a random or stochastic element, which nevertheless reflects a real but hidden distinction between those documents which are "about" the concept represented by the term and those which are not. Those documents which are "about" this concept are described as "elite" for the term. We may draw an inference about eliteness from the term frequency, but this inference will of course be probabilistic. Furthermore, relevance (to a query which may of course contain many concepts) is related to eliteness rather than directly to term frequency, which is assumed to depend *only* on eliteness. The usual term-independence assumptions are replaced by assumptions that the eliteness properties for different terms are independent of each other; although the details are not provided here, it is clear that the independence assumptions can be replaced by "linked dependence" assumptions in the style of Cooper [7].

As usual, the various assumptions of the model are very clearly over-simplifications of reality. It seems nevertheless to be useful to introduce this hidden variable of eliteness in order to gain some understanding of the relation between multiple term occurrence and relevance.

3 The 2–Poisson Model

The 2–Poisson model is a specific distributional assumption based on the eliteness hypothesis discussed above. The assumption is that the distribution of within-document frequencies is Poisson for the elite documents, and also (but with a different mean) for the non-elite documents.

It would be possible to derive this model from a more basic one, under which a document was a random stream of term occurrences, each one having a fixed, small probability of being the term in question, this probability being constant over all elite documents, and also constant (but smaller) over all non-elite documents. Such a model would require that all documents were the same length. Thus the 2–Poisson model is usually said to assume that document length is constant: although technically it does not require that assumption, it makes little sense without it. Document length is discussed further below (section 5).

The approach taken in [6] was to estimate the parameters of the two Poisson distributions for each term directly from the distribution of within-document frequencies. These parameters were then used in various weighting functions. However, little performance benefit was gained. This was seen essentially as a result of estimation problems: partly that the estimation method for the Poisson parameters was probably not very good, and partly because the model is complex in the sense of requiring a large number of different parameters to be estimated. Subsequent work on mixed-Poisson models has suggested that alternative estimation methods may be preferable [9].

Combining the 2–Poisson model with formula 4, under the various assumptions given about dependencies, we obtain [6] the following weight for a term t:

$$w = \log \frac{(p'\lambda^{tf} e^{-\lambda} + (1-p')\mu^{tf} e^{-\mu})\ (q' e^{-\lambda} + (1-q')e^{-\mu})}{(q'\lambda^{tf} e^{-\lambda} + (1-q')\mu^{tf} e^{-\mu})\ (p' e^{-\lambda} + (1-p')e^{-\mu})}, \tag{5}$$

where λ and μ are the Poisson means for tf in the elite and non-elite sets for t respectively, $p' = P(\text{document elite for } t|R)$, and q' is the corresponding probability for $\overline{R}$.

The estimation problem is very apparent from equation 5, in that there are four parameters for each term, for *none* of which are we likely to have direct evidence (because of eliteness being a hidden variable). It is precisely this estimation problem which makes the weighting function intractable. This consideration leads directly to the approach taken in the next section.

4 A Rough Model for Term Frequency

4.1 The Shape of the *tf* Effect

Many different functions have been used to allow within-document term frequency tf to influence the weight given to the particular document on account of the term in question. In some cases a linear function has been used; in others, the effect has been dampened by using a suitable transformation such as $\log tf$.

Even if we do not use the full equation 5, we may allow it to suggest the shape of an appropriate, but simpler, function. In fact, equation 5 has the following characteristics: (a) It is zero for $tf = 0$; (b) it increases monotonically with tf; (c) but to an asymptotic maximum; (d) which approximates to the Robertson/Sparck Jones weight that would be given to a direct indicator of eliteness.

Only in an extreme case, where eliteness is identical to relevance, is the function linear in tf. These points can be seen from the following re-arrangement of equation 5:

$$w = \log \frac{(p' + (1-p')(\mu/\lambda)^{tf} e^{\lambda-\mu})\ (q' e^{\mu-\lambda} + (1-q'))}{(q' + (1-q')(\mu/\lambda)^{tf} e^{\lambda-\mu})\ (p' e^{\mu-\lambda} + (1-p'))}. \tag{6}$$

μ is smaller than λ. As $tf \to \infty$ (to give us the asymptotic maximum), $(\mu/\lambda)^{tf}$ goes to zero, so those components drop out. $e^{\mu-\lambda}$ will be small, so the approximation is:

$$w = \log \frac{p'(1-q')}{q'(1-p')}. \tag{7}$$

(The last approximation may not be a good one: for a poor and/or infrequent term, $e^{\mu-\lambda}$ will not be very small. Although this should not affect the component in the numerator, because q' is likely to be small, it will affect the component in the denominator.)

4.2 A Simple Formulation

What is required, therefore, is a simple tf-related weight that has something like the characteristics (a)-(d) listed in the previous section. Such a function can be constructed as follows. The function $tf/(\text{constant} + tf)$ increases from zero to an asymptotic maximum in approximately the right fashion. The constant determines the rate at which the increase drops off: with a large constant, the function is approximately linear for small tf, whereas with a small constant, the effect of increasing tf rapidly diminishes.

This function has an asymptotic maximum of one, so it needs to be multiplied by an appropriate weight similar to equation 7. Since we cannot estimate 7 directly, the obvious simple alternative is the ordinary Robertson/Sparck Jones weight, equation 2, based on presence/absence of the term. Using the usual estimate of 2, namely $w^{(1)}$ (equation 3), we obtain the following weighting function:

$$w = \frac{tf}{(k_1 + tf)} w^{(1)}, \tag{8}$$

where k_1 is an unknown constant.

The model tells us nothing about what kind of value to expect for k_1. Our approach has been to try out various values of k_1 (values around 1–2 seem to be about right for the TREC data—see the results section 7 below). However, in the longer term we hope to use regression methods to determine the constant. It is not, unfortunately, in a form directly susceptible to the methods of Fuhr or Cooper, but we hope to develop suitable methods.

The shape of formula 8 differs from that of formula 5 in one important respect: 8 is convex towards the upper left, whereas 5 can under some circumstances (that is, with some combinations of parameters) be S-shaped, increasing slowly at first, then more rapidly, then slowly again. Averaging over a number of terms with different values of the parameters is likely to reduce any such effect; however, it may be useful to try a function with this characteristic. One such, a simple combination of 8 with a logistic function, is as follows:

$$w = \frac{tf^c}{(k_1^c + tf^c)} \, w^{(1)}, \tag{9}$$

where $c > 1$ is another unknown constant. This function has not been tried in the present experiments.

5 Document Length

As indicated in section 3, the 2–Poisson model in effect assumes that documents (i.e. records) are all of equal length. Document length is a variable which figures in a number of weighting formulae.

5.1 Hypotheses Concerning Document Length

We may postulate at least two reasons why documents might vary in length. Some documents may simply cover more material than others; an extreme version of this hypothesis would have a long document consisting of a number of unrelated short documents concatenated together (the "Scope hypothesis"). An opposite view would have long documents like short documents, but longer: in other words, a long document covers a similar scope to a short document, but simply uses more words (the "Verbosity hypothesis").

It seems likely that real document collections contain a mixture of these effects; individual long documents may be at either extreme or of some hybrid type. (It is worth observing that some of the long TREC news items read exactly as if they are made up of short items concatenated together.) However, with the exception of a short discussion in section 5.7, the work on document length reported in this paper assumes the Verbosity hypothesis; little progress has yet been made with models based on the Scope hypothesis.

The Verbosity hypothesis would imply that document properties such as relevance and eliteness can be regarded as independent of document length; given eliteness for a term, however, the number of occurrences of that term would depend on document length.

5.2 A Very Rough Model

The simplest way to incorporate this hypothesis is to take formula 8 above, but normalise *tf* for document length (d). If we assume that the value of k_1 is appropriate to documents of average length (Δ), then this model can be expressed as

$$w = \frac{tf}{(\frac{k_1 \times d}{\Delta} + tf)} \, w^{(1)}. \tag{10}$$

This function is used in the experiments described below (section 7). However, a more detailed analysis of the effect of the Verbosity hypothesis on the 2–Poisson model may reveal a more complex pattern.

5.3 Document Length in the Basic Model

Referring back to the basic weighting function 1, we may include document length as one component of the vector $\underline{\mathbf{x}}$. However, document length does not so obviously have a "natural" zero (an actual document of zero length is a pathological case). Instead, we may use the average length of a document for the corresponding component of the reference vector $\underline{0}$; thus we would expect to get a formula in which the document length component disappears for a document of average length, but not for other lengths. The weighting formula then becomes:

$$w(\underline{\mathbf{x}}, d) = \log \frac{P(\underline{\mathbf{x}}, d|R) \; P(\underline{0}, \Delta|\overline{R})}{P(\underline{\mathbf{x}}, d|\overline{R}) \; P(\underline{0}, \Delta|R)},$$

where d is document length, and $\underline{\mathbf{x}}$ represents all other information about the document. This may be decomposed into the sum of two components, $w(\underline{\mathbf{x}}, d)_1 + w(\underline{0}, d)_2$, where

$$w(\underline{\mathbf{x}}, d)_1 = \log \frac{P(\underline{\mathbf{x}}, d|R) \; P(\underline{0}, d|\overline{R})}{P(\underline{\mathbf{x}}, d|\overline{R}) \; P(\underline{0}, d|R)} \quad \text{and} \quad w(\underline{0}, d)_2 = \log \frac{P(\underline{0}, d|R) \; P(\underline{0}, \Delta|\overline{R})}{P(\underline{0}, d|\overline{R}) \; P(\underline{0}, \Delta|R)}. \tag{11}$$

These two components are discussed separately.

5.4 Consequences of the Verbosity Hypothesis

We assume without loss of generality that the two Poisson parameters for a given term, λ and μ, are appropriate for documents of average length. Then the Verbosity hypothesis would imply that while a longer (say) document has more words, each individual word has the same probability of being the term in question. Thus the distribution of term frequencies in documents of length d will be 2–Poisson with means $\lambda d/\Delta$ and $\mu d/\Delta$.

We may also make various independence assumptions, such as between document length and relevance.

5.5 Second Component

The second component of equation 11 is

$$w(\underline{0}, d)_2 = \log \frac{P(\underline{0}|R, d)\ P(\underline{0}|\overline{R}, \Delta)}{P(\underline{0}|\overline{R}, d)\ P(\underline{0}|R, \Delta)} + \log \frac{P(d|R)\ P(\Delta|\overline{R})}{P(d|\overline{R})\ P(\Delta|R)}.$$

Under the Verbosity hypothesis, the second part of this formula is zero. Making the usual term-independence or linked-dependence assumptions, the first part may be decomposed into a sum of components for each query term, thus:

$$w(t, d)_2 = \log \frac{(p'e^{-\lambda d/\Delta} + (1-p')e^{-\mu d/\Delta})\ (q'e^{-\lambda} + (1-q')e^{-\mu})}{(q'e^{-\lambda d/\Delta} + (1-q')e^{-\mu d/\Delta})\ (p'e^{-\lambda} + (1-p')e^{-\mu})}. \tag{12}$$

Note that because we are using the zero-vector $\underline{0}$, there is a component for each query term, whether or not the term is in the document.

For almost all normal query terms (i.e. for any terms that are not actually detrimental to the query), we can assume that $p' > q'$ and $\lambda > \mu$. In this case, formula 12 can be shown to be monotonic decreasing with d, from a maximum as $d \to 0$, through zero when $d = \Delta$, and to a minimum as $d \to \infty$. As indicated, there is one such factor for each of the nq query terms.

Once again, we can devise a very much simpler function which approximates to this behaviour, as follows:

$$\textit{correction factor} = k_2 \times nq \frac{(\Delta - d)}{(\Delta + d)}, \tag{13}$$

where k_2 is another unknown constant.

Again, k_2 is not specified by the model, and must (at present, at least) be discovered by trial and error (values in the range 0–2 appear about right for the TREC databases, although performance is not sensitive to this correction[1])—see the results section 7.

5.6 First Component

The first component of equation 11 is:

$$w(\underline{x}, d)_1 = \log \frac{P(\underline{x}|R, d)\ P(\underline{0}|\overline{R}, d)}{P(\underline{x}|\overline{R}, d)\ P(\underline{0}|R, d)}.$$

Expanding this on the basis of term independence assumptions, and also making the assumption that eliteness is independent of document length (on the basis of the Verbosity hypothesis), we can obtain a formula for the weight of a term t which occurs tf times, as follows:

$$\begin{aligned} w(t, d)_1 &= \log \frac{(p'(\lambda d/\Delta)^{tf} e^{-\lambda d/\Delta} + (1-p')(\mu d/\Delta)^{tf} e^{-\mu d/\Delta})\ (q'e^{-\lambda d/\Delta} + (1-q')e^{-\mu d/\Delta})}{(q'(\lambda d/\Delta)^{tf} e^{-\lambda d/\Delta} + (1-q')(\mu d/\Delta)^{tf} e^{-\mu d/\Delta})\ (p'e^{-\lambda d/\Delta} + (1-p')e^{-\mu d/\Delta})} \\ &= \log \frac{(p'\lambda^{tf} e^{-\lambda d/\Delta} + (1-p')\mu^{tf} e^{-\mu d/\Delta})\ (q'e^{-\lambda d/\Delta} + (1-q')e^{-\mu d/\Delta})}{(q'\lambda^{tf} e^{-\lambda d/\Delta} + (1-q')\mu^{tf} e^{-\mu d/\Delta})\ (p'e^{-\lambda d/\Delta} + (1-p')e^{-\mu d/\Delta})}. \end{aligned} \tag{14}$$

Analysis of the behaviour of this function with varying tf and d is a little complex. The simple function used for the experiments (formula 10) exhibits some of the correct properties, but not all. In particular, 14 shows that increasing d exaggerates the S-shape mentioned in section 4.2; formula 10 does not have this property. It seems that there may be further scope for development of a rough model based on the behaviour of formula 14.

[1] Values of this constant depend on the base of the logarithms used in the term-weighting functions

5.7 The Scope Hypothesis

As indicated above (section 5.1), an alternative hypothesis concerning document length would regard a long document as a set of unrelated, concatenated short documents. The obvious response to this hypothesis is to attempt to find appropriate boundaries in the documents, and to treat short passages rather than full documents as the retrievable units. There have been a number of experiments on these lines reported in the literature [10].

This approach appears difficult to combine with the ideas discussed above, in a way which would accommodate an explanation of document length in terms of a mixture of the two hypotheses. One possible solution is that used by Salton [11], of allowing passages to compete with full documents for retrieval. But there seems to be room for more theoretical analysis.

5.8 Document Length and Term Frequency—Summary

We have, then, a term weighting function which includes a within-document term frequency component, without (equation 8) or with (equation 10) a document-length component. We also have a document-length correction factor (equation 13) which can be applied to either 8 or 10.

6 Query Term Frequency

The natural symmetry of the retrieval situation as between documents and queries suggests that we could treat within-query term frequency (*qtf*) in a similar fashion to within-document term frequency. This would suggest, by analogy with equation 8, a weighting function thus:

$$w = \frac{qtf}{(k_3 + qtf)}\, w^{(1)}, \tag{15}$$

where k_3 is another unknown constant.

In this case, experiments (section 7) suggest a large value of k_3 to be effective—indeed the limiting case, which is equivalent to

$$w = qtf \times w^{(1)}, \tag{16}$$

appears to be the most effective. This may perhaps suggest that an S-shaped function like equation 9 could be better still, though again none has been tried in the present experiments.

The experiments are based on combining one of these *qtf* multipliers with the within-document term frequency and document length functions defined above. However, it should be pointed out that (a) the "natural symmetry" as between documents and queries, to which we appealed above, is open to question, and (b) that even if we accept each model separately, it is not at all obvious that they can be combined (a properly constructed combined model would have fairly complex relations between query and document terms, query and document eliteness, and relevance). Both these matters are discussed further by Robertson [12]. In the meantime, the combination of either *qtf* multiplier with the earlier functions must be regarded as not having a strong theoretical motivation.

7 Experiments

7.1 TREC

The TREC (Text REtrieval Conference) conferences, of which there have been two, with the third due to start early 1994, are concerned with controlled comparisons of different methods of retrieving documents from large collections of assorted textual material. They are funded by the US Advanced Projects Research Agency (ARPA) and organised by Donna Harman of NIST (National Institute for Standards and Technology). There were about 31 participants, academic and commercial, in the TREC-2 conference which took place at Gaithersburg, MD in September 1993 [2]. Information needs are presented in the form of highly structured "topics" from which queries are to be derived automatically and/or manually by participants. Documents include newspaper articles, entries from the Federal Register, patents and technical abstracts, varying in length from a line or two to several hundred thousand words.

A large number of relevance judgments have been made at NIST by a panel of experts assessing the top-ranked documents retrieved by some of the participants in TREC–1 and TREC–2. The number of known relevant documents for the 150 topics varies between 1 and more than 1000, with a mean of 281.

7.2 Experiments Conducted

Some of the experiments reported here were also reported at TREC–2 [1].

Database and Queries

The experiments reported here involved searches of one of the TREC collections, described as disks 1 & 2 (TREC raw data has been distributed on three CD-ROMs). It contains about 743,000 documents. It was indexed by keyword stems, using a modified Porter stemming procedure [13], spelling normalisation designed to conflate British and American spellings, a moderate stoplist of about 250 words and a small cross-reference table and "go" list. Topics 101–150 of the 150 TREC–1 and –2 topic statements were used. The mean length (number of unstopped tokens) of the queries derived from title and concepts fields only was 30.3; for those using additionally the narrative and description fields the mean length was 81.

Search Procedure

Searches were carried out automatically by means of City University's Okapi text retrieval software. The weighting functions described in Sections 4–6 were implemented as BM15[2] (the model using equation 8 for the document term frequency component) and BM11 (using equation 10). Both functions incorporated the document length correction factor of equation 13. These were compared with BM1 ($w^{(1)}$ weights, approximately ICF, since no relevance information was used in these experiments) and with a simple coordination-level model BM0 in which terms are given equal weights. Note that BM11 and BM15 both reduce to BM1 when k_1 and k_2 are zero. The within-query term frequency component (equation 15) could be used with any of these functions.

To summarize, the following functions were used:

(BM0) $$w = 1$$

(BM1) $$w = \log\frac{N-n+0.5}{n+0.5} \times \frac{qtf}{(k_3+qtf)}$$

(BM15) $$w = \frac{tf}{(k_1+tf)} \times \log\frac{N-n+0.5}{n+0.5} \times \frac{qtf}{(k_3+qtf)} + k_2 \times nq\frac{(\Delta-d)}{(\Delta+d)}$$

(BM11) $$w = \frac{tf}{(\frac{k_1 \times d}{\Delta}+tf)} \times \log\frac{N-n+0.5}{n+0.5} \times \frac{qtf}{(k_3+qtf)} + k_2 \times nq\frac{(\Delta-d)}{(\Delta+d)}.$$

In the experiments reported below where k_3 is given as ∞, the factor $qtf/(k_3+qtf)$ is implemented as qtf on its own (equation 16).

Evaluation

In all cases the 1000 top-ranking documents for each topic were run against the supplied relevance assessments using a standard evaluation program from the SMART projects at Cornell University. (This was the official evaluation method used in TREC–2.) The evaluation program outputs a number of standard performance measures for each query, and finally a set of measures averaged over all the queries in the run. The measures used in the tables below are average precision (AveP), precision at 5, 30 and 100 documents (P5 etc.), R-precision (RP) (precision after the number of known relevant documents for a query have been retrieved) and recall (Rcl) (final recall after 1000 documents have been retrieved).

In TREC, a distinction is made between ad-hoc (retrospective) experiments and routing (SDI or filtering). All the results reported here have been obtained using the topics and documents (and methods) used for ad-hoc experiments in TREC–2.

7.3 Results

In these experiments the weighting functions involve three parameters (k_1, k_2 and k_3 above). It was to be expected that their values would interact, so there was a large number of preliminary runs to try to determine the extent of interaction, and to give clues as to the most fruitful ranges of values for further investigation. In should also be noted that k_1 and k_3 are parameters in expressions which are coefficients of a logarithmic value, whereas the document length correction involving k_2 is not a logarithm; hence the value of k_2 depends on the base of the logarithms used.[3]

Table 1 compares two of the new models with baseline $w^{(1)}$ weighting (BM1 with $k_3 = 0$), and with coordination level (BM0). For the shorter queries (title + concepts) BM15 appears somewhat better than BM1 (the difference is greater when a document length correction is added—Table 3). But its performance on the long queries is very poor. BM11 gives a very marked improvement over the baseline, particularly for the long queries.

[2] BM = Best Match

[3] To obtain weights within a range suitable for storage as 16–bit integers, the Okapi system uses logarithms to base $2^{0.1}$

Table 1. Comparison of term weighting functions

Function	k_1	k_2	k_3	AveP	P5	P30	P100	RP	Rcl
Query term source: titles + concepts									
BM11	1.0	0.0	0.0	0.300	0.624	0.536	0.440	0.349	0.683
BM15	1.0	0.0	0.0	0.214	0.504	0.435	0.347	0.278	0.568
BM1	0.0	0.0	0.0	0.199	0.468	0.416	0.326	0.261	0.542
BM0	—	—	—	0.142	0.412	0.336	0.270	0.209	0.411
Query term source: titles + concepts + narrative + description									
BM11	1.0	0.0	0.0	0.263	0.612	0.485	0.394	0.306	0.605
BM15	1.0	0.0	0.0	0.074	0.284	0.216	0.154	0.110	0.258
BM1	0.0	0.0	0.0	0.085	0.312	0.235	0.179	0.127	0.297
BM0	—	—	—	0.035	0.220	0.139	0.099	0.066	0.153
Database : TREC disks 1 and 2. Topics: 101–150									

Document Term Frequency

In Table 2 k_1 is varied for BM11 with the other parameters held at zero. As the value of k_1 increases from zero to about 2 performance improves sharply, then deteriorates gradually. Even very small values of k_1 have a marked effect, because the wide variation in document length implies that the term $\frac{k_1 \times d}{\Delta}$ in equation 10 can be quite large even when k_1 is as low as 0.05.

Table 2. Effect of varying the document term frequency parameter k_1

Function	k_1	k_2	k_3	AveP	P5	P30	P100	RP	Rcl
Query term source: titles + concepts									
BM11	0.0	0.0	0.0	0.199	0.468	0.416	0.326	0.261	0.542
BM11	0.2	0.0	0.0	0.263	0.616	0.499	0.404	0.311	0.633
BM11	0.5	0.0	0.0	0.287	0.628	0.525	0.432	0.338	0.664
BM11	1.0	0.0	0.0	0.300	0.624	0.536	0.440	0.349	0.683
BM11	2.0	0.0	0.0	0.303	0.640	0.524	0.443	0.359	0.689
BM11	5.0	0.0	0.0	0.285	0.612	0.506	0.431	0.342	0.666
BM11	10.0	0.0	0.0	0.259	0.540	0.485	0.404	0.324	0.635
BM11	50.0	0.0	0.0	0.179	0.412	0.400	0.317	0.254	0.537
Database : TREC disks 1 and 2. Topics: 101–150									

Document Length Correction

Values greater than 1 had a small detrimental effect in the BM11 model, but small positive values improved the performance of BM15, in which the document term frequency component is not normalised with respect to document length (Table 3).

Table 3. Effect of varying the document length correction parameter k_2

Function	k_1	k_2	k_3	AveP	P5	P30	P100	RP	Rcl
Query term source: titles + concepts									
BM11	1.0	0.0	0.0	0.300	0.624	0.536	0.440	0.349	0.683
BM11	1.0	1.0	0.0	0.300	0.632	0.532	0.438	0.349	0.678
BM11	1.0	2.0	0.0	0.296	0.632	0.523	0.437	0.347	0.671
BM11	1.0	5.0	0.0	0.275	0.624	0.506	0.424	0.335	0.631
BM15	1.0	0.0	0.0	0.214	0.504	0.435	0.347	0.278	0.568
BM15	1.0	1.0	0.0	0.229	0.512	0.453	0.364	0.292	0.598
Database : TREC disks 1 and 2. Topics: 101–150									

Query Term Frequency

Table 4 illustrates the effect of increasing k_3 from zero to infinity. For all functions and for both long and short queries performance improves fairly smoothly with k_3. For BM11 the increase in average precision is 37% on the long queries and 12% on the short. It is to be expected that k_3 would have a greater effect with the long queries, in which there are many "noisy" terms and in which most of the more apposite terms are likely to occur more than once. However, high values of k_3 increase the performance of BM15 by 24% even on the short queries.

Table 4. Effect of varying the query term frequency parameter k_3

Function	k_1	k_2	k_3	AveP	P5	P30	P100	RP	Rcl
Query term source: titles + concepts + narrative + description									
BM11	1.0	0.0	0.0	0.263	0.612	0.485	0.394	0.306	0.605
BM11	1.0	0.0	1.0	0.299	0.648	0.510	0.428	0.341	0.659
BM11	1.0	0.0	3.0	0.331	0.640	0.540	0.456	0.378	0.712
BM11	1.0	0.0	8.0	0.346	0.656	0.549	0.466	0.390	0.737
BM11	1.0	0.0	20.0	0.351	0.644	0.560	0.471	0.395	0.744
BM11	1.0	0.0	100.0	0.353	0.648	0.565	0.473	0.396	0.745
BM11	1.0	0.0	∞	0.360	0.652	0.569	0.479	0.401	0.754
Query term source: titles + concepts									
BM11	1.0	0.0	0.0	0.300	0.624	0.536	0.440	0.349	0.683
BM11	1.0	0.0	∞	0.335	0.636	0.560	0.468	0.375	0.723
BM15	1.0	1.0	0.0	0.229	0.512	0.453	0.364	0.292	0.598
BM15	1.0	1.0	∞	0.284	0.560	0.485	0.416	0.336	0.685
BM1	0.0	0.0	0.0	0.199	0.468	0.416	0.326	0.261	0.542
BM1	0.0	0.0	∞	0.232	0.504	0.435	0.361	0.289	0.601
Database : TREC disks 1 and 2. Topics: 101–150									

7.4 Discussion

On the short queries, and without a query term frequency component, the best version of BM11 gives an increase of about 50% in average precision, with somewhat smaller improvements in the other statistics, over the baseline Robertson/Sparck Jones weighting BM1. On the long queries the proportionate improvement is very much greater still. To put this in perspective, the best results reported here (Table 4, row 8), are similar to the best reported by any of the TREC–2 participants at the time of the conference in September 1993.

Many experimental runs were also carried out on two other sets of 50 topics and on two other databases: TREC disk 3 and a subdatabase of disks 1 and 2 consisting entirely of Wall Street Journal articles. The absolute values of the statistics varied quite widely, but the rank order of treatments was very similar to those shown in the tables here.

Applicability to Other Types of Database

If documents are all the same length, BM15 is the same as BM11. The fact that BM11 was so much better than BM15 must reflect the very large variation in document length in the test collection. BM15 without a document length correction is not very much better than BM1 (Table 1, rows 2 and 3). For this reason, experiments are currently under way searching relatively short, uniform documents. Clearly, statistical characteristics of different databases (e.g. abstracts, controlled and/or free indexing) will vary widely in ways which may substantially affect the performance of the weighting functions discussed here.

Relevance Feedback

No experiments have yet been conducted with any form of relevance feedback. However, all the functions used contain the Robertson/Sparck Jones weight $w^{(1)}$, which includes relevance information if it is available. Therefore in principle all the functions could be used in a relevance feedback situation (with or without query expansion). Clearly there may be interaction between the values of the ks and the use of relevance information, which would have to be investigated.

Effect of the Verbose Topic Statements

The best results reported here (e.g. row 8 of Table 4) rely on the use of BM11 with a query term frequency component from the "long" queries. Without a *qtf* component results from the long queries are not good (Table 1, bottom half). Even the "short" TREC-derived queries are very long compared with the searches entered by end-users of interactive retrieval systems. However, they are not long in comparison with user need statements elicited by human intermediaries. This suggests that it might be possible to make good use, even in an interactive system, of quite long and even rambling query statements, if users can be persuaded to enter them. We might even suggest a voice-recognition system!

Individual Queries

The statistics hide the variation over individual topics. In general, different topics did best with different functions and parameters. In many cases, though, varying a parameter brings about an improvement or deterioration which is almost uniform over the set of topics. Surprisingly, we found no very large difference between the variances of the statistics obtained from different treatments.

8 Conclusions

The approach of this paper has been that a theoretical analysis of the possible effects of a variable, within the framework of the probabilistic theory of information retrieval, can give us useful insights, which can then be embodied in very much simpler formulae. This approach has shown very considerable benefits, enabling the development of effective weighting functions based on the three variables considered (term frequency within documents and queries and document length). These functions are simple extensions of the Robertson/Sparck Jones relevance weight, and therefore fit well with some other work on the development of probabilistic models.

The approach complements a number of other current approaches. In particular, it fits somewhere in between formal modelling and pure empiricism, alongside regression-based methods, to which it seems to offer some ideas.

Acknowledgements

We are very grateful to Michael Keen, Karen Sparck Jones and Peter Willett for acting as advisors to the Okapi at TREC projects. Part of this work was undertaken with the help of grants from the British Library and ARPA.

References

1. Robertson S.E. *et al.* Okapi at TREC–2. In: [2].
2. Harman D.K. (Ed.) *The Second Text REtrieval Conference (TREC–2).* NIST Gaithersburg MD, to appear.
3. Cooper W.S. *et al.* Probabilistic retrieval in the TIPSTER collection: an application of staged logistic regression. In: Harman D.K. (Ed.) *The First Text REtrieval Conference (TREC–1).* NIST Gaithersburg MD, 1993. (pp 73–88).
4. Croft W. and Harper D. Using probabilistic models of information retrieval without relevance information. *Journal of Documentation* 1979; 35:285–295.
5. Harter S.P. A probabilistic approach to automatic keyword indexing. *Journal of the American Society for Information Science* 1975; 26:197–206 and 280–289.
6. Robertson S.E., Van Rijsbergen C.J. & Porter M.F. Probabilistic models of indexing and searching. In Oddy R.N. *et al.* (Eds.) *Information Retrieval Research* (pp.35–56). Butterworths London, 1981.
7. Cooper W.S. Inconsistencies and misnomers in probabilistic IR. In: *Proceedings of the 14th Annual International ACM SIGIR Conference on Research and Development in Information Retrieval* (pp.57-62). Chicago, 1991.
8. Robertson S.E. and Sparck Jones K. Relevance weighting of search terms. *Journal of the American Society for Information Science* 1976; 27:129–146.
9. Margulis E.L. Modelling documents with multiple Poisson distributions. *Information Processing and Management* 1993; 29:215–227.
10. Moffat A., Sacks-Davis R., Wilkinson R. & Zobel J. Retrieval of partial documents. In: Harman D.K. (Ed.) *The First Text REtrieval Conference (TREC–1).* NIST Gaithersburg MD, 1993. (pp 59–72).
11. Buckley C., Salton G. & Allan J. Automatic retrieval with locality information using SMART. In: [2].
12. Robertson S.E. Query-document symmetry and dual models. (Unpublished.)
13. Porter M.F. An algorithm for suffix stripping. *Program* 1980; 14:130–137.

The Formalism of Probability Theory in IR: A Foundation or an Encumbrance?

Wm. S. Cooper

S.L.I.S.
University of California
Berkeley CA 94720
wcooper@violet.berkeley.edu

Abstract

Probabilistic theories of retrieval bring to bear on the information search problem a high degree of theoretical coherence and deductive power. In principle, this power ought to be an invaluable asset. In practice, it has turned out to be a mixed blessing. The question considered here is whether the trappings of the probabilistic formalism strengthen or encumber IR research on balance.

Introduction

Some approaches to retrieval system design are strongly guided by theory. Others have little real theoretical underpinning but are instead more experimental and ad hoc in character. Which is preferable? Obviously, theory-guidedness is a good thing if the theory leads to promising retrieval rules to try out. Good theories have inferential power, and inferential power can help minimize empirical floundering. However, having to stay within the constraints of a strict theoretical formalism can also impose costs and penalties. The true extent of these costs is not always fully recognized.

Prominent among the theory-guided methodologies encountered in IR is the so-called 'probabilistic' approach, in which the retrieval rules are derived from the formalisms of probability theory and statistics. The probabilistic paradigm has now been around for several decades, so it does not seem out of place to attempt an assessment of whether this particular form of theory-guidedness actually pays for itself. In what follows I shall try to weigh the benefits against some of the subtler limitations of the probabilistic approach to IR.

The Probability Ranking Hypothesis

The starting point of the probabilistic approach to IR is the so-called Probability Ranking Principle (or 'PRP'). As worded in an early version [1] it reads:

> HYPOTHESIS: If a reference retrieval system's response to each request is a ranking of the documents in the collection in order of decreasing probability of usefulness to the user who submitted the request, where the probabilities are estimated as accurately as possible on the basis of whatever data is available for this purpose, then the overall effectiveness of the system to its users will be the best obtainable on the basis of that data.

This is a frankly reductionist hypothesis. It claims, in essence, that the document retrieval problem is reducible to a problem in probability estimation. According to the hypothesis there is no such thing as document retrieval theory apart from probability theory and statistics, for the retrieval problem is essentially just a particular application of probability theory.

The hypothesis itself doesn't say anything explicitly about how the probability estimation should be done. However, practitioners of the probabilistic approach to IR find it natural to think that the obvious direction in which to turn for ways of estimating probabilities is probability theory. True, there is no way of knowing ahead of time whether classical probability theory and statistics will provide the most effective estimation techniques for the IR problem, but it seems a reasonable place to start looking. This belief might be stated as a sort of 'plausible corollary' of the probability ranking hypothesis.

> PLAUSIBLE COROLLARY: The most promising source of techniques for estimating the probabilities of usefulness for output rankings in IR is standard probability theory and statistics.

It is faith in this corollary that characterizes the practising IR probabilist. Is this faith justified?

Qualifying the PRP

The case for basing a methodology of IR on the probability ranking hypothesis and its plausible corollary is weakened somewhat by several considerations of which I shall here mention only three. The PRP has been examined extensively by Robertson [2], Gordon and Lenk [3,4], and others, who point out further qualifications.

First, the PRP assumes that document usefulness is a binary property. This assumption is an oversimplification of the true problem situation, for as everyone knows, the property of interest (whether called 'usefulness', 'utility', 'relevance', or whatever) is really a matter of degree. To take degree into account, the PRP would have to be appropriately generalized within a broader theoretical framework such as utility theory. When this is done it becomes the 'Expected Utility Ranking Principle' [5], a broader principle of which the PRP is only a special case. Thus the validity of the probabilistic approach, as practised on the basis of the PRP, is compromised somewhat from the start by its restriction of attention to the special case of binary utility values. Because of this a purely probabilistic theory of retrieval can never be a completely general theory of retrieval.

Secondly, even if the simplifying assumption of binariness were accepted, the PRP would still not be universally valid. A ranking of the output documents by probability of usefulness is not always optimal, even if the probabilities are estimated with perfect accuracy, for under some conditions it is possible to do better than a probability ranking. This may be counter-intuitive but it is true. Indeed the reason why the early statement of the PRP quoted above was labeled 'HYPOTHESIS' rather than 'PRINCIPLE' is that the context in which it appeared was the construction of a counterexample showing the hypothesis to be invalid as a general principle. The counterexample in question is noted in Robertson's examination of the PRP [2]. Further counterexamples of the same sort were explored by Stirling [6] along with some nonprobabilistic retrieval algorithms that might be used for producing output orderings superior to a probability ranking.

As a practical matter, the circumstances under which one would have enough data at hand to do substantially better than a probabilistic ranking are narrowly restricted. Moreover, an alarming increase in computational complexity could be involved in trying to capture all of the potentially available increase in effectiveness (Stirling op. cit.). Perhaps partly for these reasons, most probabilistic investigators have ignored the fact that a probability ranking is sometimes suboptimal. To do so is a reasonable working policy. However, the existence of the counterexamples shows that the so-called PRP is not really a 'principle' at all, if by that term is meant a universally valid law. It is more of a design 'heuristic' -- usually close enough to the truth for practical purposes, and a helpful conceptual simplification.

Thirdly, the move from the PRP to its plausible corollary becomes less compelling when it is remembered that in the IR application it is only the *order* of the output documents that is crucial, not the retrieval status values that impose the order. True, the magnitudes of the probability estimates that serve as retrieval status values can matter if they are to be displayed for the user (more on this later), but apart from that their only function is to induce a search order in the collection. For good precision and recall they need be valid only on the ordinal level. In these circumstances it becomes thinkable that there might be homely shortcut methods that do not use the usual formalisms of standard probability theory at all, yet produce ranking rules that are as effective or almost as effective as probabilistically derived rules would be. A program of patient ad hoc trial-and-error experimentation might well hit on such a successful ranking algorithm by hunch or by chance, bypassing the need for elaborate formal theory development.

None of this is intended to suggest that the PRP is of no value or should be abandoned. The point is merely that the PRP is not as complete or absolute a foundation for IR as one could wish, and that one could reasonably question the inference from it to the 'plausible corollary' that retrieval is best treated as a standard problem in probability estimation.

Probabilistic Modeling Assumptions

The estimation procedures used in probabilistic IR are usually based on statistical simplifying assumptions or 'models' of some sort. The retrieval clues that bear on a document's probability of usefulness must somehow be combined into a single relevance probability, and modeling assumptions are needed to accomplish the combining. Typically, the assumptions adopted for the task are crude and at best only approximately true. The presence of such dubious assumptions has caused some critics to challenge the soundness of the estimation procedures and the rankings based on them.

The critics have a point. The introduction of simplifying assumptions known to be less than universally valid surely compromises to some degree the accuracy of the probability estimates that result. The important question is by how much. The extent to which the accuracy of estimate is compromised by adopting various assumptions is not yet fully known, though some exploration of the question has recently been undertaken by Gey [7], and a number of attempts to weaken the common assumptions while introducing dependency data also bear on the matter. Some probabilists find comfort in the hope that there could be considerable inaccuracy in the magnitudes of the probabilities without affecting their order much.

The presence of crude simplifying assumptions in probabilistic IR models makes it all the more thinkable that nonprobabilistic ranking rules found by ad hoc experimentation might rival the probabilistic ranking rules in effectiveness. This much seems clear. But sometimes opponents of the probabilistic approach go farther than this. They seem to imply not only that probabilistic models contain damaging simplifying assumptions, but also that other approaches do not. In this latter claim I believe they are mistaken. A more accurate assertion would be that the assumptions underlying the competing approaches are simply not fully known or articulated.

The proponents of the competing approaches might dispute this. Doubtless many would say they know perfectly well what their modeling assumptions are. Those working with the vector space IR model, for instance, might say they realize that they are assuming the orthogonality of their axes, and indeed some even go so far as to try to improve on this orthogonality assumption. Fuzzy logic enthusiasts would say they know perfectly well the rules of the fuzzy calculus they have adopted. And so on. Nevertheless I would maintain that such investigators are unable to articulate *all* of their important underlying assumptions in the same strong sense in which probabilists are able to articulate theirs.

Here is the sense in which careful probabilistic investigators are able set forth their assumptions. Their starting point is the PRP, an assumption that (though in need of qualification as we have seen) is at least clearly understood and has been intensively studied. The special independence or other statistical modeling assumptions introduced to compute the probability estimates called for by the PRP can also be stated clearly. If regression or other standard statistical techniques are involved in the estimation method, their underlying assumptions can be found in statistical reference works. Thus the computation of the probability estimates proceeds via an unbroken line of deductions whose premises are made clear at every step.

This cannot generally be said for competing methods. Though their practitioners usually accept the PRP in principle, they make no attempt to lay out the assumptions by which the probability estimates it calls for are reached. The simple reason for this is that no probability estimates per se are calculated. Rather, what is computed for each document is a 'retrieval coefficient', 'similarity measure', or 'retrieval status value', and the precise relationship of that value to the probability of usefulness is left unexamined. There is an inarticulate leap from the theoretical model to the assumption that the output ranking is what one wants. The PRP doesn't connect up with anything.

The benefit of being able to articulate one's assumptions is tangible. When the underlying theoretical postulates are known and clearly stated, their plausibility can be subjected to analysis. In some cases it may be found possible to weaken them in an attempt to increase retrieval effectiveness, as has been done for instance to allow the introduction of dependency data. Or strengthen them to simplify the computations needed for the output rankings. Other improvements may also suggest themselves when the assumptions in the deductive chain are clear. Such control over each step in the theory is deeply appealing to the theoretically minded. For some, it makes IR into something approaching a genuine subscience of the science of information [8].

Of course, advocates of nonprobabilistic methods feel differently. They regard the formulation of exact statistical assumptions as an unnecessary theoretical burden on the researcher. They maintain (with some plausibility) that the time and effort spent on such analysis would be better spent on ad hoc experimentation using formalisms looser and friendlier than probability theory. So it would seem that the completeness of statement achievable in a probabilistic theory of IR is a benefit, but a benefit that comes at a price that not all are willing to pay.

Misleading Model Descriptions

I have suggested that the clear statement of modeling assumptions made possible by a probabilistic foundation is an asset. As a cautionary note it should be added, however, that it is easy for a probabilist to state his assumptions wrongly. Indeed, of the probabilistic developments of IR whose foundational assumptions are stated precisely, many or most present assumptions that are seriously flawed in some way -- that conflict either with logic or with how the model is actually applied. I shall not attempt to defend this statement here, but refer the reader to another paper on the subject [9].

The tendency has been to state assumptions that are stronger than the assumptions actually used. Assumptions that are too strong may permit the required deductions and ranking computations to be made, but they mischaracterize the theory for which they are the alleged foundation. For purposes of understanding the character of the model, this thoroughly muddies the waters. For instance, if the stated assumptions are implausible, one is misled into thinking that the model is itself implausible, when actually the model as applied in practice is founded on other, more plausible, implicit assumptions. Such misleading model statements should be weakened to the point where the required probability estimates can still be calculated, but the assumptions needed to produce them are not overstated. (The so-called 'binary independence model' is a case in point. Its assumptions as usually presented in the form of two separate conditional independence assumptions are stronger than is needed to perform the work that the model is required to do. This defect can be repaired by weakening the stated assumptions (c.f. [9]).)

In some cases modeling assumptions have been set forth that are so strong as to lead to logical inconsistencies. That is, the assumptions, when applied to actual data, give rise to anomalies symptomatic of logical self-contradiction. Now, in respectable theories, logical inconsistencies are supposed never to occur. If a logical inconsistency is discovered in a scientific theory, what is supposed to happen is that either the theory is discarded or vigorous efforts are made to expunge the inconsistency and so save the theory. It is perhaps surprising, then, that logical inconsistencies that were identified as such as early as 1974 [10] have continued to be tolerated in probabilistic IR.

Some apologists for the models in question have been inclined to excuse the inconsistencies on the grounds that they are mere 'data inconsistencies' -- i.e. they manifest themselves only when the assumptions are applied to actual observational data. In my own view, this defense is weak and does not hold up under close methodological scrutiny. An inconsistency is an inconsistency. When contradictions can be reached by applying a model to the very data to which it was designed to be applied, when out-of-range probabilities are generated for some documents in defiance of the axioms of probability theory, when an infinity of bogus answers can be deduced for the same problem, something is wrong, and the fact that actual data was involved does not set it right. The suspicion of something wrong is vindicated when one reexamines the assumptions, discovers them to be stronger than necessary, weakens them appropriately, and finds that the troubling phenomena associated with logical self-contradiction no longer occur.

The history of misidentification of modeling assumptions in probabilistic IR suggests that the logical hazards involved in setting up sound probabilistic models are greater than might have been expected. The analysis needed to get the model right is yet another burden on the probabilist -- another occasion for wondering if the effort might not be better spent in ad hoc experimentation. On the brighter side, an optimistic probabilist might hope that the worst logical problems have by now been straightened out, and that from now on it will be relatively clear sailing. Time will tell if the optimism is justified.

Displaying the Probability Estimates

Probabilistic methodologies rank documents by estimated probability of usefulness, or by quantities easily transformable into such estimates. This raises the possibility of displaying for the user retrieval status values that can be interpreted directly as probability-of-usefulness estimates. Displaying probability estimates would seem a more friendly way to treat one's users than to show them cosines values, Jaccard coefficients, Dice coefficients, fuzzy logic values, or other similarity indicators that the casual searcher has little chance of understanding. This ease of interpretation of ranking coefficients might be counted as another potential advantage of the probabilistic approach. (We say 'potential' because it has so far been achieved only crudely [11].)

Under some conditions nonprobabilistic retrieval status values can be transformed into crude probability estimates for display purposes. This can be done by performing a logistic regression on the status values to get an equation for changing them into probability estimates just before they are displayed. At Berkeley we have tried this out on cosine values with reasonable success. Apparently then, one doesn't necessarily have to adopt a fundamentally probabilistic approach in order to enjoy the superficial advantage of having status values that are interpretable as probabilities. However, probabilistic methods are potentially capable of producing the desired probability values directly as an integral part of the ranking method.

Experimental Findings

An impressive number of retrieval experiments have been carried out over the last three decades in an attempt to see what sorts of retrieval rules are most effective. Though the number designed to test out genuinely probabilistic ranking algorithms is small, still they provide some preliminary impressions of the power of the probabilistic approach vis-a-vis other looser methods. Of course, any tentative conclusions reached must be tempered by whatever doubts one harbors about the reliability and sensitivity of retrieval experiments in general, concerning which there is no lack of grounds for skepticism.

As a preliminary remark it may be noted that probabilistic methods generally bring with them some experimental efficiencies. Usually, less experimentation has to be done to optimize a probabilistic retrieval rule than a nonprobabilistic one. Indeed this is a major reason for adopting a probabilistic approach in the first place: one hopes to discover through theoretical analysis what would otherwise have to be wrung from the data by empirical exploration. Some probabilistic rules -- especially those derived theoretically as ways of exploiting relevance feedback -- require little or no experimental optimization because the theory leads to just one rule. About all there is to do experimentally is to check this rule out as it comes off the drawing board to see how well it performs. Other probabilistic retrieval equations -- for instance those obtained by applying logistic regression to a learning set -- contain fitted parameters that must be determined experimentally. Even here, though, the experimentation is efficient. For a given set of variables, a regression analysis yields all of the coefficients needed for the retrieval rule in one run of a standard statistical regression program. This contrasts favorably with the many test runs needed to make several numeric parameters converge on optimal values under traditional methods of IR experimentation.

Still, what matters most is not experimental convenience but end results. So far as I am aware, there is as yet no compelling experimental evidence indicating that currently known probabilistic methods result in significantly more effective retrieval than do competing approaches. The experiments offering the most meaningful comparisons are probably those conducted under the auspices of the recent TREC conferences [12, 13]. Under the TREC methodology, which uses traditional precision and recall figures averaged in various ways as the principal measures of effectiveness, the top few algorithms have included both probabilistically and nonprobabilistically based systems. Comparisons between these are made problematic by differences among the entries that have little to do with the probabilistic/nonprobabilistic distinction, as well as by the ongoing nature of the TREC conferences. Yet it seems fair to conclude that, while the performance of the probabilistic systems has been very respectable, it has by no means proved itself consistently superior to other methods.

A probabilist might protest that, while probabilistic means have yet to be proved superior, they have not yet been proved inferior either. Furthermore, time may be working in favor of the probabilistic approach. The argument in support of this hope is that most current probabilistic models are still fairly crude. As they become more and more refined, it may become harder and harder to find rules of comparable retrieval power using loose empirical methods.

Conclusions

The inferential power of probabilistic modeling techniques makes possible an unbroken deductive chain extending from the probability ranking heuristic all the way to the output ranking produced in response to a user's request. This logical control is impressive and ought, in principle, to be redeemable as retrieval power. To an extent, this has already been accomplished. What I have tried to suggest here, however, is that inferential power has a price. The deductive chain has some weak links. Moreover, the cost of creating and trouble-shooting probabilistic IR theories is high.

In such circumstances the question inevitably arises: Might not the effort spent on the theoretical endeavor of stating a sound probabilistic theory be better spent on looser means of rule-discovery -- methods that make fewer theoretical demands and rely more on exploratory experimentation? Probably it is beyond mortal ability to answer this question at this moment in the history of IR, but what is presently happening is just what should be happening: both probabilistic and nonprobabilistic avenues of research are being capably pursued. Time will tell whether the theoretical baggage that accompanies the probabilistic method is more a benefit or an encumbrance.

References

1. Cooper WS. The inadequacy of probability of usefulness as a ranking criterion for retrieval system output. Xeroxed, School of Library and Information Studies, University of California, Berkeley, CA 94720, 1971

2. Robertson SE. The probability ranking principle in IR. Journal of Documentation 1977; 33:294-304

3. Gordon MD, Lenk P. When is the probability ranking principle suboptimal? Journal of the American Society for Information Science 1992; 43:1-14

4. Gordon MD, Lenk P. A utility theoretic examination of the probability ranking principle in information retrieval. Journal of the American Society for Information Science 1991; 42:703-714

5. Cooper WS, Maron M. Foundations of probabilistic and utility-theoretic indexing. Journal of the Association for Computing Machinery 1978; 25:67-80

6. Stirling KH. The effect of document ranking on retrieval system performance: a search for an optimal ranking rule. PhD thesis, University of California, Berkeley, 1977 (Published as ERIC document IR 004 997, RIE Nov. 1977)

7. Gey FC. Probabilistic dependence and logistic inference in information retrieval. PhD thesis, University of California, Berkeley, 1993

8. Losee RM. The science of information: measurement and applications. Academic Press, San Diego, 1990.

9. Cooper WS. Some inconsistencies and misidentified modeling assumptions in probabilistic information retrieval. ACM Transactions on Information Systems 1994 (in press)

10. Robertson, S. E. Specificity and weighted retrieval. Journal of Documentation 1974; 30:41-46

11. Cooper WS, Chen A, Gey FC. Full text retrieval based on probabilistic equations with coefficients fitted by logistic regression. In: The Second Text Retrieval Conference (TREC-2), DK Harmon (ed). NIST, Washington DC, 1994 (in press)

12. Harman DK (ed.). The First Text Retrieval Conference (TREC-1). NIST, Washington DC, 1993

13. Harman DK (ed.). The Second Text Retrieval Conference (TREC-2). NIST, Washington DC, 1994 (in press)

Interfaces

LyberWorld – A Visualization User Interface Supporting Fulltext Retrieval

Matthias Hemmje, Clemens Kunkel, Alexander Willett
German National Research Center for Computer Science (GMD)
Integrated Publication and Information Systems Institute (IPSI)
Dolivostr. 15, D-64293 Darmstadt, FRG
e-mail: [hemmje, kunkel, willett]@darmstadt.gmd.de

Abstract

LyberWorld is a prototype IR user interface. It implements visualizations of an abstract information space – fulltext. The paper derives a model for such visualizations and an exemplar user interface design is implemented for the probabilistic fulltext retrieval system INQUERY. Visualizations are used to communicate information search and browsing activities in a natural way by applying metaphors of spatial navigation in abstract information spaces. Visualization tools for exploring information spaces and judging relevance of information items are introduced and an example session demonstrates the prototype. The presence of a spatial model in the user's mind and interaction with a system's corresponding display methods is regarded as an essential contribution towards natural interaction and reduction of cognitive costs during e.g. query construction, orientation within the database content, relevance judgement and orientation within the retrieval context.

1 Introduction and Motivation

Graphical user interfaces are nowadays state of the art within modern information retrieval computer systems. The basic metaphors for such interfaces are in most cases desktop or others derived from real world objects (e.g. library [1]). Besides these, several visualization methods for abstract information structures have been developed (e.g. [2]). However, many text retrieval user interface components like query construction and result presentation are still form- or command-based. Looking at work in the area of Scientific Visualization, highly interactive graphical user interfaces (e.g. [3]) enable users to tailor graphical information presentations, called "visualizations", to their needs and achieve insights about the information carried by sets of plain numerical data. These insights (see [4]), would be often a lot more costly, if they were achieved without visualizations.

The information retrieval process is a good example for an information search activity also executed within very large *but abstract* information spaces. While "digging for information" with the help of a computer, users have to perceive a lot of cross references between data items to achieve insights (see e.g. [5]), i.e., to perceive hidden information carried by the relations between complex and often heterogeneous data structures. Therefore it is reasonable to enable IR users to acquire abstract information similarly as Scientific Visualization allows it for numerical data. Information retrieval user interface designs published most recently head into a similar direction. The term "Information Visualization", describing a new medium for visual communication of abstract information in a human-computer information process, has been created. Different perspectives on data sets and correlations of different data dimensions into one display perspective (see e.g. [6]) are provided. Visualization components supporting the demands of a highly interactive information process (with respect to user behaviors and UI functions, see [7], [8]) are currently under research and development (e.g. [9], [10], [11] and [12]). Such visualization work was restricted to 2 or 2 1/2D graphics for a long time because graphics systems available could not cope with more dimensions. This has now changed very significantly. High-end computer systems and software tools of the most recent past provide the necessary performance to visualize real-time animated 3D scenes in reasonable qualities (e.g. [13] based on [14]). Manufacturers have committed to supply low-cost workstations with today's high end performance measures within the next two years. For such reasons designing visualizations on 3D graphics workstations offering the highest degree of freedom to visually communicate information is strongly demanded. We will outline where our work has taken advantage of such advanced graphical abilities.

IR research (see [15]) has furthermore realized that many IR user interfaces are suffering from problems concerned with the user's perception and understanding of the information dialog between user and system. The user can neither understand how the system's information offers were initiated nor can he estimate if his information requests can be satisfied by the database content. He is unable to judge the relevance of a result in accordance to his query *with a low cognitive effort* . The metaphors of spatial navigation and attraction provided in the LyberWorld prototype aim at reducing such problems. LyberWorld is the second prototype in a series of works carried out at GMD-IPSI (see also [16], [11] and [17]) aiming at 3D-visual IR user interfaces . It concentrates on visualizations of an abstract information space – fulltext. The paper describes how a model for such visualizations is derived and a design is applied within a user interface for the probabilistic fulltext retrieval system INQUERY [18]. Spatial visualization is used to communicate information search and browsing activities in a natural way by applying metaphors of a spatial navigation and attraction to abstract information spaces. Complementary visualization tools for information activities like exploring information spaces and judging relevance of information items in these spaces are introduced and an example session demonstrates the prototype. The result strengthens the working hypotheses: Visualizing database contents with spatial properties and communicating IR by means of spatial navigation metaphors supports users in developing a mental model of the db content as a "space" and the retrieval activities executed by themselves and the system's retrieval engine as navigations in this space and manipulation of its objects. We regard the presence of a spatial model in the user's mind and a system using corresponding display methods as an essential contribution towards natural interaction and reduction of cognitive costs during e.g. query construction, orientation within the content space, relevance feedback and orientation within the retrieval context. The paper will finally draw conclusions and outline further extensions and work plans evaluating the above hypotheses during our future work.

2 What has to be Visualized? – Modelling a Spatial Information Navigation

Beginning to think in spatial concepts ... Before designing an IR process as a spatial navigation, an underlying conceptual model becomes necessary. The general information sets occurring in a computer-supported information process as well as spatial interpretations of relations between them have to be determined. Concepts like the *content* of the database, the *interest* of the user, the *context* of a retrieval session and the *result* of the current dialog are outlined in the following. *Paths* and *distances* which describe navigations in spatial representations of such information sets, then regarded as "spaces", have to be specified as well as *views* achieved from different *points of view* in such *information spaces*. Before outlining appropriate representations for information spaces, we will informally introduce each of the mentioned concepts by describing spatial navigation as an information behavior in the mentioned information sets.

The database's *content space* contains all information stored in the database. The *context space* of a session is created during navigations within the content space. It contains the information the user has *explored* during his session's history. The user explores the content space by moving his *view* into areas of the content space which have not been part of the context space before, i.e. he increases the size of the context space. The "course" the user's view is moved along within the content space is regarded as a *content-oriented search path*. It consists of a sequence of *paths* between different *information items* in the content space. A path *length* (the distance between the connected items) correlates the relevance of information items with each other. The *interest space* of the user contains all information relevant to satisfy his information need. Parts of it may be contained in the content space of the database, others not. In the following, we regard the content space as static during a session, although it is necessary to later cover dynamic content spaces too (routing tasks etc.). The *result space*, i.e., the already explored part of the interest space, consists of the context space partition *relevant* to the user's interest. To satisfy his information need, the user explores the content space until he is convinced that he has covered a sufficient result space. As result spaces created by today's systems information capacities might become very big, the *kernel* of the result space is regarded as a smaller most relevant partition of the result space. To isolate it from the result space is regarded as one of the main aims of the user's navigational information behavior.

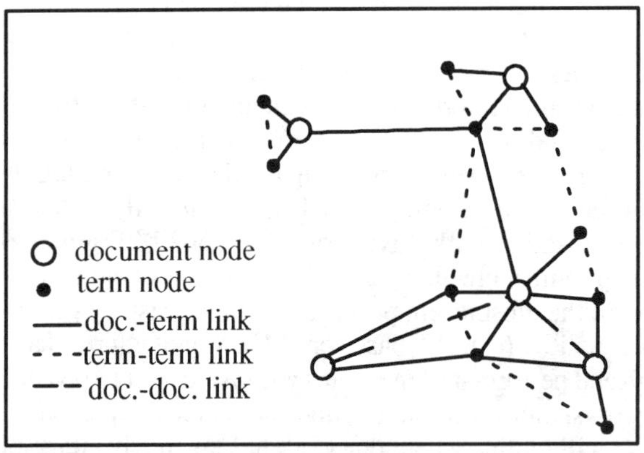

Figure 1: Document network [19]

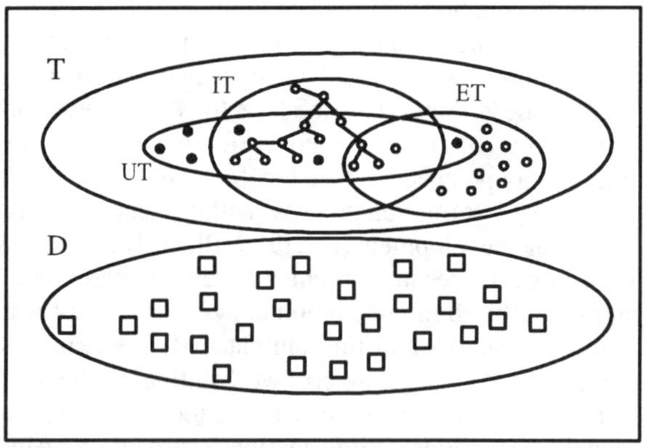

Figure 2: Two level abstraction [8]

Thinking spatially is not new, ... The above described information spaces can be represented by several kinds of data models. Useful network representations have been introduced by [19] and [8]. They are displayed in the figures 1 and 2. Such networks of terms and documents with two levels of abstraction for the content space (document and term level), and therefore with at least "document-term" relations, have been defined to establish a formal base for either retrieval tasks or user interface designs.

The integration of information and meta-information in a retrieval network is common to both approaches and helps on the one hand, the retrieval engine introduced in [18], and on the other hand the design of intelligent user interface components introduced in [20], to become more effective. Besides the mentioned probabilistic network model and the two level network representation, knowledge-based networks (e.g. [21]) and vector-based approaches ([22], [23]) have been introduced. All mentioned models could generally be considered as having "spatial" properties but they were not explicitly visualized by the resulting system's user interfaces. Although multidimensional vector space representations might appear as the most appropriate representation to be spatially visualized, we have decided to use the network representation to model relations between points in an information space. Networks can be regarded as a projection of a multidimensional vector space into a lower dimensional representation allowing a mapping onto visualizations with a maximum of three positional display dimensions. In the following we will derive visualizations revealing the metaphorical properties which a spatially interpreted network representation for information spaces can have if they are visualized at the user interface level.

... but how about interacting the way we think? The information process communicated between user and system is a sequence of interactions. As outlined above, these activities will be regarded as navigations of the user in the content space. Each step can be subject to different kinds of such navigational activities. Either the system may e.g., reveal a new view on the content space after the user has requested it, or relevance feedback becomes necessary to decide which part of the explored context space belongs to the result space. The user will request further views if he believes, that he has not explored his interest space to a satisfying amount by the current context space and similar iterations may follow. In the following, we will outline how these activities are interpreted on the representation that was chosen for the underlying retrieval system – a network.

In a fulltext retrieval application the content space contains the information that all text documents of the database deal with. If the user navigates in the content space to view information, he has to navigate in a set of documents. This set is represented by a subset of the network of [19] (see figures 1 and 3). Documents (information) may be related to each other through terms (meta-information), because they deal with information represented by identical terms within their textual content. This means that the descriptive medium to communicate navigational paths in fulltext are terms and documents. Therefore, a sequence of related terms and documents specifies a *content-oriented path* (termed *path* in the following).

We formalize the interpretations to achieve a description that is more precise. Term and document nodes within the content-space network do exist within the database and can therefore be regarded as *information items (potential points of view)* in the content space. If d is a document existing in the database and T_d is the set of terms $(t_1, t_2, t_3 \dots t_m)$ used to code the information within d, one can define T_d as the set of (meta) information items in the *view* when looking from a point d in the content space network: $view\ (d) = (t_1, t_2, t_3 \dots t_n) = T_d$ (example (see figure 3): $view\ (A) = (l,m,o))$. If t is a term existing in the database and D_t is the set of documents $(d_1, d_2, d_3 \dots d_m)$ in which t is used to represent parts of its informational content, one can define D_t as the set of information items in the *view* when looking from a point t in the content space network: $view\ (t) = (d_1, d_2, d_3 \dots d_n) = D_t$ (example (see figure 4): $view\ (o) = (A,B,C) = D_o)$. For a term t and a document d existing in the database may hold: $paths\ (t) = (t,\ view(t))$ and $paths(d) = (d,\ view(t))$. Analogously we can define a *content-oriented search path* (termed *search path* in the following) as a sequence of paths. If u is a user searching for information in the period (s,e) by performing a navigation S_u through the content space network along the nodes $(t_s, d_{s+1}, t_{s+2}, d_{s+3}, \dots t_{e-1}, d_e)$ one can define S_u as the *search path* of u: $search\ path\ (u, s, e) = (t_s, d_{s+1}, t_{s+2}, d_{s+3}, \dots t_{e-1}, d_e) = S_u$ (example (see figure 4): $search\ path\ (u,0,3) = (A,o,C) = S_u)$. If r is the numerical relevance value of a term t for a document d, the *distance* between t and d in the content-space network equals r and is called *length* of the path (t,d): $length(t,d) = length(d,t) = distance\ (t,d) = distance(d,t) = r$. If the user follows a search path, the union of all views along the path defines a context space.

The above described concepts are the starting point for an example design of tools visualizing the content network. Extending the approach to networks with several types of paths (e.g. multimedia or terminological links etc.) does not affect the generality of the design ideas described in the following.

3 What Does a Spatial Visualization Look Like? Design of Exemplar Tools

Which activities have to be supported? During an interactive information process, interpreted as a spatial search, the user has to execute at least two types of activities. The first is related to his *navigation task* during the search. It is necessary to *move*, i.e. to change position in the content space and *explore* information visible from each point of view. It is important to achieve an *orientation*, i.e. to determine the relation between a *current point of view* (e.g. from an information item) and the whole of an information space. The second category of activities is related to the *information task* that has to be executed during the search. The user has to *judge relevance* for information items in an information space partition. He has to cluster information items within an information space partition if they are similarly relevant and he has to be able to determine the *degree of exploration* of an information space to, e.g., decide if it makes sense to continue the search. Furthermore, the user needs a method to *inspect* information items in detail. In the following we will introduce exemplar visualization tools each of which support the user in some of the described activities.

NavigationCones – Context, Orientation, Exploration and History: Visualizing the development of the retrieval dialog and the extent to which the database has been searched is a basic constraint for the design of the first visualization tool, the so-called *NavigationCones*. It enables users to execute navigations in the content space along content oriented search paths. Therefore the context space explored by such search paths will be visualized.

When displaying the content network (see figure 4) directly as a graph layout by mapping it to the 3 dimensions of the Cartesian Space, a complex layout problem appears (with respect to positioning and clustering of nodes as well as avoiding the crossing of links). Solving it becomes very costly for both interaction partners, because the system has to apply costly layout algorithms (with respect to computational effort) and the user has to invest a high cognitive effort to perceive the content of the system's complex graph layout. A more efficient solution for the display of complex structures was introduced recently: *Cone Trees*. Cone Trees are horizontal or vertical three dimensional trees. Each layer of nodes is drawn below or beside the first, with their children in cones. While Robertson et al. ([24]) developed Cone Trees for a different application domain to visualize *hierarchical* information, our application of Cone Trees is different. NavigationCones transform a *non hierarchical* content network into a hierarchical Cone Tree to improve perception of complex and abstract information spaces in a text retrieval application. Cone Trees maximize the effective use of screen space and their perception by the user is cognitively more efficient, especially in combination with interactive animation (see [24]). When applying Cone Tree display methods, the above-mentioned crossing problem for the layout of links in a complex network is substituted by the optimization problem for the radii of the cone tree's circular node levels. Solutions for this problem can be calculated with low computational effort (compared to the above-mentioned network layout problem). For these reasons, the LyberWorld prototype visualizes the explored parts of the content network by using cone tree display techniques in combination with interactive animation. As the content network does not implicitly provide hierarchical properties, a mapping from the content network graph to hierarchical tree structures becomes necessary. Figure 5 displays a transformation of the network from figure 4 into a tree as it is generated when starting with document A.

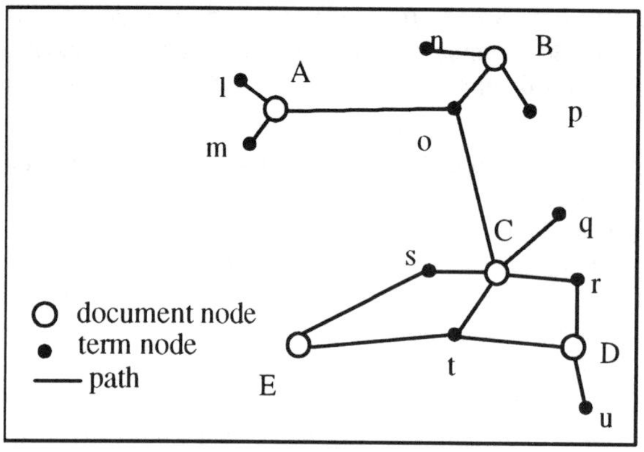

Figure 3: Content space network

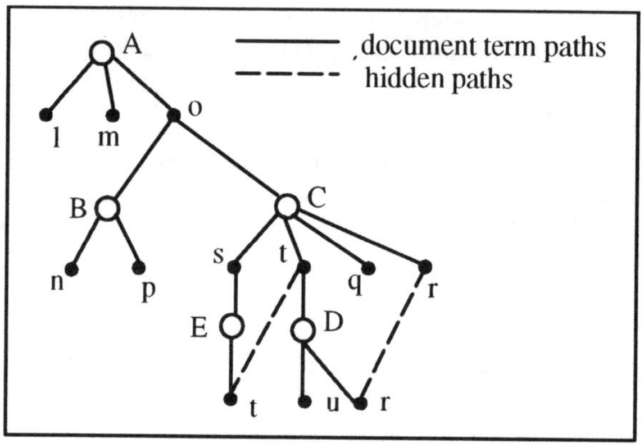

Figure 4: Tree reproducing the network

The displayed 2D-tree's topological structure is the same as the one of a corresponding NavigationCone. Every node of the tree is associated to either a term or a document node of the content network and the tree's paths correspond to the network's paths. The child nodes of a node are defined by the members of the parent nodes' view. From level to level, the tree can now be unfolded from each of its leafs according to the structure of the network. To be able to represent *all* paths of the network in the tree structure, some nodes have to be duplicated. As the consistency of the spatial metaphor (objects usually can only have one position in a physical space) has to be preserved, such multiple occurrences of identical nodes (e.g. figure 4, terms t and r) become connected by auxiliary links, so called *hidden paths*.

Interacting with NavigationCones: The above-described transformation covers the context space of a session. It is controlled by the user's navigations on paths which have not been explored before. NavigationCones implement navigations by unfolding alternating tree levels of term and document views. The different view dimensions (documents/terms) of each tree level are color coded. The so called *current view* of the NavigationCones is the tree level that is actually visited. The information items displayed on each level bear text labels displaying the term string or the document title. The order in which information items appear on a level is defined by their relevance distance towards their parent item. These relevance values are provided by INQUERY's ranking mechanisms (see [25]).

One node within the current view is the *current point of view*. It is always the one at the front, closest to the user. The current view and its point of view can be recognized by their high-lighted appearance (i.e., color coding). If the user selects a different item within the NavigationCones to be the new point of view, an animation rotates it to the front. From the selected item, the user can request the system to unfold the corresponding view by displaying all paths starting from the selected node in a new view's subtree. A NavigationCones' structure can also be reduced, if the user decides, that a viewed area is not of interest. The user is free to move between existing view levels to reach already explored regions. Nodes containing a hidden path appear differently from other items (color and shape coding). Before the view of an item with a hidden path is unfolded, an animation moves the user to the original position of the view's parent item. Visualizing hidden paths can prevent users from trying to explore a view that was already visited (search loops) or encourage them to visit it again with a different perspective/search goal. When the NavigationCones' topological structure is manipulated by unfolding or reducing, the radii of all view levels are optimized to avoid collisions.

By this means, new parts of the content network become visualized by the NavigationCones step by step, i.e. they contain more and more of the content space. Automatically creating NavigationCones that cover the whole content network at once is neither easy, because content-oriented search paths reproducing the whole content network have to be calculated, nor does it make sense, because the user could not perceive and remember the NavigationCone's structure as well as one unfolded by his own navigations.

RelevanceSpheres – Relevance Feedback and Document Clustering: To support relevance judgement, a tool that visualizes the context space and the distance between its items becomes necessary. It enables the user to identify the result space and its kernel residing in the context space. In [26], Olson et al. introduced such a tool which was implemented in the VIBE system. Apart from VIBE's intuitive visualization method, figure 5 displays a well known weakness of VIBE's layout algorithm. The term nodes A,B,C and D are applying an attraction to the relevant documents a, b, c and d. The position of each document symbol encodes the sum of all attractions, i.e. the relevance of the document towards each term of the query. As outlined in [15], it is not always clear which term's attraction is responsible for the position of a document (in figure 5: are the documents a, b relevant for the terms A&C or for A&B&C?). VIBE overcomes this problem by enabling the user to change term node positions, i.e. their distance from the center and therefore the shape of the displayed polygon itself; the layout algorithm is again applied and the new document positions are displayed. By the resulting position changes of the document symbols, the responsible attraction sources can be recognized. However, the deliberate shape of the polygon causes a perception problem for the user. The overall numerical proportions between displayed path lengths, i.e. relevance values, are not constant between differently shaped polygons.

The *RelevanceSphere* introduces a new and more appropriate visualization tool improving the situation with respect to the above described problems. It transforms the content network into a spatial visualization displaying path lengths while *preserving the numerical proportions* between themselves. Therefore path lengths of the context space are kept comparable at a glance. Taking VIBE as a starting point for deriving an appropriate visualization, each content network can be transformed into a graph with a *circular* instead of a polygonal shape. The circle radius is defined by the range of possible path lengths. Figure 6 displays a transformation of the network from figure 3 into such a graph.

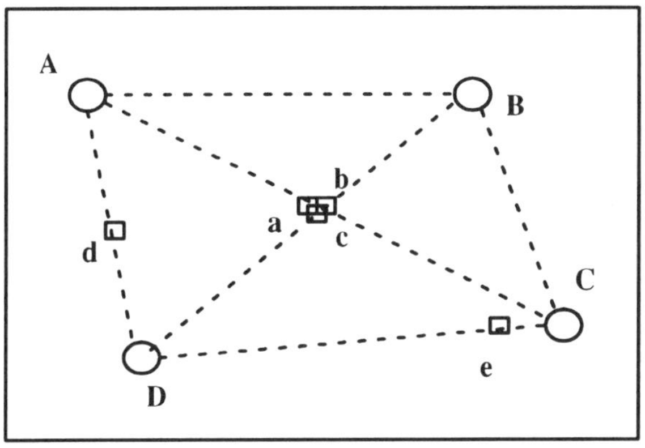

Figure 5: An unclear VIBE visualization

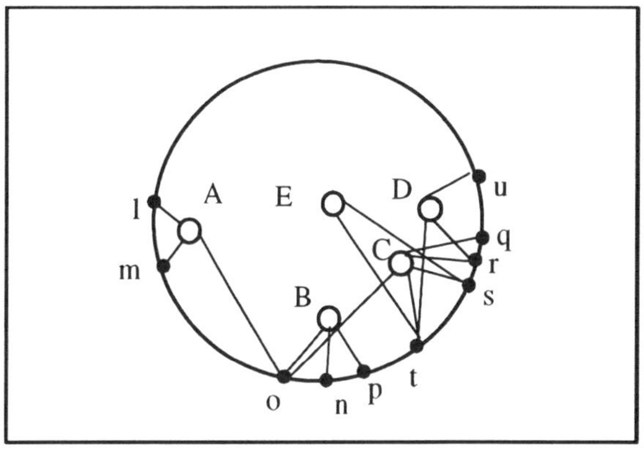

Figure 6: Circular graph

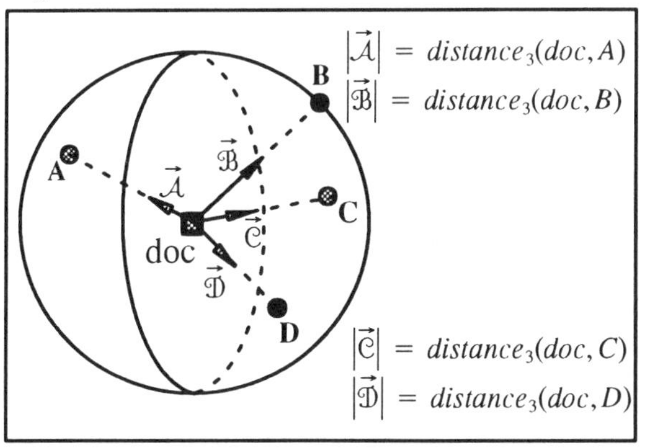

Figure 7: Attraction vectors of a documents paths

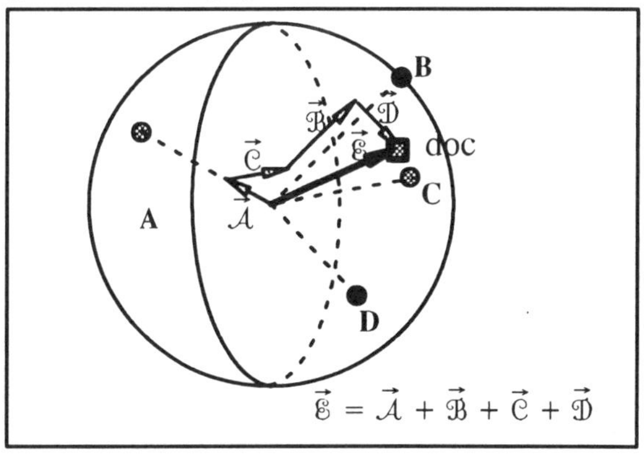

Figure 8: Document positioning along a search path

All term nodes are positioned in a circle while all paths (note that the relative lengths of the paths remains unchanged) are pointing towards the *inside* of the circle. The document nodes are positioned at the end of the appropriate paths in the inside of the circle. The relevance of the documents is now coded to its position within the circle (similar to VIBE). The closer a document is positioned to the boarder of the circle, the more relevant it is in the whole query context; the closer it is positioned to a term's position, the more relevant it is with regard to this term. However, besides preserving the relevance proportions, the scene displayed in figure 6 allows still several interpretations. Which term nodes are responsible for document position B? Terms o and p or term n? An additional degree of spatial freedom is now introduced to reduce the probability of such unclear display situations. Interactive animation provides the user a means of clearing them, i.e., the document nodes are positioned into a sphere's volume and a manipulation function for the term node's attraction factors applied along their path vectors is provided to the user.

Figure 7 displays the attraction vectors defined between a document and its paths while Figure 8 displays the generation of a document's position in the sphere with respect to the whole search path's vectors and the sphere's center as anchor point. As figure 8 outlines, the length of the attraction vectors corresponds to the length of the associated path in the content network.

The calculation applied for the displayed function $distance_3$ can be formalized as:

$distance_3\ (d,t) =$

*length(d,t) * scaling * attraction(t) *density* with *scaling = 1 / max. length of all paths in context space.*

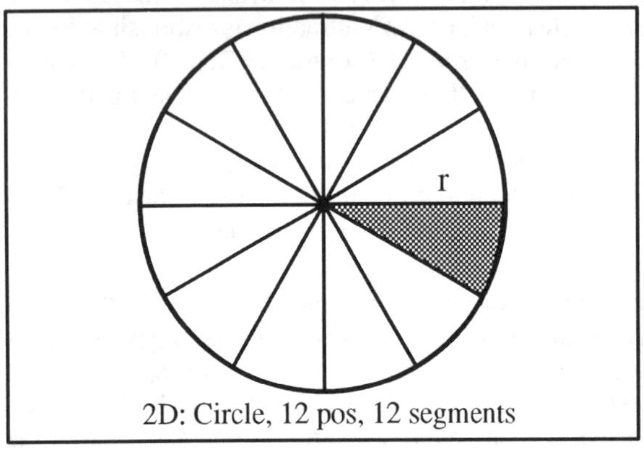

2D: Circle, 12 pos, 12 segments

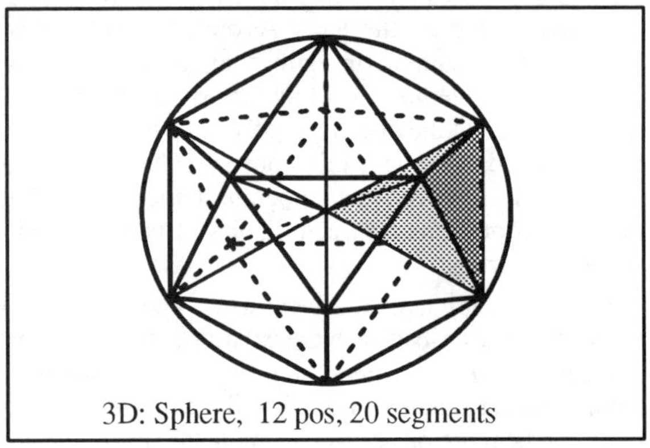

3D: Sphere, 12 pos, 20 segments

Figure 9: Segmentation in 2D

Figure 10: Segmentation in 3D

The functionality of the *density* and *attraction* factors is described later. Situations with unclear interpretation might occur in the now introduced sphere visualization too, but they are *less probable*, because position coding in the sphere has achieved a higher degree of freedom. Figures 9 and 10 display examples: segmentation of a circular 2D and 3D object under similar conditions with respect to number *npos* of node positions on the surface and radius *r*).

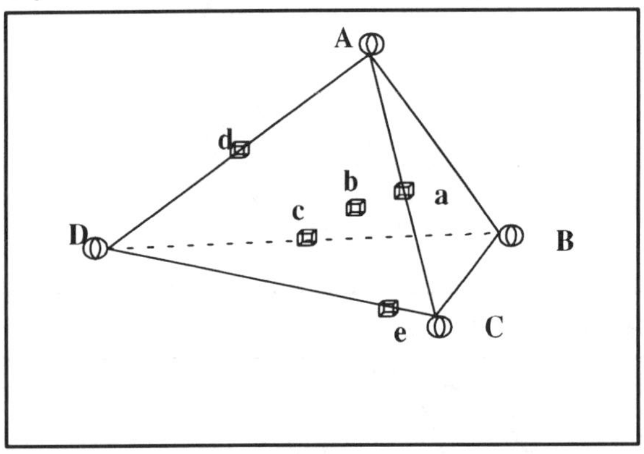

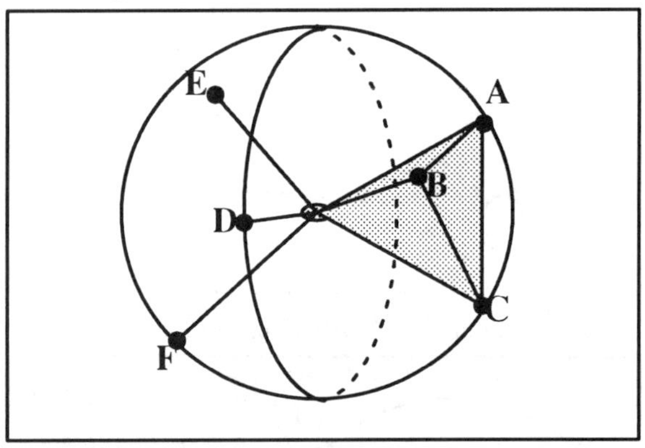

Figure 11: A RelevanceSphere example display situation

Figure 12: Interactive segmentation and clustering

To be more precise, one can formalize: Given a minimum distance of *e* between two points on the surface, the number *2Dnpos* of node positions on the surface of a circle with radius *r* is calculated by: $Dnpos(r,e)= 2*pi*r/e$. Given a minimum distance of *e* between two points on the surface, the number *3Dnpos* of node positions on the surface of a sphere with radius *r* is given by: $3Dnpos(r,e)=(4*pi*r^2)/(pi*e^2)=4r^2/e^2 \cdot 4r^2/e^2 > 2*pi*r/e$, $e<<r$. *q.e.d!* This elaborates that the sphere surface supplies a higher degree of positional freedom for terms than the boarder of the circle. For potential document positions in the inner of the compared objects a similar calculation on the basis of the circle area and the sphere volume can be done. Its result implies that the sphere provides also a higher degree of freedom for segmentation, i.e. positioning of documents. Therefore,the probability of display situations with unclear interpretations is reduced. Figure 11 displays a RelevanceSphere's solution for the situation already displayed in figure 5. The interpretation of the scene with respect to documents a, b and c has now become clear: Document *a* is attracted by term *A* and *C*, document *b* by all four terms and document *c* by term *B* and *D*.

The RelevanceSphere also supports interactive clustering of documents by manipulation of term positions. Figure 12 displays an example term distribution. Documents attracted into the highlighted segment of the sphere volume satisfy the boolean query predicate *(A & B & C)*. However, two problem situations, outlined in the following, remain. These problems indicate that a term positioning functionality on its own is not always flexible enough to achieve expressive displays. The first problem is related to the additional degree of freedom and the user's depth perception of 3D scenes displayed as projections on 2D screens without stereoscopic display equipment: Is, e.g., document b in figure 11 really positioned in the center of the 3D scene? Enabling interactive rotation of RelevanceSpheres as a whole provides the answer. Figure 13 displays the second problem. A cluster of documents with positions very close to the sphere's center is displayed. This situation has occurred because the displayed distance values are high, i.e. the relevance of the cluster is low compared to the most relevant document *x* defining the sphere radius.

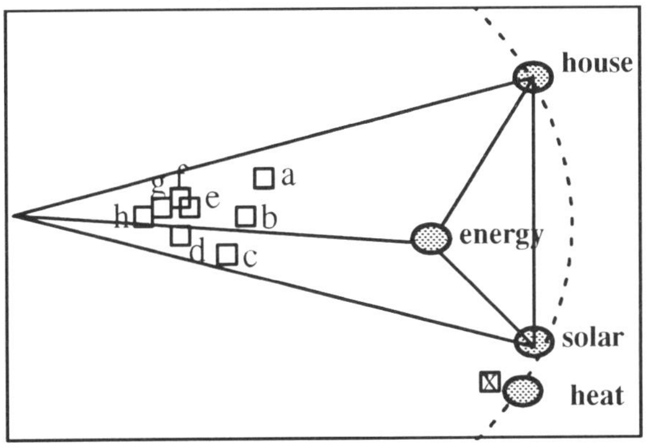

Figure 13: Display situation with high density cluster

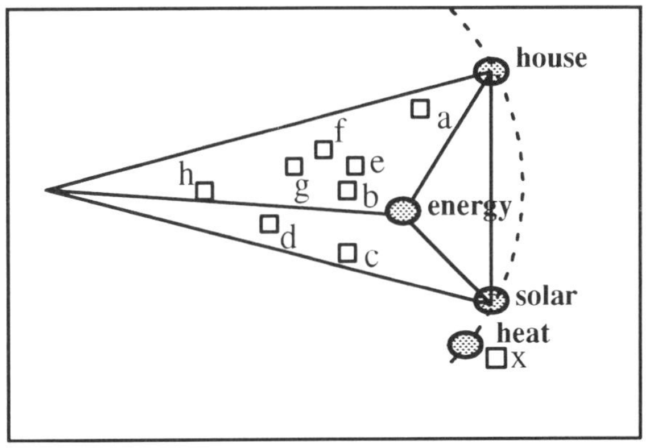

Figure 14: After decreasing the document density

To solve such problems further interactive functionalities are added to the RelevanceSphere. The above mentioned *density* factor can be manipulated by the user. It changes the overall attraction of *all* terms, i.e. the *document density* in a RelevanceSphere's volume. Figure 14 displays the same situation with a lower document density. Document *x* had to leave the inside of the sphere, but is kept closely bound to the surface. By this means the user can recognize the distance of document *x* as being no longer displayed proportional to the distances of documents residing in the inner part of the sphere. Furthermore, the user is provided with an interactive relevance feedback mechanism. He can express a higher/lower interest in a specific term and the related document cluster by in/decreasing the term symbol's attraction towards its documents. Figure 15 displays an appropriate example:

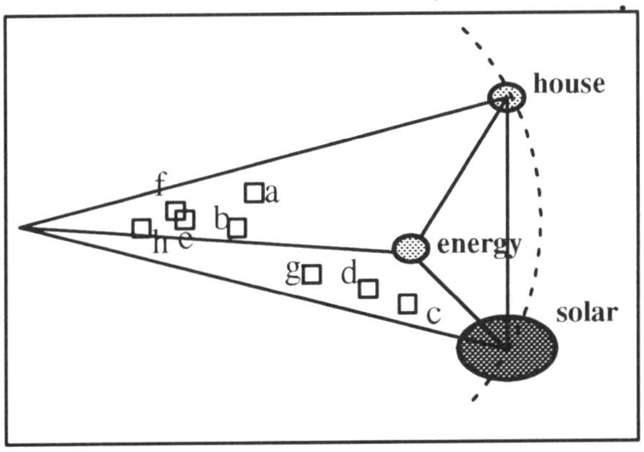

Figure 15: After increasing attraction of term "*solar*"

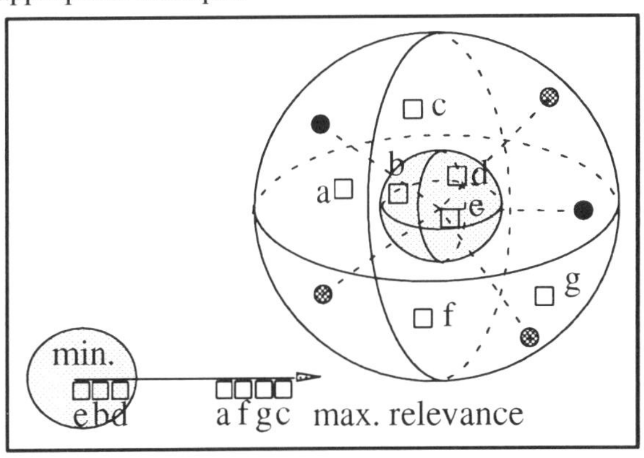

Figure 16: Partitioning of a Relevance Sphere

The interactive manipulation of a single term's *attraction* factor is implemented by manipulating a term symbol's size and color. Color coding was added to support perception of attraction size in 2D projections of 3D scenes (e.g. figure 15: is the term symbol for *solar* bigger because its size has been increased or because it is positioned to the front of the sphere). In this case the user has to note that the numerical proportions for the distance values remain no longer constant between all documents in the sphere, but proportions of the documents attracted/not attracted by the enforced term remain constant between themselves.

A partitioning mechanism for a RelevanceSphere's document set is finally introduced. It enables the user to manipulate the *scaling* factor. Figure 16 displays a RelevanceSphere with two groups of documents. One group has a very high relevance and the documents in the other group are of a lower relevance. In this case it makes sense to divide the RelevanceSphere viewing the two different areas of the relevance range separately in two disjunctive spheres. Partitioning is implemented by increasing the size of the inner sphere until it covers all documents with lower relevance and extracting it from the original outer sphere. The new scaling factor of the outer sphere is generated.

4 Examples from a LyberWorld Session

In the following we will report about *selected* situations extracted from an example retrieval session that is also provided as a video recording. In its current state, the LyberWorld prototype is applied to access documents of a database containing about 800 abstracts describing research projects. This data set is part of the larger CORDIS database (IR database of Research projects funded by the Commission of the European Communities). It was converted ([27]) from linear free-text in a relational DBMS into a format accessible for INQUERY's indexing and retrieval mechanisms. In the demonstration case, the user aims at research projects investigating alternative ways of heating houses efficiently.

Initiating a navigation: After initiating a search by entering a first keyword *heat* which is semantically associated to his interest, the user activates the NavigationCone. It displays all documents containing the keyword *heat* on a red document view level. After reading the document titles, the user decides to follow the document entitled *Courtyard Passive Solar Houses.* He selects the document to become the current item and requests to unfold its term sublevel. The resulting term view, displayed as a blue sublevel, is browsed. It contains the term *solar* which the user selects as the path to continue his search with. On the next red document level, the user selects the item *Solar Architecture in Europe* after browsing the titles of the displayed documents. He expands its blue term sublevel and browses the displayed terms. The user recognizes the terms *thermal* and *house.* The blue color of the house term is darker because it contains a hidden path into an already explored area. One of the documents in the already explored views must be dealing with the term *house.* The user requests to unfold the document view of *house* and an animation moves his point of view to the appropriate position where *house* has first appeared. The document sublevel of *house* is then unfolded.

Experiencing search loops and boundaries of interesting areas: The resulting view contains only a small number of documents. They are all colored *orange* instead of red. The user recognizes that the documents are displayed orange because they are bearing hidden paths. They were already found earlier in the history of the session. As all documents bear such hidden paths, it does not make sense to continue with one of these documents into an already searched area. The user decides to continue with the *thermal* keyword that he still remembers. As *thermal* is currently somewhere on the back side of the NavigationCones and the user does not know its exact position, he requests to add a new keyword and enters the string *"thermal"*.The system realizes that the item *thermal* was already explored and an animation moves the user to the correct view position. It also rotates the appropriate keyword label to the front where the user requests to unfold its document sublevel. The resulting document view contains quite a lot of items and only a few of them are already known (orange). As the new document titles all look a bit misleading, the user decides to stop his exploration and to start identifying the result kernel of his search. The NavigationCones are closed and the RelevanceSphere is activated.

Experiencing Relevance and Expressing Interest: The system transfers the retrieved documents into the sphere center where they appear in a cluster of little book symbols. The terms selected in the NavigationCones (constructing the query) are displayed as small blue spheres, equally distributed on the surface of the RelevanceSphere. After manipulating the RelevanceSphere's orientation and the *heat* symbol into a better display position the user starts his clustering activities. He clusters the *house* and the *solar* terms on the surface of the RelevanceSphere. One can now recognize a small subgroup of documents in the center following the movements of the two keyword spheres while two other "streams" of documents remain attracted by heat and thermal. The user wants to isolate the influenced group from the kernel in the center. He increases the size of *solar* and *house* to increase their attraction. The documents react and the cluster starts moving towards the two keywords on the surface. To enforce this effect, the user reduces the document density in the sphere and the cluster becomes fully isolated. The outmost document of the isolated cluster left the sphere while the user reduced the document-density. It is displayed as an open book, because by default the system regards it as the most relevant result. The user activates the InformationRoom icon, and the most relevant document's textual content is displayed in detail on the back wall of the room. By selecting other books of the isolated cluster to be opened and displayed in detail, the user recognizes that most of them meet the initial interests of his search. The kernel result of his information search is determined.

Complementarity of Tools: In the above-outlined example, the visualization tools have been used one after the other, but they can be changed or combined at all times. Whenever the user switches between the three tools, the context of his search is preserved and transferred into the other tools visualization metaphor. Therefore the user is free to conduct his information search using whatever information tool he chooses. The InformationRoom could have been activated at all times, too. It can, e.g., be used in combination with the NavigationCones for immediately viewing the detailed content of a selected document.

5 Conclusions and Outlook

The LyberWorld project has introduced two visualization tools offering control over a highly interactive, navigational information retrieval process. LyberWorld's visualization tools provide the system functionalities *semantic association, associative reading, sequential reading, navigation, backtracking* and *support of search strategy development* defined by [8]. They are initiated by direct manipulation techniques applied on the visualized information structures.

The NavigationCones serve as a visual history tool. The user can navigate forward and backward in the already unfolded NavigationCones for history or backtracking purposes and he will recognize when he searches an area of the content space more than once. NavigationCones provide also content-oriented terminology support (a kind of semantic association), because the term views contain only terms of the database's dictionary. By this means query construction is supported, although a "query" in the traditional sense does no longer exist explicitly. Navigation into new areas of the content is supported by unfolding new views in the NavigationCones. Reading in the Navigation-

Cones is provided in combination with the InformationRoom. Associative reading is enabled by reading a document in a certain view and by navigating over the meta-information of a related term view onto an associated document view to read in its documents. Sequential reading is provided by reading documents of the same view.

With respect to the RelevanceSpheres, we strongly believe that the function of *visualizing informational relations* in terms of e.g. relevance or similarity should be added to the list of necessary UI functions introduced by [8]. Displaying such relations, whether they exist between information or meta-information items, provides important insights for the user. Visualizations do furthermore contribute positively to the development of user's mental model of the data and the system's functionality. Besides supporting the general understanding of the systems functionality, an efficiently created and appropriate mental model is expected to reduce learning effort. Therefore the design of the visualization metaphors must be intensively proved to be intuitive. Testing the design of the introduced metaphors will be an important part of our future work. During user studies as part of the system's evaluation, it has to be analyzed if the tools are primarily used in the way the design was originally intended, if the choice of tools can be interpreted as a significant indicator for a user's search strategy, if the learning time is significantly reduced, if the users mental models corresponds to the system's data and retrieval model. The integration of additional complementary functionalities into the existing tools (as e.g. query by example and external thesauri) as well as improvements of the NavigationCones' capability to display large scale information sets are already under development. These functionalities can be implemented within the semantic of the already existing metaphors. The object oriented design of the corresponding tools will allow an easy extension of their functionality. Other functionalities like e.g. the one of displaying a content map for overview purposes, the content-oriented routing of dynamic information streams and the organizational control of large scale semi-automatic retrieval processes on such dynamic information sets will require the development of different spatial metaphors and corresponding visualization tools.

According to [7], "information seeking behavior is characterized by movement from one strategy to another within the course of a single search episode". We are convinced, that while navigating in LyberWorld, the user controls the information process in dimensions similar to *Method of Interaction, Mode of Retrieval, Goal of Interaction* and *Resource Considered* (also outlined in [7] for a user conducting a conversational information dialog). A merging of approaches for conversational and navigational information retrieval user interfaces on the base of a common conceptual model seems to be promising and encourages further work in this direction to achieve a base for comparing and integrating intelligent conversational user interfaces with advanced visualization techniques and vice versa.

Acknowledgements

The evolution of ideas embodied in the LyberWorld prototype and its implementation have been a group effort of IPSI's VISIT department (VISual Interaction Tools) headed by Heinz-Dieter Böcker. The entire team's contributions have been essential for the realization of the prototype and the ideas presented in this paper. Special thanks go to Bruce Croft and Nick Belkin for the discussions and encouragement during their visits at IPSI. Furthermore we would like to thank our colleages Adrian Müller, Adelheit Stein and Ulrich Thiel for many fruitful discussions. Last but not least we thank Arndt Steinmetz for producing the demonstration video with unbelievable patience and experience.

References

1. Pejtersen AM: a library system for information retrieval based on a cognitive task analysis and supported by an icon based interface. In: Belkin NJ, van Rijsbergen CJ (eds) Proc. of the 12th Annual Int. Conference on Research and Development in Information Retrieval (SIGIR '89). Cambridge, Mass. 1989
2. Kerner A, Thiel U: graphical support for users inferences within retrieval dialogues. In: Proc. IEEE Workshop on Visual Languages, Kobe/Japan, October 1991. Washington: IEEE Computer Society Press, 1991, pp 211-216
3. Silicon Graphics Inc.: IRIS Explorer 2.0 Technical Report. Silicon Graphics Computer Systems, Mountain View 1992.
4. Russel DM, Stefik MJ, Pirolli P, Card SK: the cost structure of sense making. In: Proc. of InterCHI '92. 1992
5. Eick SG, Wills GJ, Sumner E: who did what, when, and where? Analyzing a statistical reference database. To appear in: Proc. IEEE Workshop on Database Issues for Data Visualization at Visualization '93, San Jose, California, October 1993.
6. Keim DA, Kriegel HP: visually supporting data mining of large existing databases. To appear in: Proc. IEEE Workshop on Database Issues for Data Visualization at Visualization '93, San Jose, California, October 1993.
7. Belkin NJ, Marchetti PG, Cool C: BRAQUE: design of an interface to support user interaction in information retrieval. In: Information Processing and Management, Special Issue on Hypertext, 1993.
8. Agosti M, Gradenigo G, Marchetti PG: architecture and functions for a conceptual interface to very large online bibliographic collections. In: Intelligent Text and Image Handling, RIAO '91, Barcelona, Spain, April 1991.
9. Card SK, Robertson GG, Mackinlay JD : the information visualizer, an information workspace, In: Proc. CHI '91, New Orleans, April 1991. ACM Press, 1991, p 181
10. Boyle J, Fothergill JE, Gray PMD.: design of a 3D user interface to a database. To appear in: Proc. IEEE Workshop on Database Issues for Data Visualization at Visualization '93, San Jose, California, October 1993.

11. Hemmje M: eine inhaltsorientierte, intuitive 3D-Benutzerschnittstelle für Information-Retrieval-Systeme. In: Knorz G, Krause J, Womser-Hacker C (eds) IR'93, Proc. of the 1st German National Conference on Information Retrieval, Regensburg, Sept. 13-15. Universitätsverlag Konstanz, 1993, pp 82-99

12. Spoerri A: InfoCrystal: a visual tool for information retrieval & management. In: Proc. Information & Knowledge Management '93, Nov. 1-5, Washington D.C., 1993.

13. Silicon Graphics Inc.: IRIS Inventor Programming Guide. Silicon Graphics Computer Systems, Mountain View 1992

14. Strauss PS, Carey R: an object-oriented 3D graphics toolkit, Computer Graphics July 1992; 26:2:341-349

15. Korfhage RR: to see or not to see – is that the query?, In: Proc. of the 14th Annual Int. Conference on Research and Development in Information Retrieval (SIGIR '91), Chicago, 1991, p 134

16. Hemmje M, Böcker HD, Thiel U: Expeditionen in Informationsräume: Zur Konzeption eines graphischen Informationssystems auf der Basis dreidimensionaler Visualisierungen. In: Zimmermann HH, Luckhardt HD, Schulz A (eds) ISI '92, Proc. of 3rd International Symposiums for Information Science. Saarbrücken, November 92, Universitätsverlag Konstanz, 1992, pp 94-101

17. Hemmje M: a 3D based user interface for information retrieval systems. To appear in: Proc. of IEEE Visualization '93, Workshop on Database Issues for Data Visualization, San Jose, California, October 25–29, 1993

18. Callan JP, Croft WB, Harding SM: the INQUERY retrieval system. In: Proc. 3rd Int. Conf. on Database and Expert Systems Applications, September 1992.

19. Croft WB, Wolf R, Thompson R: A Network Organization used for Document Retrieval. Proc. of the 6th Annual Int. ACM SIGIR Conf., SIGIR Forum, Vol. 17, No. 4, 1983

20. Agosti M, Colotti R, Gradenigo G: a two-level hypertext retrieval model for legal data. In: Proc. SIGIR '91, Chicago 1991, pp 316-325

21. Thiel U, Hammwöhner R: Information Zooming: an interaction model for the graphical access to text knowledge bases. In: Yu CT, van Rijsbergen CJ (eds) Proc. of the 10th Annual Int. Conference on Research and Development in Information Retrieval (SIGIR '87), New Orleans, Louisiana 1987

22. Salton G: the SMART retrieval system – experiments in automatic document processing. Prentice Hall, Englewood Cliffs, New Jersey 1971

23. Raghavan VV, Wong SKM. A critical analysis of vector space model for information retrieval. JASIS 1986; 37:5:279-286

24. Robertson GG, Mackinlay JD, Card SK: Cone Trees: animated 3D visualizations of hierarchical information. In: Proc. CHI '91, New Orleans, April 1991, ACM Press, p 189

25. Turtle HR, Croft WB: efficient probabilistic inference for text retrieval. In: Proc. of RIAO '91, Universitat Autònoma de Barcelona, Barcelona, Spain, April 2-5 1991 , p 644-661

26. Olson KA, Kofhage RR, Sochats KM, Spring BM and Williams JG: visualization of a document collection: the VIBE system. Report LIS033/IS91001, School of Library and Information science, University of Pittsburgh, 1991

27. Gu J, Thiel U: automatically converting linear text to hypertext: a case study. To appear in: Proc. Hypermedia '93, Zurich, Switzerland, Berlin et al.: Springer 1993

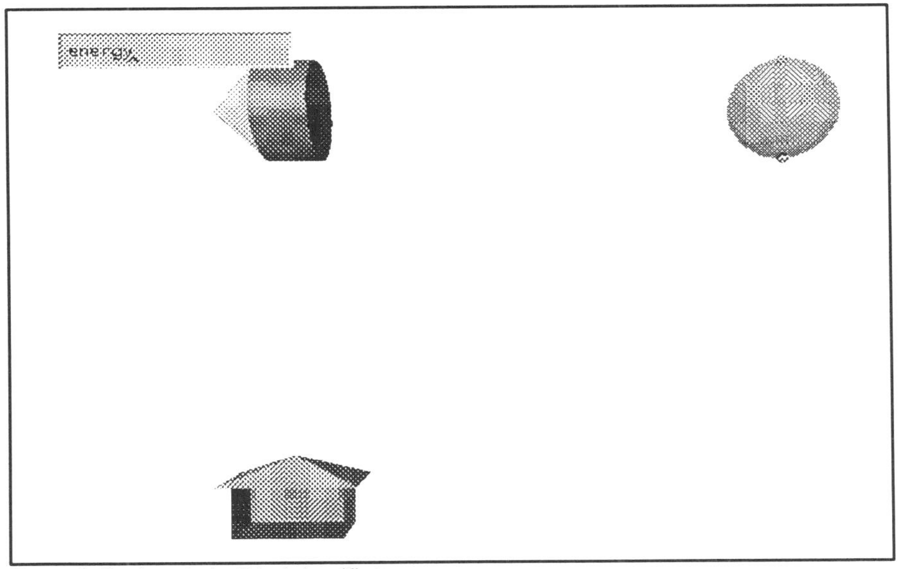

Screen 1: Session start, all tools iconified

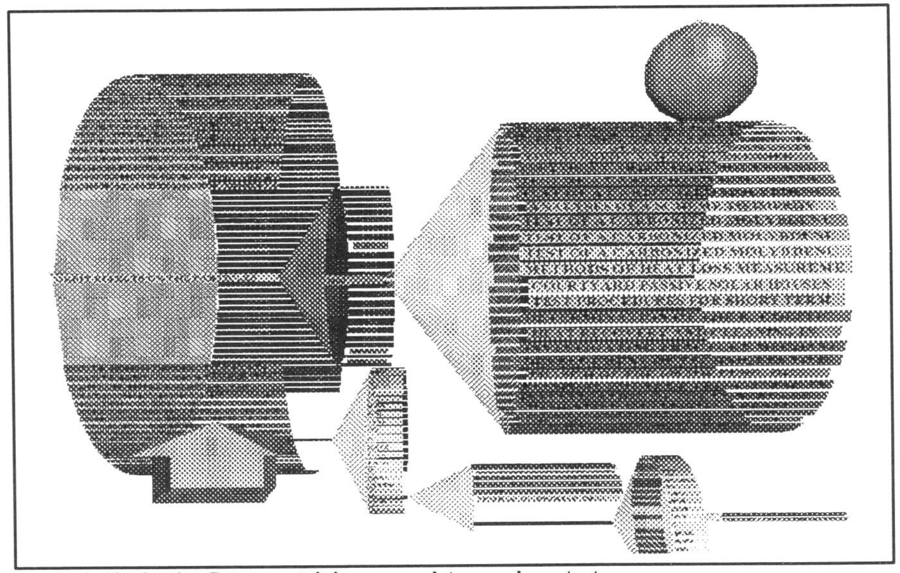
Screen 2: NavigationCones containing a complete search context

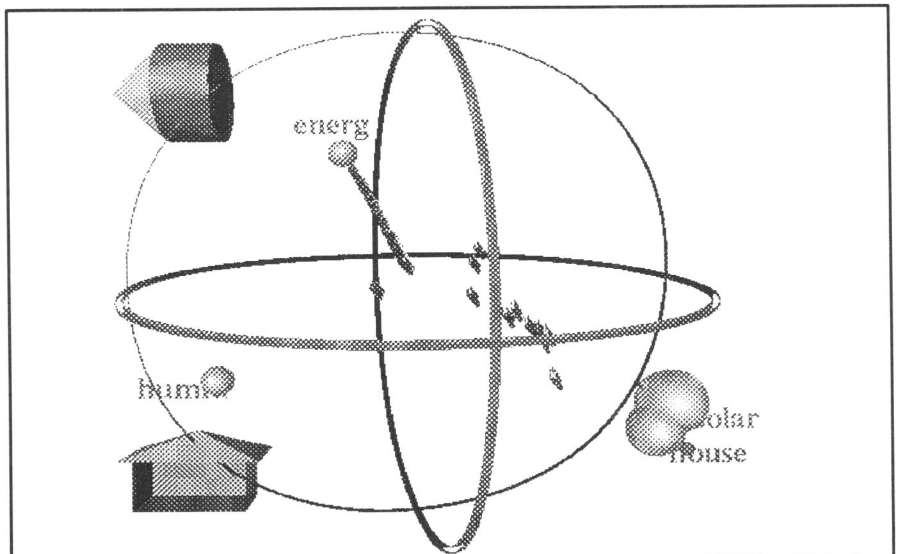

Screen 3: RelevanceSphere containing a context space, cluster of documents already isolated

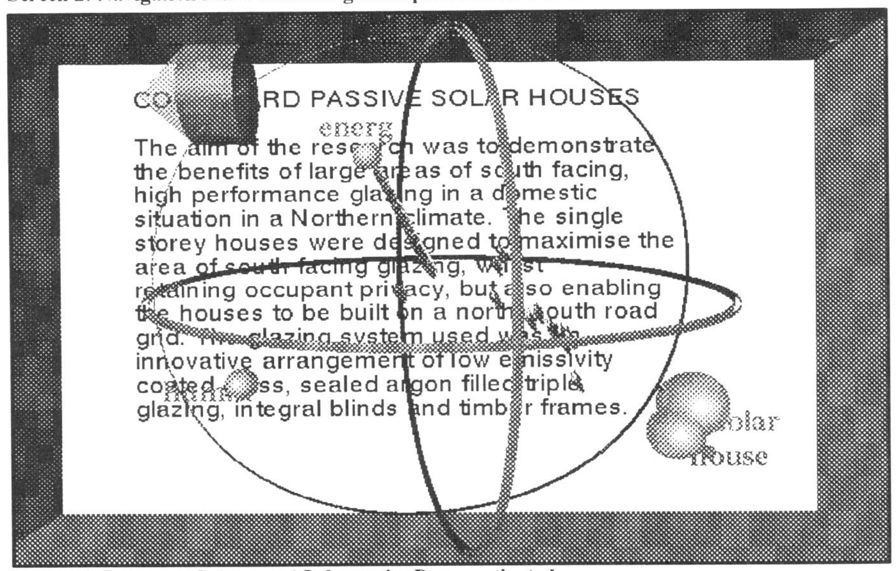

Screen 4: RelevanceSphere and InformationRoom activated

A System for Discovering Relationships by Feature Extraction from Text Databases [1]

Jack G. Conrad
West Publishing Company
St. Paul, MN 55164

conrad@research.westlaw.com

Mary Hunter Utt
Digital Equipment Corporation
Littleton, MA 01460

utt@netcur.enet.dec.com

Abstract

A method for accessing text-based information using domain-specific features rather than documents alone is presented. The basis of this approach is the ability to automatically extract features from large text databases, and identify statistically significant relationships or associations between those features. The techniques supporting this approach are discussed, and examples from an application using these techniques, named the *Associations System*, are illustrated using the *Wall Street Journal* database. In this particular application, the features extracted are company and person names. The series of tests run on the *Associations System* demonstrate that feature extraction can be quite accurate, and that the relationships generated are reliable. In addition to conventional measures of recall and precision, evaluation measures are currently being studied which will indicate the *usefulness* of the relationships identified, in various domain-specific contexts.

1 Introduction

Information retrieval systems have traditionally been *document-oriented*; that is, IR systems have been designed to store, retrieve, and display text documents such as newspaper articles or legal summaries. Furthermore, many of today's hypertext systems have inherited this paradigm of information representation to the extent that hypertext nodes are typically short text documents, possibly derived from longer sources. In some instances, browsing of index terms associated with the text documents is also supported [1, 2], but this is generally regarded as a secondary activity in relation to the primary task of identifying relevant documents (or text nodes). From the user's standpoint, however, it is usually the information contained in the text documents that is the goal of the search, not the documents themselves.

In some application domains, the target information is well-defined, for example, financial figures, transaction dates, product types, etc. In these domains, it may be possible to construct information retrieval and hypertext-like browsing systems based on the internal information rather than exclusively on the text documents that embody it. As a result, systems like these should be able to answer important categories of queries and support alternative means of access currently impossible with standard document-based systems. For example, a traditional text retrieval system could not be expected to satisfy a real-time query which requests a list of companies with which Ross Perot had business dealings in 1988. By contrast, a feature-based system could.

The techniques described in this paper have formed the basis for the *Associations System*. This implementation is an information retrieval system which pursues a concept-oriented rather than document-oriented approach; it focuses on the recognition of domain-specific features in a textual database and relationships identified between those features.

In the following sections, we describe techniques and experiments in three major areas needed to support this application:

- *Automatic feature extraction* - techniques used to recognize features in large, free-text databases.
- *Generating direct links* - techniques for quantifying the relationship between features based on their association in free text.
- *Generating indirect links* - techniques for indexing features and identifying indirect relations between features based on shared classifications, as well as offering possible starting points for browsing in a feature network.

[1] This research was performed at the Center for Intelligent Information Retrieval at the University of Massachusetts at Amherst.

Our experiments with the company and person name recognizers use a database of one year (1987) of *Wall Street Journal* articles. It consists of 46,449 articles containing 249 words on average, and is a part of the TIPSTER document collection [3]. Subsequent recall and precision experiments with the *Associations System* use as a database a more recent year (1991) of *Wall Street Journal* articles. It contains 42,652 articles averaging 232 words each, also from the TIPSTER collection. We have found that evaluating some of these proposed techniques is more difficult than a typical information retrieval experiment, and this issue will be discussed in the sections that follow.

2 Automatic Feature Extraction

The problem of feature or fact extraction from unrestricted text has been studied by a number of researchers in the context of the Message Understanding Conferences [4] and the TIPSTER project [3]. The basic approach has been to use a variety of natural language processing and statistical techniques to extract predetermined types of facts for a specific domain. In the TIPSTER joint venture domain, for example, the goal of extraction is to identify information such as the companies forming the joint venture, the name of the new company, the location of the new company, the products of the new company, and the amount of money involved.

Accurate extraction of some types of information requires either sophisticated analysis or significant amounts of training data. There are, however, a number of important and fairly general features which can be recognized using relatively simple techniques. These include the names of companies, the names of people, locations, monetary amounts, and dates. The task of collecting this information could be described as the recognition and categorization of certain noun phrases. In other words, a feature is essentially an object which falls into a special word grouping and has certain attributes associated with it [5]. High rates of accuracy are possible because of the relative simplicity of the task. It is, for example, much easier to recognize the presence of a company name in an article about a joint venture than to identify the role that company is playing. The ability to recognize these simple features can be used to develop powerful new approaches to accessing information [6].

For the application we address in this paper, the two feature recognizers required are for company names and person names. The techniques used for these feature recognizers involve a combination of lexical scanners built using *lex* [7], or a similar tool, and table lookup.

2.1 The Company Name Recognizer

The company name recognizer scans the text for proper nouns (capitalized words) that have the appropriate format for a company name. Company names often include special words such as *Inc.*, *Corporation*, or *Pty. Ltd.* that are particularly useful for recognition [8]. In a given document, the company name recognizer will use these special words to recognize the first mention of a company name and store it in a temporary table. This table permits the recognition of subsequent uses of that company name, even if the special words are not used. In newspaper articles, for example, the first use of a company name in a story generally uses the full form.

In a simple test of the company name recognizer, we applied it to a sample of the *Wall Street Journal* database and compared the results to company names identified manually. The test database consisted of 139 articles containing 29,000 words. The manual scan of the database identified 334 company names. In this test, the precision (percentage of names identified as companies that actually were companies) was 89% and the recall (percentage of company names in the sample that were identified as companies) was 79%.[2] Many of the precision errors were caused by two difficult company name formats where names are combined using 'and' and 'of', such as in *X, Y and Z Corporation* and *X of Y Inc.* Although these can be valid formats (e.g., Mutual of Omaha), they tend to introduce too many errors. We are currently revising the company name recognizer to improve recall by introducing a company name table that will contain common names and synonyms (e.g., for American Telephone & Telegraph/AT & T and Digital Equipment/DEC). This modification is based on the observation that references to well-known companies are more likely not to use the full form of the name.

[2] The tests performed were name-based rather than occurrence-based.

2.2 The Person Name Recognizer

Many application-dependent approaches to personal name identification have been developed over the last three decades [9]. Because of our application domain, the person name recognizer relies upon techniques similar to the above, but places more emphasis on table lookup. A name is recognized when a capitalized sequence of words begins with a title such as *Ms.*, *Chairman*, *President*, and so forth. In addition, lists of first names and last names are used to identify names that do not contain titles. As in the case of the company name recognizer, subsequent references to people in the same story are recognized, even if the full name is not used. Checks are made to ensure that a recognized name is not a company name (for example, that L. L. Bean Inc., referred to later in a story as "L. L. Bean" is not recognized as a person name).

Finally, because sequences of capitalized words may contain other words in addition to a name, a stop list of common problem words is maintained. For example, the *Wall Street Journal* frequently begins sentences with constructions such as *Added Joe Smith* ... or *Investor Jane Doe* ... We are investigating whether dictionary lookup may be more effective (and general) for this purpose.

To test the person name recognizer, the same database used for the evaluation of the company name recognizer was used. The manual scan identified 269 person names in the sample text. The person name recognizer achieved 92% precision and 93% recall. Many of the errors were due to unsuitable names in the first and last name tables. As an example, we are modifying the recognizer to avoid identifying locations (e.g., Santa Monica, Carson City) as person names.

Recognizing synonymous names is also a problem. For example, Bill Clinton and William Clinton are currently recognized as two different people. For two names in different stories to be recognized as the same, we have specified that the first name, middle initial (if any) and last name have to be the same. Given that we want to make connections between people and companies, the resolution of variant names needs to be addressed. A table of common synonyms will help, but it is not the complete solution. Fortunately, the company-person connections themselves can provide significant additional evidence that two names are the same. If, for example, Roger Smith and Roger B. Smith are both highly correlated with GM, it is likely that they are the same person. This technique is used to conflate person-company links after they are generated using the techniques described in the next section. Despite the complexities involved in recognizing company and person names, our experiments show that these names can be reliably recognized in textual databases.

3 Generating Direct Links

Having identified references to companies and people in the text, the next step is to identify relationships or associations between them. These associations can be used as the basis for the links in a hypertext network of companies, people, and source texts. Associations can be identified using either direct or indirect associations. A direct association occurs when the company and/or person names occur 'close' to each other in the text. Closeness can be measured either by a simple distance measure (how far apart the names are) or using some linguistic context (for example, in the same sentence or in a subject-object relationship). In previous experiments [10], word distance has been shown to be the strongest evidence for the presence of phrasal relationships, so for this study we have concentrated on name distance as the primary measure of association.

By contrast, an indirect association occurs when the company and person names have similar types of words associated with them. In the next section, we discuss how word contexts can be used to derive these indirect associations and support the additional retrieval of companies and people.

In the direct associations study, we used text *windows* to define direct links. A window refers to the number of words on either side of a target feature (i.e., company or person name). For example, a window of size 11 would include the target feature, the five preceding words, and the five succeeding words. The window sizes used here were 51 words and 201 words. These sizes were chosen empirically, and roughly approximate average paragraph-level and document-level associations.

The strength of association between two features depends on the number of associations or co-occurrences in a text window and how common the features are in the whole database. For example, a single co-occurrence of GM and IBM in a text window is not likely to be significant, given how frequently these companies are mentioned in the database. To determine significant associations (or to rank the relationships found by presumed importance), we use two statistical measures, the expected mutual information measure (*EMIM*) [11] and phi-squared (ϕ^2) [12].

The expected mutual information measure compares the probability of observing two features, x and y, together to the probability of observing the two features independently. In this paper, we use a simplified version of this measure that ignores terms involving probabilities that features do not occur. The measure used is:

$$EMIM(x,y) = \log_2 \frac{P(x,y)}{P(x)P(y)}$$

When a strong relationship exists between the features, the joint probability (P(x,y)) will be greater than chance and $EMIM(x,y)$ will be greater than 0.

The calculation of both *EMIM* and ϕ^2 makes use of a contingency table. This table can be represented as follows:

	y	$\bar{y}$
x	a	b
$\bar{x}$	c	d

The upper-left-hand cell [a] records the number of times features x and y co-occur in a window. Cell [b] records the number of times x occurs but y does not. Similarly, cell [c] records the number of times y occurs but x does not. Finally, cell [d] records the number of times neither feature occurs. Given this table to estimate probabilities, the *EMIM* calculation is:

$$EMIM(x,y) = \log_2 \frac{a(a+b+c+d)}{(a+b)(a+c)}$$

The ϕ^2 measure has been suggested as an alternative to *EMIM* and will tend to favor high-frequency events more. This is calculated as follows:

$$\phi^2 = \frac{(ad-bc)^2}{(a+b)(a+c)(b+d)(c+d)}, \quad \text{where } 0 \leq \phi^2 \leq 1$$

Feature Recognizer Window Experiments

The two measures described were used to compute associations between all features (companies and people) that co-occurred in text windows for the 1987 *Wall Street Journal* collection (Table 1).

Two different window sizes were used. For window size 51, there were 226,475 windows. For size 201, there were 54,464 windows. Since the second window size is close to the average size of a document, the number of windows is similar to the number of documents in the database.

Table 2 lists the number of pairs of features (n) that co-occurred m times within windows of size 51 and 201 respectively, for $m = 1$ to 10. The tables also list the maximum number of co-occurrences.

Evaluating the associations produced is difficult. The top ranked associations for *EMIM* and ϕ^2 appear to be very similar. For example, 58 of the top 68 ϕ^2 scores for company-person associations are also among the top 68 *EMIM* scores. When the top ranked associations are examined for a given company or person for either *EMIM* or ϕ^2, one observes that, although there are not large differences between the measures, the ϕ^2 measure does seem to favor high frequency associations. Since this often corresponds with intuition about associations, the ϕ^2 measure is probably the better choice.

The question remains, however, just how reliable or useful these discovered relationships are. It is not clear whether it would be possible to develop a list of "relevant associations" as is done with relevant documents in IR tests. Certainly, it is clear that the approach works to the extent that obvious relationships are found (such as between the CEO of a company and the company) and that all the relationships discovered have a basis in the text documents. Spurious relationships only occur at low frequency co-occurrences (mainly $m = 1$) and with larger window sizes. The data for the window size

Database:	WSJ87	WSJ91
Number of words indexed in the collection:	11,550,222	9,885,466
Number of person names identified by recognizer:	45,285	38,058
Number of company names identified by recognizer:	25,816	30,615

Table 1: Statistical Information for the 1987 and 1991 *Wall Street Journal* databases (WSJ87 & WSJ91)

Number of times (m) a pair of features co-occurred	Number of pairs of terms (n) that co-occurred m times					
	Window size = 51			Window size = 201		
	person-company and company-person	person-person	company-company	person-company and company-person	person-person	company-company
1	74,950	81,890	102,404	135,112	129,430	197,642
2	28,880	28,924	20,622	60,902	65,382	36,442
3	11,084	11,654	9,206	23,584	26,944	15,112
4	6,336	7,264	4,780	16,576	22,122	9,646
5	3,512	3,790	2,534	8,204	9,898	5,616
6	2,618	2,776	1,774	7,960	10,600	4,986
7	1,740	1,908	1,182	4,544	5,410	3,228
8	1,362	1,434	916	4,572	5,390	2,824
9	1,118	992	670	2,890	3,578	2,134
10	852	720	562	2,632	3,078	1,626
maximum value of m	149	145	150	200	200	199

Table 2: WSJ87 Co-occurrence Data

of 201 shows that many more co-occurrences are found. Some of these will be useful and some will be chance co-occurrences. The most useful window size will probably depend on the application and the users.

As an indication of the type of relationships discovered, the following are results from our *Associations System* graphical user interface.[3] It is presented as an illustration of how our techniques might be integrated into a single application. Another reason we show it here is as a means of examining whether the relations found are reasonable.

From the system's entry window, the user has the option of selecting the statistical measure of association (*EMIM* or ϕ^2) and setting the co-occurrence threshold.[4] For example, if a user is only interested in names which co-occur ten or more times, then the co-occurrence threshold would be set to 10. The default values for these parameters are ϕ^2 and 2 respectively.

The first interaction shows the companies that are associated with "Donald Trump" (Figure 1). There are four regions of the screen: *Query Entries*, *Selections* (user options), *The Listings* (containing the output produced by the query), and *History*. The first column of the output listing shown contains the association measures (ϕ^2 in this case); the second column contains the frequency of co-occurrence. Note the high degree of association between "Donald Trump" and "Golden Nugget" (a hotel-casino owed by Mr. Trump). In the second interaction (Figure 2), we see additional individuals associated with the "Golden Nugget" enterprise, one of them of course being "Donald Trump," but the list also points in new directions. This second list also illustrates how the ϕ^2 association measure tends to favor higher frequency relations. From this juncture, the user has the choice of either continuing to browse through the feature network or calling up relevant documents—by using a pair of related names in a structured query, for instance.

4 Generating Indirect Links and Entry Points for Browsing

In the last section, company names and person names were used as initial queries for the system, and the associations generated were based on direct links identified by way of the co-occurrence of the features in the documents. It is also possible to develop a more general approach to identifying associations between

[3] Our GUI is constructed using the *Tcl* interpretive command language and its X toolkit, *Tk* [13].

[4] Because the *Associations System* has been integrated with *INQUERY* [6], the user can also specify the number of documents to retrieve, as well as the size of its proximity operator (e.g., for paired names used in structured queries).

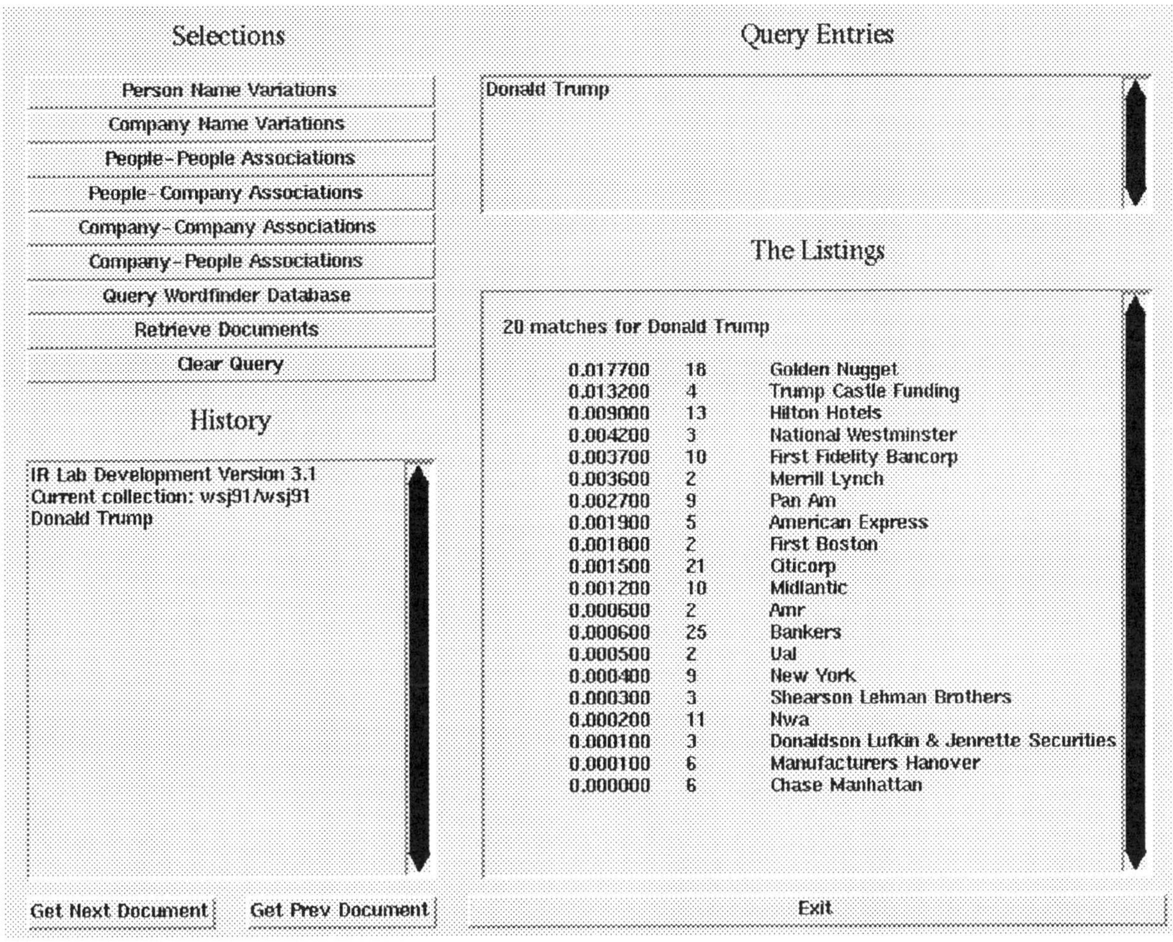

Figure 1: Companies associated with Donald Trump

features, by means of a search based on shared "attributes." This same general approach can be used to provide entry points into the system's feature network.

The basic technique involves identifying all the paragraphs in the entire database in which a given feature occurs. For each feature, a pseudo-document is created consisting of all of the paragraphs in the original database in which that feature is found. For example, if *Transamerica* (Corp.) is mentioned in 35 paragraphs in the database, the words in those paragraphs are used to create a pseudo-document for *Transamerica*. In this sense, the feature itself is treated as a special type of document and a "feature database" can be created, analogous to a document database. This approach and its resultant pseudo-documents are thus distinct from current research efforts which use local content when retrieving from large text files [14]. The types of linkages generated from this component of the system are different from normal hypertext linkages (which usually relate small text segments and, in our case, the direct links discussed above). These indirect links have provided our system with a powerful auxiliary tool, not only in terms of identifying entry points, but also in supplementing discoveries from direct-link retrieval with other new findings. In the experiments described here, the *INQUERY* text retrieval system [6] was used to store feature representations and to retrieve features.

The words that are used to represent features are all the non-stopwords in the paragraphs, weighted by their frequency of occurrence in the paragraphs and in the database as a whole. Currently, no limit is put on the number of words in the representation of a feature. Frequently occurring people and companies, therefore, may have thousands of words in their representations. It is an open research issue to determine if there are optimal representation sizes and whether the entire database or some subset of it should be used to derive these representations.

Once a feature database has been generated, at least two query mode options exist. In the first case, another feature (i.e., person or company) is used as a query, thus accessing features with similar representations. In this manner, *indirect* company-company, person-person, or company-person relations

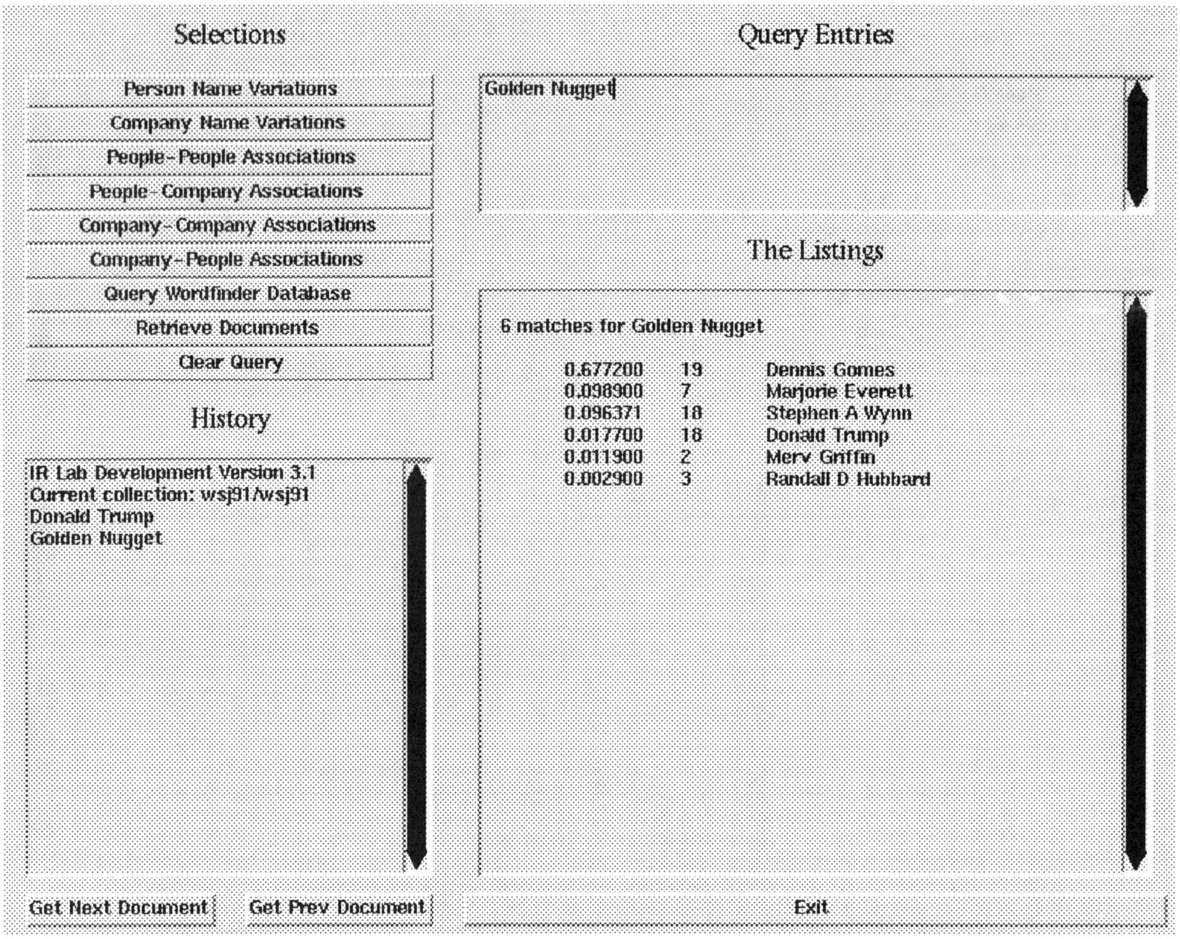

Figure 2: Persons associated with Golden Nugget (Hotel-Casino)

can be determined. Such relations could be requested by a user at any point during the user's interaction with the system.

The second mode corresponds to the use of natural language queries. Such an option provides the user with a convenient means of establishing a suitable entry point to the "feature network" at the beginning of an information search session. Natural language queries could be invoked by the feature retrieval system (in our case, *INQUERY*), and ranked lists of company and person names would be produced. The features retrieved would be those whose representations contain the words in the query with high weights. We could, for example, ask for "companies or people active in biomedical research and technology" and retrieve companies and individuals whose names have co-occurred frequently with the phrases such as "biomedical research" or "biomedical technology" in paragraphs in the database.

A feature retrieval system was generated for the WSJ92 database (with 2,275,134 indexed words) using the *INQUERY* system. The features retrieved for test cases were reasonable, based on the results of our precision experiments. That is, the company and person names retrieved using natural language queries were judged to be relevant to the topics mentioned in the queries. The output of this component of the system, however, was more difficult to evaluate for performance. More rigorous evaluation would require the participation of users in particular application domains.

Figure 3 provides an illustration of the operation of the feature retrieval system. Note that the format of the output of this system is quite different from the direct-link *Associations* program shown above. The first query is an attempt to find people and companies who are associated with the biomedical field. The first number on each line is the rank, the second is the similarity to the query, and the numbers in parentheses after the feature are related to its frequency of occurrence in the database. Note that this list contains both companies (or "enterprises") and people.

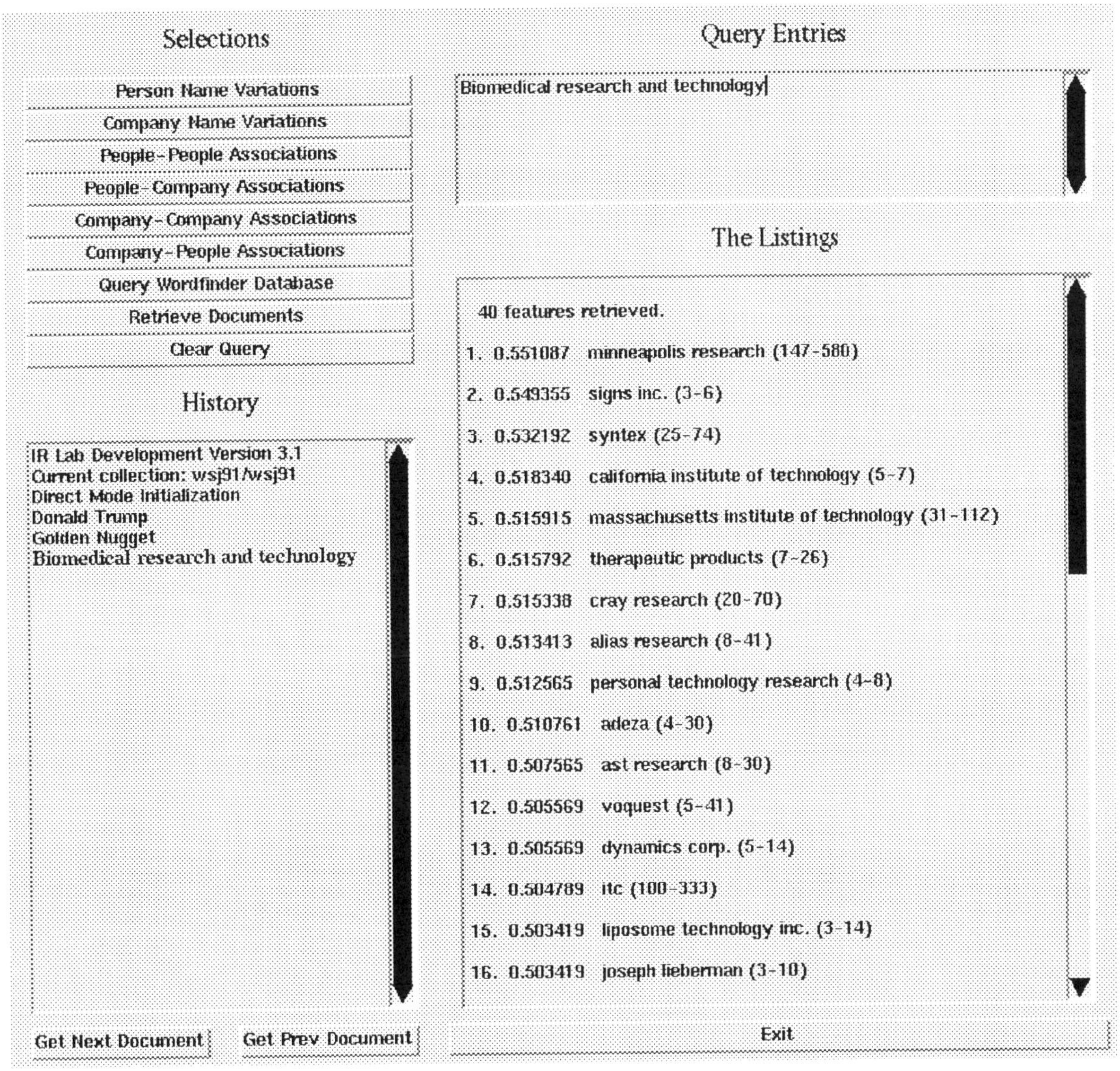

Figure 3: Enterprises and Persons associated with Biomedical research & technology

5 Development of a Feature-based System like *Associations*

The following is a summary of the processes we have developed for a system based on extracted features and relationships.

- Direct-link Generation
  1. Identify (i.e., index) features while parsing the document database. Record the position of each feature in the document/database.
  2. Compute the statistical measure of association (e.g., EMIM or ϕ^2) for direct (proximity-based) links between each of the features identified in a reasonably select co-occurrence window.
  3. Retrieve pairs of strongly associated features in response to queries consisting of features in the same domain.
- Indirect-link Generation
  1. Index all non-stopwords while parsing the document database.
  2. Generate a "feature database" consisting of pseudo-documents created using the words which are indexed near the given feature in the original database.

3. Harness a retrieval engine to provide ranked features in response to a variety of queries (e.g., either features themselves or natural language).

- System Integration—Integrate the above functionality, along with a conventional document retrieval system, to produce a hypertext-like feature browser and text retrieval system.

- Simultaneous Processing—Portions of the first two tasks above (e.g., parsing) can be performed simultaneously.

Note that given a stable parsing vehicle, these steps are free from any particular domain dependencies. In our implementation of the *Associations System*, we made a significant effort to optimize our processing of those steps which were initially computationally expensive. We can currently parse over 100 megabytes of *Wall Street Journal* text in approximately 30 minutes using a Sun 490. This is roughly equivalent to a database the size of WSJ88, which contains 39,906 articles. The computation for *Associations'* statistical measures for WSJ87, containing 46,449 articles, took approximately 4 hours. We are currently focusing on the next phase of our system development, which is to to generate one large composite *Associations* database consisting of all six years of the TIPSTER *Wall Street Journal* collection.

System Experiments

Precision Tests—To answer the question of whether the associations generated are correct, 15 company names and 15 person names from a variety of fields were chosen from the WSJ91 database (Table 1). Both company and person matches generated by the *Associations System* were recorded. Using the *INQUERY* retrieval engine, documents were then retrieved and the correctness of the relations produced was corroborated (i.e., either Yes or No).[5] In the cases studied, representing 286 company matches and 262 person matches, a precision figure of 90% was found for both categories of matches (i.e., for company names and person names), increasing to 95% when feature recognizer errors were removed (Tables 3 and 4).

In using the *Wall Street Journal* database, we have observed that in some cases up to one half of the features associated with a given company or person fall into the categories of either investment firms or their financial analysts. Whether or not these types of relations are useful depends on the information requirements of the user. As an implementation decision, some of these "financial" features could be filtered from the output, since the set of such firms is limited and identifiable. In either case, we acknowledge the need for domain-specific users to provide their assessments of the "usefulness" of these discovered relationships.

	Matches w/ Persons	%	Matches w/ Companies	%	Combined Matches	%
Initial Results	47/58	81.0%	226/249	90.8%	273/307	88.9%
Compensating for Recognizer Error	47/47	100%	226/239	94.6%	273/286	95.5%

Table 3: Precision Values for Company Name Matches

	Matches w/ Persons	%	Matches w/ Companies	%	Combined Matches	%
Initial Results	200/221	90.5%	53/53	100%	253/274	92.3%
Compensating for Recognizer Error	200/209	95.7%	53/53	100%	253/262	96.6%

Table 4: Precision Values for Person Name Matches

[5] The relevance judgements here were made by the authors.

Recall Tests—To determine whether the system misses any relations, two companies (Revlon Inc. and William Blair & Co.) and two business figures (Charles E. Exley [of NCR] and Philip E. Benton [of Ford]) were chosen. These names were also used in the precision tests above. Again using *INQUERY* as the retrieval engine, documents were retrieved, using each of these four names as queries, and a list of related persons and companies was generated for each.[6] The *Associations System* produced 49 company matches and 29 person matches for these same names. The results produced by the system and by manual verification do not include one time only co-occurrences which as often as not are due to chance (Tables 5 and 6). In addition to the observations cited earlier, we found that another reason some companies are not recognized is because they may never occur in the database with a suffix indicating their corporate status. This finding suggests that a correct combination of company name recognizer and lookup capability will produce a system which is not only more thorough in terms of recall, but more domain independent as well.

	Documents Retrieved	Matches w/ Persons	%	Matches w/ Companies	%	Combined Matches	%
Revlon Inc.	65	7/11	64%	19/28	68%	26/39	67%
William Blair & Co.	39	1/1	100%	19/26	73%	20/27	74%

Table 5: Recall Values for Company Name Matches

	Documents Retrieved	Matches w/ Persons	%	Matches w/ Companies	%	Combined Matches	%
Philip E. Benton	12	6/7	86%	4/6	67%	10/13	77%
Charles E. Exley	34	15/19	79%	7/17	41%	22/36	61%

Table 6: Recall Values for Person Name Matches

It is not completely clear how one would proceed to evaluate thoroughly a system such as *Associations*. The tests we have performed to date are preliminary. The evaluations presented above serve to illustrate some of the types of experiments we believe are essential for an initial assessment. A number of our results have been promising, especially with respect to precision, and encourage further refinement and enhancement of these techniques. An additional evaluation is currently being investigated, beyond precision and recall, which provides a measure of output *usefulness*. It is a parameter which is client-need dependent, and we think this is a part of what is required to contribute to the assessment process.

6 Conclusion

The approach presented here provides a new means of accessing information contained in textual databases. By developing techniques for extracting features and identifying relationships between features, we have begun to address types of information needs which queries in typical text retrieval systems could not handle. For instance, we may learn through the *Associations System* that NCR Corp. is related to Robert E. Allen, who is in turn strongly related to the AT & T Co. Discovering the relationship between the NCR and AT & T companies may have been difficult in a text retrieval system because the two companies are not necessarily mentioned in the same articles, and users who must formulate the query will probably not know that they are even looking for articles about the NCR and AT & T companies until they see that this relationship exists.

In the *Associations System* framework, the person-company application addresses a demonstrated user need. This is only one example, however, among many potential applications. The techniques we have described can be similarly applied to other domains such as medical or legal data systems. The implications for such a feature-supported system are far-ranging. A similar system could be developed,

[6]It is unlikely that the retrieval engine identified every document in the WSJ91 collection containing the given base names, but in the absence of a more authoritative source on these occurrences, the results produced by INQUERY are considered a reasonable starting point.

for example, to serve a public health network, providing access to a combination of information, based on ailments, billings, and dates—in a real-time capacity not addressed by current systems. Further, the influence that such a system would have on domains which still rely upon manual indexing or unintegrated software is potentially revolutionary, in terms of time and cost savings. The challenges that we currently face appear to be in designing new evaluation measures which focus on the *usefulness* of the relations generated. Measures like these are essential in order to evaluate and tune the performance of systems like *Associations*.

Acknowledgments

This work was supported in part by the NSF Center for Intelligent Information Retrieval (CIIR) at the University of Massachusetts. Bruce Croft initiated the approach used in the *Associations System* and guided its development. Mark Pezarro suggested applying these techniques to the person-company domain. Yufeng Jing contributed significantly to the implementation of the indirect link experiments described in the paper.

References

[1] R. H. Thompson and W.B. Croft. Support for browsing in an intelligent text retrieval system. *International Journal of Man-Machine Studies*, 30:639–668, 1989.

[2] P. D. Bruza and Th.P. van der Weide. Two level hypermedia. In *Proceedings of the International Conference on Database and Expert Systems Applications*, pp. 76–83. Springer-Verlag, 1990.

[3] D. Harman. The DARPA tipster project. *ACM SIGIR Forum*, 26(2):26–28, 1992.

[4] W. Lehnert and B. Sundheim. A performance evaluation of text-analysis technologies. *AI Magazine*, pp. 81–94, 1991.

[5] D. D. Lewis. Text representation for intelligent text retrieval: a classification-oriented view. *Text-based Intelligent Systems*, ed. Paul S. Jacobs, pp. 179–197, LEA Press, 1992.

[6] J. P. Callan, W.B. Croft, and S.M. Harding. The INQUERY retrieval system. In *Proceedings of the 3rd International Conference on Database and Expert Systems Applications*, pp. 78–83. Springer-Verlag, 1992.

[7] M. E. Lesk and E. Schmidt. Lex—a lexical analyzer generator. In *UNIX Programmer's Manual*, Bell Telephone Laboratories, Inc., 1979.

[8] L. F. Rau. Extracting company names from text. In *Proceedings of the Sixth IEEE Conference on Artificial Intelligence Applications*, 1991.

[9] C. L. Borgman and S.L. Siegfried. Getty's Synoname *TM* and its cousins: a survey of applications of personal name-matching algorithms. *JASIS*, 43(7): 459–476, 1992.

[10] W. B. Croft, H.R. Turtle, and D.D. Lewis. The use of phrases and structured queries in information retrieval. In *Proceedings of the ACM SIGIR Conference on Research and Development in Information Retrieval*, pp. 32–45, 1991.

[11] K. W. Church and P. Hanks. Word association norms, mutual information, and lexicography. In *Proceedings of the 27th Meeting of the ACL*, pp. 76–83, 1989.

[12] K. W. Church and W.A. Gale. Concordances for parallel text. In *Seventh Annual Conference of the University of Waterloo Centre for the New OED and Text Research*, pp. 40–62, 1991.

[13] J. K. Ousterhout. *An Introduction to Tcl and Tk*, Addison-Wesley Publishing Company, Inc., 1994.

[14] G. Salton, J. Allan, and C. Buckley. Approaches to passage retrieval in full text information systems. In *Proceedings of the Sixteenth Annual International ACM SIGIR Conference on Research and Development in Information Retrieval*, pp. 49–58, 1993.

Routing

Information Filtering Based on User Behavior Analysis and Best Match Text Retrieval

Masahiro MORITA
hiro@jaist.ac.jp

Yoichi SHINODA
shinoda@jaist.ac.jp

School of Information Science
Japan Advanced Institute of Science and Technology
15 Asahi-dai, Tatsunokuchi, Ishikawa 923-12 Japan

Abstract

Information filtering systems have potential power that may provide an efficient means of navigating through large and diverse data space. However, current information filtering technology heavily depends on a user's active participation for describing the user's interest to information items, forcing the user to accept extra load to overcome the already loaded situation. Furthermore, because the user's interests are often expressed in discrete format such as a set of keywords sometimes augmented with if-then rules, it is difficult to express ambiguous interests, which users often want to do. We propose a technique that uses user behavior monitoring to transparently capture the user's interest in information, and a technique to use this interest to filter incoming information in a very efficient way. The proposed techniques are verified to perform very well by having conducted a field experiment and a series of simulation.

1 Introduction

Recent developments in computers and computer networks interconnecting large numbers of systems have brought us convenience in many aspects, but have introduced a situation of "information overloading" also. As highly developed computer networks disseminate into our everyday life, the amount of information we create and exchange has grown by an order of magnitude. The amount is far more than a person can understand and manage, and the task of retrieving a piece of information from the magnitude of information is beginning to take considerable amount of time and effort.

A concept of *information filtering* [1] was introduced as a key technology to overcome this situation, but we are all aware that technologies such as user profile acquisition should be studied in detail before the information filtering technologies are put into any practical use.

In this paper, we propose a profile acquisition and user feedback technique to accumulate a user's preference for information, based on user behavior monitoring, as well as an information filtering technique using the acquired profile. The proposed techniques are based on an assumption that a user is performing a quick pattern matching task upon deciding if a piece of information is relevant to the user or not, before the user attempts to understand the semantics of the information any further. If this is all true, we can expect that information not of interest to the user is immediately rejected, and conversely, information of interest requires a noticeable amount of time to process.

In the following, we will briefly review the general architecture of information filtering systems and associated issues in section 2, followed by an explanation of our assumption in section 3. Section 4 describes the method and results of the field experiment we conducted with readers of NetNews, to prove the correctness of our assumption for the profile acquisition. Then, in section 5, the proposed information filtering technique using the acquired profile is described. A simulation of the proposed information filtering technique showed that the technique can retrieve relevant information for a user with sufficient precision and recall rates for casual source of information such as NetNews. Finally, in section 6, summaries of the proposals and results as well as remaining issues and directions for future research are presented.

2 Information Filtering Systems

In this section, we will give a brief explanation of information filtering systems and associated issues, based on our survey on information filtering technology [6].

In general, filtering information can be classified roughly into the following three categories[5], namely, *cognitive filtering* that does filtering by characteristics of information contents, *social filtering* that works on personal and organizational interrelationships of individuals in a community, and *economic filtering* that filters by cost-benefit assessments. While issues regarding social filtering are relatively well studied and economic filtering has the concrete measure of cost, cognitive filtering raises numerous issues which are directly or indirectly coupled with problems in natural language understanding technologies. We believe that cognitive filtering is very important, because it ac-

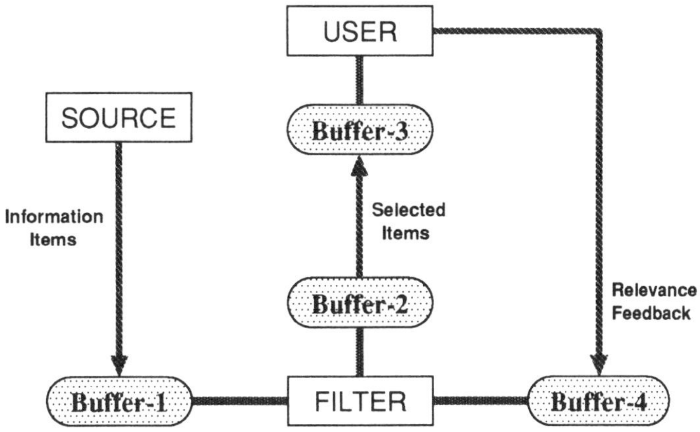

Figure 1. Generalized architecture of Information Filtering System

counts for humans' creative work by capturing potentially important information from casual information sources such as NetNews. From here on, we focus heavily on cognitive filtering systems.

Figure 1 shows a generalized architecture of information filtering systems [4]. This figure explains an information filtering system as consisting of seven logical units, namely the information source, the information filter, the user and four buffers. In this system, the source represents some descriptors of the information items to the filter, and the filter forwards to the individual user a subset of the items selected based on advance knowledge of the user's needs that is stored as the user's *profile*. The profile is like a reference database representing information needs or preferences of the user. Users may have the option of providing the filter with feedback indicating an extent to which the selection met their current information needs.

There are four buffers between the source, the filter, and the user as shown in the figure. These buffers are required in order to accommodate diverse information types or usage scenario types. For instance, buffer–4 stores the user's profile.

In our survey, we concluded that there are three important issues, listed below, that must be studied to realize any practical information filtering system.

- *Accumulation of user's preference to information*

  User's preferences must be accumulated in advance as a profile, and should be updated appropriately.

  Most of the previous work on cognitive filtering relied heavily on the user's active participation in profile accumulation and feedback. Profiles were often expressed in discrete forms such as a set of keywords possibly augmented with if-then rules, so that the user can enter and edit the profiles with an editor of some kind. However, we claim that it is generally difficult to express one's "interest", which is a non-discrete quantity, in the discrete way. Discrete profiles would result in incomplete description of the user's interest, which would lead to possible loss of potentially interesting information.

  Relying on the user's active participation in updating the profile database also have a problem in tracking temporal changes in the user's interest.

  We claim that a cognitive filtering system must be able to handle user's interest in a non-discrete fashion.

- *Representation of the profile*

  This issue is the direct product of the above issue. If a filtering system must deal with non-discrete information, the representation of the profile that stores the information will immediately be an issue.

- *Filtering mechanism*

  This issue, again, is the direct product of the first issue. Because a filtering system must deal with non-discrete profile and discrete target information, what will the best filtering technique be ?

We also point out that a practical cognitive filtering system should do its best not to filter out potentially important or stimulating information, to allow users of the system to have opportunity to be exposed to new information.

3 Information Filtering as Pattern Matching

The information filtering technique described in this paper is largely inspired by the advances in information retrieval using full-text search. In the WAIS system [3], search based on a concept of "similar to", that uses similarity among documents that uses number of words that appear commonly in the documents can be performed. This information retrieval technique based on the similarity of documents can be used as filtering mechanism in a information filtering system, if a set of documents that correctly reflect a user's preference to incoming information is given in advance.

Foltz took this approach of using similarity among documents for information filtering. He reported in [2] that using latent semantic indexing (LSI) for filtering news articles using articles pre-selected by a readers as the reader's profile can perform significantly better than filtering based on simple keyword matching on filtering performance.

Although their results are interesting, we felt that we need to study further on in following two points before directly employing the mechanism to judge similarity among documents in an information filtering system.

3.1 Semantical v.s. Syntactical Filtering

First point is the relevance of LSI upon "first impression" decision making of whether a document is interesting or not. Foltz claims that user preference will be similar for articles that are semantically similar. However, according to our experience, we all feel that when we read Japanese texts, we are not performing a deep understanding of each article upon making the decision of whether the article is important to us or not, but doing a pattern matching task looking for major keywords or combination of the keywords, and judging article's overall syntactical structure. Success in machine translation of Japanese into English text that uses only the syntactical information [11] partially justify this assumption.

It should be argued that people with languages using ideograms as mother tongue behave differently from those with languages using phonograms as mother tongue. It is natural that our assumption applies to those with languages using ideogram as a mother tongue, but we also know that there is a reading technique for phonogramic language text that picks up words diagonally from a page without considering the page's semantical structure, and still captures the semantical structure of the page. This means that certain variation of keyword search may work for phonogramic language texts also.

It is not clear that Foltz's result using LSI was compared to simple keyword count or using similarity between documents approach seen in the WAIS system. If information filtering using the syntactical similarity between documents performs as well as that based on LSI approach, it might be considered as our first choice for filtering mechanism because of its low processing overhead compared to the LSI method. It is needless to say that LSI approach deals more deeply with semantical content of documents, and when compared to "syntactical similarity" approach that only deals with one dimensional measure that is the number of keywords appeared commonly in two documents, it should perform better. But if two approach behaves almost the same, we claim that simple syntactic similarity is better for efficiency reasons. This is especially true for language texts that have no clear word break in a sentence, since breaking sentences into words require numerous machine cycles and we just can't afford them.

3.2 Profile Acquisition and User Feedback

Another is the user feedback issue, as discussed in the previous section. As Foltz pointed out in [2], in the conclusion of the paper, that we need some mechanism that reflects temporal transitions in interests of readers into the preference database. He also pointed out that his method of having users rate each article requires a lot of effort on the part of the user. That is, we need some mechanism to acquire and feedback user's preference to the profile.

Again, from our experience of reading news articles in Japanese text, as we reject uninteresting articles using our first impression of the articles, we can easily assume that articles which took considerable amount of time to read can be treated as potentially interesting articles. If we can determine whether a reader is interested in an article or not by measuring the time to read it, we might be able to capture the readers profile automatically. Foltz, although very vaguely, also pointed this out.

4 Profile Acquisition and Feedback by User Behavior Monitoring

Based on the second observation in the last section, we conducted an experiment that is similar to Foltz's experiment, to investigate the dominating factors that affects time to read an article. In this experiment, in addition to having users rate each article, we setup a system so that we could measure the time spent for each article.

We setup following hypothesis at beginning of the experiment:

- Users spend longer time to read interesting information than not-interesting ones.

In addition to the hypothesis, we decided to see if there are other factors which may affect the time spent for an article, such as the followings.

- Time spent for an article increases in proportion to size or length of the article.
- Time spent for an article is affected by the readability of the article, i.e., denseness of the article, in some degree.
- Time spent for an article is affected by a size of a back log that a user have to process, e.g. if the user have large quantity of unread articles, time spend for each article get shorter.

In the following, we will first describe how the experiment was carried out, followed by result of analyzing the collected data.

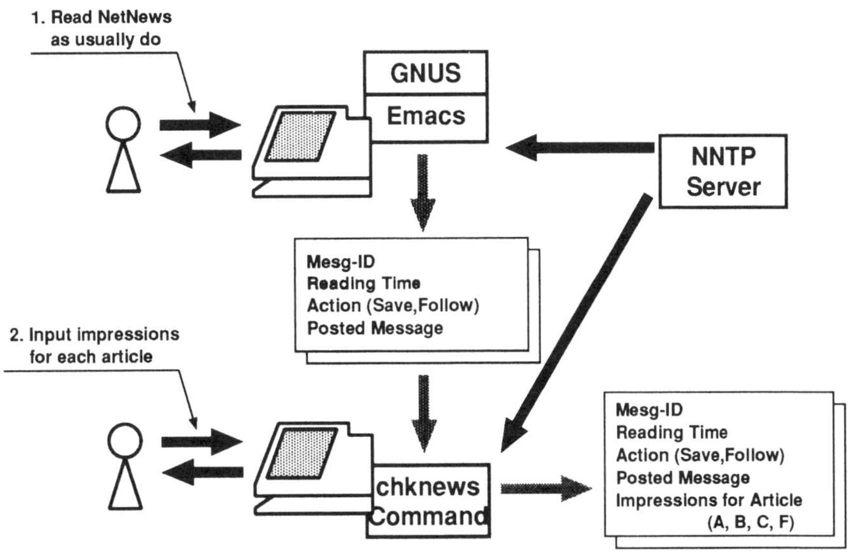

Figure 2. The Experimentation System

4.1 Experimentation

4.1.1 Subjects of the Experiment

This experimentation is aimed at NetNews (we focused on `fj.*` newsgroups, which is written mostly in Japanese) user, which is a popular Internet information service. Subjects of our experiment were recruited from actual user of NetNews by the NetNews itself, and 8 people volunteered as subjects. These 8 subjects read total of 8,000 articles during a period of 6 weeks.

4.1.2 Experimentation System

Figure 2 illustrates over all setting for the experiment. We modified GNUS, a widely used NetNews reader based on GNU Emacs, to record following information for each article that were read by subjects of this experimentation.

1. Message identifier of the article.
2. Time spend for the article (How much time was spent for the article).
3. Action for the article (The article was saved or follow-up was posted).
4. Copy of posted messages if the subject post new articles.

After a GNUS session is over, subjects rate each articles they read in the last session using **chknews** command. The **chknews** command uses the record of message identifiers to display contents of each article on users terminal and interviews subjects about impression of the article. Then it merges the records described above and the impressions about articles, and send them into a data collecting server using ordinal e-mail messages.

The impressions of article was to be answered in four grade of 'A', 'B', 'C' or 'F' where 'A' meaning very interesting, 'B' meaning interesting, 'C' meaning neither interesting nor not-interesting, and 'F' meaning not-interesting.

We requested subjects to behave as close to usual news reading session as possible during the experimental GNUS session, but also requested the followings to avoid abnormalities in the resulting data.

- During the GNUS session, subjects must wholeheartedly read articles and should not do other things such as leaving the terminal a while to get a cup of coffee or read newly arrived e-mail messages.
- During the period of experiment, subjects should read NetNews everyday as possible.
- Subjects should read all articles in registered newsgroups, e.g. subjects should not skip articles without having a glance at them or issue "catch up" commands.

Note that we separated the reading session and the rating session for the same reason.

Table 1 summarizes collected data over the period of 6 weeks. In following sections, we use the terms 'useful' or 'interesting' for those article that subject rated 'A' or 'B', and 'un-useful' or 'not-interesting' for those rated 'F'.

4.2 Analyzing Behavior of NetNews Users

From the statistical analysis on the collected data, we concluded that a major factor that influence a time spent for an article is the preference of a user to the article. Figure 3 illustrates this observation. In this figure, number of articles and time spent to read them are plotted for three groups of articles, namely all articles, those rated interesting and

Table 1. Collected Data

Subject #	# of Session	# of Article for each impressions				
		A	B	C	F	Total
1	37	91	156	209	835	1291
2	68	30	451	969	90	1540
3	40	21	528	1218	27	1794
4	11	13	28	58	201	300
5	25	3	387	208	3	601
6	38	1	19	746	7	773
7	41	35	352	233	14	634
8	30	26	162	697	14	899
Total	290	220	2083	4338	1191	7832

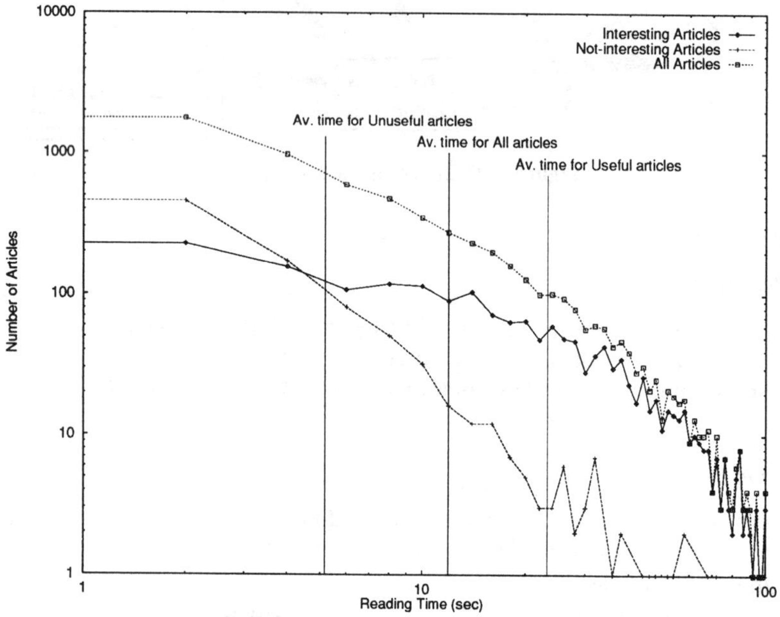

Figure 3. Distribution of Articles against Reading Time

those rated not-interesting. Other factors played only a very little role in affecting reading time of an article. The results from our analysis can be summarized as follows.

- There is a strong tendency to spend a long time to read articles those rated interesting.
- There is a tendency not to spend a long time to read articles those rated not-interesting.
- There was very low correlation of less than 0.08 between length of an article and a time to read the article. This probably indicates that not all articles are completely read, e.g. the decision of whether an article is interesting or not, especially in the not-interesting articles, are made by looking at first couple of dozens of lines.
- Readability of an article is not an important factor that affects its reading time. In our analysis, we used several metrics for denseness of characters in article, including average number of characters per line, ratio of blank lines in an article. We suspected that reading time become longer in proportion as denseness of the article become higher, but the results showed very low correlation between reading time and any of the metrics we used. The highest correlation we observed was 0.25, which was for average number of characters per line.
- Effect of back log (unread articles) was also very small. Correlation between number of unread articles and reading time is less than 0.18.

From the observation made above, we can conclude that preference of a user to an article is the dominating factor that affects time to spend reading it, meaning that it is possible, to a certain extent, to monitor the time spend for an article and know if the user is interested in the article or not. Consider for example, with some threshold time τ seconds, and treating articles which took longer than τ seconds to read as interested articles, and use these article as feedbacks, we can perform user feedback with significant precision. For example, our result indicates that with τ being 20 seconds, 30% of interesting articles can be retrieved with precision of 70%.

Table 2. % of Mutual Relation of Impression between Initial and Follow up Articles

Impression for Initial Articles	Impressions for Follow up Articles			
	Interesting	Not-interesting	Others	Total
Interesting (1447 articles)	489 (52.3%)	47 (5.0%)	400 (42.7%)	936 (100.0%)
Not-interesting (493 articles)	42 (10.5%)	271 (68.3%)	84 (21.2%)	397 (100.0%)

Table 3. % of Mutual Relation of Reading Time between Initial and Follow up Articles

Reading Time for Initial Articles	Reading Time for Follow up Articles			
	less than 10 sec	more than 20 sec	10 to 20 sec	Total
less than 10 sec (2151 articles)	1333 (77.4%)	138 (8.0%)	251 (14.6%)	1722 (100.0%)
more than 20 sec (1019 articles)	200 (35.1%)	219 (38.5%)	150 (26.4%)	569 (100.0%)

4.3 Effect of Relationship Between Articles on User Impressions

NetNews articles usually have a initial-follow relationship. During the analysis of our experiment, we examined mutual relation between impressions for initial article and it's follow up, and have found following interesting facts as shown in table 2.

This table can be interpreted as follows.

- Impressions for an initial article is inherited to follow up articles with high probability. That is, follow up articles of a not-interesting article are also not-interesting, and conversely, follow up articles of an interesting article are also interesting.
- It is a rare case that an impression for an initial article is reversed in follow up articles.

These observation suggest that if an initial article is considered to be un-useful or not-interesting, a news reader program can drop its follow up articles with very low probability of dropping potentially interesting articles.

We also examined a similar relationship between initial and follow up articles using time spent to read them, to see if they have any new indications. Table 3 shows mutual relationships between initial-follow relationship and users' behavior (reading time). From this table, we can conclude the followings.

- If a user spent short time (say, less than 10 seconds) reading an initial article, time spent for its follow up articles are also short (less than 10 seconds) with very high probability of almost 76%. This is easily expected from the above observation concerning the inheritance of impressions.
- Even if a user spent long time (say, more than 20 seconds) to read an initial article, time spent for its follow up articles vary (second row in table 3). That is, time spent for follow up articles to an initial articles having long read time are not necessarily long.

Let us examine the second point more carefully. Our result indicates that 26.5% within the 35.1% of the articles with short read time (less than 10 seconds) that are follow up to an initial article with long read time (more than 20 seconds) are rated interesting. This figure is statistically meaningful compared to the ratio of interesting articles within all articles with reading time less than 10 seconds, which is 14%. That is, follow up articles to an interesting initial article are potentially interesting even if its own reading time is short.

5 Information Filtering using Sub-String Indexing

In this section, we describe a proposed information filtering method, using the user behavior monitoring described in the previous section as user profile acquisition and feedback, and its simulation results using the collected data.

In this filtering method, we adopt following hypotheses:

- We are making a first approximation of whether an information item is interesting or not by the appearance or pattern of characters or keywords in the information item.
- There are some common or similar features in the pattern of characters or keywords within a collection of information items rated interesting, and in a collection of information items rated not-interesting also.

In traditional approach to filter information based on user model [8, 9, 12], it has been considered that deep understanding of semantical contents of the information items is a necessity. In these approach, it is proposed that information filtering system is told of users preference in a form of "user model". Then, upon arrival of an incoming information, the information is semantically analyzed and checked against the user model if the item fit the user's needs.

Our approach is quite different from the above. As already given as one of our hypotheses, it seems that we do not understand the details of information when we are getting information from information service mainly for casual use like NetNews, *etc.*, and we are mostly judging from impressions of pattern of characters or keywords to determine if the given piece of information item is interesting or not. So, we adopted the sub-string indexing method that uses only a simple syntactical information as primitive method for evaluating pattern of characters.

5.1 Sub-String Indexing Method

In our information filtering method, we use sub-string indexing method to evaluate the pattern of characters. Here, sub-string (or n-gram) refers to a product of splitting a given string into a fixed length sub-parts allowing fixed length overlapping. Figure 5 gives an example of decomposing a Japanese string into sub-string of length 2 with overlapping length of 1.

Figure 4. Decomposition of a Japanese String into Sub-strings

Sato showed in [10] that best match information retrieval method using this sub-string indexing is very powerful and efficient. The basic idea of his method is to put Japanese texts in database with its sub-strings as keys, and a search is carried out using a query key, which also is decomposed into sub-strings, by searching a text that has highest number of matching sub-string keys. Figure 5 gives an example of score calculation.

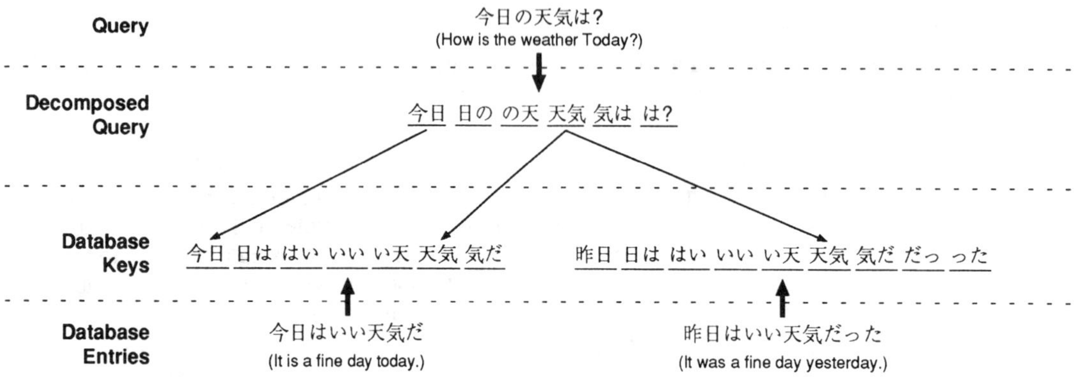

Figure 5. Best Match Text Retrieval using Sub-string Indexing

Our filtering method is a variation of the best match retrieval method. When a new article is given, we calculate its score, or occurrence count of all sub-string of the article in a sub-string database containing sub-strings made by splitting articles determined to be interesting in the past. We then use some threshold score to determine if the new article is interesting or not. Similarly, to determine if a new article is not-interesting, we can carry out the same scoring procedure using those articles that are determined not-interesting in the past.

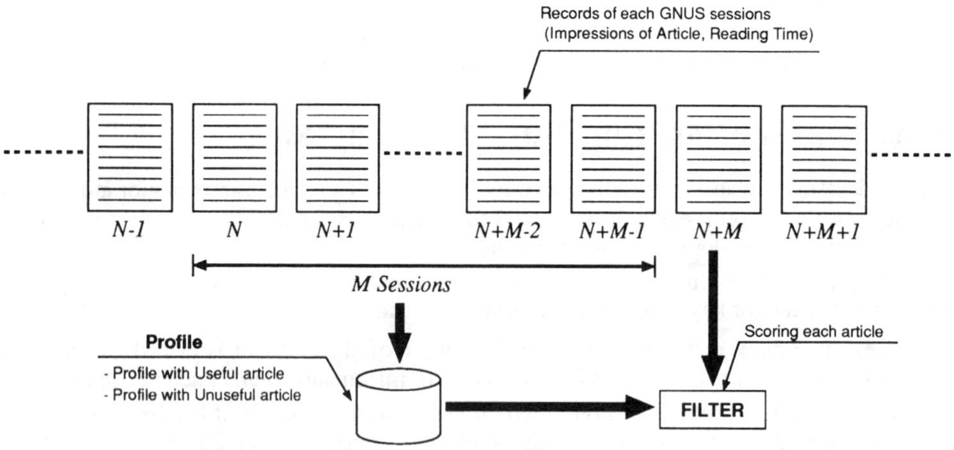

Figure 6. Evaluating Method

5.2 Evaluation

We evaluated the proposed information filtering method using the sub-string index method by a simulation using the collected data.

Figure 6 illustrates show how the simulation was carried out. We took records of M consecutive sessions starting at session N from a subject's records of GNUS interaction and rating work, and made a profile database of articles rated interesting and not-interesting by the subjects. Then, articles in $N + M$ th session was scored using the profile database. To increase the samples, we shifted the starting session N within the entire recorded session.

Table 4. Number of Articles in Evaluation Data Set

	# of Articles	Chance Performance
Rated Interesting	1956	30.1 %
Rated Not-interesting	756	11.6 %
Total	6511	

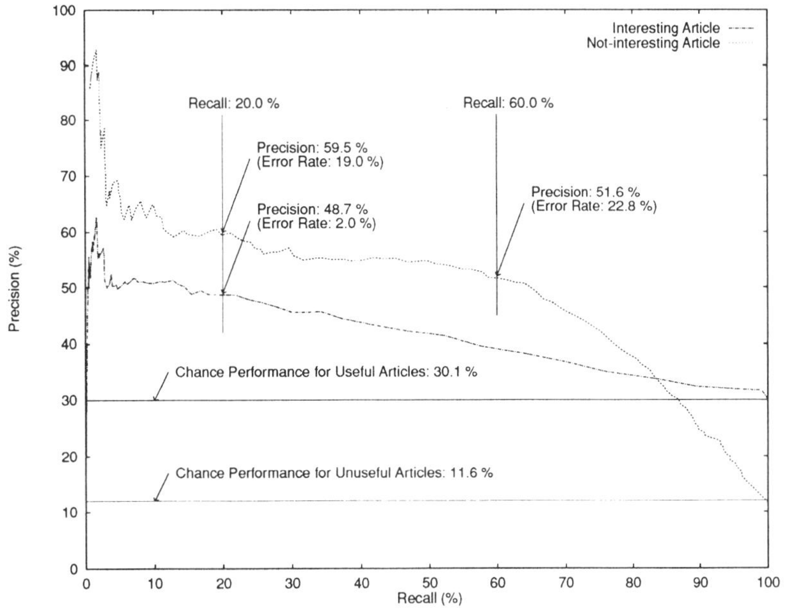

Figure 7. Precision curves of Filtering Information

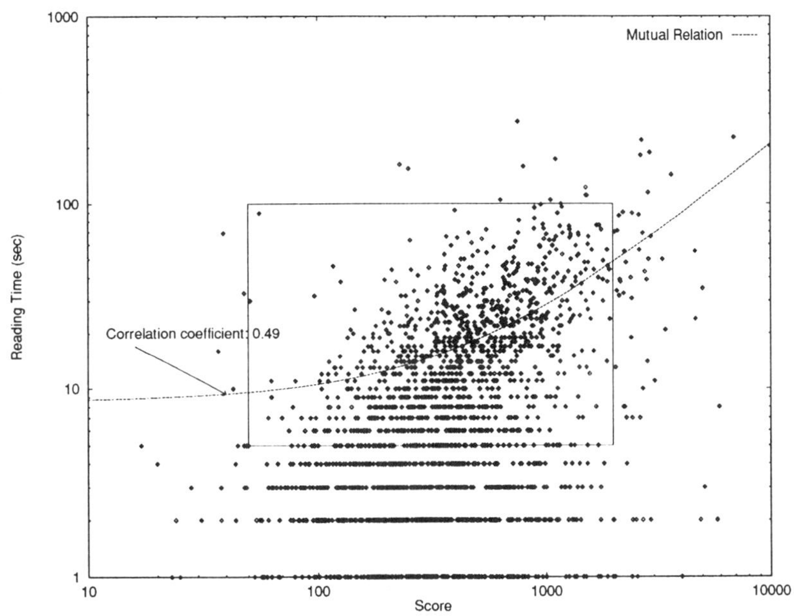

Figure 8. Correlation between Estimated Usefulness Scores and Reading Time

Table 4 shows dimension of data sets used in this evaluation. We varied the value of M in the range of 1, 2, 5, 10 and 20, and obtained best results with $M = 5$. Following discussions are based on this value of M.

Figure 7 shows precision-recall curves of predicting interesting and not-interesting articles, obtained by varying the threshold scores that determines whether the articles are interesting or not. It illustrates that the filtering for both interesting and not-interesting articles performed considerably better than their chance performance. For example, at the recall rate of 20%, precisions are 48.7% for interesting articles and 59.5% for not-interesting articles. Filtering of not-interesting articles perform well even at the high recall rate of 60% with precision of 51.6% against chance performance of 11.6%.

To further justify our hypothesis given at the beginning of this section, we examined the correlation between estimated usefulness scores and reading time for all articles. Figure 8 shows the correlation between these two values. This figure shows there is a strong correlation between them (correlation coefficient is 0.49), suggesting that the score calculated by our method can predict user's impression with very high precision.

5.3 User Feedback Methods and its Evaluation

We also carried out a similar simulation, using articles that are deemed interesting by monitoring user's behavior (reading time > 20 seconds) in the profile database, instead of articles by user's actual rating, and did the same prediction procedure using the score by sub-string indexing. With this simulation, although surprising but somewhat expected, the filtering method performed better than using a user's actual rating as the profile, in both precision and recall performance. We are interpreting this phenomenon as a result of user's mis-rating of articles. We consider this result as both interesting and encouraging, because the result suggests that articles having long read time has certain good characteristics as items in profile database.

However, we also found out that precision and recall performance degrade as we increase the degree of the feedback (increase M in figure 6). We call this phenomenon as *sub-string saturation.* When sub-string saturation occur, that is, when the profile database is saturated with too many sub-strings, any piece of information can obtain a high score. We are aware of the problem, and are still investigating the way to avoid the phenomenon.

6 Summary and Concluding Remarks

We conducted experiments to verify our assumption that (a) users' preference to NetNews articles are well reflected into the time spent to read these articles, and (b) users are carrying out simple syntactical pattern matching task upon deciding whether an article is interesting or not. Results of our experiment is very encouraging. Results presented in this report collectively suggest that our method does provide solutions for major issues of information filtering systems, namely profile acquisition/feedback without users' extra effort and filtering technique itself. Although we do not claim that the technique described here behave "semantically correct", e.g. it is not capable of picking up information that users actually do need, results presented in this paper indicates that our mechanism does perform as good as or little more than human users do in practice.

There are, however, several issues still waiting to be studied.

- *Improvement in filtering precision*

  As discussed in the last section, we observed the phenomena of sub-string saturation when we tried to increase the precision of filtering by increasing the degree of feedback. We must study further on to increase the precision without having sub-string saturation. We are looking at removing sub-strings that are obviously meaningless from the profile database.

- *Determination of uninteresting information by user behavior monitoring*

  Although our method of user behavior monitoring is highly capable of automatically determining interesting information, it does not perform as well for determining uninteresting information. As we observed that the disinterest of an initial article is inherited to its follow up articles stronger than interestingness of an initial article is inherited to its follow up articles, it is important to establish a way to determine if a certain information is uninteresting.

  In our experiment, due to the limitation in the GNUS news reader program, we were not capable of knowing if an article was completely read by a subject, or if time spent for each displayed page got shorter as the subject progress through the article. Since issuing a "next article" command or typing successive "next page" command are routinely used in our everyday NetNews life to skip uninteresting articles, monitoring these behaviors might bring a new result.

- *Effectiveness of our method for phonogramic language text*

  As discussed in section 3, it is interesting to examine if our method does perform as well for phonogramic language text. As also pointed out in section 3, we have a reason to expect our method to work as well. It is equally interesting to compare our techniques with filtering techniques using semantic processing such as LSI.

As needs for research on issues do remain, our approach seems to be quite promising as user friendly and cost effective way of information filtering, at least for ideogramic language text, especially those that are costly to carry out even a lowest level of semantical or grammatical analysis.

Acknowledgements

Results presented in this report owe a lot to those volunteered to be a subject of our experiment. Without their patience through tedious task of rating once read articles, this report would never be completed. We would also like to thank Professor Satoshi Sato of JAIST for his valuable advice in information retrieval using sub-string indexing.

Our appreciation also goes to Professor Naohito Chino of Aichi Gakuin University, department of psychology, for his advice in statistical analysis of the collected data.

References

1. Nicholas J. Belkin and W. Bruce Croft. Information Filtering and Information Retrieval: Two Sides of the Same Coin? *Communications of the ACM*, 35(12):29–38, December 1992.
2. Peter W. Foltz. Using Latent Semantic Indexing for Information Filtering. In *Proceedings of the ACM Conference on Office Information Systems*, pages 40–47, April 1990. Boston.
3. Brewster Kahle. Wide Area Information Server Concepts. Thinking Machines (FTP:/wais/doc/wais-concepts.txt@quake.think.com), 1989.
4. Shoshana Loeb. Architecting Personalized Delivery of Multimedia Information. *Communications of the ACM*, 35(12):39–48, December 1992.
5. Thomas W. Malone, Kenneth R. Grant, Franklyn A. Turbak, Stephen A. Brobst, and Michael D. Cohen. Intelligent Information-Shareing System. *Communications of the ACM*, 30(5):390–402, May 1987.
6. Masahiro Morita. A Survey of Information Filtering Technology (In Japanese). JAIST Research Report IS–RR–93–9I, School of Information Science, Japan Advanced Institute of Science and Technology, 1993. FTP: /pub/jaist/doc/93/rr/is-rr-93-9i.ps@ftp.jaist.ac.jp.
7. Masahiro Morita. Information Filtering Based on User Behavior Analysis (In Japanese). Master's thesis, School of Information Science, Japan Advanced Institute of Science and Technology, February 1994.
8. Ashwin Ram. A Knowledge goals: A Theory of Interestingness. In *Proceedings of the 12th annual conference of the cognitive science society*, pages 206–214, July 1990. Cambridge, Mass.
9. Ashwin Ram. Natural Language Understanding for Inforamtion Filtering Systems. *Communications of the ACM*, 35(12):80–81, December 1992.
10. Satoshi Sato. CTM2: A Japanese-English Example-Based Translation Aid System using N-gram Index Method (In Japanese). JAIST Research Report IS–RR–93–6I, School of Information Science, Japan Advanced Institute of Science and Technology, 1993. FTP: /pub/jaist/doc/93/rr/is-rr-93-6i.ps@ftp.jaist.ac.jp.
11. Satoshi Sato and Takeshi Kawase. A High-Speed Best Match Retrieval Method for Japanese Text. *Submitted to COLING'94*, 1994.
12. Irene Stadnyk and Robert Kass. Modeling Users' Interests in Information Filters. *Communications of the ACM*, 35(12):49–50, December 1992.

Improving Text Retrieval for the Routing Problem using Latent Semantic Indexing

David Hull

Xerox PARC and Stanford University
3333 Coyote Hill Rd. Palo Alto, CA 94304
internet: hull@parc.xerox.com

Abstract

Latent Semantic Indexing (LSI) is a novel approach to information retrieval that attempts to model the underlying structure of term associations by transforming the traditional representation of documents as vectors of weighted term frequencies to a new coordinate space where both documents and terms are represented as linear combinations of underlying semantic factors. In previous research, LSI has produced a small improvement in retrieval performance. In this paper, we apply LSI to the routing task, which operates under the assumption that a sample of relevant and non-relevant documents is available to use in constructing the query. Once again, LSI slightly improves performance. However, when LSI is used is conjuction with statistical classification, there is a dramatic improvement in performance.

1 Introduction

The vector space model (VSM) [1], which measures the similarity between the query and each document by the weighted inner product of overlapping terms, has long been a standard in information retrieval. The VSM has its flaws, since it ignores both the order and association between terms, but it is hard to find a better method with an equivalent computational complexity. The recent development of Latent Semantic Indexing (LSI) [2] opens a promising avenue of research into methods for using term associations. LSI is a method designed to refine and improve vector space retrieval by transforming the search space to a new coordinate system that captures the most important underlying structure in the association matrix between terms and documents. The method reduces the full term-document matrix to a small number of information-rich LSI vectors, which can then be used in a traditional retrieval model or as the basis for more advanced statistical classification algorithms.

In this paper, we will examine LSI and the vector space model in a slightly different setting than that of the traditional query-based retrieval problem. Instead of basing the analysis only on the initial query, we will assume that the user has a sample of relevant and non-relevant documents which can be used to construct an improved query. The goal is then to find the relevant documents in a new collection or the remaining relevant documents in the collection that the sample is drawn from. This task is equivalent to the routing problem used for system evaluation at the TREC retrieval conference [3]. One can also imagine this task as the second stage in a retrieval algorithm in place of the the traditional strategy of relevance feedback [4].

Since this approach starts with an information-rich environment, we can concentrate on overcoming the problems associated with using term frequencies as the underlying variables in the retrieval model. If our retrieval strategy does not improve performance for the routing task, then it will not produce good results for query-based information retrieval. If an improved variable set is found, it will then be possible to address the question of improving the model in an information-poor environment.

In the following sections, we: (1) present a brief overview of Latent Semantic Indexing, describing the advantages and drawbacks of using it for document retrieval; (2) evaluate the performance of LSI and the vector space model for the routing task using the Cranfield collection; (3) show how the singular value decomposition can be used to generalize the traditional form of the query for the routing problem; (4) describe a statistical classification technique for ranking the documents; (5) evaluate the statistical model on the routing task and show the conditions under which it improves retrieval performance; and (6) make suggestions for future research.

2 Latent Semantic Indexing

Since most retrieval strategies not based on natural language processing ignore the order of terms in a document, the document by term matrix, where each entry gives the term frequency in the corresponding document, is sufficient to represent the collection. However, some of the information contained there could actually hinder the process of document retrieval. A smaller, more tractable representation of terms and documents that retains only the most important information from the original matrix may actually improve both the quality and the speed of the retrieval system. The singular value decomposition (SVD) is a matrix decomposition that produces a reasonable solution to this problem by describing terms and documents as linear combinations of orthogonal (uncorrelated) indexing variables. From Deerwester et al. [2]:

> . . . these factors may be thought of as artificial concepts; they represent extracted common meaning components of many different words and documents. Each term or document is then characterized by a vector of weights indicating its strength of association with each of these underlying concepts. [. . .] Our aim is . . . to represent terms, documents, and queries in a way that escapes the unreliability, ambiguity, and redundancy of individual terms as descriptors.

The SVD represents the original document by term matrix as the product of three other matrices: $X = DST'$, where the rows of D and T represent the documents and terms respectively in the new coordinate space defined by the columns of the these matrices. The diagonal elements of matrix S assign weights to the factors according to their significance, while the off-diagonal elements are zero.

The power of this decomposition comes from the fact that the new factors are presented in the order of their importance (as measured by the diagonal of S). Therefore, the least important factors can easily be removed by truncating the matrices D, T, and S, i.e. by deleting some of the right-most columns of these matrices. The remaining columns of D will be called the LSI factors. In fact, the truncated matrix $X^* = D^*S^*T'^*$ is the matrix of reduced rank which is most similar to X in terms of the least-squares norm. In subsequent experiments, performance will be measured for varying numbers of LSI factors. The following section presents reasons why using a reduced number of LSI factors could be helpful for retrieval.

2.1 Advantages of LSI

Deerwester et al. [2] describe the three major advantages of using the LSI representation with the following labels: synonymy, polysemy, and term dependence. Synonymy refers to the fact that the same underlying concept can be described using different terms. Traditional retrieval strategies have trouble discovering documents on the same topic that use a different vocabulary. In LSI, the concept in question as well as all documents that are related to it are all likely to be represented by a similar weighted combination of indexing variables. In essence, LSI can be described as a method for automatic query expansion. It makes use of similar information to the technique proposed by Qiu and Frei [5], which performs query expansion using a term-term similarity matrix.

Polysemy describes words that have more than one meaning, which is common property of language. Large numbers of polysemous words in the query can reduce the precision of a search significantly. By using a reduced representation in LSI, one hopes to remove some "noise" from the data, which could be described as rare and less important usages of certain terms. However, using a reduced representation does not guarantee improved performance. Since the LSI term vector is just a weighted average of the different meanings of the term, when the real meaning differs from the average meaning, LSI may actually reduce the quality of the search. An SVD of the term similarity matrix can be used in conjunction with cluster analysis to directly determine the sense of a particular word as demonstrated by Schütze [6].

The traditional vector space model assumes term independence and terms serve as the orthogonal basis vectors of the vector space. Since there are strong associations between terms in language, this assumption is never satisfied. While term independence represents the most reasonable first-order approximation, it should be possible to obtain improved performance by using term associations in the retrieval process. Adding common phrases as search items is a simple application of this approach. On the other hand, the LSI factors are orthogonal by definition, and terms are positioned in the reduced space in a way that reflects the correlations in their use across documents. Some alternative methods for incorporating term associations into a retrieval model are given by Wong in [7, 18]. It is very difficult to take advantage of term associations without dramatically increasing the computational requirements of the retrieval problem. While the LSI solution is difficult to compute for large collections, it need only be constructed once for the entire collection and performance at retrieval time is not affected.

The theoretical advantages listed above will only be considered valuable if they can be translated directly into improved retrieval peformance. While Deerwester et al. have obtained some promising results, they do not show conclusively that retrieval using LSI is superior to the basic vector space model [2]. In the following section, we address this issue in the context of the routing problem. Our experiments will provide evidence that LSI slightly improves performance for the routing task.

2.2 Drawbacks of LSI

Unless LSI substantially improves retrieval performance, the storage and computational costs of the matrix decomposition may outweigh its benefits. While a reduced representation based on a small number of orthogonal variables might appear to cut storage costs substantially, the opposite is actually true. For example, the document by term matrix for the Cranfield collection used in our experiments has 90,441 non-zero entries (after stemming and stop word removal). Retaining only 100 of the possible 1399 LSI vectors requires storing 139,900 values for the documents alone. The term vectors require the storage of roughly 400,000 additional values. In addition, the LSI values are real numbers while the original term frequencies are integers, adding to the storage costs. Using LSI vectors, we can no longer take advantage of the fact that each term occurs in a limited number of documents, which accounts for the sparse nature of the term by document matrix. With recent advances in electronic storage media, the storage requirements of LSI are not a critical problem, but the loss of sparseness has other, more serious implications.

One of the most important speed-ups in vector space search comes from using an inverted index. As a consequence, only documents that have some terms in common with the query must be examined during the search. With LSI, however, the query must be compared to every document in the collection. Fortunately, several factors can reduce or eliminate this drawback. If the query has more terms than its representation in the LSI vector space, then inner product similarity scores will take more time to compute in term space. For example, if relevance feedback is conducted using the full text of the relevant documents, the number of terms in the query is likely to grow to be many times the number of LSI vectors, leading to a corresponding increase in search time. In addition, using a data structure such as the k-d tree [8] in conjuction with LSI would greatly speed the search for nearest neighbors, provided only a partial ordering of the documents is required. Most of the additional costs come in the pre-processing stage when the SVD and the k-d tree are computed, and actual search time should not be significantly degraded. Other query expansion techniques suffer even more heavily from the difficulties described above, and LSI performs relatively well for long documents due to the small number of context vectors used to describe each document. However, implementation of LSI does require an additional investment of storage and computing time. The disadvantages of LSI in terms of retrieval performance are difficult to quantify. Other useful references to LSI include [9, 10].

2.3 Comparing LSI to the vector space model

Can LSI provide better performance than the vector space model? Deerwester et al. obtain experimental results for two collections, MED and CISI, comparing LSI to SMART [1] and several other term-matching strategies. For MED, LSI improves average precision from .45 to .51 (odds of 29 to 1 of this difference happening by chance), with the largest benefits being found at high recall. The authors note that they perform no stemming or term weighting in their LSI solution. Since term-weighting has a large positive impact on retrieval performance, the improvement found due to LSI appears to be promising. However, the authors also mention that the MED data set was constructed in a way likely to produce unrealistically good results for LSI.

Their second experiment, performed on the CISI collection, found no significant differences between LSI and SMART. In this example, LSI used the same set of index terms as SMART, i.e. stemming was included. In addition, when they compared average performance to the number of LSI factors included for the MED collection, they found found that performance improved with the number of factors until 80-100 factors were used in the model. These experiments suggest that LSI has the potential to improve search performance.

3 Evaluating LSI for the routing problem

We now address the issue of whether LSI improves performance when applied to the routing task. Our experiments use the Cranfield collection, a corpus of documents on aeronautics that is routinely studied in IR experiments. The collection consists of 225 queries, each with a list of relevant documents, and a total of 1399 documents. There are two reasons for choosing this collection: (1) it is small enough that the LSI representation can be computed and stored relatively easily; (2) it has a large number of queries and is considered a fair testing ground for new retrieval methods. However, the conclusions reached in this paper should be tested on larger, more varied document collections in the future.

Unfortunately, the Cranfield collection is not ideal for experiments on the routing problem. In an ideal experiment, the corpus would be divided into a training set of known relevant and nonrelevant documents and a test set of unknown documents to use for evaluation. However, with an average of only eight relevant documents per query, the Cranfield collection does not have enough relevant documents for this strategy to be feasible. We can still conduct a reasonable analysis by using the technique of cross-validation. The strategy is to remove one document at a time from the collection, and then use the remaining documents to try to predict the relevance of the missing document. With cross-validation, we can use nearly all of the collection without biasing the results of the experiment, given a willingness to adjust the routing query to evaluate each document.

Given a set of relevant and non-relevant documents, one must determine the best way to incorporate this information into the routing query. Rocchio [11] suggests using the difference between the mean of the relevant and the mean of the non-relevant documents.

$$Q_{opt} = \frac{1}{n} \sum_{i \in rel} \frac{D_i}{|D_i|} - \frac{1}{N-n} \sum_{j \in nrel} \frac{D_j}{|D_j|}$$

where N is the size of the collection, n is the number of relevant documents, and *rel* and *nonrel* refer to relevant and nonrelevant documents respectively. Subsequent research on relevance feedback [4] has obtained good results using the difference of weighted means to update the original query.

We choose to represent the routing query simply by the mean of the relevant documents for two reasons. First, previous experiments by the author on this collection have found no evidence that using non-relevant documents in the query improves performance. Second, if the non-relevant documents are ignored, cross-validation need only be performed over the relevant documents. Because relevant documents are such a small fraction of the collection, this substantially reduces the computational cost of the experiment.

Cross-validation differs from using the mean of the relevant documents as the query only in the following manner. Each relevant document is compared to the mean of the remaining relevant documents after excluding the document being examined. Therefore, a relevant document cannot favorably influence its own performance. The different queries are normalized to have equal length, and documents are ranked according to their inner product similarity to the routing query. Performance is evaluated using precision and recall.

In this experiment, we compare the performance of LSI with different numbers of factors to the traditional vector space model. A number of pre-processing steps are applied to the data. The raw terms are analyzed using a stemming algorithm and the most frequent function words are removed using a stop list. The terms in each document are then weighted by a function which has shown good performance in previous term-weighting experiments by the author:

$$w_{ij} = \frac{\sqrt{f_{ij}} * \log \frac{N}{n_i}}{\sqrt{|D_i|}}$$

where f_{ij} is the frequency of term j in document i, $|D_i|$ is the length of document i, $\log \frac{N}{n_i}$ is the traditional inverse document frequecy (idf) weighting. This weight function strongly resembles the tf-idf weighting structure and its variants which have been used frequently in other retrieval experiments [12]. The similarity between the routing queries and the relevant documents is measured by the inner product of the corresponding weighted query and document vectors.

In order to provide the best match between our LSI solution and the vector-space solution described earlier, we apply the same weighting scheme to the elements of the term-document matrix before computing the SVD. By matching the weight functions, we insure that the LSI and term-matching solutions are directly comparable. The SVD is then computed using SVDPACK, a sparse matrix SVD program written by Michael Berry and available through NETLIB [13]. The routing query for the LSI solution is chosen to be the average of the relevant documents as represented in LSI space. The similarities are then computed directly from the LSI representation, using cross-validation to compute the scores for the relevant documents.

$$sim(Q, D) = \sum_i q_i * s_i * d_i$$

where q_i and d_i are the weights for the i'th LSI factor for the query and document respectively, and s_i is the i'th diagonal element of the matrix S.

Performance is evaluated using several different strategies. We present scores that are the average of a 10-pt (10%-100%) precision-recall curve (avg.pr.curve), the average of precision evaluated at 1-20 documents retrieved (avg.precision) and the average of recall evaluated at 21-50 documents retrieved (avg.recall) [14]. These measures represent a number of different retrieval strategies that could be adopted by the user. The first scoring method is the traditional measure of evaluation in the IR community. The second method assumes the user is only searching a few documents and is primarily interested in precision. The third method assumes the user is examining a larger sample of documents and wants to maximize recall.

Figure 1 shows the results of the first experiment. The values listed are the average of the appropriate evaluation measure over 219 queries in the Cranfield collection. The six queries with only two relevant

Evaluation Method	VSM	40	← 80	LSI 120	→ 160	200
avg.pr.curve	0.509	0.406	0.507	0.544	0.556	0.567
avg.precision	0.405	0.328	0.403	0.433	0.444	0.451
avg.recall	0.758	0.732	0.796	0.811	0.809	0.811

Figure 1. Performance of LSI and the vector space model

documents are excluded, as cross-validation means that the query would be based on only a single relevant document, which is not a good demonstration of the routing problem. The performance of LSI is measured for 40, 80, 120, 160, and 200 factors retained.

The results from Figure 1 suggest that LSI improves performance when at least 100 LSI factors are included in the model. Performance decreases rapidly as the number of factors drops below that level. Performance increases gradually but levels off as the number of factors approaches 200. The performance curve for average recall rises faster, surpassing the vector space model at fewer than 80 factors and levels off by 120 factors. The best LSI model using 200 factors produces a 5% improvement in performance.

The statistical significance of the differences observed in Figure 1 was judged using the Friedman test and the two-way ANOVA [14]. All LSI models with 120 factors or more are found to be significantly better than the vector space model. The Friedman test suggests that 200 factors is better than 120 when the results are evaluated using the average precision-recall curve, but otherwise no significant differences are found between using 120, 160, and 200 LSI factors.

These results are fairly consistent with those obtained by Deerwester et al. even though the query-based retrieval model relies more on query expansion than the routing problem. This is a bit surprising since query expansion is probably the most significant contribution of the LSI model. For the routing problem, we already use a significant number of relevant documents in the query, so query expansion should not be so helpful. Harman [15] suggests that relevance feedback can be improved by selectively choosing the most important terms to add to the query. Perhaps in the routing problem LSI performs this term selection process in reverse by eliminating the less important components from the relevant documents.

In conclusion, LSI does not greatly improve performance over the vector space model for the routing problem, although the difference is measurable. In the next section, we examine an alternative application of LSI that can be used in conjunction with statistical classification to obtain a significant improvement in retrieval performance.

4 An improved model using LSI and statistical classification

In most retrieval models, the system ranks documents according to their inner product similarity with respect to a query. Most solutions to the routing problem use the same method, although information from known relevant and non-relevant documents is incorporated into the query construction process. Ranking documents according to their inner product similarity to a query is equivalent to applying a one-dimensional linear projection to the document space. A well-constructed query will provide a nice separation between the relevant and non-relevant documents. In general, there is no a priori reason to believe that a good linear separation of the relevant documents exists. If only the original query is available, it is hard to imagine a better method for identifying relevant documents. However, the routing problem has far more information that can be exploited. In particular, we can take advantage of the distribution of the relevant documents.

Statistical classification methods are designed to distinguish between groups (relevant and non-relevant) based on the distribution of the elements (documents) within each group. The general statistical classification problem can be described as follows. A population consists of two or more groups, and there exists a training sample for which the class of each element is known and a test sample for which the class is unknown. The goal is to produce a classification rule which will predict the class of the unknown elements. The classification rule is generated from the training sample based on a number of predictor variables that have been measured for both the known and unknown populations. The routing problem is merely a special case of the classification problem, since there are only two groups, relevant and nonrelevant.

The challenge comes in producing a good set of predictor variables. If there are too many predictor variables, the classifier will overfit the training data, which will lead to poor results on the test data. To give an extreme example, consider using terms as predictor variables. It is likely that every relevant document in the training sample has one or more unique terms. If one uses these terms to define the classification rule, then the classifier will perfectly identify the relevant documents in the training sample, but it will have no power to discriminate over the test sample.

For the routing problem, there must be significantly fewer predictor variables than relevant documents before it is possible to obtain good estimates of the parameters in the classification model. Based on this criterion, terms could not be used as predictor variables for classification. The LSI decomposition substantially reduces the dimension of document space. But even when the document representation is based on 100-200 LSI factors, it is very hard to produce a good classification rule for queries with 30 or fewer relevant documents.

Current methods produce a good classification rule based on a single predictor variable, the inner product similarity score with respect to the mean. It must be possible to produce a better rule using two or more predictor variables. A variant of Latent Semantic Indexing can be used to produce these variables. One could consider using a small subset of the factors from the original LSI solution, but these variables are based on the distribution of the documents across the entire collection and thus are poorly suited to distinguish between documents in the local region that contains the majority of the relevant documents. Therefore, we choose instead to compute a new LSI decomposition based only on the relevant documents.

In order to obtain the local LSI solution, we apply the singular value decomposition to a matrix whose rows are the relevant documents and whose columns are the factors of the original LSI matrix representation. This produces a new set of local LSI factors. We can retain as many local LSI factors as we wish to have predictor variables. The document scores with respect to each predictor variable are simply the inner product of the document representation with the corresponding local LSI factor.

One might ask why these newly derived variables should effectively separate the relevant and non-relevant documents. Each LSI factor is chosen to maximize the variance explained subject to the constraint that it must be orthogonal to all previously computed factors. In a sense, we are maximizing the information about the relevant documents that can be retained in a lower dimensional representation. The effectiveness of this method is best demonstrated using a picture.

Figure 4 plots the document scores for two local LSI factors taken from the results for the first query from the Cranfield collection. The large circles are relevant documents while the smaller squares represent non-relevant documents. The x and y coordinates of the points are the inner product scores of the document with respect to the first and second local LSI factors. Since these dimensions are not particularly meaningful for the non-relevant documents, their scores tend to fall in a cluster around the origin. The relevant documents are much more widely distributed, illustrating how these dimensions manage to capture the structure of the relevant documents.

For comparison, Figure 5 shows a one-dimensional projection onto the mean of the relevant documents. The non-relevant documents are replaced by a smooth estimate of their density function to improve the clarity of the picture. It is also relatively successful at separating the relevant and non-relevant documents, although the separation is not as clean as the two-dimensional representation in Figure 4.

The local LSI method has an increased cost because a separate SVD be computed for each query. However, the SVD is only being applied to the relevant documents, which means that the matrix is far smaller than the one used in the initial LSI decomposition. In addition, since documents are being represented in LSI space, the matrix has at most a few hundred columns. For a matrix of this size, the first few singular vectors that are required can be computed in only a few CPU seconds. However, a similarity score must now be computed for each factor of the new projection, which multiplies the compute time and the storage requirement by the number of local LSI factors. We now describe how statistical classification is used to identify the relevant documents.

Discriminant analysis [16] is a commonly used statistical classification technique. Essentially, it characterizes each population by its estimated mean vector and covariance matrix measured over the known observations. Each unknown observation is classified into the group with the nearest mean vector, scaled for the shape of the covariance matrix. For observation vectors x_j and groups g_i with n_i known members, the mean vector $\bar{x}_i$ and covariance matrix S_i are defined as:

$$\bar{x}_i = \sum_{j \in g_i} \frac{x_j}{n_i} \quad \text{and} \quad S_i = \frac{1}{n_i - 1} \sum_{j \in g_i} (x_j - \bar{x}_i)(x_j - \bar{x}_i)'$$

An unknown observation x is classified into the group with the nearest mean vector based on the Mahalanobis distance metric:

$$\text{dist}(x) = (x - \bar{x}_i)' S_i^{-1} (x - \bar{x}_i)$$

In the case of text-based retrieval, we are less interested in classifying a document as relevant or non-relevant than with ranking all the documents in terms of their probability of relevance. This can be accomplished by assigning each document a score as follows:

$$\text{score}(x_p) = \text{dist}(x_p, \bar{x}_{rel}) - \text{dist}(x_p, \bar{x}_{nrel})$$

Documents are ranked in increasing order of their scores, which reflect their relative likelihood of belonging to the relevant population. For convenience, we will refer to this method as TDA, for text-based discriminant analysis. Note that any other method of classification could be substituted at the this point, such as classification trees or neural networks.

5 Testing the performance of TDA

We return to the Cranfield collection to obtain an objective evaluation of the performance of TDA. Cross-validation [16] will again be used to obtain unbiased estimates of the scores of the relevant documents. The initial experiment will compare the VSM and LSI with 200 factors to a TDA model using two local LSI factors.

Eval. Method	VSM	LSI	TDA2
avg.pr.curve	0.509	0.567	0.760
avg.precision	0.405	0.451	0.604
avg.recall	0.758	0.811	0.830

Figure 2. Performance of TDA vs. LSI and the vector space model

The results of this experiment are presented in Figure 2. When evaluation is based on average precision at fixed recall, TDA combined with local LSI achieves more than three times the amount of improvement as was attained by using LSI instead of the VSM. Precision averaged over documents retained yields similar performance. Recall averaged over documents retained shows a much smaller improvement for TDA. The differences for the first two measures are statistically significant according to both an ANOVA and the Friedman test. The difference in average recall is only significant for the Friedman test. This discrepancy indicates that TDA is performing worse than LSI for a small number of queries, but better for most of the remaining queries.

We repeated the experiment using three, four, and five local LSI factors with TDA. The results, broken down by the number of relevant documents in the query, are presented in Figure 3. The local LSI decomposition cannot produce more dimensions than there are relevant documents. Since cross-validation removes one relevant document, there must be more relevant documents than local LSI factors to obtain a valid solution. In addition, when the number of dimensions selected approaches the number of relevant documents, there is overfitting to the training data.

num.rel	queries	LSI	TDA2	TDA3	TDA4	TDA5
3	29	0.568	0.363	NA	NA	NA
4	19	0.665	0.754	0.465	NA	NA
5	26	0.560	0.854	0.693	0.433	NA
6	28	0.485	0.853	0.795	0.642	0.463
7-8	36	0.631	0.877	0.906	0.843	0.693
9-10	29	0.606	0.852	0.908	0.928	0.894
11+	52	0.515	0.747	0.811	0.855	0.880

Figure 3. Precision averaged at 10%-100% recall, broken down by number of relevant documents

Figure 3 demonstrates that performance continues to improve as additional factors are added to the model, provided that the number of dimensions is less than half the number of relevant documents. However, the improvement becomes less and less significant as more dimensions are added. If both a training and test set are available, one can estimate the optimal number of local LSI factors using cross-validation over the training set. The final results come as no surprise. TDA makes use of much more information from the sample of relevant documents than is contained in a simple one dimensional projection such as the vector mean. More information in the model translates directly into better performance.

6 Conclusions and directions for future work

The vector space model has long been used as a basic framework for developing new retrieval methods. It is difficult to devise a retrieval strategy that performs better with an equivalent amount of computation. However, the vector space model has some significant problems. It assumes that terms are independent and thus ignores term associations. Latent Semantic Indexing addresses this problem by re-expressing the term-document matrix in a new coordinate system designed to capture the most significant components of the term association structure. Experiments run on the Cranfield collection demonstrate that LSI can improve retrieval performance for the routing problem if enough LSI factors are included in the analysis. However, the small performance gains measured may not justify the additional computing and storage costs associated with constructing and maintaining the LSI factors.

However, the LSI solution only needs to be as good as the VSM in order to useful as a component of the TDA model. When we apply the SVD again to the matrix of relevant documents, we can obtain a projection of the documents into a small number of local LSI factors that nicely separates the relevant and non-relevant documents. When this document space is analyzed using discriminant analysis, retrieval performance improves significantly. Performance continues to improve when more factors are added to the model, as long as there are more than twice as many relevant documents as factors.

TDA does take considerably more time to compute than the vector space model. Even so, TDA is still much faster than many of the alternative strategies for incorporating term associations into the retrieval model such as current applications of neural networks [7, 17] or the generalized vector space model [18], since it is applied to such a low dimensional subspace. In addition, time is a much less important issue for the routing problem. Of course, the SVD of the term-document matrix must also be computed, but this need only be done once, prior to constructing any routing queries. Future research will extend this strategy to query-based information retrieval, for which far less information is available. Although TDA cannot be applied without a set of known relevant documents, one can envision a form of relevance feedback based on TDA that has the potential to substantially improve performance.

References

1. Gerard Salton, editor. *The SMART retrieval system: Experiments in Automatic Document Processing.* Prentice-Hall, 1971.
2. S. Deerwester, S. Dumais, G. Furnas, T. Landauer, and R. Harshman. Indexing by latent semantic analysis. *Journal of the American Society for Information Science*, 41(6):391–407, 1990.
3. Donna Harman. Overview of the first TREC conference. In *Proc. of the 16th ACM/SIGIR Conference*, pages 36–47, 1993.
4. Gerard Salton and Christopher Buckley. Improving retrieval performance by relevance feedback. *Journal of the American Society for Information Science*, 41(4):288–297, 1990.
5. Yonggang Qiu and H.P. Frei. Concept based query expansion. In *Proc. of the 16th ACM/SIGIR Conference*, pages 160–169, 1993.
6. Hinrich Schütze. Dimensions of meaning. In *Proceedings of Supercomputing '92*, pages 787–796, 1992.
7. S.K.M. Wong, Y.J. Cai, and Y.Y. Yao. Computation of term associations by a neural network. In *Proc. of the 16th ACM/SIGIR Conference*, pages 107–115, 1993.
8. J. Friedman, J. Bentley, and R. Finkel. An algorithm for finding best matches in logarithmic expected time. *ACM Transactions on Mathematical Software*, 3(3):209–226, 1977.
9. G. Furnas, S. Deerwester, S. Dumais, T. Landauer, R. Harshman, L. Streeter, and K. Lochbaum. Information retrieval using a singular value decomposition model of latent semantic structure. In *Proc. of the 11th ACM/SIGIR Conference*, pages 465–480, 1988.
10. B.T. Bartell, G.W. Cottrell, and R.K. Belew. Latent semantic indexing is an optimal special case of multidimensional scaling. In *Proc. of the 15th ACM/SIGIR Conference*, pages 161–167, 1992.
11. J.J. Rocchio. Relevance feedback in information retrieval. In Gerard Salton, editor, *The SMART retrieval system: Experiments in Automatic Document Processing*, pages 313–323. Prentice-Hall, 1971.
12. Gerard Salton and Christopher Buckley. Term-weighting approaches in automatic text retrieval. *Information Processing and Management*, 24(5):513–523, 1988.
13. M. Berry. Large scale singular value computations. *International Journal of Supercomputer Applications*, 6(1):13–49, 1992.
14. David Hull. Using statistical testing in the evaluation of retrieval performance. In *Proc. of the 16th ACM/SIGIR Conference*, pages 329–338, 1993.
15. Donna Harman. Relevance feedback revisited. In *Proc. of the 15th ACM/SIGIR Conference*, pages 1–10, 1993.
16. Geoffrey J. McLachlan. *Discriminant Analysis and Statistical Pattern Recognition*, pages 52–64, 341–346. Wiley, 1992.
17. Ross Wilkinson and Philip Hingston. Using the cosine measure in a neural network for document retrieval. In *Proc. of the 14th ACM/SIGIR Conference*, pages 202–210, 1991.
18. S.K.M. Wong, W. Ziarko, and P.C.N. Wong. Generalized vector space model in information retrieval. In *Proc. of the 8th ACM/SIGIR Conference*, pages 18–25, 1985.

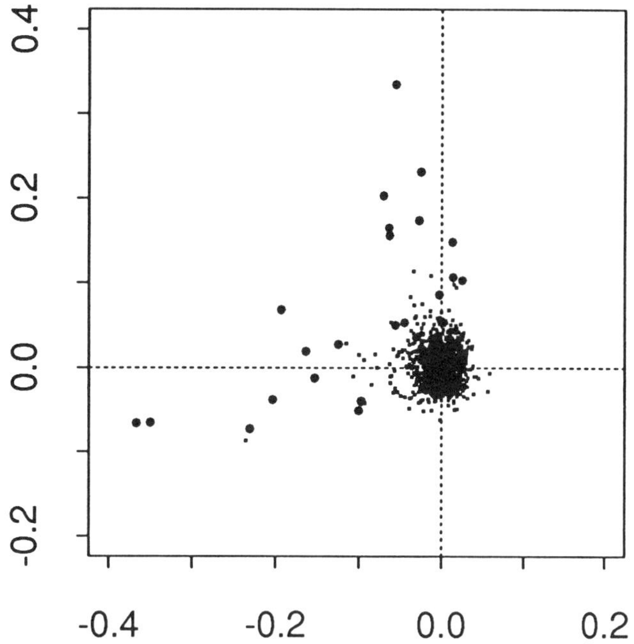

Figure 4: LSI projection

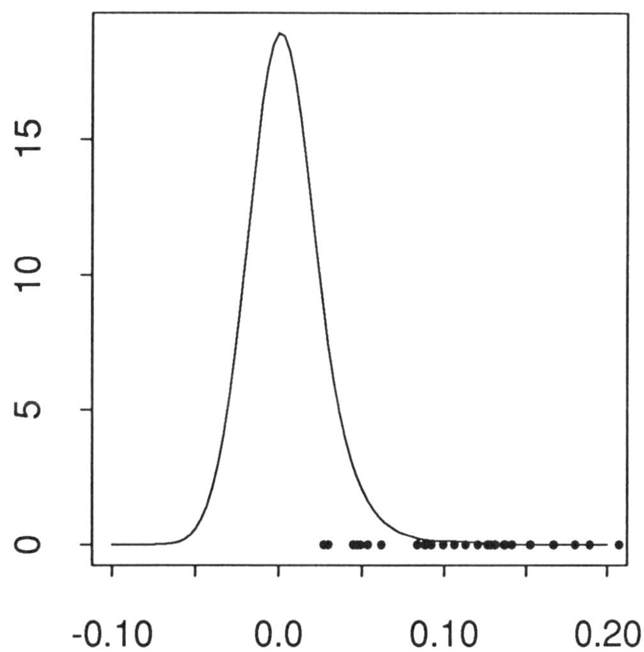

Figure 5: Mean projection

The Effect of Adding Relevance Information in a Relevance Feedback Environment

Chris Buckley*Gerard Salton, James Allan

Department of Computer Science
Upson Hall
Cornell University
Ithaca, NY 14853-7501
Internet: {chrisb,gs,allan}@ cs.cornell.edu

Abstract

The effects of adding information from relevant documents are examined in the TREC routing environment. A modified Rocchio relevance feedback approach is used, with a varying number of relevant documents retrieved by an initial SMART search, and a varying number of terms from those relevant documents used to expand the initial query. Recall-precision evaluation reveals that as the amount of expansion of the query due to adding terms from relevant documents increases, so does the effectiveness. There appears to be a linear relationship between the log of the number of terms added and the recall-precision effectiveness. There also appears to be a linear relationship between the log of the number of known relevant documents and the recall-precision effectiveness.

1 Introduction

Relevance feedback is a commonly accepted method of improving interactive retrieval effectiveness.[1, 2, 3] An initial search is made by the system with a user-supplied query, returning a small number of documents to the user. The user indicates which of the returned documents are useful (relevant). The system then automatically reformulates the original query based upon those user relevance judgements. The new "feedback query" is then compared to the collection of documents, returning an improved set of documents to the user. The process can continue to iterate until the user's information need is satisfied.

The same relevance feedback techniques can be used in the routing environment, in which a user may have a long-lived information need and is interested in any new documents that match the need. In this case the user's query can be constantly updated by the system as it receives relevance information about new documents seen by the user. Over the life of the query, thousands of documents could conceivably be returned to the user for relevance judgements.

The question of to what degree relevance information can be effectively used by a relevance feedback process has only cursorily been studied. Until very recently, there has not been a good test bed for examination of this question. The standard small information retrieval test collections do not have enough relevant documents to be able to effectively alter the amount of learning information while keeping a constant environment for testing the effects of the added information. The TREC[4, 5] routing environment solves that problem. It is possible to gather information from a learning set consisting of hundreds of thousands of documents, with an average of hundreds of relevant documents per query. The learned information can be used to alter the original query, which can then be evaluated on a separate set of hundreds of thousands of documents, with again an average of hundreds of relevant documents per query.

We study the effects of varying two sources of information from relevant documents. The first is the number of known relevant documents used for feedback. The second is the number of terms occurring in the relevant documents that are to be added to the original query. Two earlier experiments, Salton and Buckley [2] and Haines and Croft [3], on the standard small collections suggest that increasing the number of terms added can improve effectiveness, or at least does not harm effectiveness. However, the limitations of the small collection test environment precluded looking at this relationship in detail.

One of the criticisms of the TREC experimental setup is that the learning set information is gathered from the combined runs of many, very different, retrieval systems. While this is good for the completeness of the relevance judgements, it is not the environment that will be encountered in general. In practice, the relevance judgements will necessarily be gathered from one retrieval system, and thus any biases induced by that system will affect the set of relevant documents to be used for feedback. To avoid that problem,

*This study was supported in part by the National Science Foundation under grant IRI 93-00124.

Set Name	Type	Size (bytes)	Size(records)
D_{12}	documents	2.3 Gbytes	742709
D_3	documents	1.3 Gbytes	336314
Q_2	queries	52380	50
JQ_2D_{12}	judgements	–	16394
JQ_2D_3	judgements	–	10489

Table 1. TREC Collection Sets Used

the sets of relevant documents that we use for the learning information are the top documents retrieved by the SMART system itself. However, further tests here using the global set of learning information contributed by many systems show that this is not an important concern.

2 Methodology

The TREC environment offers several sets of documents, queries, and relevance judgements. The ones used for this experiment are described in Table 1.

An initial vector space run is done with queries Q_2, running on the "learning document set" D_{12}. The queries are weighted with the "ltc" weighting scheme.[6, 7] Each query term, q_k, receives a weight that increases as the number of times q_k occurs in the query increases (term frequency contribution), but decreases as the proportion of documents the term occurs in increases (the idf or inverse document frequency contribution.) The entire query vector is normalized using the cosine length of the vector.

$$q_{ik} = \frac{(\log(f_{ik}) + 1.0) * \log(N_D/n_k)}{\sqrt{\sum_{j=1}^{t}[(\log(f_{ij}) + 1.0) * \log(N_D/n_j)]^2}}$$

where f_{ik} is the number of times term k occurs in Q_i, N_D is the collection size, and n_k the number of documents with term k assigned.

The documents are weighted with the "lnc" weighting scheme which is the same as the "ltc" query scheme, except no idf factor is used. This "lnc" document weight, "ltc" query weight combination proved very effective in TREC 1 and TREC 2.

N documents are retrieved for each query, where N varies from 5 to 5000. The relevance judgements JQ_2D_{12} are used to determine which of the retrieved documents are relevant. All other documents, both retrieved and non-retrieved, are considered non-relevant. The query is then expanded by adding the X terms that occur in the largest number of relevant documents. Ties are broken by preferring those terms with the highest average weight in the relevant documents. In the experiments below, X varies from 0 to 4000.

The expanded query is weighted using the modified Rocchio formula used by Cornell in TREC 2[2, 7, 8]:

$$\begin{aligned} Q_i^{\text{new}} &= \alpha\, Q_i^{\text{old}} \\ &+ \beta \frac{1}{|\text{rel docs}|} \sum_{\text{rel docs}} wt_i \\ &- \gamma \frac{1}{|\text{nonrel docs}|} \sum_{\text{nonrel docs}} wt_i \end{aligned}$$

Query terms with overall negative weights are dropped.

This reweighting differs from the original Rocchio formula only in that the original formula used

$$-\gamma \frac{1}{|\text{known nonrel docs}|} \sum_{\text{known nonrel docs}} wt_i$$

That is, the only documents considered non-relevant were those that had been seen by the user and judged non-relevant. The modified formula makes the assumption that all unseen documents are non-relevant, an assumption which is undoubtedly false, but perhaps better than the assumption that the known non-relevant documents are representative of non-relevant documents in general.

One crucial property of the modified Rocchio approach is that the weight of a term in a query generally decreases as the amount of information known about the term decreases. A term's weight is averaged over all relevant and non-relevant documents, not just the documents in which it occurs. Thus a term that occurs comparatively infrequently in both the collection and the relevant documents will have a low value for both the contribution from the relevant documents, and the contribution from the non-relevant documents. The net contribution of the term is the (weighted) difference between those two values, which is guaranteed to be low. This property is important since random chance dictates much of the occurrence characteristics of low-frequency terms.

This can be compared with the probabilistic approaches[9, 10] in which the final contribution of a term is a ratio between a value due to relevant documents and a value due to non-relevant documents (or more precisely, the log of a ratio). The values are lower for the more infrequent terms, but since a ratio is being computed, if the relevant value and non-relevant value decrease by the same factor, the magnitude of the final contribution will not decrease. For example, with binary-weighted documents and the modified Rocchio approach, a term which occurs in 1/10 of the relevant documents and 1/100 of the non-relevant will have a weight of .09, while a term occurring in 1/100 of the relevant documents and 1/1000 of the non-relevant documents will have a weight of .009. The same two terms in the classical probabilistic model will have nearly equal weights (log (11.0) vs log (10.1)). Thus it is easy for the random effects of the infrequent terms to overwhelm the positive effects of the known good terms. A document should not be highly ranked solely because of the presence of terms occurring infrequently in the relevant documents.

The constants α, β, γ in the Rocchio formula are set to 8,16,4 respectively: the same values that were determined reasonable in TREC 2. This combination emphasizes occurrences in the relevant documents as opposed to non-relevant documents.

One subtle issue in using the Rocchio formula is that weights from documents and queries are being added together, which implies they must be based on the same factors. Thus instead of using "lnc" weights for the documents in the Rocchio formula (i.e., no idf factor for the document weights), the same "ltc" weighting scheme used by the queries is used for the documents.

Once an expanded, weighted query is constructed, it is run against D_3 (the "test document set"). D_3 again is weighted with "lnc" document weights. The relevance judgements JQ_2D_3 are used to evaluate the retrieval output. The evaluation values presented here are average recall-precision: the average precision after each relevant document is retrieved.[5] Graphically, this is the area under the well-known recall-precision graphs. A complete *relevant-rank* evaluation is done (i.e., the ranks of all relevant documents are used, not just a retrieved subset.)

Since the evaluated test runs are made on a different document collection than the learning runs, there is no need for rank freezing or residual collection evaluation.[11, 2] This is one reason why this experiment could not have been done in the past – the small collections did not have enough relevance information to be able to split collections and to both form and fairly evaluate feedback queries.

3 Results.

Table 2 shows the average recall-precision for the base case run of the original unmodified query being run against D_3 without any relevant information.

Run	Average recall-precision
"ltc" original query	0.2927

Table 2. Base-case Performance

Table 3 then gives the average recall-precision for a selected subset of values of N (number of retrieved documents to gather relevance information from) and X (number of terms from relevant documents to be added to query). Space prohibits showing the entire 10x13 table, but all values (except X=0) are plotted in Graph 1 with a logscale for the value of X.

Two additional runs are shown using relevance information gathered from many retrieval systems instead of just the SMART initial run. The run **all** uses all relevant documents found in judgement set JQ_2D_{12}. The run **all-1/4** randomly takes approximately 1/4 of all the relevant documents of JQ_2D_{12}.

Table 4 gives the average number of relevant documents (N') retrieved for each value of N, the number of initially retrieved documents. As is to be expected, the relationship is not linear: doubling the number of retrieved documents does not double the number of relevant retrieved documents. Also given in Table 4 is the average number of terms (X') by which each query is expanded for the 500 and 4000 targets. Obviously 3.1 relevant documents will not often contain 4000 unique terms that could possibly be added to the query! There were also a very few terms dropped because they would have had a negative weight.

Let X' be defined (as above) as the average number of terms added for a run, and N' be the average number of relevant documents retrieved for a run. Graph 1 plots X' on a log scale versus the resultant

N (Number Initially Retrieved)	X (Target Number of Expansion Terms) 0	5	10	50	200	500	4000
5	0.3083	0.3231	0.3291	0.3386	0.3458	0.3475	0.3475
15	0.3140	0.3285	0.3364	0.3495	0.3588	0.3618	0.3623
30	0.3161	0.3331	0.3380	0.3551	0.3657	0.3692	0.3698
50	0.3213	0.3373	0.3436	0.3635	0.3750	0.3805	0.3819
100	0.3203	0.3377	0.3455	0.3660	0.3789	0.3833	0.3855
200	0.3217	0.3419	0.3478	0.3690	0.3823	0.3878	0.3893
500	0.3237	0.3408	0.3488	0.3668	0.3827	0.3892	0.3917
1000	0.3274	0.3445	0.3553	0.3733	0.3904	0.3968	0.3993
2500	0.3311	0.3488	0.3577	0.3794	0.3993	0.4045	0.4064
5000	0.3316	0.3478	0.3576	0.3812	0.4018	0.4052	0.4062
all-1/4	0.3313	0.3468	0.3560	0.3805	0.3989	0.4046	0.4033
all	0.3314	0.3459	0.3566	0.3829	0.4026	0.4068	0.4062

Table 3. Average Recall-Precision For Selected Runs

Number Docs Seen	Avg Number Rel Docs	Number Expanded At Target 500	Number Expanded At Target 4000
5	3.1	257.9	287.8
15	8.8	376.8	573.3
30	16.9	435.1	925.0
50	27.3	473.9	1252.4
100	47.8	489.3	1766.8
200	80.2	497.9	2424.1
500	137.7	497.8	3041.7
1000	188.8	498.4	3385.9
2500	248.9	498.8	3658.0
5000	280.1	499.0	3736.5
all	327.9	499.5	3770.2

Table 4. Statistics For Selected Runs of Table 3

recall-precision for each of the possible values of N'. Graph 2 plots N' on a log scale versus the resultant recall-precision for each of the possible values of X.

4 Statistical Analysis.

The output of the Graph 1 consists of near-straight lines that appear to follow a linear relationship of the form

$$\text{Recall-precision} = A * log(N') + B * log(X') + C$$

A linear regression analysis is presented in Table 5 using log(N') and log(X') up to 500 expansion terms which shows that a reasonably close linear relationship exists.

Separate sets of linear regressions are shown in Tables 6 and 7 for each line of Graph 1 and Graph 2 (i.e., for each possible value of N in Graph 1 and each possible value for $X \leq 500$ in Graph 2)

5 Discussion of Results.

As expected from our earlier TREC 2 experiments, the more terms added from relevant documents, the better the recall-precision, up to a steady-state value. Massive query expansion works well for Rocchio feedback even if the relevance information is minimal. Expanding by 500 terms after looking at

A	B	C	R-Squared	SquaredError	F(2,77)	prob (F)
0.008118	0.01015	0.292022	0.9572	0.0041	861.1116	0.0000

Table 5. Regression Analysis for RP = A * log(N') + B * log(X') + C

N	A	B	R-Squared	SquaredError	F(1,6)	prob (F)
5	0.006139	0.315116	0.9838	0.0012	363.6741	0.0000
15	0.007559	0.319546	0.9757	0.0019	240.4660	0.0000
30	0.008408	0.320761	0.9823	0.0018	332.9829	0.0000
50	0.009793	0.322903	0.9854	0.0020	404.7223	0.0000
100	0.01018	0.323824	0.9792	0.0025	283.1230	0.0000
200	0.01037	0.326296	0.9865	0.0020	439.8625	0.0000
500	0.01064	0.325219	0.9907	0.0017	638.5675	0.0000
1000	0.01145	0.328259	0.9924	0.0017	780.6660	0.0000
2500	0.01272	0.329226	0.9897	0.0022	576.3812	0.0000
5000	0.01324	0.328358	0.9806	0.0031	303.5382	0.0000

Table 6. Regression Analysis for RP(N) = A * log(X') + B

X	A	B	R-Squared	SquaredError	F(1,8)	prob (F)
0	0.004735	0.303078	0.9447	0.0019	136.5866	0.0000
5	0.005335	0.317537	0.9674	0.0016	237.7434	0.0000
10	0.006168	0.321918	0.9714	0.0017	271.6812	0.0000
20	0.007403	0.326019	0.9735	0.0020	294.1245	0.0000
30	0.007753	0.328406	0.9592	0.0026	188.2034	0.0000
50	0.008518	0.331013	0.9511	0.0031	155.7192	0.0000
100	0.009772	0.333380	0.9567	0.0034	176.7990	0.0000
200	0.01134	0.333833	0.9643	0.0035	216.0912	0.0000
500	0.01207	0.335513	0.9756	0.0031	319.9049	0.0000

Table 7. Regression Analysis for RP(X) = A * log(N') + B

5 documents improves recall-precision by 19% as compared to the base case. This is even more impressive if one considers that six queries retrieve no relevant documents in the top 5 retrieved documents, and thus are unaltered by the feedback process.

The improvement is correspondingly stronger if much more relevance information is available. Adding 500 terms after looking at 2500 documents yields a 38% improvement. While nobody will judge 2500 documents in a relevance feedback environment, it is much more reasonable in a routing environment. 2500 documents is an average of 10 documents per working day for a year which for some long-lived routing queries may be desirable.

For all levels of relevant document information, the effectiveness increase starts to level off after 500 terms have been added. Except for minor random fluctuations after the effectiveness has reached its maximum value, there are no decreases in effectiveness due to adding more terms. Table 4 shows that only a small number of relevant documents are necessary in order to substantially expand the query. Thus the desired amount of query expansion does not depend strongly on the amount of relevant information.

The straight lines of Graph 1 and the statistical analysis of Tables 5 and 6 suggest a direct relationship between the log of the number of terms added to a Rocchio feedback query, and the effectiveness of the query. This means that doubling the number of new terms will add a constant to the recall-precision measure. For this particular set of queries and documents, with relevance information based on 100 retrieved documents, doubling the number of added terms (within the range 5 to 500) will yield about a 2.4% improvement in recall-precision over the base case. (0.01018 * log (2) / .2927).

There seems to be a similar relationship between the log of the number of relevant documents used and recall-precision effectiveness. The R-squared correlation measures of Table 7 are smaller, indicating the straight line fits are not as good as in Table 6, but they still seem to be valid. For this particular collection in the ranges of values considered, doubling the number of known relevant documents has a slightly smaller effect than doubling the number of expansion terms.

As Table 6 (or Table 7) shows, the two sources of added relevance information (X' = number of added terms, and N' = number of relevant documents used) are not truly independent. As N' grows, the slope of the lines gradually increase, as can be seen from the increasing values of column A. Thus the improvement due to doubling X' gradually increases from 1.5% at N = 5 (0.006139 * log(2) / .2927) to 3.1% at N = 5000 (0.01324 * log(2) / .2927). The relationship between N' and X' should be statistically explored further (e.g., adding a log(N')*log(X') factor into the linear regression equation improves the fit) when the current effects are better understood.

The two runs using relevance information from many systems (**all** and **all-1/4**) show that that multi-system relevant documents perform better than an equal number of single-system documents, but after a certain percentage of total relevant documents has been retrieved, the source of those documents is immaterial. This is not surprising: every system has its own weaknesses and strengths and thus some types of relevant documents will be hard to retrieve initially. If those documents can be found to be relevant using other systems, then the feedback query on the original system will be able to retrieve other documents of that type.

However, the improvement is not substantial. The **all-1/4** runs do about 3-4% better than the **N=200** run in Table 3, which uses an equal number of relevant documents. The reason for performing this comparison is that one of the criticisms of the TREC experimental setup has been that the learning set relevance judgements were derived from a pool of many different retrieval systems. This setup is unrealistic since in practice any relevance judgements available would come from one system. While 3-4% is noticeable, it is not enough improvement to warrant changes to the TREC experimental design. The extremely small differences between the **all-1/4** runs and **all** runs are also welcome news for TREC participants, suggesting that any lack of completeness of the TREC relevance judgements should have little effect upon the formation of routing queries (as long as there are not weaknesses shared by all participating systems).

6 Efficiency of massive query expansion.

The efficiency of massive query expansion depends on the environment. For interactive relevance feedback, the time needed for massive expansion in a normal vector-space model is prohibitive. Well over half the inverted file is being used for some of the runs above, with search time being slowed down by a factor of 40. The searcher or system administrator will have to judge the effectiveness/efficiency tradeoff suitable for themselves.

For routing though, reasonably massive expansion is feasible. As an extremely rough estimate, SMART handles about 100,000 extra query terms in about the same time as it takes to index a single document. Thus expanding 200 routing profiles by 500 terms apiece will at most double the amount of time needed to handle an incoming document. SMART indexes documents at 300 Mbytes/hour, so routing (in this example) could proceed at around 100-150 Mbytes/hour, which should be sufficient for many purposes.

7 Future work.

The conclusions reached here are based upon one collection with one set of queries using one relevance feedback approach. The general validity of the relationships proposed here remains to be proved. The most important immediate step is replication of the experiment in other environments. Earlier work with the small information retrieval test collections also reached the conclusion that as the number of added terms increases, so does the effectiveness, but nothing more detailed could be concluded. This work needs to be repeated in a large collection environment.

One very important question, of course, is why recall-precision effectiveness appears to be linear with the log of the number of added terms. A theoretical explanation would seem to be somewhat difficult given the large number of system-dependent decisions that take place between the initial simple concept of "adding more terms" and the final recall-precision output. A number of those decisions are crucial to even obtaining the simple result that adding more terms is beneficial. What exactly is being captured by this mathematical relationship?

The fact that any mathematical relationship at all exists between added information and effectiveness opens up an entire line of future experiments. It may be possible to isolate the effects of particular types of information, and explore weighting phenomena in much more detail than the large-scale investigations of the past.

8 Conclusions.

A large number of relevance feedback/routing runs are presented in the TREC routing environment. A modified Rocchio relevance feedback approach is used, with a varying amount of relevance information obtained from an initial SMART search.

Recall-precision effectiveness in this experiment varies linearly with the log of the number of terms added to the query from the relevant documents. Recall-precision also seems to vary linearly with the log of the number of known relevant documents. The implications of this mathematical relationship are not currently well-developed.

The overall effectiveness increase due to relevance feedback is quite impressive, ranging from 19% to 38% depending on the number of known relevant documents.

Finally, a comparison of feedback based upon an equal number of relevant documents obtained from either a single system (SMART), or a general pool of many systems, reveals a modest improvement of about 4% for using relevant documents from many sources.

References

1. Gerard Salton. *Automatic Text Processing—the Transformation, Analysis and Retrieval of Information by Computer.* Addison-Wesley Publishing Co., Reading, MA, 1989.
2. Gerard Salton and Chris Buckley. Improving retrieval performance by relevance feedback. *Journal of the American Society for Information Science*, 41(4):288–297, 1990.
3. David Haines and W. Bruce Croft. Relevance feedback and inference networks. In Robert Korfhage, Edie Rasmussen, and Peter Willett, editors, *Proceedings of the Sixteenth Annual International ACM SIGIR Conference on Research and Development in Information Retrieval*, pages 2–11, New York, 1993. Association for Computer Machinery.
4. D. K. Harman. Overview of the first Text REtrieval Conference (TREC-1). In D. K. Harman, editor, *Proceedings of the First Text REtrieval Conference (TREC-1)*, pages 1–20. NIST Special Publication 500-207, March 1993.
5. D. K. Harman. Overview of the second Text REtrieval Conference (TREC-2). In D. K. Harman, editor, *Proceedings of the Second Text REtrieval Conference (TREC-2).* NIST Special Publication (in preparation).
6. Chris Buckley, Gerard Salton, and James Allan. Automatic retrieval with locality information using SMART. In D. K. Harman, editor, *Proceedings of the First Text REtrieval Conference (TREC-1)*, pages 59–72. NIST Special Publication 500-207, March 1993.
7. Chris Buckley, James Allan, and Gerard Salton. Automatic routing and ad-hoc retrieval using SMART : TREC 2. In D. K. Harman, editor, *Proceedings of the Second Text REtrieval Conference (TREC-2).* NIST Special Publication (in preparation).
8. J.J. Rocchio. Relevance feedback in information retrieval. In Gerard Salton, editor, *The SMART Retrieval System—Experiments in Automatic Document Processing*, pages 313–323. Prentice Hall, Englewood Cliffs, NJ, 1971.
9. S.E. Robertson and K. Sparck Jones. Relevance weighting of search terms. *Journal of the American Society for Information Science*, 27(3):129–146, May-June 1976.
10. S.E. Robertson, C.J. van Rijsbergen, and M.F. Porter. Probabilistic models of indexing and searching. In R.N. Oddy, S.E. Robertson, C.J. van Rijsbergen, and P.W. Williams, editors, *Information Retrieval Research.* Butterworths, London, 1981.
11. Y.K. Chang, C. Cirillo, and J. Razon. Evaluation of feedback retrieval using modified freezing, residual collection, and test and control groups. In Gerard Salton, editor, *The SMART Retrieval System—Experiments in Automatic Document Processing*, chapter 17, pages 355–370. Prentice Hall, Englewood Cliffs, NJ, 1971.

Graph 1: Expansion vs Recall-Precision at Various Number Relevant

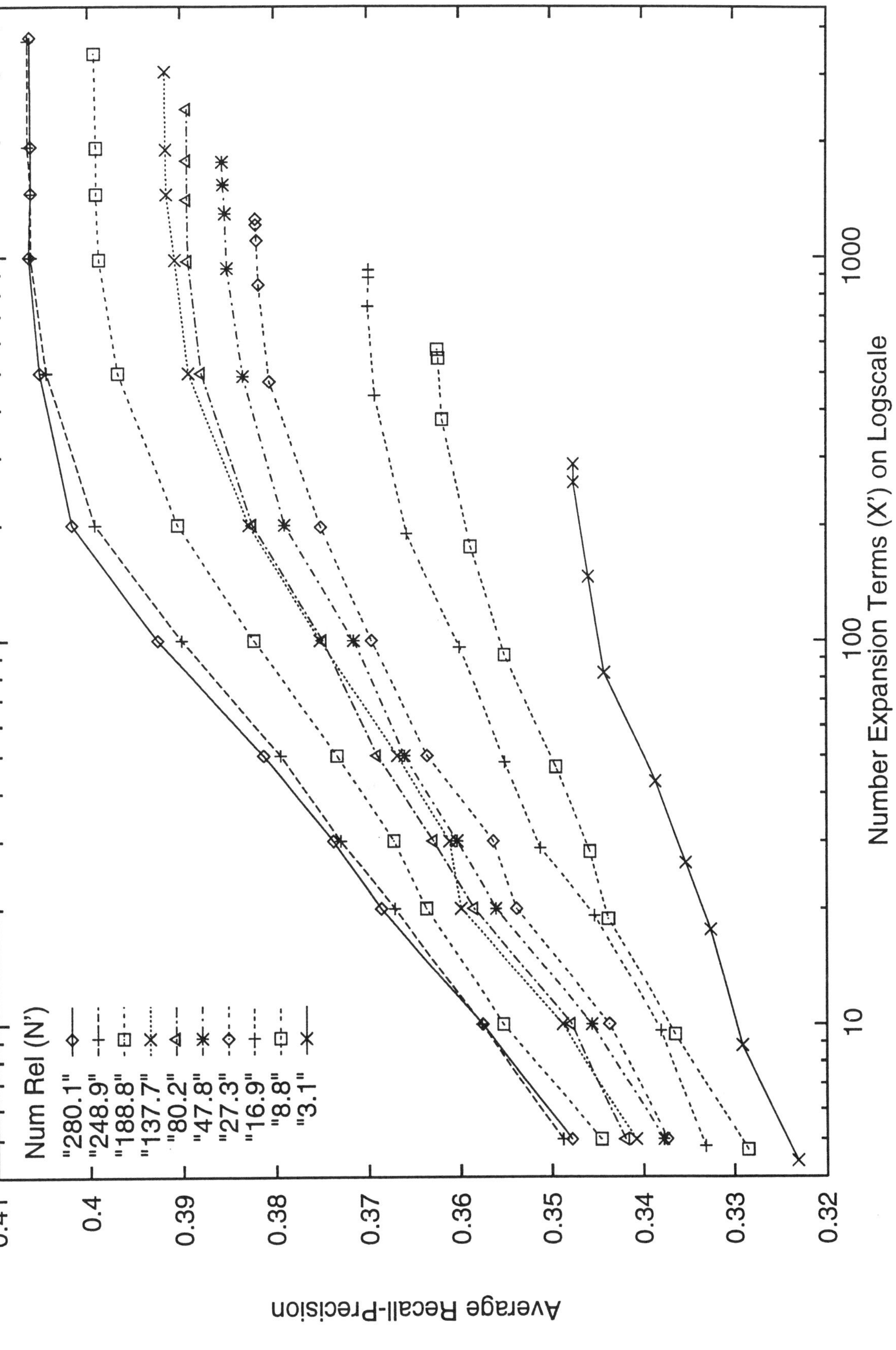

Graph 2: Number Relevant vs Recall-Precision at Various Expansion Values

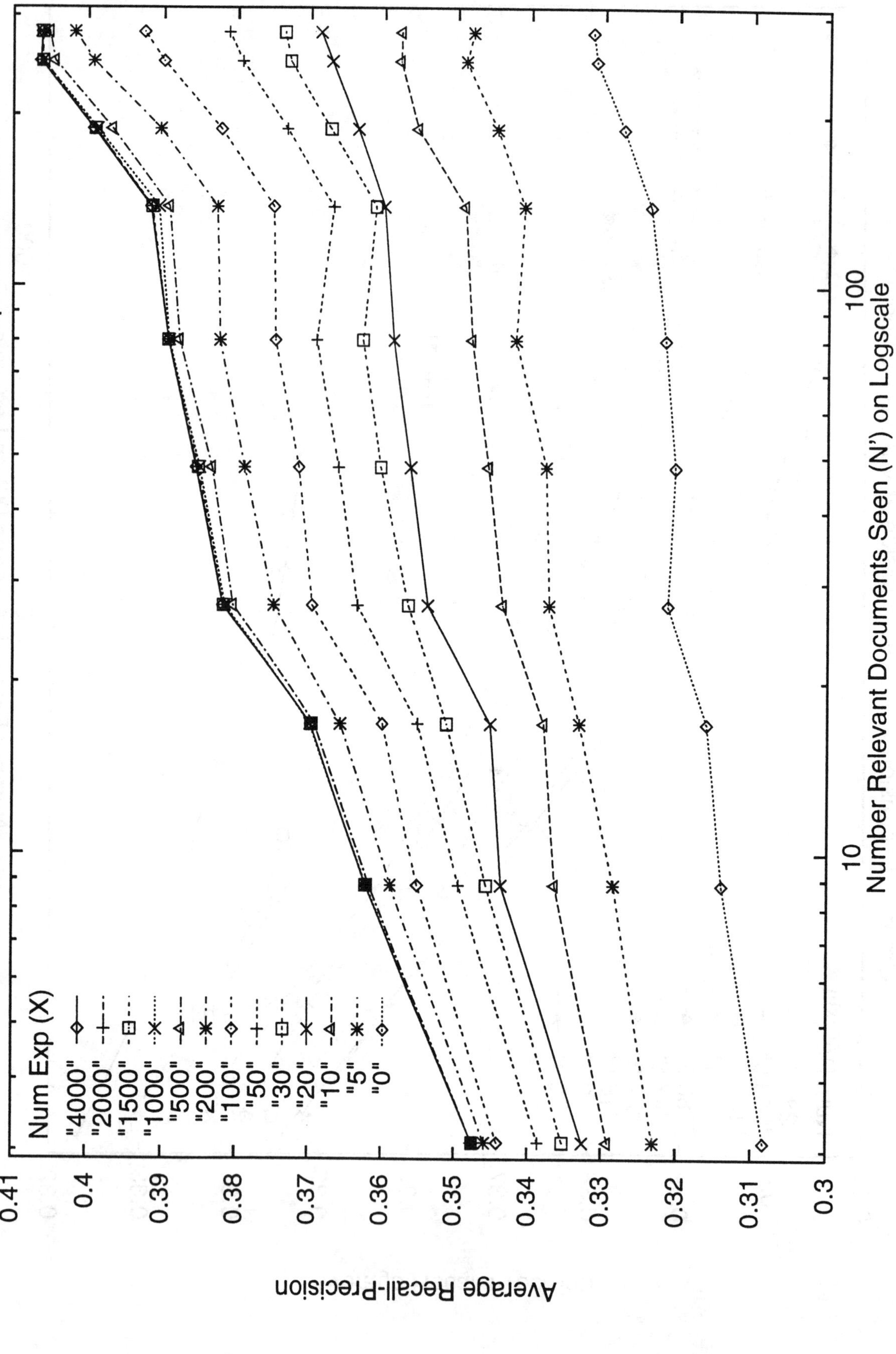

Passage Retrieval

Passage-Level Evidence in Document Retrieval

James P. Callan
callan@cs.umass.edu

Computer Science Department, University of Massachusetts
Amherst, MA 01003-4610, USA

Abstract

The increasing lengths of documents in full-text collections encourages renewed interest in the ranking and retrieval of document passages. Past research showed that evidence from passages can improve retrieval results, but it also raised questions about how passages are defined, how they can be ranked efficiently, and what is their proper role in long, structured documents.

This paper reports on experiments with passages in INQUERY, a probabilistic information retrieval system. Experiments were conducted with passages based on paragraphs, and with passages based on text windows of various sizes. Experimental results are given for three homogeneous and two heterogeneous document collections, ranging in size from three megabytes to two gigabytes.

1 Introduction

It is sometimes better to apply retrieval algorithms to portions of a document text than to all of the text. If each portion of text, or *passage*, is ranked, an interface can quickly direct a user to the relevant information in a document [11; 12]. Whether this feature is necessary or merely helpful was unclear from research using short and medium length documents. Recent work using long documents with complex internal structure suggests that passage-level evidence is an important part of document retrieval [14; 13; 15; 10; 6].

Long documents, documents with complex structure, and even short documents summarizing many subjects, are a challenge for algorithms that do not distinguish where in a document the text matches a query. If the algorithm cannot distinguish a few matches scattered across a document from a dense region of matches, it may have difficulty retrieving long documents and newswire "news summaries".

One can view information retrieval as a task of retrieving passages instead of documents [11]. During indexing, a document is divided into passages, perhaps with links maintained between its components, and each passage is stored as if it were a distinct entity [10; 9]. This approach has the advantage of simplicity, because no new algorithms are necessary. However, it creates a problem of how to recognize a small portion of relevant text that spans two passages [15]. It may also be unsuitable for very long queries, because chances are lower that short passages can match many of the query terms.

Information retrieval can also be viewed as a task of retrieving documents that have a hierarchical internal structure [14; 10]. For example, documents may contain sections, paragraphs and sentences. Each element of the document structure is a source of evidence that can be used in retrieval. Document-level matches are *global* evidence, while sentence-level matches are very *local*. Combining evidence from different levels of a document's structure may provide more accurate retrieval than will evidence from any single level [14].

The types of passages explored by researchers can be grouped into three classes: discourse, semantic, and window. *Discourse* passages are based upon textual discourse units (e.g. sentences, paragraphs and sections). *Semantic* passages are based upon the subject or content of the text (e.g. *TextTiling* [9]). *Window* passages are based upon a number of words.

One might expect discourse passages to be the most effective, because discourse boundaries organize material by content. However, discourse passages also require more consistency from writers than do semantic or window passages. If writers are sloppy or rushed, or if discourse boundaries are introduced for visual presentation, then dividing documents by textual discourse boundaries may be inappropriate. Discourse passages have been found to work well with highly structured and edited encyclopedia text [14; 13]. However, in experiments with the TIPSTER collection [8], which contains short, long, structured, and news summary documents, discourse passages sometimes worked well and sometimes did not [2; 10].

In spite of the intuitive appeal of passages, and in spite of the evidence in their favor, it remains unclear how important they are and how to use them effectively. What *is* clear is that passages present a system designer with a variety of challenging issues, ranging from how passages are defined, stored and retrieved to how they are combined with other forms of evidence. There are many more passages than documents, so in general they slow retrieval. How to use this source of evidence, and how to use it efficiently, are nontrivial problems.

This paper describes progress in adding passages to INQUERY, a probabilistic information retrieval system based upon a Bayesian inference network model [16; 4]. Two types of passages, discourse and window, are investigated. The issue of how best to use passage-level evidence, alone or in combination with document-level evidence, is also addressed. Finally, the issue of efficiently ranking passages is discussed briefly.

The work described in this paper differs from earlier work with INQUERY in which "paragraph-level" constraints were expressed with a proximity operator [3; 5]. The advantages of that approach were its precision, efficiency, and simplicity. The disadvantage was the all-or-nothing nature of the operator, which restricted its use to simple constraints formed manually. In the work reported here, a complex structured query can be applied to passages in exactly the same way it can be applied to documents. The principal difference is the amount of text involved.

2 Ranking Passages in INQUERY

Inference networks are an effective formalism for reasoning about multiple sources of uncertain evidence, which makes them particularly suited for IR. Previous research showed that INQUERY's performance, as measured by precision and recall, generally improved with the amount of evidence available. This result held for collections of short documents [16], a collection of large documents [7], and a heterogeneous collection [1].

INQUERY's effectiveness at using multiple sources of evidence is consistent with the view of IR as a task of retrieving structured documents. Multiple sources of evidence can be obtained by applying a query to various levels of a document, or by applying different queries to different levels. This approach requires adding to the query language operators that control the scope of a query or query fragment. In the work reported here, the INQUERY query language was extended slightly, to include a new operator that restricted the scope of its argument (a query or query fragment) to passages.

The implementation of a `#passage` scope operator required two restrictions on query formulation. The restrictions were 1) a slightly simplified phrase model, and 2) use of the synonym operator in place of the probabilistic OR operator. These restrictions simplified implementation, but are not inherent in the approach taken.

Two experiments investigated whether these restrictions cause any improvements in document retrieval that might be attributed mistakenly to use of passage-level evidence. Both experiments used complete and restricted query sets to retrieve documents from one volume of the TIPSTER collection (about a gigabyte text). TREC judgements were used to assess relevance. In both experiments, the restrictions caused a small loss in the average precision of document retrieval (−2.7% and −3.6%). The results suggest that relaxing these restrictions on query formulation would slightly improve the passage-level results presented below.

If passages are viewed as evidence for *document* retrieval, it makes little sense to store the score or rank of each passage in each document. The amount of memory required to do so for a collection like TIPSTER would be extremely large. Instead, it is sufficient to record the contribution of its passages to a document's score, and then to discard them. No extra memory is required. Preliminary experiments suggested that the best results could be obtained by recording only the contribution provided by a document's best passage. Others have found that adding the scores of several passages is effective [9; 17], but that was not the case in our experiments.

Ignorance of how best to divide documents into passages discouraged the use of special indices. Instead, experiments were conducted by reading the usual document-level indices and dividing documents into passages "on-the-fly" during retrieval. This approach requires only a very small index of discourse boundaries, but does slightly increase the cost of retrieval.

Three different approaches were taken to determining passage size and location: paragraphs, bounded paragraphs, and fixed-length windows. Paragraphs were recognized by heuristic rules (e.g. by indentation). Bounded paragraphs were paragraphs that were constrained to be greater than a minimum number of words and less than a maximum number of words. The sizes of fixed-length windows were specified as query-language parameters. Each approach is described in more detail below.

2.1 Paragraph Passages

A series of experiments was conducted with INQUERY to test discourse passages in the TIPSTER collection. The boundaries between paragraphs are not identified explicitly in the TIPSTER collection, so they were recognized automatically during indexing by a set of collection-specific heuristics. In preliminary experiments, paragraph boundaries performed poorly on collections of short and medium length

Table 1. TIPSTER Federal Register volume 1, selected queries, TREC-1 judgements. Paragraphs contained between 50 and 200 words.

Recall	Precision (27 queries)				
	Document (D)	Bounded Paragraph (BP)		Combined (2*D+BP)	
0	28.2	26.6	(−5.9)	28.5	(+0.9)
10	28.2	26.6	(−5.9)	28.5	(+0.9)
20	28.2	26.6	(−5.9)	27.9	(−1.3)
30	23.6	21.9	(−7.2)	23.8	(+1.1)
40	21.4	20.3	(−5.3)	21.4	(+0.1)
50	21.4	19.8	(−7.5)	20.3	(−4.9)
60	13.1	15.7	(+19.7)	12.7	(−3.6)
70	10.3	10.2	(−0.6)	11.1	(+8.2)
80	9.6	9.6	(+0.1)	10.2	(+6.0)
90	8.9	9.2	(+3.8)	9.6	(+8.1)
100	7.5	8.2	(+9.1)	8.5	(+12.6)
avg	18.2	17.7	(-2.9)	18.4	(+1.0)

Table 2. TIPSTER volumes 1 and 2, queries 101-150, TIPSTER 24 month judgements. Paragraphs contained between 50 and 200 words.

Interpolated Recall - Precision Averages:					
	Document (D)	Bounded Paragraph (BP)		Combined (2*D+BP)	
at 0.00	0.8275	0.7067	(−14.6)	0.8400	(+1.5)
at 0.10	0.5945	0.4722	(−20.6)	0.6101	(+2.6)
at 0.20	0.5383	0.4218	(−21.6)	0.5512	(+2.4)
at 0.30	0.4775	0.3673	(−23.1)	0.4985	(+4.4)
at 0.40	0.4290	0.3170	(−26.1)	0.4468	(+4.2)
at 0.50	0.3720	0.2659	(−28.5)	0.3864	(+3.9)
at 0.60	0.3133	0.2055	(−34.4)	0.3265	(+4.2)
at 0.70	0.2316	0.1393	(−39.9)	0.2482	(+7.2)
at 0.80	0.1388	0.0758	(−45.4)	0.1652	(+19.0)
at 0.90	0.0588	0.0293	(−50.2)	0.0758	(+28.9)
at 1.00	0.0095	0.0046	(−51.2)	0.0082	(−13.7)
Average precision (non-interpolated) over all rel docs					
	0.3480	0.2511	(−27.9)	0.3629	(+4.3)

documents (1987 Wall Street Journal), long documents (65 megabytes of Federal Register), and mixed documents (a combination of 1987 Wall Street Journal and 65 megabytes of Federal Register).

Manual verification of the heuristics revealed large variation in the sizes of paragraphs in the Wall Street Journal and the Federal Register. Wall Street Journal paragraphs were sometimes just one sentence long, and didn't always correspond to a shift in content. Federal Register paragraphs ranged from one line to thousands of words, and indicated more consistently a shift in content.

2.2 Bounded-Paragraph Passages

Bounded paragraphs were an attempt to solve the problems described above. The hypothesis was that one can provide more consistent paragraphs by merging short paragraphs and by dividing large paragraphs. A series of experiments suggested that 50 words be a minimum paragraph size and 200 words be a maximum paragraph size. Each paragraph smaller than the minimum was merged into the paragraph that followed it. In preliminary experiments with the 1987 Wall Street Journal, Federal Register, and combined collections described above, bounded paragraphs were more effective than "real" paragraphs.

This approach was evaluated in an experiment with 65 megabytes of TIPSTER volume 1 Federal Register documents (Table 1), and on TIPSTER volumes 1 and 2 as as part of the UMass participation in the TIPSTER project (Table 2).[1] In these experiments, retrieval of documents based on their single best

[1] TIPSTER participants were evaluated on only the top 1000 documents submitted for each query, so the results shown are not directly comparable to the full-ranking results from other tables in this paper.

matching paragraph produced losses of 2.9% and 27.9% respectively. However, combining the document-level and paragraph-level evidence produced 1.0% and 4.3% improvements in average precision.

The results from the Federal Register experiment should be viewed with caution, because there were very few relevant documents for each query. About half of the queries had just one relevant document. The results are included here because they are counterintuitive. One might expect queries with so few relevant documents to be unstable, but they were not. Instead, passage-level evidence had relatively little impact.

It is unclear from these experiments why retrieval based upon the best bounded paragraph performed so poorly with TIPSTER volumes 1 and 2. Another experiment with the 1987 Wall Street Journal and 65 megabytes of Federal Register (not included here) produced very similar results. One possibility is that the length-based criteria used for merging and dividing paragraphs produced passages that did not sufficiently organize text by content. An approach to reconstructing paragraphs based on semantic considerations (e.g. TextTiling [9]) might yield better results.

2.3 Window Passages

Discourse and semantic passages are based on the assumption that there is a single "good" organization of the information in a document. The difference between the two approaches is whether the writer is trusted to reveal that organization. However, what if there is no single division of a document into passages that is appropriate for all queries?

Passages based on fixed-length windows appear initially to have even more problems, because they impose a single division of text into passages, and because they are more likely to divide relevant text among different passages. However, both of these problems are solved easily.

The solution adopted for INQUERY was to begin the first passage in a document at the first term matching the query, creating new passages of length n every $\frac{n}{2}$ words. For example, if the passage length was 100 and the first matching term was at position 62, overlapping passages of 100 words would begin at positions 62, 112, 162, 212, etc. The use of overlapping passages reduces the chance that a small block of relevant text is split among two passages; it is similar in spirit to passage *blurring* [15].

If passage locations vary from query to query, then the formulae used to determine the evidence contributed by a term t to a document d cannot be used directly for passages. These formulae, shown below, require the frequency of the most frequent term in each document (max_tf_d).

$$ntf_{td} = 0.4 + 0.6 * \frac{\log(tf_{td} + 0.5)}{\log(max\_tf_d + 1.0)} \quad (1)$$

$$idf_t = \frac{\log\left(\frac{\text{docs in collection}}{\text{docs containing } t}\right)}{\log(\text{docs in collection})} \quad (2)$$

$$belief_{td} = 0.4 + 0.6 * ntf_{td} * idf_t \quad (3)$$

max_tf is determined easily during indexing for each document, but cannot be determined during indexing for passages whose locations depend upon queries. It is impractical to find the max_tf of a passage at runtime, so an alternative is required. The simplest solution is to use the max_tf of the document. However, better results are obtained when the term frequency of the passage (tf_{tp}) is scaled by the passage length. It is unclear why passage length, which is essentially constant for fixed-length windows, should be preferable for ranking passages.

The window-based approach to passages was tested in experiments with four collections. The collections, and their characteristics, are shown below.

Name	Size	Documents	Queries	Avg Query Length	Results (Table)
TIPSTER Fed Reg	474 MB	46,315	38	42.4	3
West	298 MB	11,953	34	11.3	4
TIPSTER vol. 1	1.2 GB	510,887	50	42.7	5
NPL	3 MB	11,429	93	10.8	6

The Federal Register experiment described in Section 2.2 found that passages based on bounded paragraphs had little effect on document retrieval (Table 1). Prior to testing the effects of window passages, a possible flaw in that earlier experiment, the small number of relevance judgements for several queries, was corrected. A new set of 38 queries was assembled, in which each query had at least 5 relevant documents. This is a better methodology, but unfortunately makes the results obtained not directly comparable to those in Table 1.

Table 3 shows the results from the experiment with window passages and the revised set of Federal Register queries. This experiment found that document retrieval based upon evidence from the single best passage was 20.7% better than retrieval based upon evidence from the entire document. A weighted

Table 3. TIPSTER Federal Register volumes 1 and 2, selected queries, TREC-1 and TREC-2 judgements. The window size was 300 words.

Recall	Precision (38 queries)				
	Document (D)	Window (W)		Combined (D+7∗W)	
0	66.4	68.1	(+2.6)	72.5	(+9.1)
10	53.1	60.1	(+13.1)	59.9	(+12.7)
20	40.4	48.9	(+21.0)	50.3	(+24.4)
30	36.2	43.5	(+20.2)	44.8	(+23.8)
40	32.5	40.1	(+23.6)	41.2	(+26.9)
50	26.7	36.1	(+35.1)	36.2	(+35.8)
60	22.7	33.6	(+47.7)	33.0	(+45.4)
70	20.2	28.1	(+39.2)	28.5	(+41.6)
80	18.4	23.2	(+25.9)	24.8	(+34.4)
90	13.4	16.4	(+21.9)	16.2	(+20.6)
100	8.9	11.2	(+25.5)	11.1	(+24.6)
avg	30.8	37.2	(+20.7)	38.0	(+23.5)

Table 4. West collection. The passage size was 200 words.

Recall	Precision (50 queries)				
	Document (D)	Window (W)		Combined (D+2∗W)	
0	87.6	95.9	(+9.5)	93.0	(+6.1)
10	81.7	86.6	(+6.0)	87.9	(+7.5)
20	77.1	79.3	(+2.9)	79.8	(+3.5)
30	72.4	74.9	(+3.4)	76.5	(+5.7)
40	64.1	65.2	(+1.8)	66.9	(+4.4)
50	59.3	58.2	(-1.9)	61.1	(+3.0)
60	52.0	51.3	(-1.4)	54.1	(+4.0)
70	43.5	43.9	(+0.9)	45.1	(+3.8)
80	35.2	37.5	(+6.7)	38.0	(+8.0)
90	21.5	23.7	(+10.2)	24.3	(+12.7)
100	12.0	12.9	(+7.5)	13.1	(+9.2)
avg	55.1	57.2	(+3.8)	58.2	(+5.5)

combination of document-level and passage-level evidence (D+7∗W) yielded a 23.5% improvement. Significant improvements were observed at virtually all recall levels. The heavy emphasis on passage-level evidence was required due to the large disparity in the performance of document-level and passage-level evidence. If the weighting were more moderate, for example D+2∗W, the combination would have been slightly worse than passage-level evidence alone.

A second experiment investigated the effect of window passages on a collection of legal documents provided by the West Publishing Company. The West documents are almost four times longer than the Federal Register documents, the queries are almost four times shorter, and the average precision from document-level evidence relatively high (55.1%).

The results were that document retrieval based upon evidence from the single best passage was 3.8% better than retrieval based upon evidence from the entire document (Table 4). A weighted combination of document-level and passage-level evidence (D+2∗W) yielded a 5.5% improvement. Once again, significant improvements were seen at most recall levels.

A third experiment investigated the effect of window passages on TIPSTER volume 1, a heterogeneous collection of about 500,000 documents. The TIPSTER documents range from 1 sentence to thousands of words in length, and contain a varied vocabulary. The earlier experiment with TIPSTER volumes 1 and 2, described in Section 2.2, found passages based upon bounded paragraph to be detrimental by themselves, and somewhat helpful when combined with document-level evidence (Table 2). The experiment with window passages used a different set of queries, a different portion of the TIPSTER collection, and a different method of evaluation, so the results of the two experiments are indicative but not directly comparable.

Table 5 shows the results from the experiment with window passages on TIPSTER volume 1. This experiment found that document retrieval based upon evidence from the single best passage was about the same as retrieval based upon evidence from the entire document. Combining document-level and

Table 5. TIPSTER volume 1, queries 51-100, TREC-1 judgements. The passage size was 200 words.

Recall	Precision (50 queries)				
	Document	Window		Combined	
	(D)	(W)		(D+2∗W)	
0	82.7	86.6	(+4.7)	86.5	(+4.5)
10	60.3	62.5	(+3.6)	65.0	(+7.8)
20	52.6	51.1	(-2.9)	55.9	(+6.2)
30	46.7	44.4	(-4.9)	49.4	(+5.9)
40	40.4	39.7	(-1.9)	43.6	(+7.8)
50	34.8	34.6	(-0.7)	37.4	(+7.5)
60	30.4	30.0	(-1.3)	32.8	(+8.0)
70	25.4	24.6	(-3.3)	27.7	(+9.1)
80	19.8	18.5	(-6.3)	21.4	(+8.6)
90	12.1	12.4	(+2.6)	13.9	(+14.6)
100	2.4	2.9	(+17.8)	2.9	(+21.0)
avg	37.1	37.0	(-0.1)	39.7	(+7.1)

Table 6. NPL collection. The passage size was 50 words.

Recall	Precision (93 queries)				
	Document	Window		Combined	
	(D)	(W)		(D+2∗W)	
0	71.1	72.3	(+1.7)	73.9	(+3.9)
10	57.5	61.1	(+6.3)	62.2	(+8.3)
20	47.5	48.8	(+2.8)	50.8	(+6.9)
30	39.0	39.7	(+1.6)	41.7	(+6.8)
40	32.4	32.5	(+0.3)	34.7	(+7.2)
50	25.2	26.4	(+4.9)	27.1	(+7.8)
60	18.1	18.7	(+3.4)	19.6	(+8.2)
70	13.4	14.6	(+9.0)	14.8	(+10.5)
80	10.5	10.9	(+4.6)	11.2	(+6.9)
90	6.3	6.5	(+3.2)	6.6	(+4.9)
100	3.2	3.2	(-1.9)	3.2	(-1.0)
avg	29.5	30.4	(+3.3)	31.4	(+6.7)

passage-level evidence yielded a 7.1% improvement. Significant improvements were seen at almost every level of recall for the combination retrieval.

The fourth and final experiment investigated the effect of long window passages on a collection of very short documents. The goal was to determine whether use of window passages, with the slightly different method of calculating belief, had a negative effect on short documents. The NPL collection of short physics abstracts was used for this fourth experiment.

One result was that the passage-level and document-level approaches to calculating belief yielded similar results, although small differences were apparent at all recall levels (Table 6). However, combining the results of the two approaches yielded a 6.5% increase in average precision, with significant improvements occurring at most recall levels. This result was unexpected, and bears further study. It may suggest ways of improving INQUERY's method of combining evidence, or it may mean that considering the same evidence from two points of view, even if they are only slightly different, yields some advantage.

2.3.1 Window Size

The four experiments described above were conducted with window sizes of 300 for Federal Register, 200 for West, 200 for TIPSTER volume 1, and 50 for NPL. These sizes were chosen to provide the best results for each collection. However, they raise the question of whether there is a single "right" passage size.

Experiments were conducted with a wide variety of passage sizes for each collection, ranging from 25 words to 10,000 words. Tables 7 and 8 show some of the results. Passages of 150-300 words yielded the best results. Performance was reasonably consistent in that range. If one had to choose a single size for all collections, a window of 200 or 250 words provides consistently good results.

Two experiments were conducted to determine the effects of combining the results of document-level evidence with evidence from 2 passages of different sizes. Both experiments yielded further improvements of about 1%, over all recall levels and in average precision, on the West collection. One can view this

Table 7. Effect of passage size on document retrieval, using only passage-level evidence. Values shown are 11-point average precision.

	Size of Passage											
Collection	25	50	75	100	150	200	250	300	400	500	750	1000
FR	32.0	33.9	33.4	34.8	36.0	36.0	36.6	37.2	36.5	35.7	35.2	34.9
West	51.6	54.1	55.6	56.0	56.5	57.2	57.3	56.5	56.6	56.2	55.9	55.0
Tip1	30.0	32.1	33.9	35.2	36.2	37.0	37.6	37.6	37.6	37.2	37.0	36.1
NPL	29.6	30.4	29.8	29.7	29.6	29.6	29.6	29.7	29.8	29.7	29.8	29.8

Table 8. Effect of passage size on document retrieval, using a combination of document and passage-level evidence (D+2*P). Values shown are 11-point average precision.

	Size of Passage											
Collection	25	50	75	100	150	200	250	300	400	500	750	1000
FR	35.2	36.2	35.6	35.8	36.6	36.8	36.8	36.9	35.9	35.6	35.2	34.8
West	57.3	57.8	57.7	57.9	58.0	58.2	58.0	57.6	57.5	57.4	56.7	56.0
Tip1	39.0	39.3	39.7	40.0	40.0	39.7	39.6	39.6	39.3	38.8	38.3	37.8
NPL	31.2	31.4	31.2	31.1	31.0	31.0	31.1	31.1	31.1	31.1	31.2	31.2

result as either diminishing returns or an indication that further improvements are possible. With careful implementation, this improvement might come at little additional cost.

3 Implementation and Efficiency

The original implementation of INQUERY repeatedly read from disk the complete inverted record for a term, merged the evidence into its accumulating store of evidence for each document, and then discarded the inverted list. This approach minimizes I/O, but requires increasing amounts of memory as a collection grows. Treating passages like documents would require at least an order of magnitude more memory.[2]

INQUERY now reads inverted lists in blocks, in parallel, computing a complete score for one document before proceeding to the next. This approach is known to slow I/O [18], but scales well, and enables optimizations that are impossible with the previous "term at a time" approach. Several commercial IR vendors also use this technique.[3]

The window-based approach to passages described above requires that a document be divided into passages after the query is available. Many document passages contain few or no query terms, so it makes little sense to evaluate the entire query once per passage. Instead, INQUERY assigns a default belief to each passage, and then each query operator updates the belief of any passage for which it has evidence. The result is a relatively fast ability to rank every passage in a document. The cost of ranking passages for 50 queries on TIPSTER volume 1 is about 25% higher than the cost of ranking documents.

One can avoid ranking every passage by ranking every document and then ranking passages for only those documents that exceed some threshold [14]. However, this technique runs the risk of missing a highly relevant passage in a long, mostly irrelevant document. One might expect this problem to become more serious as document length increases.

The results of experiments with the Federal Register collection, described above (Table 3), were examined to determine whether ranking passages only in the top-ranked documents would cause the system to overlook some relevant documents. The hypothesis was that if the system were required to retrieve n documents, it would be better to rank all documents by their best passages and then return the top n documents than to rank all documents and then rerank the top n based on their best passages. This collection was chosen because the documents are long and because passage-level evidence yielded significantly better results than document-level evidence (Table 3). There were 38 queries, and 1085 relevant documents (28.6 relevant documents per query, on average).

If the threshold n is 250 documents, the approach based on ranking all passages finds 33 more relevant documents. If the threshold is 500, ranking all passages finds 28 more relevant documents. The difference drops to 7 with a threshold of 1000 documents, and 4 with a threshold of 2000 documents. This result suggests that ranking all documents and then reranking the top n by passages may cause relatively little loss in recall, as long as n is large relative to the average number of relevant documents.

[2] Assuming 10 passages per document, which is conservative for the TIPSTER and West collections.
[3] Personal communications.

4 Conclusions

This paper describes experiments with paragraph-based and window-based methods of defining passages. The experiments were conducted with three relatively homogeneous collections (Federal Register, West, and NPL) and two relatively heterogeneous collections (TIPSTER volume 1, and TIPSTER volumes 1 and 2).

The experiments were intended to help understand how passages should be defined, how they should be ranked, and how they should be used in retrieval. Although the experiments raise new questions, some general conclusions can be drawn from the results reported here.

Passages based upon paragraph boundaries were less effective than passages based upon overlapping text windows of varying sizes. This result held for both document retrieval based on a single best passage, and document retrieval based upon combining document-level and passage-level evidence. This result may be due to inconsistent use of paragraphs by the authors of TIPSTER documents, or it may be that there is no single division of documents into passages that is appropriate for all queries. It may also be that paragraphs are too small, and that a larger unit of discourse (e.g. section or subsection) would yield better results.

A slight variation of the formulae for ranking documents was effective for ranking passages. However, it is not clear why scaling the term frequency in the passage (tf_p) by a constant value should be more effective than scaling it by the maximum term frequency in the document (max_tf_d). Improvements may also be possible by finding an alternative to idf_t that reflects inverse passage frequency. Finally, the improvement seen in the NPL experiment suggests that further improvements may also be possible in the formulae for ranking documents.

Perhaps the clearest result of the experiments is that it was always best to combine document-level evidence and passage-level evidence. This result confirms some of the previous research on passages, and also confirms that the effectiveness of the inference network generally improves with the amount of evidence available. The experiments leave open the question of how best to weight the different sources of evidence, and whether it is appropriate to conduct retrieval by gathering and combining evidence from several levels of a document's structure.

Acknowledgements

I thank the West Publishing Company for providing the West collection of legal texts. This research was supported by the NSF Center for Intelligent Information Retrieval at the University of Massachusetts.

References

1. N. J. Belkin, C. Cool, W. B. Croft, and J. P. Callan. The effect of multiple query representations on information retrieval system performance. In R. Korfhage, E. Rasmussen, and P. Willett, editors, *Proceedings of the Sixteenth Annual International ACM SIGIR Conference on Research and Development in Information Retrieval*, pages 339–346, Pittsburgh, PA, June 1993. Association for Computing Machinery.

2. C. Buckley, J. Allan, and G. Salton. Automatic routing and ad-hoc retrieval using SMART: TREC-2. In D. Harman, editor, *Proceedings of the Second Text REtrieval Conference (TREC-2)*. National Institute of Standards and Technology Special Publication 500-215, 1994.

3. J. P. Callan and W. B. Croft. An evaluation of query processing strategies using the TIPSTER collection. In R. Korfhage, E. Rasmussen, and P. Willett, editors, *Proceedings of the Sixteenth Annual International ACM SIGIR Conference on Research and Development in Information Retrieval*, pages 347–356, Pittsburgh, PA, June 1993. Association for Computing Machinery.

4. J. P. Callan, W. B. Croft, and S. M. Harding. The INQUERY retrieval system. In *Proceedings of the Third International Conference on Database and Expert Systems Applications*, pages 78–83, Valencia, Spain, 1992. Springer-Verlag.

5. W. B. Croft, J. Callan, and J. Broglio. TREC-2 routing and ad-hoc retrieval evaluation using the INQUERY system. In D. Harman, editor, *Proceedings of the Second Text REtrieval Conference (TREC-2)*. National Institute of Standards and Technology Special Publication 500-215, 1994.

6. Cary Griffith. WESTLAW's winning ways. *Law Office Computing*, pages 31–38, February/March 1993.

7. David Haines and W. B. Croft. Relevance feedback and inference networks. In R. Korfhage, E. Rasmussen, and P. Willett, editors, *Proceedings of the Sixteenth Annual International ACM SIGIR Conference on Research and Development in Information Retrieval*, pages 2–11, Pittsburgh, PA, June 1993. Association for Computing Machinery.

8. D. Harman. The DARPA Tipster project. *SIGIR Forum*, 26(2):26–28, 1992.

9. M. A. Hearst and C. Plaunt. Subtopic structuring for full-length document access. In R. Korfhage, E. Rasmussen, and P. Willett, editors, *Proceedings of the Sixteenth Annual International ACM SIGIR Conference on Research and Development in Information Retrieval*, pages 59–68, Pittsburgh, PA, June 1993. Association for Computing Machinery.

10. A. Moffat, R. Sacks-Davis, R. Wilkinson, and J. Zobel. Retrieval of partial documents. In D. Harman, editor, *Proceedings of the Second Text REtrieval Conference (TREC-2)*. National Institute of Standards and Technology Special Publication 500-215, 1994.

11. J. O'Connor. Answer-passage retrieval by text searching. *Journal of the American Society for Information Science*, 31(4):227–239, 1980.

12. J. S. Ro. An evaluation of the applicability of ranking algorithms to improve the effectiveness of full-text retrieval. I. On the effectiveness of full-text retrieval. *Journal of the American Society for Information Science*, 39(2):73–78, 1988.

13. G. Salton, J. Allan, and C. Buckley. Approaches to passage retrieval in full text information systems. In R. Korfhage, E. Rasmussen, and P. Willett, editors, *Proceedings of the Sixteenth Annual International ACM SIGIR Conference on Research and Development in Information Retrieval*, Pittsburgh, PA, June 1993. Association for Computing Machinery.

14. G. Salton and C. Buckley. Automatic text structuring and retrieval – Experiments in automatic enclopedia searching. In A. Bookstein, Y. Chiaramella, G. Salton, and V. V. Raghavan, editors, *Proceedings of the Fourteenth Annual International ACM/SIGIR Conference on Research and Development in Information Retrieval*, Chicago, IL, October 1991. Association for Computing Machinery.

15. C. Stanfill and D. L. Waltz. Statistical methods, Artificial Intelligence, and Information Retrieval. In P. S. Jacobs, editor, *Text-based intelligent systems*, pages 215–225. Lawrence Erlbaum, 1992.

16. H. R. Turtle and W. B. Croft. Evaluation of an inference network-based retrieval model. *ACM Transactions on Information Systems*, 9(3):187–222, 1991.

17. R. Wilkinson. Effective retrieval of structured documents. In *Proceedings of the Seventeenth Annual International ACM SIGIR Conference on Research and Development in Information Retrieval*, Dublin, Ireland, July 1994. Association for Computing Machinery.

18. P. Willett. A nearest neighbor search algorithm for bibliographic retrieval from multilist files. *Information Technology*, 3(2):78–83, 1984.

Effective Retrieval of Structured Documents

Ross Wilkinson
ross@cs.rmit.edu.au

Dept. of Computer Science, RMIT,
GPO Box 2476V, Melbourne, Victoria, Australia 3001

Abstract

Information systems usually retrieve whole documents as answers to queries. However, it may in some circumstances be more appropriate to retrieve parts of documents. We consider formulas for retrieving whole documents and parts of documents from a large structured document collection. We consider what information is needed to retrieve effectively and show that knowledge of the structure of documents can lead to improved retrieval performance.

1 Introduction

Provision of answers to informally phrased questions is a central part of information retrieval. These answers traditionally take the form of documents retrieved from a text database, but documents will often be unsatisfactory as answers. They may be large and unwieldy; the answer they represent may be diffuse, and therefore hard for the user to extract; and word-based retrieval systems may be misled by the breadth of vocabulary of a long document into believing it to be relevant. Moreover, the structure of these large documents may be relevant to determining the relevance of the documents as a whole.

It is important to decide whether to index whole documents, parts of documents or both. Our approach to the problem of partial documents was to regard documents as hierarchical structures. We conducted a set of experiments that attempted to determine whether large documents should be indexed as single objects, and whether the documents' structure could be used in conjunction with the contents of its elements. We also experimented with retrieval of partial documents and investigated whether context, in particular the rank of the whole document, helped improve ranking of sections. In these experiments, rather than determine a definitive formula appropriate to any particular retrieval environment, we have attempted to determine what factors were important in ranking large structured documents.

2 Structured Document Databases

Many document collections contain documents that have significant structure. This structure has been regarded as very important in hypertext databases as a navigation aid, but has not been thoroughly explored in document retrieval. There has been some interesting work on combining hypertext and information retrieval [1, 4, 3, 6], however this work has typically taken the approach of finding relevant documents or fragments using standard retrieval techniques, and then exploring the retrieved information using browsing.

Little work has been carried out on developing a similarity measure or algorithm that uses structure. The retrieval formula may be designed to retrieve whole documents using their structure or to retrieve parts of documents that take into account the context of the parts. Macleod [10] describes a query language that retrieves documents using the structure of documents in an exact matching algorithms but does not attempt to combine evidence using similarity. Salton and colleagues [13, 2] have demonstrated that the use of local information, namely individual sentences, can help determine the relevance of whole documents. Hearst [8] has shown how structure can be discovered and has advocated queries based on content in context. Sometimes the structure is explicitly available via markup such as SGML. In most retrieval methods, the characteristics of the document database and the content of the documents are considered. A retrieval formula might also take into account document structure - the hierarchy of parts that form the document, the type of these parts, and their content.

Our investigation of this problem grew out of the TREC conference sponsored by NIST [7]. Many of the documents in the TREC collection are very large and have explicit structure, and it is possible to use this structure to break documents into parts. In particular, many documents can be broken up into a set of sections, each section having a type. We used a database consisting of 4,503 documents extracted from the Federal Register sub-collection of the TREC database. These documents were selected as being the 2,500 largest documents which were relevant to a least one of the queries used for the TREC experiment. Another 2,000 documents were randomly selected from the Federal Register collection to provide both smaller documents and non-relevant documents. The average number of words in these documents was 3,260. These documents were then split into sections based on their internal markup. The documents had a number of tags inserted that defined an internal structure. Each of these sections had a type based on its tag. The types were ⟨purpose⟩, ⟨abstract⟩, ⟨start⟩, ⟨summary⟩, ⟨title⟩, ⟨supplementary⟩, and a general category ⟨misc⟩ that included all remaining categories.

Having made the document selections, there were 24 queries for which there was a relevant document in the collection. Each of the sections of documents that had been judged as relevant was judged for relevance by a member of our research group with no special expertise against these queries so that finer grained retrieval experiments were possible. One difficulty that arose was that quite a few documents that had been judged relevant appeared to have no relevant sections—there were relevant key terms in the documents but the documents themselves did not appear to address the information requirement. To be consistent, we took these document to be irrelevant. There were an average of 23 relevant sections per query.

3 Experiments

There were four broad questions that were considered in the experiments that were carried out.

1. Can retrieval of whole documents be carried out effectively using just their parts?
2. Can retrieval of whole documents be enhanced using both global and local information?
3. Can retrieval of document parts be based on retrieval of whole documents?
4. Can retrieval of document parts be enhanced using both global and local information?

The information available was:

- frequency of terms in both documents and sections
- document content
- section content
- section type
- section–document inclusions

A standard form of the cosine measure was selected to obtain the similarity of the content [12], and the text retrieval system described by Moffat et al. [11] was used to carry out the retrieval. The term weights used were the common tf.idf weights: the weight of the jth term in the ith "document" is given by $tf_{ij} log(N/d_j)$, where tf_{ij} counts the number of times the jth term occurs in the ith "document", N is the number of documents, and d_j is the number of documents containing the jth term. Note that if the content of documents was being compared the document frequency gave the number of documents containing the relevant term and $N = 4,503$, whereas if the content of sections were being compared the "document" frequency gave the number of sections containing the relevant term and $N = 39,724$.

Experiments were evaluated by obtaining precision figures after viewing 5 documents, 10 documents, 15 documents, etc. These figures were averaged over the query set to give a set of results. These results were not combined into a single number, since an average of these results seems to be of little use. Recall results are not given as the collection in question does not have complete relevance judgements.

To answer our first question, we first carried out a baseline experiment of retrieval of whole documents using the standard cosine measure. Our next experiment measured section similarity, and ranked documents according to their highest ranked section. Since each section has a type we tried to provide a weight associated with each type. This is described in Experiment 11. Having obtained the weights for sections, we ranked documents according to the product of the similarity of the content and the weight of the type. There are many ways of combining the significance of all of the sections that comprise a document. We considered the two most significant sections, the sum of the weights of all sections, this sum divided by the number of sections, and a sum that decays for the less significant sections. This last formula (Experiment 4) had the advantage of a fixed upper value, $\alpha/(1-\alpha)$, and gave the best results. A decay factor of $\alpha = 0.5$ was found to be most effective. Finally we combined these two approaches to use section content, type and structure to retrieve documents without using whole documents. The results of these experiments (1–5) are given in Table 1.

Experiment 1: Rank full documents against the queries using standard cosine measure.

$$E1 = \left(\sum d_{ij} q_j\right) / \left(\sqrt{\sum d_{ij}^2 q_j^2}\right)$$

Experiment 2: Split documents into sections. Measure similarity of each section against the queries using standard cosine measure. Order documents based on the highest ranked section.

$$E2 = max_{s_k \in d_i} \left[\left(\sum s_{kj} q_j\right) / \left(\sqrt{\sum s_{kj}^2 q_j^2}\right)\right]$$

Experiment 3: Repeat experiment 2, where the weight of section types is included.

$$E3 = max_{s_k \in d_i} \left[\left(wt(type(s_k)) \sum s_{kj} q_j\right) / \left(\sqrt{\sum s_{kj}^2 q_j^2}\right)\right]$$

Experiment 4: Split documents into sections. Measure similarity of each section against the queries using standard cosine measure. Order documents based on

$$E4 = \sum_{s_n \in d_i} \left(0.5^{n-1} \sum s_{kj} q_j\right) / \left(\sqrt{\sum s_{kj}^2 q_j^2}\right)$$

where s_n is the nth highest ranked section in the document.

Experiment 5: Combine E3 and E4.

$$E5 = \sum_{s_n \in d_i} \left[\left(0.5^{n-1} wt(type(s_k)) \sum s_{kj} q_j\right) / \left(\sqrt{\sum s_{kj}^2 q_j^2}\right)\right]$$

We next addressed the issue of enhancing document retrieval using global and local information. We tried two approaches: combining ranks and combining similarities. To combine the ranks, we simply summed the inverse inverse of the ranks. To combine similarities we performed a test similar to Salton et al.'s experiment [13, 2], first using the results of Experiment 3 and then of Experiment 5. To combine, we first

Documents / Experiment	5	10	15	20	25	30	50	200
1	0.242	0.229	0.208	0.202	0.200	0.193	0.169	0.087
2	0.200	0.179	0.178	0.175	0.163	0.154	0.143	0.076
3	0.200	0.200	0.194	0.192	0.183	0.174	0.161	0.070
4	0.208	0.208	0.192	0.179	0.173	0.169	0.157	0.077
5	0.250	0.225	0.203	0.192	0.173	0.171	0.162	0.075

Table 1. Comparison of ranking formulae for fixed number of documents returned

normalised so that the maximum similarity using one measure is equal to the maximum similarity of the other. The relative significance of each component can be varied, and optimised, as has been described by Fuhr and Buckley [5]. However, we give simply one such variant to indicate its potential significance. The results of these experiments are given in Table 2.

Experiment 6: Combine rankings.

$E6 = 1/(1/Rank1(d_i) + 1/Rank5(d_i))$

where Rank$i$ is the numeric order of documents ranked using formula Ei

Experiment 7: Add normalised weights of experiments 1 and 3.

$E7 = \widehat{E1} + \widehat{E5}$

Experiment 8: Add weighted normalised weights of experiments 1 and 3.

$E8 = \widehat{E1} + 0.16\widehat{E5}$

Experiment 9: Add normalised weights of experiments 1 and 5.

$E9 = \widehat{E1} + \widehat{E5}$

Documents / Experiment	5	10	15	20	25	30	50	200
6	0.250	0.233	0.208	0.202	0.197	0.187	0.176	0.085
7	0.275	0.213	0.206	0.196	0.193	0.199	0.186	0.082
8	0.267	0.229	0.211	0.196	0.202	0.196	0.171	0.084
9	0.275	0.221	0.208	0.204	0.200	0.197	0.183	0.084

Table 2. Combining evidence for retrieving a fixed number of documents returned

The most obvious way of retrieving relevant sections is to build a database of sections and retrieve them on the basis of the similarity of their content to the queries. This provides a baseline for section retrieval. Now sections, unlike documents, are not all equivalent a priori as each section has a type. A section of type ⟨summary⟩ might be more likely to be relevant than a section of type ⟨misc⟩. We investigated weighting by type. The weights of the types of sections were obtained by conducting a set of experiments where all types but one were given a weight of 1, and in turn, each type was given a weight of 2. Using these experiments it was determined that ⟨purpose⟩ and ⟨summary⟩ were each more helpful, and that ⟨misc⟩ was less helpful. As a result, after further experiments on the comparative weights, $wt(\langle\text{purpose}\rangle) = wt(\langle\text{summary}\rangle) = 2$, $wt(\langle\text{misc}\rangle) = 0.5$, and other weights were set to 1.

If sections to be retrieved and only document ranking is available, there seems little else to do than rank documents and then view sections in order of appearance. However it may be possible to rank the sections within each document as it is retrieved. Thus global ranking only occurs once. It is further possible to introduce a threshold so that lowly ranked sections are not viewed at all, even though they are in highly ranked documents. The results of these experiments are given in Table 3.

Experiment 10: Rank each section on content.

$$E10 = \sum s_{ij} q_j / \sqrt{\sum s_{ij}^2 q_j^2}$$

Experiment 11: Rank each section on content and type.

$$E11 = wt(type(s_i))E10$$

Experiment 12: Rank each section based solely on containing document (E1).

$$E12 = \sum d_{kj} q_j / \sqrt{\sum d_{kj}^2 q_j^2}$$

where document d_k contains section s_j and ties (being in the same document) are broken by order of appearance in document.

Experiment 13: Rank each section by document first, and then by section using E11.

Experiment 14: Using document ranking, then section ranking, but discarding those sections below a threshold. The threshold used for this experiment was the 201st value of E11.

Sections / Experiment	5	10	15	20	25	30	50	200
10	0.167	0.146	0.150	0.142	0.138	0.142	0.137	0.097
11	0.175	0.192	0.183	0.179	0.168	0.160	0.143	0.103
12	0.050	0.054	0.064	0.077	0.078	0.072	0.072	0.061
13	0.100	0.104	0.108	0.106	0.112	0.112	0.103	0.072
14	0.158	0.167	0.172	0.175	0.175	0.169	0.160	0.103

Table 3. Comparison of ranking formulae for fixed number of sections returned

To answer our final question of whether combined evidence is useful for section retrieval, we will assume that we have rankings provided by E1 and E11 available. We again combine evidence by normalising E1 and E11 so that the most similar section has the same weight as the most similar document. We then varied the importance of each component by varying β and γ in the formula:

$$\beta\widehat{E1} + \gamma\widehat{E11}$$

The results of these experiments are given in Table 4.

Experiment 15: $E15 = 1.0\widehat{E1} + 1.0\widehat{E11}$

Experiment 16: $E16 = 0.5\widehat{E1} + 1.0\widehat{E11}$

Experiment 17: $E17 = 0.2\widehat{E1} + 1.0\widehat{E11}$

Experiment 18: $E18 = 1.0\widehat{E1} + 0.5\widehat{E11}$

4 Discussion

We have earlier argued that retrieval of parts of documents may be desirable. At the same time it may be equally desirable to retrieve whole documents. It is thus of importance to decide whether to index whole documents, parts of documents, or both. In analysing the results of these experiments, we hope to provide data that allows a more informed decision.

Sections / Experiment	5	10	15	20	25	30	50	200
15	0.208	0.183	0.167	0.169	0.165	0.158	0.153	0.111
16	0.217	0.183	0.186	0.173	0.173	0.171	0.159	0.114
17	0.183	0.192	0.186	0.175	0.168	0.169	0.160	0.112
18	0.158	0.163	0.161	0.148	0.148	0.147	0.126	0.095

Table 4. Combining evidence for retrieving a fixed number of sections

The first set of experiments showed that acceptable retrieval effectiveness can be obtained when whole documents are desired by using section information only. The formula E5 combines content, type and hierarchical information to effectively replicate retrieval of whole documents. We may thus consider indexing sections only. Note however that there are many more sections than documents. This means that retrieval will be slower, although this increase in speed can be ameliorated to a degree [11].

Combining evidence using both local and global information to retrieve documents has shown limited benefits using the techniques that we have explored. Unless a cheap way of providing both levels of comparisons is available, it would appear that the cost may outweigh the benefits. Note however that techniques that retrieve only a very few highly related documents or fragments may be appropriate for one of the components if a high precision search is required. It remains open what would happen if paragraph and sentence level retrieval was combined as well.

We started with the premise that retrieval of large documents is not always desirable. In a typical existing retrieval system, this may be the default. By examining the relevance of each section of every relevant document, we were able to determine how effective document retrieval is when sections are required. Experiment 12 shows just how poor this strategy is. It seems to be absolutely necessary to rank sections once documents have been retrieved. If we assume that this must take place dynamically on the text of the retrieved documents, a large amount of processing may be required. The alternative of using E11 for section retrieval appears more attractive.

Should both document and section similarities be available, Experiment 16 shows that there may be benefit in combining evidence compared to the best section similarity measure described by E11. Again the benefit is most obvious for high precision searches.

These experiments have been carried out on only one database. We have had a limited set of queries and the form of these queries is quite specialised. The results thus need to be treated with caution. nevertheless Experiment 12 gives a clear indication of how important it is not to treat documents as homogeneous objects, and the consistent evidence is that knowledge of structure improves retrieval.

5 Conclusions

In this paper, we have considered formulas for retrieving whole documents and parts of documents from a large structured document collection. We have identified that as well as the content of whole documents, the type of the parts, the content of the parts, and the structure of the parts can be usefully considered.

We have shown that retrieval of whole documents can be carried out using just knowledge of their parts. However retrieval of relevant parts cannot proceed using solely knowledge of whole documents. We have seen that knowledge of both the whole and the parts can be combined to provide additional useful information. This has led to better high precision performance, but has shown no gains for high recall retrieval.

We believe that we have shown that knowledge of the structure of documents can lead to improved retrieval performance.

Acknowledgements

I would like to thank Daniel Lam for his assistance with the experiments described here, an in particular for making the relevance judgements for a very large number of sections. I would like to acknowledge the valuable environment of the Hypermedia group at the Collaborative Information Technology Research Institute. This work was supported by the Australian Research Council and the Centre for Intelligent Decision Systems.

References

1. M. Agosti, R. Colotti, and G. Gradenigo. A two-level hypertext retreival model for legal data. In A. Bookstein, Y. Chiaramella, G. Salton, and V. V. Raghavan, editors, *Proceedings of the 14th Annual International Conference on Research and Development in Information Retrieval*, pages 316-325, Chicago, Illinois USA, 13-16 October 1991. ACM Press.
2. J. Allan, C. Buckley, and G. Salton. Automatic routing and ad-hoc retrieval using SMART: TREC 2. In Harman [7]. To appear as a NIST Special Publication.
3. W. B. Croft, N. J. Belkin, M.-F. Bruandet, R. Kuhlen, and T. Oren. Hypertext and information retrieval: what are the fundamental concepts? pages 362–366, INRIA, Versailles, France, November 28 – 30 1990. Cambridge University Press, The Cambridge Series on Electronic Publishing.
4. D. B. Crouch, C. J. Crouch, and G. Andreas. The use of cluster hierarchies in hypertext information retrieval. In *Proceedings of the ACM Hypertext '89 Conference*, pages 225–237, Pittsburgh, Pennsylvania, November 5–8 1989. ACM.
5. N. Fuhr and C. Buckley. Optimizing document indexing and search term weighting based on probabilistic models. In D. Harman, editor, *Proceedings of the First Text Retrieval Conference*, Gaithersburg, Maryland, 1993. NIST Special Publication 500-207.
6. M. Fuller, E. Mackie, R. Sacks-Davis, and R. Wilkinson. Coherent answers for a large structured document collection. In Korfhage et al. [9], pages 204–213.
7. D. Harman, editor. *Proceedings of the Second Text Retrieval Conference*, Gaithersburg, Maryland, 1994. To appear as a NIST Special Publication.
8. M.A. Hearst and C. Plaunt. Subtopic structuring for full-length document access. In Korfhage et al. [9], pages 59–68.
9. R. Korfhage, E. Rasmussen, and P. Willett, editors. *Proceedings of the 16th Annual International Conference on Research and Development in Information Retrieval*, Pittsburg, U.S.A., June 27 – July 1 1993. ACM.
10. I.A. Macleod. Storage and retrieval of structured documents. *Information Processing and Management*, 26(2):197–208, 1990.
11. A. Moffat and J. Zobel. Fast ranking in limited space. In *Proc. IEEE International Conference on Data Engineering*, 1994. (To appear).
12. G. Salton. *Automatic Text Processing*. Addison-Wesley, Reading, Massachusetts, 1989.
13. G. Salton, J. Allan, and C. Buckley. Approaches to passage retrieval in full text information systems. In Korfhage et al. [9], pages 49–58.

Document and Passage Retrieval Based on Hidden Markov Models

Elke Mittendorf
mittendorf@inf.ethz.ch

Peter Schäuble
schauble@inf.ethz.ch

Swiss Federal Institute of Technology (ETH)
CH-8092 Zürich (Switzerland)

Abstract

Introduced is a new approach to Information Retrieval developed on the basis of Hidden Markov Models (HMMs). HMMs are shown to provide a mathematically sound framework for retrieving documents—documents with predefined boundaries and also entities of information that are of arbitrary lengths and formats (passage retrieval). Our retrieval model is shown to encompass promising capabilities: First, the position of occurrences of indexing features can be used for indexing. Positional information is essential, for instance, when considering phrases, negation, and the proximity of features. Second, from training collections we can derive automatically optimal weights for arbitrary features. Third, a query dependent structure can be determined for every document by segmenting the documents into passages that are either relevant or irrelevant to the query. The theoretical analysis of our retrieval model is complemented by the results of preliminary experiments.

1 Introduction

We introduce a new approach to Information Retrieval, i.e. document retrieval and passage retrieval. Documents are considered as being produced by stochastic processes. A first stochastic process generates text fragments that are relevant to a certain query. A second stochastic process generates text fragments independent of any particular query. The generation of text fragments by the two stochastic processes is modeled by means of two Hidden Markov Models (HMMs). Whether one of these two HMMs generates a text fragment with a high probability or with a low probability depends on the distribution of the query features within the text fragment.

In the case of document retrieval, the documents are assigned scores that depend on the ratio of the probability that the document was generated by the first stochastic process and the probability that the document was generated by the second stochastic process. As usual, the documents are presented to the user in decreasing order of their scores. In the case of passage retrieval, the score of a passage depends on the probability that the passage itself was generated by the first stochastic process and the text fragments before and after the passage are generated by the second stochastic process.

There are three problems, that are considered difficult in Information Retrieval. First, it is not well known how complex features (e.g. phrases, proximity data, negations, cooccurrence and cocitation data etc.) should be used for indexing. Second, we lack a general weighting scheme for arbitrary indexing features and for arbitrary document collections. Third, the optimal segmentation of a long document into segments that are either relevant or irrelevant to a query is another open problem. Our approach encompasses promising capabilities to solve these three problems at least partially. First, information about positions of features can be conserved, because in our approach a document is considered as being produced by a stochastic process. Conventional retrieval models do not take into account the positions where the indexing features occur. Second, the problem of feature weighting is partially solved by an effective and efficient algorithm (Baum–Welch) which determines automatically the stochastic parameters of the model. These stochastic parameters depend on the domain but not on the queries. Third, the retrieval method proffers itself as a method well suited for retrieving passages of arbitrary lengths and formats. Furthermore our approach is based on a theoretically sound framework of probabilistic retrieval. A theoretical analysis and some preliminary experiments show that our approach to passage retrieval works well.

The approach described in this paper is a second attempt to employ HMMs (which play an important role in speech recognition at the present time). A first attempt by Schäuble and Glavitsch [21] had several drawbacks. The new approach presented in this paper is similar to a recently proposed method for spotting keywords in a speech recording [18]. It would seem that in the future, HMM matching will also become popular in fields other than speech recognition [7], [4], [9], [10]. HMM matching may supersede dynamic programming techniques as used for instance in [25] because in contrast to the dynamic programming approach, with its intuitive and empirical characteristics, HMMs are mathematically more sound and they encompass dynamic programming as a special case [1].

In what follows we summarize *related work* on passage retrieval. Methods for retrieving passages of predefined lengths (e.g. sentences, paragraphs, sections, pages, 30-word segments, etc.) are described in: [8], [13], [14], and [22]. As already mentioned, methods for retrieving passages of arbitrary lengths and formats are preferable due to their greater effectiveness.

O'Connor [15] enhances his original method by "compound passages" which consist of several adjacent sentences. A rather complicated system of rules specifies whether a single sentence or a compound passage should be retrieved, e.g. if every sentence of the compound passage matches the query in a specific way and if the sentences are connected by phrases like "however" or "on the other hand." O'Connor's approach is domain independent whereas the knowledge based approach of Hahn [3] heavily depends on the domain of discourse. The approaches by O'Connor and Hahn lack a procedure to optimize automatically the characteristics of their retrieval model.

Salton, Allan, and Buckley [19] describe a hierarchical approach. They first retrieve entire documents by means of a global/local text comparison where it may be difficult to find necessary thresholds for this first step. In subsequent steps, the retrieved units are divided into subunits, where a subunit is retrieved iff its score is higher than the score of the unit to which it belongs. Another yet interesting method for retrieving passages of arbitrary lengths and formats is described in [5] where the similarities of consecutive text blocks are computed, graphed, and smoothed. The local minima of the resulting graph are assumed to be the boundaries of the passages. In contrast to our approach, the passage retrieval methods mentioned above lack a theoretical framework, e.g. a formal justification within the framework of probabilistic retrieval.

The paper is organized as follows. In Section 2, a short introduction into the theory of HMMs is given. In Section 3, a document retrieval method is introduced which is based on HMMs. In addition, it is shown under which assumptions, this retrieval method is consistent with the probability ranking principle. In Section 4, the document retrieval method is generalized to passage retrieval. In Section 5, the results of our experiments are presented. In Section 6, some conclusions are drawn.

2 Hidden Markov Model Theory

In this section, we present a short introduction into the HMM theory. Readers who are familiar with HMMs may skip this section while other readers who are interested in a thorough presentation of the theory are referred to [6] or to [11].

The structure $\lambda = \langle S, V, a, b\rangle$ represents a discrete *Hidden Markov Model* (or HMM for short) iff the following conditions are satisfied.

1. $S = \{s_0, \dots, s_{n-1}\}$ is a finite set of *states* where s_0 always denotes the so-called *initial state.*
2. $V = \{v_0, \dots, v_{m-1}\}$ is a finite set of *output symbols.*
3. $a : S \times S \to [0,1], (s_i, s_j) \mapsto a_{i,j}$ is a function determining the *transition probabilities* $a_{i,j}$ such that $\sum_{j=0}^{n-1} a_{i,j} = 1$ for all $i = 0, \dots, n-1$.
4. $b : S \times V \to [0,1], (s_j, v_k) \mapsto b_{j,k}$ is a function determining the *output probabilities* $b_{j,k}$ such that $\sum_{k=0}^{m-1} b_{j,k} = 1$ for all $j = 0, \dots, n-1$.

A HMM defines a stochastic process that generates output symbols step by step. Every step consists of a state transition from a state s_i to a state s_j and of the generation of an output symbol v_k upon arriving at state s_j.

The transition probability $a_{i,j}$ is the probability that s_j is the next state, given that s_i is the current state. The output probability $b_{j,k}$ is the probability that v_k is generated upon arriving at s_j. In this way, the so-called *Markov assumptions* are satisfied, i.e. these probabilities do not depend on the previously visited states and on the previously generated output symbols.

Every HMM λ is assigned a probability space $\langle \Omega, P_\lambda\rangle$. The sample space Ω consists of pairs (σ, ν) where the function $\sigma : \mathsf{N}^+ \to S, t \mapsto \sigma_t$ determines an infinite sequence $\sigma_1, \sigma_2, \dots$ of states and the function $\nu : \mathsf{N}^+ \to V, t \mapsto \nu_t$ determines an infinite sequence $\nu_1, \nu_2, \dots$ of output symbols. Let $x = (s_0, x_1, \dots, x_T)$ be a finite sequence of states that starts with the initial state s_0 and let $y = (y_1, \dots, y_T)$ be a finite sequence of output symbols. We define the following three events.

$$A(x) := \{(\sigma, \nu) \,|\, x = (s_0, \sigma_1, \dots, \sigma_T)\} \tag{1}$$

$$B(y) := \{(\sigma, \nu) \,|\, y = (\nu_1, \dots, \nu_T)\} \tag{2}$$

$$E(x, y) := A(x) \cap B(y) \tag{3}$$

The set $A(x)$ denotes the event where at the outset the state sequence x is traversed while generating any sequence of output symbols. The set $B(y)$ denotes the event where at the outset the sequence of output symbols y is generated by traversing any state sequence. Finally, the set $E(x,y)$ denotes the event where at the outset y is generated by traversing the state sequence x.

When defining

$$P_\lambda(E(x,y)) \quad := \quad \prod_{t=1}^{T} c(x_{t-1}, x_t, y_t) \tag{4}$$

where

$$c(s_i, s_j, v_k) := a_{i,j} b_{j,k}, \tag{5}$$

it can be shown that $\langle \Omega, P_\lambda \rangle$ is a probability space. For simplicity we will subsequently write $P_\lambda(x,y)$, $P_\lambda(y)$, and $P_\lambda(x)$ instead of $P_\lambda(E(x,y))$, $P_\lambda(B(y))$, and $P_\lambda(A(x))$ respectively.

When using HMMs, there are three problems of interest:

1. Given a HMM $\lambda = \langle S, V, a, b \rangle$ and a sequence of output symbols y, find the probability $P_\lambda(y)$ that y was generated along *any* state sequence.
2. Given a HMM $\lambda = \langle S, V, a, b \rangle$ and a sequence of output symbols y, find a state sequence x along which y is generated with the highest probability $P_\lambda(x,y)$.
3. Given a set Y consisting of sequences y, find a HMM which generates these sequences y with high probabilities.

The first problem is solved by means of the *forward algorithm* that computes the probability

$$P_\lambda(y) \quad = \quad \sum_x P_\lambda(x,y) \tag{6}$$

with a time complexity $O(T*(n+\langle\#\text{positive } a_{i,j}\text{'s}\rangle))$ even though the sum in (6) consists of n^T summands. The second problem is solved by means of the *Viterbi algorithm* that computes

$$\operatorname{argmax}\{P_\lambda(x,y) \,|\, x\} \tag{7}$$

with a time complexity $O(T*(n+\langle\#\text{positive } a_{i,j}\text{'s}\rangle))$ even though a most probable sequence out of n^T different sequences has to be found. The last problem is solved by the elegant *Baum-Welch algorithm* which is based on the following proposition.

Proposition: Let $\lambda = \langle S, V, a, b \rangle$ and $\overline{\lambda} = \langle S, V, \overline{a}, \overline{b} \rangle$ be two discrete HMMs that are based on the same set of states and on the same set of output symbols. In addition, let Y be a set of training sequences where T_y denotes the length of $y = (y_1, \ldots, y_{T_y})$ for every $y \in Y$. Assume that the transition probabilities a and $\overline{a}$ and the output probabilities b and $\overline{b}$ are related by the following reestimation formulas

$$\overline{a}_{i,j} \quad = \quad \frac{\sum_{y\in Y}\sum_{t=1}^{T_y}\gamma_{i,j}[y](t)}{\sum_{y\in Y}\sum_{j=0}^{n-1}\sum_{t=1}^{T_y}\gamma_{i,j}[y](t)}, \quad \overline{b}_{j,k} = \frac{\sum_{y\in Y}\sum_{i=0}^{n-1}\sum_{t:y_t=v_k}\gamma_{i,j}[y](t)}{\sum_{y\in Y}\sum_{i=0}^{n-1}\sum_{t=1}^{T_y}\gamma_{i,j}[y](t)} \tag{8}$$

where $\gamma_{i,j}[y](t)$ is the probability that the process generates y along any state sequence such that the states s_i and s_j are visited at time $t-1$ and at time t respectively.

$$\gamma_{i,j}[y](t) \quad := \quad \alpha_i[y](t-1)c(s_i, s_j, y_t)\beta_j[y](t)$$

$$\alpha_j[y](t) \quad := \quad \begin{cases} 0 \text{ if } j \neq 0 \text{ and } t = 0 \\ 1 \text{ if } j = 0 \text{ and } t = 0 \\ \sum_i \alpha_i[y](t-1)c(s_i, s_j, y_t) \text{ if } 0 < t \end{cases}$$

$$\beta_i[y](t) \quad := \quad \begin{cases} 1 \text{ if } t = T_y \\ \sum_j c(s_i, s_j, y_{t+1})\beta_j[y](t+1) \text{ if } t < T_y \end{cases}$$

If the reestimation formulas yield the same probabilities (i.e. $\overline{a} \equiv a$ and $\overline{b} \equiv b$), then

$$\sum_{y\in Y} P_\lambda(y) \tag{9}$$

is a *local maximum* with respect to a and b. This local maximum is the probability that λ generates a sequence y of the training set Y. Otherwise (i.e. if $\exists i,j : a_{i,j} \neq \overline{a}_{i,j}$ or $\exists j,k : b_{j,k} \neq \overline{b}_{j,k}$), the strong inequality

$$\sum_{y\in Y} P_\lambda(y) \quad < \quad \sum_{y\in Y} P_{\overline{\lambda}}(y) \tag{10}$$

holds. *End of proposition.*

This proposition leads to the Baum-Welch algorithm to find a HMM which generates the sequences y of a given set Y with high probabilities. First, an appropriate initial HMM is chosen. Second, the transition probabilities and the output probabilities are reestimated by using the reestimation formulas and the training set Y. According to the proposition, the new HMM generates the training sequences with a higher probability than the original HMM does (unless we are already in a local maximum). The second step can be repeated until an appropriate convergence criterion is met.

3 Document Retrieval Based on Hidden Markov Models

In this section we introduce a document retrieval method based on HMMs. In the next section we show that this document retrieval method lends itself well to passage retrieval. At the outset of this section, we describe how documents are converted into sequences of output symbols. We then come to the key idea of our approach where we use HMMs generating such sequences of output symbols. Finally, we conclude this section by showing that our document retrieval method based on HMMs encompasses a conventional retrieval method that is based on a well known weighting scheme and on a simple normalization scheme.

When using HMMs, the documents have to be considered as sequences of certain output symbols. If we would define the set of output symbols V to be the set of all terms Φ in a document collection, the cardinality of this set makes any estimation of parameters unfeasible and the whole model would also be very sensitive to changes in the document collection. Pattern recognition solves this problem by extracting significant features and by comparing them to the query. This idea is not new in information retrieval; for instance, it is used to estimate parameters of probabilistic retrieval models. In our case we need a mapping $\vec{v} : \Phi \times Q \rightarrow \mathsf{R}^k$,

$$\vec{v}(\varphi, q) \quad := \quad \begin{pmatrix} sim_0(\varphi, q) \\ \vdots \\ sim_{k-1}(\varphi, q) \end{pmatrix}. \tag{11}$$

such that a vector $\vec{v}(\varphi, q)$ describes the similarity between a token φ and a query q in a way that preserves information about relevance. That means if φ_1 and φ_2 both seem equally relevant to the query they should be mapped to vectors very close to each other with respect to an appropriate distance measure.

The image set $\vec{v}(\Phi, Q) \subseteq \mathsf{R}^k$ may contain infinitely many elements. These elements are grouped into disjoint clusters by means of an appropriate vector quantization technique [12]. Every cluster is uniquely represented by a centroid and the (finite) set of centroids (or their indexes) serves as an output alphabet. In this way, every pair (q, d) consisting of a query q and of a document d is assigned a sequence $Y(q, d) = y$ where

$$Y : Q \times D \rightarrow V^*, (q, d) \mapsto y \tag{12}$$

denotes the corresponding function and every element y_t of the sequence

$$Y(q, d) = y = (y_1, \ldots, y_T) \tag{13}$$

denotes an output symbol v_k representing a centroid which approximates a vector $\vec{v}(\varphi, q)$

We now describe the *key idea* of our approach. At the same time we disclose the relationship between our retrieval method based on HMMs and a probabilistic retrieval method based on the probability space $\underline{Q} \times \underline{D}$ containing simple events $(\underline{q}, \underline{d})$ as described in [2]. Such a simple event $(\underline{q}, \underline{d})$ consists of an individual usage (or an interpretation) of the query q and of an individual usage (or an interpretation) of the document d. Depending on the interpretation, d may be considered as relevant to q (i.e. $(\underline{q}, \underline{d}) \in R$) or d may be considered as irrelevant to q (i.e. $(\underline{q}, \underline{d}) \in \overline{R}$).

We assume a person π sitting in a room and generating sequences y in the following way. In a first step, π selects an information need expressed by a query q. In a second step, π writes a document he or she considers as relevant to q. In probabilistic retrieval, these two steps correspond to a random selection of a simple event $(\underline{q}, \underline{d}) \in R$. In a third step, π applies the function Y and he or she submits the sequence $y := Y(\underline{q}, \underline{d})$ to the outer world who does not know to which query and to which document the sequence y corresponds. Within the framework of probabilistic retrieval,

$$P(y \mid R) \quad = \sum_{(q,d):Y(q,d)=y} P(q, d \mid R) \tag{14}$$

is the probability that y was generated by π.

Similarly, we assume another person π' sitting in a different room and generating sequences y in the following way. In first step π' selects an information need expressed by a query q. In a second step, π' writes a document independent of whether he or she considers d as relevant to q or not. In probabilistic retrieval, these two steps correspond to a random selection of a simple event $(\underline{q}, \underline{d}) \in \underline{Q} \times \underline{D}$. In a third step, π' applies the function Y and he or she submits the sequence $y := Y(\underline{q}, \underline{d})$ to the outer world who does not know to which query and to which document the sequence y corresponds. Within the framework of probabilistic retrieval,

$$P(y) \quad = \sum_{(q,d):Y(q,d)=y} P(q, d) \tag{15}$$

is the probability that y was generated by π'.

The sequences y produced by the person π are considered as being generated by a stochastic process which we approximate by means of a HMM λ such that

$$P_\lambda(y) \quad \approx \quad P(y \mid R). \tag{16}$$

Similarly, the sequences y produced by the person π' are considered as being generated by a stochastic process which we approximate by means of a HMM λ' such that

$$P_{\lambda'}(y) \quad \approx \quad P(y). \tag{17}$$

The HMM λ is called the *passage model* and the HMM λ' is called the *background model* for reasons that will become clear in the next section. Using the HMMs λ and λ' we define a retrieval method by

$$RSV(q,d) := \log\left(\sqrt[T]{\frac{P_\lambda(Y(q,d))}{P_{\lambda'}(Y(q,d))}}\right). \tag{18}$$

This definition can be justified if we make three assumptions. First, the approximations (16) and (17) are assumed to be exact. Second, we assume that all queries and all documents are mapped to sequences $Y(q,d)$ of the *same* positive length T. This assumption implies that we can restrict ourselves to the scoring function

$$RSV'(q,d) := \log\left(\frac{P_\lambda(Y(q,d))}{P_{\lambda'}(Y(q,d))}\right). \tag{19}$$

Third, we assume that Y is injective such that $P(Y(q,d)\,|\,R) = P(q,d\,|\,R)$ and $P(Y(q,d)) = P(q,d)$. This assumption facilitates the simplification

$$RSV'(q,d) = \log\left(\frac{P(q,d\,|\,R)}{P(q,d)}\right) = \log\left(\frac{P(q,d,R)}{P(q,d)P(R)}\right) = \log\left(P(R\,|\,q,d)\right) - \log\left(P(R)\right)$$

which shows that under the three assumptions made above, RSV and $P(R\,|\,q,d)$ induce the same weak ordering of the documents because both the Tth root and the logarithm log are strictly monotonic on the open interval $(0,\infty)$. Thus, our retrieval method based on HMMs is consistent with the probability ranking principle by Robertson [17]. For the case where the image $Y(Q,D)$ consists of sequences of *different lengths*, the Tth root in (18) provides a normalization such that short sequences do not have preference over long sequences. The same normalization is successfully used in keyword spotting systems [18], [24]. This completes the presentation of a document retrieval method based on HMMs and its relationship to probabilistic retrieval.

We conclude this section by showing that our document retrieval method based on HMMs encompasses a conventional retrieval method that is based on a well known weighting scheme and on a simple normalization scheme. For we assume that both λ and λ' are based on constant Markov chains. Thus, we have $S = \{s_0\}$, $S' = \{s'_0\}$, $a_{0,0} = 1$ and $a'_{0,0} = 1$. The similarity function $\vec{v} : \Phi \times Q \rightarrow \mathrm{R}$ is chosen to be a mapping into the set of one dimensional vectors (i.e. into the real numbers).

$$\vec{v}(\varphi,q) := ff(\varphi,q)\cdot idf^2(\varphi), \tag{20}$$

where ff denotes the features frequency and idf denotes the inverse document frequency as explained in [20]. If the feature frequencies in all queries are assumed to be bounded, and if the collection is as small as e.g. MEDLARS, the image set $\vec{v}(\Phi,Q)$ is small enough to serve as an output set for λ and λ'. We therefore define $V := \vec{v}(\Phi \times Q) = \{v_0,\ldots,v_{m-1}\}$. The output probabilities of the background model λ'

$$b'_{0,k} \quad := \quad u(v_k) \tag{21}$$

are initialized by an arbitrary probability function $u : V \rightarrow [0,1]$, e.g. such that $u(v_k)$ is the relative frequency of the symbol v_k in some training collection. The output probabilities of the passage model λ are initialized as follows.

$$b_{0,k} \quad := \quad \frac{u(v_k)\exp(\kappa v_k)}{c(\kappa)} \tag{22}$$

where

$$c(\kappa) \quad := \quad \sum_{i=0}^{m-1} u(v_k)\exp(\kappa v_k). \tag{23}$$

Let us now consider the representation of a document d consisting of T tokens, represented relative to a query as in (13). By definition we have for $\vec{v}(\varphi,q) = y_t$ that $y_t = ff(\varphi,q)\cdot idf^2(\varphi)$, $i := 1,\ldots,T-1$. We then can show that

$$RSV(q,d) \quad = \quad \frac{\kappa\sum_{\varphi\in\Phi} ff(\varphi,d)ff(\varphi,q)idf^2(\varphi)}{T} - \log c(\kappa). \tag{24}$$

Thus, this retrieval model yields the same list of ranked documents as vector space retrieval with the scalar product of $ff * idf$-vectors and with a normalization by the number of tokens.

For larger collections the set $\vec{v}(\Phi,Q)$ must be compressed to a codebook with a reasonable size. That leads to a small quantization error in (24) which has marginal effects on the ranking order.

4 Passage Retrieval Based on Hidden Markov Models

In this section, we present a simple passage retrieval method based on HMMs. We use the passage model λ and the background model λ' to build a larger HMM called document model μ. We describe how the

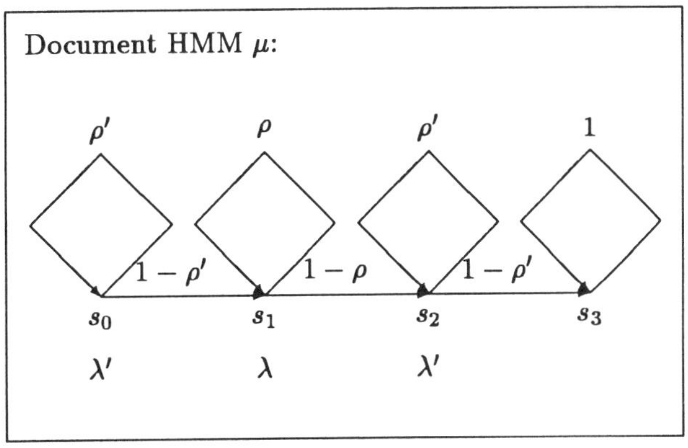

Figure 1. Structure of the document HMM μ, i.e. a simple HMM for passage retrieval.

Viterbi algorithm is used to assign scores to passages of a document. Finally, we show how this passage retrieval method is related to vector space retrieval.

The main idea is that the passage model λ and the background model λ' are concatenated to obtain a document model μ which generates relevant text fragments while traversing λ, and which generates arbitrary text fragments while traversing λ'.

We started with a simple structure for μ as shown in Figure 1. In state s_3, only end-of-document markers are generated. The probability that an end-of-document marker is generated in another state equals to zero.

Suppose we are given a query q and a long document, say a book d. The query and the document are mapped by (12) to a sequence of output symbols $Y(q,d) =: y$. Every path x through the document model μ with positive probability $P(x,y)$ has the form

$$x = (s_0, \ldots, s_0, s_1, \ldots, s_1, s_2, \ldots, s_2, s_3).$$

The paths of this form correspond bijectively to the passages of the book in an obvious way.

We use the Viterbi algorithm to trace for a path through the document model μ, i.e. for a path that has produced y with maximal probability. We call such a path a *best path*. The passage that corresponds to a best path is assumed to be a best (i.e. a most probable) passage with respect to the query.

The following algorithm yields a list of disjoint passages that are ranked in an appropriate order. We will call this algorithm *Viterbi ranking*. The top ranked passage is a passage that corresponds to a best path. We then cut off the top ranked passage, we consider the book without this passage, and again, we trace for a best path. This is repeated until there are as many passages on the list as needed by the user.

Problems might occur with the Viterbi ranking, since a retrieved "passage" may contain a gap due to a cut off in a previous step. This problem did not occur in our experiments.

We now analyze this passage retrieval method in detail. Again we investigate a relationship with vector space retrieval. Consider this particular document HMM μ (Figure 1), the similarity function defined in (20), and the output probabilities defined in (21) and (22), where the document frequencies are obtained from an appropriate training collection. Let p be a passage consisting of T_p tokens and let x_p be the corresponding path. We can show that

$$\log\left(P(x_p, Y(q,d))\right) \;=\; \kappa \sum_{\varphi\in\Phi} ff(\varphi,p)ff(\varphi,q)idf^2(\varphi) - T_p \log\left(c(\kappa)\frac{\rho}{\rho'}\right) + \log G, \tag{25}$$

where G is a value that is constant for all possible paths x_p. The probability $P(x_p, Y(q,d))$ can be regarded as the score for a passage p. After each step of the Viterbi ranking, the passage with the highest score (25) is appended to the list.

Equation (25) discloses the following properties. First we note that the score only depends on

1. the scalar product of the $ff * idf$-vectors, representing the passage p and the query q,
2. the parameter $c(\kappa)$ times the ratio ρ/ρ'.

For every token φ in the passage, the score is incremented by $\kappa \cdot ff(\varphi,q)\cdot idf^2(\varphi)$ and it is decremented by $\log(c(\kappa)\rho/\rho')$. If $\kappa ff(\varphi,q)idf^2(\varphi) > \log(c(\kappa)\rho/\rho')$ the token ϕ causes an increase of the score; otherwise, it causes a decrease of the score. By changing κ and the ratio ρ/ρ', the expected length of the retrieved passages can be manipulated. The larger $c(\kappa)\rho/\rho'$, the shorter is the average length of the retrieved passages. We also can see that for this particular passage retrieval method a retrieved passage always starts and ends with a token that occurs in the query. To avoid this we are deliberating on other HMM structures as well as on other similarity functions, i.e. other than the function (20).

We have presented simple HMMs for passage retrieval and we have shown that in this case the Viterbi ranking provides meaningful scores. Based on the experience we get from our experiments, we hopefully will be able to design more sophisticated HMMs.

5 Experiments

In this section, we describe three experiments. The first two experiments are about passage retrieval based on HMMs with different output probability distributions. The third experiment is about retrieving passages of fixed formats (sentences) which is used as a reference method.

Evaluating passage retrieval is problematic, since appropriate evaluation methods do not exist. It is not clear how to consider the percentage of the retrieved passage that is relevant and the percentage of the relevant passage that is covered by the retrieved passage. Moreover, we lack relevance judgements containing detailed information about relevant passages.

To get an idea of the effectiveness of our passage retrieval method, the following framework for experiments has been designed. Standard document collections are considered as one large document without document boundaries. The concatenation of all documents of a particular collection is called a book d. The set Φ is the set of terms, consisting of word classes obtained by Porter's reduction algorithm [16] after removing the stop words listed in [23, pp. 18–21]. The similarity function is defined by (20). The models λ and λ' are concatenated as shown in Figure 1.

Using the Viterbi ranking, the documents d_j of the book d are ranked as follows. A document d_j is ranked next if the currently best passage starts in d_j. The whole document d_j is then cut off from the book d. We decided to rank only this document, even if the retrieved passage covers more than one document of the collection. This can be justified by the fact that a user usually starts reading a retrieved passage from the beginning.

Below we describe three different experiments. Two experiments are based on HMMs and one experiment serves as a reference method.

Experiment 1: (HMM0) For testing the initialization analyzed in Section 4, λ is defined by (22) and λ' by (21). Thus in the model μ we have $b_{0,k} = b_{2,k} = u(v_k)$ and $b_{1,k} = u(v_k)\exp(\kappa v_k)/c(\kappa)$, k=0,..., m-1. The parameter κ is set to 0.2. No training is performed.

Experiment 2: (HMM1) The output probabilities of λ and λ' are optimized by means of the reestimation formula (8). The training data for λ consists of $\{(q,d) \mid d \text{ relevant to } q\}$ and the training data for λ' consists of $\{(q,d) \mid d \in D,\, q \in Q\}$.

For all experiments the transition probabilities ρ and ρ' are set to be equal, $\rho = \rho' = 0.9999$.

A comparison of vector space retrieval and our method of passage retrieval would not be fair, since vector space retrieval uses the information about the document boundaries and passage retrieval does not. For that reason, we let the vector space retrieval perform a primitive kind of passage retrieval in the following way: all documents d_j of a collection are segmented into sentences, since this is the smallest reasonable unit for a passage. After stopwording and stemming, a conventional vector space retrieval with cosine measure and $ff * idf$-weights is performed on the sentences. From the list of ranked sentences a document ordering is built in the following way: the top ranked document is the one which contains the top ranked sentence. Then we append the document to the list in which the sentence occurs that is ranked next, but only if this document has not already been ranked.

Experiment 3: (sent) Vector space retrieval of sentences with standard cosine measure.

Each experiment is performed on two disjoint subsets of the test collection to have the possibility to separate a test set and a training set.

Setting A: The tests are performed on odd numbered queries. For experiment 2 the even numbered queries and their relevance assessments are used to train the HMMs.

Setting B: The tests are performed only on even numbered queries. Training is performed with odd numbered queries.

We show the recall-precision graphs determined by the experiments on the MEDLARS test collection. Figure 2 shows the recall-precision graphs for test setting A and Figure 3 shows the recall-precision graphs for test setting B.

From experiment 2 one can see that the Baum–Welch algorithm is able to assign appropriate weights to extracted similarity features. Another observation is that the results for experiment 2 did not depend on the initializations of the HMMs before training. Experiments with different initializations have shown the same results. That shows that the reestimation formula (8) is not trapped by inappropriate local maxima.

Furthermore, we can see that HMM based retrieval is clearly more effective in adjusting the right size of a passage than a rigid presegmenting into sentences. In other experiments, in which passages were

Figure 2. Effectiveness of HMM based passage retrieval on the MEDLARS test collection using odd numbered queries, (setting A).

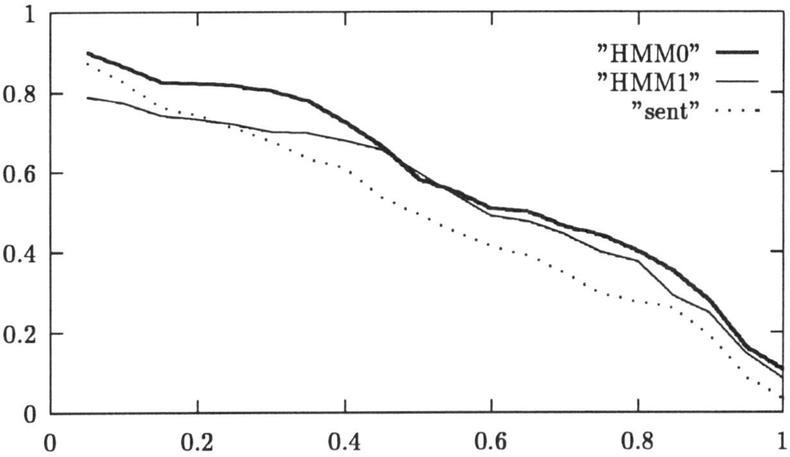

Figure 3. Effectiveness of HMM based passage retrieval on the MEDLARS test collection using even numbered queries, (setting B).

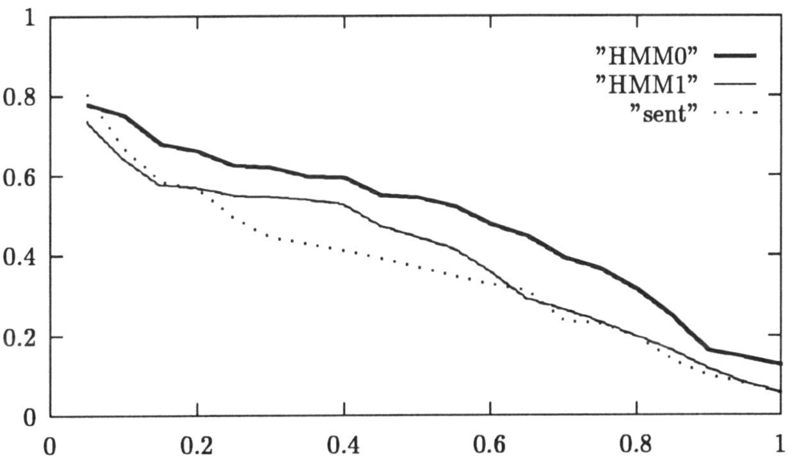

presegmented to contain a fixed number of tokens, the retrieval effectiveness was at best as good as that in experiment 3, but usually worse.

Due to the lack of appropriate relevance judgements and evaluation measures, our evaluation framework does not measure, how much information relevant to the query is covered by and contained in a retrieved passage. However, it was interesting to observe that very often—when consecutive documents are relevant to a query—the most relevant passage consisted exactly of those adjacent documents. For instance, in the MEDLARS test collection, the consecutive documents 164–172 are relevant to query 1. Interestingly, our passage retrieval method identified these consecutive documents as a single passage and it assigned this passage the highest score.

6 Conclusions and Outlook

The analysis presented in Section 4 as well as the experiments presented in Section 5 show that our approach to passage retrieval based on HMMs is feasible. In addition, we have shown that HMMs provide a mathematically sound framework for passage retrieval which can be explained in terms of probabilistic retrieval.

We described a rather simple way to use HMMs, since the passage model and the background model are based on constant Markov chains. Despite this simple approach, the results of the experiments are absolutely encouraging. Even more importantly, this simple approach provides a better understanding of both document retrieval based on HMMs and passage retrieval based on HMMs, because both types of retrieval could be interpreted in terms of conventional vector space retrieval.

Having shown the feasibility of HMM based retrieval and having understood the relationship between HMM based retrieval, probabilistic retrieval, and vector space retrieval, we look forward to using more sophisticated HMMs that model non-trivial structures of the running text (stochastic grammars). We hope that the Baum–Welch algorithm is able to estimate appropriate weights for the various syntactic structures that can be identified by state-of-the-art natural language processing devices.

References

1. J. S. Bridle. Stochastic Models and Template Matching: some Important Relationships Between Two Apparently Different Techniques for Automatic Speech Recognition. In *Institute of Acoustics, Autumn Conference*, pages 452a–452h, 1984.
2. N. Fuhr. Probabilistic Models in Information Retrieval. *The Computer Journal*, 35(3):243–255, 1992.
3. U. Hahn. Topic Parsing: Accounting for Macro Structures in Full-Text Analysis. *Information Processing & Management*, 26(1):135–170, 1990.
4. Y. He, N.Y. Chen, and A. Kundu. Handwritten Word Recognition Using HMM with Adaptive Length Viterbi Algorithm. In *International Conference on Acoustics, Speech, and Signal Processing*, pages III–153–III–156, 1992.
5. M. A. Hearst and C. Plaunt. Subtopic Structuring for Full-Length Access. In *ACM SIGIR Conference on R&D in Information Retrieval*, pages 59–68, 1993.
6. X. D. Huang, Y. Ariki, and M. A. Jack. *Hidden Markov Models for Speech Recognition.* Edinburgh University Press, Edinburgh, 1990.
7. J. J. Hull. A Hidden Markov Model for Language Syntax in Text Recognition. In *11th IAPR International Conference on Pattern Recognition. Vol.II*, pages 124–127, 1992.
8. R. Kuhlen and M. Hess. Passagen-Retrieval–auch eine Möglichkeit der automatischen Verknüpfung in Hypertexten. In *Information Retrieval'93*, pages 100–115, Konstanz, Deutschland, October, 1993. Hochschulverband für Informationswissenschaft (HI).
9. J. Kupiec. Hidden Markov Estimation for Unrestricted Stochastic Context-Free Grammars. In *International Conference on Acoustics, Speech, and Signal Processing*, pages I–177–180, 1992.
10. J. Kupiec. Robust Part-of-Speech Tagging Using a Hidden Markov Model. *Computer Speech and Language*, 6:225–242, 1992.
11. L. W. Levinson, L. R. Rabiner, and M. M. Sondhi. An Introduction to the Application of the Theory of Probabilistic Functions of Markov Process to Automatic Speech Recognition. *The Bell System Technical Journal*, 62(4):1035–1075, 1983.
12. Y. Linde, A. Buzo, and R. M. Gray. An Algorithm for Vector Quantizer Design. *IEEE Transactions on Communication*, 28(1):84–95, 1980.
13. A. Moffat, R. Sacks-Davis, R. Wilkinson, and J. Zobel. Retrieval of Partial Documents. In *TREC-2 Proceedings*, 1993.
14. J. O'Connor. Retrieval of Answer-Sentences and Answer-Figures from Papers by Text Searching. *Information Processing & Management*, 11(5/7):155–164, 1975.
15. J. O'Connor. Answer Passage Retrieval by Text Searching. *Journal of the ASIS*, 31(4):227–239, 1980.
16. M. F. Porter. An Algorithm for Suffix Stripping. *Program*, 14(3):130–137, 1980.
17. S. E. Robertson. The Probability Ranking Principle in IR. *Journal of Documentation*, 33(4):294–304, 1977.

18. R. C. Rose and D. B. Paul. A Hidden Markov Model Based Keyword Recognition System. In *International Conference on Acoustics, Speech, and Signal Processing*, pages 129–132, 1990.

19. G. Salton, J. Allan, and C. Buckley. Approaches to Passage Retrieval in Full Text Information Systems. In *ACM SIGIR Conference on R&D in Information Retrieval*, pages 49–58, 1993.

20. G. Salton and C. Buckley. Term Weighting Approaches in Automatic Text Retrieval. *Information Processing & Management*, 24(5):513–523, 1988.

21. P. Schäuble and U. Glavitsch. A Probabilistic Hypermedia Retrieval Model Based on Hidden Markov Models. Workshop Intelligent Access to Information Systems, Darmstadt, Nov. 1990.

22. C. Stanfill and D. Waltz. Statistical Methods, Artificial Intelligence, and Information Retrieval. In P. S. Jacobs, editor, *Text-Based Intelligent Systems: Current Research and Practice in Information Extraction and Retrieval*, pages 215–226. Lawrence Erlbaum Associates, 1992.

23. C. J. van Rijsbergen. *Information Retrieval.* Butterworths, London, second edition, 1979.

24. L. D. Wilcox and M. A. Bush. HMM-Based Wordspotting for Voice Editing and Indexing. In *European Conference on Speech Communication and Technology (EUROSPEECH)*, pages 25–28, 1991.

25. P. Willet and A. M. Robertson. Searching for Historical Word-Forms in a Database of 17th-Century English Text Using Spelling-Correction Methods. In N. Belkin, P. Ingwersen, and A. M. Pejtersen, editors, *ACM SIGIR Conference on R&D in Information Retrieval*, pages 256–265, 1992.

Implementation

Synthetic Workload Performance Analysis of Incremental Updates *

Kurt Shoens
IBM Almaden[†]

Anthony Tomasic
Stanford University[‡]

Hector Garcia-Molina
Stanford University[§]

Abstract

Declining disk and CPU costs have kindled a renewed interest in efficient document indexing techniques. In this paper, the problem of incremental updates of inverted lists is addressed using a dual-structure index data structure that dynamically separates long and short inverted lists and optimizes the retrieval, update, and storage of each type of list. The behavior of this index is studied with the use of a synthetically-generated document collection and a simulation model of the algorithm. The index structure is shown to support rapid insertion of documents, fast queries, and to scale well to large document collections and many disks.

1 Introduction

As the costs of processors, main memories, and disks have fallen, full-text indexing has become an increasingly popular tool. These costs trends have also encouraged the storage of increasing numbers of documents on-line. As a result, there is renewed interest in efficient document indexing techniques.

The underlying index structure for most document retrieval systems is the *inverted list* [6]. The inverted list for a particular word w contains a sequence of *postings*, each reporting the occurrence of w in a document. Each posting may include a variety of information, such as the word offset (within the document) where w occurs or the region where w occurs (title, abstract, author list, etc.) In a full text index, every word occurring in documents (minus perhaps some *stop* words) has an inverted list. The size of the inverted lists for a full text index varies from perhaps 25% to 100% the size of the text document database itself.

In an information retrieval system, users submit queries that consist of a set of words and some condition. The exact form of the condition varies among systems. Boolean systems support boolean expression conditions such as "(cat and dog) or mouse." Proximity systems support additional conditions, such as requiring that "cat" and "dog" occur within so many words of each other, or that "mouse" occur within a title region. In a vector model system, the query specifies weights for the words, and the system locates documents that maximize the weighted sum of occurring words. All of these query models are well served by inverted lists.

Traditional information retrieval systems, of the type used by libraries (e.g., Stanford University's FOLIO or the University of California's MELVYL) or information vendors (e.g., Dialog Inc. or Mead Data Central Inc.), assume a relatively static body of documents. Given a body of documents, these systems build the inverted list index from scratch, laying out each list sequentially and contiguously to others on disk (with no gaps). (They also build a B-tree or hash table that maps each word to the locations of its list on disk.) Periodically, e.g., every weekend, new documents are added to the database and a new index is built. Rebuilding the index is a massive operation, but its cost is amortized over multiple days of operation.

In many of today's environments, such full index reconstruction is unsatisfactory. One reason is that text document databases are more dynamic. For instance, if one is indexing news articles, electronic mail, or stock information, the latest information is required. Thus, one would like to update the index in place, as new documents arrive. (Updating the index for each *individual* arriving document is inefficient, as we will discuss later. Instead, the goal is to batch together in memory small numbers of documents for each in-place index update. The in-memory batch can be searched simultaneously with the larger index.)

*This research was sponsored by the Advanced Research Projects Agency (ARPA) of the Department of Defense under Grant No. MDA972-92-J-1029 with the Corporation for National Research Initiatives (CNRI). The views and conclusions contained in this document are those of the authors and should not be interpreted as necessarily representing the official policies or endorsement, either expressed or implied, of ARPA, the U. S. Government or CNRI.

[†]IBM Almaden Research Center. e-mail: shoens@almaden.ibm.com
[‡]Department of Computer Science, Stanford, CA 94305-2140. e-mail: tomasic@cs.stanford.edu
[§]Department of Computer Science, Stanford, CA 94305-2140. e-mail: hector@cs.stanford.edu

A second reason why in-place updates are desirable is that they eliminate (or at least postpone) resource consuming reorganizations. Massive reorganizations may be acceptable in conventional systems where user load is minimal over weekends, but in today's world of 7 days a week, 24 hours a day continuous operation, degradation of service for prolonged periods is not acceptable.

A third reason why in-place updates may be desirable is that the index may simply be too massive for reorganization. As the volume of documents grows in some applications, it may be more desirable to have a dynamic index that can grow and dynamically migrate to new disk drives, without ever being fully reorganized.

To address these issues, in a previous work [8] we proposed and experimentally analyzed a new dynamic dual-structure for inverted lists. Lists are initially stored in a "short list" data structure; as they grow they migrate to a "long list" data structure. Our proposed algorithm dynamically selects lists to migrate. Our previous work also studied a family of disk allocation policies for long lists. Each policy dictates, among other things, where to find space for a growing list, whether to try to grow a list as an in-place update or to migrate all or parts of it, and how much free space to leave at the end of a list. Finally, we did a detailed performance evaluation of the dual-structure lists and the various allocation policies. The evaluation is based on a collection of 64 days worth of NetNews indexed according to our algorithms. Our experimental system generates the exact sequence of disk block updates that each policy produces and executes them on real disks. Based on the resulting disk layout, we also computed disk space utilization and estimated query performance.

In the previous work, we used real text data and measured performance on real disks. While this approach has the advantage of being grounded in reality, it has some disadvantages. First, a given text collection has specific characteristics such as size and type of indexing. Our collection was relatively small (686 MB). We only studied an abstracts index of our text collection where duplicate occurrences of a word in a document are dropped. Our synthetic document generator will permit us to study larger text collections of documents. As we shall see, some effects in our system can only be observed with larger text collections. In addition to abstracts indexes, we will study the effect of full text indexing of those collections. Second, in real experiments, we are dependent on the specific hardware characteristics of our test system. Performing experiments with real disks takes a long time – a typical graph can take a day of computation time to produce. And those results depend on a disk with specific characteristics such as seek time and transfer rate. Our simulations take only a few minutes to run, permitting us to explore a much larger range of parameters. In addition, our simulation is calibrated to the results of our real disks, so we are sure that the simulation is accurate. Our synthetic disk simulation permits us to vary multiple parameters of the I/O architecture to study a parameter's effects.

In summary, the new contributions of this paper are:

- a method for generating synthetic documents that are representative of a real document collection,
- a performance evaluation of our algorithms to show the effects of data structure tuning, disk performance, and index scale, and
- a comparison between our dynamic approach of building incremental indexes and a static approach typically found in existing systems.

The next section describes the dual-structure index and algorithms introduced in our previous work. The following two sections describe our experimental design and results. We wrap up with related work and conclusions.

2 Dual-Structure Index and Algorithms

In this paper we assume that when a new document arrives it is parsed and its words are inserted into an in-memory inverted index. At some point the in-memory inverted index must be written to disk. Our objective is to update the disk incrementally with the in-memory inverted index as efficiently as possible.

The lengths of the inverted lists for a database of text documents have a roughly exponential distribution (the Zipf curve [10]). This presents a dilemma for the in-place update of inverted lists since some inverted lists (corresponding to frequently appearing words) will expand rapidly with the arrival of new documents while others (corresponding to infrequently appearing words) will expand slowly or not at all.

In our scheme there are two data structures for lists. We place short inverted lists (of infrequently appearing words) in a fixed size region of disk where the region contains postings for multiple words. These lists are referred to as *short lists* and the fixed size regions are known as *buckets*. The idea is that every inverted list starts off as a short list; when a bucket fills up with inverted lists, the longest inverted list becomes a long list. We place the long inverted lists (of frequently appearing words) in variable length contiguous sequences of blocks on disk. We refer to these inverted lists as *long lists*. Each block of a long list contains postings for only one word. Given a word w, we examine a *directory* which determines if the word has a long inverted list. If the word does not have a long inverted list, it has a short inverted list or no inverted list at all. In this case, a function $h(w)$ (e.g., a hash function or a tree search) returns the bucket where the short inverted list, if any, for the word is stored.

2.1 Buckets and Short Lists

At some point, an in-memory list L for word w (generated from arriving documents) must be moved to disk. First, if w already has a long list (on disk), L is appended to the long list as discussed in the next section. Otherwise, we assume L is a short list and insert it into bucket $h(w)$. If the bucket is not already in memory, it is read in, and L inserted. (If a list for w already existed in the bucket, L is added to it; else a new short list is created in the bucket.) If the bucket overflows, we then pick the longest short list[1] in the bucket, say M, remove it, and make M a long list. Once M is removed, the bucket will be partially empty. The updated bucket $h(w)$ is written to disk (eventually), and list M is written to disk as discussed in the next section. Note that a word w never has both a short list and a long list associated with it. The buckets dynamically determine which words have inverted lists containing only a few postings, since these words are unlikely to grow enough to overflow into a long list. (Assuming that the bucket data structure is large enough to hold all the infrequent words.)

In our simulations we assume that the bucket data structure is maintained in memory across incremental updates, which saves one read of the entire bucket data structure. Our scheme can be adapted to use a very small amount of memory by sorting the in-memory lists into bucket order, then merging with the buckets. This requires only one bucket to be in memory at any time, at an approximate doubling of the cost of managing the bucket data structure. This is a classical space time trade-off which we do not investigate further here.

2.2 Long list data structure

Once a short inverted list L for a word w overflows from a bucket, L is written out to disk and the directory is updated with the existence of w and the location of L. On a subsequent update, an in-memory list L' for a word w is directly appended to L without accessing a bucket. The append is accomplished as follows. If L' fits in the reserved space at the end of L, then L' is added as an in-place update. That is, the last block of L is read, L' is concatenated to the tail of L and the result is written out as an in-place update. If L' does not fit in the reserved space at the end of L, then L' is appended to L in a new region of disk. That is, L is read from disk, L' appended to L, and the result written to a new region of disk with a 10% reserved space at the end of the new region. The old version of L on disk is then freed to be reused. The value of 10% was determined to give good performance by experimental analysis [8]. The long list management policy we have described here is called "whole, limit = y, proportional allocation" in [8]. This is the only policy we consider here. Others are described and compared in [7].

In summary, the dual-structure index allows us to apply different storage structures to the huge number of infrequent words and to the relatively few frequent words. Through the use of fixed-size buckets, this approach dynamically discovers the frequent words that require their own long list. Updates to the large number of infrequent words are amortized into a relatively small number of disk operations, since the buckets are small enough to fit in memory. In addition, coalescing infrequent words reduces wasted disk space by packing multiple very short inverted lists into a disk block. Long lists are kept contiguous to insure good query performance.

3 Experimental Design

This section describes our experimental framework, which consists of three parts. The first part is the synthetic document generator. The output of the generator is given to a simulation of the algorithms and data structures described in Section 2. The result of this simulation is a sequence of disk operations. This sequence is synthetically simulated by our disk simulation. The result of the disk simulation is a set of timings for incremental updates.

---

[1] If there are multiple longest short lists, we choose one arbitrarily.

3.1 Batch update generator

The synthetic document generator creates batches of updates that we use to drive our algorithm simulations. The document generator uses an arbitrary profile of word-occurrence frequences, represented by variable *Profile*, an estimate function f of vocabulary growth, and some document characteristic variables. From our real document collection, we found that each document has on average 350 unique words and that there are 2,124 documents on the average day. We generated 200 days worth of documents totalling 151 million postings.

3.2 Design of the Generator

The synthetic document generator operates as follows. Since the growth in the vocabulary of the database does not go to zero over time (because new words are constantly introduced to the database with each update e.g., family names, company names, misspellings, etc.), two types of words are generated. One are words that are already in the index and the other are synthetic words that are new to the index.

First, the simulator constructs a *synthetic final index* (SFI) representing the final index at the end of all batch updates based on three arguments:

- a *Profile* of a word-occurrence distribution, which is a set of words and the number of times each word occurs,
- the total postings *TotalPostings* in the synthetic final index, and
- a function $f(x)$ that, given a parameter x representing the number of postings, $f(x)$ estimates the number of unique words a document collection of size x.

To construct SFI, the generator proceeds by first basing the distribution on *Profile*. It then adds new synthetic to bring the vocabulary to that estimated by $f(\mathit{TotalPostings})$. The base distribution is expanded to accommodate the new words by assigning 1 posting to each new synthetic word in the distribution, giving SFI.

Next, random documents are created by the generator by selecting *UniqueWords* random words from the SFI. The probability that a word is chosen is proportional to its frequency distribution, e.g., if the word "cat" occurs x times in the SFI, then its probability of being chosen is $x/\mathit{TotalPosting}$. *Documents* random documents are generated and then a synthetic batch update is constructed from the documents. The generator repeatedly creates new random documents and constructs synthetic batch updates until *Updates* batch updates are generated. The form of each synthetic batch update is a set of words and the number of times that each word occurs. This corresponds to the lengths of the inverted lists in an actual implementation of an information retrieval system.

Some information systems index all occurrences of a word, rather than just the count of the occurrences in each document. Indexing all occurrences supports efficient query proximity operators such as finding terms adjacent to one another or within some specified number of words of each other. In [7], we model the index for a full text indexing system by using the (larger) size of the complete inverted lists. We also model the effects of using a "stop list" of very frequent terms that are presumed to offer limited search discrimination.

3.3 Determining Parameters

For our experiments, we supplied arguments to our batch document generator to emulate the characteristics of a collection of 64 days of NETNEWS articles occupying 686 megabytes. Our collection is based on all the articles at our local newsfeed. We then eliminated all nontext articles and articles of short length [8].

To provide the proper parameters to our synthetic document generator, we follow these steps.

1. Estimate the growth in the vocabulary of the text document database.
2. Estimate the number of documents in a batch update.
3. Estimate the number of unique words in a document.
4. Verify that the generator is accurate.

In studying the vocabulary of our document collection, we found a continued introduction of new words into the index for each incremental update. To predict the size of the vocabulary as the number of postings grows beyond 48 million postings, we generate a function $f(x)$ by a curve fit to the data. To

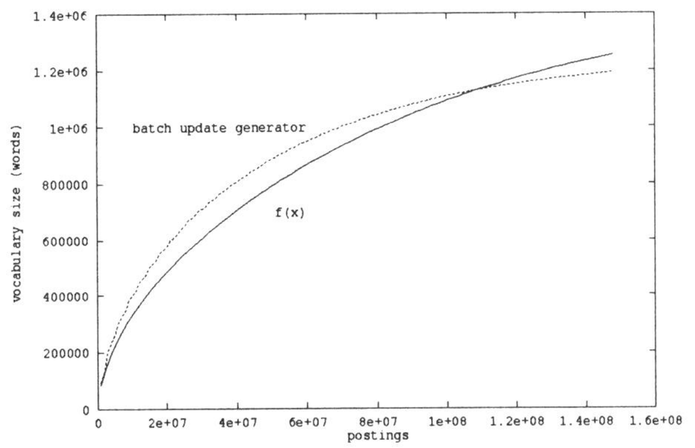

Figure 1: Comparison of the batch update generator to the curve fit function

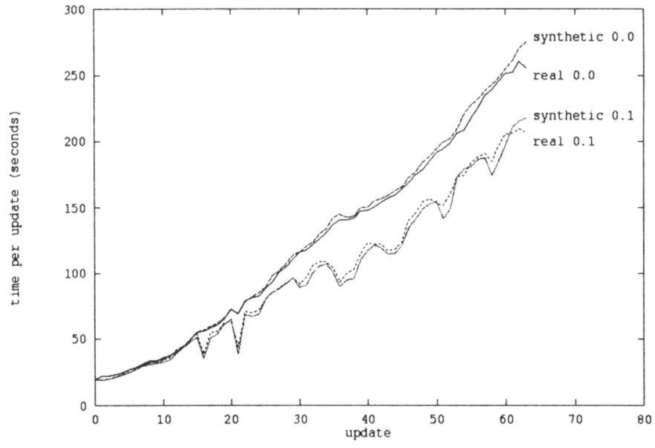

Figure 2: Comparison of traces run on real disks vs. synthetic disks

determine the form of f, we start with the function $x \ln x$ (analytically derived in [1]) and then add all combinations of lower order terms. The result of fitting the data to the equation $a + bx + c \ln x + dx \ln x$ using [9] is the equation

$$f(x) = -436739.2 + 0.09494688x + 35499.8 \ln x - 0.004679559x \ln x. \tag{1}$$

(We also tried curve fits for every subexpression of the function. The function above had the lowest least-squares error of all the curve fit equations.) We found close agreement between the growth in the vocabulary size and the function f.[7] However, the curve fit equation has a limited range of utility since it eventually produces negative numbers as x approaches infinity (due to a negative value of d – the constant for the dominate term of the function). We limit the scaling of our database to just over 3 times, or *Updates*= 200, the number of postings in the real text collection. Within this range the curve fit function behaves reasonably.

To estimate the behavior of documents in a batch, we assume that the number of documents per batch and the number of unique words per batch are about equal to the averages of the 64 known batches, so we let each batch have *Documents*= 2124 documents and each document have *UniqueWords*= 350 unique words. To compute *TotalPosting* for our SFI, we linearly scale the experimental final index of about 48 million postings for 64 batch updates to predict *TotalPosting*= 151 million postings for 200 updates. Using f, the SFI has an estimated total vocabulary of about 1.26 million words. The resulting synthetic text collection represents 430,000 documents occupying 2.1 GB.

To verify that the batch generator is accurate, we compare the vocabulary size of the function f with the vocabulary size produced by the generated documents. Figure 1 shows that the batch update generator initially overestimates the vocabulary size. This is due to the fact that the selection of a word for a batch update is over the entire range of words in the SFI. Eventually the generator underestimates the vocabulary size. This indicates that not every possible word was chosen for some batch update. However, we believe the generator is good enough to qualitatively compare the behavior of databases scaled to larger sizes.

3.4 Dual-structure index simulation

To study the behavior of the dual-structure index, we wrote a simulation of the algorithms and data structures described in Section 2. The simulation reads a list of document batches and writes a trace of the disk I/O operations required to update the bucket data structure and the long lists. At the end of each batch update, we simulate the flushing of all data structures to disk. More detail on the simulation is available in [7].

In comparing our simulation to an implementation of the bucket data structure in an information retrieval system, we note that an implementation would perform a similar computation using inverted-lists as our simulation does using the document representation generated by the synthetic document generator. Thus, our simulation generates exactly the same sequence of disk requests as an actual information retrieval system, but the *contents* of the lists differ. In our simulation the contents of the disk requests are empty, in an actual information retrieval system, the contents are inverted lists.

In our model, the bucket structure is striped over all available disks. We also assume that the buckets all fit in memory so no disk I/O's are simulated to read the buckets.

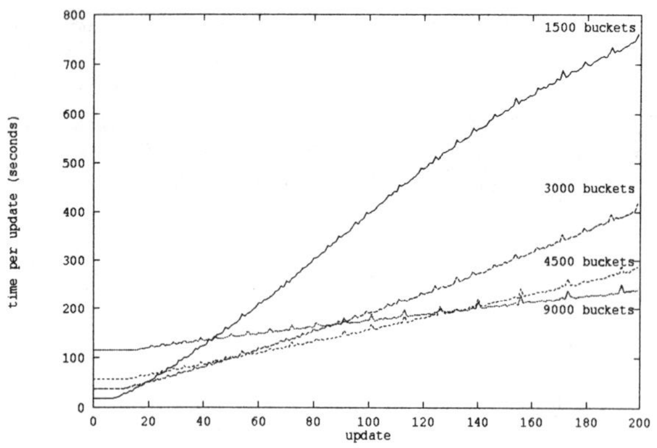

Figure 3: Update time per batch for the dual scheme vs. bucket size

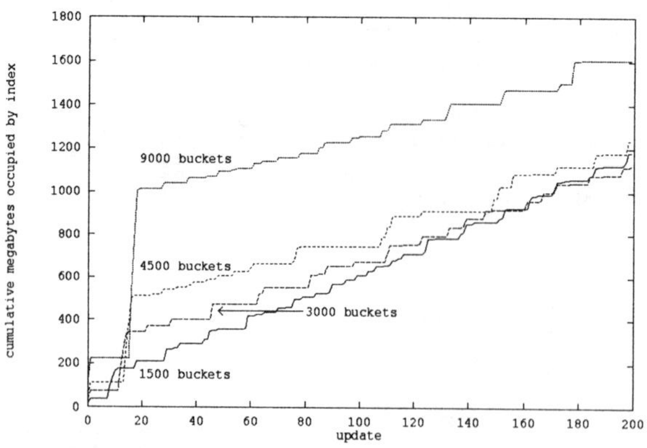

Figure 4: Disk space occupied for the dual structure index vs. bucket size

For our simulation, we used 4 disks, 4500 buckets, 6500 postings per bucket, and 4096 byte blocks.

3.5 Synthetic Disks

Our synthetic disk model replaces execution of traces on disks with the evaluation of an analytic function. It reads the disk I/O trace and predicts how long it would take to perform the inserts for a given number of disks with a given performance. This model can accommodate various seek times and data rates, as well as varying numbers of disks run in parallel.

Our model is based on an average time to read or write the first block of a request, plus an additional charge for each subsequent block in the request. This model takes into account the relatively large time to seek to a block and the relative efficiency of reading or writing many blocks at a time. Read and write data rates are modeled separately, because real disks exhibit significantly different rates (especially optical disks).

We use a simple formula to estimate the time to perform a disk operation. Let x be the number of blocks to read or write. For read operations, we use $Seek + ReadBlock \cdot x$ as the number of milliseconds required for the read operation. For write operations, we use $Seek + WriteBlock \cdot x$, as the number of milliseconds required for the write operation. We measured three disks on a single controller for workloads like those used in this study to determine the values $Seek = 20.0$, $ReadBlock = 3.8$, and $WriteBlock = 4.0$, all values in milliseconds. The synthetic disk model reads a disk trace, computes the time taken by each disk using the read and write formula, and then reports the maximum of these times as a prediction of the total time need to execute the disk trace by actual hardware.

To verify the accuracy of the model, we compared the actual times encountered in running the disk traces on real hardware to those predicted by the synthetic disk model. The results are shown in Figure 2. Two sets of curves are shown. Each set compares real to synthetic. The top set is the time taken for each batch update when no additional reserved space is allocated at the end of a long inverted list. The second set is when 10% reserved space is allocated. We see from the graph that the synthetic disk model does a good job of estimating the time taken by real disks in performing the disk traces.

4 Results

This section describes some of the results of our study (additional results can be found in [7]). One of our goals is to analyze how the dual structure scheme scales; hence, we explore its behavior as the number of batches (days of operation) grows from the 64 in our real collection to 200, representing over half a year of operation. A second goal is to study the impact of various key system parameters, such as the number and speed of the disks, and the number of buckets.

4.1 Choosing the Number of Buckets

The size of the bucket data structure in our dual-structure index is important. Too little bucket space results in many long lists, slower batch insertions, and increasing internal fragmentation due to the allocation of disk blocks to relatively short lists. Too much bucket space results in internal fragmentation in the bucket structure and a higher fixed cost per batch insertion.

In this section, we apply our synthetic batch generator to examine the behavior of buckets as the index grows. We use the batch update generator and the synthetic disk process to estimate the per batch update time for 200 batch updates. Figure 3 shows this situation for several different sizes of the bucket data structure. (We vary the number of buckets and keep the size of each bucket constant.) Examining the curves for the first 20 updates, we see that as the bucket data structure grows in size, the update time per batch is higher. This is due to the need to write out a larger bucket data structure. Over the entire set of updates, however, the larger bucket data structure eventually has the lowest per batch update time since the smallest number of long lists exist for the index with the largest number of buckets. The spikes in the curves correspond to an unusual amount of moving of lists for that update. This is to be expected since each batch update is of a fixed size. This means that many of the long lists are growing at a constant rate and consequently they all overflow the 10% reserve space at the same time. The slight bend in the curve for 1500 buckets is due to the flattening out of the vocabulary size for the index as it grows.

For the same situation as the previous figure, Figure 4 shows the space occupied by the index for each of the bucket sizes. The jump in the space occupied in each curve is due to the update in which the largest lists overflow from the bucket data structure. Since each of these very long lists has a 10% reserved space, a tremendous amount of space is reserved for these lists. We see that the slope of the curve for the 1500 bucket scenario is higher than the slope for the 9000 bucket scenario. Eventually, these curves will converge to points separated only by the size of the bucket data structure. This is due to the bucket data structure filling up with words containing short lists with only a few postings.

4.2 An Alternative Scheme for Comparison

For the remaining experiments we will describe in this section, it is useful to contrast our dual-structure index to a simple "old master/new master" index structure, which we refer to as the *alternative* scheme. This alternative scheme is what current information retrieval systems typically use. In this scheme, the postings for each word are stored contiguously and there is no free space allocated between the lists for different words. On each batch update, the entire existing database is read sequentially, the updates in memory are applied, and the database is written out. Note that the database need not be read completely into memory, but can be processed in convenient-sized chunks. In our comparison, we assume that the time to perform an update in the alternative scheme is mostly disk I/O time and that the I/O time to write the database can be completely overlapped with the time to read it.

The alternative scheme as described above requires about twice as much disk space to store the index, since a copy of the old and new index must exist simultaneously. It is possible to design schemes that break the index into several large pieces to reduce the storage overhead. We assume in our simulation of the alternative scheme that such designs will have little effect on the batch build time if the pieces are kept reasonably large (e.g., 8 to 32 megabytes).

Since the alternative scheme's update time is controlled by disk data rate, we assume that the index is laid out so that the index can be read in parallel from half the disks and written in parallel to the other half.

The alternative scheme offers a couple of advantages. First, since there are no gaps between the lists for different words, there is no space overhead due to internal fragmentation. The postings for words are stored contiguously, so they can be read quickly for queries. Finally, all of the disk I/O during an update is sequential, which typically yields a factor of ten faster data rate than random I/O.

On the negative side, the alternative scheme has to re-read the entire database, even when applying a small batch update. We expect the index build time of the alternative scheme to suffer as the database grows. These features will become apparent when we present our performance results in the following sections.

4.3 Disk Performance

In this section, we show the effects of disk performance on index building time. In our measurements on a real system, we used disks that took about 20 milliseconds to read or write the first block and could sustain a data rate of about 1 megabyte/second. We considered these disks to be "medium speed." We also modeled optical disk-like parameters (slow seek, somewhat slower read data rate, significantly slower write data rate) and current best-performance magnetic disks (faster seek and data rate).

To compare seek times, we modeled four disks with 10, 20, and 50 millisecond times to read or write the first block plus the data rates that we measured on our real disks. The results of this comparison are shown in Figure 5. There is a strong component of seek time. Initially, most of the I/O operations are for rewriting the buckets and are strongly sequential. As the trace progresses, the average size of the data of an I/O operation falls to only a few blocks as more long words are created. Since the average number of blocks written for each long word is small, the average size of the data of an I/O operation

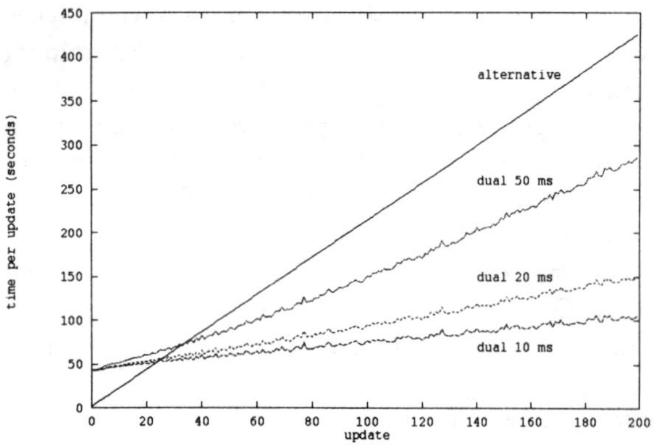

Figure 5: Comparison of varying seek times

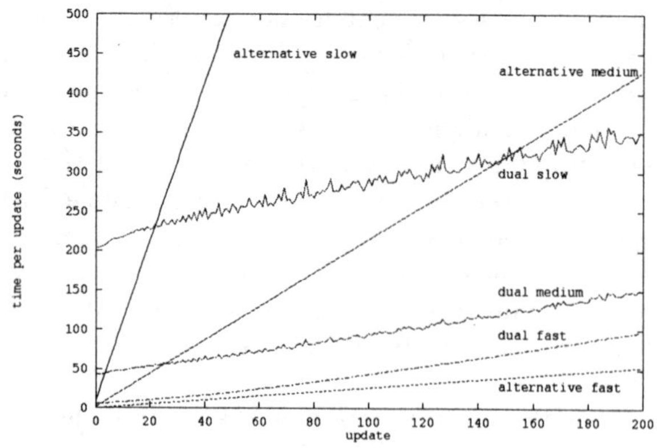

Figure 6: Comparison of varying data rates

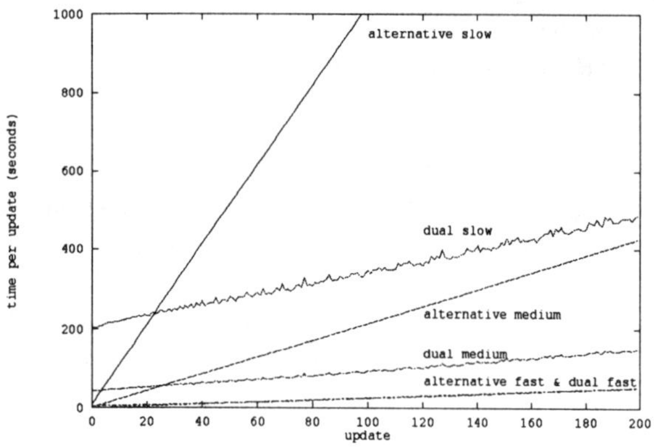

Figure 7: Comparison of varying disks

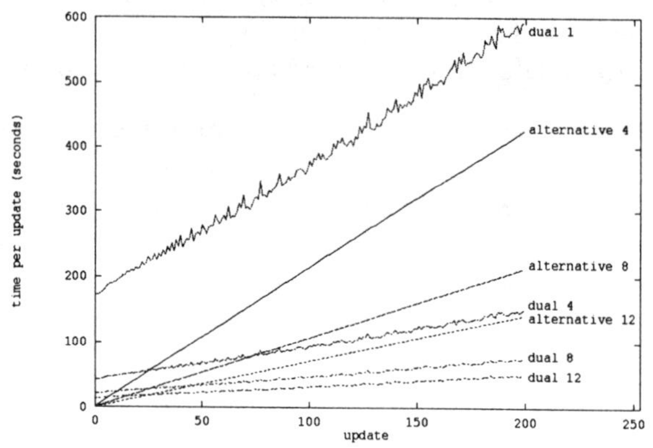

Figure 8: Comparison of varying number of disks

falls and the seek time begins to dominate the total I/O time required to add a batch to the data base. Since the number of seeks is proportional to the number of long words, the faster seek time disks have a smaller slope of increased update time as batches are added.

The alternative scheme is not affected by seek time; a single line is shown for four 1 MB/second disks. The alternate scheme is clearly more time consuming than the dual structure one, even with slow disks, except when the index is very small. Because of its high cost, the alternate scheme would probably not be used after each relatively small batch as we have done here. Instead, larger batches would be constructed. The update cost would still be very high, but it would not be paid as frequently.

To compare the effects of data rate, we model disks with 20 millisecond seeks as seen on our real disks and used a variety of data rates, as shown in Figure 6. The slow transfer curve has a data rate based on optical disks (660 KB/sec reads, 210 KB/sec writes). The medium transfer curve has a data rate based on our disks (1 MB/sec to read and write). The fast transfer curve has a data rate based on current high end disks (8 MB/sec to read and write).

For the dual-structure index, two effects are visible from the figure. First, the slower data rate device exhibits far larger variations in update times. The spikes in the update times are due to update batches that move many long lists. Second, faster transfer times significantly reduce the update times. This variation is mostly due to the reduced time to rewrite the buckets on each disk. That difference is seen on the time required to process the first batch.

The time to perform a batch update in the alternative scheme is the database size divided by the data rate. Therefore, higher data rates result in a flatter line.

Note that the best build performance in this set is given by the alternative scheme. This is due to the combination of a high data rate and only "nominal" seek performance. The poor seek performance hurts the dual structure index but does not affect the alternative scheme. Should technology trends provide disks with significantly faster data rates but only somewhat faster seek times, the dual structure index should be tuned with a larger bucket data structure. As seen earlier, a larger bucket structure increases the amount of sequential I/O per update but decreases the amount of seeking.

To provide a complete picture of the differences in index time caused by disks of various performance, we compare various specific devices directly. The slow disk curve represents optical drive parameters (50 millisecond seek, 660 KB/sec read, 210 KB/sec write). The medium disk curve represents our disk parameters (20 millisecond seek, 1 MB/sec read and write). The fast disk curve represents the latest generation disk parameters (10 millisecond seek, 8 MB/sec read and write). The results are shown in Figure 7. For the dual structure index, the effects of the previous two studies are combined. The fastest seek time provides a more gradual slope coupled with the fastest data rate giving the lowest base update time. For the alternative index, seek time is irrelevant and the results from the data rate study are repeated.

Again, note that for the fastest disk drives, the alternative scheme and the dual structure index produce nearly identical performance. The fast disk has 8 times the data rate but only 2 times the seek performance as our nominal drives.

Another important variable in the configuration of a system is the total number of disks. As the number of disks grows, more I/O's can occur concurrently. In particular, the buckets will reside on more disks and can be thus updated in less time. Each long list is still written to a single disk, but more lists can be updated concurrently.

To study the effect of this variable we fix the single disk parameters to those of our current disk drives. The maximum system disk throughput we assumed for this study is 12 MB/second and is well within the capabilities of current workstations. Given a properly spread I/O load, the use of multiple disks simulates a smaller number of disks that support a high data rate and fast seek time. This effect is borne out in this study, shown in Figure 8. As more disks are used, the slope of the lines for the dual structure index flatten out and the variations in batch time are reduced, as seen in the seek study. In addition, more disks reduce the base time to rewrite the buckets, as seen in the data rate study.

For the alternative scheme, more disks means more aggregate throughput so the lines flatten out accordingly. Note that increasing the number of disks helps the dual structure index more than it helps the alternative scheme. This is because the dual-structure scheme can take advantage of the larger number of seeks per second that can be performed with more drives.

To summarize, we have shown that the time to update the dual structure index is roughly a linear combination of the size of the bucket data structure divided by the aggregate disk data rate and the number of long words time the seek time. Since increasing the size of the bucket structure reduces the number of long words, the dual structure index can be tuned to accommodate the data rate and seek time for the disks used to store the index.

For the alternate scheme, the time is proportional to the database size divided by the aggregate disk data rate. Both of the schemes split well over multiple disks.

5 Related Work

Cutting and Pedersen [1] consider incremental updates of inverted lists where a B-tree is used to organize the vocabulary. Updates are optimized by storing short inverted lists directly in the B-tree. In our framework this optimization can be represented by a very small bucket for approximately each word in the text document database. However, in Section 4 we show that using few, larger, buckets offers better performance. In addition, our scheme dynamically determines a threshold value for determining if an inverted list is stored in a fixed sized structure or a variable length one. Cutting and Pedersen also described a buddy system for the allocation of long lists. This approach deserves further experimental study since it offers comparable space utilization and it is not clear if it offers better update performance than the methods presented here.

Faloutsos and Jagadish [3] extensively analyze the physical organization of long list. Performance comparisons between our work and the schemes presented there are difficult since updates are not batched in that paper. In another work, Faloutsos and Jagadish [2] extensively analyze a dual-structure scheme based on signature schemes for long lists and inverted lists for short lists. The division in the structure is static as opposed to a dynamic scheme presented here. In addition, we believe that using inverted lists for short lists is computationally expensive since many I/O operations, each containing only a few postings, are required to update this structure.

Zobel, Moffat and Sacks-Davis [11] consider several issues in inverted file indexing. The compression methods presented there complement this paper well. They also consider fixed size buckets for storing inverted lists but do not discuss techniques for handling long lists.

An interesting and entirely different approach, by Fox and Lee, based on preprocessing of document representations and a merge update of inverted lists is described in [4]. The scheme is non-incremental.

Harman and Candela [5] also describe an update method and cite an indexing time of 313 hours for 806 MB of documents on a minicomputer with six Intel 80386 processors. Finally, our own measurements[2] show that freeWAIS version 0.202 requires 12.2 hours to incremental index the month of December (298 MB) of our experimental text document database.

6 Conclusion

For dynamic, time critical text document databases, it is important to modify index structures in place, as batches of documents arrive. We have presented a dual structure index strategy to address this problem. Comparing the results presented here with the literature, we have argued that the dual-structure index has better performance than existing implementations with the added bonus of providing incremental updates. The principle source of our improvement is the dynamic division of postings into short and long inverted lists and the application of appropriate data structures to each type of list.

We have described a means of creating large synthetic document collections and have described a simple model of parallel disks. The synthetic document model can be tuned to model the statistics of an existing text collection and can be scaled to model varying numbers and sizes of documents. We adjusted our disk model to conform to our existing real disks; the disk model can also be modified to model slower disks, such as optical, or the faster disks that have been recently announced.

We studied the I/O subsystem extensively and determined that the time required to write the bucket data structure to disk is dominated by the subsystem data rate, whereas the time to incrementally update the long lists is dominated by the disk seek time. We quantitatively describe the performance improvements due to speeding up disk or adding more disks. In particular, we showed that the inverted file organization described in this paper stripes across multiple disks well.

We also showed the effects of varying the amount of disk space allocated to the bucket data structure and suggested a way to scale the number of buckets as the size of the inverted file grows.

Acknowledgments: Thanks to Mendel Rosenblum for discussions on file system mechanisms related to this paper.

References

[1] Doug Cutting and Jan Pedersen. Optimizations for dynamic inverted index maintenance. In *Proceedings of SIGIR '90*, pages 405–411, 1990.

[2] Christos Faloutsos and H. V. Jagadish. Hybrid index organizations for text databases. In A. Pirotte, C. Delobel, and G. Gottlob, editors, *Proceedings 3rd International Conference on Extending Database Technology - EDBT '92*, Vienna, 1992. Springer–Verlag.

[3] Christos Faloutsos and H. V. Jagadish. On B-tree indices for skewed distributions. In *Proceedings of 18th International Conference on Very Large Databases*, pages 363–374, Vancouver, British Columbia, Canada, 1992.

[4] William B. Frakes and Ricardo Baeza-Yates. *Information Retrieval: Data Structures and Algorithms.* Prentice-Hall, 1992.

[5] Donna Harman and Gerald Candela. Retrieving records from a gigabyte of text on a minicomputer using statistical ranking. *Journal of the American Society for Information Science*, 41(8):581–589, 1990.

[6] Donald E. Knuth. *The Art of Computer Programming.* Addison-Wesley, Reading, Massachusetts, 1973.

[7] Anthony Tomasic, Hector Garcia-Molina, and Kurt Shoens. Incremental updates of inverted lists for text document retrieval. Technical Note STAN-CS-TN-93-1, Stanford University, 1993. Available via FTP from db.stanford.edu as /pub/tomasic/stan.cs.tn.93.1.ps.

[8] Anthony Tomasic, Hector Garcia-Molina, and Kurt Shoens. Incremental updates of inverted lists for text document retrieval. In *International Conference on Management of Data (SIGMOD 94)*, 1994.

[9] Stephen Wolfram. *Mathematica.* Addison-Wesley, Redwood City, California, 2nd edition, 1991.

[10] George Kingsley Zipf. *Human Behavior and the Principle of Least Effort.* Addison-Wesley Press, 1949.

[11] Justin Zobel, Alistair Moffat, and Ron Sacks-Davis. An efficient indexing technique for full-text database systems. In *Proceedings of 18th International Conference on Very Large Databases*, Vancouver, 1992.

[2] We use a DEC 5000 Model 240 (32 MB memory) with an external disk on a SCSI-I bus under ULTRIX V4.2A (Rev. 47) operating system.

Document Filtering for Fast Ranking

Michael Persin
mp@kbs.citri.edu.au

CITRI, Dept. of Computer Science, RMIT
723 Swanston St., Carlton Victoria 3053, Australia

Abstract

Ranking techniques are effective for finding answers in document collections but the cost of evaluation of ranked queries can be unacceptably high. We propose an evaluation technique that reduces both main memory usage and query evaluation time, based on early recognition of which documents are likely to be highly ranked. Our experiments show that, for our test data, the proposed technique evaluates queries in 20% of the time and 2% of the memory taken by the standard inverted file implementation, without degradation in retrieval effectiveness.

1 Introduction

Ranked queries are used to retrieve documents from a database and show them to the user in order of estimated relevance to the user's query [11]. Estimation of relevance is based on the statistical similarity of document and query. For existing ranked query evaluation techniques, even documents that contain only one of the terms in the query has some perceived relevance to the user's query [1, 3, 4, 13]. As a consequence, the set of answers to a query can contain a large number of documents, almost the whole database for some queries. For this reason, only the top-ranked documents are retrieved for presentation to the user—most of the candidate documents are discarded.

Since for typical queries large numbers of documents are candidate answers, the amount of main memory needed for storing information about these answers can be prohibitively high, as can the time for processing lists of documents containing terms in the query. In particular the majority of both main memory expenditure and processing time is spent on the most common (and hence uninformative) terms in queries. Such terms are by definition encountered in many of the documents in a collection, and processing the inverted indexes for these terms—that is, processing the lists of document identifiers for documents containing these terms—takes much time. Moreover, these common terms give rise to a large number of candidate documents and hence a large number of similarity values to be kept in main memory.

We propose a technique for filtering documents that allows a significant reduction in both the volume of main memory required and the time of query evaluation. Our approach is based on processing only the most informative parts of inverted lists. Our experiments in applying this technique to the cosine measure show that it allows evaluation of the queries on a large document collection in approximately 20% of the time and in 2% of memory of previous techniques, and without deterioration in retrieval effectiveness. Such savings make information retrieval possible for small machines such as PCs, and for large multi-user document systems such as library systems, which can have thousands of simultaneous users.

We describe the cosine measure and the structure of our document database in Section 2. The technique of document filtering is described in Section 3. Practical results are discussed in Section 4. Conclusions are presented in Section 5.

2 Ranked queries

2.1 Cosine measure

The technique of evaluation of ranked queries we use in this paper is the *cosine measure* [11]. This technique is used to evaluate the similarity of a document and a query and is determined by

$$cosine_{q,d} = \frac{\sum_t sim_{d,q,t}}{\sqrt{\sum_t w_{q,t}^2} \cdot \sqrt{\sum_t w_{d,t}^2}} , \tag{1}$$

where q is the query, d is the document, and $w_{x,t}$ is the weight of the term t in a document or query x.

The expression $sim_{d,q,t}$ is the *partial similarity* of the query q and the document d given by the term t, and is determined by

$$sim_{d,q,t} = w_{q,t} \cdot w_{d,t} \tag{2}$$

Several term weighting systems have been proposed and explored [8, 11]. We assign the weight to a term in a query or a document using the frequency-modified inverse document frequency, described by

$$w_{x,t} = f_{x,t} \cdot \log(N/f_t) , \tag{3}$$

where $f_{x,t}$ is the number of occurrences of the term t in x, N is the number of documents in the collection, and f_t is the number of documents containing t. This function assigns a high weight to terms which are encountered in only a small number of documents in a collection. It is supposed that rare terms have high discrimination value and the presence of such a term in both a document and a query is a good sign that the document is relevant to the query.

2.2 Database structure

The inverted file organisation [10, 11, 12] was chosen for implementation of our system. The main advantage of the inverted file organization is the speed of query evaluation. No search operation is carried out on the documents themselves; the documents are identified using only pointer lists in the inverted file. Disk space overheads on index storage can be substantially reduced by usage of compression techniques such as those described by Moffat & Zobel [5].

To evaluate ranked queries efficiently, the following structures are required: the vocabulary, containing terms and for each term a corresponding pointer to the inverted file entry; the inverted file, consisting of, for each term, the list of document identifiers for documents that contain the term; the term weights; the document lengths; and the set of accumulators (usually one accumulator for each document in the database) containing the similarity values for each document with respect to a query.

Each distinct term t in a collection is stored in a vocabulary together with a pointer to a term entry and the value f_t, which is the total number of documents containing t. Knowledge of f_t allows the terms in a query to be processed in order of decreasing weight [1, 4], which is necessary for the technique we shall describe. The term entries are stored in the inverted index. A term entry for each term consists of pairs of values (document number d, term frequency $f_{d,t}$). Document number d is a unique number identifying a document and term frequency $f_{d,t}$ is the number of occurrences of the term t in the document d.

Evaluation of the cosine measure also requires a file containing the values of document lengths for each document. The document length $W_d = \sqrt{\sum_t w_{d,t}^2}$ describes the total weight or the length of a document. These values are independent of a query and need to be computed only once, at database creation time, for a static database. The document lengths are stored independently to allow effective compression of the inverted file. Storage of the within-document frequencies normalised by the document lengths would mean storage of float numbers rather than small integers which can be effectively compressed and hence, sharp increase in the size of the inverted file.

2.3 Processing of ranked queries

A common technique for evaluation of a ranked query is to simultaneously compute the cosine correlation between each document in a collection and the query, and then choose the k documents with the highest cosine value [2, 6, 10, 11]. The basic algorithm uses a set of accumulators, one accumulator for each

1. For each document d in the collection, set accumulator A_d to zero.
2. For each term t in the query,
   (a) Retrieve the term entry for t from the disk.
   (b) For each (document number d, term frequency $f_{d,t}$) pair in the term entry, add $w_{q,t} \cdot w_{d,t}$ to A_d.
3. Divide each non-zero accumulator A_d by the document length W_d.
4. Identify the k highest values of accumulators (k is the number of documents to be presented to the user) and retrieve the corresponding documents.

Figure 1. Simple algorithm for computing a cosine measure

document in a collection, and an inverted index. For each query term the inverted index is used to identify both the documents containing the term and the contribution to the cosine value for the document made by the term; this contribution is added to the document's accumulator. A simple version of this algorithm, as given by Moffat & Zobel [6], is shown in Figure 1.

Two problems of this simple approach are the high number of query-document comparisons that must be carried out and the large volume of main memory occupied by the set of accumulators. Algorithms have been proposed to minimize the percentage of term entries to be inspected and the volume of main memory to be used [6, 8]. Our approach to solution of these problems is described in the next sections.

3 Document filtering

In this section we describe our approach to evaluation of ranked queries, based on processing only the most informative parts of term entries.

3.1 Reducing the number of documents processed

As we have described above, the usual approach to the evaluation of ranked queries is consecutive processing of every term in a query and of the whole index entry for each term. With this technique, we determine, for each query term and each document containing the term, a partial similarity of the document and the query.

The described technique has some shortcomings. Usually, a large part of all accumulated partial similarities are given by common terms and thus have very low weight. Processing of these values produces very little increase in accuracy and takes time. It is particularly important in the systems that use compression for storage of term entries, since, to evaluate queries, large volumes of data have to be decompressed. Moreover, the most common terms in a typical query are contained in a large proportion of the documents in a collection. Processing of all documents in these term entries leads to a steep increase in the number of accumulators kept in main memory.

There have been previous attempts to improve the efficiency of the basic algorithm. Elimination of "stop-words"—that is, of very frequent words or closed-class words such as "and" and "of"—is often used to reduce the number of uninformative terms processed. However, even a stop-word can influence the final rank of a document in the set of answers if the number of its occurrences in the document is large. Another problem with the elimination of stop-words is that it is often difficult to determine the list of stop-words. For example, in our test database the word "text", which is not especially common in English, is encountered in every document in the collection and hence does not have any discrimination value. Another word, "computer", is also very common in the collection, but does seem to provide useful discrimination.

More sophisticated algorithms implement some dynamic stopping condition. The typical scheme of these algorithms is to order terms in a query by decreasing weight and process terms from most to least important until some stopping condition is met [1, 3, 4, 6]. Moffat & Zobel [6] implemented the stopping condition by limiting the number of accumulators. They tested two versions of the algorithm.

In the first version, processing of a query was stopped as soon as the number of accumulators exceeded a certain limit. In the second, processing of query was continued after reaching the limit number of accumulators but no new documents were inserted into the set of candidates. The first version of this algorithm showed noticeable improvement in response time but at the cost of significant deterioration in retrieval effectiveness. The second version gave the same retrieval effectiveness as a basic version which processed all term entries but the processing time did not decrease significantly.

Harman & Candela [3] experimented with another pruning algorithm. They accumulated partial similarities given by all documents in all term entries (like the second algorithm by Moffat & Zobel) but limited the number of accumulators by setting a condition for the insertion of new documents into the set of relevant documents. They inserted, into the set of relevant documents, only those documents which contained terms with inverse document frequency more than a certain fraction of the maximum inverse document frequency of any term in the database. An overview of pruning algorithms and some additional references are given by Salton [10] and Frakes & Baeza-Yates [2].

These algorithms allow reduction of the number of processed document-term pairs but usually lead to deterioration in retrieval effectiveness. The reason for this is that the decision to stop is based only on global parameters of the data set. These algorithms select, for processing or rejection, whole term entries rather than separate documents within these entries, and as a consequence these algorithms cannot provide a gradual transition from processing terms to rejection of terms. For example, a document with a high within-document frequency for a term can be discarded because the term has low inverse document frequency, whereas a document with a low within-document frequency for a term that has only slightly greater inverse document frequency may be considered.

3.2 Filtering documents

The essence of our approach, to decrease the time of query evaluation and main memory expenditure, comprises more sensitive processing of term entries, taking into consideration both the global parameter of term importance across the whole collection and the local parameter of the number of occurrences of a term in each document. We modified the basic algorithm of Figure 1 in the following way.

We determine two thresholds, an insertion threshold k_{ins} and an addition threshold k_{add}, where $k_{ins} \geq k_{add}$. These thresholds are recomputed before processing of each query term. As we process a term entry for term t we compare the partial similarity $sim_{d,q,t}$ of a query q and each document d in the entry to each threshold. If $sim_{d,q,t}$ is more than k_{ins} we consider that this document is important enough to be one of the candidates. If this document is already present in the set of relevant documents we add $sim_{d,q,t}$ to the value of the accumulator corresponding to this document. If the document is not present in the set we insert it. If $sim_{d,q,t}$ is less than k_{ins} but more than k_{add} we consider that the document is not important enough to be interesting to the user by itself but it can affect the final order of documents. So if the document is already present in the set of accumulators then $sim_{d,q,t}$ is added to the accumulator. And, finally, if $sim_{d,q,t}$ is less than k_{add}, the information is regarded as unimportant and we go to the next document.

The rationale for our use of thresholds is that, if we have a large enough number of candidate documents with high values of similarity to the query, it is not profitable to consider small partial similarities; they will not be able to change the final rank of answers. Skipping these documents saves CPU time spent on computation and accumulation of partial similarities. The threshold k_{add} allows us to ignore these partial similarities. Likewise, when we already have many documents with high similarities, there is no reason to consider a new document with a lesser partial similarity given by a more common term. The threshold k_{ins} allows us to discard such documents. Thresholds have previously been used to decide whether to process or reject whole term entries [3], but not to decide whether to process or reject individual documents.

The values of both thresholds are determined as a product of a predefined constant and the accumulated partial similarity of the currently most relevant document S_{max}. This heuristic supposes that if the current most relevant document has a high weight then we do not need to process a document that has a small value of similarity to a query, as it unlikely changes the final rank of relevant documents or identifies an important document that is not yet included in the set of relevant documents. Another possibility is to use the average similarity of several top documents instead of the highest one, but the overheads for implementation of this version are larger than for use of current maximal similarity. The values of the thresholds are determined as

$$k_{ins} = c_{ins} \cdot S_{max} \quad \text{and}$$

$$k_{add} = c_{add} \cdot S_{max} ,$$

where $c_{ins} \geq c_{add} \geq 0$ are constants.

We shall process document d containing term t only if the partial similarity of d and the query given by t is more than the current value of threshold k_{ins}:

$$\omega_{d,t} \cdot \omega_{q,t} > k_{ins}$$

(Recall that k_{ins} is never less than k_{add}.) Having substituted the definition of the weight of a term in a document from Equation 3 in Section 2.1, we obtain

$$f_{d,t} \cdot \log \frac{N}{f_t} \cdot f_{q,t} \cdot \log \frac{N}{f_t} > k ,$$

where k is either k_{ins} or k_{add}. The final condition is

$$f_{d,t} > \frac{k}{f_{q,t} \cdot \log^2 N/f_t} \tag{4}$$

We expressed the condition of processing of the document d as a condition for a within-document frequency of the term t in the document. Let us denote the threshold frequencies, determined by the right part of Equation 4, as f_{ins} and f_{add} for the insertion and addition thresholds respectively:

$$f_{ins} = \frac{c_{ins} \cdot S_{max}}{f_{q,t} \cdot \log^2 N/f_t} \tag{5}$$

$$f_{add} = \frac{c_{add} \cdot S_{max}}{f_{q,t} \cdot \log^2 N/f_t} \tag{6}$$

We have created a filter that rejects or accepts the document d contained in the term entry for the term t depending on: the frequency of the term across a database f_t; the number of term occurrences in this document $f_{d,t}$; and the importance of the term in a query $f_{q,t}$.

Note that the values of f_{ins} and f_{add} in Equations 5 and 6 are computed at the beginning of processing of the term t. The decision, whether we process the document d containing the term t or not, depends only on the number of occurrences of the term in d. This means that during processing a term entry we have to execute only one comparison per document to decide whether to process or ignore the document.

Formulas 5 and 6, which determining the values of the filters for each term, provide a smooth transition from processing to rejection of documents in term entries. For the document d containing the term t, the more common the term t in a collection the higher must be the within-document frequency of t in d if d is to be considered as a relevant document. This approach allows a gradual increase of the cut-off threshold, in contrast to the global pruning of terms in queries used by other approaches. This is an essential difference in comparison to the algorithms that use the "everything or nothing" strategy for rejection of terms in the query and stop processing upon achieving a certain limit [1, 3, 4, 6].

The constants c_{ins} and c_{add} in the definition of the value of the threshold are used for tuning the algorithm. By increasing the constant c_{add} we decrease the number of document-term pairs (and, correspondingly, the number of partial similarities of documents and a query) inspected and accumulated by the algorithm. By increasing the constant c_{ins} we decrease the number of documents which can be candidates.

3.3 Fast processing of term entries

For our ranking technique, the decision about whether to process or reject a document depends only on the number of occurrences of the term in the document. Using the usual structure of inverted file entries, where document identifiers are numerically ordered [6, 12], we have to process the whole entry, comparing the number of term occurrences in every document to the current value of the threshold. However, a different structure of the inverted file provides much faster processing of term entries. By sorting the documents in the term entries in order of decreasing number of term occurrences in a document, we process the most important documents in each entry first. As soon as we find the first document in

1. Create an empty structure of accumulators.
2. Sort the terms in the query in order of decreasing weights.
3. Set the value of the weight of the current most relevant document S_{max} to 0.
4. For each term t in the query,
    (a) Compute the values of the filters f_{ins} and f_{add}.
    (b) If $f_{max} \leq \max(f_{ins}, f_{add})$, go to step 4.
    (c) Retrieve the term entry for t from the disk.
    (d) For each (document number d. term frequency $f_{d,t}$) pair in the term entry,
        i. If $f_{d,t} > f_{ins}$, add $w_{q,t} \cdot w_{d,t}$ to A_d and add A_d to the set of accumulators if necessarily.
        ii. Else, if $f_{d,t} > f_{add}$ add $w_{q,t} \cdot w_{d,t}$ to A_d if A_d is present in the set of accumulators.
        iii. Otherwise, go to step 4.
        iv. Set $S_{max} = \max(S_{max}, A_d)$.
5. Divide each non-zero accumulator A_d by the document length W_d.
6. Identify the k highest values of accumulators (k is the number of documents to be presented to the user) and retrieve the corresponding documents.

Figure 2. Filtering algorithm for computing a cosine measure

which the number of term occurrences is less than the addition threshold, we can stop processing this term entry because all the rest of the documents have the same or less importance as the first rejected document.

We need to compute and to store in the vocabulary the values of maximal within-document frequencies for each term in a database in order to support efficient skipping of term entries. As the vocabulary is kept in main memory, the time of access to this information is insignificant. Before commencing the processing of each term in a query we compute the threshold frequencies f_{add} and f_{ins} and compare them to the maximal within-document frequency of the term f_{max}. If the maximal frequency is less than or equal to the values of both f_{add} and f_{ins} then no document containing this term will be processed and we can process the next term in the query without retrieving the current term entry from the disk. The final version of the filtering algorithm, using this structure of the inverted file, is shown in Figure 2.

The modified inverted file, which stores document identifiers in term entries ordered by the term frequency, is smaller than a usual inverted file, as we do not store the term frequency for every document. It is sufficient to store the term frequency for all the set of documents with the same frequency and the number of documents in this set. A detailed description of experiments with restructured inverted files can be found elsewhere [9].

4 Experimental results

The database we have used in our experiments is a collection of *Wall Street Journal* articles, extracted from the TIPSTER collection for the TREC project [7]. The size of this database is 532 Mb; it contains 173,000 documents; average document size is 510 terms; the longest document consists of 22,200 terms. We have used queries 1–100 from the TREC experiment; the length of the queries ranges from 35 to 130 terms. We measured effectiveness of algorithms by averaging precision for 11 values of recall (0%, 10%, ..., 100%). For consistency with the TREC experiments, we only retrieved the top 200 documents for each query, and pessimistically assumed all recall values outside the top 200 to be zero. All results shown in the graphs are average values over all 100 queries.

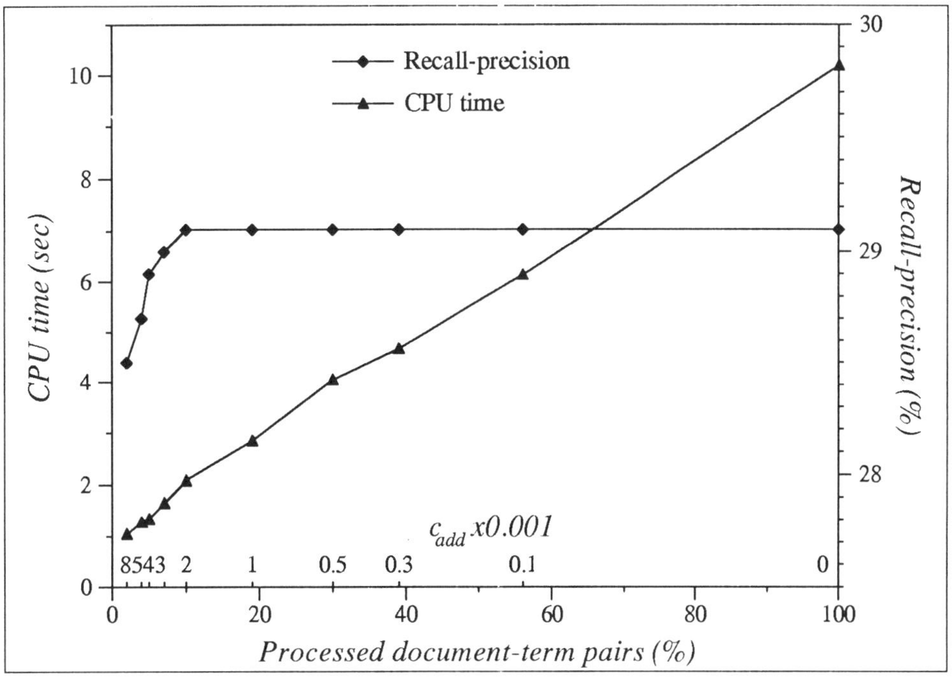

Figure 3. Time of query evaluation for different values of c_{add} ($c_{ins} = 0.07$)

Query evaluation time and retrieval effectiveness are shown as a function of the addition threshold in Figure 3. We depict two parameters on the horizontal axis: the value of the constant c_{add} and the percentage of (document number, term frequency) pairs processed by the algorithm for this value of c_{add}. The value of the insertion threshold was fixed in this experiment. Prior to these experiments we measured retrieval effectiveness for different values of c_{ins}, and chose the value 0.07 because it gave good retrieval effectiveness using a small number of accumulators. For this value of c_{ins}, we can obtain an answer to a ranked query with the same retrieval effectiveness as the basic algorithm (28.9%) having processed only 5% of the contents of all term entries in only 20% of the time needed for processing of all entries. Interestingly, processing only 10% of the contents of all term entries, we obtain even better retrieval effectiveness in comparison to the standard algorithm. The reason for this is the pruning of common terms that are encountered in almost every document and that create informational noise rather than help discriminate between documents. Note that it is only necessary to process a very small part of all term entries to obtain a decent level of retrieval effectiveness. While processing only 1% of term entries, which takes 17% of the time taken by the previous implementation, we obtain an answer to a query with deterioration in retrieval effectiveness of only 2.7%. Note that there are processing overheads that are independent on the number of processed documents; hence the decrease in the time of queries evaluation is not a linear function of the number of the quantity of index processed.

We found that the described technique saves not only the cpu time spent processing of term entries, but also the number of disk accesses. Making a decision about whether to reject a term does not require a disk access, as all the necessary information is kept in memory. Moreover, if we accept a term for processing we do not necessarily have to read the whole term entry into main memory. Term entries for common terms usually occupy more than one disk block. As the rejection threshold for these terms is quite high we usually have to read only the first block of each term entry.

Figure 4 shows the dependency of retrieval effectiveness on the number of accumulators. The number of accumulators was varied by changing the insertion threshold. Both the value of the constant c_{ins} and the corresponding number of accumulators is depicted on the horizontal axis. We used the zero value of the addition threshold in this experiment to prevent the skipping of common terms, that is for each of document included in the set of candidate documents we accumulated all partial similarities given by all terms. Note that using a relatively small number of candidate documents we obtain better retrieval effectiveness in comparison to the basic algorithm. Interestingly, this phenomenon is consistent

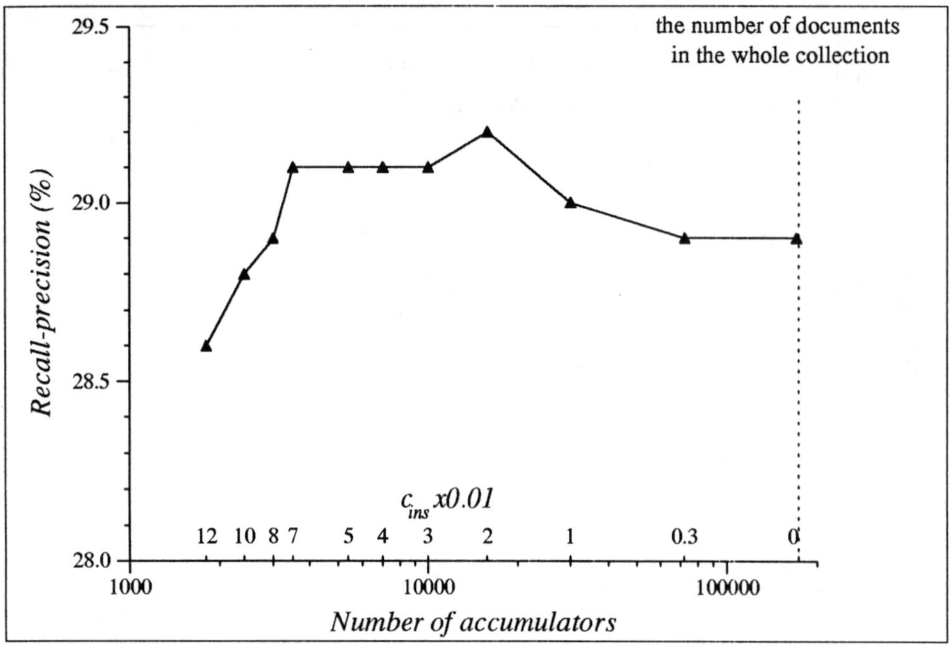

Figure 4. Number of accumulators for different values of c_{ins} (c_{add}=0)

for different techniques and different document collections: similar results were obtained by Moffat & Zobel in their experiments with an explicit limit on the number of accumulators [6].

Using a value of the threshold that does not deteriorate retrieval effectiveness (in this case we process 5% of all term-document pairs), we reduce the number of accumulators by a factor of over fifty. The filtering algorithm is reasonably insensitive to c_{ins}, providing good performance across a wide range of values; we are currently conducting experiments to determine whether similar thresholds apply to different databases. Moreover, the largest number of accumulators used in our experiments was no more than 3 times the average value, so that performance of the filtering algorithm does not greatly depend on characteristics of individual queries.

Moffat & Zobel experimented with a pruning algorithm based on an explicit limit on the number of accumulators [6]. Comparison of our algorithm to their technique shows that a precise selection of documents allows faster evaluation of ranked queries using half of the memory.

4.1 Other term weighting systems

The cosine measure as described in Section 2.1 is not the only similarity measure. There are other similarity measures, for example those described by Lucarella [4] and Harman & Candela [3]. We tested the robustness of document filtering by applying it to these similarity measures.

Lucarella determined the similarity of a document and the query using the formula:

$$S_{d,q} = \frac{\sum_t w_{q,t} \cdot w_{d,t}}{\sqrt{\sum_t w_{q,t}^2} \cdot \sqrt{\sum_t w_{d,t}^2}}, \qquad (7)$$

where q is the query, d is the document, and $w_{x,t}$ is the weight of the term t in a document or query x. The weight of a term is determined as

$$w_{x,t} = (0.5 + 0.5 \cdot f_{x,t}/f_{max_x}) \cdot \log_2(N/f_t)\,, \qquad (8)$$

where $f_{x,t}$ is the number of occurrences of the term t in x, f_{max_x} is the maximum occurrence frequency among the terms associated with the document or query x, N is the number of documents in the collection, and f_t is the number of documents containing t. This measure is similar to our form of the cosine measure, but the importance of the within-document frequency of a term in a document is much smaller in Lucarella's measure since it is normalized.

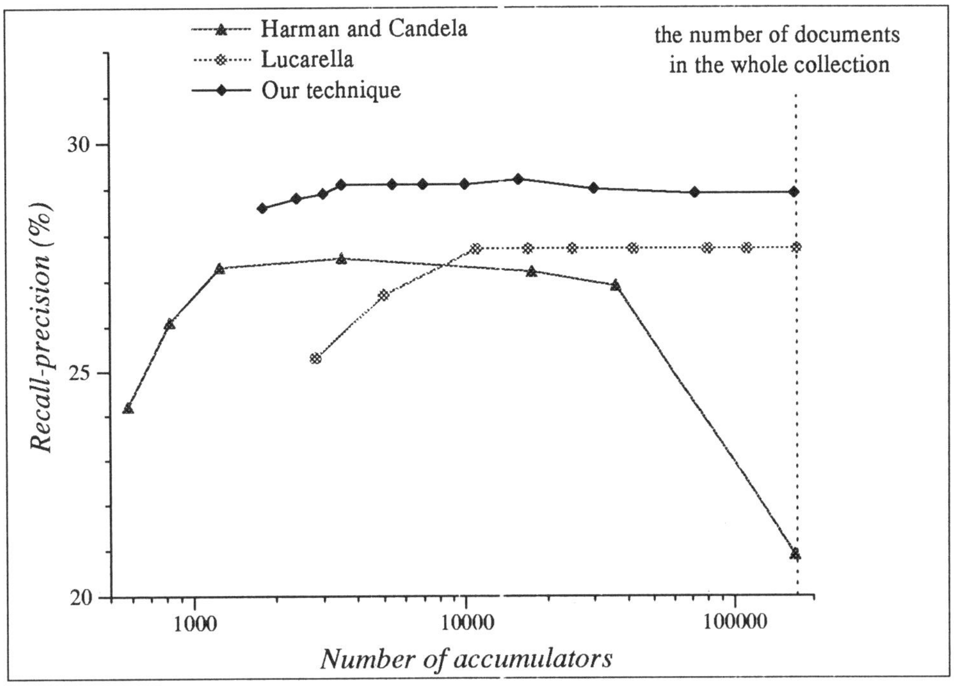

Figure 5. Retrieval effectiveness for different number of accumulators

Harman & Candela employed the following similarity measure:

$$S_{d,q} = \sum_t \frac{\log_2 f_{d,t} \cdot (\log_2(N/f_t) + 1)}{\log_2 M_d}, \tag{9}$$

where M_d is the total number of significant terms (including duplicates) in the document d. This similarity measure considers only a frequency of a term in documents, not taking into account the number of term occurrences in a query.

We were not able measure time savings that our technique would yield for these similarity measures, as this would demand a reimplementation of the inverted index. We measured only the reduction in the number of accumulators. As the volume of computation required for evaluation of the similarity of the query and documents is approximately the same both for our similarity measure and for the measures used by Harman & Candela and by Lucarella, we expect that the time savings should be the same as for the similarity measure used in our system.

Figure 5 shows the dependency of retrieval effectiveness, given by the two similarity measures, on the number of accumulators. The number of accumulators was varied by changing the constant c_{ins}. As can be seen, for all of the similarity measures use of the technique of document filtering allows obtaining an answer to a query without deterioration in retrieval effectiveness, using only about 1% and 6% of main memory for Harman & Candela's and Lucarella's algorithms respectively.

5 Conclusion

A technique has been presented that allows fast evaluation of ranked queries; in less main memory; and without any deterioration in retrieval effectiveness. The technique uses an inverted file representation of the document collection and examines the minimum number of documents in inverted lists in order to improve the speed of query evaluation.

The technique is especially suitable for databases used on small computers with acute limitations on the size of main memory, CPU speed and disk access time. Time saving given by this technique is more noticeable for the systems which use compression for storage of data, since for such systems decompression of long inverted file entries is a substantial overhead on processing time.

The experimental results show that significant improvement both in time (5 times faster) and in the volume of main memory used (over 50 times smaller) can be achieved without deterioration in retrieval effectiveness. The algorithm was tested on several term weighting schemes proposed by other researchers. Experiments showed a consistent steep decrease in the volume of main memory required (40–100 times) and improvement in retrieval effectiveness (up to a factor of 1.3). The results suggest that the proposed technique is a practical optimisation for evaluation of ranked queries in systems based on inverted files.

Acknowledgements

I would like to thank Ron Sacks-Davis and Justin Zobel. I would also like to thank Anthony Botham and Neil Sharman for their advice. This research was supported by the Key Center of Knowledge Based Systems and the Collaborative Information Technology Research Institute.

References

1. C. Buckley and A.F. Lewit. Optimisation of inverted vector searches. In *Proc. ACM-SIGIR International Conference on Research and Development in Information Retrieval*, pages 97–110, Montreal, Canada, June 1985.
2. W.B. Frakes and R. Baeza-Yates, editors. *Information Retrieval: Data Structures and Algorithms.* Prentice-Hall, New Jersey, 1992.
3. D. Harman and G. Candela. Retrieving records from a gigabyte of text on a minicomputer using statistical ranking. *Journal of the American Society for Information Science*, 41(8):581–589, 1990.
4. D. Lucarella. A document retrieval system based upon nearest neighbour searching. *Journal of Information Science*, 14:25–33, 1988.
5. A. Moffat and J. Zobel. Parameterised compression for sparse bitmaps. In *Proc. ACM-SIGIR International Conference on Research and Development in Information Retrieval*, pages 274–285, Copenhagen, Denmark, June 1992. ACM Press.
6. A. Moffat and J. Zobel. Fast ranking in limited space. Technical Report 93/11, Department of Computer Science, The University of Melbourne, 1993. Submitted to the 1994 Data Engineering conference.
7. National Institute of Standards and Technology. *Proc. Text Retrieval Conference (TREC)*, Washington, November 1992. Special Publication 500-207.
8. S.A. Perry and P. Willett. A reniew of the use of inverted files for best match searching in information retrieval systems. *Journal of Information Science*, 6:59–66, 1983.
9. M. Persin, J. Zobel, and R. Sacks-Davis. Fast document ranking for large scale information retrieval. Technical Report 94/1, Collaborative Information Technology Research Institute, Department of Computer Science, Royal Melbourne Institute of Technology, Australia, 1994.
10. G. Salton. *Automatic Text Processing: The Transformation, Analysis, and Retrieval of Information by Computer.* Addison-Wesley, Reading, MA, 1989.
11. G. Salton and M.J. McGill. *Introduction to Modern Information Retrieval.* McGraw-Hill, New York, 1983.
12. J. Zobel, A. Moffat, and R. Sacks-Davis. An efficient indexing technique for full-text database systems. In *Proc. International Conference on Very Large Databases*, pages 352–362, Vancouver, Canada, August 1992.
13. J. Zobel, A. Moffat, and R. Sacks-Davis. Memory-efficient ranking of document collections. Technical Report TR-92-53, Collaborative Information Technology Research Institute, RMIT and The University of Melbourne, Melbourne, Australia, August 1992.

Adapting a Full-text Information Retrieval System to the Computer Troubleshooting Domain

Peter G. Anick
Digital Equipment Corporation, Marlboro, MA. USA
and
Brandeis University, Waltham, MA. USA

Abstract

There has been much research in full-text information retrieval on automated and semi-automated methods of query expansion to improve the effectiveness of user queries. In this paper we consider the challenges of tuning an IR system to the domain of computer troubleshooting, where user queries tend to be very short and natural language query terms are intermixed with terminology from a variety of technical sublanguages. A number of heuristic techniques for domain knowledge acquisition are described in which the complementary contributions of query log data and corpus analysis are exploited. We discuss the implications of sublanguage domain tuning for run-time query expansion tools and document indexing, arguing that the conventional devices for more purely "natural language" domains may be inadequate.

1 Introduction

Prior to the advances in computer and IR technology that made full-text indexing and retrieval possible, IR applications relied on manual keywording of documents for indexing and retrieval. In many cases, extensive effort was put into developing classification schemes for specific domains, like medicine and law, to insure that all the important concepts of an application domain were indexed and hence retrievable. In full-text indexing, the words of the documents take the place of a controlled vocabulary, eliminating the labor of manual keywording and the need for users to understand a controlled vocabulary. Because full-text retrieval does not require explicit domain tuning, it has been possible to apply information retrieval techniques readily to on-line documents on any available subject.

Nevertheless, full-text retrieval suffers from the difficulty of matching the uncontrolled vocabulary of the user to the ambiguous and varied language of the documents, and much effort has gone into attempts to improve the recall and precision of full-text methods [1]. Stemming is commonly used to improve recall by collapsing across morphological variants of words. Numerous techniques have been devised to automatically construct clusters of words from document collections for expanding queries at run-time [2]. Relevance feedback techniques are employed to extend queries with words from documents users select at run-time as relevant to their needs [3,4].

Such techniques have the merit of being automatic and domain independent. However, they do not necessarily make further domain tuning unnecessary or irrelevant. Some full-text systems, for example, supply an on-line thesaurus to help users pick out related query terms or to automatically add synonyms into a query. Likewise, recent IR research in the domains of financial and microelectronics news stories has showed the advantages of fine tuning an IR system in order for it to be responsive to specific constructs of the application domain (e.g. [5]).

In this paper, we outline the methodology we are developing for tuning a help-desk information retrieval system to the domain of computer troubleshooting. The approach is data driven, based on logs of actual query behavior by the end-user community. We describe the algorithms we have developed for acquiring data about the use of the application and deciding what kinds of domain tuning should be done. We argue that the mix of natural language and technical sublanguage vocabulary motivates query expansion techniques different from those employed for more conventional natural language textual databases. We then discuss the suite of tools we use in our run-time system for instantiating domain tuning and present several alternative approaches to indexing in the computer troubleshooting domain.

2 The Domain of Computer Troubleshooting

Information Retrieval technology is fast becoming a standard tool at computer troubleshooting help-desks and there is a growing interest in the research problems posed by this application domain [6,7,8]. Characteristics peculiar to the help-desk domain are that users are typically in a hurry to get at information (to solve a pressing problem) and they are apt to have their information need satisfied by a single document. In addition, the language of computer troubleshooting is an ever-growing mélange of technical terms, product names, and acronyms.

Digital's Customer Support Centers use the internally developed STARS V2 system to access over 200,000 technical documents. The STARS V2 system accepts queries entered in natural language; query terms are stemmed and noisewords are removed; then a Boolean expression is composed by ORing each remaining query term with any stored synonyms and then ANDing these clusters together. If this expression produces no matches, the most restrictive term is removed and the query is retried.

While users have found the STARS V2 system to be effective for finding on-line problem solutions, they also encounter difficulties when query behavior does not match their expectations or articles known to be in the database prove elusive. Often this reflects a lack of understanding about how the underlying system works. For example, stemming can inadvertently give rise to a large number of false alarms. Sequences of query terms that users may perceive as phrases are instead being interpreted as independent terms. The way strings containing numerics and punctuation are tokenized and indexed can lead to confusion over what form of a technical term to enter in a query.

In response to these and other issues, we initiated a parallel advanced development effort, AI-STARS, to look into ways of improving the natural language processing of queries and utilizing a graphical interface to make the system's behavior visible to and directly manipulable by end-users [9]. The AI-STARS system includes tools for an on-line lexicon, linguistically accurate morphological analysis, a flexible thesaurus allowing user-defined relationships, phrase recognition, and a pattern matcher for recognizing special expressions like version number variants.

For such query enhancing tools to add value to a specific application, they must be populated with data relevant to the application domain. We therefore began an effort to explore automated and machine-aided techniques for domain knowledge acquisition. At first, we looked to techniques from the field of computational linguistics, applying morphological tagging, syntactic pattern matching [10], lexical semantics [11] and collocational analysis [12] to the textual databases in order to acquire new vocabulary items, a phrasal lexicon, and collections of statistically and syntactically related terms. However, such corpus-based techniques, aside from being unwieldy simply due to corpus scale (over 200,000 documents), provided no guarantee of addressing the issues of greatest impact to our user community. We therefore decided to look into knowledge acquisition from another potentially rich source of collocational data, logs of actual STARS V2 query sessions.[1]

3 Domain Knowledge Acquisition

3.1 User Query Analysis

The STARS V2 system logs event records containing the user-id, time, user query, and number of matches in response to the query. Given some time period, we may produce from this log data a snapshot of user behavior as follows:

- Sorting log entries by user id and time, we group as a single user "session" all queries issued within three minutes of the previous query in the sesssion. We have empirically found that a query issued shortly after another is generally a restatement of the same information need. This grouping into sessions allows us to

[1] We chose to look at STARS V2 logs rather than AI-STARS logs because AI-STARS, in its pilot stage, was being used by a relatively small number of internal users in an experimental setting, while STARS V2, as the Customer Support Centers' production system, was servicing thousands of internal and customer queries daily, providing a steady stream of log data captured under realistic circumstances.

measure the degree of query reformulation done by users.

- To construct a profile of the terminology used in queries, we make use of an on-line lexicon of roughly 20,000 "common" English words to divide query terms into known and unknown word categories. The known words are further categorized as to part of speech and whether or not the query term is an inflected or uninflected form. Those terms which do not appear in the generic English dictionary are divided into five categories, based on the character sets they are made up of:
  - alpha (only alphabetic characters)
  - numeric (only digits)
  - alphanumeric (only alphabetic and digits)
  - numeric-punc (only digits and punctuation characters)
  - alphanumeric-punc (alphabetic, digits, and punctuation characters)
- For each query in a session, we count the number of non-noiseword terms[1] in that query. Additionally, we compute the number of unique non-noiseword terms appearing across all the queries of a given session. This latter figure provides a sense of the total number of different terms users feel they must generate in the course of trying to satisfy a single information need.

3.2 Usage Profile

We collect log data for both internal Digital Customer Support Specialists and external customers accessing STARS V2 data via a modem connection. This allows us to compare query behavior between groups with different levels of familiarity with the system. The example data cited in this paper was derived from a 3 day sample of external queries produced in December 1993. It encompasses 4,671 query sessions, comprised of 9,754 individual queries. When we analyzed the lengths of queries, calculating percent of queries at each length, we found that 56% of the queries contained a single search term, 20% contained only 2 terms and another 11% contained 3. Totalling the number of unique terms used within a query *session*, we found that 33% contained a single term, 23% 2 terms, and 30% contained 3-5 terms. Looking at the number of reformulation attempts per session, we learned that, while a handful of sessions contained over 10 reformulation attempts, over 50% of the sessions involved no reformulation and 40% of the sessions involved 2-4 reformulations of the query.

It should be pointed out that because STARS V2 does stemming and (a modest degree of) automatic synonyming, the effective query length may be slightly longer. However, it is clear that users opt to enter minimal queries and see what they get back before generating more terms.[2] We found very similar results with log data from internal users, indicating that familiarity with the system did not affect behavior regarding the number of terms used in queries. Examining the size of the result sets, we found that 16% of queries returned 0 matches; 45% returned 1-50 matches; 9% returned 51-100 matches; and 30% returned over 100 matching documents. From this data, we concluded that the use of query expansion techniques both to improve precision/recall and to enable meaningful ranking of the result list is probably warranted.

In Figure 1, we present the distribution of terms in our sample sessions. The total number of query terms is 19,181, of which 4,928 are unique strings. All words, including noisewords, are included in these totals. It is clear from the low number of prepositions, articles, and inflected forms that users are well aware that there is no need to make a query look like natural language to be effective. Two other interesting observations from this distribution are (1) that the majority of string *types* (unique terms) and 43% of the *tokens* (instances of terms) are terms that do not appear in the generic dictionary and (2) that a significant percentage of these "unknown" terms contain digits and/or punctuation. These latter sets include much of the technical sublanguage of the domain, as in the following examples:

- "vaxstation3100" - product name
- "32MB" - unit quantity
- "backup-i-readywrite" - informational message

[1] Our noiseword list contains 84 English function words, primarily pronouns, determiners, and prepositions.

[2] Apparently, this behavior is not due to the STARS V2 search engine per se. Debili et al [13], reporting on the SPIRIT IR system deployed at a large French computing center, note that users "give less information in their queries to the system than they use in their explanatory messages to the database manager." Chmaj [14] reports that help-desk users querying a probabilistic search engine often used around 3-4 terms even though longer queries would have produced better search results. Nor does the help-desk domain appear to be the key factor, for Stanfill [15] observes that users of the DowQuest (vector space) engine typically entered 1-3 word queries to retrieve news stories.

"KNOWN" WORDS	inflected forms				all forms			
	types		tokens		types		tokens	
	count	%	count	%	count	%	count	%
noun	81	1.64	248	1.29	497	10.08	3870	20.17
verb	142	2.88	419	2.18	244	4.95	862	4.49
noun/verb	136	2.75	1155	6.02	537	10.89	4786	24.95
adjective	4	.08	5	.02	120	2.43	539	2.81
preposition	0	0	0	0	54	1.09	486	2.53
pronoun	4	.08	33	.17	5	.10	34	.17
article	0	0	0	0	2	.04	91	.47
conjunction	0	0	0	0	1	.02	183	.95
adverb	0	0	0	0	8	.16	112	.58
interjection	0	0	0	0	0	0	0	0
total	367	8	1860	10	1468	30	10963	57

"UNKNOWN" WORDS	types		tokens	
	count	%	count	%
alpha	1716	34.82	5592	29.15
numeric	169	3.42	377	1.96
alpha-numeric	236	4.78	353	1.84
punc	341	6.91	201	1.04
numeric-punc	88	1.78	334	1.74
alpha-punc	910	18.45	1361	7.09
total	3460	70	8218	43

Figure 1. Term distribution data for sample of 4,671 customer query sessions. Percentages are based on a total of 19,181 "known" and "unknown" word terms comprising 4,928 types (unique strings). The *all forms* section of the "known" words table includes both inflected and uninflected word forms. The noun/verb row in the "known" words table represents terms that are ambiguous in part of speech between noun and verb.

- "reply/username" - command language command
- "errlog.sys" - file name
- "sys$check_access" - system service routine
- "ps205-aa" - part number
- "v4.1" - version number

3.3 Knowledge Acquisition from Queries

Upon inspecting the log data to determine what users did when reformulating a query, we found that much of their effort appeared to involve attempts to improve recall by substituting variants of these technical terms and expressions. Indeed, such technical sublanguage terms are often very good search terms, given their specificity. However, because they typically occur in many variant forms, they pose a retrieval problem not unlike that posed by morphological variants of non-technical English words. Unfortunately, whereas the rules of English morphology are fixed and well known (and thus can be dealt with in IR systems using stemming or morphological analysis), the rules and linguistic behaviors for words and phrases in the technical sublanguage must first be discovered and then somehow applied to user queries within the constraints of the run-time tools offered by the retrieval engine.

Several researchers have proposed automatic or semi-automatic approaches to acquiring domain knowledge. The STAIRS IR system, for example, generates thesaurus terms on the fly on the basis of suggestions made by the user at query time [1]. Güntzer et al [16] describe TEGEN, a rule-based system for acquiring possible thesaurus relationships among terms. Their system observes the sequence of steps a user takes during a query session and tries to infer term relationships based on the query reformulations the user undertakes in response to the results of a search. TEGEN is able to capitalize extensively on the use of explicit Boolean operators in user queries, and utilizes on-line interaction with the end-user wherever possible to refine hypotheses. In the case of the STARS V2 help-desk system, there is no system initiated interaction with the user other than prompting the user to enter a query. However, because users do enter new or altered queries when the result of an earlier query is inadequate, we undertook an experiment with a variant of the TEGEN approach to acquire related term information from the STARS V2 query session logs.

Our algorithm examined each new query within a session to identify which new terms were being added by that query. Each added term was then compared to terms appearing in earlier queries of the same session. This comparison was based on orthographic similarity and was used to identify any of five orthographic conditions:

- prefix(term1, term2) - term1 is a prefix of term2
- suffix(term1, term2) - term1 is a suffix of term2
- shared-prefix(term1, term2) - term1 and term2 share a 4-character prefix
- shared-suffix(term1, term2) - term1 and term2 share a 3-character suffix
- middle(term1, term2) - term1 appears as an internal substring of term2

The assumption behind this algorithm was that any new query terms which orthographically resembled previous query terms within the same session were likely to have been added to serve as synonyms, similar to the way a user might explicitly add inflectional variants to improve recall in a system that did no morphological analysis.

3.4 Results of Query Log Analysis

Applying this algorithm to our sample 3-day customer query log generated 1,288 potential pairs of variants (potentially related terms) out of the 4,671 query sessions. Because of the volume of data produced, we classified the variant pairs into cells in a three-dimensional matrix. The first dimension captures the character set composition of the two variants, indicating whether each string is alphabetic, numeric, alphanumeric, alphabetic with punctuation, numeric with punctuation, or alphanumeric with punctutation. The second dimension defines the kind of relationship found between the two strings (prefix, shared-prefix, suffix, etc.) The third dimension captures the types of of the characters at the boundary of the two words. For example, in the pair ("setdir" "setdir_enable"), the boundary between the shorter and longer strings consists of an alphabetic character (the "r") and a punctuation character (the "_"). The intent of this 3 dimensional categorization was to bring similar semantic categories together, assuming that semantic categories shared linguistic behaviors, and to expose what rules of word variation might exist which were sensitive to character type transitions.

The categorization scheme produces 1,530 possible cells. However, most variants fell into a small fraction of these, around 20, a sampling of which are shown in Figure 2. What is more, a number of the cells do correspond rather closely to identifiable semantic categories. The cell for the ((ALPHA ALPHA-NUMERIC), PREFIX, ALPHA-DIGIT) situation contains primarily product names, in which the second string satisfies the "specialization of" relation to the first string. The ((ALPHA ALPHA), SUFFIX, ALPHA-ALPHA) cell contains mostly compound words, in which the second word is again a specialization of the first. In the cell for ((ALPHA ALPHA-PUNC), SUFFIX, PUNC-ALPHA), we find a number of system messages linked to their primary concept.

The largest cell, ((ALPHA ALPHA), PREFIX, ALPHA-ALPHA), is composed primarily of five different kinds of relationships: abbreviations, compound words, inflections, morphological derivations, and spelling errors. By using the on-line text corpus and our morphological analysis tools, we have been able to devise heuristics for automatically partitioning these variant pairs into these respective sets:

- Inflections are recognized using the morphological analyzer. If the word is known to the lexicon, no further acquisition step is necessary. If the word is unknown, the morphological analyzer can be run in "guess" mode to hypothesize the word's citation form and part of speech. This hypothesis can be tested against the corpus by (1) checking for the existence of other inflected forms of the same hypothetical word

cell: ((ALPHA ALPHA), PREFIX, ALPHA-ALPHA) 295 22.90%
"condition" "conditionhandler"
"image" "images"
"dump" "dumpfile"
"perform" "performance"
"vol" "volume"
"time" "timeout"
"init" "initialize"
"datatrieve" "datatrievev"

cell: ((ALPHA ALPHA-NUMERIC), PREFIX, ALPHA-DIGIT) 13 1.00%
"nas" "nas200"
"dsm" "dsm062"
"tty" "tty01"
"hsc" "hsc50"

cell: ((ALPHA ALPHA, SUFFIX, ALPHA-ALPHA) 123 9.54%
"windows" "decwindows"
"laser" "declaser"
"mailbox" "netmailbox"
"vms" "openvms"
"reachable" "unreachable"

cell: ((ALPHA ALPHA-PUNC), SUFFIX, PUNC-ALPHA) 100 7.76%
"attributes" "get_attributes"
"unreachable" "system-f-unreachable"
"access" "ms*access"
"blocking" "record_blocking"
"zone" "sys$time_zone"
"sysverdif" "system-w-sysverdif"
"gblbufquo" "rms_gblbufquo"
"unsupported" "lnk$gl_unsupported"

cell: ((ALPHA ALPHA), SHARED-PREFIX, ALPHA-ALPHA) 83 6.44%
"priners" "printers"
"upgrae" "upgrade"
"nickname" "nickkname"
"motiv" "motif"

cell: ((NUMERIC-PUNC ALPHA-PUNC), SUFFIX, ALPHA-DIGIT) 14 1.08%
"5.0" "v5.0"
"6.0" "v6.0"
"5.5" "v5.5"

Figure 2. Sample output of cells derived from the variant acquisition algorithm. For each cell, its classification labels, the number of variants in the cell, and the percent of total variants are shown.

and (2) attempting to resolve noun/verb ambiguities through simple syntactic collocations, such as a preceding "the" or "a".

- Derivations are recognized using derivational morphological rules after inflectional suffixes have been removed. Unlike some systems, in which stemming collapses derivational and inflectional forms into a single stemmed index term, we chose to treat derivations as unique index terms which can be related, if justified in the application domain, by a link in the thesaurus. Finding collocated derivational variants in query log data provides a strong indication that a thesaurus link is indeed justified for this pair.
- Compound words are those for which both the prefix and the remainder of the second word exist as inde-

pendent strings in the text corpus. Often, such a compound can be expressed as well by a two word phrase. This can be verified by checking the corpus.

- Spelling errors are identified as those strings which do not appear in the lexicon and appear very infrequently in the text corpus. Since misspellings are rampant in queries and relatively rare in on-line databases, log and corpus data nicely complement each other. Query-time rule-based spell checking in a technical domain can be problematic, as the vocabulary is effectively infinite and very irregular, but run-time checking of unrecognized query terms against a list of actual misspellings, derived from the logs, may provide a pragmatic alternative which both improves over time and avoids generating annoying false alarms.
- Abbreviations are assumed by default to account for those cases that do not fit into any of the other categories.

These heuristic techniques differ from traditional corpus analysis by using the log data as a mechanism for focusing attention and launching hypotheses which corpus data can then help to confirm or deny.

3.5 Acronyms and Phrases

Another phenomenon evident in the log data is the widespread use of acronyms and phrases. Among the "unknown" alphabetic query terms in the sampled log data were 548 2-4 letter strings, many of which, on manual inspection, proved to be acronyms. The corpus data can be used here as well to help verify the hypothesis that a string is an acronym, and additionally supply the acronym's expansion for inclusion in the thesaurus. The document collection can be queried for all items containing the potential acronym. Then the returned documents can be individually searched for the closest occurring string of words that begins with the same sequence of letters. The number of documents supporting the same interpretation, as well as more stringent tests, such as capitalization of the candidate word sequence or its appearance in parentheses, can be used to reduce the number of false alarms. Still, determining good a priori statistical criteria for differentiating between hits and false alarms has proved difficult. Currently, we produce sorted lists of acronym expansions for review by a database administrator.

Adjacent words appearing in queries are often intended by users to act as multi-word phrases. However, because users tend to simply concatenate sequences of nouns into queries, without using function words or verbs to separate them, the percentage of false alarms from any phrase acquisition strategy based solely on log data would be overwhelming. We experimented, for example, with the heuristic that pairs of words which only co-occurred in queries in a specific adjacent order would be more likely to be true phrases. However, the results from our sample log data were unsatisfactory, producing many false alarms in addition to misses. We are now looking instead into using the corpus as the filtering device, using syntactic parsing and frequency of adjacency in the corpus itself to "validate" candidate phrases extracted from query data.

4 Application Tuning

In the previous sections, we outlined a suite of heuristic techniques for acquiring domain knowledge in the computer troubleshooting domain, using a combination of query and corpus data. As these methods are only heuristic, the results should be manually reviewed to eliminate false alarms and recategorize relationships when appropriate. The next step in application tuning is to add the domain knowledge to the IR system so that it can be applied at run-time. This step can take a number of forms.

4.1 Tools for Incorporating Domain Knowledge

In STARS V2, the primary method of automated query refinement is the ORing in of synonyms. Thus, tuning the V2 application means adding those relationships that can be construed as synonyms into the STARS V2 synonym database. With AI-STARS, however, we have a wider range of run-time tools with which to implement application tuning. Specifically, these are

- a word lexicon, containing morphological paradigms for each word
- a phrasal lexicon, for storing and recognizing known phrases
- a thesaurus, allowing words and phrases to be related according to user-defined link types
- a special expression handler for detecting non-lexicalized patterns in a query

AI-STARS also supports a graphical user interface that optionally exposes the system's query refomulation results to the user to explain the system's behavior and allow the user to augment and override the system's defaults [17]. The visual display can be used to present not only the terms actively used in the match expression, but also potentially related terms, generalizations, specializations, etc. which the user can activate via mouse clicks.

4.2 Encoding Term Relationships

The choice of which tool to use to encode term relationships depends on a number of factors, including ease of entering/representing the data, the manner in which the tool is applied at run-time, and the degree of precision desired during query expansion. Since the word lexicon is based on declaratively represented inflectional rulesets (or "paradigms") [18], it is possible to add new rulesets to the lexicon to handle cases of systematic orthographic variation in a technical sublanguage. For example, VMS system service routine names (and their abbreviations) often comprise a predictable family of variant forms (e.g., SYS$UNWIND, $UNWIND_S, $UNWIND_G, UNWIND_S, etc.). By treating such forms as inflectional variants, one need only add a single root form to the lexicon, specifying its paradigm, and at run-time, all variants of the user's query term will be used for matching against documents.

Where few variants exist or where there is no regular orthographic pattern among the related terms, each term can be explicitly linked to other terms via thesaurus links. By specifying the run-time behavior associated with different kinds of thesaurus links, one can exercise control over how the variants are to be employed during query expansion. For example, synonyms might be added to a query by default, whereas specializations might be added only at the user's explicit request.

In some cases, a regular pattern of syntactic variations exists but the set of variants is not finite. A good example of this is version numbers, which form a potentially infinite set (making it inappropriate to expand variants via thesaurus entries) but which conform to readily identifiable rules. The rules for recognizing and acting upon such expressions can be encoded by the "special expression" handler. The special expression handler must be able to strip version numbers off of product names (as in "vms5.0"), recognize multi-word phrases (as in "vms 5.0"), and parse compound tokens (as in "v5.0-a"). It is possible to use such a facility at indexing time to derive canonical index keys for these expressions, similar to doing stemming at index time. However, given the expectation that such rules will require future refinements and augmentation, we prefer to apply the rules at run-time to (1) recognize the expression in the query, (2) produce a canonical form from which all variants can be generated, and (3) match the generated variants against the raw index using ordered proximity constraints.

4.3 Indexing and Tokenization

Domain sublanguage has also had an impact on our indexing strategy. As the data in figure 1 amply illustrate, STARS V2 queries consist of roughly equal parts of English and technical sublanguage symbols. Unfortunately, in many cases, English and technical symbols are ambiguous, as in command names, components of file names, etc. When the strings are intended as English words, they conform to the rules of English morphology. But when used as part of the technical sublanguage, different (or no) rules may apply. For this reason we have chosen not to index on stemmed forms, but rather on the strings as they appear in the text. At run-time, we can use the lexicon and a morphological generator to produce all the inflected forms when we want to match on a string as an English word.[1]

The proliferation of strings composed of alpha, numeric, and punctuation characters complicates the matter of indexing in yet another way. What is the right unit to index on to permit the desired range of substring variant and special expression matching? The simplest option is to always index on the longest string bounded by whitespace or terminal punctuation. This has the drawback that a query term which is a semantically related substring of some longer term will not match the longer indexed term. This can be compensated for to some degree by implementing suffix wildcarding (assuming a B-tree index) and seeing to it that any other meaningful substring-superstring combinations are supplied by the thesaurus at run-time. This would result in a very large (and hopelessly incomplete) thesaurus.

A second option, recognizing the importance of character set boundaries in the construction of sublanguage vocabulary, is to use character set transitions as token boundaries and indexing a string on all its component parts. This accommodates the matching of subcomponents but requires that matching on any query term com-

[1] Alternatively, we could enlarge the size of the index and store both unstemmed and stemmed keys.

posed of a concatenation of subcomponents do the equivalent of a phrase match (ordered proximity match) on all the components of the string. As a number of these components are likely to be punctuation characters, some of the indexed sets can be quite large, incurring I/O and set intersection overhead in addition to the space overhead for storing the concordance data for all the subcomponents. It should also be noted that it may be necessary with this scheme to mark index keys with information specifying whether the token is completely whitespace bounded or appears as the start, middle, or end of a larger substring. This information would allow a query to distinguish between "natural language" occurrences of a term, which can inflect and are typically whitespace bounded, and sublanguage uses of a term, which are likely to include embeddings but not to inflect. A hybrid variant of this approach is possible as well, in which a subset of character set transitions are pragmatically chosen to break up tokens. At query time, the appropriate chunking factor must be applied to input tokens to match them against index keys.[1]

A third option is to index on the full strings but provide a supplementary permuted index to support the matching of substrings. This has the cost of considerable index space overhead as well as the additional I/O's needed to fetch the index sets for each superstring matched, but it is clearly the most flexible approach, as it supports full wildcard matching in the index. It has the additional benefit that the superstrings themselves can be retrieved and shown to the user, allowing the user to choose explicitly which superstrings to include in a query.

5 Conclusions

While the very high frequency of terse queries makes query expansion important for full-text retrieval in the computer troubleshooting domain, pervasive sublanguage vocabulary adds both complexities and opportunities with respect to domain tuning. We have outlined here a set of strategies for acquiring domain knowledge which make complementary use of query log and corpus data to generate and test hypotheses about potentially related terms. We find that mixing English and sublanguage terminology adds a new level of ambiguity to users' queries and that a rich set of run-time tools and a properly tokenized index are necessary for putting application domain knowledge fully to work during query expansion.

Having a range of tools to choose from does not necessarily make it easy to decide which representational approach to use to implement a specific domain construct. In some cases variant handling could be accomplished via adding a new morphological paradigm, populating the thesaurus with a set of linked terms, or writing more general expression recognition and handling rules. Future work is needed to evaluate the tradeoffs in manual encoding effort, system response time performance, and recall/precision value. Likewise, our knowledge extraction algorithms will need to be refined and augmented. We are particularly interested in investigating techniques based on query and corpus data that could help to relate English expressions of concepts to their relevant technical vocabulary.

Finally, given the potential value of query log data for keeping an IR system's knowledge base "up to date" in a linguistic domain as dynamic as computer troubleshooting, we are interested in exploring how to improve the quality of information logged without intruding on the user at run-time. We believe that a direct manipulation visual interface like that of AI-STARS [17] may encourage a style of user query reformulation which can contribute directly to knowledge acquisition without engaging the user in a more explicit question-answer oriented dialogue.

Acknowledgements

I would like to thank Lynn Beckner for her help in acquiring the query log data, Jim Moore for his assistance with the query log analysis, and Rex Flynn for his always insightful comments on earlier drafts of this paper.

References

1. Salton G. Another look at automatic text-retrieval systems. Comm. of the ACM 1986, 28(7): 648-656.
2. Spark-Jones K. Notes and references on early classification work. SIGIR Forum 1991; 25(1): 10-17.

[1] This is the approach we have currently chosen for our AI-STARS pilot, although we are interested in investigating the benefits and trade-offs of the other solutions.

3. Salton G, Buckley C. Improving retrieval performance by relevance feedback. J. of the ASIS 1990; 41(4): 288-297.
4. Harman D. Relevance feedback revisited. SIGIR'92, pp. 1-10.
5. Callan J. P, Croft W. B. An evaluation of query processing strategies using the TIPSTER collection. SIGIR'93, pp. 347-355.
6. Maarek Y. S, Smadja, F. A. Full text indexing based on lexical relations, an application: software libraries. SIGIR'89, pp. 198-206.
7. Weinberg M. Adapting information retrieval techniques for customer support and service. Proceedings of IEEE CAIA-92 Workshop on AI for Customer Service and Support, 1992, pp. 199-207.
8. Broglio J, Callan J. P, Chmaj J, Croft W. B, Derosa M. Information retrieval for customer support. AAAI-93 Workshop working notes for AI in Service and Support: Bridging the Gap between Research and Application, 1993, pp. 17-23.
9. Anick P. Integrating natural language processing and information retrieval in a troubleshooting help-desk. IEEE-Expert, Dec. 1993, pp 9-17.
10. Church K. A stochastic parts program and noun phrase parser for unrestricted text. Proceedings of Second Conference on Natural Language Processing (ACL), 1988, pp. 136-143.
11. Pustejovsky J, Bergler S, Anick, P. Lexical semantic techniques for corpus analysis. Computational Linguistics, 19(2): 331-358.
12. Smadja F. Retrieving collocations from text: Xtract. Computational Linguistics, 19(2): 143-177.
13. Debili F, Fluhr C, Radasoa P. About reformulation in full-text IRS. Proceedings of RIAO'88, pp. 343-359.
14. Chmaj J. personal communication, 1993.
15. Stanfill C. personal communication, 1993.
16. Güntzer U, Jüttner G, Seegmüller G, Sarre F. Automatic thesaurus construction by machine learning from retrieval sessions. Information Processing and Management. 1989. 25(3): 265-273.
17. Anick P, Brennan J, Flynn R, Hanssen D, Alvey B, Robbins J. A direct manipulation interface for boolean information retrieval via natural language query. Proceedings of SIGIR'90. 135-150.
18. Anick P, Artemieff S. A high-level morphological description language exploiting inflectional paradigms. Proceedings of COLING-92, Nantes, 1992.

Panel Sessions

Panel:
Integration of Information Retrieval and Database Systems

Moderator: Norbert Fuhr, University of Dortmund, Germany

Panelists: Ray R. Larson, University of California at Berkeley, USA
Peter Schäuble, ETH Zurich, Switzerland
Joachim W. Schmidt, Hamburg University, Germany
Ulrich Thiel, GMD-IPSI Darmstadt, Germany

The panelists will report on their current work as well as on their experience they have gained in the following projects.

- Lassen/SEQOIA 2000
- MIND
- NOSFERATU
- SPIDER
- Tycoon

Among others the following issues will be discussed.

1. *Extensible database systems* supporting text retrieval by means of user defined functions and/or triggers.
2. *Data models and retrieval models* for semistructured data incorporating best-match retrieval and exact-match retrieval as special cases.

Panel: Evaluating Interactive Retrieval Systems

moderator: Susan Dumais, Bellcore

Nicholas Belkin
Rutgers University
New Brunswick, NJ USA
belkin@cs.rutgers.edu

Christine L. Borgman
University of California Los Angeles
Los Angeles, CA USA
IIN4CLB@mvs.oac.ucla.edu

Susan Dumais
Bellcore
Morristown, NJ USA
std@bellcore.com

Micheline Hancock-Beaulieu
City University
London UK
mmhb@is.city.ac.uk

Most current information retrieval systems are highly *interactive*. Users ask queries, get immediate feedback, refine their queries, and so on. Methods for evaluating these dynamic systems have not kept pace with the rapid advances in system design. It is no longer enough to use the standard precision-recall measures to evaluate and to improve interactive retrieval systems. There is often no single final query to evaluate, with useful information being gathered from many different queries along the way. In addition, interfaces play a critical role in building effective retrieval systems. The best retrieval algorithm can be rendered functionally useless if the interface to it is unusable. Conversely, of course, the spiffiest new interface is not worth much without a good retrieval engine behind it. It would be easy if one could study interfaces and retrieval engines separately and take the best of both worlds. Unfortunately, there are important *interactions* that cannot be evaluated by studying components in isolation – e.g., how do you incorporate ranking or relevance feedback for a Boolean retrieval engine, or how do you highlight matching terms if complex syntactic and semantic processing of queries is used? The design of effective interactive retrieval environments will require careful attention to the larger *human - interface - retrieval-engine* system.

Systematic, generalizable evaluations of these larger interactive systems are possible both in the laboratory and in the field. The panelists will describe interactive retrieval experiments and experiences, focusing on: a) why it is important to study interaction, b) how interactive retrieval performance should be measured, and c) how the methods for evaluation and findings generalize to other systems. Belkin will begin with an overview of some of the problems in evaluating interactive retrieval systems and will present a new framework characterizing IR as interaction with text. The remaining talks will describe end-user experiments involving highly interactive retrieval systems. The focus of these talks will be on the approaches, methods and instruments used to evaluate retrieval effectiveness and ease of use as well as the relationship between system functionality and the interface. Dumais will describe the importance of interfaces in retrieval, and will present examples of successful iterative interface design with the SuperBook and X-LSI systems. Hancock-Beaulieu will review a series of experiments on the Okapi system to systematically examine the effectiveness of different retrieval aids. Borgman will describe the multiple evaluation methods employed to study children's information-seeking behavior using the Science Library Catalog, a graphical browsing system supplemented by keyword searching tailored to children's skills, and attempts to generalize these evaluation methods to other IR environments.

Author Index